PRINCIPLES
OF
PAYMENT SYSTEMS

By

James J. White
Professor of Law, University of Michigan
Member, Michigan Bar

Robert S. Summers
Professor of Law, Cornell University
Member, Oregon and New York Bars

CONCISE HORNBOOK SERIES®

Mat #16525227

Concise Hornbook Series, *WESTLAW* and West Group are trademarks registered in the U.S. Patent and Trademark Office.

© 2008 Thomson/West
  610 Opperman Drive
  St. Paul, MN 55123
  1–800–313–9378

Printed in the United States of America

ISBN: 978–0–314–23944–0

 *TEXT IS PRINTED ON 10% POST CONSUMER RECYCLED PAPER*

Preface

This work is a modified and much reduced version of the relevant parts of the 5th Edition of J. White and R. Summers, The Uniform Commercial Code, Volumes 2 and 3 (2008).

*

Summary of Contents

Table of Contents

*

PRINCIPLES
OF
PAYMENT SYSTEMS

*

Chapter 1

THE NEGOTIABLE INSTRUMENT

Analysis

1

§ 1–1   Introduction

In this chapter we consider the contractual liability of parties to a negotiable instrument and the effects of the transfer and payment of a negotiable instrument upon any underlying obligation between the parties. We discuss the liability of the maker of a promissory note, of the drawer of checks and other drafts, and of indorsers generally. We also examine the liability of more exotic animals of the forest, accommodation parties and guarantors.

Consider a simple example. Assume that Seller sells fifty steers to Rich Buyer and fifty steers to Poor Buyer. The contract of sale in each case is "the underlying obligation." At the time of tender Rich Buyer gives Seller his check. On signing it in the lower right hand corner, Rich Buyer becomes the "drawer." Assume that the check is payable to the order of Seller, who thus becomes the "payee," and that it is drawn on Rich Buyer's bank, the "drawee." However, Poor Buyer has insufficient money in the bank to pay by check, nor can he pay in cash. Accordingly Poor Buyer gives Seller a note. He too signs in the lower right hand corner and so becomes the "maker" or "issuer" and he too names the Seller as the one to whom payment is to be made and so makes the Seller the "payee." While he has possession of either of these two documents, Seller is also the "holder" of each of them.

Although courts often use the terms maker and drawer interchangeably, the Code uses the word "maker" to designate the party in the position of Poor Buyer and the word "drawer" to designate the party in the position of Rich Buyer, the signer in the lower right hand corner on a check or other draft. Sections 3–412 to 3–415 of the Code set out the "statutory contract" of each. While our focus in this chapter is on these stereotyped statutory contracts, we also consider matters related to the contractual liability of parties to negotiable instruments, such as the effect of a signature by the agent and, of course, the effect that the issuance of an instrument and its ultimate payment has upon the underlying obligation. Finally we examine the various ways in which a party's liability on a check and on the underlying obligation can be discharged. We postpone our discussion of noncontractual liabilities of parties to a check (warranty, tort, etc.) until later chapters on lost and stolen instruments.

One must first understand that a negotiable instrument is a peculiar animal and that many documents calling for the payment of money and others loosely called "commercial paper" are not negotiable instruments and not subject to the rules of Article 3.

Since one can be a "holder in due course" of only a negotiable instrument, the question whether an instrument is "negotiable" becomes most acute when one is trying to determine whether a party is a "holder in due course" who takes free of prior claims and defenses. For that reason we reserve intensive discussion of the difficulties in determining whether an instrument is negotiable for Chapter 2 on the holder in due course. For now a brief summary of the requirements of negotiability will suffice. Section 3–104(a) gives the basic definition of negotiable instrument:

> Except as provided in subsections (c) and (d), "negotiable instrument" means an unconditional promise or order to pay a fixed amount of money, with or without interest or other charges described in the promise or order, if it:
>
> (1) is payable to bearer or to order at the time it is issued or first comes into possession of a holder;
>
> (2) is payable on demand or at a definite time; and
>
> (3) does not state any other undertaking or instruction by the person promising or ordering payment to do any act in addition to the payment of money, but the promise or order may contain (i) an undertaking or power to give, maintain, or protect collateral to secure payment, (ii) an authorization or power to the holder to confess judgment or realize on or dispose of collateral, or (iii) a waiver of the benefit of any law intended for the advantage or protection of an obligor.

While a negotiable instrument contains a promise to pay a fixed amount of money, the instrument may provide for the payment of interest as long as it is described in the promise or order. Finally, under section 3–401(a) a person is only liable on an instrument signed by that person or an authorized representative. Consider, for example, the typical installment contract. Will it be a negotiable instrument subject to the rules of Article 3? Most installment contracts will fail on two grounds. First, they are usually not payable to "order or to bearer" and thus fail the test in (a)(1). Secondly, they usually include additional promises by the maker and thus fail the "unconditional promise" test in subsection (a)(3). However, section 3–106 authorizes certain additional conditions and promises notwithstanding section 3–104. As we explain in Chapter 2, one cannot safely give an opinion on whether a document is negotiable without examining that section in addition to 3–104.

What policy supports Article 3's narrow concept of negotiability? One policy is to put persons who deal with negotiable instruments on notice of their negotiability. Many business people and some consumers appreciate the unique legal liabilities associated with negotiable instruments and conduct their affairs accordingly.

If the variety of instruments that qualify as negotiable were allowed to proliferate, the expectations of such persons would be frustrated: those who thought they had undertaken one of the stereotyped Article 3 liabilities might have quite another liability, and those who expected to be able to assert contract defenses might be denied that right.

§ 1–2 Recent Revisions to Article 3

Article 3 underwent a major overhaul in 1990. Even cosmetic changes introduced the possibility for uncertainty, confusion and error. These revisions introduced two significant new elements into Article 3. First, the drafters changed the rules having to do with the personal liability of a person claimed by the holder to be a principal and characterized by himself as a mere agent.

The most important change in the 1990 revision was the modification of the liability of accommodation parties on negotiable instruments.

At this writing in 2008, all of the states except for New York and South Carolina have adopted the 1990 amendments to Articles 3 and 4. The amendment process has overtaken itself, for new amendments to Articles 3 and 4 were promulgated in 2002. The 2002 amendments have been adopted only in Arkansas, Kentucky, Minnesota, Nevada and Texas. The 2002 amendments are being considered in other states, and it is too soon to know whether those amendments will be widely adopted. The 2002 amendments started life as a relatively extensive revision but, in the end, the 2002 effort only made large changes in one section (3–605, and in 3–605's fellow traveler 3–419), proposed controversial changes to a couple of others (3–305, 3–416 and 4–208), and proposed mostly modest changes to another handful of sections and comments.

Consider some of the 2002 changes. First, 3–309 now makes clear that a party seeking to enforce a lost instrument does not have to be in possession of the instrument at the time it was lost. For example, when the FDIC takes on the portfolio of a failed bank, it may be unable to find some notes on which the bank is the payee.

Second, 3–602 would address the situation where a person entitled to enforce an instrument transfers it without giving notice to the obligated parties. The new rule is in line with the Restatement of Mortgages and the Restatement of Contracts. The new section will force transferees of notes to notify the makers or risk discharge by payment to the transferor.

Third, the drafters have completely rewritten section 3–605 on the discharge of secondary obligors to bring it in line with the Restatement of Suretyship and Guaranty. These changes could have a significant impact on the obligations of accommodation parties. The new rule parallels the modern interpretation of the common law on suretyship.

Fourth, the 2002 revision deals with two controversial issues. The first has to do with items known as "remotely-created items"; the second deals with the consumers' liability on debt obligations that should but do not contain the FTC restriction on the rights of a holder in due course.

Remotely-created items are checks that are drawn not by the drawer but by the payee. In the typical transaction, a debt collector, speaking to the debtor on the telephone, gets authority to draw on the debtor's account. The debtor on the telephone tells the payee his account number and other data to allow the payee's agent to make out a check to be transmitted to the drawer's bank for payment. Of course, the drawer will never see this check nor will his own manual signature appear on it. The line for the drawer signature will contain some indication that the drawer has authorized the check. Because the debtor does not see the check before it is presented for payment, this process offers opportunity for fraud and error.

To give drawers some leverage in this transaction, the 2002 amendments proposed additions to the transfer warranties in Articles 3 and 4 (3–416 and 4–208). These new warranties, coming from the payee, the depositary bank, and other transferees, warrant (with respect to a "remotely created consumer item") that "the person on whose account the item is drawn authorized the issuance of the items in the amount for which the item is drawn." This new warranty is intended to make depositary banks monitor their debt collecting customers.

Since this warranty could impose burdens on hometown depositary banks vis-à-vis out-of-state payor banks, some states have been hesitant to adopt the warranty unless the home state of the payor bank who will benefit from the warranty has adopted a similar rule. Some have also been concerned with the possibility that debt collectors might avoid giving the warranty by moving their operations to Canada or to a Caribbean country.

Federal Trade Commission rules now require many consumer creditors to put a legend on their debt obligations that allows the consumer to assert most of his defenses on the obligation even against a holder in due course. But what of the cases where the creditor is obliged to include the legend but does not do so? Do transferees of such notes and other obligations take free of the consumer debtors offenses or are such notes to be treated as though they contain the legend? New section 3–305(e) specifies that an instrument that should contain the legend under the FTC rule will be treated as though it does contain the legend. Some might see this as uncontroversial, but of late, the American Bankers Association has made it a practice to oppose any new uniform legislation that could cause liability, however slight, to any of its members.

Finally, several changes have been made to ease the implementation of UETA and notes have been added that outline the consequences of any future implementation of the United Nations Convention on International Bills of Exchange and International Promissory Notes.

§ 1–3   Liability of Principals and Agents on Negotiable Instruments: Rules, Symbols, and Proof

Section 3–401(a) of the Code states the general rule for liability on an instrument: a person is not liable unless the person signed the instrument, or unless the person is represented by an agent who signed the instrument. This is a departure from long-established law, which, in the words of old Article 3, found one was not liable on an instrument "unless his signature appears thereon." Now, a principal can have liability on a negotiable instrument even though there is no "signature" that is "his." That is to say, if Roger Smith is the authorized agent of General Motors and he signs the words "Roger Smith," General Motors may well have liability even though the words "General Motors" nowhere appear on the instrument. Comment 1 to 3–401 states: "It is not necessary that the name of the obligor appear on the instrument so long as there is a signature that binds the obligor."

In Triffin v. Ameripay, LLC,[1] a payroll services company signed and issued invalid checks on behalf of an employer company without indicating its agency status. Since the name and address of the represented entity appeared prominently on the checks, it did not matter that the payroll company managed the account and the only signatories on the account were representatives of the payroll company. The obvious intent to have an agency relationship controls and therefore the employer company, and the employer company alone, was liable on the checks, even if the agent signed its own name.

Comment 2 to 3–401 tells us that a person may make his signature in a variety of ways: "handwritten, typed, printed or made in any other manner." Under this broad view an imaginative plaintiff might argue that preprinted forms (for instance, checks) with the name of a corporation or individual inscribed on them are "signed" instruments. Before rushing to tear up one's supply of preprinted checks, the reader should consider section 1–201(b)(37): " 'Signed' includes using any symbol executed or adopted with

§ 1–3

1.   368 N.J.Super. 587, 847 A.2d 628, 53 UCC2d 573 (App. Div. 2004).

present intention to adopt or accept a writing." One would be hard pressed to maintain that a party had "present intention to adopt" whatever might later be written on a check when one orders a batch of checks with a name printed on them.

In a modernizing touch, revised section 3–401(b) specifically indorses a "device" or "machine" as a way of putting a "signature" on a negotiable instrument.

§ 1–4   Agency: Principal's Liability

Commerce demands, and the Code provides, that agents may sign negotiable instruments and thus bind their principals. Section 3–402 states that the principal is bound by the agent's signature "to the same extent the represented person would be bound if the signature were on a simple contract." This explicitly invites consideration of common law agency cases. Presumably the reference to establishing agency and principal status as would be done on a simple contract invokes not only the substantive law of agency in a particular state, but also its parol evidence rule together with other rules and presumptions on what symbols are necessary and what symbols are sufficient.[1] For example, in Carelli v. Hall,[2] the court found that parol evidence (the debtor told the plaintiff he was using the funds for partnership purposes) should not have been consid-

---

§ 1–4

1. § 3–402 reads as follows:

(a) If a person acting, or purporting to act, as a representative signs an instrument by signing either the name of the represented person or the name of the signer, the represented person is bound by the signature to the same extent the represented person would be bound if the signature were on a simple contract. If the represented person is bound, the signature of the representative is the "authorized signature of the represented person" and the represented person is liable on the instrument, whether or not identified in the instrument.

(b) If a representative signs the name of the representative to an instrument and the signature is an authorized signature of the represented person, the following rules apply:

(1) If the form of the signature shows unambiguously that the signature is made on behalf of the represented person who is identified in the instrument, the representative is not liable on the instrument.

(2) Subject to subsection (c), if (i) the form of the signature does not show unambiguously that the signature is made in a representative capacity or (ii) the represented person is not identified in the instrument, the representative is liable on the instrument to a holder in due course that took the instrument without notice that the representative was not intended to be liable on the instrument. With respect to any other person, the representative is liable on the instrument unless the representative proves that the original parties did not intend the representative to be liable on the instrument.

(c) If a representative signs the name of the representative as drawer of a check without indication of the representative status and the check is payable from an account of the represented person who is identified on the check, the signer is not liable on the check if the signature is an authorized signature of the represented person.

2. 279 Mont. 202, 926 P.2d 756, 33 UCC2d 513 (1996).

ered since the note and security agreement unambiguously identified the debtor as the sole debtor.

Section 3–402(a) makes it plain that one who is not "identified in the instrument" is liable if that person is truly the principal and if the instrument was signed by that person's agent. In QAD Investors, Inc. v. Kelly,[3] a partner who did not sign a note was liable when another partner signed with apparent authority to bind the partnership and the non-signing partner's acts after the execution of the note confirmed that his partner had authority to sign the note for the partnership.

Comment 1 to 3–402 points out that under some interpretations of the pre–1990 Code, it was possible to have an instrument on which no one was liable. The agent might have escaped by showing he or she signed only as the agent and did not have personal liability, and the actual principal might have escaped because he or she was not identified on the instrument. That is no longer possible.

a. *Unauthorized Signatures*

Under revised section 3–403 an agent's unauthorized signature is generally ineffective to bind a presumed principal. For example, in Citizens Bank of Maryland v. Maryland Industrial Finishing[4] an employee used one-half of a stamp given her by her employer to indorse checks that were payable to the company; she omitted the restrictive indorsement "For Deposit Only." She then deposited the checks into her own account. The court remanded the case for consideration whether the omission of the restrictive language was unauthorized.

An unauthorized signature may be ratified, and, when so, binds the ratifying principal. What acts constitute the ratification of an unauthorized signature?[5] Generally, ratification is found when the principal knowingly assents to the unauthorized signature by express statement or conduct.[6] In Rehrig v. Fortunak,[7] a Pennsylvania

---

3. 2001 ME 116, 776 A.2d 1244, 46 UCC2d 480 (2001).

4. 338 Md. 448, 659 A.2d 313, 26 UCC2d 1009 (1995).

5. § 1–201(b)(41) defines unauthorized signature:

"Unauthorized signature" means a signature made without actual, implied or apparent authority. The term includes a forgery.

6. Restatement (Second) of Agency § 82 (1957) defines ratification:

Ratification is the affirmance by a person of a prior act which did not bind him but which was done or professedly done

on his account, whereby the act, as to some or all persons, is given effect as if originally authorized by him.

Restatement (Second) of Agency § 83 (1957) states:

Affirmance is either

(a) a manifestation of an election by one on whose account an unauthorized act has been done to treat the act as authorized, or

(b) conduct by him justifiable only if there were such an election.

7. 39 Pa. D. & C.2d 20, 3 UCC 636 (Com.Pl. 1966).

court held that a wife's retention of benefits from a note constituted ratification of her allegedly unauthorized signature made by her husband. Mere delay in complaining about an unauthorized signature may not be enough to cause a ratification. Also, a defendant is required by section 3–308 "specifically" to deny in the pleadings the validity of any signature the defendant wants to contest.

The pre–1990 Code contained two provisions under which a principal might be precluded from denying an unauthorized signature, even if the principal did not ratify the signature. As is explained in Comment 1 to the new section 3–403, both of these provisions could have been applied to certain cases of forgery, but the two sections were subject to different standards of liability. This overlap created confusion, according to the comment. To avoid confusion, the post–1990 Code drops the reference to "preclusion."

b. Burden of Proof

Because an undisclosed principal can now be liable "on an instrument signed by an authorized representative," section 3–308 places the burden on the person seeking enforcement to show that an undisclosed principal should be the one to pay. This rule, explained in Comment 1 to section 3–308, makes obvious sense. It would be too easy for an obligee to claim that a third party not mentioned on the instrument was liable and very difficult for that third party to prove a negative—that he or she was not meant to be liable or had nothing to do with the transaction. Section 3–308(a) reads, in part:

> If an action to enforce the instrument is brought against a person as the undisclosed principal of a person who signed the instrument as a party to the instrument, the plaintiff has the burden of establishing that the defendant is liable on the instrument as a represented person under Section 3–402(a).

Section 3–308(a) first provides that if the authenticity of a signature is to be contested it must be specifically denied in the pleadings. Once denied, the party claiming validity has the burden of proof, but this will almost always be met prima facie since there is a rebuttable presumption under 3–308(a) that the signature is "authentic and authorized." This rule changes, however, if a plaintiff seeks to establish liability of a purported signer who is dead or incompetent. In that case, the plaintiff has the burden of establishing validity.

Finally, subsection 3–308(b) states that once the validity of signatures is admitted or proved ("and there is compliance with subsection (a)") several more steps may be required for plaintiff to prevail. The plaintiff must prove entitlement to payment under 3–

301. Usually this is easy, since 3–301 states that any "holder of an instrument" is a person entitled to enforce it. Therefore, merely by producing a properly indorsed or issued instrument the plaintiff proves that he is entitled to enforce it as a holder. See section 1–201(b)(21) defining "holder." Once this is accomplished, the burden shifts back to the defendant to prove a defense or claim in recoupment.[8] If no such defense or claim is proved, the plaintiff is entitled to recover on the instrument. If the defendant, however, establishes a defense or claim in recoupment, the defendant is discharged unless the plaintiff can prove status as a holder in due course or has the rights of a holder in due course. A successful showing that one is a holder in due course or has the rights of one, as discussed in Chapter 2, will bar the defendant's claims and defenses (save the real defenses) and allow the plaintiff to recover.

§ 1–5   Personal Liability of the Agent

One of the weeds that flourishes in modest-sized corporations is the question of the personal liability of a corporate employee who claims to be only an agent. The typical defendant either signed twice on the front without indicating representative capacity or signed a second time on the back of the instrument, leaving matters ambiguous. In the usual case, when the corporate debtor fails to pay, the creditor sues the signer individually, and argues that the separate signature was not as an agent, but as one who intended to be personally liable as a guarantor. It is hard to imagine why a corporate employee would sign twice if he did not intend to be personally liable. Of course, it is possible that a clever creditor—understanding the law better—simply said, "Sign here, here and here," and the debtor's employee blindly complied. Whatever the reason, defendants sometimes argue that they signed as agents even though the instrument neither specifies that status nor identifies the principal.

In addressing this problem, section 3–402 abandons earlier Code attempts to identify general symbols that make one "unambiguously" an agent and symbols that do not. The Code now leaves those decisions to the court. In Comment 2, the drafters explain their position as follows:

> Subsection (b) concerns the question of when an agent who signs an instrument on behalf of a principal is bound on the instrument. The approach followed by former Section 3–403 was to specify the form of signature that imposed or avoided liability. This approach was unsatisfactory. There are many ways in which there can be ambiguity about a signature. It is

---

8. U.S. Bank Nat'l Ass'n v. Scott, 2003 S.D. 149, 673 N.W.2d 646, 52 UCC2d 554 (2003) (makers failed to deny the validity of the note so it was admitted and the burden of proof shifted to the makers to prove payment).

better to state a general rule. Subsection (b)(1) states that if the form of the signature unambiguously shows that it is made on behalf of an identified represented person (for example, "P, by A, Treasurer") the agent is not liable. This is a workable standard for a court to apply. Subsection (b)(2) partly changes former Section 3–403(2). Subsection (b)(2) relates to cases in which the agent signs on behalf of a principal but the form of the signature does not fall within subsection (b)(1). The following cases are illustrative. In each case John Doe is the authorized agent of Richard Roe and John Doe signs a note on behalf of Richard Roe. In each case the intention of the original parties to the instrument is that Roe is to be liable on the instrument but Doe is not to be liable.

Case #1. Doe signs "John Doe" without indicating in the note that Doe is signing as agent. The note does not identify Richard Roe as the represented person.

Case #2. Doe signs "John Doe, Agent" but the note does not identify Richard Roe as the represented person.

Case #3. The name "Richard Roe" is written on the note and immediately below that name Doe signs "John Doe" without indicating that Doe signed as agent.

In each case Doe is liable on the instrument to a holder in due course without notice that Doe was not intended to be liable. In none of the cases does Doe's signature unambiguously show that Doe was signing as agent for an identified principal. A holder in due course should be able to resolve any ambiguity against Doe.

Two conditions must exist for the agent to escape scot free under 3–402(b)(1). First the signature must show "unambiguously" that it is made on behalf of the represented person. Second, the represented person must be "identified in the instrument." Thus, in the examples given in Cases 1 and 2 in the comment quoted above, the agent could not fit within (b)(1) because the represented person is not identified in the instrument. We would think that a signature matching the form "John Jones Company, by Rebecca Taylor, Agent," would "unambiguously" show that Rebecca Taylor was the agent and would free her from liability under (b)(1). Having read a number of cases in this area that have come to mysterious outcomes, we hesitate to predict that every court would go along with our conclusion.

In Dewberry Painting Centers, Inc. v. Duron, Inc.,[1] two instruments were at issue. On the first instrument, the defendant's

1. 235 Ga.App. 40, 508 S.E.2d 438,

signature was preceded by name of the corporation and followed by "President." The court found representative capacity on this instrument as a matter of law. On the second instrument, the name of the corporation was not written on the face of the instrument and the words "personally guarantee" were crossed out once but left in at another place on the note. This ambiguous message made liability a matter for the jury to determine.

The post–1990 subsection 3–402(b)(2) has potential to surprise an unwary agent. If the plaintiff is a holder in due course, the plaintiff takes free of the claim (presumably unfettered by any extrinsic evidence) that the agent was not personally liable. Thus, one who signs in an ambiguous capacity or who omits the name of the principal when signing an instrument may become liable to a holder in due course even where the original parties intended this party to be an agent only.

A careless agent may escape liability to holders other than holders in due course, but the agent will have to work at it. The last sentence in subsection 3–402(b)(2) reads:

> With respect to any other person [i.e., non-holders in due course], the representative is liable on the instrument unless the representative proves that the original parties did not intend the representative to be liable * * *.

Where the represented person is not identified or the form of the signature does not show unambiguously that it is made in a representative fashion (that is, if either of those is true), then the agent is personally liable unless the agent proves "that the original parties did not intend the representative to be liable." One might regard this sentence as a presumption of liability. Certainly the consequence is to make the agent liable unless the agent shows the requisite intent of the original parties. Comment 2 to 3–402 suggests that almost any relevant evidence, parol or not, is to be admitted to show the intention of the parties. For example, a defendant who signed as an agent would be permitted to testify to his or her own intention. If that testimony were persuasive, it would carry the day. The comment makes the point as follows:

> In some of the cases the court refused to allow proof of the intention of parties and imposed liability on the agent based upon former section 3–403(2)(a) even though both parties to the instrument may have intended that the agent not be liable. Subsection (b)(2) changes the result of those cases, and is consistent with section 3–117 which allows oral or written agreements to modify or nullify apparent obligations on the instrument.

The case of Wang v. Wang[2] is a good example of a lawsuit that would probably come out differently under the 1990 Code. In *Wang*, the trial court admitted parol evidence establishing that the signer on a note had intended to sign only as a representative and held that the signer was not liable. The South Dakota Supreme Court reversed, holding that parol evidence could not be admitted to show representative capacity because the note showed neither representative capacity nor the principal's name.

This result was correct under the former Code, but a brief review of the facts shows how discomforting the outcome. Victor Wang, a third party to the suit, had taken out a loan from the Rosebud Federal Credit Union for $97,425.09. RFCU was associated with the Farmer's Cooperative Oil Company (Coop), another business from Winner, South Dakota. As part of the ongoing association, the Coop guaranteed many of the loans taken out by patrons of RFCU. Albert Schramm, an officer of both organizations, would sign a note that had been executed by a patron, and a stamp was later affixed above Schramm's signature reading "Farmer's Cooperative Oil Association of Winner By-." The stamp was never placed on the particular note involved, so that Schramm's signature stood alone. Victor Wang subsequently defaulted on the loan and some of the collateral held by RFCU was sold to cover part of the loss. The Coop paid the remaining $43,344 to RFCU.

When Schramm later called to talk to Victor, he learned that Victor's brother Robert was interested in acquiring some of the unsold collateral. RFCU reached an agreement with Robert Wang, transferring to him the note and security agreement for $8,000. Robert Wang then filed suit demanding payment of $106,193.37 (principal and interest) from Schramm, who found out for the first time that his signature stood naked on the note. With the state Supreme Court's ruling, Schramm could not introduce parol evidence to show his representative status.

Article 3 now admits parol evidence to prove an individual did not sign personally in all instances where the holder is not a holder in due course. It is no longer necessary for an instrument to bear some evidence that it was signed in a representative capacity. If the *Wang* case were decided today, parol evidence would be permitted since Robert was not a holder in due course (he had notice that the note was overdue). Schramm would be presumed liable, but he would have the opportunity to prove that the original parties did not intend him to be liable, and, instead, that he had signed in a representative capacity. Needless to say, a person faced with personal liability may not be the most reliable or honest arbiter of the "parties' intent." Exactly how the courts will navigate here, we are uncertain.

2. 393 N.W.2d 771, 2 UCC2d 972 (S.D. 1986).

a. Parol to Hold Principal

There is a second parol evidence question that arises when a creditor attempts to prove an undisclosed principal liable. That may occur, for example, where the alleged agent has fled, is insolvent, or when the principal is comparatively wealthy and the agent is comparatively poor. Greyhound Lines, Inc. v. First State Bank of Rollingstone[3] presents this problem. In that case, the plaintiff payee was offered a check to cover a debt. The payee would not accept the check unless the payor bank confirmed that there were sufficient funds in the drawer's account. The drawer returned with the check after it had been signed by Klein, a vice president of the First State Bank, the drawee. The payee called Klein and was assured that there were sufficient funds to cover the check. When the check was later dishonored for insufficient funds, the payee asserted that Klein had signed as an agent of the bank (meaning the bank had accepted). In attempting to prove this assertion, the payee introduced parol evidence to impose liability on the bank for the agent's signature. The appellate court found the bank liable under the pre–1990 Code's section 3–403(2)(b).[4] That section stated when an authorized representative was personally liable and, by implication, also identified the remaining situations in which the signature of an authorized representative bound the principal. The section made an agent personally liable if the agent signed an instrument that failed to name the represented party and failed to indicate the agent's representative status. An agent who satisfied only one prong of the test would also be personally liable "except as otherwise established between the immediate parties." Klein satisfied the first prong by showing that the check "name[d] the person represented," since the bank's name and logo were printed on the check. Klein then had to introduce parol evidence to show an agreement between the parties—a Greyhound official had spoken to Klein at the bank and "understood [Klein] signed the check for the Bank." The appellate court approved the use of parol evidence, saying: "Study of a note and the circumstances surrounding execution of an instrument is appropriate to determine the liability of the principal, as between the immediate parties."

Although Klein managed to prove in court that the check "named" the principal, the bank was, for all practical purposes, an undisclosed principal. For the reasons stated below, we believe that

---

3. 366 N.W.2d 354, 40 UCC 1757 (Minn.App. 1985).

4. § 3–403(2)(b) reads:

An authorized representative who signs his own name to an instrument

(b) except as otherwise established between the immediate parties, is personally obligated if the instrument

names the person represented but does not show that the representative signed in a representative capacity, or if the instrument does not name the person represented but does show that the representative signed in a representative capacity.

in these cases (where the creditor is seeking to hold an undisclosed principal liable) the court should treat questions of admissibility of parol evidence the same way the court treats evidence offered to prove an individual's agency status.

First, recall that under 3–401 a principal can be liable on an instrument even though that principal's name does not appear on it. Thus the drafters must have contemplated that evidence other than the instrument would be introduced in order to show a principal liable. Second, 3–402(a) and Comment 1 to that section insure that there can never be an instrument on which no one is liable. Consequently, if it is established at trial that the signature on an instrument was made in a representative capacity—and thus that the agent is not liable—it must also have been established that there is a principal liable on the instrument. Finally, as we demonstrated above, almost any type of evidence is admissible to show that a person who signed an instrument is an agent and so not personally liable. If this evidence is admissible to show that the individual whose signature appears on the instrument is not liable (because he is an agent), then it must also be admissible to demonstrate that an undisclosed principal exists and is liable. Any other conclusion would create the possibility of an instrument on which no one was liable. Logic leads to the same conclusion. It would make little sense to have a rule which admitted parol evidence to establish that one person was involved in a special two-person relationship, but did not admit it to show that the second person was involved in the same relationship.

The final provision of 3–402(c) is a special rule for checks drawn on the checking account of the principal.

> (c) If a representative signs the name of the representative as drawer of a check without indication of the representative status and the check is payable from an account of the represented person who is identified on the check, the signer is not liable on the check if the signature is an authorized signature of the represented person.

The comment explains this section as follows:

> Virtually all checks used today are in personalized form which identify the person on whose account the check is drawn. In this case, nobody is deceived into thinking that the person signing the check is meant to be liable.

Assume Rebecca Taylor is an authorized drawer on the Johnson Company's account. She signs a check "Rebecca Taylor." The check is on the account of Johnson Company and contains the printed name "Johnson Company," showing that the account is that of the company. Subsection 3–402(c) puts the Code's legal stamp of approval on the obvious intent of the transaction—that the company's check binds only the company, even if an agent signs in her own name.

b. Conclusion

In summary, the 1990 version of section 3–402 frees courts from strange and improper results dictated from law. The section invites the courts to hear more evidence than was formerly the case and clearly and correctly favors the agent in printed check cases.

PROBLEM

Assume that Donald Fox is the sole shareholder of a Delaware corporation, Fox Automotive, that operates a car dealership in California. Fox signs the following documents:

1. Fox makes out a note under which "Fox Automotive promises to pay $500,000 to the order of First Bank." Fox signs the note "Donald Fox, Pres." He then signs his name a second time beneath his first signature.

   Is Donald Fox personally liable on the note? Yes, for sure, to a holder in due course. This note does not show unambiguously that Fox made the second signature in a representative status.

   Is Fox liable to a non-holder in due course? Almost surely yes, but at least he could introduce parol evidence to show that the parties intended otherwise. Of course, it is hard to imagine any reason for the second signature except to create personal liability as a guarantor of the corporation's debt.

2. What if the note read "The undersigned promises to pay $500,000 to First Bank or order one year after date" and was signed "By Donald Fox, Pres." Is Fox personally liable to a holder in due course? The comment to 3–402 says yes; the name of the represented corporation is not stated on the note. But shouldn't the holder be put on notice by the preposition "by" and by the title "pres" after the signature? We think so, but the comments and the text of 3–402 say no.

   Here Fox could show that First Bank knew that the loan was to the corporation and not to him personally. (For this purpose, First Bank should not be recognized as a holder in due course even if we might recognize payees as HDIC's for some purposes.)

3. What if the note says "Fox Automotive promises to pay ..." and is signed "Donald Fox?" Here we think there is no personal liability to either a non HDIC or to an HIDC because the note gives the name of the represented person. So we think this shows "unambiguously" that Fox is signing as a representative even though it is not a perfect articulation. (But we can imagine some taking the opposite position by

drawing negative inferences from subsection 3–402(c) discussed below.)

4. And if Fox signs his name to a check that shows itself to be a check of "Fox Automotive?" Here subsection (c) protects Fox from personal liability.

5. How do you do it right? "Fox Automotive Inc promises ..." signed "By Donald Fox, Pres."

§ 1–6   Basic Liabilities of the Parties to a Negotiable Instrument, Drawers, Makers, Indorsers, Acceptors

The contract liability of the maker of a note is as easy to understand as the words "I promise to pay...." Section 3–412 requires the issuer of a note or cashier's check or other draft to pay the instrument "according to its terms" either at the time of issue or at the time it first came into possession of the holder. The issuer's promise is unconditional, unless, under 3–106, the instrument states expressly that the promise is controlled by another writing or that obligations under the instrument are described in another writing.

The maker owes the obligation "to a person entitled to enforce the instrument." But the 1990 Code required the drawer and indorser of an instrument to pay "the holder or any indorser who takes it up." The post–1990 phrase, "a person entitled to enforce the instrument," is defined as follows in section 3–301:

"Person entitled to enforce" an instrument means (i) the holder of the instrument, (ii) a nonholder in possession of the instrument who has the rights of a holder, or (iii) a person not in possession of the instrument who is entitled to enforce the instrument pursuant to Section 3–309 or 3–418(d). A person may be a person entitled to enforce the instrument even though the person is not the owner of the instrument or is in wrongful possession of the instrument.

This provision recognizes that the person actually entitled to enforce an instrument often does not fit comfortably within the definition of holder, indorser, or the like. An example given in the comments to 3–301 is a person entitled to enforce a lost or stolen instrument. Those entitled to enforce an instrument might also include one in possession of an instrument who is not a holder because the person acquired rights by subrogation or by assignment from the holder in a form that did not make the possessor or "a holder." An example is a bona fide transfer where the payee (transferor) forgot to indorse.

a. Issuers, Drawers, Makers

The drawer of a draft drawn on a bank or other third party is only "secondarily" liable on the instrument. That is, the holder must make an attempt to collect elsewhere before the drawer must pay. Put another way, the drawer of a check, like the maker of a note, signs the instrument in the lower right-hand corner, but the drawer's contract is unlike the maker's in that the drawer orders another to make payment and promises to pay only if the order bears no fruit. (See section 3–414.) Thus, in common experience, the holder of a check looks first to the bank for payment,[1] and if it cannot be had there, to the drawer. According to 3–104(f), a check is a draft "other than a documentary draft, payable on demand and drawn on a bank," or a cashier's or teller's check. The legal basis for the obligation of the drawer is set out in 3–414(b):

> If an unaccepted draft is dishonored, the drawer is obliged to pay the draft (i) according to its terms at the time it was issued or, if not issued, at the time it first came into possession of the holder * * *.

The Code no longer requires that the holder give the drawer notice of the dishonor. This change sounds striking but will have little impact, since the drawer of a draft was rarely discharged under the pre–1990 Code, even where there was no timely notice.

Under section 3–414(b), the drawer owes its obligation "to a person entitled to enforce the draft or to an indorser who paid the draft under section 3–415." This replaces the less definite language of former section 3–413(2) under which the obligation ran to the "holder or to any indorser who takes it up."

Section 3–414(f) frees the drawer from an obligation to pay a check if it is not presented for payment within 30 days or given to a depositary bank for collection within that time, but this discharge applies only where (1) the drawee bank fails and (2) because of the delay the drawer is deprived of funds. The drawer is then discharged only "to the extent deprived of funds." For example, Bob buys a rare clarinet from Tom and pays with a $110,000 check drawn on good funds. Tom is disorganized and leaves the check under a stack of papers for two months. During that time, the drawee bank fails. In most cases, Bob would collect $100,000 in federal bank deposit insurance. His obligation to pay Tom the remaining $10,000 would be discharged, since Bob would otherwise be deprived of funds that he could have withdrawn from the bank before it failed. Bob would assign to Tom his drawer's rights

1. The bank has no obligation to the holder to pay a check. § 3–408 provides:

" * * * the drawee is not liable on the instrument until the drawee accepts it."

against the drawee, and it would be up to Tom to try to collect the $10,000.

"Issuers" of notes or cashier's checks or other drafts drawn on the drawer are covered by section 3–412. We do not believe that inclusion of cashier's checks in the section with notes will materially change the problem (discussed in Chapter 2) concerning the bank's right to raise its, or a third party's, defenses when it is sued on a cashier's check by one who is not a holder in due course.

b. Acceptance

A party who takes a check in payment of a debt expects the bank on which it is drawn to pay it. However, without more, the drawee bank is not obligated to the *payee* to pay even a nickel. The drawee has made no promise on an unaccepted check. In the words of 3–408:

> A check or other draft does not of itself operate as an assignment of funds in the hands of the drawee available for its payment, and the drawee is not liable on the instrument until the drawee accepts it.

Even if the drawee arbitrarily dishonors a check, the payee or holder ordinarily has no cause of action against the drawee bank on the instrument.

In Messing v. Bank of America,[2] a presenter sued a payor bank for conversion when the bank refused to pay unless the presenter placed his thumbprint on the check. Although the teller had printed the time, date, amount, account number and teller number on the check, the presenter had indorsed the check, and the teller had requested the presenter to put his thumbprint on the check, the bank had not accepted the check. The court held that although a bank must receive presentment of a check for payment, it is under no obligation to accept or pay the check and it could not be liable for conversion of the cash proceeds of a check it never accepted.

Accordingly, a payee may wish assurance that the drawee will carry out the drawer's order. In particular, the payee or other holder may demand that the drawee "accept" the draft and thus become liable upon the instrument. "Acceptance" is defined in section 3–409 to mean "the drawee's signed agreement to pay a draft as presented." A drawee who "accepts" usually does so by signing vertically across the face of the instrument, but since the drawee has no other reason to sign, a signature anywhere else on the instrument, even on the back, is sufficient to show acceptance.[3] Drafters of acceptances should look at 3–413(b). By authorizing an

---

2. 373 Md. 672, 821 A.2d 22, 50 UCC2d 1 (App. 2003).

3. Comment 2 to § 3–409 discusses the formalities required for accepting an instrument.

acceptor to state the amount certified or accepted, the section protects an acceptor from owing a greater amount to a holder in due course. It is most uncommon for a certified check to be raised and then passed to a holder in due course; a bank that processes many acceptances can easily protect itself against this small risk by modifying its procedure to fit within 3–413(b).

When a bank on which a check is drawn accepts the check, the bank is said to certify the check, under 3–409(d). If a draft is accepted by a bank, the drawer is discharged under 3–414(c) and prior indorsers are discharged under 3–415(d).

Under the pre–1990 Code's section 3–411, the drawer and prior indorsers were discharged "where a holder procures certification." Arguably this language meant that if the drawer of a check (who is not the holder because it is typically not payable to the drawer's order) procured a certification, the drawer was not discharged. The Code drafters eliminated the distinction with the following language in 3–414(c): "If a draft is accepted by a bank, the drawer is discharged, regardless of when or by whom acceptance was obtained."

Under section 3–414(d), acceptance of a draft by a non-bank does not discharge the drawer, but in effect turns the drawer into an indorser:[4]

> (d) If a draft is accepted and the acceptor is not a bank, the obligation of the drawer to pay the draft if the draft is dishonored by the acceptor is the same as the obligation of an indorser under Section 3–415(a) and (c).

c. Indorsers

"Indorsement" is a formal act that has several distinct purposes. The definition acknowledges that the act of indorsement and accompanying symbols may fulfill three functions. First, indorsement and accompanying symbols are the means—by far the best means with respect to an order instrument—for transferring title, i.e., of negotiating the instrument. Second, they comprise the stereotypical way of incurring a guarantor's liability on the instrument. Third, they are a way of protecting against conflicting claims downstream by "restricting payment of the instrument." Thus, the indorsement "for deposit only" is not merely to pass title or to incur a guarantor's liability, it is to prevent the local liquor store who takes a stolen check from later claiming that it is a holder in due course.

These functions are described in the definition of indorsement:

> (a) "Indorsement" means a signature, other than that of a signer as maker, drawer, or acceptor, that alone or accompa-

---

4. This process is sometimes called certification.

nied by other words is made on an instrument for the purpose of (i) negotiating the instrument, (ii) restricting payment of the instrument, or (iii) incurring indorser's liability on the instrument, but regardless of the intent of the signer, a signature and its accompanying words is an indorsement unless the accompanying words, terms of the instrument, place of the signature, or other circumstances unambiguously indicate that the signature was made for a purpose other than indorsement. For the purpose of determining whether a signature is made on an instrument, a paper affixed to the instrument is a part of the instrument.

Section 3–204(a) tells us that every signature that does not "unambiguously" fit in some other cubbyhole is an indorsement. This is true irrespective of the "place of the signature." Thus, an indorsement need not be in its usual place on the back of the instrument.

All indorsements fall into two broad categories, special and blank. A special indorsement ("pay to the order of Joe Jones, /s/ John Peterson") makes the instrument into an "order instrument" if it is not already one. A blank indorsement on the other hand (/s/ "John Peterson") makes an instrument into a "bearer instrument." Thus, section 3–205 provides:

(a) If an indorsement is made by the holder of an instrument, whether payable to an identified person or payable to bearer, and the indorsement identifies a person to whom it makes the instrument payable, it is a "special indorsement." When specially indorsed, an instrument becomes payable to the identified person and may be negotiated only by the indorsement of that person. The principles stated in Section 3–110 apply to special indorsements.

(b) If an indorsement is made by the holder of an instrument and it is not a special indorsement, it is a "blank indorsement." When indorsed in blank, an instrument becomes payable to bearer and may be negotiated by transfer of possession alone until specially indorsed.

(c) The holder may convert a blank indorsement that consists only of a signature into a special indorsement by writing, above the signature of the indorser, words identifying the person to whom the instrument is made payable.

(d) "Anomalous indorsement" means an indorsement made by a person who is not the holder of the instrument. An anomalous indorsement does not affect the manner in which the instrument may be negotiated.

The recipient of a bearer instrument may convert it into an order instrument by specially indorsing. Similarly, under 3–205(b) the holder of an order instrument may transform it into a bearer instrument by indorsing it in blank. For example, an instrument that recites "Pay to the order of John Jones" becomes a bearer instrument when John signs the back "John Jones." Note that a thief's signature in the name of the true owner does not constitute a blank indorsement under 3–205 (because the thief is not a holder) and therefore does not convert order paper into bearer paper.

PROBLEM

An important but not obvious role of an indorsement is to change the status of negotiable paper from "bearer paper" to "order paper" and vice versa. Since the rights of a good faith taker of stolen order paper are different from those of a good faith taker of stolen bearer paper, the distinction is important for the understanding of the rules on stolen instruments discussed in Chapter 3.

1. Kristen receives a check for $4300 payable to her order. Intending to deposit the check she signs her name on the reverse. Later that day the check is stolen and ultimately deposited in a bank and paid by the payor bank. Kristen's signature was an indorsement "in blank," 3–205, and it turned the check into a "bearer" instrument. Since anyone in possession of bearer paper is a holder, 1–201(b)(21), and since a holder's transfer to a person who takes in good faith and value makes that taker a holder in due course, the depositary bank gets to keep the funds, and Kristen goes hungry.

2. Kristen receives a check payable to the order of "cash." This is a bearer instrument, 3–109(a). Kristen signs the check on the back, "pay to the order of First Bank, Kristen." She has now turned the check into an order instrument by her "special indorsement," 3–205. When this check is stolen and transferred to a good faith holder, we will see in Chapter 3 that Kristen's rights will not be defeated and she will be able to recover from downstream takers even if they acted in good faith and gave value.

3. In case 1 what if the thief forged Kristen's indorsement and a later good faith taker then argued that he (the later taker) was an HIDC? The later taker is not a "holder" and therefore not an HIDC because of the first sentence in 3–201(b). Read it carefully; the thief was not himself a holder because the order paper was not to his order. His attempt at a blank indorsement was not sufficient to make his good faith taker into a holder because it was not "an indorsement by the **holder**" as required by 3–201. In effect 3–201 immunizes order paper

> from ever becoming bearer paper by the act not only of the thief but of every subsequent taker.

d. Indorser's Contract

Section 3–415 deals with the contract obligation of the indorser.[5] The indorser's obligation is discharged if any notice of dishonor required by 3–503 is not timely given. One can readily grasp the policy reasons underlying the Code provisions that require notice of dishonor before an indorser is held liable while extending no comparable favor to the drawer. Consider, for example, the position of the drawer who has received goods, services, or cash in return for his promise to pay embodied in his check. After the check's transfer and before it is paid, the drawer is in a net positive position: he has received goods but he has not yet advanced cash from his account. Failure of the payee to make timely presentment injures the drawer only if in the interim the drawee has become insolvent and funds on deposit are lost before they could be applied against the instrument. There, the drawer is and ought to be discharged, but if he is discharged in other cases he may get a windfall; that is, he will get goods or services for which he pays nothing.

On the other hand, the ordinary indorser is one who gave up money, goods, or services when he received the instrument. Of course, he received an equivalent amount when he transferred the check, but that leaves him in a net zero position with respect to the transaction. If he is excused by the holder's delay (or other noncompliance), he does not receive a windfall. Accordingly, the Code requires the holder to act promptly if he hopes to hold the indorser liable.

---

5. § 3–415. Obligation of Indorser.

(a) Subject to subsections (b), (c), (d), (e) and to Section 3–419(d), if an instrument is dishonored, an indorser is obliged to pay the amount due on the instrument (i) according to the terms of the instrument at the time it was indorsed, or (ii) if the indorser indorsed an incomplete instrument, according to its terms when completed, to the extent stated in Sections 3–115 and 3–407. The obligation of the indorser is owed to a person entitled to enforce the instrument or to a subsequent indorser who paid the instrument under this section.

(b) If an indorsement states that it is made "without recourse" or otherwise disclaims liability of the indorser, the indorser is not liable under subsection (a) to pay the instrument.

(c) If notice of dishonor of an instrument is required by Section 3–503 and notice of dishonor complying with that section is not given to an indorser, the liability of the indorser under subsection (a) is discharged.

(d) If a draft is accepted by a bank after an indorsement is made, the liability of the indorser under subsection (a) is discharged.

(e) If an indorser of a check is liable under subsection (a) and the check is not presented for payment, or given to a depositary bank for collection, within 30 days after the day the indorsement was made, the liability of the indorser under subsection (a) is discharged.

Section 3–503(c) gives a non-bank party 30 days after dishonor to give notice to an indorser. Section 3–503(c) requires banks to give notice of dishonor "before midnight of the next banking day following the banking day on which the bank receives notice of dishonor of the instrument." Given Regulation CC's stimulus to rapid transfer of the instrument back upstream after dishonor, rarely will an indorser on a dishonored instrument escape because he or she did not receive timely notice from the payor or an intermediary bank.

Because section 3–605 discharges not only an accommodation party, but also an "indorser," whatever that party's other status, it will sometimes be important for a party to establish status as an indorser entitled to a discharge under 3–605. That party can turn to section 3–204 for help.

§ 1–7 Restrictive and Qualified Indorsements

The clever indorser can subscribe his or her name under a variety of magic phrases. The Code specifies the legal effect of some of these phrases. Qualified indorsements ("without recourse") limit the liability of the indorser if the instrument is dishonored. Restrictive indorsements such as "for deposit only," "pay any bank," and the like set the terms for further negotiation of the instrument. Their main purpose is to prevent thieves and embezzlers from cashing checks. Some phrases may constitute offers or terms of underlying agreements between the parties (for instance, "in full satisfaction of all claims"). Some are only friendly messages ("kiss my foot"), and more than a few have clouded legal effect.

If an indorser adds the words "without recourse" to his or her indorsement and so makes a "qualified" indorsement, the indorser does not assume the full obligations under 3–415(a), as spelled out in subsection (b). That is, the indorser transfers title to the instrument, but does not promise to pay should the instrument be dishonored upon presentation.

To keep restrictive indorsements from clogging the flow of checks through the banking system, section 3–206 limits the effect of restrictive indorsements in several ways. An indorsement that seeks to limit payment to a particular person, such as "pay to John only," or otherwise to prohibit further transfer or negotiation, is ineffective under section 3–206(a).

Although an indorsement claiming to prohibit further transfer is ineffective, the power of the "for deposit" or "for collection" restrictions are substantial and clear. Clarity in the law is, of course, no guarantee. Clarity of expression is equally important when it comes to a restrictive indorsement. In Franzese v. Fidelity

New York FSB,[1] writing an account number following a signature was not a restrictive indorsement. But woe to the person who takes an instrument that is part of a theft or fraud scheme over an indorsement that should have provided notice of the misbehavior. Section 3–206(c) provides:

> (c) If an instrument bears an indorsement (i) described in Section 4–201(b), or (ii) in blank or to a particular bank using the words "for deposit," "for collection," or other words indicating a purpose of having the instrument collected by a bank for the indorser or for a particular account, the following rules apply:

> (1) A person, other than a bank, who purchases the instrument when so indorsed converts the instrument unless the amount paid for the instrument is received by the indorser or applied consistently with the indorsement.

> (2) A depositary bank that purchases the instrument or takes it for collection when so indorsed converts the instrument unless the amount paid by the bank with respect to the instrument is received by the indorser or applied consistently with the indorsement.

> (3) A payor bank that is also the depositary bank or that takes the instrument for immediate payment over the counter from a person other than a collecting bank converts the instrument unless the proceeds of the instrument are received by the indorser or applied consistently with the indorsement.

> (4) Except as otherwise provided in paragraph (3), a payor bank or intermediary bank may disregard the indorsement and is not liable if the proceeds of the instrument are not received by the indorser or applied consistently with the indorsement.

Observe that subsection (c)(1) makes a non-bank who buys an instrument bearing a "for deposit" indorsement into a converter unless that person pays the real owner or applies the money consistently with the instrument. Similarly subsection (c)(2) forces the depositary bank (but not other banks, see (c)(4)) to pay careful attention to such indorsements and normally, therefore, to deposit the money into the account of the indorser. Subsection (c)(3) makes the bank who is "payor and depositary bank" into a converter if it does not behave. Subsection (c)(4), as we have indicated, permits payors (other than depositary payors) and intermediary banks to disregard the indorsement.

§ 1–7

1.   214 A.D.2d 646, 625 N.Y.S.2d 275, 28 UCC2d 584 (N.Y.A.D. 1995).

To summarize, the consequence of placing a restrictive indorsement on an instrument is to prevent the depositary bank and any nonbank takers from becoming holders in due course if they fail to respect the restriction. Since these parties lack good title, they are personally liable in conversion to the owner, usually the payee who restrictively indorsed.

For example, assume that Tom Swift, Inc. (T.S.I.) receives a $150,000 check. T.S.I.'s treasurer indorses the check with the inscription "for deposit only, T.S.I." and mails the check to its bank. However, the postman steals the check, adds his name below T.S.I.'s indorsement and deposits the check in his account at First National Bank. First National forwards the check to Second National who transfers it to the payor bank, Third National, where the check is finally paid. What right of recovery does T.S.I. have against the various banks? Second National is an intermediary bank,[2] and under 3–206(c)(4), has no obligation to respect a restrictive indorsement. Third National, the payor bank, also faces no liability under 3–206(c)(4) and need only concern itself with indorsements placed on the check by Second National. It is equally clear under pre-Code law and 3–206(c)(2) that T.S.I. has a cause of action in conversion against First National, the depositary bank. The only proper indorsement immediately following an indorsement "for deposit" should be that of a bank.

When an item[3] has been indorsed "pay any bank," then only a bank can become a holder of it.[4] A "pay any bank" indorsement makes the bank an agent of the indorser; the latter does not give up his ownership rights.

A step beyond "for deposit" restrictions leads to confusion. What does section 3–206(b) mean? It reads:

> (b) An indorsement stating a condition of the right of the indorsee to receive payment does not affect the right of the indorsee to enforce the instrument.

2. § 4–105(4) defines "intermediary bank" as a bank "to which an item is transferred in course of collection except the depositary or payor bank[.]"

3. An item is not necessarily a negotiable instrument. § 4–104(a)(9) defines an "item" as "an instrument or a promise or order to pay money handled by a bank for collection or payment. The term does not include a payment order governed by Article 4A or a credit or debit card slip[.]"

4. § 4–201(b) states:

After an item has been indorsed with the words "pay any bank" or the like, only a bank may acquire the rights of a holder until the item has been:

> (1) returned to the customer initiating collection; or

> (2) specially indorsed by a bank to a person who is not a bank.

When a bank does specially indorse the item to a nonbank party, according to Comment 7 to § 4–201, "the bank would be liable to the owner of the item for any loss resulting therefrom if the transfer had been made in bad faith or with lack of ordinary care."

Assume, for example, that Jane, the payee of a check, indorses the check "pay to the order of John provided John repairs my car's generator." Assume further that there is no other express contract. John fails to repair, Jane causes the drawer to stop payment, and John sues Jane. Does section 3–206(b) mean that Jane cannot raise the defense that John failed to perform his end of the contract? One might reach that conclusion from the unadorned language of section 3–206(b), but common sense and the comments indicate otherwise. The next to the last sentence in Comment 2 to 3–206(b) states that: " * * * Section 3–206(b) * * * makes the conditional indorsement ineffective with respect to parties *other than the indorser and indorsee*" (emphasis added). We read this to mean that failure of the condition could be asserted by Jane as a defense to the suit on the indorsement contract by John even though it would not be a defense to any other party's right to sue, and even though any other party could safely take the check from John without inquiry about whether he had fixed the generator. This, of course, facilitates negotiability.

Note that the comment says the condition is "ineffective with respect to parties other than the indorser and indorsee"—that is, with respect to both of them. The underlying policy is apparently that the indorsee should not be able to circumvent a condition he or she accepted in a contract, at least in dealings with the indorser who was the other party to the contract. Thus, the comment points out that a person in the position of Jane would be able to assert the defense of a broken contract, regardless of whether the condition was expressed in her indorsement.[5] Outside the immediate confines of the contract between John and Jane, however, the conditional indorsement might as well be written in invisible ink.

Let us imagine two possibilities. First, say John waited 100 days after receiving the check and then transferred it to his friend Fred in exchange for several cases of beer. Fred would not be a holder in due course—the instrument would be overdue. The terms of 3–206(b) do not require, however, that the person taking the instrument be a holder in due course, only that the person take the instrument "for value or collection." Thus, Fred would be able to enforce the instrument against Jane, regardless of the apparent infirmities.

Second, say John decides to side-step Jane, who was the payee, and instead sue the drawer. Once again, under 3–206(b), the

---

5.   Comment 2 to 3–206 says in part:

If the check was negotiated by the payee to A in return for a promise to perform a contract and the promise was not kept, the payee would have a defense or counterclaim against A if the check were dishonored and A sued the payee as indorser, but the payee would have that defense or counterclaim whether or not the condition to the right of A was expressed in the indorsement.

conditional indorsement by Jane would be ineffective in preventing enforcement of the instrument.

In practical terms, the hypothetical dispute between John and Jane is likely to unfold as follows: John will deposit his third-party check in his bank, the bank will pay John, as it should, and the bank will debit the drawer's account. Jane, aggrieved that her generator is still broken, may try to persuade the drawer to stop payment on the check, but such a move would not withstand legal challenge from John. Instead, Jane should sue John on the contract.

All this raises a perplexing policy question: Why should John have greater rights against the drawer of the check than against the indorser with whom he dealt? We see no clear answer. Of course, after the drawer paid John, and Jane sued John on the contract, the money would ultimately be distributed properly. This resolution, however, would hardly be efficient.

Subsection 3–206(d) walks the narrow line between protecting the beneficiaries of a trust from fraud by their trustee while at the same time allowing an honest trustee or agent the flexibility required to do business. It reads as follows:

(d) Except for an indorsement covered by subsection (c), if an instrument bears an indorsement using words to the effect that payment is to be made to the indorsee as agent, trustee, or other fiduciary for the benefit of the indorser or another person, the following rules apply:

(1) Unless there is notice of breach of fiduciary duty as provided in Section 3–307, a person who purchases the instrument from the indorsee or takes the instrument from the indorsee for collection or payment may pay the proceeds of payment or the value given for the instrument to the indorsee without regard to whether the indorsee violates a fiduciary duty to the indorser.

(2) A subsequent transferee of the instrument or person who pays the instrument is neither given notice nor otherwise affected by the restriction in the indorsement unless the transferee or payor knows that the fiduciary dealt with the instrument or its proceeds in breach of fiduciary duty.[6]

Subsection (d)(2) protects subsequent transferees and (d)(1) protects those who were not given notice under the terms of revised 3–307. In effect (d)(1) says that one who pays an instrument over the indorsement of the trustee has no liability even though the trustee is stealing the money, unless the beneficiary can somehow

---

6. In Chapter 4 we deal with § 3–307 in so far as it deals with notice of breach of fiduciary duty.

show that the one making payment is on notice under, or otherwise violates, 3–307. Comment 4 explains the operation of subsection (d) as follows:

> Subsection (d) replaces subsection (4) of former Section 3–206. Suppose Payee indorses a check "Pay to T in trust for B." T indorses in blank and delivers it to (a) Holder for value; (b) Depositary Bank for collection; or (c) Payor Bank for payment. In each case these takers can safely pay T so long as they have no notice under Section 3–307 of any breach of fiduciary duty that T may be committing. For example, under subsection (b) of Section 3–307 these takers have notice of a breach of trust if the check was taken in any transaction known by the taker to be for T's personal benefit. Subsequent transferees of the check from Holder or Depositary Bank are not affected by the restriction unless they have knowledge that T dealt with the check in breach of trust.

What is the bank to do when a father appears at the teller's window with a $30,000 check that is payable or indorsed to his order as trustee for his daughter, Melissa? Clearly he is authorized to indorse the check. It is equally obvious that he would be permitted to deposit it in an account titled "Jones as Trustee for Daughter." But what if he wishes to cash the check and take the cash away from the teller window or to deposit it in his personal account? In both of those cases, one can expect the bank to argue that it has no knowledge that such a transaction is "for his own benefit" and that the Code permits it to presume that he will do what he is supposed to with the money that he has procured. Conversely, a subsequent guardian for little Melissa will point out that the bank had knowledge of the trust arrangement. The new guardian will also point out that, if the trustee deposited the check in his personal account, the bank actually had knowledge of the payees to whom funds were paid out of that account, and that this information suggested that the money was not being used for Melissa.

Courts have faced disputes over such questions, and they are instructive even though the decisions were issued under the old Code. Two courts came to different conclusions on slightly different facts. In Smith v. Olympic Bank,[7] the Washington Supreme Court held that a bank that allowed the father to deposit the money in his personal account and then to draw it out for his personal use was not a holder in due course and was liable to the beneficiary for the full amount. The court noted that because the father had failed to deposit the funds in a trust account, the beneficiary lost certain legal protections as to this money ($30,588.39) that such an account

---

7.   103 Wash.2d 418, 693 P.2d 92, 40 UCC 519 (1985).

would have provided. The father could not have paid off a personal unsecured loan to the bank for $3,000, the father's new wife could not have written checks against the funds without court approval, and the bank could not have exercised a setoff of $12,500. Because the bank had notice that the father had breached his fiduciary duty, the bank could not be a holder in due course of the check. Perhaps the court was influenced by the fact that the bank accepted more than half of the proceeds of the check for what it knew were the personal obligations of the father.

In a similar case, In re Knox,[8] the New York Court of Appeals found that a bank was not liable in circumstances in which the trustee cashed a check for approximately $15,000 at one branch of the defendant's bank and then deposited the cash in a personal account at another branch. The court pointed out that there was nothing in the nature of the transactions to alert the bank that the trustee was misappropriating the funds, and also that the funds were used for family purposes although not exclusively for the use of the beneficiary child. Relying upon prior New York cases and upon the Code sections cited above, the court concluded that the bank had no liability: "[i]n general, a bank may assume that a person acting as a fiduciary will apply entrusted funds for the proper purposes and will adhere to the conditions of the appointment * * *."

Perhaps the two cases can be distinguished based on the knowledge of the two banks. In the former, there was a direct deposit of the check payable to the trustee into his personal account; in the latter, there was merely a cashing of the check. The proceeds were then deposited in another branch and presumably the personnel at the second branch had no knowledge of the origin of the funds.

We believe the New York case was correctly decided under the old Code, and that the post–1990 Code's section 3–307 would produce the same result. We would not prohibit a trustee from taking cash and, if the trustee deposited it in a trust account, we would argue that a bank has no responsibility to monitor checks drawn on the account to determine whether or not the trustee was violating his or her fiduciary duty. Surely it is undesirable in effect to make the bank a trustee for every amount put in a deposit account and to require the bank to undertake responsibilities of inquiry for every single transaction. Such costs would be borne by the beneficiary and might well overstate and outweigh the risks under a more lenient policy.

Today, section 3–206(d) says the bank is not liable unless it has notice of a breach of fiduciary duty under 3–307. Section 3–307

8. 64 N.Y.2d 434, 488 N.Y.S.2d 146, 477 N.E.2d 448, 40 UCC 927 (1985).

holds the bank liable only if the trustee uses the instrument to pay a debt the bank knows is personal, uses it for personal benefit with the bank's knowledge, or deposits the instrument in a non-trust account. The trustee in the New York case performed none of these forbidden moves by cashing the check and later depositing cash.

We are less certain about the correctness of the Washington case, but 1990 section 3–307 apparently dictates the same conclusion as was reached by the court. Perhaps as an empirical matter the bank is put more clearly on notice of a trustee's violation of his or her obligation when the trustee deposits the funds in a personal account than when the trustee receives them in cash. But we are uncertain of that. To the extent that the case supports an inference that the bank has a responsibility to trace the funds after they have been deposited in a personal account, we are doubtful. Despite our misgivings, however, 3–307(b)(2) says a bank has notice of breach of fiduciary duty if a trustee deposits an instrument payable to the beneficiary or to the trustee as such in "an account other than an account of the fiduciary, as such, or an account of the represented person."

Although certain indorsements may now be made by nonholders under 3–204(a), it is doubtful that 3–204 would recognize the inscription by a drawer or a stranger as a restrictive indorsement.[9] This means that it is not possible to give someone a check and force that person, by means of a "for deposit only" indorsement (already on the check) to deposit the check. Another fruitless strategy is to require the payee of a check to promise to indorse it "for deposit only" to insure that the payee will deposit the check instead of cashing it. Although it might be a breach of contract with a third party, the holder is free to modify his or her indorsement. In Handley v. Horak,[10] the payee of a check indorsed it "for deposit only" at the request of another party; later, the payee crossed out the indorsement and cashed the check. The bank was not liable for paying the check.

§ 1–8   Presentment, Notice of Dishonor, and Protest

Article 3, Part 5 defines "dishonor," "presentment," and related terms, specifies when presentment is necessary, and tells when one must give notice of dishonor—all in boring and incessant detail. At the risk of oversimplifying, but in the interest of lightening the reader's load, we will outline the pertinent provisions. Section 3–502 tells us that an instrument is dishonored when the holder makes presentment and payment is refused on the day of presentment of a note payable on demand or a note that has become

9. See § 3–204(a).

10. 370 N.Y.S.2d 313, 82 Misc.2d 692, 17 UCC 483 (1975).

payable. Presentment and dishonor occur, for instance, when the holder of a check attempts to cash it at the drawee bank, but payment is refused because the drawer lacks sufficient funds on deposit. The demand for payment is presentment. The bank's refusal to pay is dishonor. The pre–1990 Code's section 3–503 required presentment within a reasonable time, depending on the type of instrument. The post–1990 Code omits that language, but contains a new section, 3–118, laying out the statute of limitations for enforcing various obligations. We discuss 3–118 below.

Section 3–501(b)(1) specifies how a holder may make presentment; it embraces "any commercially reasonable means, including an oral, written or electronic communication." (We are doubtful that an "oral communication" would be a "commercially reasonable" presentment absent an explicit agreement to permit it.) The presentment is effective when the demand for payment or acceptance is received. The person to whom presentment is made may demand that the instrument be exhibited, under 3–501(b)(2). Section 4–108 permits the payor to set a cut off hour after 2 p.m. for receipt of items and to treat those items received after that time as having been received on the next banking day.

The obligation of an indorser to pay an instrument kicks in only after the instrument has been dishonored and the indorser has been given notice of that fact under 3–503. There are exceptions in 3–504(b) where the instrument specifies that notice is not necessary or there has been a waiver of notice. As with presentment, notice of dishonor can be by "any commercially reasonable means," according to 3–503. A person seeking to enforce an instrument against a maker must also give notice, but only in the narrow circumstance of a dishonored "draft accepted by an acceptor other than a bank," as described in Comment 1 to 3–503, which says:

> There is no reason why drawers should be discharged on instruments they draw until payment or acceptance. They are entitled to have the instrument presented to the drawee and dishonored (Section 3–414(b)) before they are liable to pay, but no notice of dishonor need be made to them as a condition of liability.

The rationale behind the exception is explained in Comment 4 to 3–414. Once a draft is accepted by a drawee other than a bank, the drawee, as acceptor, becomes primarily liable and "the drawer's liability is that of a person secondarily liable as a guarantor of payment." In this case, the drawer's liability is identical to that of an indorser. (Of course, if a bank accepts an instrument, the drawer is discharged under section 3–414(c).)

The fact that an instrument has been dishonored can be formally stated in a protest, which is, according to 3–505(b), a certificate of dishonor made by a United States consul or vice consul, or a notary public or other person authorized to administer oaths by the law of the place where dishonor occurs. Protests were once required in certain situations, under the pre–1990 Code's section 3–501, but the reference to necessary protests is gone from the post–1990 Code. The Comment to 3–505 explains the drafters' thinking:

> Protest is no longer mandatory and must be requested by the holder. Even if requested, protest is not a condition to liability of indorsers or drawers. Protest is a service provided by the banking system to establish that dishonor has occurred. Like other services provided by the banking system, it will be available if market incentives, inter-bank agreements, or governmental regulations require it, but liabilities of parties no longer rest on it. * * *

The Comment goes on to note, however, that a protest may still be required for liability on international drafts governed by foreign law.

§ 1–9   Excuse: Section 3–504

A lawyer representing a client who has missed a step in the ritual of presentment and dishonor should not panic until he or she has consulted section 3–504–a restatement of the pre–1990 Code's section 3–511. In many circumstances, section 3–504 forgives the holder for delay or failure in complying with the requirements of Part 5, Article 3.

In particular, 3–504(a) excuses lapses in presentment where the person "cannot with reasonable diligence make presentment," where the maker or acceptor has repudiated his obligation to pay or is dead or insolvent, where the instrument specifies that presentment is not necessary, where the drawer or indorser has waived presentment "or otherwise has no reason to expect or right to require that the instrument be paid or accepted," or where "the drawer instructed the drawee not to pay or accept the draft or the drawee was not obligated to the drawer to pay the draft."

The simplest case is one in which the indorser has expressly waived the right to have the instrument presented or to receive notice of dishonor. If the indorser has waived presentment or notice of dishonor, there will be no basis for the indorser to complain if there is some defect in the holder's performance of these duties. An express waiver may take a number of forms and appear on the body of the instrument as well as on the back. Many standard form printed notes contain waivers of notice and the like. Note that 3–504(b) provides that a waiver of presentment is also a waiver of notice of dishonor. Similarly, under the old Code, a waiver of protest was also a waiver of presentment and notice of dishonor, even if a protest was not required. An indorser can waive dishonor and notice by implication as well as by express language. Thus in Wiener v. Van Winkle,[1] defendant indorsers were found liable despite plaintiff's failure to make presentment because the indorsers waived presentment when they requested an extension of time for payment.

When an indorser has played an active role in causing an instrument to be dishonored, there is little reason to force the holder to go through the formality of presentment and dishonor. Presentment is excused under 3–504 when the maker or acceptor has repudiated an obligation to pay ((a)(ii)), when the drawer or indorser has waived presentment "or otherwise has no reason to expect or right to require that the instrument be paid or accepted" ((a)(iv)), and when the drawer instructs the drawee not to pay or accept the draft.

A problem arises when the indorser played no active role, but had access to facts from which he or she could infer that the instrument would not be paid. For instance, does the indorser's knowledge of the maker's insolvency excuse presentment and notice of dishonor? Both pre-Code cases and cases decided under the Code hold that mere knowledge of insolvency does not excuse presentment and notice of dishonor. For example, in Makel Textiles, Inc. v. Dolly Originals, Inc.,[2] the payee of a corporate promissory note sought payment from the corporation's president and another person, both of whom had signed as individual indorsers. The defendants maintained that they were not liable because plaintiff had not made presentment or given notice of dishonor. The New York Court responded to the corporation president's argument:

> By virtue of his active participation in the affairs of Dolly Originals, Inc., it was obvious that the defendant Nathan Goldberg well knew that the notes could not be and were not paid from corporate funds. Under these circumstances the obligation to serve Goldberg with notice of dishonor and nonpayment must be deemed unnecessary, at least impliedly, within the meaning of the Uniform Commercial Code. Plaintiff's failure to present the notes for payment and give the said defendant notice of nonpayment could not and did not injure nor prejudice his rights in any way. Formal notice of presentment and dishonor to Mr. Goldberg would be merely a useless gesture of advising him of a fact with which he was most

§ 1–9

1. 273 Cal.App.2d 774, 78 Cal.Rptr. 761, 6 UCC 819 (1969).

2. 1967 WL 8938, 4 UCC 95 (N.Y.Sup. 1967).

familiar [citing the pre–1990 Code's sections 3–511 and 3–507 and several pre-Code cases].[3]

The other indorser, however, convinced the court that presentment and notice of dishonor were required to hold him liable. The court said:

> As to said defendant Kushner, the record is void of any testimony, or proof of notice of presentment and dishonor as required under the Uniform Commercial Code. Nor is there any evidence of any activity or participation in the affairs of the corporation so as to excuse presentment or notice of dishonor.[4]

The court dismissed the suit against the indorser who did not participate in the corporate affairs and held the corporate president liable.

Under pre-Code law, a party's insolvency or bankruptcy did not excuse presentment and notice of dishonor, but the UCC has changed that rule. In the Code's current form, section 3–504 includes insolvency among the excuses for failure to make presentment. Note however that insolvency does not excuse a failure to give notice of dishonor. (Under section 3–502(e), it is possible to have dishonor without presentment. That subsection provides that, if presentment is excused under 3–504, then "dishonor occurs without presentment if the instrument is not duly accepted or paid.") Unless the indorser comes under the "or otherwise having no reason to expect" language of 3–504(a), the holder must meet the notice requirements in order to hold the indorser liable. This is understandable, for even if the party primarily liable is insolvent, it is not certain that he will lack sufficient assets to pay the instrument. Moreover, undue delay may make it impossible for the indorser to recover from the insolvent person or other prior parties.

As mentioned above, a person seeking to enforce an instrument need not give notice of dishonor, under 3–504(b), if the instrument specifies that notice is not required or if the party whose obligation is being enforced has waived notice.

The Code excuses a party who was unable to make presentment after exercising "reasonable diligence." The Code does not elaborate, but the comment to 3–504 notes that the section is "largely a restatement" of the former section 3–511. Comment 5 to that provision of the old Code explained the section as follows:

> The excuse is established only by proof that reasonable diligence has been exercised without success, *or that reasonable*

---

3. *Id.* at 97.   **4.** *Id.*

diligence would in any case have been unsuccessful (emphasis added).

The emphasized language of the comment considerably expanded the scope of the subsection, and the post–1990 Code has not repudiated this interpretation. The New York Law Revision Commission expressed approval of the broader version indicated by the comment, but we have found no cases on point.

Where an item is dishonored because of a failure to make timely acceptance, section 3–502(f) sometimes provides an excuse:

> If a draft is dishonored because timely acceptance of the draft was not made and the person entitled to demand acceptance consents to a late acceptance, from the time of acceptance, the draft is treated as never having been dishonored.

PROBLEM

Here consider the contracts (or some might say the statutory liability) of five persons: drawers of drafts, makers of notes, indorsers, payors of drafts and acceptors of drafts. A check is a draft payable on demand and drawn on a bank; here we consider only those drafts.

1. Eliot draws a check to the order of Emperor's. When it is presented, the check bounces. Of course Eliot would have liability as a drawer whose check had been presented to the drawee (payor), but assume that Eliot cannot be found or has no money. So Emperor's sues the payor, Chase. Emperor's does not recover, 3–408. Even though Chase has a contract with its depositor, Eliot, Emperor's is not a third party beneficiary of that contract and as 3–408 states, the check does not operate as an assignment of any of the funds that Eliot has on deposit.

2. What if Emperor's held the check for several months before it presented the check to Chase? Not to worry; unless Chase failed in the interim (see 3–413(f)), a delay short of three years (or more likely here, 10 years) is irrelevant, 3–118.

3. The result would be different if Emperor's had passed Eliot's check to its customer who had held it for three months and then sought to recover, not from Eliot, but from Emperor's on Emperor's indorsement contract. Under 3–415 Emperor's is discharged by the delay.

    Why the indorser but not the drawer? Because the indorser is really only a backup, a guarantor of the drawer's promise. By hypothesis Eliot has received the services that the check represents and will be enriched if there is no payment, but that is not true of Emperor's who has performed the services and has not been paid. Note the similar distinction between the greater liability of the drawer and the lesser liability of the indorser recognized by the rules in 3–503 on Notice of Dishonor.

4. Eliot draws a check for $4430 and takes it to Chase for "certification." Chase signs across the front of the check and has so "accepted." Now Chase has an "acceptor's" liability and is obliged to pay the check, 3–409; it is no longer a mere bystander-payor. According to 3–103 acceptors are a subclass of drawees of drafts. The certified check will act much like a cashier's check, and when the drawee signs, it will set aside funds from Eliot's account to insure that it has sufficient funds if it is called on to pay on its acceptance.

5. Finally, Eliot goes to Chase to procure a "cashier's" check payable to Emperor's for $4300. Cashier's checks are treated by laymen like money and the bank's liability is like the liability of anyone on a note, 3–412. It is an unconditional obligation—no need to present or to let time pass—and is payable on presentation without more.

But assume that Chase refuses to pay when the check is presented. Now this does not look quite like "money" to the layman. So Emperor's gets interest and perhaps even consequential damages, 3–411.

§ 1–10 Liability of Accommodation Parties

One with money to lend, goods to sell or services to render may have doubts about a prospective debtor's ability to pay. In such cases the creditor is likely to demand more assurance than the debtor's bare promise of payment. The prospective creditor can reduce its risk by requiring some sort of security. One form of security is the Article 9 security interest in the debtor's goods; another takes the form of joining a third person on the debtor's obligation. A third party who thus takes on an obligation to answer for the debt or default of the debtor is called a surety.

Suretyship is a three party relationship involving the creditor, the principal debtor and the surety.[1] The debtor's obligation as a purchaser of goods or borrower of money is already familiar. So, too, is its obligation as a signer of a negotiable instrument. The surety's obligation is somewhat different. In effect the surety

§ 1–10

1. Throughout this discussion we most often use the generic terms (surety, debtor, creditor). Occasionally we use specific Code terminology (e.g., accommodation party, guarantor). Note that § 1–201(40) specifies that " '[s]urety' in-

cludes guarantor." See Peters, Suretyship Under Article 3 of the Uniform Commercial Code, 77 Yale L.J. 833 (1968). For a lengthy discussion of 1990 3–605, see PEB Commentary 11, 16 Feb. 1994.

undertakes to "back up" the performance of the debtor and thereby gives the creditor the added assurance of having another party to the obligation. It is common practice for a surety to appear on a note either as a co-maker or as an indorser.[2] Assume, for example, that a father is going to be the surety on his son's contract to pay for a new car. The father may sign the note as co-maker or he may simply indorse the note. As we will see, in either case the Code calls him an "accommodation party," and he owes the obligation of a maker or an indorser, as the case may be (although he will have certain defenses not normally available to makers or indorsers against all but holders in due course without notice of his accommodation status).

As between the surety and the debtor, it is clear that the debtor has the primary obligation to pay the debt.[3] Since the creditor is entitled to only one performance and the debtor receives the benefit of the transaction, the surety's obligation is undertaken with the expectation that the debtor will meet his commitment to the creditor. Thus, if the surety is made to pay the principal's debt, the surety has the right to recover from the principal. If the creditor releases the principal debtor without insisting on full payment, or if the creditor fails to perfect a security interest in collateral given by the debtor and so is unable to recover his debt out of the collateral, the surety's burden will be increased. The law assumes that the surety has not assented to such increased burdens. Consequently, the law has traditionally held that conduct by the creditor which increases the surety's risk discharges the surety or reduces the surety's obligation pro rata.

In this section we deal with the legal consequences when a surety joins with the debtor on a negotiable instrument.[4] One

---

2. Uniwest Mortgage Co. v. Dadecor Condominiums, Inc., 877 F.2d 431, 9 UCC2d 577 (5th Cir.1989) (mere reference to a guaranty in an instrument is not enough to bring it within Article 3, it must be written on the instrument itself).

3. See Restatement of Security § 82 (1941):

Suretyship is the relation which exists where one person has undertaken an obligation and another person is also under an obligation or other duty to the obligee, who is entitled to but one performance, and as between the two who are bound, one rather than the other should perform.

* * *

Comment f. When the statement is made that the principal should perform,

or that the principal has the principal or primary duty and the surety an accessorial or a secondary duty, it does not mean that the creditor's assertion of his right against the surety must be postponed until some action is taken against the principal. So far as the creditor is concerned, the surety may be the primary obligor. Where principal and surety are bound jointly, from the standpoint of the creditor there is no secondary liability.

4. One of the vexatious problems raised by the Code provisions governing Article 3 suretyship is determining the extent to which the Code incorporates or modifies the pre-existing law of suretyship. The problem principally comes up when the surety wishes to assert a right or defense against the principal debtor or the creditor.

should not be intimidated by the vocabulary of suretyship law. Under the Code the word "surety" includes all "guarantors"[5] and all "accommodation parties." A "guarantor" differs from an "accommodation party" only because the guarantor has added some words to its signature and has so altered (slightly or greatly) the liability it would have had if it had simply put its signature on the instrument as a mine-run accommodation party. The comment to section 3–419 defines an accommodation party as "a person who signs an instrument to benefit the accommodated party either by signing at the time value is obtained by the accommodated party or later, and who is not a direct beneficiary of the value obtained."[6] Consideration does not have to be received by an accommodation party to make the party's obligation enforceable. Section 3–419(b) tells us an accommodation party is "obliged to pay the instrument in the capacity in which the accommodation party signs." Thus an accommodation party may appear on the instrument as a maker, acceptor, drawer or indorser, and its liability is governed by the Code sections on the contracts of parties who sign in these capaci-

The legislative history of 3–415(1), the predecessor of 3–419(a), is not particularly enlightening. § 3–415(1) (1952 Official Draft) originally provided:

An accommodation party is one who signs the instrument in any capacity as surety for another party to it.

Comment 1 to 3–415 (1952 Official Draft) explained:

The word "surety" is intended to incorporate the entire background of the law of suretyship as applied to negotiable instruments.

The section was criticized as confusing and complicated because it introduced the law of suretyship into negotiable instruments. 1 N.Y. State Law Revision Comm'n, 1954 Report 208–209, 428 (1954). Professors Sutherland, Mentschikoff, and Gilmore responded that the section merely codified prior law and that the obligation of an accommodation party could not be understood as other than a suretyship obligation. Id. at 253, 274, 461 (1954); Vol. 2, 1954 Report at 1168 (1954). The original language of the statute and the comment were deleted and the old § 3–415(1) substituted as the result of the debate before the New York Law Revision Commission. Perm. Ed.Bd. for UCC, 1956 Recommendations 113 (1956).

The 2002 amendments generally conform the Code rules to the Restatement of Suretyship and Guaranty.

5. § 1–201(b)(34) provides, " 'Surety' includes a guarantor or other secondary obligor."

6. Sureties who undertake their obligation by executing an instrument to which the debtor is not a party cannot claim the advantages of 3–419. See Bank of America Nat. Trust & Sav. Ass'n v. Superior Court, 4 Cal.App.3d 435, 84 Cal.Rptr. 421, 7 UCC 713 (1970), where plaintiff-bank sought and obtained a writ of mandamus ordering grant of summary judgment against the agent of a corporation who in return for a loan to the corporation gave his own note. Defendant claimed status as an accommodation party and alleged defenses under former § 3–415(3). The appellate court concluded that since the corporation was not a party to the note, defendant was not an accommodation party.

Conversely, guarantees that are not written on the negotiable instrument itself may be governed by Article 3 if they are closely related to an instrument that falls under Article 3. See Cusimano v. First Maryland Sav. and Loan, 639 A.2d 553, 23 UCC2d 14 (D.C. App. 1994) (holding a guarantee and the accompanying documents are subject to Article 3 even where the obligation arises from documents that are not themselves negotiable instruments).

ties.[7] An accommodation maker's basic liability to a holder is identical to that of any other maker, and the rules requiring presentment and notice of dishonor apply to an accommodation indorser in the same manner that they apply to a regular indorser. As we will see, however, surety status of an accommodation party may give that person special defenses unavailable to the general run of parties on instruments.

The legal relations between the surety and the debtor are not complex. Since the surety must pay only if the debtor is unable to do so, it is no surprise that the debtor, having paid, has no right to make the surety share its cost even if both are co-makers on a note. It also follows from the nature of the surety's undertaking that it is entitled to recover from the debtor any payment it is called on to make to the creditor. If a friend agrees to sign another's note and is ultimately made to pay that note to the creditor, curbstone equity tells us that he should have a cause of action against the person who actually benefited from the creditor's loan. The surety has two traditional rights of recovery: subrogation and reimbursement. The surety's right of subrogation is its equitable right to assert the rights of the creditor against the debtor. In common parlance the surety upon payment "stands in the shoes" of the creditor. That is to say, the surety can assert the rights that the creditor had against the debtor. If, for example, a surety co-maker paid a note in full, the surety would be "subrogated" to the holder's right to sue its co-maker (debtor) on the note. The surety's right of "reimbursement" does not, however, depend upon the rights of the creditor; rather it rests upon the debtor's express or implied promise to indemnify the surety or upon grounds of unjust enrichment.[8]

---

7. The 2002 amendments also address the situation of anomalous signatures. New 3–419(e) provides:

If the signature of a party to an instrument is accompanied by words indicating that the party guarantees payment or the signer signs the instrument as an accommodation party in some other manner that does not unambiguously indicate an intention to guarantee collection rather than payment, the signer is obliged to pay the amount due on the instrument to a person entitled to enforce the instrument in the same capacity as the accommodated party would be obliged, without prior resort to the accommodated party by the person entitled to enforce the instrument.

8. See L. Simpson, Handbook on the Law of Suretyship, § 48 (1950).

According to PEB Memorandum 11, the accommodation party's right to recourse may be cut off in some cases where the party accommodated would have had a complete defense:

The juxtaposition of the accommodated party's duty to reimburse the accommodation party (§ 3–419(e)) with the accommodated party's right to raise defenses (§ 3–305(b)) raises important policy issues. If a duty to reimburse exists even when the accommodated party had a defense, that duty could be said to obviate the value of the defense. On the other hand, if no duty to reimburse exists in such circumstances, the cost of performance will be borne ultimately by the accommodation party rather than the accommodated party.

There are a number of different contexts in which the situation may arise. Generally speaking, the accommodation party may raise as a defense to its obligation the defense of the accommodated party to its obligation. See § 3–305(d).

Section 3–419(e)[9] recognizes the surety's rights of subrogation and reimbursement as follows:

> An accommodation party who pays the instrument is entitled to reimbursement from the accommodated party and is entitled to enforce the instrument against the accommodated party. An accommodated party who pays the instrument has no right of recourse against, and is not entitled to contribution from, an accommodation party.

Under general suretyship law imported by 1–103, the surety may have the creditor's rights not only on the instrument, but also on the underlying obligation. Comment 5 to 3–419 notes the surety's right to the creditor's collateral.

To this point we have considered only the rights of the surety against the principal after the surety has paid the principal's debt. Occasionally it will be important that the principal debtor have no claim against the surety when the tables are turned and the debtor has paid. Section 3–419(e) puts it as follows: "An accommodated party who pays the instrument has no right of recourse against, and is not entitled to contribution from, an accommodation party." Indeed, a surety has no such liability even though it signs in the capacity which would apparently make it liable to the principal debtor. For example, in Gibbs Oil Co. v. Collentro & Collentro, Inc.,[10] the payee of a promissory note sought to recover from one who had indorsed the note. The defendant had signed as an accommodation indorser to enable the payee to discount the note. The court found that the indorser was not liable to his principal.

Suretyship law on the right of a surety to assert defenses of the principal debtor against the creditor has always been opaque, and the pre–1990 Article 3 did not help. The post–1990 Code clears the

---

There are three exceptions. The accommodated party's defense of discharge in insolvency proceedings, infancy, and lack of legal capacity are not available to the accommodated party. If the accommodation party pays the instrument when the accommodated party had one of these defenses, the accommodated party has no duty to reimburse the accommodation party. The accommodation party has, in a sense, assumed the risk that such defenses will exist.

Occasionally, an accommodation party will pay an instrument even though the accommodated party has a defense that is available to the accommodation party. In such cases, the existence of the duty to reimburse may depend on whether the accommodation party was aware of the defense at the time it paid the in-strument. If the accommodation party was unaware of the defense, there is a duty to reimburse. Thus, there is an incentive for the accommodated party to make the accommodation party aware of any defenses it may have. If the accommodation party pays the instrument while aware of a defense of the accommodated party, however, reimbursement would ordinarily not be justified but might be justified in some circumstances. Resolution of this issue is left to the general law of suretyship through § 1–103.

The addition of Comments 6 and 7 to § 3–419 reflect this discussion.

9. Now (f) in the 2002 amendment.

10. 356 Mass. 725, 252 N.E.2d 217, 6 UCC 1237 (1969).

air by specifying in section 3–305(d) that the accommodation party has all defenses of the principal except for those of insolvency, infancy and lack of capacity.[11] It is only sensible that the accommodation party should be permitted to advance some defenses of the principal debtor, but should be prohibited from using other defenses that are available to the debtor alone. For example, the principal debtor's bankruptcy and discharge from its obligations is the very case where the accommodation party should pay. No accommodation party should be permitted to assert the bankruptcy discharge defense of the principal debtor.[12] On the other hand, if the principal debtor has a defense because he was sold shoddy goods and has a breach of warranty claim, the accommodation party should be able to assert that same defense. Similarly, the accommodation party may assert breach of contract, breach of warranty, and other defenses that the principal debtor could also make against a wide array of claims.

Section 3–305(c) limits the power of one party to raise the defense of another (*jus tertii* claims). Because of a specific exception in subsection (d) for accommodation parties, 3–305(c)'s limitation on raising another's defense does not apply when the accommodation party is asked to fulfill the obligation of the principal debtor.

The conventional surety's rights should be distinguished from the rights of the issuer of a letter of credit. Although the letter of credit fulfills much the same economic function as a guarantee, the critical difference is the "independence" of the letter of credit issuer's obligation under Article 5 and other law. To say that the obligation of the issuer is "independent" is to say that the issuance of a letter of credit—unlike a guarantor or conventional surety—cannot assert the defenses on the underlying deal that would be available to the debtor. Thus the bargain that a creditor makes with the conventional surety is different from the bargain that the creditor makes with the issuer of the letter of credit. In the former case the creditor knows that the surety can assert some defenses arising out of the underlying contract that could be asserted by the debtor. In the latter case, involving a letter of credit, the creditor enjoys greater rights. In that transaction the creditor expects to be paid even though it has broken its contract with the debtor and it expects to be able to take the money home and to be the defendant in a law suit, not the plaintiff in a suit against the issuer or other

---

11. Of course purported defenses of the *principal* which would be ineffective in the principal's hands will also be ineffective in the surety's hands. Accordingly, individuals who sign as sureties for corporations cannot raise the defense of usury in states where usury is not a defense available to a corporation.

12. A minor who has in fact disaffirmed and returned the consideration may get a more sympathetic reception and raise such defenses. See McKee v. Harwood Automotive Company, 204 Ind. 233, 183 N.E. 646 (1932), cited in L. Simpson, Handbook of the Law of Suretyship § 59 at 289 (1950); Restatement of Security § 125 (1941).

guarantor. This is the fundamental difference between a letter of credit obligation under Article 5 and the obligation of a conventional guarantor or surety.

§ 1–11   Suretyship Defenses, Section 3–605

Part I: The post–1990, pre–2002 Code

Section 3–605 (which replaced 3–606) codified the so-called suretyship defenses; every commercial lawyer needs to learn that section, new in 1990. It is especially important to the drafter of guarantee contracts because there are things that can be done for a creditor to hold onto accommodation parties and there are things that can be done for accommodation parties to loosen the creditor's grip. It is also important for the workout lawyer and for the litigator.

The section is much more detailed than its predecessor, and it makes careful distinctions not drawn under the old section. It also clarifies who is entitled to the protection of the various sections. It distinguishes not only between an accommodation party and all others, but among accommodation parties, nonaccommodation parties, indorsers, and those who, though not accommodation parties, are nevertheless "jointly and severally liable." Unfortunately, the 1990 section conflicted with the Restatement (Third) of Suretyship and Guaranty, and was again substantially redrafted in 2002 to conform to the Restatement.

First, let us identify the players under 3–605.[1] Subsections (b)-(e) apply to accommodation parties and indorsers. Subsection (f)

---

§ 1–11

1. The first six subsections of 3–605 read as follows:

(a) In this section, the term "indorser" includes a drawer having the obligation described in Section 3–414(d).

(b) Discharge, under Section 3–604, of the obligation of a party to pay an instrument does not discharge the obligation of an indorser or accommodation party having a right of recourse against the discharged party.

(c) If a person entitled to enforce an instrument agrees, with or without consideration, to an extension of the due date of the obligation of a party to pay the instrument, the extension discharges an indorser or accommodation party having a right of recourse against the party whose obligation is extended to the extent the indorser or accommodation party proves that the extension caused loss to the indorser or accommodation party with respect to the right of recourse.

(d) If a person entitled to enforce an instrument agrees, with or without consideration, to a material modification of the obligation of a party other than an extension of the due date, the modification discharges the obligation of an indorser or accommodation party having a right of recourse against the person whose obligation is modified to the extent the modification causes loss to the indorser or accommodation party with respect to the right of recourse. The loss suffered by the indorser or accommodation party as a result of the modification is equal to the amount of the right of recourse unless the person enforcing the instrument proves that no loss was caused by the modification or that the loss caused by the modification was an amount less than the amount of the right of recourse.

applies to anyone who is "jointly and severally liable with respect to the secured obligation" even though not an accommodation party. Thus, for the purpose of the main sections (b) through (e), it is necessary to figure out who is an indorser. This problem has been solved for us by section 3–204(a) discussed above. It tells us to treat as indorsers not only typical indorsers (those signing at the top on the back of the document), but also nearly anyone who signs a document in an ambiguous capacity unless that person proves he or she is something else.

a. Accommodation Party Defined

Which are accommodation parties and which not? Almost always this question arises with respect to a co-maker of a note.[2] If the co-maker is an accommodation party and if any of the events that discharge accommodation parties in (c) through (e) occur, the co-maker is discharged to the extent provided in those sections. If, on the other hand, our co-maker is not an accommodation party, this party is almost certainly a party "jointly and severally" liable and may still enjoy a limited discharge under (f). The latter, however, will be rare.

Under the post–1990 Code—as under the old—the principal battle will be whether a particular co-maker is an accommodation

(e) If the obligation of a party to pay an instrument is secured by an interest in collateral and a person entitled to enforce the instrument impairs the value of the interest in collateral, the obligation of an indorser or accommodation party having a right of recourse against the obligor is discharged to the extent of the impairment. The value of an interest in collateral is impaired to the extent (i) the value of the interest is reduced to an amount less than the amount of the right of recourse of the party asserting discharge, or (ii) the reduction in value of the interest causes an increase in the amount by which the amount of the right of recourse exceeds the value of the interest. The burden of proving impairment is on the party asserting discharge.

(f) If the obligation of a party is secured by an interest in collateral not provided by an accommodation party and a person entitled to enforce the instrument impairs the value of the interest in collateral, the obligation of any party who is jointly and severally liable with respect to the secured obligation is discharged to the extent the impairment causes the party asserting discharge to pay more than that party would have

been obliged to pay, taking into account rights of contribution, if impairment had not occurred. If the party asserting discharge is an accommodation party not entitled to discharge under subsection (e), the party is deemed to have a right to contribution based on joint and several liability rather than a right to reimbursement. The burden of proving impairment is on the party asserting discharge.

For discussion of a number of complex issues that have been raised by the enactment of § 3–605 but were not fully anticipated by the drafters, see PEB Commentary No. 11. The commentary deals with eleven different issues raised by § 3–605. The Commentary proposes a series of amendments to the comments that appear in editions of the Uniform Code published after February 10, 1994 when PEB Commentary No. 11 was promulgated.

2. Since the indorser is covered by name, we need not ask whether he or she is an accommodation party; if there is but one maker, that person is obviously the party primarily liable and not an accommodation party—except in the most strange and unusual cases.

party. (Because Section 3–605 treats "indorsers" as accommodation parties, we need not ask whether indorsers would otherwise qualify as sureties.) Section 3–419(a) restates the test routinely used by courts to distinguish between accommodation and nonaccommodation parties. An accommodation party is one who "signs the instrument for the purpose of incurring liability on the instrument without being a *direct beneficiary* of the value given for the instrument * * *." (emphasis added).

But who is and who is not a "direct beneficiary"? The cases show many of the kinds of disputes one can expect here, but they hardly bound the universe or tell us every possible variation. A husband or wife who signs a spouse's note can be expected to claim at trial that he or she is only an indirect beneficiary, even if the profits from the business, where the funds were used, put food on the table or provided shelter and clothing for the co-maker. Whether the co-maker will be a direct beneficiary may depend on factors as diverse as whether that person actually worked in the business, had a hand in making decisions for the business, was an owner of stock and the like. We despair of answering all possible questions; we are confident only that new variants will arise again, again, and again, no matter how careful the drafting of the relevant documents and how obvious the appearance at the time the documents were signed and the deal made.

The drafters who revised Article 3 were circumspect. They have provided us only one example in the comments to section 3–419, and this is an example of an indirect benefit:

> For example, if X co-signs a note of Corporation that is given for a loan to Corporation, X is an accommodation party if no part of the loan was paid to X or for X's direct benefit. This is true even though X may receive an indirect benefit from the loan because X is employed by Corporation or is a stockholder of Corporation, or even if X is the sole stockholder so long as Corporation and X are recognized as separate entities.

In Plein v. Lackey,[3] Cameron signed a promissory note both in his corporate capacity and individually to purchase property. Later, Cameron paid off the note and sought to enforce the instrument and foreclose on the property so that he would have a secured interest in the corporation's assets upon dissolution. The court reasoned that this situation closely paralleled the comment to 3–606 and Cameron was an accommodation party. Therefore, he was entitled to subrogation on the original instrument.

However, not every case fits so easily. To understand our despair, consider two cases that have irreconcilable—even per-

---

3. 149 Wash.2d 214, 67 P.3d 1061 (2003).

verse—conclusions. In Godeaux v. Godeaux[4] the court found accommodation party status where the benefit involved seemed to be direct. There, in a post-divorce settlement, Ms. Godeaux sued her ex-husband for reimbursement of payments she had made on a note to purchase a mobile home. The court found any benefit to her to be indirect because the mobile home was found to be the separate property of the husband. This was the case even though the wife had lived in the house for a month before separation and then for one and a half years after separation while she made payments on the note. Since the court seems to judge directness of benefit as of the time of execution of a note rather than in light of subsequent events, the decision seems questionable.

By contrast, cases like Nelson v. Cotham[5] have found a direct benefit where the signer was merely the officer of a corporation. In *Nelson*, the defendant half-owner of a corporation signed for a loan to help make payments for construction costs on a house the corporation was building. The court held that the defendant was not an accommodation party because he received a direct benefit from the loan in that it benefited his business interest by keeping the corporation afloat.

It is hard to say just what constitutes a direct benefit. The status of many cosigners of notes claiming to be accommodation parties will remain unpredictable as the courts continue to wrestle with this problem.

b. Joint and Several

Who are the parties identified in 3–605(f) as "jointly and severally liable with respect to the secured obligation"? Mostly, perhaps exclusively, they are co-makers of notes in cases where neither party is an accommodation party for the other because each receives a direct benefit from the loan.[6] Assume that John and Jane are partners in operating a flower shop. Each works there, and each shares the profits and losses. Neither John nor Jane would be an accommodation party or an indorser if both co-signed a note, and therefore, neither would be covered by any of the earlier subsections of 3–605, but only by subsection (f).

In subsection (f), the drafters reject the case law that found the suretyship defenses applicable to those whose "rights of recourse or

4. 488 So.2d 434, 1 UCC2d 843 (La. App. 1986), cert. denied, 493 So.2d 636 (La. 1986).

5. 268 Ark. 622, 595 S.W.2d 693, 28 UCC 1070 (App.1980).

6. § 3–116(a) reads as follows:

Except as otherwise provided in the instrument, two or more persons who have the same liability on an instrument as makers, drawers, acceptors, indorsers who indorse as joint payees, or anomalous indorsers are jointly and severally liable in the capacity in which they sign.

Courts applying the predecessor section, 3–118(e), have freely found joint and several liability.

reimbursement" consisted only of the contribution claim of a joint and several party and not the reimbursement claim of an accommodation party as specified in 3–419.

c. Suretyship Defenses

After determining whether a potential defendant is an indorser, an accommodation party or jointly and severally liable, one can turn to the various suretyship defenses laid out in 3–605. For reasons mysterious to one of your authors, sureties have been ancient favorites of the courts. Thus, if the creditor and debtor agreed to any modification in their agreement, the courts would often discharge the surety. The policy behind such discharge is easy to see in the starkest case: assume that debtor pays creditor a small sum under the table in return for debtor's release from the obligation on a note. Creditor then sues the surety, an accommodation maker on the note. Curbstone equity requires us to discharge the surety in such a case.

But real life rarely takes this form of payment under–the-table. The creditor may grant an extension because the debtor, who honestly hopes to pay the debt, needs an extra month or two to gather the money. In theory the surety calculated and undertook the probability of debtor default on the original term, but did not undertake the supposedly greater probability of default over the longer term. In fact, the extension could just as well leave the accommodation party better off, since the debtor might ultimately pay the debt and discharge the liability of the accommodation party. Or, a creditor may settle with the debtor for half the amount owed, which at least frees the accommodation party from half the obligation should the debtor default. These twists and turns, and more, are handled in the subsections of 3–605. The subsections are self-contained units that apply to discrete events. Because the subsections apply to somewhat different persons, the burdens of proof are different in the various sections. It is vital to identify the specific subsection that applies to a particular dispute. We analyze each subsection in turn below, but first consider one defense that does not work. An accommodation party's failure to receive cash from the creditor is not a defense. Time and again sureties respond to a holder's suit by arguing, "I am a surety, and I did not receive consideration for my contract." This is a losing argument, as the Code now says explicitly in section 3–419(b).

d. Section 3–605(b)—The Effect of Release of a Principal

Before 1990, a holder discharged any party to the instrument to the extent that the holder—

releases or agrees not to sue any person against whom the party has to the knowledge of the holder a right of recourse or agrees to suspend the right to enforce to such person, the instrument or collateral, or otherwise discharges such person * * *.[7]

The pre–1990 Code also provided that a holder discharged a party to the instrument if the holder unjustifiably impaired any collateral given by the person who would be discharged.

Keeping the pre–1990 Code in mind for comparison, turn now to 3–605(b). It reads in full as follows:

(b) Discharge, under Section 3–604, of the obligation of a party to pay an instrument does not discharge the obligation of an indorser or accommodation party having a right of recourse against the discharged party.

This is not a suretyship defense; it is the reverse. It tells that an event that might have caused a discharge of an accommodation party under the old 3–606 does not cause one under revised 3–605. Referring to 3–604, section 3–605(b) tells us that a release, an agreement not to sue, or a renunciation of rights against one party does *not* free the indorsers or accommodation parties. How remarkable! In the words of Comment 3, the subsection "is designed to allow a creditor to settle with the principal debtor without risk of losing rights against sureties." The Comment gives the following example:

If Borrower is unable to pay all creditors, it may be prudent for Bank to take partial payment, but Borrower will normally insist on a release of the obligation. If Bank takes $3,000 and releases Borrower from the $10,000 debt, Accommodation Party is not injured. To the extent of the payment Accommodation Party's obligation to Bank is reduced. The release of Borrower

---

7. § 3–606 of the pre–1990 Code which reads as follows:

§ 3–606. Impairment of Recourse or of Collateral.

(1) The holder discharges any party to the instrument to the extent that without such party's consent the holder

(a) without express reservation of rights releases or agrees not to sue any person against whom the party has to the knowledge of the holder a right of recourse or agrees to suspend the right to enforce against such person the instrument or collateral or otherwise discharges such person, except that failure or delay in effecting any required presentment, protest or notice of dishonor with respect to any such person does not discharge any party as to whom presentment, protest or notice of dishonor is effective or unnecessary; or

(b) unjustifiably impairs any collateral for the instrument given by or on behalf of the party or any person against whom he has a right of recourse.

(2) By express reservation of rights against a party with a right of recourse the holder preserves

(a) all his rights against such party as of the time when the instrument was originally due; and

(b) the right of the party to pay the instrument as of that time; and

(c) all rights of such party to recourse against others.

by Bank does not affect the right of Accommodation Party to obtain reimbursement from Borrower if Accommodation Party pays Bank. * * *

The comments at various places indicate the policy behind this rule: a creditor will not "gratuitously release" a debtor, but will typically insist on partial payment and that partial payment may well facilitate the most sensible and efficient outcome. The comments also point out that under 3–606 of the pre–1990 Code, the creditor could accomplish the same result merely by "reserving its rights" in the discharge agreement. The principal consequence of this change in the law, therefore, will be to protect creditors who are ignorant or hasty and do not include a reservation of rights clause of the kind that would have protected them under the pre–1990 Code.

Rarely will the creditor conspire with the principal debtor to the disadvantage of the accommodation party. Where there is a continuing relationship between the accommodation party and the principal debtor, that alone will protect against such conspiracy. In the rare case where the principal debtor and the creditor conspire to release the principal debtor for less than he or she should fairly pay and with the intention of taking advantage of the accommodation party, the agreement can be attacked as lacking good faith. We would not expect such attacks to be often made and we would expect them to be successful even less often. To prove good faith, the creditor need not show that the last drop has been taken out of the debtor's cup. Bad faith here would include an active conspiracy between the principal debtor and the creditor to take advantage of a rich or foolish accommodation party.

In summary, the creditor can discharge the principal debtor for nothing or for whatever larger sum the debtor can pay and still hold the indorsers or accommodation parties. But beware, the 2002 3–605 default rule reverts to the old rule and frees the accommodation party unless the creditor takes action to hold him.

Note that there was a lively debate under the pre–1990 Code on the question whether co-makers who were not accommodation parties should have the benefit of the suretyship defenses. Some courts held yes, others held no. Section 3–605 is more explicit than the rules in the pre–1990 Code. It rejects the proposition that a co-maker is *ipso facto* an accommodation party and, as we have noted above and consider below, the section gives only limited protection to co-makers who are not accommodation parties. Subsection (f) gives only limited rights and then only in case of impairment of collateral to such a co-maker. So, under the post–1990, pre–2002 Code, a co-maker who is not an accommodation party does not get the benefit of the suretyship defense but gets some limited protection under subsection (f).

e. Section 3–605(c)—Effect of Extension of the Due Date

Section 3–605(c) covers "extension of the due date" of the principal obligation. An extension discharges an indorser or accommodation party who "proves" that the extension caused loss to the indorser or accommodation party with respect to the "right of recourse." Presumably this right of recourse is the right specified in 3–419(e), which states that an accommodation party paying the instrument is "entitled to reimbursement from the accommodated party and entitled to enforce the instrument against the accommodated party." This sentence states the traditional equitable rights of the accommodation party to reimbursement and subrogation.

Returning to subsection (c), how can an extension of time cause loss with respect to the "right of recourse"? Comment 4 to section 3–605 confesses:

> In relatively few cases the extension may cause loss if deterioration of the financial condition of the principal debtor reduces the amount that the surety will be able to recover on its right of recourse unless default occurs.

The comment notes that the pre–1990 section 3–606 did not take into account the loss to the accommodation party and, indeed, courts have sometimes allowed accommodation parties to escape liability even in circumstances where it appears there was no injury to them from the note's cancellation or modification.

The burden here is on the accommodation party who must show not only loss but also the "extent" of the loss, for there is discharge only to that "extent." What evidence could the accommodation party offer and under what circumstances would it be successful? Assume a case in which the principal debtor, Sara, has a net worth of $1,000,000 at the time the note becomes due, but the note for $500,000 is extended for a year. A year later Sara is worth $0. Presumably that proof alone would be enough to show loss and to allow the accommodation party to escape from the entire $500,000 liability because Sara would have paid the entire note had payment been demanded at the original due date, but can pay none of it now.

In life, the numbers will seldom be so stark and the accommodation parties and indorsers will have an uphill climb. The actual case is likely to be further complicated by testimony that the principal creditor spoke to the accommodation party and—without getting a formal agreement to the extension—received assurances that the accommodation party was not interested in paying the obligation at the time the extension was discussed. Thus the accommodation party's own behavior and motivation is likely to be equivocal and this will bear upon the determination of what loss was suffered.

Since no creditor will ordinarily extend a note's maturity unless the debtor would have difficulty making current payments, we expect that the burden on the accommodation party to show not only "loss," but also "its extent" will be hard to carry. As with all these cases, there is the possibility that the debtor will have two obligations to the creditor: one that is guaranteed and one that is not. When the creditor extends the guaranteed obligation but insists on the payment of the unguaranteed obligation, the courts are certain to listen closely to complaints from accommodation parties. Of course, insisting on payment of non-guaranteed obligations while extending guaranteed obligations is not alone evidence of bad faith. Indeed, if there is a reasonable prospect of payment in the future and a high likelihood the guarantor would have to fork money over if the debt were called at once, there will not be any injury to the accommodation party by the extension.

f. Section 3–605(d)—Effect of Material Modification

Section 3–605(d) deals with "material modification" of the principal obligation other than extension. Material modification has the same consequence as extension of time, with one procedural difference. Here the burden is on the creditor to prove a negative, namely, to prove that no loss was caused by the modification, or that the loss caused was an amount less than the amount of the right of recourse. Where there are complicated facts, the burden of proof may be critical. It may prove significant that the burden is on the debtor in (c), but on the creditor in (d).

But what modifications are we speaking of here? The assumption of the drafter appears to be that modifications other than extensions or complete cancellations are likely to be particularly injurious to accommodation parties. The Comments contain the Delphic statement: "Modification of the obligation of the principal debtor without permission of the surety is unreasonable unless the modification is benign."[8]

Presumably the most significant modification other than extension of time is reduction in the amount owed. This can take the form of forgiveness of past due interest, modification of the principal amount, or even alteration of the rate of interest. A reduction in the rate of interest would be to the benefit of the accommodation party. It is hard to see why forgiveness of half of the principal should discharge the accommodation party under 3–605(d) when forgiveness of all of it yields no discharge under 3–605(b).

Further complicating the picture, it may not be entirely clear whether a modification to a debtor's contract is properly evaluated under 3–605(b) or (d). Subsection (b) covers discharges under 3–

---

8. § 3–605, Comment 5.

604—cases in which the creditor gives back or tears up the note, or renounces his or her rights in writing. So far so good, but then comes subsection (d), which covers all modifications of a party's obligations except for the extension of the due date. Presumably the drafters meant to treat complete cancellation of obligation under (b) and lesser changes under (d), but the language does not quite say so. Thus, one might argue that a partial discharge in writing should be governed by the terms of (b).

Given the ominous statement about "benign" modifications in Comment 5, a creditor would be well advised to get the accommodation party's agreement to anything other than an extension or a complete cancellation. In most workouts the strong hand is with the creditor—at least when the creditor is dealing with the accommodation party—and if the accommodation party is unwilling to go along with what appears to be reasonable modification, the creditor is always free to declare a default and sue the accommodation party.

Professor Cohen has suggested that the dire consequences of a material modification in 3–605(d) will drive the creditor back to (b), cause cancellation of the entire liability, and so leave the accommodation party worse off. We wonder whether that is true. Presumably, the creditor lent to the principal debtor because the creditor thought that debtor could pay. Where there remains some possibility of payment by the debtor, the creditor will be hesitant to give a complete discharge. That is why the typical workout is "a workout," and not a complete discharge of the kind contemplated by 3–604 and 3–605(b).

g. Section 3–605(e), (f), and (g)—Effects of Impairment of Collateral, etc.

On occasion, a person entitled to enforce an instrument will impair the collateral securing the obligation of a party to pay an instrument. Such an impairment will obviously displease accommodation parties who find themselves farther out on the limb than they intended. The Code deals with such situations in two stages. First is section 3–605(e), discharging indorsers and accommodation parties, and second is section 3–605(f), discharging those jointly and severally liable. Like subsection (c) they put the burden of proving impairment on the party asserting discharge and they incorporate the case law limiting the discharge to the extent of the impairment.

Section 3–605(g) identifies four separate events that may constitute impairment of collateral:

> (g) Under subsection (e) or (f), impairing value of an interest in collateral includes (i) failure to obtain or maintain perfection or recordation of the interest in collateral, (ii) release of collateral without substitution of collateral of equal value, (iii)

failure to perform a duty to preserve the value of collateral owed, under Article 9 or other law, to a debtor or surety or other person secondarily liable, or (iv) failure to comply with applicable law in disposing of collateral.

Probably the most common impairment is failure to perfect a security interest. In Shaffer v. Davidson,[9] the principal debtor gave the creditor a security interest in his automobile. The debtor sold the car to a third party and disappeared. When the creditor sued, the accommodation party argued that the creditor's failure to perfect the security interest impaired the collateral and discharged her. The trial court set off the value of the auto against the face amount of the note, accrued interest and attorney's fees. On appeal, the creditor argued that "impairment of collateral" in 3–606(1)(b) refers only to diminishment of the value of the physical property subject to the security interest and not to impairment of the security interest itself. The Wyoming Supreme Court rejected this argument and held that the accommodation party was discharged by the creditor's failure to perfect. The court also concluded that since the value of the automobile was equal to the principal amount of the debt, the award of interest and attorney's fees was improper.

Failure to perfect a security interest signifies that the asset goes to the great unwashed on the debtor's bankruptcy and not to the secured creditor. Typically in such case the loss is equal to the difference between the pro rata distribution received by the creditor (now unsecured) and the amount that the secured creditor would have received if this creditor had been a perfected secured creditor.

Note too that subsection (g)(iv) invites to this affair all of the troublesome fellows found in Part 6 of Article 9. Thus, it invites a surety to argue that the secured creditor who repossessed and resold did not do so in a commercially reasonable way. This, of course, merely cements the proposition that the duties under Part 6 of Article 9 are owed not merely to the principal debtor, but to an accommodation party as well.

The only difference that we can see between (e) and (f) is that the amount of discharge will usually be larger in (e) than in (f). This is because the claim for reimbursement under (e) (of an indorser or accommodation party) is invariably larger (assuming the same transaction) than would be the claim of one who was jointly and severally liable with another party under (f) in a similar transaction.

To see how (e) and (f) might operate, consider the following examples:

9. 445 P.2d 13, 5 UCC 772 (Wyo. 1968). Accord, Port Distributing Corp. v. Pflaumer, 880 F.Supp. 204, 28 UCC2d 235 (S.D.N.Y. 1995) (Port's failure to perfect in a timely manner discharged Pflaumer entirely).

A and B are jointly and severally liable co-makers on a note for $1000. A puts up collateral worth $500 to partially secure the debt. Creditor later makes an agreement with A to return the collateral and instead replaces it with collateral worth $350. A subsequently goes into bankruptcy. What is the extent of B's obligation? If Creditor had not impaired collateral, B could have paid a debt of $1000 and gained rights to the collateral by subrogation. B would then have been able to recover up to $500 from A's collateral based on rights of contribution. Now, since the collateral is only worth $350, B has lost out on $150 worth of contribution rights from A's collateral. Consequently, B has been damaged by $150 and this is the extent of his discharge. He must pay $850 and then can proceed against A for contribution.

Suppose instead that B was an accommodation party. In this case B would be discharged "to the extent of the impairment," which subsection (e)(ii) informs us is equal to the "increase in the amount by which the amount of the right of recourse exceeds the value of the interest." Originally, the right of recourse ($1000) exceeded the interest by $500 ($1000 - $500). Now it exceeds the interest by $650 ($1000 - $350). Thus the extent of B's discharge is the difference between these two ($650 - $500 = $150).

h.   Section 3–605(h)

Section 3–605(h) denies the discharge that would otherwise be available under 3–605 when the person enforcing the instrument was without knowledge of the accommodation party's status, or without notice under 3–419(c) that the instrument was signed for accommodation. Section 3–419(c) provides a presumption of accommodation status and indicates at least some of the circumstances in which there is "notice" that a person signed for accommodation:

> A person signing an instrument is presumed to be an accommodation party and there is notice that the instrument is signed for accommodation if the signature is an anomalous indorsement or is accompanied by words indicating that the signer is acting as surety or guarantor with respect to the obligation of another party to the instrument. * * *

This section establishes a presumption that an indorsement that shows it is not made for the purpose of transfer is made as an accommodation for another party. To see how this provision works in the typical case, assume that Rocky has agreed to become an accommodation party for Bullwinkle's note which is payable to Boris. Bullwinkle executes the note as maker with Boris as payee. Rocky indorses the note prior to its delivery to Boris. When Boris negotiates the note to Natasha, she has notice under section 3–415(4) of the pre–1990 Code that Rocky is an accommodation party. Rocky's signature is outside the chain of title, because it appears above that of the payee who would normally be the first indorser. Because an indorsement out of the chain shows accommodation status without the need for any words, signature as an indorser is a desirable way for the accommodation party to sign the instrument. When the instrument contains such notice, (i.e., the indorsement is anomalous or is accompanied by words indicating the signer is acting as a surety or guarantor), even a holder in due course must respect the surety's rights under section 3–605(c), (d), and (e). Since all indorsers enjoy most of the rights under 3–605—whether or not that indorser is technically an accommodation party—we do not see much significance here in the fact that one might be proved to be an anomalous indorser.

i. *Waiver of Suretyship Defenses*

Finally, to what extent can the suretyship defenses be waived by agreement? Section 3–605(i) deals with that question.

If the waiver is to be effective, either it must be obtained contemporaneously with a workout by a "consent,"[10] or there must be an earlier waiver in the accommodation or other agreement. Sometime, somehow, the accommodation party must agree.[11] This is a change from the pre–1990 Code, under which a party could save its claims against an accommodation party merely by "reserving them," unilaterally and without the consent of the accommodation party.

Section 3–605(i) authorizes waivers not only "specifically" but also "by general language." This is expansive language that will certainly make creditors' lawyers reach for their pens. We see no reason why accommodation parties ought not to be able to waive their defenses. Were we judges, we would quite willingly follow the instructions of the legislature, even in circumstances where the waiver language were only "general."

Almost certainly 1990 3–605(i) will come into conflict with the antiwaiver provisions in Part 6 of Article 9. Section 9–602 limits the power of a debtor to waive its Part 6 rights (foreclosure protection in Article 9). The courts have been diligent in protecting debtors against such waivers, and we wonder whether they will read 3–605(i) to grant the creditor greater rights vis à vis an accommodation party than the creditor would have against the principal debtor

---

10. The surety's consent may take the form of conduct that shows assent to the creditor's action.

11. An express statement of consent incorporated in the instrument is effective against the surety.

on a secured loan. We hope so, for that is what the legislature seems to have said. But we are not sure.

Quaere, would it be possible for the creditor to make the following case to the accommodation party? "I am telling you now that I might take security for this loan and that if I take security, I might perfect the security interest, and if I take it I may or may not look to it on default, but I do not promise to do any of these and I expect you to sign an agreement that makes you liable even if I do not take security or, if I do take it, even if I fail to perfect my interest in it." If an accommodation party, so informed, signs a guarantee that contains similar language and waives any defenses arising under 3–605, including those having to do with impairment of collateral or somehow arising out of Article 9, is this enforceable against the accommodation party? At this writing the Permanent Editorial Board has issued a commentary that would restrict the impact of any such waiver on the rights that the accommodation party would otherwise have under Part 6 of Article 9 because of acts that might constitute impairment of collateral. As we indicate above, we think a waiver of the kind described should be effective, but the PEB appears to have wimped out.[12] Thus, notwithstanding

---

12. See PEB Commentary No. 11, February 10, 1994. The Commentary reads in part as follows:

What sort of language is sufficient to waive discharge under § 3–605?

DISCUSSION

Section 3–605(i) provides that a party is not discharged under that section if the instrument or a separate agreement of the party waives such discharge "either specifically or by general language indicating that parties waive defenses based on suretyship or impairment of collateral." Thus, no particular language or form of agreement is required, and the standards for enforcing such a term are the same as the standards for enforcing any other term in an instrument or agreement. There is no requirement of particularity in referring to the four grounds for discharge established by § 3–605 so long as the language used indicates that suretyship defenses are waived. By allowing the use of general language, the rule recognizes that the use of lengthy provisions containing detailed waivers or even separate identification of each ground for discharge does not necessarily promote greater understanding of an instrument's terms. Yet, the requirement that the language indicate that defenses are being waived assures that a diligent indorser or accom-

modation party will, at the least, not be unjustly surprised when it is asserted that the terms of the instrument or agreement delete protections that would otherwise be available. In adopting this course, § 3–605 is consistent with the general law of suretyship. See Restatement of the Law Third, Suretyship § 42 (Tent. Draft No. 2, 1993).

ISSUE 11

As a result of § 3–605(i), may an accommodation party waive whatever protections it may have pursuant to Part 5 of Article 9?

DISCUSSION

Section 3–605(e) provides that impairment of an interest in collateral for the obligation of the accommodated party may discharge the accommodation party. Section 3–605(g) defines impairment of an interest in collateral as including, *inter alia*, failure to comply with applicable law in disposing of collateral. In the case of personal property or fixtures, applicable law includes, of course, Article 9. Thus, failure to comply with the rules in part 5 of Article 9 concerning disposition of collateral constituted impairment of an interest in collateral. In addition, under Article 9, an accommodation party may qualify as a debtor. See § 9–105. In some jurisdictions, the

an expansive waiver under 3–605(i) that freed the creditor from impairment of collateral claims, the accommodation party who signed such a waiver could argue, for example, that it was discharged under Article 9 as a "debtor" who had been injured by the secured creditor's failure to conduct a commercially reasonable resale which constituted an "impairment of the collateral." As we have said before, an accommodation party is sometimes defined as a fool with a pen and thus deserving of judicial protection.

In summary, not only the poodles present at the inception of guarantee liability, but also junkyard dogs attending workouts and lawsuits, should know section 3–605 inside and out. It presents interesting possibilities both for doing it wrong and right. It presents multiple opportunities for creditors' lawyers to protect their clients' interests at the time the documents are prepared and even more possibilities for doing it right or wrong at the time of the workout. We have set out all of the main issues and problems we see. We are certain that the courts will find others.

Part II: The 2002 Amendments

Section 3–605 of the 2002 amendments[13] generally conform to the rules of the Restatement (Third) of Suretyship and Guaranty. A

limits placed by § 9–105 on the power of a debtor to waive the protections of §§ 9–504 and 9–505 have been interpreted so as to limit the power of an accommodation party to waive those protections. Section 3–605(i), on the other hand, provides that an accommodation party may waive discharge under this section (including discharge for impairment of an interest in collateral pursuant to § 3–605(e)). This does not mean that the accommodation party may waive *all* protections it may have concerning disposition of collateral; rather, it provides for the waiver of protections created by § 3–605. To the extent that Article 9 also provides the accommodation party similar protections, waiver of those protections is governed by Article 9 as interpreted in each jurisdiction.

13. 2002 § 3–605:

(a) If a person entitled to enforce an instrument releases the obligation of a principal obligor in whole or in part, and another party to the instrument is a secondary obligor with respect to the obligation of that principal obligor, the following rules apply:

(1) Any obligations of the principal obligor to the secondary obligor with respect to any previous payment by the secondary obligor are not affected. Unless the terms of the release preserve the secondary obligor's recourse, the principal obligor is discharged, to the extent of the release, from any other duties to the secondary obligor under this article.

(2) Unless the terms of the release provide that the person entitled to enforce the instrument retains the right to enforce the instrument against the secondary obligor, the secondary obligor is discharged to the same extent as the principal obligor from any unperformed portion of its obligation on the instrument. If the instrument is a check and the obligation of the secondary obligor is based on an indorsement of the check, the secondary obligor is discharged without regard to the language or circumstances of the discharge or other release.

(3) If the secondary obligor is not discharged under paragraph (2), the secondary obligor is discharged to the extent of the value of the consideration for the release, and to the extent that the release would otherwise cause the secondary obligor a loss.

(b) If a person entitled to enforce an instrument grants a principal obligor an extension of the time at which one or more payments are due on the instrument and another party to the instrument is a secondary obligor with respect to the obligation of that principal obligor, the following rules apply:

(1) Any obligations of the principal obligor to the secondary obligor with respect to any previous payment by the secondary obligor are not affected. Unless the terms of the extension preserve the secondary obligor's recourse, the extension correspondingly extends the time for performance of any other duties owed to the secondary obligor by the principal obligor under this article.

(2) The secondary obligor is discharged to the extent that the extension would otherwise cause the secondary obligor a loss.

(3) To the extent that the secondary obligor is not discharged under paragraph (2), the secondary obligor may perform its obligations to a person entitled to enforce the instrument as if the time for payment had not been extended or, unless the terms of the extension provide that the person entitled to enforce the instrument retains the right to enforce the instrument against the secondary obligor as if the time for payment had not been extended, treat the time for performance of its obligations as having been extended correspondingly.

(c) If a person entitled to enforce an instrument agrees, with or without consideration, to a modification of the obligation of a principal obligor other than a complete or partial release or an extension of the due date and another party to the instrument is a secondary obligor with respect to the obligation of that principal obligor, the following rules apply:

(1) Any obligations of the principal obligor to the secondary obligor with respect to any previous payment by the secondary obligor are not affected. The modification correspondingly modifies any other duties owed to the secondary obligor by the principal obligor under this article.

(2) The secondary obligor is discharged from any unperformed portion of its obligation to the extent that the modification would otherwise cause the secondary obligor a loss.

(3) To the extent that the secondary obligor is not discharged under paragraph (2), the secondary obligor may

satisfy its obligation on the instrument as if the modification had not occurred, or treat its obligation on the instrument as having been modified correspondingly.

(d) If the obligation of a principal obligor is secured by an interest in collateral, another party to the instrument is a secondary obligor with respect to that obligation, and a person entitled to enforce the instrument impairs the value of the interest in collateral, the obligation of the secondary obligor is discharged to the extent of the impairment. The value of an interest in collateral is impaired to the extent the value of the interest is reduced to an amount less than the amount of the recourse of the secondary obligor, or the reduction in value of the interest causes an increase in the amount by which the amount of the recourse exceeds the value of the interest. For purposes of this subsection, impairing the value of an interest in collateral includes failure to obtain or maintain perfection or recordation of the interest in collateral, release of collateral without substitution of collateral of equal value or equivalent reduction of the underlying obligation, failure to perform a duty to preserve the value of collateral owed, under Article 9 or other law, to a debtor or other person secondarily liable, and failure to comply with applicable law in disposing of or otherwise enforcing the interest in collateral.

(e) A secondary obligor is not discharged under subsection (a)(3), (b), (c), or (d) unless the person entitled to enforce the instrument knows that the person is a secondary obligor or has notice under Section 3–419(c) that the instrument was signed for accommodation.

(f) A secondary obligor is not discharged under this section if the secondary obligor consents to the event or conduct that is the basis of the discharge, or the instrument or a separate agreement of the party provides for waiver of discharge under this section specifically or by general language indicating that parties waive defenses based on suretyship or impairment of collateral. Unless the circumstances indicate otherwise, consent by the principal obligor to an act that would lead to a discharge under this section constitutes consent to that act by the secondary obligor if the sec-

secondary obligor is limited to those who are parties to the instrument. It does not include persons who make a guarantee in a separate agreement. Section 3–605 in 2002 is substantially different from 1990 3–605.

Under 2002 3–605, a discharge without reservation of rights against secondary obligors discharges both the borrower and guarantor under 3–605(a)(1) and (2). Otherwise the release to the borrower could be illusory, for the guarantor could demand immediate recourse and a creditor's desire to keep the borrower solvent by reducing the debt owed would be frustrated. Should the lender wish to retain the right to pursue the guarantor, he may do so and the guarantor will then be discharged only to the extent of any loss caused by the release of the debtor under 3–605(a)(2) and (3). According to Comment 4, holding the guarantor does not require the use of any particular "magic words." Any statement that the rights against secondary obligors is retained will suffice. If the creditor preserves both the right to pursue the guarantor and the right of recourse of the guarantor against the borrower, then there is no loss to the guarantor and no defense under 3–605(a)(3).

Comment 4 to section 3–605 illustrates the reservation rule with the following four cases:

> *Case 1.* D borrows $1000 from C. The repayment obligation is evidenced by a note issued by D, payable to the order of C. S is an accommodation indorser of the note. As the due date of the note approaches, it becomes obvious that D cannot pay the full amount of the note and may soon be facing bankruptcy. C, in order to collect as much as possible from D and lessen the need to seek recovery from S, agrees to release D from its obligation under the note in exchange for $100 in cash. The agreement to release D is silent as to the effect of the release on S. Pursuant to Section 3–605(a)(2), the release of D discharges S from its obligations to C on the note.

ondary obligor controls the principal obligor or deals with the person entitled to enforce the instrument on behalf of the principal obligor.

(g) A release or extension preserves a secondary obligor's recourse if the terms of the release or extension provide that the person entitled to enforce the instrument retains the right to enforce the instrument against the secondary obligor; and the recourse of the secondary obligor continues as though the release or extension had not been granted.

(h) Except as otherwise provided in subsection (i), a secondary obligor asserting discharge under this section has the burden of persuasion both with respect to the occurrence of the acts alleged to harm the secondary obligor and loss or prejudice caused by those acts.

(i) If the secondary obligor demonstrates prejudice caused by an impairment of its recourse, and the circumstances of the case indicate that the amount of loss is not reasonably susceptible of calculation or requires proof of facts that are not ascertainable, it is presumed that the act impairing recourse caused a loss or impairment equal to the liability of the secondary obligor on the instrument. In that event, the burden of persuasion as to any lesser amount of the loss is on the person entitled to enforce the instrument.

Case 2. Same facts as Case 1, except that the terms of the release provide that C retains its rights to enforce the instrument against S. D is discharged from its obligations to S pursuant to Section 3–605(a)(1), but S is not discharged from its obligations to C pursuant to Section 3–605(a)(2). However, if S could have recovered from D any sum it paid to C (had D not been discharged from its obligation to S), S has been harmed by the release and is discharged pursuant to Section 3–605(a)(3) to the extent of that harm.

Case 3. Same facts as Case 1, except that the terms of the release provide that C retains its rights to enforce the instrument against S and that S retains its recourse against D. Under subsection (g), the release effects a preservation of recourse. Thus, S is not discharged from its obligations to C pursuant to Section 3–605(a)(2) and D is not discharged from its obligations to S pursuant to Section 3–605(a)(1). Because S's claims against D are preserved, S will not suffer the kind of loss described in Case 2. If no other loss is suffered by S as a result of the release, S is not discharged pursuant to this section.

Case 4. Same facts as Case 3, except that D had made arrangements to work at a second job in order to earn the money to fulfill its obligations on the note. When C released D, however, D canceled the plans for the second job. While S still retains its recourse against D, S may be discharged from its obligation under the instrument to the extent that D's decision to forgo the second job causes S a loss because forgoing the job renders D unable to fulfill its obligations to S under Section 3–419.

If the creditor extends the time for payment without reservation of rights, the guarantor is discharged to the extent of loss and may choose either to pay at the original time or to wait until the new due date. However, should the guarantor pay immediately, he will be required to wait until the extended due date to collect from debtor for the debtor's obligations to guarantor are deferred under 3–605(b)(1). Should the creditor wish to reserve the right to pursue the guarantor while extending the due date for the borrower, the guarantor is discharged to the extent of loss and to the extent not discharged the guarantor will have the same option as above—to pay immediately and wait until the due date to seek recourse. If the right to recourse by the guarantor is also reserved, the debtor's obligation to guarantor is not extended under 3–605(b)(1).

Comment 5 illustrates the application of these rules with the following hypotheticals:

Case 5. A borrows money from Lender and issues a note payable to the order of Lender that is due on April 1, 2002. B signs the note for accommodation at the request of Lender. B signed the note either as co-maker or as an anomalous indorser. In either case Lender subsequently makes an agreement with A extending the due date of A's obligation to pay the note to July 1, 2002. In either case B did not agree to the extension, and the extension did not address Lender's rights against B. Under paragraph (b)(1), A's obligations to B under this article are also extended to July 1, 2002. Under paragraph (b)(3), if B is not discharged, B may treat its obligations to Lender as also extended, or may pay the instrument on the original due date.

Case 6. Same facts as Case 5, except that the extension agreement includes a statement that the Lender retains its right to enforce the note against B on its original terms. Under paragraph (b)(3), B is liable on the original due date, but under paragraph (b)(1), A's obligations to B under Section 3–419 are not due until July 1, 2002.

Case 7. Same facts as Case 5, except that the extension agreement includes a statement that the Lender retains its right to enforce the note against B on its original terms and B retains its recourse against A as though no extension had been granted. Under paragraph (b)(3), B is liable on the original due date. Under paragraph (b)(1), A's obligations to B under Section 3–419 are not extended.

When an alteration is made to the agreement between the debtor and the creditor that is not a complete or partial release or an extension of the due date, the secondary obligor is discharged to the extent of the resulting loss and the secondary obligor can choose to pay the note in accordance with either the original or modified terms and the obligation of the borrower to the guarantor is modified, regardless of any language of reservation, under 3–605(c)(1).

Section 3–605(h) usually places the burden of proof on the secondary obligor for both the occurrence of acts alleged by the secondary obligor and the loss or prejudice thereby caused by those acts. However, 3–605(i) provides that if prejudice caused by an impairment of recourse is proven and the amount of loss is not reasonably ascertainable, the loss is presumed to be equal to the liability of the secondary obligor on the instrument unless proven otherwise by the creditor.

PROBLEM

1. George and Donald co-sign a note to First Bank for $400,000. George pays the entire note when it is due. George sues

Donald for the full $400,000. What does he recover? There are three possibilities: 0, $200,000 and $400,000.

George recovers nothing if he is the principal obligor and Donald is an accommodation party. George and Donald split the liability if each one is a principal debtor and neither is an accommodation party for the other, or if both are accommodation parties and there is no recovery from the principal, 3–116. In that case George has a cause of action for "contribution." If George is the accommodation party and Donald the principal debtor, George has a cause of action against Donald for "reimbursement" and that claim is for the full $400,000 that he has paid, 3–419(f).

2.   Assume now that George is the maker of the note and that Donald indorses the note. When George falls on hard times he convinces First Bank to take $50,000 in full satisfaction of the $400,000 note. Bank then turns to Donald (who as an anomalous indorser is presumed to be an accommodation party, 3–419(c)).

If the 1990 version of 3–605 applies, the release of George does not change Donald's liability and First Bank can recover $350,000 from Donald, 3–605(b). Can Donald recover anything from George if the $50,000 payment did not empty his pockets? Yes, 3–419 and comment 3 to 3–605. So the "release" that George gets may not mean much.

If the 2002 version of 3–605 applies, the release of George by the Bank also releases George from any duty to pay Donald, 3–605(a)(1), unless the "terms of [George's] release preserve [Donald's] recourse." The release also releases Donald from his indorser's liability to Bank unless the release specifically states otherwise.

So the drafters of 2002 saw life quite differently than did the drafters of 1990. The 2002 version follows the Restatement 3d of Suretyship.

3.   What if First Bank merely extends George's time to pay by 6 months? Here the 3–605's are about the same. Donald is discharged to the extent that he is injured by the extension of time (as when he can show that George could have paid $200,000 on the original due date but could pay nothing 6 months later).

§ 1–12   Discharge on the Instrument and on the Underlying Obligation

The events that discharge one's liability on a negotiable instrument are many; the Code addresses these with the blanket statement in 3–601(a): "The obligation of a party to pay the instrument is discharged as stated in this Article or by an act or agreement with the party which would discharge an obligation to pay money under a simple contract." Part 6 identifies several sources of discharge for individual treatment. The Code discusses payment (3–602), tender of payment (3–603), cancellation and renunciation (3–604), and discharge of indorsers and accommodation parties. Section 3–601 allows a party to become a holder in due course despite discharge, but provides that a holder in due course who takes with knowledge of the discharge is subject to that discharge. For example, as the comment to 3–601 says, a person who takes an instrument bearing a cancelled indorsement would have notice that the indorser has been discharged, so that discharge would be effective even if the person was a holder in due course.

In the normal course of events, the liability of a party to a negotiable instrument will terminate via discharge under 3–602: a holder of a check presents it to a bank for payment or a holder of a note presents it to the maker for payment; the holder is paid and relinquishes the instrument.

The language of section 3–602 is worth noting. The section states that an instrument is paid when a party obliged to pay does so, and when the money is transferred to "a person entitled to enforce the instrument." This language replaces more general references in the pre–1990 Code about the discharge by payment to "the holder" of a negotiable instrument. This fine tuning by the drafters of the 1990 revisions makes it clear that the party "entitled to enforce the instrument"—the one who should be paid and whose payment will discharge the instrument—may not be a holder. This would be true, for example, in the case of a payee from whom an instrument is stolen. The payee would be the one entitled to payment and that payment should discharge the liability except as against a potential holder in due course of the instrument. The party "entitled to enforce the instrument" is defined in section 3–301.[1] In addition, courts may be willing to supplement the Code with agency law and allow payment to an agent of a party entitled to enforce the instrument to discharge the liability, even when that agent absconds with the payment. For example, when an instrument is payable jointly and one payee is the agent of the other, courts have found the principal is in a better position to prevent the loss than the maker and the note is therefore discharged by the agent's receipt of the funds despite the use of a forged indorsement.

§ 1–12

1. § 3–301. Person Entitled to Enforce Instrument.

"Person entitled to enforce" an instrument means (i) the holder of the instrument, (ii) a nonholder in possession of the instrument who has the rights of a holder, or (iii) a person not in possession of the instrument who is entitled to enforce the instrument pursuant to Section 3–309 or 3–418(d). A person may be a person entitled to enforce the instrument even though the person is not the owner of the instrument or is in wrongful possession of the instrument.

Note that this does not prevent the principal from making a conversion claim against the depositary bank.

Section 3–602 plays a small role in establishing the responsibility of the issuer of a cashier's check. We discuss that issue in section 1–14.

2002 Amendments

The 2002 amendment to section 3–602 addresses the situation where an obligor pays a party who was entitled to enforce the note but who assigned the note to another before the payment. This situation could arise where a mortgagor continues to make payments to the bank where he obtained the original mortgage loan despite the fact that the bank assigned the mortgage to another entity. In order to protect these mortgagors, 2002 3–602 allows the debtor to pay the transferor until proper notice has been given to the debtor that a transfer has taken place and payments are to be made to a new person. Even after notice has been received by the debtor, he may request reasonable proof that the transfer took place and may continue to pay the transferor until that proof is provided. A new Comment 4 explains that this does not prevent a transferee from becoming a holder in due course for all other purposes.

§ 1–13 Discharge: Cancellation and Renunciation, Section 3–604

Section 3–604 provides that a person entitled to enforce an instrument may discharge the instrument, even without consideration, by an intentional voluntary act demonstrating the discharge, or by a written renunciation of rights. The section provides the following examples of acts that would adequately show intent to discharge: "surrender of the instrument . . ., destruction, mutilation or cancellation of the instrument, cancellation or striking out of the party's signature, or the addition of words to the instrument indicating discharge."

Section 3–604(b) provides that cancellation or striking out an indorsement "does not affect the status and rights of a party derived from the indorsement."

Section 3–604 makes it clear that surrender of an instrument acts as a discharge only if the instrument is surrendered with the intention of discharging it. This could be important in common disputes arising after old notes are exchanged for so-called renewal notes. On occasion, through inadvertence or for some other reason, the new notes will omit the signature of a co-maker or indorser of the original notes, or bear a forged signature. The typical dispute will then center on whether the original note remains effective or is discharged by surrender of the instrument to the original maker. In such cases, the party whose signature appeared on the old notes, but not on the renewal notes, can be expected to make two arguments.

One argument is that the holder discharged the omitted party by surrendering the original notes. This defense was not particularly successful even under the old Code, which provided in old section 3–605 that a surrender could effect a discharge even without intent to do so. The Code now specifically requires intent, and the argument will be even less often successful.

Even before the 1990 revision, courts usually required intent and surrender for discharge. In American Cement Corp. v. Century Transit Mix, Inc.,[1] plaintiff held notes made by Century and individually indorsed by a corporate officer. When the maker changed banks, plaintiff agreed to surrender the original notes and take new notes on the condition that the new notes duplicated the terms of the originals. Due to clerical error, the new notes did not have the signature of the individual indorser. Upon the maker's default, plaintiff sued the maker and the individual indorser. The indorser argued that he was not liable on the new notes because he had not signed them, and that the surrender of the original notes discharged him under the pre–1990 Code's section 3–605(1)(b). The New York court held that there was no surrender or discharge of the original notes because the plaintiff-holder did not intend to discharge anyone when it agreed to exchange the notes.

The second argument in the omitted party's defense is to claim that the new notes were taken in payment of the old ones. To this, the payee can be expected to cite 3–310, which provides that an exchange of one instrument for another does not discharge liability under the first instrument, but merely suspends it.

When the obligor has possession, the party suing on the instrument has to overcome a presumption that the instrument was discharged. Proof of the fact that the debtor never satisfied the underlying obligation, or that after the alleged cancellation the parties believed the obligation still existed, or even a credible denial by the creditor of intent to cancel the instrument can meet this burden.

§ 1–14   Suspension: Section 3–310

Section 3–310, a tidying up provision, states the legal effects on the underlying obligation when one takes a negotiable instrument for that obligation. The section also states the legal effects on the

1. 1966 WL 8946, 3 UCC 424 (N.Y. Sup. 1966).

underlying obligation when the obligation on the instrument is discharged. The "underlying obligation" is the original obligation between the parties which led to issuance of the negotiable instrument in the first place. In most cases, this obligation will be a contract, perhaps a contract for the sale of goods or services, and if no negotiable instrument were issued, this obligation would alone be enforceable by one party against the other. It is the issuance of the instrument that muddies the water with respect to the underlying obligation. Section 3–310 replaces the pre–1990 Code's section 3–802.

Usually, when one takes a negotiable instrument for an underlying obligation, the legal effect is not to discharge that obligation but merely to suspend it until the instrument is paid or dishonored.[1] Obviously, the obligation is discharged when the instrument is paid. The obligation is also discharged when a check is certified, under 3–310(b)(1).

The underlying obligation is discharged, not merely suspended, if the instrument is exchanged for a certified, cashier's, or teller's check. This exception brings 3–310[2] into conformance with 3–414(c), which says: "If a draft is accepted by a bank, the drawer is discharged, regardless of when or by whom acceptance was obtained." Doubtless these rules are consistent with normal business

---

§ 1–14

1. § 3–310(b): Unless otherwise agreed and except as provided in subsection (a), if a note or an uncertified check is taken for an obligation, the obligation is suspended to the same extent the obligation would be discharged if an amount of money equal to the amount of the instrument were taken, and the following rules apply:

(1) In the case of an uncertified check, suspension of the obligation continues until dishonor of the check or until it is paid or certified. Payment or certification of the check results in discharge of the obligation to the extent of the amount of the check.

(2) In the case of a note, suspension of the obligation continues until dishonor of the note or until it is paid. Payment of the note results in discharge of the obligation to the extent of the payment.

(3) Except as provided in paragraph (4), if the check or note is dishonored and the obligee of the obligation for which the instrument was taken is the person entitled to enforce the instrument, the obligee may enforce either the instrument or the obligation. In the case

of an instrument of a third person which is negotiated to the obligee by the obligor, discharge of the obligor on the instrument also discharges the obligation.

(4) If the person entitled to enforce the instrument taken for an obligation is a person other than the obligee, the obligee may not enforce the obligation to the extent the obligation is suspended. If the obligee is the person entitled to enforce the instrument but no longer has possession of it because it was lost, stolen, or destroyed, the obligation may not be enforced to the extent of the amount payable on the instrument, and to that extent the obligee's rights against the obligor are limited to enforcement of the instrument.

2. § 3–310(a):

Unless otherwise agreed, if a certified check, cashier's check, or teller's check is taken for an obligation, the obligation is discharged to the same extent discharge would result if an amount of money equal to the amount of the instrument were taken in payment of the obligation. Discharge of the obligation does not affect any liability that the obligor may have as an indorser of the instrument.

expectations. A cashier's check mimics cash and it is likely that the expectation of the parties is that the obligation is extinguished when such a check is passed. On the other hand, it is a rare and foolish business executive who treats a personal check as identical to cash. The drawer still has the power to stop payment and many a check is drawn against insufficient funds. In reality, taking a personal check is no more than trading one promise for another by the same party.

In a typical uncertified-check case, "suspension" of the underlying obligation has little practical significance, for the parties contemplate that the check will be presented promptly and that the drawer will pay promptly.[3] The same is not true if one party gives the other a note due in 90 or 120 days. Suspension of the payee's right to sue on the underlying obligation for the period until the note becomes due is significant for both parties. The payee gives up a valuable right to insist on the immediate payment and the maker acquires valuable time to get his payment together.

Note that 3–310 is prefaced by the phrase "unless otherwise agreed," so the rules just discussed can be overturned by agreement of the parties. If the parties agree that one of them will take the other's check in satisfaction of a debt, then the underlying obligation is discharged. Occasionally a defendant will argue that the circumstances surrounding the taking of the check evidenced an "agreement otherwise" to discharge the obligation. What circumstances constitute an agreement is not clear from the cases discussed in Section 1–13 *supra*. In those cases, a set of checks is exchanged for a set of notes or a set of notes is renewed by the maker's execution of new notes. In these exchanges the question arises, as we have seen, whether the obligation on the originals (in this case the underlying obligation) was discharged as to one who was a party to the first set but not to the second when the creditor took the second. In the *Slaughter*[4] case (in which one maker on the first set refused to sign the second set), the court found that the second set extinguished the obligation. Similarly, in *Cipra*[5], the court held that the second note discharged the obligations of both the corporate maker and individual indorsers of the first note (where the latter were not parties to the second note, and were thus entirely discharged). Where, on the other hand, one signer was inadvertently omitted from the second set or where the first set was

---

3. Long v. Cuttle Const. Co., 60 Cal. App.4th 834, 70 Cal.Rptr.2d 698, 34 UCC2d 418 (1998) (creditors cannot recover interest for 5 day period between time received an uncertified check and time bank paid the check. Discharge of the debt related back to the time the creditors took the check as payment for the debt).

4. Slaughter v. Philadelphia Nat. Bank, 290 F.Supp. 234, 5 UCC 856 (E.D.Pa. 1968), rev'd on other grounds, 417 F.2d 21 (3d Cir.1969).

5. Cipra v. Seeger, 215 Kan. 951, 529 P.2d 130, 16 UCC 461 (1974).

cancelled without knowledge of two of the original signers, and their signatures were forged on the second set, the courts found no intention that the second set be taken in satisfaction of the first. Suffice it to say that the lawyer should be aware of the possibility of an agreement between the parties that the giving of the instrument extinguishes the underlying obligation.

Subsections 3–310(b)(3) and (4) deal in greater detail with the unusual circumstances where the underlying obligation and the obligation on the instrument are somehow divided. This would arise, for example, when a buyer takes a third-party's check or note, payable to the buyer, and transfers it to a seller in payment for goods. Subsection (b)(4) deals with the case in which the instrument is stolen or lost and the obligation so potentially divided. The comments describe the effect of the last sentences of (b)(3) and (b)(4) as follows:

> The last sentence of subsection (b)(3) applies to cases in which an instrument of another person is indorsed over to the obligee in payment of the obligation. For example, Buyer delivers an uncertified personal check of X payable to the order of Buyer to Seller in payment of the price of goods. Buyer indorses the check over to Seller. Buyer is liable on the check as indorser. If Seller neglects to present the check for payment or to deposit it for collection within 30 days of the indorsement, Buyer's liability as indorser is discharged. Section 3–415(e). Under the last sentence of Section 3–310(b)(3) Buyer is also discharged on the obligation to pay for the goods.

> * * * There was uncertainty concerning the applicability of former Section 3–802 to the case in which the check given for the obligation was stolen from the payee, the payee's signature was forged, and the forger obtained payment. The last sentence of subsection (b)(4) addresses this issue. If the payor bank pays a holder, the drawer is discharged on the underlying obligation because the check was paid. Subsection (b)(1). If the payor bank pays a person not entitled to enforce the instrument, as in the hypothetical case, the suspension of the underlying obligation continues because the check has not been paid. Section 3–602(a). The payee's cause of action is against the depositary bank or payor bank in conversion under Section 3–420 or against the drawer under Section 3–309. In the latter case, the drawer's obligation under Section 3–414(b) is triggered by dishonor which occurs because the check is unpaid. Presentment for payment to the drawee is excused under Section 3–504(a)(i) and, under Section 3–502(e), dishonor occurs without presentment if the check is not paid. The payee cannot merely ignore the instrument and sue the drawer on the underlying contract. This would impose on the drawer the

risk that the check when stolen was indorsed in blank or to bearer.

The problem posed later in the same comment, that of a lost check, provides a nice view of the effect of subsections (b)(3) and (b)(4). If one loses a check given to settle an obligation, what actions should one pursue?

First, you should ask the issuer of the check to issue a replacement check and to stop payment on the lost one. This provides the best assurance for both parties. Having failed in this, the party losing the check could proceed as if the check had been stolen. Recall that the taking of the check suspended the underlying obligation, but did not discharge it. Therefore, it is fruitless to proceed against the issuer of the check on the underlying obligation. Instead the action must be brought on the instrument itself. Under 3–309, our unlucky friend would qualify as a person entitled to enforce the instrument. If this person can further prove the terms of the instrument, he is treated (under 3–309(b)) as though he had actually presented the instrument and was entitled to payment—provided the court concludes that the issuer of the lost check is adequately protected against a later claim on the instrument by a third party.

Most of the cases under pre–1990 3–802 are strictly mine-run specimens. In Goblirsch v. Heikes,[6] plaintiff, an eccentric seller of tractors, held checks from purchaser for five years before attempting to cash them. Defendant purchaser had placed a stop payment order on the checks approximately six months after the purchase. Since plaintiff did not establish that he had presented the checks within a reasonable time, defendant was discharged from liability on the checks. However, discharge from liability on the checks was not discharge from the underlying obligation, and defendant was still obliged to pay for the tractors. Tendering the checks suspended the underlying obligation, but once the checks were dishonored, the liability for the obligation returned.

U.S. for Use and Benefit of D'Agostino Excavators, Inc. v. Heyward–Robinson Co.,[7] has gossip value owing to the fact that some crafty or lucky lawyer induced the eminences of the Second Circuit (Friendly, Kaufman, and Lumbard, JJ.) thoroughly to misinterpret the Code discharge provisions. In that case, Heyward, the appellant, gave promissory notes in a face amount of $36,250 to D'Agostino. Later, D'Agostino negotiated the notes to third parties at less than their face amount. Heyward, the maker, later "reacquired" the notes from the third party holders (that is, satisfied his obligations under them) for $18,500. At trial Heyward argued

6. 547 N.W.2d 89, 31 UCC2d 1049 (Minn.App.1996).

7. 430 F.2d 1077, 7 UCC 1331 (2d Cir.1970), cert. denied, 400 U.S. 1021, 91 S.Ct. 582, 27 L.Ed.2d 632 (1971).

his liability to D'Agostino was so discharged to the extent of the full $36,250. The trial court allowed the jury to determine "as a question of fact the amount which should be credited to Heyward on these notes." Judge Lumbard, sitting as the trial judge, instructed the jury that Heyward should be credited with the full amount "only if the parties intended the notes as payment at the time they were received." On appeal, the Second Circuit noted in passing that appellant had not pointed out the provisions of the pre–1990 Code's 3–802 to the trial court; nevertheless the court found that 3–802 was consistent with the instructions in fact given to the jury. If (as appears, though not clearly) Heyward in fact satisfied the notes for something less than their face value to their holders, his obligation on the notes was discharged under 3–603. Under 3–802(1)(b) that discharge also discharged him on the underlying obligation. All of this follows irrespective of the intentions of the parties at the time Heyward gave the notes to D'Agostino. If the inference we draw from the opinion, that the maker paid the notes, is not correct, the court's analysis of 3–802 would be inartful but accurate. The only fact at issue in that case would be whether the parties had originally "agreed" to transfer the notes in full satisfaction of the underlying obligation.

The court found that Heyward "was entitled to credit against the payee, D'Agostino, only for the amount it paid to the transferees." That finding makes no sense, for it would mean that the payee on the note, D'Agostino, could have sold the notes for $30,000 and then insisted upon additional payment from Heyward amounting to the difference between $36,000 and the amount Heyward paid (in this case a difference of approximately $18,000). It makes no sense to peg Heyward's obligation by reference to the amount he paid to reacquire the notes for he should have been discharged either under 3–603 (payment) or by virtue of 3–601(3)(a) (one who reacquires the instrument in his own right). In defense of the eminent judges of the Second Circuit and their clerks—all apparently ignorant of Parts 6 and 8 of Article 3—Heyward's lawyer must have been equally ignorant of those provisions.[8]

§ 1–15 Accord and Satisfaction Through Use of an Instrument

Offering a check for less than the full amount claimed by the creditor but in "full settlement" is a common practice. If the amount offered is not grossly insufficient, it presents the creditor with an exquisite dilemma: Will I accept the $9,000 and forfeit the other $1,000 that he really owes me, or do I refuse it all in the hope

---

8. In 2002, the PEB amended comment 3 to 3–310 to explain that the underlying obligation is not revived in the situations under (b)(4) even after the note is dishonored. Only the obligation to pay the instrument remains.

I can get $10,000 later? Traditional legal analysis has treated the tender of the check as the offer of an accord and satisfaction. The payee who indorses a check and receives payment has accepted the contract and so discharged any claim for a larger amount.[1]

Before the Code, a payee's attempt to modify the proposed contract by scratching out the full satisfaction language or by adding some supplementary language was ineffective to change the result. By cashing the check, the payee was bound by the drawer debtor's offer. With the passage of the Code, the rules of the game arguably changed. Former Section 1–207 reads in part as follows:

A party who with explicit reservation of rights performs or promises performance or assents to performance in a manner demanded or offered by the other party does not thereby prejudice the rights reserved. Such words as "without prejudice", "under protest" or the like are sufficient.

But this language brought its own uncertainty. Did 1–207 permit creditors who added some form of disclaimer (e.g., "all rights reserved") to keep the money without forfeiting claims to additional sums from debtors? Or, as some argued, did 1–207 apply only in a particular, narrow circumstance, where two parties to a continuing contract disagree over some aspect of their contract but do not want the disagreement to disrupt work under the contract? Under the latter interpretation, a creditor, seeking only to enforce an obligation to pay could not amend the instrument, deposit a full-payment check and reserve the right to sue for more money. Courts divided on this question. Some courts interpreted 1–207 as inapplicable to "full satisfaction" checks and followed the common law rule, thus finding an accord and satisfaction, and denying effect to the creditor's disclaimer. Other courts read 1–207 to permit the creditor to cash the check while rejecting the offer of full settlement. The latter courts found that the creditor retained its unpaid part of its claim.

The 1990 Code revisions resolved this debate in favor of those who argued that 1–207 did not apply to full satisfaction checks. First, the drafters of revised Article 3 amended section 1–207, adding the following provision as subsection (2): "Subsection (1) does not apply to an accord and satisfaction." The Comment describes the purpose of 1–207 as follow:

This section provides machinery for the continuation of performance along the lines contemplated by the contract despite a pending dispute, by adopting the mercantile device of going ahead with delivery, acceptance, or payment "without preju-

1. See 6 A. Corbin, Contracts, sections 1277–78 (2d ed. 1962).

dice," "under protest," "under reserve," "with reservation of all our rights," and the like.

All of this has now moved to Section 1–308 with the 2001 revision of Article 1. The 1990 revisions included section 3–311; that section finds an accord and satisfaction even in circumstances where the creditor signs "under protest" or "with reservation of rights." The section reads in full as follows:

(a) If a person against whom a claim is asserted proves that (i) that person in good faith tendered an instrument to the claimant as full satisfaction of the claim, (ii) the amount of the claim was unliquidated or subject to a bona fide dispute, and (iii) the claimant obtained payment of the instrument, the following subsections apply.

(b) Unless subsection (c) applies, the claim is discharged if the person against whom the claim is asserted proves that the instrument or an accompanying written communication contained a conspicuous statement to the effect that the instrument was tendered as full satisfaction of the claim.

(c) Subject to subsection (d), a claim is not discharged under subsection (b) if either of the following applies:

(1) The claimant, if an organization, proves that (i) within a reasonable time before the tender, the claimant sent a conspicuous statement to the person against whom the claim is asserted that communications concerning disputed debts, including an instrument tendered as full satisfaction of a debt, are to be sent to a designated person, office, or place, and (ii) the instrument or accompanying communication was not received by that designated person, office, or place.

(2) The claimant, whether or not an organization, proves that within 90 days after payment of the instrument, the claimant tendered repayment of the amount of the instrument to the person against whom the claim is asserted. This paragraph does not apply if the claimant is an organization that sent a statement complying with paragraph (1)(i).

(d) A claim is discharged if the person against whom the claim is asserted proves that within a reasonable time before collection of the instrument was initiated, the claimant, or an agent of the claimant having direct responsibility with respect to the disputed obligation, knew that the instrument was tendered in full satisfaction of the claim.

Note first, the written communication of full satisfaction need not be on the instrument itself, but can be on an "accompanying written communication."[2]

Second, this communication must be "conspicuous." In Gelles & Sons General Contracting, Inc. v. Jeffrey Stack, Inc.,[3] Gelles submitted an invoice for $26,175 for brick laying work provided to JSI. JSI responded with a schedule of account making adjustments to the total provided by Gelles to reflect work and material provided by JSI to "properly complete the work." These calculations were disputed by Gelles. JSI sent a check for $13,580 to Gelles along with a letter which in its final paragraph stated that the check was the final payment on the contract. Gelles negotiated the check and then filed suit against JSI for the difference. The court found that the UCC requires an objective determination whether a reasonable person would understand that the payment was meant to discharge the obligation. The court further held that it could properly take into account the circumstances of the transaction and conduct of the parties. The court therefore found that the entire course of conduct and the communications between the parties made it clear that JSI offered the check as final payment.

Third, 3–311(a) incorporates the standard common law rules regarding an amount that is unliquidated or subject to "bona fide dispute,"[4] and requires good faith. The issue of good faith has been troublesome. We believe that good faith in this context refers to the manner in which the tender is offered, not to conduct related to the underlying claim.

In Webb Business Promotions, Inc. v. American Electronics & Entertainment Corp.,[5] Webb entered into a contract to deliver 300,000 blank videotapes to AE & E. AE & E attempted to cancel the order by notifying Webb that the order was canceled and it would thereafter place orders on a weekly basis. AE & E then ordered 85,000 units. AE & E paid by a check explicitly referring to the original order for 300,000 units and including the words "Please be aware that this is a final check, AE & E will have no obligation to Webb as long as the check is cashed by Webb." Webb deposited the check.

AE & E cancelled its contract with Webb because Target Corp. cancelled its contract with AE & E. Webb did not know that Target

2. Havard v. Kemper Nat'l Ins., 945 F.Supp. 953, 31 UCC2d 828 (S.D. Miss. 1995) (precise words "full payment" not required, courts will look to overall thrust of the writings).

3. 264 Va. 285, 569 S.E.2d 406 (2002).

4. Employers Workers' Compensation Ass'n v. W.P. Industries, 925 P.2d 1225, 31 UCC2d 833 (Okla. App. 1996) (dispute over whether liable for more than 50% of partnership's assessment does not make amount of assessment subject to good faith dispute).

5. 617 N.W.2d 67, 42 UCC2d 534 (Minn. 2000).

Corp. could cancel anytime prior to delivery for any reason. Despite the fact that this could have represented bad faith regarding the original contract for 300,000 units, the court held that the good faith element of accord and satisfaction is violated when bad faith is directly related to the tender of the accord and not violated when bad faith is purely related to the actions (i.e., misrepresentation, concealment of facts) with respect to the underlying contracts.

The outmaneuvered creditor, who loses the right to money he or she was owed, deserves sympathy, but there is some compelling logic from 1–207 to current 3–311. The logic rests on the common law foundation, generally unassailable, that the offeror is the "master of his offer."[6] By this reasoning, the drawer has made an offer, namely that of full payment, and allowing the payee to accept the money without the other terms of the offer is not only unfair, but also in direct conflict with the traditional notions of contract formation. But, of course, there is another side to this coin; the debtor who knows he owes $10,000 and offers $9,000 is a chiseler.

Subsections 3–311(b), (c), and (d) deal with two other complications. First, what happens with respect to Commonwealth Edison when its customers offer "full satisfaction" checks claiming that they owe less than the full amount of their electric bill? Commonwealth Edison and other utilities receive thousands of checks every day, process them mechanically and cannot be expected to give careful thought to messages on the back of each check. Section 3–311(c)(1) is for these payees. Under this provision, a utility can send a conspicuous statement to its customer to the effect that "communications concerning disputed debts, including an instrument tendered as full satisfaction of a debt, are to be sent to X" (a designated person, office or place.) If the customer then submits the "full satisfaction" check in the normal manner, declining to send it to the person in charge of disputed debts, the offer of discharge for less than the full amount claimed is ineffective.

Note that section 3–311(d) is an exception to the exception. If the debtor does not send the check to the specially designated office, and if the employees of the utility are exceptionally diligent and notice the full settlement language on the back of the check, the payee is then bound by its notice, and the debt is fully discharged if the payee cashes the check. The comments make clear that even persons at a collection agency or others collecting accounts receivable may qualify as agents of the claimant "having direct responsibility" under section 3–311(d):

6. Note that § 2–207 has changed the common law rule that the offeror is the master of his offer. In many cases under 2–207 the offeror will find himself bound to a contract that omits terms that were in his offer to which he never explicitly agreed.

With respect to an attempted accord and satisfaction the "individual conducting that transaction" is an employee or other agent of the organization having direct responsibility with respect to the dispute. For example, if the check and communication are received by a collection agency acting for the claimant to collect the disputed claim, obtaining payment of the check will result in an accord and satisfaction even if the claimant gave notice, pursuant to subsection (c)(1), that full satisfaction checks be sent to some other office. Similarly, if a customer asserting a claim for breach of warranty with respect to defective goods purchased in a retail outlet of a large chain store delivers the full satisfaction check to the manager of the retail outlet at which the goods were purchased, obtaining payment of the check will also result in an accord and satisfaction. On the other hand, if the check is mailed to the chief executive officer of the chain store, subsection (d) would probably not be satisfied. The chief executive officer of a large corporation may have general responsibility for operations of the company, but does not normally have direct responsibility for resolving a small disputed bill to a customer. A check for a relatively small amount mailed to a high executive officer of a large organization is not likely to receive the executive's personal attention. Rather, the check would normally be sent to the appropriate office for deposit and credited to the customer's account. If the check does receive the personal attention of the high executive officer and the officer is aware of the full-satisfaction language, collection of the check will result in an accord and satisfaction because subsection (d) applies. In this case the officer has assumed direct responsibility with respect to the disputed transaction.

If full satisfaction check is sent to a lock box or other office processing checks sent to the claimant, it is irrelevant whether the clerk processing the check did or did not see the statement that the check was tendered as full satisfaction of the claim. Knowledge of the clerk is not imputed to the organization because the clerk has no responsibility with respect to an accord and satisfaction. Moreover, there is no failure of "due diligence" under Section 1–201(27) if the claimant does not require its clerks to look for full satisfaction statements on checks or accompanying communications. Nor is there any duty of the claimant to assign that duty to its clerks. Section 3–311(c) is intended to allow a claimant to avoid an inadvertent accord and satisfaction by complying with either subsection (c)(1) or (2) without burdening the check-processing operation with extraneous and wasteful additional duties.

Section 3–311(c)(2) offers a 90 day safety valve to a creditor who has received a "full satisfaction" check on a large amount and wishes not to forfeit its claim. Assume, for example, that a debtor about to be involved in litigation with the creditor sends a $2,000,000 check in satisfaction of a $5,000,000 claim, with a stamp on the reverse side "in full settlement." Assume that the check is deposited and paid without the creditor's noticing the legend. Any time within 90 days the creditor can undo the possibility of an accord and satisfaction under 3–311 by tendering repayment. In any event, it would be wise to establish a policy to look at the back of every large check. Those who routinely receive large numbers of small checks (such as utilities) should surely accept the drafters' offer in revised 3–311(c) and send a "conspicuous statement" to their customers identifying the person to whom they should send communications concerning "disputed debt."

§ 1–16 Statute of Limitations

Section 3–118, an elaborate statute of limitations, was added to the Code as part of the 1990 revisions. The section does not state when a cause of action accrues, but it generally states the time after which a lawsuit may not be filed. Comment 1 also points out that the section does not attempt to state all rules with respect to a statute of limitations. For example, questions concerning tolling of the statute of limitations and other similar matters are left to the common law. The statutory time for various liabilities is summarized in the following chart:

Type of Instrument	Must Commence Action to Enforce	
Note payable at definite date	1)	6 years after due date
Demand Note	1)	Must make demand within 10 yrs.
	2)	6 more years once dishonored
Unaccepted Draft	1)	Must make demand within 10 yrs.
	2)	3 more years once dishonored
Certified, Teller's,	1)	No time limit to make demand
Cashier's and Traveler's Checks	2)	3 years once demand made and dishonored
Certificates of Deposit	1)	Action to enforce must begin with six years of demand for payment
	2)	dated: within 6 years after due date

Type of Instrument	Must Commence Action to Enforce
Other Accepted Drafts (drawn on nonbanks)	1) Demand: 6 years after acceptance 2) dated: 6 years after due date
Action for Conversion, Breach of Warranty, etc.	1) 3 years after action accrues

Depending on the circumstances, the period of limitations is ten years, six years, or three years. In general, the maker of a note has a liability for six years after the due date or after the date of acceleration, whichever is earlier. Liability on a conventional check runs out three years after dishonor or, if there is never a dishonor, ten years after the date of the draft.

In Penagos v. Capital Bank,[1] plaintiff held a certificate with a maturity date of December 27, 1988. On November 30, 1991, Plaintiff made a written demand for payment and in February of 1995 filed suit. Applying a Florida statute outside the Code, the court found that the statute of limitations began running at the time of written demand, not at the date of maturity. The Court notes that 3–118(e) commands the same result.

Section 3–118(b) makes issuers of certified, teller's, cashier's and traveler's checks potentially liable for an indefinite period if there has never been a demand for payment. That is to say, they have the same liability of the drawer of a conventional draft except the ten year outside limit does not apply to them.

Notes payable on demand are a special case. Assume that the payee on such a note makes no demand and receives no payments. The statute would run ten years after the note was issued. Assume, however, that the payee makes a demand for payment in the ninth year. That demand would give the payee six additional years in which to sue; there would then be a fifteen year liability on the note. If the demand note provided for interest and if interest were paid at least once within each ten years, the liability would continue indefinitely under the last sentence of revised section 3–118.

The new statute of limitations provisions will be useful clarifications and will help minimize problems formerly associated with pawing around in a state's disorganized body of statutory and case law on limitations. But the most significant subsection in the new section 3–118 may be (g) which reads in full as follows:

§ 1–16

1. 766 So.2d 1089, 42 UCC2d 751 (Fla.App. 2000).

(g) Unless governed by other law regarding claims for indemnity or contribution, an action (i) for conversion of an instrument, for money had and received, or like action based on conversion, (ii) for breach of warranty, or (iii) to enforce an obligation, duty, or right arising under this Article and not governed by this section must be commenced within three years after the [cause of action] accrues.

Note first that the "governed by other law" clause at the beginning of the subsection applies only to claims for indemnity or contribution. It does not apply to conversion, warranty or the like. The sentence establishes a three-year statute of limitations on conversion (3–420), restitution (3–418), and other obligations, duties or rights arising under the article and not otherwise governed by this section. All of these "must be commenced within three years after the [cause of action] accrues."

When does the cause of action accrue? On the "event," or on plaintiff's notice or discovery of the event? Section 3–417(f) states that the cause of action for breach of warranty accrues "when the claimant has reason to know of the breach." On the other hand, section 2–725 on sale of goods embraces the time of the breach, not the time of discovery. Beyond the cases specifically covered by 3–416(d) and 3–417(f), reasonable people can differ about the meaning of "accrues." We prefer the time of the events giving rise to liability, not the time such events are discovered. Many courts adopt this rule (i.e., that the discovery rule does not apply unless the defendant fraudulently concealed the transaction so as to prevent its discovery by the plaintiff).[2]

Does section 3–118(g) apply to claims pursuant to the underlying obligation (for which a check or note is given)? Section 3–118(g) applies to an "obligation arising under this Article." But the underlying obligation does not "arise" under Article 3 and is therefore subject to the statute of limitations in Article 2 on the sale of goods or in the common law of a particular state, not to 3–118.[3] We believe that the same is not true of a conversion cause of action under section 3–420, even though that section begins with the sentence: "The law applicable to conversion of personal proper-

2. Bradley v. National City Bank of Kentucky, 2004 WL 3017297, 55 UCC2d 613 (Ky. App. 2004). See also Estate of Hollywood v. First Nat. Bank of Palmerton, 859 A.2d 472, 54 UCC2d 343 (Pa. Super. 2004) (rejected discovery rule absent any proof banks fraudulently concealed conversion of checks); Quilling v. Compass Bank, 2004 WL 2093117, 54 UCC2d 975 (N.D. Tex. 2004) (discovery rule did not apply because bank did not fraudulently conceal transactions); New Jersey Lawyers' Fund for Client Protection v. Pace, 374 N.J.Super. 57, 863 A.2d 402, 55 UCC2d 729 (App. Div. 2005) (discovery rule did not apply where there was no assertion of fraud against bank).

3. Because § 3–118 merely states the latest time one may "commence" an action and does not "discharge" the obligation, we do not believe that § 3–118 causes a discharge of the underlying obligation.

ty applies to instruments." In our view, the rights on conversion of the instrument arise under "this Article" and thus, are covered by 3–118(g).

The same is true of the cause of action set forth in 3–406(b). Under the old Code, negligence under section 3–406 operated merely by way of preclusion or defense. Section 3–406(b) introduces comparative negligence and allows the one who has borne the loss to recover a portion of that loss from another because of that person's negligence. This section states an affirmative cause of action arising under "this Article" and should also be governed by 3–118(g).

Because section 4–111, the statute of limitations in Article 4, also uses a three-year limitation, the danger of conflict between the two articles with respect to negligence and warranty causes of action is minimal.

Chapter 2

THE HOLDER IN DUE COURSE

Analysis

§ 2–1 Introduction

In Chapter 1 we considered the *prima facie* liability of various parties to commercial paper, makers, acceptors, indorsers, and drawers in actions "on the instrument." *Prima facie* liability is one thing; ultimate liability after parties have asserted their contract and other defenses is another. Among these defenses are failure of consideration, the failure of a condition, fraud and so on. In this branch of the law, the legal effectiveness of those defenses varies with the plaintiff's status, and the party able to attain the status of holder in due course qualifies as Superplaintiff. With some exceptions, the holder in due course is immune to defenses, claims in recoupment, and claims of title that prior parties to commercial paper might assert. The holder in due course always enjoys certain pleading and proof advantages.[1]

In theory at least, the holder in due course doctrine facilitates all kinds of transactions. First, it facilitates the flow of capital from large lenders to the seller to an individual consumer. In theory it does that by causing the lenders to purchase consumer paper and thus to use their capital to allow individual lenders and merchants to do business with the consumer. Second, the doctrine theoretically facilitates the transfer of checks and arguably makes one more willing to accept the checks if he or she knows he or she can be a holder in due course of that instrument and take it free of defenses that might have existed between the buyer and the seller in the underlying transaction. Over the past fifty years there has been a continuing debate about the importance of the holder in due course doctrine in facilitating these transactions. Some argued that the abolition of the holder in due course doctrine in consumer transactions would substantially restrict the flow of credit and thus diminish the purchase options available to consumers. Others argued that the holder in due course doctrine was not important for such transactions and that they would continue notwithstanding its abolition. It now appears that the latter arguments were correct. The Federal Trade Commission's Rule (16 CFR 433.1–.3) effectively abolished the holder in due course doctrine in most consumer credit transactions. In section 2–9 we discuss that doctrine and its application. Suffice it to say that the FTC reached farther in abolishing the holder in due course doctrine than even the doctrine's most virulent opponents could have hoped as recently as forty years ago. Not only has it effectively wiped out the holder in due course doctrine as to consumer paper transferred among sellers and lenders, but it has rendered many lenders who make direct loans to consumers subject to the defenses that those consumers have against third-party sellers. Its passage has caused some adjustments in the market, largely unseen, but it surely has not had the catastrophic impact upon the consumer market that some predicted.

Since the FTC rule has substantially reduced the significance of the holder in due course doctrine, one might ask why study it? Despite its virtual extinction in the realm of consumer debt obligations, the holder in due course doctrine lives on in many commercial settings and in some consumer settings, particularly those involving checks and notes that are secured by real estate. Every

§ 2–1

1. See generally Lewis v. Opstein, 1 Neb.App. 698, 510 N.W.2d 382, 23 UCC2d 767 (1993) (burden of proof of holder in due course status); Weinberg, Pleading and Practice in Commercial Paper Cases: Burdens of Proof, 72 Ky. L.J. 575 (1983).

year many takers of checks that are dishonored (because payment has been stopped or for other reasons) sue drawers claiming freedom of defenses on the underlying contract. In an equal number of cases, purchasers of commercial paper rely upon their holder in due course status to protect them against claims arising out of the underlying transaction. These, of course, are the traditional beneficiaries of the holder in due course doctrine. In other cases, the takers seek the protection of the doctrine in order to cut off prior defenses or enjoy priority under 9–331. Finally, one needs to understand the holder in due course doctrine to be a self-respecting lawyer. Like knowledge of a variety of other doctrines of marginal utility (such as the rule against perpetuities), knowledge of the holder in due course doctrine remains a badge of the lawyer.

Finally, we mention one last wrinkle in the holder in due course doctrine—the last major modifications were part of the 1990 revision of Article 3. Some of these modifications clarify; others respond to recent changes in commerce. The 2002 revision of Article 3 has not affected the holder in due course doctrine much except as related to the Federal Trade Commission Rule mentioned above. The 2002 revisions have not yet been widely adopted (and may never be), so the 1990 revisions continue to be important. We point out the changes, as we did in the previous chapter, to alert readers familiar with the pre–1990 Code and to flag those provisions least tested by the courts.

The most notable change in 1990 was to modify the "sum certain" requirement so that variable rate notes can be negotiable. Under the pre–1990 Code, many courts held that variable rate notes did not contain a sum certain, were therefore not negotiable, and thus were incapable of being held by a holder in due course. A second change in the conditions for holder in due course status was in the definition of "good faith." The change has caused some confusion in the courts and inconsistency in applying the new definition despite the drafters' official comments explaining the changes, as we will see in 2–6. What long-term impact that change will have, or whether it will have any impact at all, remains to be seen.

The drafters also modified the language of Article 3 in both 1990 and 2002 to make the holder in due course doctrine and the concept of negotiable instruments fit together with the Federal Trade Commission rules concerning consumer notes. In addition, the drafters changed the operational language concerning the rights of holders in due course so that now one must worry not only about real defenses and other defenses and claims, but also about "rights in recoupment." These changes are probably insignificant.

§ 2–2   Holder in Due Course Defined

A holder in due course must meet five conditions:[1]

1. a holder

2. of a negotiable instrument who took it

3. for value

4. in good faith

5. without notice of certain problems with the instrument.

The drafters modified three of the basic conditions in 1990. They redefined "instrument" and "good faith," and slightly modified the kind of notice that will keep one from being a holder in due course.

PROBLEM

Thief steals two checks. Check One has been indorsed in blank and so becomes bearer paper, 3–205(b). Check Two is payable to the order of George Fox and has not been indorsed. Thief forges Fox's name and adds a fictitious signature to both checks before cashing them at Check Cashing Service. Service pays Thief the face amount of both checks and takes them without notice of the forgeries and in good faith. Both are dishonored because both drawers issue stop orders. When the checks are returned to Service, it sues each of the drawers on their drawers' contracts. Drawers, of course, defend by challenging Service's title and asserting theft as a defense, 3–305(c), 3–306.

Service recovers on Check One but does not recover on Check Two because it is a holder in due course as to Check One but not even a holder of Check Two. Do you recall the reasons from Chapter 1? Remember that one becomes a holder only by "negotiation" and that negotiation of an order instrument requires the indorsement of the "holder." Thief is a holder of the bearer check but not of the order check, 1–201(b)(21). So the "indorsement" on

---

§ 2–2

1. § 3–302(a) provides in part:

"holder in due course" means the holder of an instrument if:

(1) the instrument when issued or negotiated to the holder does not bear such apparent evidence of forgery or alteration or is not otherwise so irregular or incomplete as to call into question its authenticity; and

(2) the holder took the instrument (i) for value, (ii) in good faith, (iii) without notice that the instrument is overdue or has been dishonored or that there is an uncured default with respect to payment of another instrument issued as part of the same series, (iv) without notice that the instrument contains an unauthorized signature or has been altered, (v) without notice of any claim to the instrument described in Section 3–306, and (vi) without notice that any party has a defense or claim in recoupment described in Section 3–305(a).

the order paper by Thief is not the indorsement "by the holder" as 3–201(b) requires for the "negotiation" of an order instrument.

These rules explain why one sees few bearer instruments in life and why we can be so casual in the mailing and keeping of order instruments.

§ 2–3   Holder in Due Course Defined—Holder

Obviously only a holder can be a holder in due course. To be a holder, one must meet the two conditions in 1–201(b)(21):

(1) he must have possession (2) of a negotiable instrument payable to him or to bearer.

Section 3–201 is also relevant. It provides:

(a) "Negotiation" means a transfer of possession, whether voluntary or involuntary, of an instrument by a person other than the issuer to a person who thereby becomes its holder.

(b) Except for negotiation by a remitter, if an instrument is payable to an identified person, negotiation requires transfer of possession of the instrument and its indorsement by the holder. If an instrument is payable to bearer, it may be negotiated by transfer of possession alone.

The ambiguity in the word "possession" has caused little trouble. With rare exceptions, those claiming to be holders seem to have had physical possession of the instrument in question. Lost, destroyed, or stolen notes can also be enforced in some cases under 3–309. The second requirement is also clear in most cases but has posed real interpretive difficulties—particularly in cases in which an instrument has passed through the hands of a thief before reaching the hands of the putative holder in due course. If an instrument is payable to bearer, either because it was issued that way and continued its life as a bearer instrument ("pay to the order of Cash") or because it was indorsed in blank by a holder ("Joe Jones"), the possessor of the instrument will be a holder and, if he meets the other tests, a holder in due course. This is so even though the instrument may have passed through the hands of a thief; the holder in due course is one of the few purchasers in Anglo–Saxon jurisprudence who may derive a good title from a chain of title that includes a thief in its links.

The same rule does not apply to a stolen order instrument ("Pay to the order of Joe Jones"). In order to transfer a stolen order instrument, a thief must forge the indorsement of the party to whose order it is drawn. The thief himself is not a holder under 1–201(b)(21) because the instrument is not payable to his order or to bearer; by hypothesis it is payable to the order of another, the true owner. Under section 3–201 quoted above, this instrument may be "negotiated" (i.e., passed to a person who thereby becomes its "holder") only if it is indorsed "by the holder." Since the thief is not a holder, any writing he puts on the back is not an "indorsement by the holder;" therefore the transaction—however voluntary with a third party who is fooled by the thief—does not constitute a negotiation under 3–201 and does not therefore render that third party himself a holder. The upshot of these rules stated in 1–201(b)(21) and 3–201 is that none of the transferees downstream from the thief—however much value they have given and however good their faith—can be a holder or a holder in due course. Each will have taken by a process that is not "negotiation" and each will in turn not be a holder and accordingly lack the power to make a negotiation under 3–201. Absent preclusion of the owner to deny the forgery à la 3–404 through 3–406, no party can ever be a holder of an order instrument stolen prior to indorsement by the owner of the instrument.

Prior to the 1990 revisions, section 3–110 stated that a check payable to both bearer and order was payable to order under some conditions. Revised 3–109(b) now requires that an instrument payable to order must not be payable to bearer, and Comment 2 is explicit in explaining that when an instrument is payable both to bearer and to order, the instrument is treated as payable to bearer. In State of New Mexico v. Herrera,[1] the defendant was found not guilty of forgery when he modified a check payable to "cash" by adding his name to the payee line because he did not change the legal effect of the check. A special indorsement pursuant to section 3–205(a) allows an instrument payable to bearer to be converted into an order instrument.

Sometimes one claiming to be a holder in due course will not have possession of the instrument at the time of the suit. When a collecting bank holds the check, the solution is simple, for section 4–201 makes that bank the agent of the owner of the check.[2] Under traditional analysis, the agent's possession would be the owner's possession and thus the owner would have "possession." But section 4–201 applies only to collecting banks, not to payor banks or others who are not banks. What of the case in which the payor has paid a check by mistake against insufficient funds, retains posses-

§ 2–3

1. 130 N.M. 85, 18 P.3d 326, 44 UCC2d 186 (App. 2001).

2. § 4–201(a) states: "Unless a contrary intent clearly appears and before the time that a settlement given by a collecting bank for an item is or becomes final, the bank, with respect to an item, is an agent or sub-agent of the owner of the item and any settlement given for the item is provisional. * * * "

See United Credit Corp. v. Necamp, 1976 WL 23622, 19 UCC 1197 (Pa.Com. Pl. 1976) (holder of check can still sue as holder in due course after he has deposited check in bank, because under 4–201 bank acts as agent of holder).

sion of it, and then sues the payee in restitution? The payee might try to defeat this restitution claim by citing 3–418. That section does not bar recovery by a person who took the instrument "in good faith and for value or who in good faith changed position in reliance on the payment or acceptance." The quoted language was added in 1990 and removed a stumbling block lurking in the pre–1990 Code under which the payee in our example had to prove he or she was a holder in due course in order to defeat the restitution claim. The legal gymnastics of making that proof are no longer necessary; now the payee has to satisfy only two conditions of the holder in due course, namely that he or she took in good faith and for value.

On occasion, the drawer of a check will intend to make the instrument payable to a particular person, but will neglect for some reason to insert that person's name in the blank space. Such an instrument is treated under sections 3–109 and 3–115(b) as payable to bearer, and the one in possession of the check is a holder. Section 3–109(a) states, in part: "A promise or order is payable to bearer if it: * * * (2) does not state a payee; * * *." This is a change from the pre–1990 Code, under which such an incomplete check would have been ineffective until completed. The change is unlikely to have much significance, however. Under the pre–1990 Article 3, the owner could reach the same result by filling in his or her own name as payee.

Even though an instrument listing an "ambiguous payee" (e.g., a fictitious entity such as Superman) is not considered payable to bearer, section 3–404(b)(1) makes any person in possession of such an instrument its holder and section 3–404(b)(2) makes any indorsement by any person in the name of the stated payee effective.

§ 2–4 Holder in Due Course Defined—Negotiable Instrument

One of the least obvious requirements in section 3–302 is that the holder in due course take an "instrument." As used by Article 3, "instrument" means "negotiable instrument." This term is defined in section 3–104(a) which imposes seven requirements. For an item to be a negotiable instrument it must be (1) an unconditional (2) promise or order (3) to pay a fixed amount of money (4) with or without interest or other charges described in the promise or order (5) payable to bearer or to order at the time it is first issued or first comes into possession of a holder (6) on demand or at a definite time (7) which does not state any other undertaking or instruction by the person promising or ordering payment to do any act in addition to the payment of money. (The requirement that an instrument be payable to bearer or order has an exception for certain checks. This exception is described below.)

Some of these requirements cause little difficulty. Few problems result, for example, from the requirement that an instrument be payable on demand or at a definite time. The date requirement is fairly flexible: provisions for extension or acceleration do not affect negotiability,[1] and courts construe instruments with a missing date as payable on demand.

External references to due dates are also allowed, as long as the date is definite at the time the instrument is executed. For example, in Regent Corp., USA v. Azmat Bangladesh, Ltd.,[2] the need to refer to another document for payment instructions did not prevent the instrument from being negotiable. Regent contracted with Azmat, a textile company located in Bangladesh, for the purchase of bed sheets and pillowcases for import. An essential condition of the sale was that the goods be manufactured in Bangladesh since such goods were not subject to quota restrictions. Azmat required payment by "confirmed irrevocable letter of credit" before shipping the textiles. Regent sent the letters of credit, and each draft indicated that payment was to be made "at 90 days deferred from bill of lading date." Azmat's advising bank, International Bank, presented these drafts along with the bill of lading to Regent's bank for payment. After Regent's bank had made partial payments, United States Customs detained the textiles for inspection and soon afterward determined that they had actually been manufactured in Pakistan. Regent sought to enjoin his bank from further payments and commenced an action against Azmat and International Bank. The court held that a draft indicating that payment was to be made "at 90 days deferred from bill of lading date" and accompanied by a dated bill of lading met the "definite time" requirement of pre–1990 3–104(1)(c).[3] The note was negotiable: "mere reference to the bill of lading date does not impair the note's negotiability."

To be negotiable, an instrument must require payment of "a fixed amount of money, with or without interest or other charges." This language, added during the 1990 revisions, embraces variable rate notes. Before the revisions, the Code required payment of a "sum certain," and that language produced some uncertainty.

The words chosen by the drafters of post–1990 section 3–104(a) make variable rate notes negotiable (as long as the notes meet the

§ 2–4

1. § 3–108(b) provides that "A promise or order is 'payable at a definite time' if it is payable * * * at a time or times readily ascertainable at the time the promise or order is issued, subject to rights of (i) prepayment, (ii) acceleration, (iii) extension at the option of the holder, or (iv) extension to a further definite time at the option of the maker or acceptor or automatically upon or after a specified act or event."

2. 253 A.D.2d 134, 686 N.Y.S.2d 24, 38 UCC2d 131 (App.Div. 1st Dept.1999).

3. Section 3–104 was renumbered in the 1990 revisions, and the definite time requirement can now be found in 3–104(a)(2).

other requirements of negotiability). Now consider the language of current section 3–104(a). In the reference to "a fixed amount of money, with or without interest or other charges," the adjective "fixed" modifies only "amount of money"; "interest" is added in the prepositional phrase "with or without interest" and is not modified by "fixed." By this choice of words the drafters indorse variable rate notes as complying with the 3–104 requirements for negotiable instruments. That conclusion is supported by section 3–112 on interest; it reads in full as follows:

> (a) Unless otherwise provided in the instrument, (i) an instrument is not payable with interest, and (ii) interest on an interest-bearing instrument is payable from the date of the instrument.

> (b) Interest may be stated in an instrument as a fixed or variable amount of money or it may be expressed as a fixed or variable rate or rates. The amount or rate of interest may be stated or described in the instrument in any manner and may require reference to information not contained in the instrument. If an instrument provides for interest, but the amount of interest payable cannot be ascertained from the description, interest is payable at the judgment rate in effect at the place of payment of the instrument and at the time interest first accrues.

All of this is also confirmed by Comment 1 to 3–112:

> Under Section 3–104(a) the requirement of a "fixed amount" applies only to principal. * * * If a variable rate of interest is prescribed, the amount of interest is ascertainable by reference to the formula or index described or referred to in the instrument.

These sections and comments plainly permit a variable rate note to be a negotiable instrument.[4]

A similar issue arises when a document promises to pay in a foreign currency with a floating exchange rate. Is such a promise not a negotiable instrument because it is not a promise to pay a "fixed amount of money?" 1990 Article 3 does not specifically address the issue, but we think such a document should be negotiable. "Money," defined by section 1–201(24), includes foreign currency, so a note payable in foreign currency can be covered by Article 3. Revised section 3–107 further states that an instrument

---

4. Under the pre–1990 section 3–106 this outcome was hard to reach. The courts treated variable rate notes as non-negotiable because they do not call for the payment of a "sum certain." (See cases cited supra note 7). This result was difficult to avoid in the face of Comment 1 to old 3–106, which read in part: "The computation must be one which can be made from the instrument itself without reference to any outside source," and "this section does not make negotiable a note payable with interest 'at the current rate.' "

payable in foreign currency can be paid either in that currency or in U.S. dollars, using the current bank-offered spot rate at the place of payment on the date the instrument is paid. So, for example, if an instrument calls for payment on June 1 in Bonn where the exchange rate is 60 cents to the Mark, the payor may pay either 100,000 DM or 60,000 U.S. dollars. The fact that the precise number of U.S. dollars required to satisfy the contract fluctuates should not make the instrument nonnegotiable if the number of Deutsche Marks required is fixed.

Outside the consumer credit context, where the FTC rule has rendered it unimportant, section 3–104(a) will present a persistent problem for the drafter of a note where one party (usually the payee) wants a reference in the note itself to separate agreements. One might wish a note to disclose its relationship to a capitalization agreement, to a mortgage, or to a variety of other contractual obligations. Here, the drafter of the note must walk a fine line through section 3–106, which describes elements of a promise that might make it conditional and therefore not a negotiable instrument under 3–104. The drafter may, without rendering the promise conditional, refer to another writing "for a statement of rights with respect to collateral, prepayment, or acceleration." The drafter of a note may also specify that payment will come from a particular fund or source. The drafter may not, however, violate the three taboos in 3–106(a): (i) the promise must not state an express condition of payment, (ii) the promise may not be subject to or governed by another writing, and (iii) the promise must not be affected by rights or obligations stated in another writing.

Quite clearly, any note which says it is "subject to" or "governed by" a separate agreement is thus rendered nonnegotiable. Likewise, it would seem that any other reference that incorporates a separate agreement by a reference deprives a note of its negotiability. A note that states that it is "non-negotiable" on its face is also non-negotiable.

After 1990, the Code refers only to undertakings or instructions by the maker. Pre–1990 3–104(1)(b) was broader; it forbade any "other promise, order, obligation or power given by the maker or drawer * * * ." In Ameritrust Co., N.A. v. White[5] this clause was used to find a note nonnegotiable where the note gave the payee additional rights. In this case, defendant White had executed a note as part of the purchase price of a share in a limited partnership. White made the note payable to the partnership, and it was eventually indorsed to the plaintiff bank, Ameritrust, as security for a loan. The note contained a forfeiture clause which provided that if payments were not timely made, the partnership would have no obligation to account for any previous payments made. When

5. 73 F.3d 1553, 28 UCC2d 1277 (11th Cir.1996).

the limited partnership defaulted on its loan with Ameritrust, White decided not to continue making payments on his note. Ameritrust sued White to collect on the unpaid note. Prior to trial, the parties requested the district court to rule on the negotiability of the note. The court determined the forfeiture clause to be an impermissible "other power" under pre–1990 revision 3–104(1)(b) and found the note nonnegotiable. The determination was upheld on appeal:

> A situation could develop, by mistake or otherwise, wherein the partnership exercises its option before the holder declares a default. The maker might well decline to cure an overdue payment or to make future payments because of the forfeiture. This exemplifies the reason why negotiable instruments may contain no other power except as authorized by the statute.....
> To be negotiable, a note must be a courier without luggage; it must move unencumbered. However unlikely the scenario described above, this potential created by the forfeiture clause destroys the note's negotiability.

Since the 1990 revisions, section 3–104 prohibits only an "undertaking or instruction by the person promising or ordering payment to do any act in addition to the payment of money" and 3–106 prohibits only governance by "another record." The 1990 Code does explicitly forbid the giving of additional powers to the payee. We are hesitant to say that the outcome in this case would have been different under the post–1990 Code, but since the language the court relied on has been changed, the result might have been different.

The permission to specify a particular fund from which payment will come is new with the 1990 Code. The old Code provided that most promises or orders that specified a particular fund for payment were conditional. Comment 1 to revised 3–106 recognizes that there is "no cogent reason why the general credit of a legal entity must be pledged to have [an item qualify as] a negotiable instrument." Rather the drafters surmised that the market will insist upon general liability where that is appropriate and apply an appropriate discount where it is not:

> Market forces determine the marketability of instruments of this kind. If potential buyers don't want promises or orders that are payable only from a particular source or fund, they won't take them, but Article 3 should apply.[6]

A second recurring issue under 3–104 and its predecessor concerns the meaning of subsection (a)(1), which requires that a negotiable instrument be "payable to bearer or to order at the time

---

6. § 3–106, Comment 1.

it is issued or first comes into possession of the holder." More than any other symbols, the words "order" and "bearer" are supposed to put parties on notice that they are dealing with negotiable instruments. For this reason, courts have been slow to recognize substitutes for these symbols. The drafters of the 1990 revisions exempt certain checks from the "payable to bearer or to order" requirement, as explained below, but otherwise they continue the policy of discouraging alternate language in negotiable instruments. The drafters explain their reasoning in Comment 2:

> Total exclusion from Article 3 of other promises or orders that are not payable to bearer or to order serves a useful purpose. It provides a simple device to clearly exclude a writing that does not fit the pattern of typical negotiable instruments and which is not intended to be a negotiable instrument. If a writing could be an instrument despite the absence of "to order" or "to bearer" language and a dispute arises with respect to the writing, it might be argued that the writing is a negotiable instrument because the other requirements of subsection (a) are somehow met. Even if the argument is eventually found to be without merit it can be used as a litigation ploy. Words making a promise or order payable to bearer or to order are the most distinguishing feature of a negotiable instrument and such words are frequently referred to as "words of negotiability."

The Code fleshes out the clause "payable to bearer or to order" in section 3–109. An instrument is payable to bearer if it indicates that the person in possession is entitled to payment, if it does not specify a payee, or if it says it is payable to cash or uses some other indication that no particular person is entitled to payment. A promise is payable to order if it is not payable to bearer, and is payable to the "order of" an identified person or to that person "or order." Thus, either of the following are payable to order: "to order of Brian" (3–109(b)(i)), and "to Brian or order" (3–109(b)(ii)), but "pay to Brian" is not.

We deal here with the exception noted above that allows an item to be negotiable even though it is not payable to bearer or order. The exception, described in 3–104(c), is for checks that fail the "payable to bearer or to order" requirement but otherwise satisfy the criteria of a negotiable instrument and meet the definition of a check in 3–104(f):

> "Check" means (i) a draft, other than a documentary draft, payable on demand and drawn on a bank or (ii) a cashier's check or teller's check. * * *

A document might say, for example, "pay to Jones," instead of "pay to the order of Jones." Such a document would be neither payable to bearer nor payable to the order of Jones and would not therefore be a negotiable instrument. However, if the document was a check, subsection 3–104(c) makes it negotiable. Comment 2 to section 3–104 explains:

> Subsection (c) is based on the belief that it is good policy to treat checks, which are payment instruments, as negotiable instruments whether or not they contain the words "to the order of." * * * Absence of the quoted words can easily be overlooked and should not affect the rights of holders who may pay money or give credit for a check without being aware that it is not in the conventional form.

The definition of a check in section 3–104 further says that an instrument "may be a check even though it is described on its face by another term, such as 'money order.'" This language should resolve the uncertainty that arose under the pre–1990 Code with regard to money orders, a hybrid instrument that fell somewhere in the borderland between negotiable instruments and ordinary contracts.

Other cases that turn on the "payable to bearer or to order" language are contracts for payment or other documents of clearly recognized legal status. Frequently, such documents do not qualify as "negotiable" instruments within the meaning of 3–104(a) because they are not unconditional promises to pay money or because they demand that the maker do some act in addition to the payment of money. Consequently, no holder of such nonnegotiable documents may assume holder in due course status. For example, in All Lease Co. v. Bowen,[7] Bowen had granted a security interest in some of its property to an entity named Colorback. Colorback assigned the contract to All Lease. When Bowen ceased making the payments, All Lease sued. Bowen asserted failure of consideration as a defense, and All Lease claimed to be a holder in due course. The court rejected this argument, stating:

> Clearly this document is replete with promises and obligations in addition to the promise to pay. Among others, these include the payment of a late charge for delinquent payments, the requirement that the buyer obtain the written consent of the seller before transferring the buyer's obligation while keeping the seller's interest freely transferable, the promise to insure the goods sold, and the retention of the right to take possession of the goods sold without judicial process. Each of these has been held to represent the type of additional promise that renders an instrument non-negotiable. [citations omitted]. Therefore, since the document is not a negotiable instrument,

7. 1975 WL 22864, 20 UCC 790 (Md. Cir.Ct. 1975).

the holder in due course doctrine and exceptions to it cannot apply.

Note also that arguments that an instrument is not negotiable are subject to waiver and estoppel.

§ 2–5 Holder in Due Course Defined—Value

Having determined that the plaintiff is in possession of a document that qualifies as a negotiable instrument, one must still find that he took it "for value in good faith and without notice" in order to find him a holder in due course under 3–302.[1] Section 3–303 defines value as follows:

(a) An instrument is issued or transferred for value if:

(1) the instrument is issued or transferred for a promise of performance, to the extent the promise has been performed;

(2) the transferee acquires a security interest or other lien in the instrument other than a lien obtained by judicial proceeding;

(3) the instrument is issued or transferred as payment of, or as security for, an antecedent claim against any person, whether or not the claim is due;

(4) the instrument is issued or transferred in exchange for a negotiable instrument; or

(5) the instrument is issued or transferred in exchange for the incurring of an irrevocable obligation to a third party by the person taking the instrument.

Note first that "value" (as defined by 3–303, 4–210 and 4–211) has a different meaning in Articles 3 and 4 than it does in the other Code articles. Under 3–303 an executory promise is not itself value, but under 1–204 an executory promise constitutes value.[2] In the

---

§ 2–5

1. Therefore, someone who finds a note has not given value and cannot qualify as a holder in due course. See Griffith v. Mellon Bank, N.A., 328 F.Supp.2d 536, 54 UCC2d 373 (E.D.Pa. 2004) (Holder of a 29–year–old certificate of deposit who brought action against bank, demanding payment of principal and interest, was not entitled to holder in due course status because he did not take CD for value but found it in a book purchased from an unnamed source. He admitted he did not know the CD was in the book when he purchased it. Although he bought the book in which the CD was found, he did not pay any value in return for the CD itself).

2. § 1–204: Except as otherwise provided in Articles 3, 4, [and] 5, [and 6], a person gives value for rights if the person acquires them:

(1) in return for a binding commitment to extend credit or for the extension of immediately available credit, whether or not drawn upon and whether or not a charge-back is provided for in the event of difficulties in collection;

(2) as security for, or in total or partial satisfaction of, a preexisting claim;

(3) by accepting delivery under a preexisting contract for purchase; or

comment to 3–303 the Code suggests that a person who has given only an executory promise does not need the protection of holder in due course status because the promise can be revoked in the event of a problem. Comment 2, addressing the provision in subsection (a)(1) that a person can give value by performing part of a promise, says:

> The policy basis for subsection (a)(1) is that the holder who gives an executory promise of performance will not suffer an out-of-pocket loss to the extent the executory promise is unperformed at the time the holder learns of dishonor of the instrument.

In contrast, Comment 5 discusses the provisions of subsections (a)(4) and (5), which provide that a person does give value by exchanging an instrument for a negotiable instrument or by exchanging it for an irrevocable obligation to a third party. The comment says:

> They state generally recognized exceptions to the rule that an executory promise is not value. A negotiable instrument is value because it carries the possibility of negotiation to a holder in due course, after which the party who gives it is obliged to pay. The same reasoning applies to any irrevocable commitment to a third person, such as a letter of credit issued when an instrument is taken.

In words of one syllable, the person who has given only a promise is not yet out on the limb and he does not pose the typical bona fide purchaser problem in which two people have committed their assets and the intervening person—always a scalawag of some sort—has disappeared with the money. In that typical case the loss must inevitably fall on one of two innocent parties. Such is not the case when a potential bona fide purchaser has not yet paid the scalawag, but only has promised to do so. Assume, for example, that a thief has stolen a bearer instrument from Templeton and has made a contract to sell the instrument to Cicero. If Cicero discovers that the thief has no title, he will be free of his obligation to pay, for there will be a failure of consideration and the thief will not be able to deliver what he promised. Thus Cicero has given no "value"; he has not yet irrevocably committed himself to the transaction. The owner from whom the instrument has been stolen is irrevocably committed in the sense that his right to payment will be discharged by a payment of the instrument. The Code should not instruct Cicero to go forward; he should return the instrument to its owner.[3]

(4) in return for any consideration sufficient to support a simple contract.

3. Note that a person can be a holder in due course to the extent of a partial

A holder who buys all of the seller's rights to a $1000 note is a holder in due course of the entire $1000 claim whether he gives value of $1 or $1100. Even where notes with large face amounts have been purchased at a discount, courts have been satisfied that value was given for each note. In Cadle Co. v. Ginsburg,[4] the holder had purchased more than 100 promissory notes for a lump sum. Although the holder could not specify the amount of the total which had gone towards the single disputed note, the court found that the holder had given value.

A transferee for an antecedent debt or as collateral for a loan also takes the note for value. In Groner v. Regency Federal Savings & Loan Association,[5] Groner had invested in a real estate development partnership, RRII. When RRII needed a large real estate loan, it received one from defendant bank, Regency. The real estate was not enough collateral for the loan, so RRII agreed to give Regency various notes as collateral. From time to time Regency allowed substitution of notes for the original notes. Plaintiff's note was later given to Regency in one of these substitutions by RRII. RRII defaulted on its loan, and Regency sent a letter to Groner notifying him that all future payments on his note should be sent to Regency. Groner continued to make payments and sent them to Regency. When Groner became dissatisfied with his investment, he sued Regency for return of his note and all payments he had made. Groner alleged that Regency was not a holder in due course and thus took the note subject to Groner's claim that the note had been procured through fraud, of which Regency knew or should have known. The appellate court upheld the lower court's decision that Regency took plaintiff's note for value as payment of or security for an antecedent claim under 3–303(a)(3) and qualified as a holder in due course.

In Godat v. Mercantile Bank of Northwest County,[6] Godat, an injured customer of Hasty, attempted to recover from the issuing bank on a cashier's check that Hasty had procured to repay some of the injury that he had done to his customer. Hasty procured the cashier's check by fraud from the bank; by operating a kite he built up his balance sufficiently to get the bank to issue the $200,000 check.

When Godat received the check he immediately arranged for presentation to the bank by courier. Noting that Hasty did not have

---

interest in the instrument if, for example, the person performs half of his or her obligation. Section 3–303(a)(1) makes one a giver of value if the instrument is issued or exchanged for some promised performance "to the extent the promise has been performed."

4. 51 Conn.App. 392, 721 A.2d 1246, 37 UCC2d 684 (1998).

5. 248 Ill.App.3d 574, 188 Ill.Dec. 64, 618 N.E.2d 634, 23 UCC2d 127 (1st Dist. 1993).

6. 884 S.W.2d 1, 24 UCC2d 385 (Mo. App. 1994).

sufficient funds to cover the check, the bank refused to pay its cashier's check, and Godat sued. Since Hasty had stolen the money long before the cashier's check was issued, the bank argued that Godat had not given value. Noting that Godat was not injured by the dishonor (since he had lost his investment long before), the court denied Godat's claim that he was a holder in due course.

It seems likely that Godat would have had a conversion claim or some other claim against Hasty. If that were so, Godat would have given value for the cashier's check in the form of satisfaction of an antecedent debt. So we are doubtful about the court's analysis. On the other hand, the fact that Godat hustled the check to the bank via courier belies his claim to be in good faith. So maybe the outcome is right even if the reasons are wrong. For an extensive discussion of the rights of the holder of a cashier's check against the issuing bank, see section 11 below.

The real battleground on which the "value" issues are being fought is a place far removed from 3–303. It is sections 4–210 and 4–211 in circumstances like these: Jones, a shady customer and broke as well, procures a check payable to his order for work to be performed and materials to be delivered. Jones takes the check to his bank, deposits it and so procures a credit in his checking account. Before the check is presented to the payor bank, the drawer finds that Jones will not perform and stops payment. Sometimes at once, sometimes only after the depositary bank has received notice of the infirmity, Jones draws on the credit. Unable to procure reimbursement from Jones, the depositary bank sues the drawer of the check and maintains that it is a holder in due course. The drawer defends on the ground that Bank is not a holder in due course, for Bank has not given value—or at least had not given value at the time it received notice of a defense. The questions presented by these cases may be stated as follows:

(1) Under what circumstances is the mere granting of a credit the giving of value?

(2) If in some circumstances the granting of a credit in a bank account is not giving of value, what additional events must occur for the bank to have given value?

(3) If withdrawal is the crucial point, how does one determine whether specific funds have been withdrawn from a commingled bank account over a period of time when there are several deposits and many withdrawals?

Sections 4–210 and 4–211 make it clear that when the depositor has withdrawn his money, the bank has given value and has so become a holder in due course if it otherwise qualifies. A bank has also given value when it has "applied" a credit given for a check. The most obvious case of "applying" is to take a check for deposit in an account that is overdrawn. By using the check to reduce the debt owed to the bank by the customer (the overdraft), the amount deposited is "applied" and the bank instantaneously gives value.

One must read 4–210(a)(2) with great care to determine the outcome in a case in which the credit has not been withdrawn. At first reading, 4–210(a)(2) seems to say that any giving of credit causes a security interest which in turn constitutes the bank's giving of value. Such a reading is in direct conflict with the comment to 3–303 quoted above and it would render 4–210(a)(1) superfluous. On close reading, one finds that the giving of a credit is itself the giving of value only when the credit is "available for withdrawal *as of right*." Whether a customer has the "right" to withdraw a credit will be determined by agreement with the bank or, in the absence of such an agreement, by 4–215 and Regulation CC.[7]

Under 4–215(e) the credit is available "for withdrawal as of right" in the usual case when the bank itself receives final settlement and has reasonable time to learn that settlement is final or when "applicable law" (i.e., Regulation CC) dictates earlier withdrawal rights. The negative implication is that such credit is not available as of "right" before that time. Thus in the absence of a contrary agreement between the depositor and his bank, 4–210, 4–211 and 4–215 mean that the bank, which gives its depositor a provisional credit, still does not give value until final payment of the item deposited or until the credit is withdrawn or otherwise applied. For the reasons stated in the comment to 3–303, it makes sense to keep the depositary bank from being a holder in due course until the credit is withdrawn or until the bank is committed to give the credit to its customer. Until that time, the depositary bank can protect itself by debiting the account and can thus put the loss on the evil middle party (in this case the depositor) and avoid the dilemma present in all true bona fide purchase cases.

Perhaps because the question is complex and because the path among the Code sections is by no means clear, the courts have had some difficulty under 4–210, 4–211 et seq. in arriving at the results suggested above. They are in agreement that a depositary bank at least gives value at the time the customer withdraws the funds from his account. The courts also generally agree that giving a mere provisional credit does not constitute the giving of value. The First Circuit, in an alternate holding, has strayed from the flock and found that a revocable credit not yet drawn on nevertheless gave rise to a security interest which would be regarded as the

---

7. Under the terms of § 4–214(a) the depositary bank has the right to revoke the settlement and charge back the customer's account, if the bank fails by reason of dishonor or for any other reason to "receive settlement for the item which is or becomes final."

giving of value under the pre–1990 Code's 4–208(1)(b) and 4–209. (The Code provisions relied on by the court are now numbered 4–210(a) and 4–211.) In Banco Espanol de Credito v. State Street Bank & Trust Co.,[8] the correspondent bank-plaintiff credited "the amounts specified in the letters of credit against debts" owed it by two beneficiaries under the letter of credit. The plaintiff then forwarded the draft to a Boston bank which was obliged to pay under the letter of credit, and the Boston bank refused to pay on the ground that there was fraud in the transaction. Banco Espanol responded that it was a holder in due course and that fraud could not be raised against it. The district court, in an opinion affirmed by the First Circuit, found that Banco Espanol had in fact given value, was a holder in due course and was entitled to recover from the Boston bank. The lower court held that Banco Espanol had given value because the credit given was not subject to revocation under the terms of the agreement between it and its Spanish customers. The appellate court affirmed on this ground and on the alternate ground that Banco Espanol gave "value" under the old Code's 4–208(1), now 4–210(a), "even if the credit were revocable." In support of that statement the First Circuit cited Waltham Citizens National Bank v. Flett,[9] a 1968 Massachusetts case.

In the *Waltham Bank* case the plaintiff, depositary bank, sued on a check deposited with it and for which it had given its customer a credit. According to the opinion the customer had had an $11,000 overdraft at the time the $9,000 check was deposited and the bank caused the customer to draw a check on his own account immediately after the deposit to pay off a note he owed the bank. The bank then lent him an additional $6,000 in return for his new note and credited $5,963 of the new loan proceeds to his checking account. It is unclear what happened to the $11,000 overdraft in the course of this transaction. In no event, however, does the case stand for the proposition that the mere granting of a revocable credit constitutes the giving of value. Rather the $9,000 was immediately withdrawn ("applied") to pay off a note and to the extent that an additional $6,000 credit was given, it was given for a new note and, implicitly at least, was "available for withdrawal as of right" as the proceeds of a new loan. Moreover to the extent that some or all of the $9,000 value was used to obliterate the overdraft, the bank would have given value under the pre–1990 Code's 3–303(b) by taking the check in satisfaction of an antecedent indebtedness.[10] (The pre–1990 Code's 3–303(b) is essentially the same as revised 3–303(a)(3).)

---

8. 409 F.2d 711, 6 UCC 378 (1st Cir.1969).

9. 353 Mass. 696, 234 N.E.2d 739, 5 UCC 186 (1968).

10. A bank's provisional credit for an item can satisfy the value require-

ment if the item covers an overdraft in a depositor's account. Such credit amounts to payment of an antecedent claim. See Union Bank & Trust Co. v. Polkinghorne, 801 P.2d 735, 13 UCC2d 445 (Okl.App. 1990).

Thus, the First Circuit's reliance upon the *Waltham* case is misplaced. Note that the First Circuit's misuse of authority did not change the outcome, for there were at least two sound bases for its decision that Banco Espanol had given value. The first is that relied upon by the district court which held that the terms of the agreement between the Spanish customer and Banco Espanol permitted the credit to be drawn upon as of right. Secondly, the credit in Banco Espanol was used to satisfy "debts," and presumably the bank therefore could have qualified under pre–1990 3–303(b), now 3–303(a)(3).

A bank may give value prior to the time of final payment in ways other than by granting an absolute right to draw. In Bowling Green, Inc. v. State Street Bank & Trust Co.,[11] the bank had a perfected security interest in a variety of the assets and proceeds of the assets of its depositor. The depositor deposited a $15,000 government check and State Street argued that it had become a holder in due course by giving value prior to the time when it found out about its customer's bankruptcy. The First Circuit agreed that State Street had complied with 4–209 (now 4–211) and by its security agreement with the debtor had procured a security interest in the check prior to the time of collection, for the check was a 9–306 proceed under the secured transaction between the bank and its customer. The court also relied upon 3–303(b) and 4–208(1)(c), now 3–303(a) and 4–210(a)(3).

How does one determine when the withdrawal of the specific item is made from an account consisting of commingled funds? Assume for example, that customer's account stands at zero at 9:00 a.m.; at 10:00 a.m., she deposits check one in the amount of $2000 and at 11:00 a.m., deposits check two in the amount of $3000. Depositor withdraws $2500 and disappears. Thereafter both checks bounce since payment has been stopped on each of them and the bank debits the remaining $2500 from the account. Since its customer has disappeared without a trace, the bank sues the drawer on check one and argues that it is a holder in due course and not subject to whatever defense drawer has against the bank's customer. Drawer of check one argues that bank did not give value, for the credit was never withdrawn. Under the provisions of 4–210(b) the bank wins: "For the purpose of this section, credits first given are first withdrawn." Since the $2000 check was the first one deposited, it is presumed to have been the amount first withdrawn under the FIFO rule when the customer took $2500 out of the account. Therefore bank will have a security interest in that check, will have given value for it and will be able to recover only $500 from the other drawer, for $2000 of the $2500 which the bank set off is presumed to be attributable to that check.

11. 425 F.2d 81, 7 UCC 635 (1st Cir.1970).

The first sentence of 4–210(b) reads:

If credit given for several items received at one time or pursuant to a single agreement is withdrawn or applied in part, the security interest remains upon all the items, any accompanying documents or the proceeds of either.

Presumably under this language, the bank would have a right only to a prorata recovery if both checks had been deposited simultaneously. It would be a holder in due course of check one to the extent of $1000 and a holder in due course of check two to the extent of $1500. Admittedly the quoted sentence does not specify proration in so many words, but there is no reason to believe that the drafters intended, by the quoted language, to give the bank the right to recover the entire $5000 when it paid out only $2500 in reliance upon the two checks.

In the usual case a depositary bank will not have become a holder in due course until an item deposited for collection is drawn upon, otherwise "applied or at final payment by the payor." Different rules apply when the item is not deposited for collection but is taken in payment for an antecedent indebtedness or when the credit is payment for a discounted note. The latter case is presumably covered by 4–210(a)(3) in that the depositor has a legal "right" to withdraw such a credit.

PROBLEM

Eliot has $40,000 in his account when he deposits a $5000 personal check (payable to his order from a third party) on Monday at 9:00 a.m. The check is drawn on a bank in the same town where the depositary bank is located. A check drawn by Eliot for $41,000 clears the account on Tuesday. The payor bank makes final payment on the $5000 check on Thurs. True or False:

1. Depositary bank gives value by crediting Eliot's account on Monday.

2. Depositary bank gave value on Tuesday when the $41,000 check cleared.

3. Depositary bank gave value on Wednesday morning when the amount became available as of right.

4. Depositary bank gave value on Thursday when final payment was made and the $5000 became available as of right.

Answers:

1. False. Crediting the account is not the giving of value unless the account is already overdrawn and the amount is automatically "applied" against the overdraft.

2. Partly true. Under the "first in first out" rule in 4–210(b) the $41,000 withdrawal is treated as having come first from the earlier deposited $40,000 and only $1000 of the withdrawal is treated as coming from the $5000 check. So, on Tuesday, the bank is an HIDC to the extent of $1000 of the $5000 check but not as to the rest.

3. True. Under Reg CC 229.12 and 229.19 and 4–215(e), the entire amount is available as of right at 9:00 a.m. on Wednesday.

4. If one disregards Reg. CC or if the amount of the check is over $5000 so that Reg CC allows a longer time, this is true.

§ 2–6   Holder in Due Course Defined—Good Faith

The good faith requirement has been the source of an ancient and continuing dispute. Should the courts apply a so-called objective test, and ask whether a reasonably prudent person, behaving the way the alleged holder in due course behaved, would have been acting in good faith? Or should the courts instead apply a subjective test and examine the person's actual behavior, however stupid and irrespective of the reaction a reasonably prudent person would have had in the same circumstance? The legal establishment has steered a crooked course through this debate. For a time the English law under the case of Gill v. Cubitt[1] applied the objective test of good faith. Under the NIL the American courts generally applied the subjective test and rejected the doctrine of *Gill v. Cubitt.*[2] This dispute between the backers of the objective and the subjective test carried through to the early days of the Uniform Commercial Code, and 3–302(1)(b) of the 1952 Code which was enacted in Pennsylvania, required not just that the holder be "in good faith" but "in good faith including observance of the reasonable commercial standards of any business in which the holder may be engaged."[3] Whether the language beginning with the word "including" fully implemented the objective standard was the subject of dispute; some argued before the New York Law Revision Commission that it did so.[4] In apparent response to these concerns, the drafters deleted the offending language[5] and left the bare words "in good faith."

§ 2–6

1. 3 B & C 466, 107 Eng.Rep. 806 (K.B.1824).

2. F. Beutel, Beutel's Brannon Negotiable Instruments Law § 56 at 772–74 (7th ed.1948), lists more than two pages of cases supporting the proposition that "suspicious circumstances sufficient to put a prudent man on inquiry * * * are not sufficient of themselves to prevent recovery * * * "Three cases are cited contra. *Id.*

3. § 3–302(1)(b)   (1952   Official Draft).

4. See, e.g., 1 N.Y.Law Revision Comm'n, 1954 Report 198, 203 (1954).

5. Perm.Ed.Bd. UCC, 1956 Recommendations 102 (1956).

They stated "the omission is intended to make clear that the doctrine of an objective standard of good faith, exemplified by the case *Gill v. Cubitt*, is not intended to be incorporated in Article Three." However, the subjective rule never prevailed in Article 2 with respect to merchants.[6]

With the redraft of the various other articles of the Code there has been a movement from subjective to objective definitions of good faith. The 1990 drafters tilted back toward the Code's early preference for the objective good faith standard. Depending upon the jurisdiction, the definition of good faith can be found in 3–103(a)(4) or 3–103(a)(6) or 1–201(a)(20). Good faith "means honesty in fact and the observance of reasonable commercial standards of fair dealing." Some of the issues arising from this new definition will have to do with the meaning of "fair dealing," but more likely, in our view, are questions concerning the definition of "commercial standards." Comment 4 to 1990 3–103 reads in part as follows:

> Although fair dealing is a broad term that must be defined in context, it is clear that it is concerned with the fairness of conduct rather than the care with which an act is performed. Failure to exercise ordinary care in conducting a transaction is an entirely different concept than failure to deal fairly in conducting the transaction. Both fair dealing and ordinary care, which is defined in Section 3–103(a)(7), are to be judged in the light of reasonable commercial standards, but those standards in each case are directed to different aspects of commercial conduct.

What does all of that mean? And what evidence is likely to be introduced to prove lack of reasonable commercial standards? Note that under section 3–308(b) a plaintiff confronted with defenses or claims has the burden of proving "rights of a holder in due course," and thus the burden will be on the creditor plaintiff to show good faith.

Where might this arise? One can imagine many variations on this basic theme: a depositary bank takes a check, only to have other banks say *they* would not have taken such a check and that to do so violated commercial standards. For example, would it violate commercial standards for a bank to take a $100,000 check to open an account and, shortly after, to allow the depositor to withdraw the funds? If not, the bank could be a holder in due course who might take free of a drawer's claim to that instrument even though the person with whom it dealt was a thief, not so? For reasons stated below we think the bank here would be in good faith. Can a payee violate commercial standards by demanding payment on a

---

6. See § 2–103(1)(b).

"demand note" where there has been no default in the underlying obligation?

Similar arguments might well arise at the closing of a kite, where one of the banks seeks to defend itself against a restitution claim by arguing it gave value in good faith and is protected by 3–418. That bank might be met with the argument that it was not a good faith holder of the checks passing through its hands because, by observing reasonable commercial standards, it should have understood the checks to be part of a kite. As we indicate elsewhere, we hope that few people are successful in asserting restitution causes of action after kites, but we anticipate that those arguments will be made.

Before one concludes that the banks described in the preceding paragraphs are not in good faith, return to the definition. A bank that fails to follow commercial standards is not in good faith only if it deviates from commercial standards of "fair dealing." Deviating from such standards on the side of generosity and gullibility rather than venality does not render one's act in bad faith. So beware: good faith does not require general conformity to "reasonable commercial standards," but only to "reasonable commercial standards of fair dealing." The issue is one of "unfairness" not of "negligence." If the Code is tilting back toward an objective standard, it is going only so far. We are clear on that point, but the courts are divided. As we see below, some courts insist on confusing negligence with unfairness. Some also find a duty for a depositary bank to consider the interests of all parties involved, including the drafter of the note with whom the bank has never had dealings.

What about good faith in cases such as Farmers & Merchants State Bank v. Western Bank?[7] There, two banks sued one another in the aftermath of a kiting scam conducted by OK Livestock and Fred Currey. OK maintained an account at a bank in Idaho (Farmers & Merchants) while Currey had an account at a bank in Oregon (Western). The scam began in 1980: Currey would write a check to OK larger than his account balance, OK would deposit it, and write a return check to Currey larger than its balance, which Currey would use to cover the first check before he issued another check for an even larger amount. The kite involved small amounts at first, but grew so that by July of 1981, OK and Currey were exchanging over $700,000 between the two accounts on a daily basis. As early as June Farmers & Merchants suspected that something was awry when OK's account continually appeared on a list of accounts with unusual activity. In addition, Farmers & Merchants sent two officers to talk to OK about the problems with the account in early June. One of the bank's officers, Soren Anderson, told an OK executive that he "sure as hell hope[d] there

7. 841 F.2d 1433, 5 UCC2d 372 (9th Cir.1987).

[was] not a kite situation going on," and was assured there was not.

After several more weeks of similar activity—including daily calls to the bank by OK to find out how much was needed to cover outstanding checks—Farmers & Merchants management decided to shut down the OK account. Anderson wrote to Western to find out the status of Currey's account, and was informed that he was maintaining an average median balance of six figures. Meanwhile, Western sent Farmers & Merchants checks drawn by OK payable to Currey, in an amount of $703,634.65. Farmers & Merchants decided to dishonor the checks, and sent them back to Western by mail. At the same time, Anderson went in person to Western with 13 checks Currey had written to OK, which OK had just deposited. Anderson proposed to exchange them for Western's cashier's check for $708,133.07. After verifying that Currey had made a night deposit of OK checks also in the amount of $708,133.07, Western issued its cashier's check to Anderson in payment for the $708,133.07 of checks Anderson brought from Farmers & Merchants. Western soon found out what was going on and, after Anderson refused to return the cashier's check, informed Farmers & Merchants that the cashier's check would be dishonored. After the dust cleared both banks were left with accounts overdrawn by more than a million dollars, and Farmers & Merchants sued Western to obtain payment of the cashier's check.

Because Western had defenses of fraud, lack of consideration and the like available, one question at trial was whether Farmers & Merchants had taken the cashier's check as a holder in due course and so free of those defenses. The district court held that Farmers & Merchants was a holder in due course because it had exhibited honesty in fact and had therefore taken the check in good faith. The Ninth Circuit disagreed, finding that Farmers & Merchants knew the cashier's check was issued in reliance on the checks just deposited in Currey's account, checks that Farmers & Merchants intended to dishonor. The case raises an interesting problem regardless of whether a subjective or objective standard of good faith is used. Assuming that Anderson and Farmers & Merchants had been honest in fact, did their behavior constitute "observance of reasonable commercial standards of fair dealing"?

In Farmer & Merchants' defense one might note that in kites the usual rule is to take yours and may the devil take the hindmost. Most cases find no duty by one bank to another when a kite is closed. Indeed the two employees at Western should have been put on notice by the serious man from Idaho with $700,000 of checks waiting when they opened the door, not so? Cases like this bring out our social Darwinist instincts. Why should a court find bad faith to save lost souls who gave a $700,000+ cashier's check to the waiting man? Really!

While the debate continues over subjective good faith, judicial infiltration erodes the standard on another front. A 1981 Florida case, Seinfeld v. Commercial Bank & Trust Co.[8] illustrates the point. In that case, Rachel Wolfson, whose account at the bank was overdrawn by $57,000 procured three checks from Seinfeld for a total of $160,000. These checks were payable to Wolfson's corporation and Wolfson had assured Seinfeld that she would not negotiate the checks. She did so anyway. The depositary bank first charged them against her overdraft, then allowed her to withdraw a total of $157,000 prior to the time the checks cleared. The checks were dishonored and the depositary bank sued Seinfeld. In response to Seinfeld's argument that there was a breach of the underlying agreement with Wolfson, the bank claimed it was a holder in due course and took free of that defense. The trial court granted summary judgment for the bank, and the Florida Court of Appeals reversed. The court found that there was at least a factual issue about whether the bank had acted in "good faith." It was implicitly critical of the bank for allowing a chronically overdrawn customer to draw against such an amount and suggested that one might draw the inference that the bank had acted in bad faith.

The case seems wrong. In the first place, today, banks are to be praised, not criticized, for allowing a depositor to draw on uncollected funds. In the second place, Seinfeld is hardly free of odor. If Wolfson "was not to negotiate" the checks, why were they given to her? Did he give them to her as part of a scheme to mislead third parties? By suggesting that the trial court could infer lack of good faith from such flimsy evidence, the court undermines the idea of subjective good faith. It also gives the bank good reason to be hesitant to allow depositors to draw uncollected funds at a time when the Congress in Regulation CC has directed banks to permit draws against such funds at the earliest possible time.

Despite Comment 4 to 3–103, cases continue to blur the line between "reasonable commercial standards of fair dealing" and negligence. In Maine Family Federal Credit Union v. Sun Life Assurance Company of Canada,[9] Sun Life had issued three separate

---

8. 405 So.2d 1039, 32 UCC 1137 (Fla.App. 1981). See also e.g. Choo Choo Tire Service, Inc. v. Union Planters Natl. Bank, 231 Ga.App. 346, 498 S.E.2d 799, 35 UCC2d 924 (1998) (summary judgment for bank reversed due to factual issue regarding its good faith. Court held that a jury may decide that the bank acted in bad faith when, acting inconsistently with its own normal business practices, it allowed a customer to draw against a deposited check even though the customer's account had been frequently overdrawn in the past 6 months. Court found that the bank perhaps should have put a hold on the account instead). Most courts do not characterize banks that cash checks for a depositor who is overdrawn as acting in bad faith.

9. 727 A.2d 335, 37 UCC2d 875 (Me. 1999).

checks in the amount of $40,759.35–one to each of Elden Guer-
rette's life insurance policy's beneficiaries upon his death. The
checks were given to Sun's agent, Hall, for delivery to each of
Elden's three adult children. Hall fraudulently induced the Guer-
rettes to indorse the checks in blank and to transfer them to Hall,
purportedly to be invested in a corporation formed by Hall. Hall
gave the checks to an accomplice who deposited them into his
account at the credit union. The credit union immediately made the
funds available for withdrawal. The children, regretting having
negotiated the checks to Hall, contacted Sun the next day and
requested a stop payment on the checks. Sun immediately issued a
stop order to Chase Manhattan, the drawee bank. When the checks
were presented to Chase for payment, it returned them to the
credit union. The credit union had received notice that the checks
had been dishonored on the sixth business day following their
deposit. By that time, however, Hall's accomplice had withdrawn all
of the funds. The credit union was able to recover almost $80,000
from Hall, but there remained an overdraft of over $42,000.

The credit union sued Sun as drawer of the checks and moved
for summary judgment on the ground that it qualified as a holder
in due course and took the checks free of any defenses. The trial
court found a genuine issue of material fact remained as to whether
the credit union had acted in "good faith" when it gave value for
the checks. The matter proceeded to trial and a jury found that the
credit union had not acted in good faith and therefore did not
qualify as a holder in due course.

On appeal, the Maine Supreme Court found that under the
pre–1990 rules the credit union would have no doubt met the
"honesty in fact" test for good faith, but concluded that the
legislature had intended on toughening the standard when it passed
Revised Article 3. The court interpreted revised 3–103(a)(4) as
requiring a determination of (1) whether the credit union had
observed the banking industries' commercial standards relating to
the giving of value on uncollected funds, and if so, (2) whether
those standards are reasonably designed to result in fair dealing.

The credit union's internal policy was to make provisional
credit available immediately upon the deposit of a check by one of
its members. (The credit union's policy had been approved by the
National Credit Union Administration.) The credit union also presented expert testimony that most credit unions in Maine followed
similar policies. In certain circumstances—where the check was for
a large amount and was drawn on an out-of-state bank—its policy
and Regulation CC both allowed for, but did not require, a hold to
be placed on the uncollected funds for up to nine days.

In upholding the jury's verdict, the Supreme Court rejected
these arguments and held that the credit union had not observed

"reasonable commercial standards of fair dealing" when it granted immediate availability on the three checks. The court held that the credit union should have, when allowing its member to access provisional credit on checks totaling over $120,000 drawn on an out-of-state bank: (1) investigated further to assure the deposited checks would be paid by the drawee bank, or (2) held the instruments to allow any irregularities to come to light.

The case seems wrong. Unlike Seinfeld where the bank's customer had an overdrawn account, in this case there are few indications to warn the credit union that this could be a problematic transaction. Everything on the face of the check was in order: it was drawn by a large insurance company on a well-known bank and payable to the beneficiaries of an insurance policy in satisfaction of legitimate claims. The payees had properly indorsed the checks to the credit union's regular customer. Large checks from insurance companies are not rare, and most checks from insurance companies are drawn on banks not located in Maine. That the court held that a jury could have rationally concluded that the credit union did not act according to commercial standards of fair dealing is surprising. The credit union dealt only with its customer, Hall's agent, and it followed its usual practice of allowing quick availability. Many have questioned this case; some calling it "dead wrong."

Other courts are made of sterner stuff. In Mid Wisconsin Bank v. Forsgard Trading,[10] in an appeal from a summary judgment granted in favor of Mid Wisconsin Bank, one of the defendants argued that Mid Wisconsin was not a holder in due course of a check written by Lakeshore because the bank did not take the check in good faith. Lakeshore had written a check for $18,500 to Forsgard. The next day Forsgard deposited the check at Mid Wisconsin and was given immediate credit on the deposit. That same day, Lakeshore issued a stop-payment order on the check. Mid Wisconsin received notice that payment on the check had been stopped a week later. Mid Wisconsin deducted the amount of the check from Forsgard's account. Due to transactions made by Forsgard during the week after depositing the check, the deduction resulted in a negative balance on the account. Forsgard never covered the shortfall.

Forsgard had frequently been overdrawn at Mid Wisconsin over the two years the account had been open. However, on each of these occasions Forsgard deposited money to cover the overdrafts when the bank contacted the company. Mid Wisconsin's policy allowed it to place holds on checks if it had reasonable doubts about

---

10. 266 Wis.2d 685, 668 N.W.2d 830, 53 UCC2d 898 (App. 2003). See also Wachovia Bank, N.A. v. Federal Reserve Bank of Richmond, 338 F.3d 318 (4th Cir.2003) ("To determine whether Wachovia Bank acted in conformity with reasonable commercial standards of fair dealing, we consider the fairness of Wachovia's actions, rather than any negligence on its part").

a check, but no holds were applied to Forsgard's deposits in this case.

Lakeshore claimed that Mid Wisconsin was not a holder in due course of the check Forsgard deposited because it did not take the instrument in good faith as required by 3–302(1). The court held that the practice of extending immediate credit on deposited checks was consistent with reasonable banking standards. It was unmoved by the facts that Forsgard had bounced checks previously.

How does one distinguish good faith from due care? Justice Easterbrook gets the standards right in State Bank of the Lakes v. Kansas Bankers Surety Co.:[11]

> [G]ood faith is in a different phylum from "due care." ... Article 3 of the UCC, which contains a definition of "good faith" ... links commercial reasonableness to "fair dealing." Avoidance of advantage-taking, which this section is getting at, differs from due care.

Check cashing companies appear to be the pariahs of holder in due course law. In Buckeye Check Cashing, Inc. v. Camp,[12] a check cashing company sued drawer for payment after drawer contacted his bank and ordered the bank to stop payment. Drawer of check had negotiated with a contractor for services to be completed over the next three days and drawer drafted a post-dated check as payment. (The check bore the date of the projected date of completion of the services.) Contractor immediately cashed check with plaintiff, who submitted the check for payment. The drawer, fearing services would not be completed, contacted his bank the same day and ordered it to stop payment. The court held that the future date on the check should have put the check cashing company on notice that the check might not be good. The court also held that the company failed to act in a commercially reasonable manner and did not take the check in "good faith" when it did not attempt to verify the check. We are less certain than the court is about the commercial practice with respect to postdated checks. In some circumstances it might be commercially unreasonable to take a postdated check over-the-counter without some explanation from the customer, but that surely would not be true of a check presented to an ATM.

In Any Kind Checks Cashed, Inc. v. Talcott,[13] a court held that the check cashing service did not act in good faith and should have verified a $10,000 check drawn on a 93 year-old's account when presented for cashing by a financial broker. "[The] procedures followed were not reasonably related to achieve fair dealing, ...

---

11. 328 F.3d 906 (7th Cir.2003).

12. 159 Ohio App.3d 784, 825 N.E.2d 644, 56 UCC2d 484 (2nd Dist. 2005).

13. 830 So.2d 160, 48 UCC2d 800 (Fla. 4th Dist.App. 2002).

taking into consideration all of the participants in the transaction." The court held that the financial broker was not the typical customer of a check cashing outlet because small businessmen rarely use a check cashing service that charges a 5% fee instead of a traditional bank. The business check is not the welfare or payroll check usually cashed at such an establishment. The court held that the need for speed in cashing a large business check is consistent with a drawer who might stop payment and fair dealing requires that the $10,000 check be approached with caution. "The concept of 'fair dealing' includes not being an easy, safe harbor for the dishonest."

Both the Buckeye Check–Cashing case and the Any Kind Checks Cashed case show courts that are quick to deny holder in due course status to check cashing facilities. We wonder how these courts would have handled these cases had the plaintiffs been banks and not check cashing facilities. In effect the courts are asking check cashers to adhere to a higher standard than might be required of a bank. Given the clientele of check cashing facilities, the courts' skepticism might be justified, but we would like to see a little more evidence that check-cashing facilities are a home for persons engaged in fraudulent behavior before we would subject them to higher standards than might be applied to a bank.

§ 2–7   Holder in Due Course Defined—Lack of Notice

The same facts that call a party's "good faith" into question may also give that party "notice" that the instrument has one of the problems listed in section 3–302 (e.g., the instrument is overdue or has been dishonored). Note, however, that lack of "good faith" and "notice" of a defense are not the same. For example, knowledge of a defense would prevent a holder from being a holder in due course of that instrument, but it would not necessarily prevent that same holder from being a holder in due course of other instruments of the same party. If, on the other hand, the holder knew that makers had asserted good defenses to their liability against a given payee in 50 out of the last 100 instruments made payable to that payee, the holder might fail to be a holder in due course for lack of good faith as to a particular instrument, even though the holder did not know of a specific defense on any given instrument.

A party can acquire notice of a defense in a variety of ways. He can observe that the instrument is crudely altered; he can see that its date for payment has already passed; he can note that it has been stamped "paid;" or he may even have actual knowledge of a contract defense of the drawer or maker. In all such cases, a would-be holder in due course does not deserve to take free of such defenses, for he could have refused to take the instrument.

Under 1–202, "a person has 'notice' of a fact if the person:

(a) has actual knowledge of it;

(b) has received a notice or notification of it; or

(c) from all the facts and circumstances known to the person at the time in question, has reason to know that it exists."

A court's power to find notice when the holder "has reason to know" that something exists on the basis of the "facts and circumstances known to him" introduces at least the flavor of the objective-subjective fight. It is a short step from that definition to say that one is on notice of what a reasonably prudent person in these circumstances has notice of. As we will see, courts vary substantially in their willingness to find notice of claims or defenses on the basis of facts known to holders. Some who are willing to find "notice" may be edging toward objective good faith under a new name.

In E. Bierhaus & Sons, Inc. v. Bowling,[1] an Indiana court used the objective notice standard to circumvent the subjective good faith rule. In that case a retail grocer, who was in deeply over his head, procured first a loan and ultimately a blank check from a friend, Bowling. Bowling claimed that the check was to be made out only to a new supplier, not to Bierhaus, the current supplier, and for security only. The grocer used the check to pay Bierhaus, to whom he owed $400,000. Conceding that Bowling was negligent, the court nevertheless confirmed the trial court's finding that Bierhaus was not a holder in due course because it had "notice." The court put it as follows: "Under an objective standard where a holder comes into possession of information which would dictate further inquiry by a reasonably prudent person, he may be denied holder in due course status if he fails to make such inquiry." The court goes on: "[t]he court could easily have inferred that Bierhaus, facing a $400,000 loss, either knew of the circumstances, or closed its eyes and in bad faith simply did not seek the truth in order to get its money." While the court is technically applying an objective good faith test, it seems in the quoted language almost to slip into a discussion of subjective good faith. That is particularly so when the court asserts not that the plaintiff had knowledge of certain facts from which a defense could be inferred, but that knowledge of certain facts placed it under an obligation to inquire further. How is such a conclusion different from applying a standard of objective good faith? We doubt that it is different.

Some courts have attributed notice to holders through the "close connection" doctrine. In the days before the Federal Trade Commission abolished holder in due course status for consumer

1. 486 N.E.2d 598, 42 UCC 920 (Ind. App. 1985).

notes, courts often looked for ways to protect consumers from parties who apparently conformed to all of the requirements for a holder in due course. One particularly offensive problem was that presented by a parent and subsidiary corporation in which the subsidiary might sell shoddy goods to a consumer and then sell the negotiable paper to the parent. Technically, the parent was a holder in due course because it gave value, had no notice, and took in good faith. Under the "close connection" doctrine, the courts attributed the subsidiary's knowledge to the parent if the two were sufficiently closely-connected. Some courts still restrict the doctrine to consumer transactions, but others have applied it in commercial transactions.

Standards for detecting a close connection are necessarily fuzzy, since the problem is frequently not as obvious as in the parent-subsidiary situation. For example, in one case a bank was "closely-connected" with a company when it took many notes from the company at a substantial discount, provided forms used by the company, and had a former employee working as a salesman for the company.[2] In another case, overlapping management supported a finding of close connection.[3] In Unico v. Owen,[4] the New Jersey Supreme Court stated a general approach to close connection cases:

> [W]hen it appears from the totality of the arrangements between [seller] and financer that the financer has had a substantial voice in setting standards for the underlying transaction, or has approved the standards established by the [seller], and has agreed to take all or a predetermined or substantial quantity of the negotiable paper which is backed by such standards, the financer should be considered a participant in the original transaction and therefore not entitled to holder in due course status.[5]

Section 3–302 subdivides "notice" into two broad categories—a presumption of notice for documents that are obviously suspect, and a subsection dealing with cases in which the holder did not know of various defects to the instrument.[6] Subsection (a)(1) keeps

---

2. Security Central Nat. Bank v. Williams, 52 Ohio App.2d 175, 368 N.E.2d 1264, 22 UCC 1196 (1976).

3. Arcanum Nat. Bank v. Hessler, 69 Ohio St.2d 549, 433 N.E.2d 204, 33 UCC 604 (1982).

4. 50 N.J. 101, 232 A.2d 405, 4 UCC 542 (1967).

5. 4 UCC at 558.

6. Subsection 3–302(a)(2) reads as follows:

(a) Subject to subsection (c) and Section 3–106(d), "holder in due course"

means the holder of an instrument if:
* * *

(2) the holder took the instrument (i) for value, (ii) in good faith, (iii) without notice that the instrument is overdue or has been dishonored or that there is an uncured default with respect to payment of another instrument issued as part of the same series, (iv) without notice that the instrument contains an unauthorized signature or has been altered, (v) without notice of any claim to the instrument described in Section 3–306, and (vi) without notice that any party

one from being a holder in due course in any case in which the instrument bears "such apparent evidence of forgery or alteration" or is "otherwise so irregular or incomplete as to call into question its authenticity." In effect, the subsection is a conclusive presumption of notice. Conceivably one should think about this presumption not as a notice provision at all but rather as a part of the definition of "instrument." That is to say, an instrument having any of these qualities—irregularity, incompleteness, or screaming alterations—is not a negotiable instrument at all and one cannot be a holder in due course of that instrument whether he has notice or not.[7] The pre–1990 Code, in section 3–304, was less clear on the status of a person who took such a defective instrument. The reason for the change is explained by Comment 1 to revised 3–302 as follows:

> Under subsection (1) of former Section 3–304, irregularity or incompleteness gave a purchaser notice of a claim or defense. But it was not clear from that provision whether the claim or defense had to be related to the irregularity or incomplete aspect of the instrument. This ambiguity is not present in subsection (a)(1).

Thus, any irregularity as specified in (a)(1) is not merely notice of a defense to which a holder might take subject, but is a fact that keeps anyone from being a holder in due course of that particular instrument. Every claimant is open to all defenses that could be raised on a simple contract whether or not the defense is related to the defect on the instrument.

Some courts have found a duty to examine checks and discover evidence of forgery, even when an instrument looks sound. Failing to look puts the holder on notice and precludes holder in due course status. In Triffin v. Pomerantz Staffing Services, LLC[8], a check cashing company was negligent in failing to examine the forged

---

has a defense or claim in recoupment described in Section 3–305(a).

7. See e.g. Northwestern Nat. Ins. Co. of Milwaukee v. Lutz, 71 F.3d 671, 28 UCC2d, 226 (7th Cir.1995) (investor purchased one unit of a partnership with a note made out for $68,308 but left the quantity field blank on the note. Someone else filled in the blank for the number of partnership units with the number three, inserted the words "per unit" with a carat after the amount of the note and handwrote "$68,308 x 3 units = $207,924" below. The note also included a payment schedule dictating the dates of four payments totaling $68,308. The alterations to the note were in two shades of ink different from that of defendant's signature. Court found that the changes made to the note were sufficient to put the bank on notice that it had been altered, and bank was not holder in due course); but see Barclays Bank, P.L.C. v. Conkey, 695 So.2d 931, 35 UCC2d 946 (Fla. 2d Dist.App. 1997) (court reversed trial court's finding that holder of undated promissory note could not be holder in due course since note was not payable at a definite time. Section 3–302 requires the instrument to be sufficiently complete so its authenticity is not called into question. Even though the instrument was incomplete, the omission of the date did not call into question its authenticity).

8. 370 N.J.Super. 301, 851 A.2d 100, 53 UCC2d 927 (App.Div. 2004).

checks presented to it. Friendly Check Cashing Corp. was presented with 18 counterfeit checks purporting to have been issued by Pomerantz. The checks bore the full name and address of Pomerantz and a facsimile of an authorized signature. Each check also directed the holder to touch the check to confirm its authenticity and advised that, because of heat sensitive ink, the logo "should fade when touched." Friendly cashed the checks without examining the heat sensitive ink on the back and the bank returned them unpaid and stamped "COUNTERFEIT". Friendly assigned its rights to Triffen who sued Pomerantz, asserting holder in due course status. The court held that Friendly did not meet reasonable commercial standards of fair dealing when it failed to fully examine the front and back of the check and use the method provided on the instrument for verifying its authenticity. The cashier failed to make an inquiry reasonably required by the circumstances and remained ignorant of a fact that might have disclosed a defect. Furthermore, the court implied that because Friendly was in the business of cashing checks, it might be held to a higher standard. We doubt the wisdom of this case. The court seems to be stretching here.

Above we noted that courts seem to be holding check cashing facilities to higher standards than to banks. We suspect that this case falls into that category. We note that banks routinely take checks by mail, ATM deposit or night deposit with little or no examination. It is possible that check cashing facilities should be held to a higher standard, but insistence upon too much could cause these facilities to refuse to serve their poor and working-class clientele who need a place to cash checks.

Doubtless the message on the face of an instrument that most often deprives the holder of holder in due course status is that the instrument is overdue. Under 3–304(a)(2), a check is overdue 90 days after its date. Such a check thus bears notice under 3–302 that will keep a holder from being a holder in due course. This replaced the "presumption" under the pre–1990 Code's section 3–304(3)(c) that a check was overdue 30 days after its issue. The good news is that a party can now take a check up to 90 days after its issue; the bad news is that the 90 day cutoff appears to be more than a presumption. The Code simply states that a check becomes "overdue," and is no longer merely "presumed to be" overdue. Other demand items are covered under 3–304(a)(3): they are overdue if they have been outstanding for an "unreasonably long" period of time, based on circumstances of the case, the nature of the instrument and usage of the trade. Under 3–304(b), an instrument payable at a definite time is overdue on the day after the due date or, for instruments payable in installments, upon default for nonpayment of an installment.

A second kind of information which may put a purchaser on notice derives from documents transferred concurrently with a negotiable instrument. For example, in HIMC Investment Co. v. Siciliano,[9] the court pointed out that certain of the terms on a second mortgage accompanying the note revealed a violation in the New Jersey second mortgage law. When a mortgage or other such document accompanies a note, that document may reveal violations of the state usury law, or of state or federal disclosure acts. Whether courts will find a purchaser of these documents to be on notice of all facts a lawyer-accountant might thus discover in an hour's work with a calculator, remains to be seen. The HIMC case suggests at least that holders will have notice of any gross legal defects that such documents reveal.

A third kind of information that may prevent a purchaser from being a holder in due course is his knowledge of the business practices of his payee. If the holder's knowledge of a transferor's generally shoddy business practices constitutes "notice of a defense" with respect to every instrument he transfers, this would exceed the wildest hopes of those who argued for an objective standard; but the courts show no desire to go that far. However, in several cases courts seem to have been influenced by the holder's knowledge of business practices of the transferor. For example, in Norman v. World Wide Distributors, Inc.,[10] the court stressed that the purchaser of the note "knew enough of the seller's referral plan to require it to inquire further" and secondly that he knew that the seller had been doing business under three different names during the year in which the note was transferred. Those two facts in addition to a substantial discount, led the court to find the purchaser was not a holder in due course.

In Agriliance, LLC v. Farmpro Svcs., Inc.,[11] the court found that knowledge of unscrupulous behavior was enough to impose a duty to inquire and that failure to inquire forestalls holder in due course status. Defendant-creditor had agreed to subordinate an interest in debtor-farmer's year 2001 crops to plaintiff-creditor and plaintiff-creditor provided a loan based on the crop. Defendant still had outstanding loans that debtor had defaulted on, and defendant was routinely in the business of loaning money to farmers. Since defendant's business was lending money to farmers, defendant should have known that a large cashier's check in the possession of a farmer in January must have been the payment for the prior year's crop. (Traditionally undercapitalized, farmers do not walk

---

9. 103 N.J.Super. 27, 246 A.2d 502, 5 UCC 846 (1968). The court also found facts which suggest a close relationship between plaintiff and lender, although the court did not discuss it at length.

10. 202 Pa.Super. 53, 195 A.2d 115, 1 UCC 234 (1963).

11. 328 F.Supp.2d 958, 52 UCC2d 36 (S.D. Iowa 2003).

around town with large cashier's checks unless they have just sold a crop.) The court concluded that the defendant's knowledge of these facts should have put them on notice that they were taking the payment in violation of their subordination agreement and that the payment belonged to the other creditor to whom the defendant had subordinated its security interest.

On the other hand, the court in O.P. Ganjo, Inc. v. Tri–Urban Realty Co.,[12] found that knowledge of suspicious circumstances was not enough and specifically affirmed the objective good faith test in the face of grave suspicions on the part of the purchaser about the veracity and credit standing of the subcontractor who transferred the note. Likewise, in Waterbury Sav. Bank v. Jaroszewski,[13] a Connecticut court found that knowledge of defects in three or four transactions out of five or six hundred prior transactions did not constitute notice. Thus what notice of defenses or lack of good faith courts will infer from knowledge of a transferor's shoddy business practices is still unsettled. It is clear that the courts give some weight to this knowledge when it is associated with other information, but so far no court seems willing to rely exclusively on such knowledge to find that a purchaser has notice of a claim or defense.

In some cases the courts find notice not on the basis of information available to the purchaser, but on the basis of the purchaser's behavior. Examples are cases in which purchasers discount notes by a very large margin and those where purchasers actually contact the payees on notes to disclaim any complicity in shoddy business practices of the payee. Illustrative of large discount cases is United States Finance Co. v. Jones,[14] in which the Alabama Supreme Court found that the sale of a note with a face value of $2,575.44 for $1,360 was an important factor indicating that the plaintiff had notice of a defense. In Norman v. World Wide Distributors, Inc.,[15] a representative of the purchaser called the maker of a note and informed him that he as holder had nothing to do with the referral-purchase plan. The court inferred knowledge of the referral plan's illegality from this careful disclaimer of any association with it. Whether the star of the holder in due course is waxing or waning on questions of notice and good faith is difficult to say. It seems that courts in the past were quicker to find notice on the part of a purchaser of a consumer note than they are on the part of a purchaser of a business person's note.

For most purposes there need be no connection between the defense or claim that the party on the instrument is attempting to assert and the flaw that allegedly deprives one of holder in due

---

12. 108 N.J.Super. 517, 261 A.2d 722, 7 UCC 302 (1969).

13. 4 Conn.Cir.Ct. 620, 238 A.2d 446, 4 UCC 1049 (1967).

14. 285 Ala. 105, 229 So.2d 495, 7 UCC 204 (1969).

15. 202 Pa.Super. 53, 195 Pa.2d 115, 1 UCC 234 (1963).

course status. Thus, if one takes an overdue note, the maker can assert defenses such as failure of consideration that have nothing to do with time and the fact that the note was overdue. Note also that notice is determined as of the time of taking the instrument (more precisely, when the taker gives value). Thus in Allison–Kesley AG Center, Inc. v. Hildebrand,[16] the defendant was treated as a holder in due course who took free of the plaintiff's conversion claims because the defendant did not know of the conversion at the time it took the PIK certificates, although it later did a considerable investigation and discovered the fraud not long after.

Finally, subsection 3–302(b) deals with notice of discharge. It is technically different from the old pre–1990 Article 3 because it permits one to be a holder in due course even with notice of discharge, but makes the discharge "effective" only against the one who became a holder in due course with knowledge of the fact of discharge. See also section 3–601(b). Comment 3 gives an example of the case in which there might be a discharge of one party, yet the instrument might still have vitality in the hands of a holder: a check certified after it came into the possession of the payee and on which the drawee was discharged because of the certification. The holder in due course might or might not be subject to that discharge depending upon whether the holder knew of the discharge at the time of the transfer.

§ 2–8   Payee as a Holder in Due Course

A payee can be a holder in due course. The Code used to say so explicitly, in section 3–302(2), but the drafters deleted that language during the 1990 revisions because it was "surplusage and may be misleading."[1] The drafters added the language to the pre–1990 Code, according to comment 4 to section 3–302, because of a split in authority among courts about whether a payee could be a holder in due course. The NIL provided that a "transferee" could become a holder in due course. This provision led some courts to conclude that a payee, to whom the instrument was normally "issued" rather than "transferred," could not be a holder in due course. Since the Code abandoned the NIL language that caused the uncertainty, the redrafters in 1990 said, it was no longer necessary to spell out the common-law rule that a payee could be a holder in due course.

Assume a payee named John purchases a cashier's check from a bank in exchange for a personal check that John knows is drawn on insufficient funds. The bank would have a defense to its obli-

---

16. 485 N.W.2d 841, 19 UCC2d 480 (Iowa 1992).

§ 2–8

1. Pre 1990 § 3–302(2) read: "A payee may be a holder in due course."

gation to pay the check. If John used his cashier's check to buy a car from Jane, and indorsed the check to her, Jane would take the check free of the bank's defenses. Now, assume instead that Jane and John went to the bank together and John had the cashier's check made out directly to Jane, making her the payee. Jane could be said to have "dealt" with the bank, but she should still take free of the bank's defenses. There is no good reason why a person in Jane's position should be free from the bank's defenses in one case and bound by those defenses in the other. (See Comment 4 to section 3–302 and Comment 2 to section 3–305.)

In our first example, John was the holder of a check that he indorsed to Jane. In our second example, John was not a holder but a remitter—a person who purchases an instrument from its issuer, which instrument is payable to a third person. The comment to 3–302 points out that the rights of the seller (Jane, in our case) should not be affected by whether she took the instrument from a holder or a remitter.

The pre–1990 Code might have produced different outcomes in the two cases. The Code provided in section 3–305(2) that a holder in due course "takes the instrument free from all defenses of any party to the instrument with whom the holder has not dealt." This language could be read to say that a person in the position of Jane in our second example "dealt" with the bank and would be out of luck. To avert this result, the drafters in 1990 deleted the language specifying that a holder in due course takes free of the defenses of any party "with whom the holder has not dealt."

Nevertheless, according to Comment 2 to section 3–305, the holder in due course doctrine "applies only to cases in which more than two parties are involved." Comment 4 to section 3–302 makes a similar point: when a payee of a check or note takes the instrument from the drawer or maker and has not transferred the instrument, the holder in due course doctrine is "irrelevant in determining the rights" between the two of them.

The comment to 3–302 gives four cases in which a payee might claim the status of holder in due course and, if that status were established, should be entitled to take free of the defenses of the principal obligor. As in our example of Jane and John and the cashier's check, all the cases in the comment involve three parties, but for various reasons the third party, asserting the holder in due course status, is the payee.

So far so good, but what replaces the omitted language for cases when a payee should not have the rights of a holder in due course? The language is hidden in the bowels of 3–305(b). Section 3–305 provides, in part:

(a) Except as stated in subsection (b), the right to enforce the obligation of a party to pay an instrument is subject to the following:

* * *

(3) a claim in recoupment of the obligor against the original payee of the instrument if the claim arose from the transaction that gave rise to the instrument; but the claim of the obligor must be asserted against a transferee of the instrument only to reduce the amount owing on the instrument at the time the action is brought.

(b) The right of a holder in due course to enforce the obligation of a party to pay the instrument * * * is not subject to * * * claims in recoupment stated in subsection (a)(3) against a person *other than the holder*. (Emphasis added).

* * *

We think that the prepositional phrase at the end of post–1990 3–305(b) means that a typical drawer of a check can always assert its defense against its own payee—even if the payee is technically a holder in due course—because a holder in due course takes free only of claims and defenses "against a person other than the holder" (i.e., against someone other than me). In the classic two-party case the defense will be by the drawer or maker against the payee. When the payee sues, the drawer asserts the defense against the *payee* holder, not against a person "other than" the payee holder.

Now apply revised 3–305(b) to a cashier's check where the remitter fraudulently procures the check from the bank and delivers it to the payee. In this case the payee is again technically a holder in due course. Does the payee take free of the defense of fraud that the remitter committed against the drawer bank in procuring the cashier's check? Yes, because the defense of fraud is a defense against a person other than the holder (i.e., the defense is against the remitter, not against the payee holder who is asserting the claim against the bank).

To test your understanding of these problems, consider the following case. A bank issues a note to Target Company. Having received the note, Target Company sells the assets of one of its divisions, including this particular note, to Acquiring Company in a bulk transfer. When the note becomes due, the bank refuses to pay on the ground that it was fraudulently induced by Target Company into issuing the note. At trial can the bank assert this defense to Acquiring Company's action to enforce the obligation?

Recall first that because the note was obtained through a bulk transfer, Acquiring Company can acquire only the rights of a holder in due course to the extent that its predecessor had them, see 3–302(c). One buying in a bulk transfer does not take in the ordinary course and cannot be a holder in due course in its own right. Acquiring Company, therefore, must take the note subject to the same defenses to which Target Company would be subject. But according to 3–305(b), Target Company, as a holder in due course, is only immune to defenses of the bank if the defenses are against a party "other than the holder." The defense of fraud here is against the Target Company as payee, and thus is not against a "person other than the holder." Consequently, Target Company, as payee, would be subject to the defense that it had fraudulently induced the Bank into issuing the note. Because Acquiring Company cannot take rights greater than what Target Company can through a bulk transfer, Acquiring Company is also subject to the bank's defense of fraud.

§ 2–9   Rights of a Holder in Due Course: The Effect of the Federal Trade Commission Legend and of Similar State Laws on Holder in Due Course Status

The stimulus for a limitation on the holder in due course doctrine came from consumer representatives. Those representatives correctly argued that the consumer was often left holding the bag, when, for example, she received shoddy house siding and signed a negotiable note or a retail installment contract with a "waiver of defense clause." The note or contract could quickly be transferred to a legitimate lender who would then insist upon full payment. Since the lender would be a holder in due course or a beneficiary under the waiver of defense clause, the consumer could not raise the legitimate defenses she might have, and would have to pay notwithstanding her failure to receive what she bargained for. In such a case her recourse against the house-sider who had since moved on to a new town was not satisfactory. Either she could not find the house-sider, or the house-sider would be insolvent. Amid a great deal of debate about the frequency of such fraudulent transactions and about the consequences for legitimate transactions, the legislatures in many states passed some restriction upon the holder in due course doctrine in consumer transactions. Such restrictions were embodied in the Uniform Consumer Credit Code and have been a part of most modern state consumer credit protection acts.

A number of courts have held that because a purchaser of commercial paper was "closely connected" to the seller of the goods or services, the purchaser did not enjoy holder in due course status.

One should note, as did most of the statutes, that it is not enough simply to limit the holder in due course doctrine in consumer transactions. The so-called waiver of defense clause, explicitly authorized by the Code's 9–403, must also be dealt with. Under such a clause a consumer waived her right to assert underlying defenses against the *bona fide* buyer of the paper. Thus even though that buyer of the paper was not a holder in due course, he enjoyed the same legal status. In addition, the reformers feared that if the holder in due course doctrine was abolished, the sellers of shoddy goods and services would "drag the body," i.e., would take the consumer to a lender, there arrange for the loan, the proceeds of which were to be paid directly to the seller of the goods or services, and leave the consumer with no right of setoff for her damages. She would lack such a right under the common law because the lender in that case would not be a transferee of the debtor's obligation to the original seller but would simply be one who had made a direct loan to the consumer, a loan apparently unrelated to any specific transaction. For those reasons, the most sophisticated state laws dealt not only with the holder in due course status, but also with waiver of defense clauses and, in varying degrees, with the "straight loan" that was somehow induced by the seller of the goods or services.

In 1971 representatives of the Federal Trade Commission proposed to change substantially the traditional holder in due course rules by promulgating their first FTC rule on the subject. The second rule was promulgated in 1973 and the third in 1975; the third rule became effective in May of 1976. One might properly ask who gave the FTC authority to help tear down one of the pillars of commercial law. It is odd that its federal dismantling occurred not through federal legislation, but through regulations of an administrative agency. Generations of lawyers and law teachers are surely turning in their graves at the thought that a mere federal regulation could bring down this long established doctrine.

Here is not the place for extensive debate on the power of the FTC. We share the view that the FTC has, at the least, far exceeded its appropriate reach. Indeed, one might ask what are the bounds of FTC rulemaking. If it can abolish the holder in due course doctrine, can the FTC effectively enact its own consumer credit code? Set the speed limit in Keokuk? All this has occurred without a single Representative or Senator putting a pen to paper or voting on so much as a word of this quasi-legislation.

One should distinguish between the process by which the consequence was accomplished and the consequence itself. We are not advocates of the holder in due course doctrine in consumer transactions. While we do not share the belief of FTC zealots that it was the most awful thing in Western jurisprudence, we believe that on balance the world is better off with abolition of the holder in due course doctrine in consumer transactions. Moreover, one's distaste for the process should not obscure his or her judgment about the cleverness of the rascals at the FTC. They did not mount a frontal assault on the holder in due course doctrine; they did not purport to have the power to render any state law invalid; they did not submit their proposal to the winds in the halls of Congress (a place where they might have lost). Rather, they simply required that a legend be placed on most consumer paper. Having studied the Uniform Commercial Code carefully, they correctly concluded that paper which included such a legend might not *under state law* be negotiable or, even if negotiable, could not be the basis for a suit by one immune from consumer defenses.

a. Scope and Application of the FTC Rule

The heart of the FTC rule reads as follows:

In connection with any sale or lease of goods or services to consumers, in or affecting commerce as "commerce" is defined in the Federal Trade Commission Act, it is an unfair or deceptive act or practice within the meaning of Section 5 of that Act for a seller, directly or indirectly, to:

(a) Take or receive a consumer credit contract which fails to contain the following provision in at least ten point, bold face, type:

NOTICE

ANY HOLDER OF THIS CONSUMER CREDIT CONTRACT IS SUBJECT TO ALL CLAIMS AND DEFENSES WHICH THE DEBTOR COULD ASSERT AGAINST THE SELLER OF GOODS OR SERVICES OBTAINED PURSUANT HERETO OR WITH THE PROCEEDS HEREOF. RECOVERY HEREUNDER BY THE DEBTOR SHALL NOT EXCEED AMOUNTS PAID BY THE DEBTOR HEREUNDER.

or,

(b) Accept, as full or partial payment for such sale or lease, the proceeds of any purchase money loan (as purchase money loan is defined herein), unless any consumer credit contract made in connection with such purchase money loan contains the following provision in at least ten point, bold face type:

NOTICE

ANY HOLDER OF THIS CONSUMER CREDIT CONTRACT IS SUBJECT TO ALL CLAIMS AND DEFENSES WHICH THE DEBTOR COULD ASSERT AGAINST THE SELLER OF GOODS OR SERVICES OBTAINED WITH THE PROCEEDS HEREOF. RECOVERY HEREUNDER BY THE

DEBTOR SHALL NOT EXCEED AMOUNTS PAID BY THE DEBTOR HEREUNDER.[1]

Thus, if the seller includes the required notice in its written contract, or if it is incorporated in the paper used in a covered transaction written as a direct loan by the creditor, no subsequent holder of that paper will have the rights of a holder in due course. Moreover, the original creditor-writer of the direct paper will be subject to the claims and defenses which the debtor could have asserted against the seller. These results followed because any promise bearing the legend was probably a conditional promise, and therefore not a negotiable instrument under section 3–104 in the pre–1990 Code. That also meant such documents were not even covered by Article 3.

In 1990 the drafters of revised Article 3 wanted to retain the FTC rule's effect and prohibit subsequent holders from being holders in due course, but they otherwise wished to include these instruments within Article 3. To accomplish that purpose they added revised 3–106(d), which reads in full as follows:

> If a promise or order at the time it is issued or first comes into possession of a holder contains a statement, required by applicable statutory or administrative law, to the effect that the rights of a holder or transferee are subject to claims or defenses that the issuer could assert against the original payee, the promise or order is not thereby made conditional for the purposes of Section 3–104(a); but if the promise or order is an instrument, there cannot be a holder in due course of the instrument.

In a bow to other consumer law, section 3–302(g) renders the holder in due course doctrine "subject to any law limiting status as a holder in due course in particular classes of transactions." Comment 7 to 1990 3–302 explicitly states that this provision means that the holder in due course rules in revised Article 3 are subject to "state statutory and case law."

b. *Transactions Covered*

Before considering all of the legal consequences of the FTC rule, examine the transactions that it will cover and those that it will not cover. In the first place, the rule covers no transactions that deal exclusively with business credit; it reaches only "consumer credit."

The key word is "consumer." For the transaction to be covered, the debtor must be "a natural person who seeks or acquires

§ 2–9

1. FTC Holder in Due Course Regulations, 16 C.F.R. § 433.2 (1978).

goods or services for personal, family or household use." Thus, one who borrows money to purchase a washing machine for use in a washeteria would not be covered by the rule. A doctor who borrowed money for use in her practice would not be covered by the rule nor would the millions of other credit transactions unrelated to personal, family or household use. In some cases (as with the doctor's car which might be used in part for practice of medicine and part for her own personal use) one might have difficulty in determining whether or not the transaction was covered. Such transactions are likely to be few and far between.

Note second that the definition[2] of consumer includes only the acquisition of "goods or services"; it thus includes contracts for the use of health spas (presumably as a service) and time payment contracts for schools, but it does not include contracts for the sale of real property. One might argue that a contract for the use of a health spa is a contract for the use of real property; however, it is certain that the FTC would take the position that the contract was for the sale of services, and it seems likely that the FTC would win.

A final preliminary, probably insignificant limitation upon the rule, is that it applies only when "credit" is granted. By use of the words "purchase money loan" and "financing a sale," the rule

2. Applicable definitions for the FTC rule are in the section preceding it. FTC Holder in Due Course Regulations, 16 C.F.R. § 433.1 (1978), reads as follows:

Definitions

(a) *Person.* An individual, corporation, or any other business organization.

(b) *Consumer.* A natural person who seeks or acquires goods or services for personal, family, or household use.

(c) *Creditor.* A person who, in the ordinary course of business, lends purchase money or finances the sale of goods or services to consumers on a deferred payment basis; *Provided,* such person is not acting, for the purpose of a particular transaction, in the capacity of a credit card issuer.

(d) *Purchase money loan.* A cash advance which is received by a consumer in return for a "Finance Charge" within the meaning of the Truth in Lending Act and Regulation Z, which is applied, in whole or substantial part, to a purchase of goods or services from a seller who (1) refers consumers to the creditor or (2) is affiliated with the creditor by common control, contract, or business arrangement.

(e) *Financing a sale.* Extending credit to a consumer in connection with a "Credit Sale" within the meaning of the Truth in Lending Act and Regulation Z.

(f) *Contract.* Any oral or written agreement, formal or informal, between a creditor and a seller, which contemplates or provides for cooperative or concerted activity in connection with the sale of goods or services to consumers or the financing thereof.

(g) *Business arrangement.* Any understanding, procedure, course of dealing, or arrangement, formal or informal, between a creditor and a seller, in connection with the sale of goods or services to consumers or the financing thereof.

(h) *Credit card issuer.* A person who extends to cardholders the right to use a credit card in connection with purchases of goods or services.

(i) *Consumer credit contract.* Any instrument which evidences or embodies a debt arising from a "Purchase Money Loan" transaction or a "financed sale" as defined in paragraphs (d) and (e).

(j) *Seller.* A person who, in the ordinary course of business, sells or leases goods or services to consumers.

incorporates the doctrine set out in the Truth in Lending law[3] and Regulation Z.[4] Several cases under the law have raised serious and interesting questions as to whether certain kinds of installment contracts are in fact credit contracts or whether, since the debtor prepays in some of those, there is no extension of credit by the seller. For example, where the buyer is to receive goods or services in installments and where he pays before he receives such performance by the seller, there is arguably no credit granted by the seller. In any case, the basic transaction reached by the rule is one in which the seller writes paper and sells it to a creditor.

The transaction that raises the most legal problems is one which is written as a direct loan by the creditor to the buyer. In that case, the seller's name may not even appear on the loan document (except perhaps as an indorser). Although there is no transfer of the credit instrument in that case, and theoretically the transaction is only a loan by a creditor to a debtor, the creditor's right to repayment will often be subject to defenses of the debtor-buyer that arise out of the purchase of the services or goods.

Under the terms of the rule, the seller who accepts "proceeds of any purchase money loan" must see to it that the notice concerning defenses is included in the contract. The rule itself[5] defines purchase money loans as follows:

> (d) *Purchase money loan.* A cash advance which is received by a consumer in return for a "Finance Charge" within the meaning of the Truth in Lending Act and Regulation Z, which is applied, in whole or substantial part, to a purchase of goods or services from a seller who (1) refers consumers to the creditor or (2) is affiliated with the creditor by common control, contract, or business arrangement.

How does one distinguish this case from one where a bank customer routinely borrows money from his bank? Even the consumer zealots could not have intended that the bank be responsible for all the foolish bargains that each of its borrowers might make. The answer lies in the last part of the definition of purchase money loan. It includes only loans that are made for the purchase of the goods from a seller who refers consumers to the creditor or to a seller who is "affiliated" with the creditor in ways which we will discuss below.

First the rule is designed to forestall evasion of the holder in due course limitation by "dragging the body" of the consumer from seller's place of business to the bank. It is sufficient if the creditor

---

3. Consumer Credit Protection Act, 15 U.S.C.A.§ 1601 et seq. (1976).

4. Truth in Lending Regulations, 12 C.F.R.§ 226.1 (1978).

5. 16 C.F.R.§ 433.1(d) (1978).

and the seller are related by "common control, contract, or business arrangement." Business arrangement is defined most broadly to include "[a]ny understanding, procedure, course of dealing, or arrangement, formal or informal, between a creditor and a seller, in connection with the sale of goods or services to consumers or the financing thereof." At minimum the quoted language would include the following transactions:

(1) Any direct loan written by a financing subsidiary such as GMAC, Ford Motor Credit, or General Electric Credit, for the purchase of goods manufactured by their parent company or sold by a franchisee of the parent.

(2) All cases in which there is an explicit agreement that the seller of the goods or services will send its buyers to a specific creditor.

Some cases are less clear. What if the creditor, a bank, "floor plans" the inventory of seller, an automobile dealer? Although the bank has provided the dealer with no forms, more than one third of the dealer's customers get their loans from the bank. There is no evidence of an agreement that the dealer will send his customers to the bank; there is no kickback of the interest charge. In such a case, the FTC might argue that there must be referrals, and that thus the bank's loans are "purchase money loans" within section 433.1(d), or the customers would not go to the bank in such numbers. Nevertheless, the FTC's proposed enforcement guide-lines[6] state that they are not referrals if there is "no communication whatsoever between the seller and a lender."[7] The numbers themselves may be evidence of referrals, but they are probably insufficient standing alone.

The second FTC argument will be that the floor plan amounts to a contract between the parties that brings the transactions within the rule. The guidelines state that "a commercial lease, the factoring of accounts receivable or a general business loan * * * do not by themselves invoke the Rule,"[8] but they also state that a floor plan that "contemplates" the assignment of paper on the referral of customers does invoke the rule.[9] Thus, arguably a floor plan is not enough alone.

However, if the floor plan was written at a lower interest rate than would prevail on a similarly secured but free standing loan, the FTC might have a third argument, namely that the favorable interest rate is the "payment of a consideration"[10] for referrals.

---

6. Guidelines on Trade Regulation Rule Concerning Preservation of Consumers' Claims and Defenses, 41 Fed. Reg. 20022 (1976).

7. *Id.* at 20025.

8. *Id.* at 20026.

9. *Id.*

10. *Id.*

Consider also a situation where there is no financing arrangement between the creditor and the seller, but the creditor is one of four financing institutions whose names are routinely given to the seller's customers who seek financing. Also, assume that one of the loan officers of the creditor routinely goes to the local auto dealers' monthly meeting and that he occasionally buys lunch for the sales managers at the different agencies. Do these various contacts amount to a "business arrangement" sufficient to invoke the rule? Under the guidelines, one may give buyers a list of creditors[11] but may not do so according to an "arrangement."[12] The FTC could argue in any case that the lunch and the other contacts amounted to a "course of dealing."[13]

At least this much is clear: many consumer transactions, whether written as direct loans or as the purchase of paper written by the seller, are within the reach of the rule. Surely, it is an unusual case today where, despite a significant number of common customers, there is no floor plan nor any agreement to purchase paper, nor any referral, nor any drafting of loan application documents by the creditor for the seller.

PROBLEM

Consumer debtor buys a car from dealer and a house from seller. In both cases he signs a note for the purchase price—to the car dealer in the first case and to the bank/mortgagee in the second.

1. The auto note contains the FTC legend ("subject to claims and defenses") but the mortgage note does not. Has the mortgagee violated the FTC rule? No; the rule applies only to sales to consumers of goods and services and the house is neither.

2. Dealer proposes to evade the FTC rule as follows: I will not be a party to the transaction and my name will not appear on the note. I propose to take the customer to a bank with whom I do business and have the buyer take out a loan directly with the bank (who, of course, will pay the money directly over to me).

    This will not work because if there is a "business arrangement" between the dealer and the bank, then the note must contain the legend so making the bank and all subsequent takers subject to the defenses even if the dealer's name is not on the note.

A year after the car loan was made and after buyer has paid $10,000, buyer stops paying, asserts a right to reject the car and

---

11. *Id.* at 20025.   **13.** 16 C.F.R. § 433.1(g).
12. *Id.*

asks for its entire $50,000 purchase price from bank. What is bank's liability?

Bank's liability is capped at $10,000, the amount paid. But it will be liable for that amount only if buyer can make a case under 2–714 and 2–715 for damages in that amount. Unless the buyer can fit his case within a lemon law, it is unlikely that it will have a right to reject and so get to cancel the contract because too much time has passed. Bank will note that the FTC rule only leaves the parties where they would have been had there been a sales contract between them. If buyer cannot prove his case or qualify for a particular remedy under Article 2, he loses whether the defendant is a HIDC or not.

c. Consequences of Failure to Comply with the FTC Rule

The code was again revised in 2002 to clarify the situation where the seller did not include the required FTC notice on a consumer contract. Revised 3–305(e) and Comment 6 specify that a consumer contract that has omitted the required notice will be treated as if the notice was included and the holder will be subject to the same claims and defenses that would have been available had the notice been included.

The states have been slow to embrace 2002 Article 3, but some courts adopted similar rules even before then. In Gonzalez v. Old Kent Mortgage Company,[14] the court treated a contract without the notice as though it had the notice. Gonzalez hired a contractor for some home improvement projects. The contractor hired to do the work brought Gonzalez to Old Kent and arranged for a mortgage on her home to pay for the improvements. The mortgage mentioned Gonzalez and Old Kent only and, once the mortgage was signed, the contractor received a check directly from Old Kent. Gonzalez was unhappy with the contractor's work, and sued to hold Old Kent liable for the damages. Gonzalez wanted to offset her damages from her payments to Old Kent. Old Kent argued at trial that, since the FTC notice was omitted from the mortgage contract, the FTC rule did not apply and Old Kent was not subject to plaintiff's claims for damages. The court held that "it would turn the law on its head" if Old Kent was allowed to avoid the consequences of its own failure to include the required FTC notice. The court held that public policy required the note be treated as though it included the notice even though it had been omitted, and that Old Kent could be held

14. 2000 WL 1469313 (E.D.Pa. 2000). See also Associates Home Equity Svcs., Inc. v. Troup, 343 N.J.Super. 254, 778 A.2d 529 (App.Div. 2001).

liable for plaintiff's claims against the home improvement contractor.

If the seller does not include the notice on the consumer contract, what other consequences will it suffer? By its omission the seller has committed an unfair trade practice and is then subject to the sanctions that follow from a suit by the FTC for violations of the FTC Act.[15] The power of the FTC to sanction violations of the Act, and the methods by which such sanctions may be accomplished, were expanded by the passage of Title II of the Magnuson–Moss legislation, entitled the "Federal Trade Commission Improvement Act."[16] Among other things, the amendments authorize the Commission immediately to institute a civil penalty suit for knowing violations and so avoid the three-to-five year delay which traditionally preceded the filing of a civil penalty suit under the original Act. In addition, Title II creates a new section 19 which allows the FTC to institute consumer redress suits in certain circumstances. It should be noted that under the current phrasing of the holder in due course rule the creditor has no liability.

Will the sellers be subject to private remedies in the form of class action or individual suits by consumers for omission of the legend? If a bank and an automobile dealer are routinely writing paper without the notice, is there any private liability for violation of the rule to the debtors on that paper? With one recent exception, the courts have consistently refused to interpret the FTC Act to grant a private right of action. The most comprehensive statement of the basis for denying a private right of action under the FTC Act is found in Holloway v. Bristol–Myers Corp.[17] The *Holloway* court based its denial of a private right of enforcement upon the ground that private enforcement would pose serious problems to the enforcement activities of the FTC and that such enforcement was inconsistent with the Congressional intent that an administrative agency, with an expertise in dealing with commercial practices, proceed against violators of the Act.[18] An early case, however, took a position contrary to the *Holloway* decision, Guernsey v. Rich Plan of the Midwest.[19] Stating that the "efficacy of the Federal Trade Commission in acting to deter consumer fraud is suspect,"[20] the *Guernsey* court found an implied right to seek a private remedy for unfair and deceptive trade practices, at least in the circumstances of *Guernsey* where the FTC had previously issued a cease and desist order against defendant's franchisor. The D.C. Circuit has explicitly rejected *Guernsey* and upheld *Holloway* in Bott v. Holiday Univer-

15. 16 C.F.R. § 433.2.

16. 15 U.S.C.A. § 57(a) (1976).

17. 485 F.2d 986 (D.C.Cir. 1973).

18. *Id*. at 1002.

19. 408 F.Supp. 582 (N.D.Ind. 1976).

20. *Id*. at 586.

sal, Inc.[21] The D.C. Circuit decision represents the weight of authority. And the fact that Congress has granted private remedies to consumers in certain analogous cases (e.g., the Magnuson–Moss Warranty provisions)[22] suggests that it intended no such remedy here.

If a dishonest seller has taken and negotiated a consumer installment contract without including the FTC notice, is the consumer without recourse in a suit for payment? Not necessarily. The assignee may fail to be a holder in due course for lack of good faith as required by section 3–302. Obviously, sophisticated purchasers of negotiable instruments know the status of consumer paper in the post-FTC rule era. Arguably one will not be "in good faith" when he purchases paper that omits the FTC notice but that shows its consumer origin by the name of the payee on the note (i.e., "pay to the order of Acme Car Sales").

d. Creditor Responses to the FTC Rule

Before one decides to leave the lending business for having lost his status as a holder in due course, a lender should consider the probable consequences of the FTC rule. Laymen, particularly retail sellers, are wont to complain that under the rule any microscopic defect in the goods will give the buyer a right to quit paying, return the goods and demand a refund.

That is not an accurate statement of the law. The denial of the holder in due course status only puts the creditor or other holder of the paper in the same position the seller would have been in. The rights between the buyer and the seller of goods are governed principally by Article 2. A buyer's general remedies are catalogued in section 2–711 and a buyer's right to reject or revoke acceptance is set out in section 2–602 et seq.

If there is a minor defect in a product sold and if the buyer chooses to retain the product, he has the right under sections 2–711, 2–714, and 2–717 to set off his damages against the seller. Whether he can set off all of these damages in the first installment or whether he must prorate them is not clear under 2–717.[23] It is clear that he cannot stop paying entirely. Rather, he simply reduces the total amount of his payments by the amount of his damages. Assume for example that a windshield cracked two months after the buyer purchased a car. Assume further that it would cost $300 to replace the windshield and that the buyer chose to keep the car. In those circumstances buyer's damages under 2–714 would not normally exceed $300 and the buyer would typically be permitted to set off that amount—if indeed it could be proven that the wind-

---

21. 1976 WL 1283 (D.D.C. 1976).

22. See 15 U.S.C.A. § 2310(d).

23. See § 2–717 and Comment thereto.

shield broke because it was defective and not because it was subjected to improper use.

Thus the creditor usually has at least two arguments against someone who wishes not to pay. First the creditor need not accept the buyer's argument that a defense exists. Second, absent revocation or rejection, the creditor can limit the setoff to the amount of damages and can insist that the buyer pay the remaining amount of the purchase price.

Under what circumstances can the buyer entirely escape paying? Assuming there is fraud in the transaction, typically the buyer can rescind and get restitution of money paid. Assuming less than fraud in the transaction, the buyer who gives notice and acts properly can reject defective goods, provided the seller makes no effective cure under section 2–508. The cumulative impact of the seller's right to cure and of the limits on notice and use mean that the buyer usually will not have a right to reject or to revoke acceptance unless there is a substantial defect in the goods sold and the buyer acts before the goods have undergone significant change.

Only when there is nondelivery or the delivered goods are rejected or their acceptance revoked does section 2–711 give the buyer the right to "cancel" and to recover "so much of the price as has been paid" together with damages. Thus it is important to emphasize that most defects in the underlying transaction do not give the buyer the right to stop paying entirely.

If the underlying transaction involves a sale of services and not goods, Article 2 does not govern the transaction. Typically the common law of contract will give the right to stop paying entirely only if there is a material breach. Otherwise the buyer will be left in the same circumstances as one who had not rejected. He will probably have a right to set off an amount equal to the damages he has suffered but will have to pay the rest of the price.

Note finally that even if the buyer rejects and proves substantial damages, the maximum exposure of the creditor under the FTC rule is the amount already paid by the debtor. If, for example, the debtor buys an $8,000 car, pays $200 down and suffers $20,000 of damages as a result of breach of warranty, he can recover only $200 from the creditor and must turn to the seller for the additional $19,800.

Beyond this, how should one faced with a loss of holder in due course status in the area of consumer paper respond? Depending upon the market circumstances, the type of consumers with whom it is dealing and type of seller whose paper it is buying, a creditor may choose not to buy certain kinds of paper previously purchased. Presumably, one will follow that course only when the paper is bad because the seller, the buyer, or both are not good risks.

In other circumstances, the creditor has a variety of more acceptable options. First and most obvious is to buy the paper with recourse. Whether the creditor can achieve that goal will of course depend upon the market. In some circumstances the creditor may simply decide to buy the paper without recourse and to eat the losses. Conceivably a creditor can protect against those losses by some sort of insurance or by raising the interest rate. As creditors are well aware, there are a variety of recourse arrangements and quasi-recourse arrangements that can be arranged. Thus, the recourse contract can be tailored as the market dictates.[24]

§ 2–10   Rights of a Holder in Due Course: Freedom From Claims in Recoupment, Defenses, and Claims of Title

The legal battles fought over the holder in due course doctrine typically focus on whether a given party is a holder in due course. Once that issue is determined, the battle is usually finished and the legal consequences usually clear.

Section 3–305 divides the obligor's defenses into two main categories: those that stand up against even a holder in due course, and those that do not. Defenses of the durable variety—so-called real defenses—are limited in 3–305(a)(1) to four circumstances. We note them here and discuss them in more detail below. They are:

(1) infancy,

(2) duress, lack of legal capacity or illegality of the transaction,

(3) fraud that induced the obligor to sign the instrument without knowing its terms and without reasonable opportunity to find them out, and

(4) discharge of the obligor through insolvency.

A holder in due course takes free of the obligor's other claims and defenses, which are laid out and further subdivided in sections 3–305 and 3–306. Those "defenses" come in two basic flavors— defenses of the obligor (section 3–305(a)(2)), and a new feature of the 1990 Code labeled a "claim in recoupment" of the obligor (section 3–305(a)(3)).[1] In addition, section 3–306 addresses a "claim of a property or possessory right in the instrument or its proceeds."

---

24. The seller might try to add a limitation to the FTC-required legend (e.g., * * * "But the holder is responsible only to the extent of the first $50 in damages."). However, as well as incurring the wrath of the FTC, this ploy would undoubtedly be unsuccessful as it is an obvious evasion of the spirit of the rule.

§ 2–10

1. (a) Except as stated in subsection (b), the right to enforce the obligation of a party to pay an instrument is subject to the following: * * *

(2) a defense of the obligor stated in another section of this Article or a defense of the obligor that would be available if the person entitled to enforce the

The defenses of the obligor can be summed up neatly as follows: all defenses provided elsewhere in Article 3 and all defenses that would be available to the obligor who was attempting to enforce the instrument as a simple contract, that is to say, at common law. By tradition, the defenses from which a holder in due course takes free are called "personal defenses" and include: failure or lack of consideration, breach of warranty, unconscionability and garden variety fraud (fraud in the inducement). Recall that a holder in due course does not necessarily take free of all "personal" defenses. Rather, the holder in due course is sure to take free only of the personal defenses that do not arise from his own behavior. As we have seen, the payee of a note can be a holder in due course and yet, if the maker has a defense against *him*, be subject to all of the maker's defenses.

Note how this differs from the result under the pre–1990 Code. Old 3–305(2) provided that a holder in due course "takes the instrument free from all defenses of any party to the instrument with whom the holder has not dealt." Before the drafters deleted this language in 1990, it created confusion about when a holder had "dealt with" the obligor and thus was subject to the obligor's defenses. For example, in A.I. Trade Finance, Inc. v. Altos Hornos de Vizcaya, S.A.[2] Delta agreed to supply and install a line of equipment at Altos Hornos' plant. Delta invited A.I. to participate in financing the transaction, and a representative of A.I. took active part in negotiating the financing terms with Delta and Altos Hornos. Altos Hornos gave Delta ten promissory notes to pay for the equipment, and Delta then sold the notes to A.I. for a discounted price. However, Delta did not ship all of the promised equipment and Altos Hornos ceased payment on the notes. When A.I. sued for payment on the notes, Altos Hornos asserted the defense of breach of contract. A.I. claimed to be a holder in due course who took free of such defense. Altos Hornos responded that by participating in financing the transaction between Delta and Altos Hornos, A.I. "dealt with" Altos Hornos within the meaning of 3–305(2), and was subject to its breach of contract defense.

The court found A.I. had not dealt with Altos Hornos. Since the provisions of 3–305 were intended to facilitate commercial transactions, and since it was a common business practice for financing companies to become involved in a transaction shortly after the commercial terms are worked out, the court decided that a

instrument were enforcing a right to payment under a simple contract; and

(3) a claim in recoupment of the obligor against the original payee of the instrument if the claim arose from the transaction that gave rise to the instrument; but the claim of the obligor may be asserted against a transferee of the instrument only to reduce the amount owing on the instrument at the time the action is brought.

2. 840 F.Supp. 271, 22 UCC2d 790 (S.D.N.Y. 1993).

finding that A.I. "dealt with" defendants would discourage the sort of transaction the statute was supposed to promote, an undesirable result. The post–1990 Code reaches the same result by an easier route.

What is the difference between a "defense" and a "claim in recoupment"? Comment 3 to 3–305 illustrates a claim in recoupment by posing a case in which a buyer accepts defective goods and sues for damages arising from the defect. In the words of the drafters, this buyer has no "defense" because, under Article 2, buyer is obligated to pay for the goods. Buyer has only a claim in recoupment. Having accepted the goods, the buyer has an obligation under Article 2 to pay the price, but also has a right under Article 2 to recover damages suffered because of the defect. In the comment, this is contrasted with a case where the buyer rejects the goods, or they are never delivered. In that case, the buyer's rights are characterized as a "defense" to the seller's action for the price. The buyer has no duty to pay under Article 2.

The language of section 3–305(a)(3) on recoupment performs an additional service. Even if the transferee of the instrument is not a holder in due course, the transferee takes the instrument subject only to the claims of recoupment that "arose from the transaction that gave rise to the instrument; * * *." In UMLIC–Ten Corp. v. Jones,[3] the defendant Jones had applied for a 20–year mortgage with New Haven Savings Bank and signed a note for $46,400. Nine years later Jones stopped making payments on the note and New Haven took possession of the mortgaged property by changing the locks and boarding up the property. The house was damaged by vandals and required $20,000 of repairs. New Haven assigned the note to UMLIC who sued for payment of the note. Claiming that New Haven's mismanagement after taking possession of the property caused the damage, Jones filed a special defense of setoff and recoupment. UMLIC conceded that it was not a holder in due course. Under revised 3–305(a)(3) the court held that the claim in recoupment "arose from the transaction that gave rise to the instrument," and that the creditor breached its duty to preserve collateral in its possession from waste, injury or loss. Boarding up the property in the neighborhood where this house was located, only encouraged the wholesale plundering and vandalism. The $20,000 in damages suffered by the defendants must be subtracted from the damages of $48,892.90 established by the plaintiff.

Assume, for example, that Sara made five purchases from Benjamin and that the fifth one was on credit for which she gave a note for $10,000. After the note becomes due, Benjamin transfers it to a third party at a considerable discount and the third party sues

---

3. 2000 WL 804706, 41 UCC2d 1187 (Conn.Super.Ct. 2000).

Sara. Because the note was overdue at the time of the transfer, the transferee is not a holder in due course and, if Sara has a defense or a claim in recoupment arising out of the fifth transaction, she can clearly assert it against the plaintiff transferee. But what if her claim arises out of the first or second or third transaction? Since that claim would not "ar[i]se from the transaction that gave rise to the instrument," the right to enforce it is not "subject" to it and she cannot assert it against the transferee. Moreover, modern notions of counterclaims will not help Sara because she has no affirmative cause of action against the transferee. Rather, she will have to commence an independent suit against the original party, Benjamin.

Exactly why claims of title or property were given a separate section, 3–306, to be distinguished from conventional "defenses" and "claims in recoupment" is not clear. Perhaps part of the reason was to enable the drafters to include more detail and to elaborate somewhat on the rights to be protected. The section reads in full as follows:

> A person taking an instrument, other than a person having rights of a holder in due course, is subject to a claim of a property or possessory right in the instrument or its proceeds, including a claim to rescind a negotiation and to recover the instrument or its proceeds. A person having rights of a holder in due course takes free of the claim to the instrument.[4]

The section makes explicit what was only implicit in the former law, namely, that it covers possessory as well as more extensive property rights and that it reaches also to claims for rescission, replevin, or the like. In any event, section 3–306 makes it clear that the holder in due course takes free not only of defenses or contract claims, but also of title and other defects, and of other claims that might be regarded as defects in title.

With regard to the "real defenses," a pre-Code question still with us is whether a given fraud involves so-called fraud in the factum (a real defense) or fraud in the inducement (a personal defense). Both section 3–305(a)(1) of 1990 and its predecessor specified and limited the circumstances under which fraud may be raised as a defense against a holder in due course. Note that subsection 3–305(a)(1)(iii) can be divided into several conditions, each of which a party must meet to raise a defense against a holder in due course:

(1) The fraud must have induced the signature;

(2) the signer must not have known the "character" or "essential terms" of the instrument; and

---

4. § 3–306.

(3) the signer must have lacked a reasonable opportunity to obtain this knowledge.

Thus presumably if an uneducated party signs a document that another misrepresents as a receipt and it turns out to be a note, that party can raise a defense of fraud against a holder in due course, at least if he was so ignorant that he could not have determined that it was a note, and if no one else was nearby who could have assisted him in determining its character. But if, for example, an uncle with a high school education was nearby, his presence would offer a "reasonable opportunity" and this might preclude the misrepresentation defense against a holder in due course.

Most cases arise because the defendant was tricked into signing another document different from the one which he read, or because he did not read the document he signed. Sometimes the fraud is not on the document but arises in the dealings between parties. In Union Planters Nat. Bank v. Crook,[5] defendant made arrangements to buy a truck from Southway and gave Southway two checks totaling over $44,000 to hold the truck until Crook could arrange financing from a third-party. The agreement was that the checks would not be cashed and the money would be returned when Crook returned to buy the truck. Southway deposited the checks with plaintiff-Union bank, on the next day it was given immediate credit and withdrew the amount from its account. When Crook returned with financing the next day, Southway notified him that the checks had been deposited "accidentally" and advised Crook to stop the checks. Crook issued a stop-payment order. The next day Southway declared bankruptcy. When Union sued Crook, Union's motions were denied because it was not a holder in due course. The jury found for Crook and Union appealed. Appellate court held that even if Union was holder in due course, under pre–1990 3–305(b) and (c) there was enough evidence of a real defense presented to the jury that the depositing of the checks by Southway was fraudulent and theft by deception. Therefore denial of motion for directed verdict does not require reversal and judgment was affirmed. We disagree.

Many cases quote with approval the factors now set forth in Comment 1 of section 3–305, which contains slight changes in wording from its predecessor. The comment now reads:

> The test of the defense is that of excusable ignorance of the contents of the writing signed. The party must not only have been in ignorance, but must also have had no reasonable opportunity to obtain knowledge. In determining what is a reasonable opportunity all relevant factors are to be taken into account, including the intelligence, education, business experi-

---

5. 225 Ga.App. 578, 484 S.E.2d 327, 33 UCC2d 129 (1997).

ence, and ability to read or understand English of the signer. Also relevant is the nature of the representations that were made, whether the signer had good reason to rely on the representations or to have confidence in the person making them, the presence or absence of any third person who might read or explain the instrument to the signer, or any other possibility of obtaining independent information, and the apparent necessity, or lack of it, for acting without delay. Unless the misrepresentation meets this test, the defense is cut off by a holder in due course.

There is one minor modification in the substance of the comment—the signer's age and sex are no longer considered relevant to the signer's ability to learn the terms of the instrument. The defense of tender age now ends at infancy.

Another interpretative problem arises with respect to subsection (a)(1)(ii), which allows a defendant to raise the defenses of duress, lack of legal capacity and illegality against a holder in due course when these nullify the obligation "under other law," meaning state law. The Code does not clarify how one tests whether these defenses nullify an obligation under state law. Comment 1 to 3–305 states:

> Such incapacity is largely statutory. Its existence and effect is left to the law of each state. If under the state law the effect is to render the obligation of the instrument entirely null and void, the defense may be asserted against a holder in due course. If the effect is merely to render the obligation voidable at the election of the obligor, the defense is cut off.

Comment 1 also deals with "duress" and "illegality" (which are also modified by "which, under other law, nullifies the obligation of the obligor") and states:

> Duress, which is also covered by subsection (a)(ii), is a matter of degree. An instrument signed at the point of a gun is void, even in the hands of a holder in due course. One signed under threat to prosecute the son of the maker for theft may be merely voidable, so that the defense is cut off. Illegality is most frequently a matter of gambling or usury, but may arise in other forms under a variety of statutes. The statutes differ in their provisions and the interpretation given them. They are primarily a matter of local concern and local policy. All such matters are therefore left to the local law. If under that law the effect of the duress or the illegality is to make the obligation entirely null and void, the defense may be asserted against a holder in due course. Otherwise it is cut off.[6]

---

6. What is duress? See Randall v. Rapoza, 2001 WL 863546, 46 UCC2d 182

In Unified School District No. 207 v. Northland National Bank[7] the school district sued to cancel lease-purchase agreements for copying machines when the school did not get good service. The agreement failed to meet the mandatory disclosures, such as total capital cost of equipment and the effective interest cost, as required by Kansas Cash–Basis Law which prohibits transactions that create indebtedness in excess of funds in the school district's treasury. The court held that the agreements were void for failing to make the required disclosures and even if bank was holder in due course, it was not immune from illegality defense under revised 3–305(a)(1)(ii). While we are hardly in a position to second-guess the Kansas court about the meaning of Kansas law, the Court seems to be reaching pretty far in finding that other Kansas law made this transaction "void."

Readers familiar with the old Code may notice that the 1990 revision greatly increased the number of words devoted to the rights of the holder in due course, which might be thought to signify some major change in the law. We do not see great changes in policy or substance.

PROBLEM

Construction Co. buys ten large trucks in ten separate transactions and signs a negotiable note for each. The notes are all transferred to various banks who claim to be Holders in Due Course.

1. Construction has a claim for $50,000 for a defect in truck 1, but it has paid off the note on truck 1 and wishes to setoff the amount against the liability to the same holder on the note for truck 8. Bank responds that Construction may not setoff this amount even if Bank is not a HIDC because of 3–305(a)(3). Bank is right.

2. Construction argues that dealer from whom it bought the trucks committed fraud by knowingly misrepresenting their horsepower and performance. Construction points to the right to recover even from a HIDC for "fraud" in 3–305(a)(1). Bank responds that the fraud in (a)(1) is a narrow and unusual form of fraud such as fraud practiced on one incapable of reading the documents or otherwise disabled from understanding the deal. Bank wins.

3. When Construction defaults, Bank sues Construction's president who co-signed the notes as an accommodation party.

(Mass.App.Div. 2001) (maker claiming that he executed note due to holder's attitude, demeanor, harassment, and as a result of marital difficulties and effects of medication he was taking were insufficient to establish defense of duress).

7. 20 Kan.App.2d 321, 887 P.2d 1138, 26 UCC2d 1185 (1994).

President seeks to assert a breach of warranty claim against
Bank. Bank asserts that even if it is not a HIDC (because it
may have had notice as President alleges), he cannot assert
the defense of a third party. If it is not a HIDC, Bank loses, 3–
305(d).

§ 2–11 Bona Fide Holders Not in Due Course: Jus Tertii and Other Defenses

The rights of a transferee who is not a holder in due course
usually (but not always) rise no higher than those of the transferor.
Thus, if one takes a negotiable instrument by assignment from the
payee where the transferee does not become a holder in due course,
the transferee is likely to be met by the same claims and defenses
the obligor could put up against the original payee. However, that
is not always true.

In section 2–10 we recognized one claim in recoupment that
the obligor could usually assert against the original payee (by
counterclaim), but could not assert against the transferee: the claim
in recoupment arising out of a transaction *other than* the one that
spawned the instrument. Recall the example above of Ben and Sara
and see section 3–305(a)(3).

By far the most significant claims and defenses that cannot be
asserted against a transferee (even though not a holder in due
course) are claims of third parties, *jus tertii* claims. This rule is
stated as follows in section 3–305(c):

> Except as stated in subsection (d), in an action to enforce the
> obligation of a party to pay the instrument, the obligor may not
> assert against the person entitled to enforce the instrument a
> defense, claim in recoupment, or claim to the instrument
> (Section 3–306) of another person, but the other person's claim
> to the instrument may be asserted by the obligor if the other
> person is joined in the action and personally asserts the claim
> against the person entitled to enforce the instrument. * * *

This is a revision and clarification of the pre–1990 section 3–306(d),
which reads as follows:

> * * * The claim of any third person to the instrument is not
> otherwise available as a defense to any party liable thereon
> unless the third person himself defends the action for such
> party.

The former Code was unclear as to whether it barred claims in
recoupment, defenses, and also claims to the instrument. Section 3–
305(c) makes clear that all three are barred. However, Section 3–
305 permits a third party's *claim* to the instrument (but not his

defenses or claims in recoupment) to be asserted if the claimant is joined and personally asserts it.

Cashier's and Teller's Checks and the Like

To see how the *jus tertii* claim is most frequently presented and how a court might analyze the rights of a particular party to assert its own defense, consider the common battleground where banks that have issued cashier's or other bank checks seek to assert their own defenses or, more commonly, the defenses of their remitters.

For the purpose of the discussion, assume that the remitter buys a cashier's check, payable to Howard Cooper Porsche Audi. The remitter gets his Porsche, Howard Cooper presents the $60,000 cashier's check for payment, and the bank refuses to pay. Now assume two alternatives. In the first alternative, the bank refuses to pay because the personal check with which the remitter purchased the cashier's check proved to be no good. Also assume that for the purpose of this example, payee, Howard Cooper, is not a holder in due course. In the second alternative, the bank refuses to pay because the good customer, the remitter, called to say that he does not want the Porsche that he bought or that it is somehow defective.

In the first case the bank will be asserting its own defense, albeit a defense that it has against the remitter, a third party, and not directly against Howard Cooper. In the second case the bank will be asserting a third party's defense, namely the defense of the remitter against Howard Cooper. In general, courts have not been sympathetic to banks in their assertion of either of these two defenses, but the courts' analyses of these problems have often been deficient. Sometimes courts simply conclude that cashier's checks were "accepted when issued" and therefore the bank must pay. Other courts analogize cashier's checks to cash and force the banks to pay, presumably on the unarticulated assumption that the law should carry out the reasonable expectations of the parties.

Logically the two problems require different analyses. In the second example, when the bank seeks to assert the remitter's (buyer's) claim against the payee seller, Howard Cooper, we have a true *jus tertii* case. The defendant obligor is attempting to assert a claim that belongs to a third party. We believe that section 3–305(c) is the place to look for an answer to this case; it tells us that the bank must pay, that it may not assert the remitter's defense, however valid. Moreover, as we read section 3–305(c), it does not matter whether the remitter is joined in the suit. Note that joining the remitter in the suit merely gives the bank the right to raise "the other person's claim to the instrument," i.e., its title claim, not its contract defenses.[1]

For reasons stated in Chapter 1 the bank's position here is quite precarious. If it guesses wrong about its right to defend, section 3–411 may make it liable to Howard Cooper for incidental expenses, possibly including attorney's fees, and perhaps also for consequential damages.

What about the first case, where the bank is asserting its own defense, namely, the defense that the remitter passed an NSF check and possibly committed fraud in procuring the cashier's check? (Remember we are assuming for the purpose of the example that payee Howard Cooper is not a holder in due course.) To determine whether the bank can assert this defense, we must return not to 3–305(c) (for this is not a *jus tertii* case) but to 3–305(a)(2) to see whether this is " * * * [A] defense of the obligor that would be available if the person entitled to enforce the instrument were enforcing a right to payment under a simple contract. * * * "

The rule for a "simple contract" concerning defenses based on misrepresentation or fraud is stated in Restatement of Contracts 2d, section 164(2). The bank could not assert its own defense of fraud (arising out of the third party's act) under the Restatement if the payee in good faith either "gave value" or relied "materially on the transaction." Howard Cooper would have given value by giving up possession of the automobile. Therefore it would take free of the related defense arising out of the underlying transaction between the bank and the remitter—even though we assumed it was not a holder in due course.

To see how all of this might arise in a real case, consider Guaranty Federal Savings & Loan Ass'n v. Horseshoe Operating Co.[2] On July 23, 1985, Donald Rubin, a customer at Guaranty Savings and Loan, came to the Dallas branch and informed an employee that two associates, Leo Merkow and Alan Parmet, would be in later to make a large deposit. Shortly thereafter Merkow and

---

§ 2–11

1. This conclusion is supported by Comment 4 to 3–305, which analyzes the similar case of a bank refusing to pay a cashier's check after the buyer using it learns he has been defrauded by the seller. The comment reads:

Bank has no defense to its obligation to pay the check and it may not assert defenses, claims in recoupment, or claims to the instrument of Buyer, except to the extent permitted by the "but" clause of the first sentence of subsection (c). Buyer may have a claim to the instrument under Section 3–306 based on a right to rescind the negotia-

tion to Seller because of Seller's fraud. Section 3–202(b) and Comment 2 to Section 3–201. Bank cannot assert that claim unless Buyer is joined in the action in which Seller is trying to enforce payment of the check.

As one can see, this language implies that the only type of claim belonging to the buyer that may be asserted by the bank is a title claim to the instrument.

2. 748 S.W.2d 519, 6 UCC2d 774 (Tex.App. 1988), rev'd sub nom., Guaranty Fed. Sav. Bank v. Horseshoe Operating Co., 793 S.W.2d 652, 11 UCC2d 571 (Tex. 1990).

Parmet came in with a $1,990,000 check drawn on the account of Royal Chevrolet & Buick Company at Citizens State Bank of Malakoff, Texas, and signed by Nick Zaika. The check, payable to Merkow and indorsed by him, was deposited in an account opened up by Parmet. Parmet returned 30 minutes later to draw $900,000 of the newly deposited money, with which he purchased an "official check" of Guaranty. This teller's check was drawn on Citibank in New York, and payable to "Binnon & Co." (misspelled).

Later that day Rubin telephoned Ted Binion in Las Vegas, owner of Binion's Horseshoe Casino there. Rubin informed Binion that he and "some other gentlemen" were coming to Las Vegas with a bank check for $900,000 and that they intended to do some serious gambling. Binion got the check number and bank name from Rubin and telephoned Guaranty to verify the existence and authenticity of the check. After two calls Binion was able to verify that a check for that amount had been issued by Guaranty. The credit manager of the Horseshoe Casino also called to verify that the check had been issued.

Rubin, Parmet, Merkow and Zaika arrived by private jet in Las Vegas. They presented Binion with the check and received $900,000 worth of chips. By betting an average of $80,000 per hand of blackjack, they lost $890,000 in less than four hours. A gracious host, Binion reimbursed Rubin for the cost of the chartered jet, set the four men up in a hotel, provided them limousine service and gave them $5,000 for "some walking around money."

The next morning, Parmet was back in Dallas waiting at the door when Guaranty opened. Claiming that the $1,900,000 check he deposited had been drawn on insufficient funds, he told the bank he wanted to stop payment on the "official check" drawn the day before. Guaranty immediately contacted Citibank and instructed it to stop payment on the check. Shortly thereafter, Horseshoe called Citibank to inquire about the check. Citibank informed Binion that Guaranty had stopped payment. The lawsuit followed.

In deciding the case, the Texas Court of Appeals assumed, but did not decide, that Horseshoe was not a holder in due course because of the possibility it had notice of a defense. Instead, the court relied on the fact that the "official check" was essentially a cashier's check and should be considered the equivalent of cash. As such, it was accepted upon issuance and payment could not be refused. Furthermore, the court concluded that Guaranty had no defense of failure of consideration available to release itself from an obligation to pay the check.

On appeal, the Texas Supreme Court reversed the grant of summary judgment for Horseshoe, holding instead that there was an issue of fact as to whether the casino was a holder in due course. Horseshoe's status should determine the outcome of the case, the court held, since if Horseshoe was just an ordinary holder, it would be subject to the bank's defense of fraud committed against the bank by Parmet and the others.

If there is ever a case where the payee on such a check should be victorious, this is it. Of all the people in this transaction, Binion was the most careful. He took more than reasonable steps to verify the check was not a fake and that it had been actually issued by the bank. As between two innocent parties, Guaranty and Horseshoe, surely the bank should bear the loss.

The bank might bear the loss under either of two theories. First, if Binion proves to be a holder in due course, as seems quite possible, he will have taken free of the defense that the bank would have had against Parmet and others. In the words of section 3–305(b), this is a defense "against a person other than the holder."

Second, we would hope that the Texas court would reconsider its judgment about the right of somebody in the position of the bank to raise its fraud defense against a third party who is not a holder in due course. Applying Restatement of Contracts 2d, section 164(2), to this case leads to the conclusion that Binion changed his position in reliance upon the instrument, gave value to the remitter, and therefore should be protected even if he did not qualify as a holder in due course.

Surely the decision of the Texas Supreme Court cannot be justified as new-found Calvinism from a court that sits in one of our most yeasty jurisdictions.

PROBLEM

Collector buys a painting from Gallery for $100,000. Collector pays with a cashier's check that he has procured from his bank by giving his bank his own personal check. Assume that Bank refuses to pay on the cashier's check when it is presented. Assume also that Bank justifies its refusal because: 1) of defects in the painting's lineage that suggest it to be a counterfeit, or 2) Collector's personal check bounced.

1. In the first case Bank is asserting its customer's defense (i.e., defects in lineage). Bank cannot raise this defense; it must pay. 3–305(c). By giving a cashier's check, Collector implicitly abandoned the right to abort payment. Collector must pursue its claim in a separate suit.

2. In the second case Bank is asserting its own defense; i.e., that Collector committed fraud on it by knowingly giving Bank a bad check. Since 3–305(c) only forecloses the assertion of defenses of others, it does not speak to this case. We think Bank cannot assert the defense here either because of Section

> 164(2) of the Restatement of Contracts 2d where the instrument went to someone in good faith and, of course, if Gallery is a holder in due course then certainly Bank may not refuse payment.

§ 2–12   Special Transactions

Section 3–302(c) lists some circumstances that *dis*qualify a holder who might otherwise qualify as a holder in due course:

> [A]   person does not acquire rights of a holder in due course of an instrument taken:
>
> (i) by legal process or by purchase in an execution, bankruptcy, or creditor's sale or similar proceeding,
>
> (ii) by purchase as part of a bulk transaction not in ordinary course of business of the transferor, or
>
> (iii) as the successor in interest to an estate or other organization.

In these unusual circumstances, the purchaser of the instrument is treated as a successor in interest to the prior holder and can acquire no better rights. If the holder purchases the instrument from a holder in due course, then the holder would acquire the holder in due course status of the seller by means of the "shelter rule" in 3–203(b)[1] even though he made the purchase at a judicial sale.

The meaning of 3–302(c)(i) is clear on its face, as is that of 3–302(c)(iii). Subsection 3–302(c)(ii) is not as plain: it does not simply refer to unusually large sales. Rather, it concerns the transfer in bulk of the assets of one entity to another. According to Comment 5 to section 3–302:

> For example, it applies to the purchase by one bank of a substantial part of the paper held by another bank which is threatened with insolvency and seeking to liquidate its assets. Subsection (c) would also apply when a new partnership takes over for value all of the assets of an old one after a new member has entered the firm, or to a reorganized or consolidated corporation taking over the assets of a predecessor.

§ 2–12

1. § 3–203(b) reads as follows:

Transfer of an instrument, whether or not the transfer is a negotiation, vests in the transferee any right of the transferor to enforce the instrument, including any right as a holder in due course, but the transferee cannot acquire rights of a holder in due course by a transfer, directly or indirectly, from a holder in due course if the transferee engaged in fraud or illegality affecting the instrument.

Chapter 3

BASIC LIABILITY ARISING FROM STOLEN INSTRUMENTS AND FORGED SIGNATURES

Analysis

---

§ 3–1 Introduction

The drawer or payee of a check need not be paranoid to fear that a check may be stolen. A thief dressed as a mailman may steal the check, the thief may be the drawer's trusted employee, or the thief may simply be a burglar or other intruder. If the stolen check is an order instrument, (that is, one drawn "pay to the order of Cicero" or indorsed "pay to the order of Cicero, Repeunzel"), the thief will have to forge the indorsement of the payee or indorsee in order to pass it along to an innocent party. A greedy thief may even alter the instrument by, for example, moving the decimal point a few places so that $10.00 check becomes a $1,000.00 check. Theft, forgery and alteration of negotiable instruments have generated thousands of litigated cases.

Whether the thief intervenes between the drawer and the payee or further down the stream, the stolen check will usually

144

move from the thief down to the drawee bank who might or might not pay (depending upon whether it discovers the wrongdoing). Generally a drawee is not entitled to charge the drawer's account when it pays over a forged drawer's signature or over a forged indorsement or when it pays an altered instrument (except to the extent of its original tenor). But there are exceptions to these rules, and we will discuss the rights of the drawer against his bank in Chapter 6.

To utter a truism, when the curtain rises on the last act, the wrongdoer will either be off stage or insolvent. Yet he, or more often she, will have pocketed the proceeds of the check received from someone or some bank and that party in turn may not be successful in procuring payment from the drawee. In any event, the party that has paid money to another for the check but has not received payment on it will initially bear the loss. Inevitably that party will look for a potential defendant on whom to thrust the loss. We find it useful to divide such plaintiffs into two classes: those who sue "downstream" and those who sue "upstream." In what then seemed a flash of intuitive brilliance, the stream metaphor occurred to one of us several years ago. In theory each check flows like a stream from the drawer to the payee to the depositary bank and so on down to the drawee bank. Despite considerable friendly, and some hostile, student criticism of our metaphor, we persist in its use, for we know no better one to describe the check collection process.

In chart form our stream appears as follows:

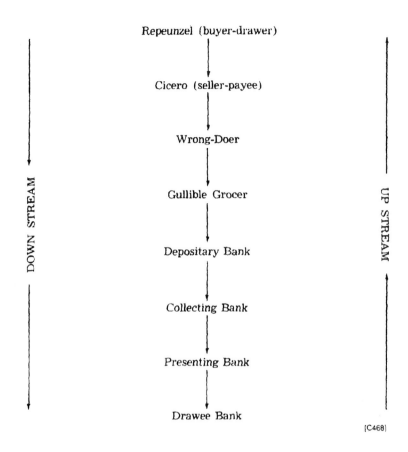

Repeunzel (buyer-drawer)

Cicero (seller-payee)

Wrong-Doer

Gullible Grocer

Depositary Bank

Collecting Bank

Presenting Bank

Drawee Bank

DOWN STREAM

UP STREAM

[C468]

The wrongdoer might appear between Repeunzel and Cicero. Conceivably he could follow Gullible Grocer; there is nothing inevitable about the wrongdoer's position on the chart set out above. In the diagram, the first class of potential plaintiffs, those suing downstream, will frequently include the Ciceros of the world and sometimes the Repeunzels, too. As a seller-payee whose check is stolen and ultimately paid over a forged indorsement, Cicero might, for example, sue downstream against the drawee for its paying the wrong party. Similarly Repeunzel, the buyer-drawer, might find that the drawee has paid over a forged indorsement in exceptional circumstances where the drawee is entitled to charge the drawer's account (for example, because of 3–406). In that event Repeunzel would be motivated to become a plaintiff and to try, on some theory, to throw the loss "downstream" on, perhaps, Gullible Grocer, the party who dealt with the wrongdoer.

Members of the second class of plaintiffs sue "upstream." This class consists mostly of drawee banks who make payment and then discover that they have no right to charge the drawer's account.

These drawees commonly try to throw their loss back upstream onto prior banks or onto the party who dealt directly with the wrongdoer. Another familiar member of "upstream" plaintiffs is a presenting bank to whom the drawee refuses payment and who then seeks reimbursement upstream.

Assume first the following situation: Repeunzel (drawer) issues a check "payable to the order of Cicero"; thief steals the check and forges Cicero's indorsement. Thief then cashes the check at a depositary bank which passes it to a collecting bank which ultimately receives payment from drawee bank. The drawee wrongfully charges the check to Repeunzel's account. The principal lawsuits that might arise from this case are as follows:

1. *Payee v. Drawer on a stolen instrument (3–309).*[1] In the limited cases covered by 3–309 the payee may sue upstream against the drawer on a stolen (or lost) instrument, provided the payee indemnifies the drawer against the possibility of a second claim on the stolen check.

2. *Drawer v. Drawee.* The drawer is likely to sue downstream against the drawee only if the drawer issues a second check to the payee and the drawee refuses to recredit the drawer's account (after having paid the first check over a forged indorsement). The drawer's argument is that the drawee has (1) violated its statutory duty implicit in 4–401 to pay only checks "properly payable," and (2) its contractual obligation to the same effect implicit in the deposit contract.

3. *Payee v. Drawee or Depositary Bank.* Here payee sues downstream as owner of the check on the theory that those who have dealt with the check after the thief are guilty of conversion under 3–420(a).[2]

---

§ 3–1

1. § 3–309 reads in part as follows:

(a) A person not in possession of an instrument is entitled to enforce the instrument if (i) the person was in possession of the instrument and entitled to enforce it when loss of possession occurred, (ii) the loss of possession was not the result of a transfer by the person or a lawful seizure, and (iii) the person cannot reasonably obtain possession of the instrument because the instrument was destroyed, its whereabouts cannot be determined, or it is in the wrongful possession of an unknown person or a person that cannot be found or is not amenable to service of process.

Note that possession includes that of agent as well. See A.I. Credit Corp. v. Gohres, 299 F.Supp.2d 1156, 52 UCC2d 733 (D.Nev. 2004).

2. § 3–420(a) provides that:

The law applicable to conversion of personal property applies to instruments. An instrument is also converted if it is taken by transfer, other than a negotiation, from a person not entitled to enforce the instrument or a bank makes or obtains payment with respect to the instrument for a person not entitled to enforce the instrument or receive payment. An action for conversion of an instrument may not be brought by (i) the issuer or acceptor of the instrument or (ii) a payee or indorsee who did not receive delivery of the instrument either directly or through delivery to an agent or a co-payee.

4. *Drawer v. Collecting Bank.* The drawer might sue a collecting bank downstream either on a conversion theory or, under the pre–1990 Code, on the theory that the drawer is somehow a beneficiary of the warranty that the transferor was a person entitled to enforce the item under 4–207(a)(1).[3] After the 1990 revisions, it is now clear that the 4–207 warranty does not run through the drawee and back to the drawer.

5. *Drawee v. Depositary or other bank.* If the drawee has decided or has been forced to recredit the drawer's account, the drawee might then sue back upstream for breach of the warranty under 4–207(a)(1) that the transferor was a person entitled to enforce the item. In turn, the defendant in the drawee's suit may seek to cast the liability further upstream by suing the party who gave it the check. Thus, the drawee may shift the loss upstream onto the presenting bank, the presenting bank onto the collecting bank, the collecting bank onto the depositary bank, and perhaps the depositary bank onto the forger (a rarity).

One theft sometimes spawns two or three lawsuits of the foregoing kinds. More often all such suits are impleaded into one case and that case winds up with the payee or drawee on one side and the party who took from the thief on the other. Absent negligence or the like on the part of the owner of a check and irrespective of the sequence of suits or settlements, the loss should normally come to rest upon the first solvent party in the stream after the one who forged the indorsement. Thus in our hypothetical case the depositary bank should ultimately wind up with the loss unless the payee or drawer substantially contributed to the loss by negligent behavior.[4]

Another way to look at this entire area is to apply the concept of least-cost avoider and understand that the Code seeks to place the loss on the party who could most easily have avoided it. For example, the depository bank is in the best position to check the identification of the depositor and identify a forged indorsement,

3. § 4–207 provides that:

(a) A customer or collecting bank that transfer an item and receives a settlement or other consideration warrants to the transferee and to any subsequent collecting bank that:

    (1) the warrantor is a person entitled to enforce the item; * * *.

4. The following chart shows the Code provisions that various actors might cite as they sue other persons in a dispute over a stolen check. This chart comes courtesy of White, and is provided despite the misgivings of Summers.

In the accompanying chart the check traveled from the upper lefthand corner (drawer) around the outside of the rectangle to the bottom lefthand corner where it is paid by the drawee payor. Each of the arrows runs from a potential plaintiff to a potential defendant and is intersected with the section that contains the potential cause of action. The chart omits the comparative negligence causes of action, 3–404, 3–405, and 3–406, that are discussed in the next chapter.

while the drawee bank is theoretically in the best position to check the signature of its own client.

As a student once put it, the material in this chapter and the next one is "for adults only." This material is abstract, difficult and interrelated. We have done our best to make it clear, but we are certain that the student and the neophyte lawyer will have to proceed slowly and back-track frequently.

The material in this chapter cannot be read independently of the material on negligence and imposture in the next chapter. Virtually every case discussed in this chapter involves issues in the following one as well. We justify our division of basic liability and negligence only on the basis that one cannot consider all of these questions simultaneously. As jugglers of limited and declining abilities, we can only keep a few balls in the air at once.

This chapter will look at the default rules that apply in the absence of actual or implied negligence by any of the parties. The next chapter addresses situations where the drafters of the Code would believe that another party is actually in a better situation to prevent the theft than the party that would otherwise bear the loss, such as when the thief is an employee of the drawer.

As in the previous chapters, we must address the differences between the three versions of the Code resulting from the uneven enactment of the 1990 and 2002 amendments to Articles 3 and 4. We find no major substantive changes in the basic liabilities. There are many changes that clarify the law, some that indorse one line of cases and reject another, and a variety of modifications to eliminate technical deficiencies in the language of their previous counterparts.

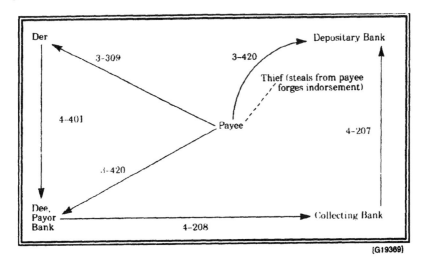

[G19369]

§ 3–2   Lost or Stolen Instruments, Section 3–309

If a thief steals a check from a payee, the payee might turn to his or her drawer for payment. Section 3–309 allows a person who loses an instrument by misplacing it or theft to enforce it in certain circumstances. The person must have been entitled to enforce the instrument at the time it was lost. Subsection 3–309(a) states:

> A person not in possession of an instrument is entitled to enforce the instrument if (i) the person was in possession of the instrument and entitled to enforce it when loss of possession occurred, (ii) the loss of possession was not the result of a transfer by the person or a lawful seizure, and (iii) the person cannot reasonably obtain possession of the instrument because the instrument was destroyed, its whereabouts cannot be determined, or it is in the wrongful possession of an unknown person or a person that cannot be found or is not amenable to service of process.

Note that the person described in section 3–309 is the prototypical "person entitled to enforce the instrument" defined in 3–301. Technically this person is not a holder in due course because a holder must have possession. It also seems awkward to describe the person as an owner, though there is no reason not to recognize the person's "ownership" rights, at least if they can be proved. Section 3–309 is a more careful articulation of the rules that were formerly contained in 3–804 of the pre–1990 Code.

Thus, a payee who receives a check in payment for services, and then loses the check while walking home, can still enforce the instrument. Similarly, if the payee was the victim of a mugging on the way home and the thief made off with the payee's wallet containing the check, the payee remains entitled to enforce the instrument. If, on the other hand, the drawer had entrusted a messenger with delivery of the check to the payee, and the messenger instead chose to flee to Jamaica with the check, the payee would not be able to enforce the instrument because the payee would not have had possession at the time of the loss. (The payee, not having been paid, could still enforce the underlying obligation, however.) So too if the payee received the check, but inadvertently left it at his out-of-state grandmother's home after a visit, the payee would not be entitled to enforce the instrument because the check's whereabouts can be determined. If Granny decides to appropriate the check for herself, and due to her out-of-state residence is not amenable to service of process, then the payee's right to enforce the instrument is revived.

This requirement of possession at the time of loss in the 1990 Code has caused trouble where an instrument is lost prior to assignment so that the assignor never had possession of the note. To resolve this dispute, section 3–309 was amended in 2002 to omit the possession requirement and to require only an entitlement to enforce the instrument when the instrument was lost, or the acquisition of ownership from a person who was so entitled.[1] The person seeking enforcement of the lost instrument must prove its terms.[2]

A drawer sued under 3–309 can legitimately ask how to avoid double liability. This drawer has already issued one instrument that has been stolen (or lost), and the payee (or other transferee) by suing under 3–309 now demands in effect that the drawer issue a second one. If a holder in due course should turn up with the stolen check, the drawer would have to pay the holder in due course even if the drawer had issued a second check to the payee (or the payee's transferee). Of course, if the instrument was an order instrument when stolen, no subsequent possessor of that instrument could be a holder and therefore no subsequent possessor could be a holder in due course of it. Neither a thief of an order instrument nor a transferee from the thief has power to indorse. This is so because of section 3–201. Section 3–201(a) makes negotiation the exclusive method of making a person a holder. Section 3–201(b) requires that, with the exception of remitters, the only way to negotiate a non-bearer instrument is to have the current holder indorse it and transfer possession.[3]

Thus, the drawer of a stolen instrument can stop payment or, if the drawee has paid it, can insist that the drawee recredit the

---

§ 3–2

1. 2002 Revised 3–309 states in part:

(a) A person not in possession of an instrument is entitled to enforce the instrument if:

(1) the person seeking to enforce the instrument:

* * *

(B) has directly or indirectly acquired ownership of the instrument from a person who was entitled to enforce the instrument when loss of possession occurred; * * *

2. Yanoff v. Muncy, 688 N.E.2d 1259, 35 UCC2d 1278 (Ind. 1997) (defendant's testimony regarding the amount of the debt and the schedule of payments was sufficient to prove the essential terms of the note).

3. § 3–201 says:

(a) 'Negotiation' means a transfer of possession, whether voluntary or involuntary, of an instrument by a person other than the issuer to a person who thereby becomes its holder.

(b) Except for negotiation by a remitter, if an instrument is payable to an identified person, negotiation requires transfer of possession of the instrument and its indorsement by the holder. If an instrument is payable to bearer, it may be negotiated by transfer of possession alone.

A thief will not be able to convert an order instrument into a bearer instrument and then take advantage of the last sentence of 3–201. Only the holder can transform the character of an instrument in this way, under section 3–205(b), which reads:

If an indorsement is made by the holder of an instrument and it is not a special indorsement, it is a "blank indorsement." When indorsed in blank, an instrument becomes payable to bearer and may be negotiated by transfer of possession alone until specially indorsed.

drawer's account. If the drawer is sued by one who purports to be a holder in due course taking free of the defects in the title, the drawer can defend on the ground that the plaintiff could not be a holder in due course and is thus subject to the defense described in 3–305(c). That subsection says: "An obligor is not obliged to pay the instrument if the person seeking enforcement of the instrument does not have rights of a holder in due course and the obligor proves that the instrument is a lost or stolen instrument."

If the instrument was bearer paper on its face or was converted into bearer paper before it was stolen (e.g., indorsed "pay to the order of Cash" or indorsed in blank "Cicero"), then a taker from the thief could be a holder in due course and could successfully sue on the drawer's contract under 3–414(b), for the defense of theft is not valid against a holder in due course.[4] Section 3–309(b) permits the court to require a bond or some other form of adequate protection to insure that the drawer or maker will not have to pay a second time if a holder in due course later arrives on the scene. Presumably that security is to indemnify not only against that possibility, but also against legal fees and other costs the drawer would incur in showing that a plaintiff is not a holder in due course. Thus in Chase Manhattan Bank v. Concord Utilities Corp.,[5] a depositary bank that had credited its customer's account with the amount of a check and had then lost the check (apparently without ever presenting it for payment) sued the drawer under the pre–1990 Code's section 3–804, the predecessor of 3–309. The court required that the depositary bank put up security equal to twice the amount of the check and gave judgment in favor of the plaintiff-depositary against the drawer for the amount of the check under 3–804. Before 1990, several states went beyond the Code by requiring indemnification. Whether these states will adopt the uniform rule that makes indemnification discretionary, or will amend the revision to require it, remains to be seen.

We suspect that section 3–309, like its predecessor, will be seldom invoked. For reasons that are obvious upon a moment's thought, the pre–1990 Code's section 3–804 was rarely used by payees from whom checks were stolen. Assume, for example, that an employee of Dr. Ellen Jones steals patients' checks worth $50,000 from Dr. Jones. Theoretically the doctor could sue each of

---

4. Section 3–305(b) says:

The right of a holder in due course to enforce the obligation of a party to pay the instrument is subject to defenses of the obligor stated in subsection (a)(1), but is not subject to defenses of the obligor stated in subsection (a)(2) or claims in recoupment stated in subsection (a)(3) against a person other than a holder.

The claims in (a)(1) are infancy, duress, lack of legal capacity or illegality of the transaction, fraud and discharge of the obligor in insolvency proceedings. Theft is not among the defenses.

5. 1969 WL 11038, 7 UCC 52 (N.Y. City Ct. 1969).

the drawers under section 3–309(a), but think of the consequences. She would be forcing *her patients* to pay her a second time for services for which they had already paid. For that reason, if for no other, Dr. Jones is likely to look downstream to the depositary and payor banks and not back upstream at her patients. Note that 3–309 allows the entitled person only to "enforce the instrument." This is not a suit on the underlying liability. Section 3–310(b)(4) makes it clear that the suit is on the instrument and cannot be on the underlying obligation.

§ 3–3 Drawee's Liability for Paying Instruments That Are Not Properly Payable, Section 4–401

In Chapter 6 we will discuss the relationship between customer and the customer's bank in greater detail. Here, an introduction will do. Section 4–401, like its predecessor of the same number, states when a bank "may" charge the customer's account. By implication the section tells when a bank "may not" charge the account. The drafters in 1990 added the following sentence: "An item is properly payable if it is authorized by the customer and is in accordance with any agreement between the customer and bank." This is a small step forward for the customer. Comment 1 makes it clear that the bank does not "properly pay" over a forgery: "An item containing a forged drawer's signature or forged indorsement is not properly payable."[1] Thus a customer can proceed here against a bank.

Whether one regards the cause of action by the drawer against its bank (for paying an item bearing a forged indorsement or a forged drawer's signature) as a contract claim under the deposit contract or a statutory claim under section 4–401 could be important for the purpose of deciding which statute of limitations to apply. Section 4–111 contains a three-year statute for obligations "arising under this Article." Probably a claim for breach of the deposit contract does arise under this Article. Yet it might be in the interest of a tardy plaintiff to argue that this is a contract claim governed by other statutes on claims under written contracts. The statute of limitations on a claim for breach of a written contract is usually longer than three years.

Elsewhere we discuss what is and what is not properly payable. For now it is enough to know that a check that is altered, bears a forged indorsement, or bears a forged drawer's signature is not properly payable. Section 4–401(d) authorizes a drawee bank acting

---

§ 3–3

1. § 4–401, Comment 1. Note that § 3–407(c), which authorizes a payor bank to enforce an altered instrument "according to its original terms," indicates that the payor may not charge the drawer's account in accordance with the altered terms.

in good faith to charge its customer according to "the original terms of the altered item," or according to the terms of the completed item "unless the bank has notice that the completion was improper." However, as we will see in the next chapter, saying a bank may not charge its customer according to the altered terms of an instrument is not the same as saying the bank is liable for paying on such a document. In many cases the customer is precluded from asserting forgery or alteration. Some courts require a customer to show damage if he is to gain recredit for improperly paid checks. These courts characterize the recredit payment as a consequence of the bank's failure to exercise reasonable care subject to standards set out in sections 4–103 and 1–106.

Upon considering the drawee's liability on a check bearing a forged drawer's signature, one should distinguish the drawee's liability before it makes final payment from its liability afterwards. Before final payment, and absent acceptance, the drawer is merely a person to whom an order has been issued. In the words of 3–408: "A check or other draft does not of itself operate as an assignment of funds in the hands of the drawee available for its payment, and the drawee is not liable on the instrument until the drawee accepts it." If the drawee's clerk discovered the forgery before final payment and before accepting the check (for example, certifying it), the drawee is not obligated to pay the presenter, for the drawee's contract with the depositor obliges the drawee to pay only over the depositor's authorized signature. Therefore the drawee can and should dishonor. On dishonor the presenter may then seek recovery from his or her transferor either on the indorsement or on the warranty in 4–207(a)(2).[2]

Suppose, however, that employees of the drawee do not discover the forged signature but make final payment on the check by paying it over the counter. In the absence of drawer's negligence substantially contributing to the forgery, the drawee may not charge the drawer's account, for the drawer did not sign the check (see Chapter 6). If the drawee does charge the drawer's account, the drawer may insist that the account be recredited under 4–401, for the item is not "properly payable." A drawee who has paid in cash or by an irrevocable credit, and who cannot take affirmative action against some other party to recover the funds is in a dismal spot. Since it has no cause of action against the drawer, the drawee may wish to pursue the presenter or others who transferred the check down the collection stream. With rare exceptions, the drawee will have no warranty cause of action against any of these prior parties. The person presenting the draft to the drawee for payment makes

2. Under 4–207(a)(2) the transferor warrants that "all signatures on the item are authentic and authorized."

only the warranty described in 4–208(a)(3), that the presenter "has no knowledge that the signature of the purported drawer of the draft is unauthorized." Furthermore, the previous transferors of the draft make the same limited warranty to the drawee. (Warranties made to transferees under 4–207 are considerably broader than warranties to payor banks. For our full discussion of warranties, see 3–7).

A variation on this regime is made when a company decides to use an automated signature system. Agreements to use such a system invariably include a provision that authorizes the bank to pay any check that appears to be so authorized. Courts have approved this arrangement.

In summary, the liability under section 4–401 for payment of forged or altered instruments is straightforward. The arguments here will not be over 4–401 but over preclusion, negligence and the like. We deal with those below.

§ 3–4 Conversion, Section 3–420

When dealing with conversion, one should think of a check as if it were goods, and consider the party to whom the check is payable as the "owner." If, for example, Repeunzel makes a check payable to the order of Cicero and gives it to Cicero, Cicero is not only the holder but also the owner. After the check is stolen from Cicero, he is no longer the holder (no more possession), but continues to be the owner. Theft does not divest him of title. When a bank or some other party subsequently cashes the check for the thief or a party who traces title through the thief, that party is like a buyer of stolen goods; notwithstanding that party's good faith, it may be guilty of converting the check by paying the thief or the party who traces title through the thief.

The second sentence of section 3–420 provides a partial statutory definition of conversion: a convertor is one who takes an instrument "by transfer, other than negotiation, from a person not entitled to enforce the instrument."[1] That means that the liquor store operator is guilty of conversion for taking a stolen check from a customer. The same is true of a bank who "makes or obtains payment with respect to the instrument for a person not entitled to enforce the instrument or receive payment." If a thief deposits a stolen check in the bank and the depositary bank receives payment from the drawee, both the depositary bank who obtains the payment and the drawee who makes it commit conversion under 3–420(a).

---

§ 3–4

1. This includes paying one joint payee if the instrument is not indorsed by all other payees.

Section 3–420's opening sentence incorporates common law conversion: "The law applicable to conversion of personal property applies to instruments." It is conceivable, therefore, that the law of Minnesota or New York or Florida might make one guilty of conversion for dealing with an instrument in ways not described by the statutory definition (second sentence). When that is so, there will be liability under the common law introduced into Article 3 by the first sentence of 3–420.

The incorporation of the common law of conversion together with certain amendments to Article 3 from 1990 lead us to speculate about the expansion of the conversion cause of action. Most conversion cases arise from forged signatures—chiefly forged indorsements. But what about the case covered by section 3–307 in which a fiduciary with authority to sign (and by hypothesis, not a forger) violates its fiduciary duty and the bank pays the fiduciary in circumstances covered by 3–307(b) (where the bank knows of the fiduciary status and of the breach of the fiduciary duty)? Section 3–307 says merely that the bank is "on notice." The bank is therefore not a holder in due course, but surely the bank must have some liability to the check's true owner. The most obvious liability is for conversion. As we indicate below, that conclusion causes problems when the injured party is the drawer of the check.

Consider the case where the check bears a signature that is not authorized, but is not forged. As we indicate below, a signature by an authorized signer for an unauthorized purpose apparently is not forgery under the Code, but could be part of an embezzlement. Assume that an employee has authority to sign as agent for the purpose of depositing checks; instead he signs, cashes the check and takes the money. Clearly the employee has committed conversion.

Has bank also converted? In most of those cases the transfer would be a "negotiation" and therefore would not violate the second sentence of 3–420(a), but the act could violate the common law incorporated by the first sentence. Since the second sentence is supplementary (an instrument is "*also*" converted), that an act is not a conversion under the second sentence does not imply freedom from common law liability. As we indicate in Chapter 4 in the discussion concerning 3–405 and 3–406, the conclusion that a bank might be guilty of conversion when it pays over an unforged, but unauthorized signature may seriously disrupt the loss allocation scheme that depends on the comparative negligence rules in 3–404 et seq. None of the revised sections deals with unauthorized signatures unless those signatures are forgeries. Therefore, as we indicate below, one set of events arising out of a series of signatures that are held to be "forgeries" will lead to an allocation scheme that depends heavily on comparative negligence. Yet nearly identical disputes arising out of signatures that are unauthorized but technically not forgeries will bypass the comparative negligence rules found in 3–404 et seq. and will instead leave 100 percent of the loss on the downstream bank, or on the upstream employer of the embezzler.

Despite this danger, several courts have decided that an action for conversion exists for unauthorized as well as forged signatures. Courts have handled authorization determinations on a case by case basis and looked to agency law to determine whether there was either actual or apparent authorization. In Citizens Bank of Maryland v. Maryland Industrial Finishing Co.,[2] Pauline Paganni embezzled money from Maryland Industrial by using one-half of a stamp given her by her employer to indorse the checks and deposit them in her own account. One stamp contained MIFCO's name, the second stamp was "For Deposit Only." She omitted the latter and deposited checks payable to MIFCO in her personal account. MIFCO sued the depository bank for conversion. The court held that an unauthorized omission of restrictive language in an indorsement would be sufficient to make the indorsement unauthorized for purposes of conversion action and sent back the case for a hearing to determine whether the omission of the restrictive language in the case was unauthorized.

Embezzlers occasionally steal from their employers by opening accounts at the employer's bank or at another bank in a name similar to that of the employer. The embezzler then either properly indorses the checks or indorses them in the name of the fictitious company. In Calray Gas Service Inc. v. Berry,[3] Keith Berry was the bookkeeper of a company known as "Calray Gas Service, Inc." Berry opened an account with Manufacturers Hanover Trust under the name "Calray Gas Service." The true Calray kept its account at Citibank. Berry's duties included making deposits in the Citibank account. When checks came in payable to the order of Calray Gas Service, Inc., he forged the indorsements on the checks and deposited them into the newly opened Calray account at Manufacturers Hanover Trust. Eventually Berry withdrew over $107,000.

The employer, Calray Gas Service, Inc., sued Manufacturers for conversion at common law under pre–1990 3–419 and for negligence. Among other things, Calray argued that Manufacturers acted in a commercially unreasonable manner by allowing Berry to open an account in the name "Calray Gas Service" upon the production of a business certificate only, unaccompanied by any references. Bank responded that it had no duty to conduct any such investigation and it was well within its rights and common practice to open such an account. The court declined to grant Calray's motion for summary judgment.

2. 338 Md. 448, 659 A.2d 313, 26 UCC2d 1009 (1995).

3. 1990 WL 251683, 12 UCC2d 1130 (N.Y.Sup. 1990).

The question remains: when and to what extent should a bank in the position of Manufacturers Hanover be liable? In some of these cases it will be easy to make out a forged indorsement and the name will not be identical to the actual name of the employer. However, in other cases the thief will have authority to sign and the name may be identical. In the latter case, one would conclude there is a forged indorsement only by finding that the thief did not have authority to sign these checks in this way. In either case there has been a conversion by the thief. As a matter of policy and fairness, should this loss rest with the employer, with the depositary bank or with some other party?

Assume for the purpose of the argument that a bank does nothing wrong by opening an account in whatever name that a depositor chooses. As we read 3–420, the depositary bank may still be liable, at least in some states. The operative section states: "[t]he law applicable to conversion of personal property applies to instruments." Subsection (c) states that a representative "other than a depositary bank, who has in good faith dealt with an instrument," is not liable in conversion. That language would seem to make a depositary bank liable even for relatively innocent acts at least if the common law of conversion of the particular state would make such an innocent converter liable. It appears likely that Article 3 now puts a burden on the bank to determine that one opening the account has a real business and is not simply setting up a sham with the same name as his or her employer.

There is a split of authority on the question of whether the misappropriation of the funds and the unauthorized indorsement are one act or whether the indorsement and the later misappropriation should be divided into two acts. Some courts take the former view. Other courts take the view that these cases can consist of authorized indorsements followed by "unauthorized" theft of the money.

In the typical embezzlement the embezzler has made up her mind to steal the money at the time she signs her employer's indorsement. If that is true, the indorsement exceeds her "actual or apparent authority" and so is unauthorized under the definition of 1–201(43) and Comment 1 to 3–403. As a signature unauthorized under 3–403, there is no signature of the employee and therefore "no negotiation" under 3–201. Therefore, the "except" clause under 3–420 for transfers involving "negotiation" does not apply. Thus, in the conventional embezzlement, we think the Kansas court has the better part of the argument and that it is artificial to view the indorsement as one act (possibly authorized) and subsequent theft of money as another. The two are part and parcel of each other; surely neither act is authorized, at least if one attributes to the employee the evil intent at the time the indorsement is made.

Moreover, the fault of the depository bank is the same in both cases—it knows well that it should not take corporate checks for deposit into the account of the employee, particularly not into the account of a low level employee. The culpability of the depository bank is the same whether the employee decided to steal the money before she signed the employer's signature or afterwards.

In summary, we think a corporate employee signing a check with the present intention of stealing the money is making a signature under 1–201(b)(41) without "actual or implied apparent authority." That is so even if the inscription on the check is identical to one that would be authorized and within the actual authority of the embezzling agent if the agent intended to deposit the check in the employer's account. Of course, in the embezzlement case we are considering here, the bank's normal practice to refuse to take corporate checks for deposit into an individual's account undermines any argument by the depository bank that the signature is made with applied or apparent authority as regards the bank.

More complex questions arise about proper parties. We deal below with three of these questions: (1) May the drawer ever sue in conversion? (Is the drawer an "owner" of its own check?) (2) Of the parties who deal with the stolen check in good faith, which are liable in conversion? (Are depositary or collecting banks who innocently take checks from or through a thief guilty of conversion?) (3) Are parties who deal with stolen bearer instruments, and with stolen checks after they have been restrictively indorsed, liable in conversion?

a. *Who Is a Proper Plaintiff?*

With the 1990 addition of section 3–420, the conversion action is no longer available to drawers of stolen checks or to payees who never had actual or constructive possession of stolen instruments bearing their names.[4] Under pre–1990 section 3–419, some courts found drawers of stolen checks to be proper plaintiffs in conversion actions; most courts found otherwise. Courts also divided on whether a payee who never had actual or constructive possession of an instrument had a cause of action in conversion when an instrument bearing his or her name was stolen.

Comment 1 elaborates on the new policy:

---

4. The final sentence of 3–420(a) says: "An action for conversion of an instrument may not be brought by (i) the issuer or acceptor of the instrument or (ii) a payee or indorsee who did not receive delivery of the instrument either directly or through delivery to an agent or a co-payee."

Under former Article 3, the cases were divided on the issue of whether the drawer of a check with a forged indorsement can assert rights against a depositary bank that took the check. The last sentence of Section 3–420(a) resolves the conflict by following the rule stated in Stone & Webster Engineering Corp. v. First National Bank & Trust Co., 345 Mass. 1, 184 N.E.2d 358 (1962). * * *

In the conventional case, there is no reason why a drawer should have an action in conversion. On a doctrinal basis, one's own check is an obligation, not a right. It is a liability that cannot be stolen, not an asset that can be stolen. In many cases a drawer has an adequate remedy against the payor bank in cases of unauthorized payment.

When one moves a few steps beyond the *Stone and Webster* case, the prohibition of the drawer from suing in conversion presents difficulties. Assume that an authorized person draws a check payable to the order of his bank. This person is known to be a fiduciary and he causes the bank to deposit the check in his personal account. Under section 3–307(b)(4) the bank is "on notice" and is therefore not a holder in due course. As we note elsewhere, section 3–307 seems pregnant with meaning but it fails to show the legal consequences of the notice and denial of holder in due course status. Perhaps the drafters intend such a bank to be liable to the drawer in conversion.

But notice the inconsistency between sections 3–307 and 3–420. As we note above, section 3–420 says specifically that the drawer has no cause of action in conversion. Looking at the comments to 3–307, it appears that the drafters envisioned a cause of action in conversion. On the other hand, comments to 3–420 clearly indicate that drawers cannot have a cause of action in conversion. We are uncertain of the proper cause of action. The drafters must have intended some consequence from notice in 3–307(b); the most likely one is that our bank is liable for taking a check payable to *it* yet allowing its deposit in the fiduciary's personal account. Perhaps the last sentence of 3–420(a) can be limited to the *Stone and Webster* situation or maybe the prohibition upon drawer as plaintiff could be limited to the cases stated in 3–420(a) and ought not to apply the common law cases referred to in 3–420(a). Some states recognize a separate cause of action for breach of fiduciary duty. In any event, we see a conflict between the prohibition of drawers as plaintiffs and the implicit grant of a cause of action to drawers in 3–307(b)(4).

Comment 1 to new 3–420 goes on to consider the rights of a payee who never had possession:

There was also a split of authority under former Article 3 on the issue of whether a payee who never received the instrument is a proper plaintiff in a conversion action. The typical case was one in which a check was stolen from the drawer or in which the check was mailed to an address different from that of the payee and was stolen after it arrived at that address. The thief forged the indorsement of the payee and obtained payment by depositing the check to an account in a depositary bank. The issue was whether the payee could bring an action in conversion against the depositary bank or the drawee bank. In revised Article 3, under the last sentence of Section 3–420(a), the payee has no conversion action because the check was never delivered to the payee. Until delivery, the payee does not have any interest in the check. The payee never became the holder of the check nor a person entitled to enforce the check. Section 3–301. Nor is the payee injured by the fraud. Normally the drawer of a check intends to pay an obligation owed to the payee. But if the check is never delivered to the payee, the obligation owed to the payee is not affected. If the check falls into the hands of a thief who obtains payment after forging the signature of the payee as an indorsement, the obligation owed to the payee continues to exist after the thief receives payment. Since the payee's right to enforce the underlying obligation is unaffected by the fraud of the thief, there is no reason to give any additional remedy to the payee. The drawer of the check has no conversion remedy, but the drawee is not entitled to charge the drawer's account when the drawee wrongfully honored the check. The remedy of the drawee is against the depositary bank for breach of warranty under Section 3–417(a)(1) or 4–208(a)(1). The loss will fall on the person who gave value to the thief for the check.

There are limits to this exclusion, too. The Comment makes it clear that delivery of a check to an agent for the payee is delivery to the payee, and thus, gives the payee a cause of action if the check is stolen.

What evil could result from allowing a payee who never had possession of a check to sue in conversion? Allowing that cause of action might deprive a payor from raising a negligence defense that it could otherwise use as an estoppel if the proper plaintiff sued the payor. Consider the following example. A paralegal steals a check from the possession of her employer, a lawyer. The check is drawn by the lawyer on her trust account and made payable to the order of the lawyer's client in settlement of a lawsuit. (The lawyer has received the settlement and put it in her trust account.) If the lawyer was negligent in hiring and supervising the paralegal, the embezzled money should ultimately come out of the lawyer's pocket. Yet if the client (payee)—who has never had actual or constructive possession—is recognized as a proper plaintiff here, the payor may never have a chance to assert its estoppel against the negligent lawyer because the sole plaintiff (the client) would have committed no wrong.

Difficult questions about actual and constructive possession and about agency remain, and they are unavoidable. For example, in Lund v. Chemical Bank,[5] a person by the name of Laidlaw gave a $400,000 check to F.T.C., the corporate seller of an aircraft. The check was then properly indorsed to Lund's, Inc., the owner of the aircraft that had been sold. At that point Mr. Lund's partner, William Rubin, purported to indorse the check with the aid of a forged power of attorney. Ultimately, Lund's Inc. sued the person to whom the check was transferred and the payor bank, Chemical. Chemical argued Lund's had no conversion cause of action because it had never possessed the check. The District Court agreed, finding no actual or constructive delivery. Constructive delivery occurs only when the check is physically delivered into the hands of a co-payee or an agent of the payee. Here, Rubin was neither the payee nor the co-payee, and Lund's Inc. presented no evidence that he was their agent.

In Hartzell Fan, Inc. v. Waco, Inc.,[6] plaintiff entered into an agreement which provided that a third party would act as a sales representative for its products in exchange for a commission. Customers made five (5) checks payable to plaintiff for product purchases and the third party improperly indorsed and deposited them in its account. Another customer of plaintiff gave a check to the third party naming it as the payee. Judgment creditor of the third party attempted to garnish its commissions; plaintiff defended by attempting to set off the value of the checks that the third party allegedly converted. Regardless of the fact that the third party was designated an "independent contractor" in the sales agreement, it was acting as plaintiff's special agent for the limited purpose of receiving customer payments and forwarding them to plaintiff. Because the checks were delivered to plaintiff's agent, plaintiff could maintain a cause of action in conversion and the amount stolen could be deducted from the commissions owed. Because there was insufficient evidence that the check made payable to the third party was for the purchase of plaintiff's products, there was no support for a conversion claim and the amount of that check could not be set off.

5. 665 F.Supp. 218 (S.D.N.Y. 1987), reh'g denied, 675 F.Supp. 815, 5 UCC2d 651 (S.D.N.Y. 1987), aff'd, 870 F.2d 840, 8 UCC2d 731 (2d Cir.1989), on remand, 1990 WL 17711 (S.D.N.Y. 1990), aff'd, 760 F.Supp. 51, 15 UCC2d 203 (S.D.N.Y. 1991).

6. 256 Va. 294, 505 S.E.2d 196, 36 UCC2d 641 (1998).

b. *Who Is a Proper Defendant?*

Assume that a check is stolen from the payee and is then "cashed" at a depositary bank. The item then passes through various collecting banks and ultimately to the drawee who pays. Here, the plaintiff payee might have several potential defendants. First, there is the thief, a notoriously unpromising defendant. Second, there is the drawee bank.[7] Presumably the drafters intended the drawee to remain an appropriate defendant when the drawee pays over a forged indorsement. Because the pre–1990 section 3–419(1)(c) (identifying the drawee as a proper defendant) was dropped from 3–420, one might argue that even the drawee is a "representative" who is freed from liability under 3–420(c). That is wrong. The comment and the history show that the drawee bank converts when it pays over a forged indorsement and that the drawee is not merely a "representative." Still one ignorant of 3–419 can wander off the path here.

A third defendant is the depositary bank. Much can be said in favor of the depositary bank as a defendant, for it will often be located in the plaintiff's forum, will invariably be solvent, and in many cases should ultimately bear the loss—whatever the outcome of the conversion claim.

Under the pre–1990 Code's 3–419, depositary banks that took checks bearing forged indorsements could be held accountable, but only through a process that often required two lawsuits. The misbehaving depositary bank often escaped liability initially under the pre–1990 Code's section 3–419(3), which read:

> Subject to the provisions of this Act concerning restrictive indorsements a representative, including a depositary or collecting bank, who has in good faith and in accordance with the reasonable commercial standards applicable to the business of such representative dealt with an instrument or its proceeds on behalf of one who was not the true owner is not liable in conversion or otherwise to the true owner beyond the amount of any proceeds remaining in his hands.

---

7. Note one 1990 amendment to the Code regarding drawee banks as potential defendants: Comment 1 to § 3–420 explains why the drafters deleted the pre–1990 Code's subsections 3–419(1)(a) and (b). Those subsections said that a drawee to whom an instrument was delivered for acceptance committed conversion if the drawee refused to return the instrument on demand, and that any person to whom an instrument was delivered for payment committed conversion if the person refused to return the instrument or pay it on demand. The drafters thought these provisions conflicted with the proper legal outcome "in cases of noncash items that may be delivered for acceptance or payment in collection letters that contain varying instructions as to what to do in the event of nonpayment on the day of delivery." The succeeding sentences of Comment 1 to § 3–420 suggest that the invocation of personal property common law is intended for such unusual cases, not for the more routine cases that we face in this chapter.

The payee could sue the drawee, and the drawee could sue back upstream against the depositary bank on warranty. The depositary bank ultimately incurred liability. (Some courts turned a blind eye on the limitations of 3–419(3) and permitted conversion actions against depositary banks).

The drafters of the 1990 amendments altered the rule by changing the phrase "including a depositary * * * bank" to "other than a depositary bank" to subsection (c), (which replaced 3–419(3)) describing a representative's liability in conversion. The post–1990 subsection, 3–420(c), says in full:

> A representative, other than a depositary bank, who has in good faith dealt with an instrument or its proceeds on behalf of one who was not the person entitled to enforce the instrument is not liable in conversion to that person beyond the amount of any proceeds that it has not paid out.

Others who have dealt with the instrument in good faith but are not depositary banks are not liable in conversion beyond the amount of proceeds still held. Thus neither the liquor store who cashes a stolen check in good faith nor an intermediary bank that handles it has liability in conversion. The logic of permitting a conversion cause of action against depositary banks but not intermediary banks is clear enough. The depositary bank is the one who dealt with the thief, and that bank might have prevented the loss by more diligently examining the thief's credentials.

Why the conversion cause of action is not permitted against other representatives who dealt with the thief (i.e., the liquor store) is unclear. Since the liquor store will make a warranty of no forgery, it will ultimately bear the loss. The new language should probably read: "other than a representative who takes the instrument from a thief" not "other than the depositary bank." For example, consider the facts of O & K Construction v. Gresham State Bank. In that case the embezzler cashed a series of checks at a local store. The store deposited the checks at Gresham Bank—the "depositary bank." Gresham never dealt with the thief, yet the literal terms of 3–420(c) would free Zimmerman's Store from liability (assuming it is a "representative") but impose liability on Gresham. Even though Gresham never dealt with the thief, had no chance to stop the theft and, presumably, dealt routinely with Zimmerman's deposits, it could have conversion liability as a "depositary bank representative." To make Gresham liable and to free Zimmerman seems wrong. The exception to the exception should allow prosecution of the party who dealt with the thief, whether that party is, as usual, the depositary bank, or whether, as exceptional, it is a store that cashes checks for an embezzler.

Of course, the payee may still proceed directly against the liquor store in conversion if the liquor store has not acted in good faith. As defined in Section 3–103(a)(4), "good faith" means "honesty in fact and the observance of reasonable commercial standards of fair dealing." The liquor store owner who knows that the person attempting to cash the check is not the named payee, but takes the check anyway, may not be acting in good faith because the "honesty in fact" standard has not been satisfied. In that case, the liquor store owner cannot claim the protection offered in 3–420(c) to representatives who have dealt with an instrument in good faith, and will remain liable to the payee in conversion beyond the amount of any proceeds that the liquor store has not paid out.

A depositary bank may overcome its conversion liability by asserting defenses of ratification or apparent authority. For example, in Kuwait Airways Corp. v. American Security Bank, N.A.,[8] the depositary bank allowed an unauthorized employee to open an account and deposit corporate checks. Several years later, the bank notified the company of the existence of the account but the company waited two years to inquire further. The court held that the depositary bank would not necessarily be liable for its commercially unreasonable acts because it could still assert common law defenses of ratification or apparent authority.

§ 3–5   Conversion: Bearer Instruments and the Effect of Restrictive Indorsements, Section 3–420

Consider theft of bearer instruments. For reasons indicated below, a plaintiff is not likely to find a solvent defendant liable in conversion for dealing with a stolen bearer instrument unless that instrument bore a restrictive indorsement at the time of its theft (e.g., "Joe Jones for deposit only"). Assuming that the stolen bearer instrument does not bear a restrictive indorsement, the thief will be a holder.[1] Whether or not the thief is a holder, the thief can make his or her transferee a holder simply by transfer to one who gives value in good faith.[2] If the thief's transferee cashes the check and so gives value in good faith and without notice of any defense, that transferee will be a holder in due course under 3–302, free of all claims to the instrument on the part of any person and free of all personal defenses of any prior party. Therefore, the holder in due

---

8. 890 F.2d 456, 10 UCC2d 21 (D.C.Cir. 1989), on remand, 1991 WL 155784 (D.D.C. 1991).

§ 3–5

1. See the discussion of holder status, § 2–3, *supra*.

2. See § 3–201:

(a) "Negotiation" means a transfer of possession, whether voluntary or involuntary, of an instrument by a person other than the issuer to a person who thereby becomes its holder.

(b) * * * If an instrument is payable to bearer, it may be negotiated by transfer of possession alone.

course will not be liable in conversion to the true owner. Likewise if the check is passed downstream (depositary bank to collecting bank to drawee bank) and the drawee bank ultimately pays it to a party who is a holder, that payment will discharge the drawer's liability on the check and on the underlying obligation as well.[3] Of course, the owner of the check will have a good cause of action against the thief, but no other cause of action.

If in the foregoing situation a depositary bank takes a check from the thief but does not become a holder in due course, (as, for example, because the check bore a date more than ninety days prior to the date on which the bank took it), the bank would be liable of conversion under 3–420(a).

Suppose a payee indorses a check in blank but indorses it restrictively:[4] Jean Smith indorses a check payable to her order "Jean Smith for deposit only," and the check is then stolen by the mailman, cashed at a depositary bank and ultimately paid by the drawee bank. Here 3–206[5] exempts all of the banks but the depositary bank from liability on the theory that intermediary banks and the drawee bank should not be expected to examine the chain of indorsements. In Jean Smith's case, the position of the thief's signature (which would undoubtedly be procured by the depositary

---

3. See § 3–602(a) which says:

* * * an instrument is paid to the extent payment is made (i) by or on behalf of a party obliged to pay the instrument, and (ii) to a person entitled to enforce the instrument. To the extent of the payment, the obligation of the party obliged to pay the instrument is discharged even though payment is made with knowledge of a claim to the instrument under Section 3–306 by another person.

This section should be read in conjunction with subsection 3–310(b)(1) and (2), which provide:

(b) * * * if a note or an uncertified check is taken for an obligation, the obligation is suspended to the same extent the obligation would be discharged if an amount of money equal to the amount of the instrument were taken, and the following rules apply:

(1) In the case of an uncertified check, suspension of the obligation continues until dishonor of the check or until it is paid or certified. Payment or certification of the check results in discharge of the obligation to the extent of the amount of the check.

(2) In the case of a note, suspension of the obligation continues until dishon-

or of the note or until it is paid. Payment of the note results in discharge of the obligation to the extent of the payment.

4. See § 3–205, Comment 2:

"For deposit only" followed by the signature of the payee of a check is a restrictive indorsement. It is also a blank indorsement because it does not identify the person to whom the instrument is payable.

Restrictive indorsements are described in § 3–206.

5. Subsection 3–206(c) provides that if an indorsement is restrictive, the following rules apply:

(3) A payor bank that is also the depositary bank or that takes the instrument for immediate payment over the counter from a person other than a collecting bank converts the instrument unless the proceeds of the instrument are received by the indorser or applied consistently with the indorsement.

(4) * * * a payor bank or intermediary bank may disregard the indorsement and is not liable if the proceeds of the instrument are not received by the indorser or applied consistently with the indorsement.

bank) immediately beneath the "for deposit only" indorsement should put the depositary on notice of some irregularity. The only indorsements below the words "for deposit only" should be those of the payee or of a bank; the rear side of the check reading from top to bottom would appear as follows: (1) "For deposit only" (2) "Jean Smith" (3) "Thief." (The Jean Smiths of the world put "for deposit only" on their checks only when they send them to banks.) Accordingly, the Code imposes liability in such a case on a depositary bank. As we mentioned above, section 3–420(c) provides that "a representative, other than a depositary bank," who dealt with an instrument in good faith on behalf of one who was not entitled to enforce the instrument, is not liable in conversion. In plain English, good faith is a good excuse, unless you are a depositary bank. Section 3–206(c) says:

> If an instrument bears an indorsement (i) described in Section 4–201(b) ["pay any bank"], or (ii) in blank or to a particular bank using the words "for deposit," "for collection," or other words indicating a purpose of having the instrument collected by a bank for the indorser or for a particular account, the following rules apply:
>
> * * *
>
> (2) A depositary bank that purchases the instrument or takes it for collection when so indorsed converts the instrument unless the amount paid by the bank with respect to the instrument is received by the indorser or applied consistently with the indorsement.

Western Assurance Co. v. Star Financial Bank of Indianapolis[6] involves a depositary bank that was saved from conversion liability despite its facilitation of a misappropriation. Western, a California corporation, entered into a joint venture with CCG, an Indiana corporation. Western opened an account at Star. The corporate resolution authorized the owner of CCG to indorse for deposit to the credit of Western. However, the signature card for the account also authorized the CCG owner to indorse any item payable to Western "for deposit to this account or any other transaction with [the bank]." CCG then opened a bank account in its name at Star. Customers of Western sent checks payable to Western directly to CCG's office. The owner of CCG indorsed these checks "for deposit only" and deposited them into the CCG account. When Western sued Star for conversion, the court of appeals concluded that there could be no conversion because the Western signature card authorized CCG's owner to deposit Western checks, even into CCG's account. As to Western's argument that Star paid the checks

---

6. 3 F.3d 1129, 21 UCC2d 327 (7th Cir.1993). See also O'Petro Energy Corp. v. Canadian State Bank, 837 P.2d 1391, 18 UCC2d 813 (Okl. 1992).

contrary to the restrictive indorsements, the court found that since the indorsements stated "for deposit only" and did not require deposit into *Western's* account, depositing into *CCG's* account was consistent with the restriction.

The other provisions of 3–206(c) (on restrictive indorsements discussed in 1–7) explicitly grant a conversion cause of action against certain other parties who deal with instruments bearing restrictive indorsements in transactions inconsistent with the restrictive indorsement.

§ 3–6 Conversion, Measure of Damages

Damages for conversion are explicitly defined in subsection 3–420(b): "the measure of liability is presumed to be the amount payable on the instrument, but recovery may not exceed the amount of the plaintiff's interest in the instrument." In addition, section 1–106 provides a more imprecise formulation for remedies in general under Articles 3 and 4. It insures that the "aggrieved party may be put in as good a position as if the other party had fully performed but neither consequential or special nor penal damages may be had except as specifically provided in this Act or by other rule of law." The implication of both 3–420(b) and 1–106 is that the plaintiff should not receive as damages more than its actual injury. This actual injury may include damages in excess of the face amount of the converted check. At the opposite end of the spectrum, conversion or breach of warranty may cause no damages or damages substantially less than the amount of the check. We address both possibilities below.

Damages Greater or Less Than Face Amount of Check

One of the more common damages awarded on top of the face amount of the check is interest from the time of conversion until recovery. In Pamar Enterprises, Inc. v. Huntington Banks of Michigan,[1] an iron company eventually obtained the full amount it was due from a check that was initially paid without its required indorsement. The court allowed an action for conversion against the depositary bank solely to recover interest on the funds for the time between the initial conversion and Pamar's full payment.

Of course, it is possible for parties to a check to suffer loss in a related transaction that might be greater than the face amount of the check. For instance, in Patterson v. Livingston Bank,[2] the plaintiff alleged that a relative of his had forged his indorsement on a check payable to him and deposited it in her account. In his

---

§ **3–6**

1. 228 Mich.App. 727, 580 N.W.2d 11, 35 UCC2d 1298 (1998).

2. 509 So.2d 6, 5 UCC2d 134 (La. App. 1987).

conversion action against the depositary bank, the court found the plaintiff was entitled to recover the face amount of the check and other damages, including those arising from injury to his credit rating, the effect on his family at Christmas time, and those from the time, effort and expense of preparing an affidavit and making repeated phone calls to the bank.

Despite a bank's conversion or breach of warranty, the payee may suffer damages far less than the face amount of the check. One example is Atlantic Bank v. Israel Discount Bank Ltd.[3] There Atlantic issued a check drawn on itself as the proceeds of a loan to Hans Eichler. The check was for the purchase of a car from Queensboro Leasing Co., and was made payable to Queensboro and Eichler. Eichler forged Queensboro's indorsement on the check and the check was finally paid. Eichler then paid Queensboro out of other funds. Atlantic suffered injury because the check bore an instruction for the indorser, Queensboro, to perfect Atlantic's lien on the automobile. When Eichler short-circuited that transaction, the security interest was never perfected and he later sold the automobile free of Atlantic's security interest. The appellate court granted summary judgment for Atlantic against the depositary and collecting banks on a warranty theory and sent the case back for trial on the amount of damages. It concluded that the presumptive damage was the face amount of the check. But the defendants were free to show that the injury was some lesser amount equal to the value of the car at the time it would have been repossessed had the security interest been perfected. It seems to us that the court too hastily rejected the defendant's argument that any damage caused by the breach of warranty was too remote and not "proximately" caused by the breach of warranty.

Ed Stinn Chevrolet, Inc. v. National City Bank[4] well demonstrates a situation where a bank, though technically at fault, did not proximately cause the injury and ought not to be held liable. The embezzler at the drawer automobile dealership stole money out of the cash drawer at the dealership, and covered up the loss by depositing checks bearing a forged drawer's signature in the dealership's bank account. In effect, the theft was completed at the dealership (an employee stealing out of the cash fund), and the

3. 108 Misc.2d 342, 441 N.Y.S.2d 315, 31 UCC 1057 (1981). Cf. Trust Co. v. Refrigeration Supplies, Inc., 241 Ga. 406, 246 S.E.2d 282, 24 UCC 646 (1978). In that case, a general contractor issued a check jointly payable to its subcontractor and a creditor of the subcontractor (a materialman). The materialman had no interest in the check; he was a joint payee simply so that he could force the subcontractor to pay him. The subcon-

tractor forged the materialman's signature, cashed the check, and did not pay the materialman. The court held that the materialman could sue in conversion as a payee even though he had no interest in the check.

4. 28 Ohio St.3d 221, 503 N.E.2d 524, 2 UCC2d 1565 (1986), reh'g en banc, 31 Ohio St.3d 150, 509 N.E.2d 945, 3 UCC2d 1850 (1987).

checks bearing the forged drawer's signature were merely a cover-up. Nonetheless it was true that if the bank had discovered the forged drawer's signature, it would have uncovered the embezzlement and stopped it. Because there was a causal connection between the bank's failure to discover the signature and the ultimate loss, the dealer had a prima facie claim against the bank. Properly, in our view, the court rejected the argument and concluded that the loss should rest on the automobile dealer who clearly had the best opportunity to discover and avoid the loss.

Cartwright Van Lines, Inc. v. Barclays Bank of New York[5] is another case where conversion damages are less than the face amount of the check. Connecticut Marketing & Investment Company (CMI) had entered into an agency agreement with Cartwright that gave CMI the right to 87 percent of certain amounts remitted to Cartwright. Barclays Bank allowed checks made payable to Cartwright to be deposited into a CMI bank account although the checks were indorsed with variations of the following: "Cartwright Van Lines, Inc., For Deposit Only, Connecticut Marketing Investors." The court found Barclays liable to Cartwright in conversion for paying over a forged indorsement. However, the court concluded that damages are only presumed to be the face amounts of the converted instruments, and a depositary bank may defend by showing that the plaintiff was not entitled to all of the proceeds of the checks. Since Cartwright was entitled to only 13 percent of the proceeds of the checks under its agency agreement with CMI, the court permitted the bank to set off 87 percent of the face value of the checks.

The more common case where the payee's damages are less than the face amount of the check arises with joint payees. Often a joint payee will indorse his own and the other payee's name and take all of the money. The other payee, whose money has been stolen, then sues the drawee bank. The question, before 1990, was whether the bank was liable for the entire sum or for only the plaintiff joint-payee's interest. That question is now answered in section 3–420(b), which says that in actions for conversion, "the measure of liability is presumed to be the amount payable on the instrument, but recovery may not exceed the amount of the plaintiff's interest in the instrument." Some courts had reached the same conclusion under the pre–1990 Code,[6] but others permitted a joint payee to recover the full amount of the instrument.[7] If our

5. 502 N.Y.S.2d 33, 120 A.D.2d 478 (1986), appeal denied, 68 N.Y.2d 608, 500 N.E.2d 874, 508 N.Y.S.2d 1025 (1986).

6. Thigpen v. Allstate Indem. Co., 757 F.Supp. 757, 14 UCC2d 1140 (S.D.Miss. 1991) (co-payee whose in-

dorsement was forged on check by other party entitled only to actual loss sustained, not face amount of check).

7. E.S.P., Inc. v. Midway Nat'l Bank, 466 N.W.2d 417, 14 UCC2d 824 (Minn. App. 1991) (drawee bank that made full payment to one party still liable to co-

guess is correct, many of these forged indorsement lawsuits arise after the relationship between the co-payees sours. Because most co-payees are either married couples or partners in business, typically both payees will benefit in some way from the proceeds of the check: making home improvements, paying bills, financing business operations, and so on. Then, after the partnership dissolves on hostile terms, one co-payee claims he or she did not receive the money. If the co-payee has benefitted in some way from the proceeds of the check, allowing recovery for the full value of the check without inquiry would give the co-payee a windfall at the bank's expense.

Only a small minority of the check theft cases present damage issues. We are certain that we have not exhausted the possibilities.[8] We indorse judicial adoption of the proposition that there should normally be no recovery when check proceeds come into the hands of the person for whom they are intended. A number of cases stand for the proposition that neither the drawer nor an intended payee of a check that is paid over a forged or inadequate indorsement may maintain a conversion action when the funds ultimately reach or benefit the intended payee. Likewise we think it important for courts to apply traditional ideas about proximate causation to the end that the loss be put on the one who could most cheaply avoid it.

PROBLEM

Doris is the office manager at an insurance agency (Agency) in Lansing, Michigan. Doris has authority to deposit checks and she examines Agency's paid checks that are returned each month. She embezzles by stealing checks that are payable to Agency, forging the indorsement of the president on them and then depositing them in her own account through an ATM. Because they are deposited through an ATM, the depositary bank does no more than to see that there is some indorsement on each and that each is signed. When Doris' activities come to light, Agency commences

---

payee for full face value of check if indorsement forged).

8. Recoveries may also be affected by the statute of limitations discovery rule, in that a plaintiff who fails to act in time may be barred from recovering any damages. For cases discussing the discovery rule, see First Investors Corp. v. Citizens Bank, Inc., 757 F.Supp. 687, 14 UCC2d 1146 (W.D.N.C. 1991), aff'd, 956 F.2d 263 (4th Cir.1992); Husker News Co. v. Mahaska State Bank, 460 N.W.2d 476, 13 UCC2d 46 (Iowa 1990) (discovery rule does not apply in conversion

action by payee against drawee bank); Wang v. Farmers State Bank, 447 N.W.2d 516, 13 UCC2d 459 (S.D. 1989) (statute of limitations in conversion claim on forged indorsement commences to run from the date the instrument is paid); Kuwait Airways Corp. v. American Security Bank, N.A., 890 F.2d 456, 10 UCC2d 21 (D.C.Cir. 1989), on remand, 1991 WL 155784 (D.D.C. 1991) (discovery rule does not apply in conversion action by payee against depositary bank).

the following suits: (For the purposes of this problem ignore the argument that every potential defendant will make—that Doris was authorized to do what she did. If the defendants win on that, Agency eats the loss.)

1. Using section 3–309, it sues each of its clients whose checks were stolen and cashed over Doris' forgery.

    NOT. (Even if it could meet the requirements of 3–309(a)(3), which it may not be able to do, Agency will not welcome a lawyer's suggestion that it sue its own customers who have suffered a loss because of the act of Agency's dishonest employee.) So Agency will likely ask for lawyer's next suggestion rather than sue its own customers who have already paid once.

2. Agency takes an assignment from each customer of his right against his own payor bank and sues each bank for paying an item that is not properly payable under 4–401.

    Probably not. This has most of the same issues as are involved in suing the customers directly and, worse, it means suits against multiple defendants (the customers' various payor banks) that may be located in different jurisdictions.

3. Agency sues the payor banks for conversion under 3–420.

    This is a legitimate possibility but it has the multiple suit defect described above.

4. If Agency sues payor for conversion, payor will join depositary bank in a claim that depositary broke its warranty under 4–208(a)(1). As a non holder—a taker of order paper without a holder's indorsement—the depositary bank is not a "person entitled to enforce the draft. . . ."

    Payor has a good cause of action.

5. Agency sues the bank where Doris made the ATM deposits for conversion under 3–420.

    This is a legitimate possibility. Since this is the "depositary bank," the claim is not limited to the amount still held by the bank, 3–420(c).

6. What if Doris had cashed the checks at a check cashing service?

    Since that service would not be the "depositary bank," the suit might be blocked by (c). (But we could argue that (c) applies only to "representative[s]" and that the service is not a "representative".)

7. Assume that on half of the checks, Agency President (who has full authority) signed "Mid Michigan Ins Agency by RP Agassi, pres" before Doris stole them.

    Now these instruments are bearer paper and the depositary bank is probably a HIDC who takes free of the title defects and who does not commit conversion 3–305, 3–306. If that is

> so, there is no good claim by Agency against depositary bank, customer or payor bank. The loss remains on Agency.

§ 3–7   Warranty, Sections 3–416, 3–417, 4–207, 4–208

In many cases, conversion liability, liability under 3–309 and drawee liability under 4–401 tell only part of the story. After the drawee recredits the drawer's account for a check improperly paid over a forged indorsement, or after the drawee is sued in a conversion action, the drawee will seek recovery from parties up the collection stream between it and the thief. Possible defendants include the following: Gullible Grocer, who cashes the check for the thief; depositary bank, who takes the check from Gullible Grocer or who itself cashes the check for the thief; or collecting banks, who present the check to the drawee or pass it along for others to present to the drawee. Each party in this stream between the thief and the drawee bank will normally make an implied warranty, directly to the drawee bank, that it is "entitled to * * * payment."[1] We should note that under pre-Code law the liability of Gullible Grocer et al. was not normally based upon implied warranty but was regarded as quasi-contractual. The theory was that the drawee had paid money by mistake and so had a quasi-contractual right to restitution, to recover the loss from the one who had benefitted. Some pre-Code cases involved suits on express warranties of title. (The indorsement stamps of many banks included the symbols "P.E.G." These symbols expressly warranted "prior endorsements guaranteed.") Only rarely did pre-Code courts base liability on an implied warranty.

The Code imposes separate transfer and presentment warranties; these can be best understood by reviewing the Code before the 1990 amendments. The pre–1990 Code's sections on warranty, 3–417 and 4–207, were a mess, in part because earlier drafters tried to do too much in a single section of the Code. (Sections 3–417 and 4–207 were nearly identical, with one applying to Article 3 and one to Article 4.) In this single section of the UCC, the drafters included one set of warranties that ran to transferees who were not payor banks (mostly collecting banks), and a different set of warranties that ran to drawees and other payors. A principal purpose of this distinction was to uphold the rule of Price v. Neal.[2] This rule says that a payor who pays over a forged drawer's signature may not normally recover that payment. Accordingly, such a payor receives no warranty that the drawer's signature is valid. Yet those up-

---

§ 3–7

1. See 3–417(a)(1). Before 1990, the parties warranted under the pre–1990 Code's section 3–417 that they had "good title" to the instrument.

2. 3 Burr. 1354 (1762).

stream from the payor bank (depositary and collecting banks) make a warranty that there is no forged drawer's signature to all *but* the payor.

We suppose it would have been too much to ask the drafters of revised Article 3 to repeal the ancient doctrine of *Price v. Neal* and to leave us with but one rule concerning forged signatures.[3] However, they have done the next best thing. They have divided "transfer" warranties from the "presentment" warranties and given each of them its own section in Article 3 and Article 4.

To understand what we have said, compare section 4–207 with 4–208.[4] The warranty to a transferee, other than a payor, (4–207)

3. The NACHA rules do that.

4. § 4–207 Transfer Warranties

(a) A customer or collecting bank that transfers an item and receives a settlement or other consideration warrants to the transferee and to any subsequent collecting bank that:

(1) the warrantor is a person entitled to enforce the item;

(2) all signatures on the item are authentic and authorized;

(3) the item has not been altered;

(4) the item is not subject to a defense or claim in recoupment (Section 3–305(a)) of any party that can be asserted against the warrantor; and

(5) the warrantor has no knowledge of any insolvency proceeding commenced with respect to the maker or acceptor or, in the case of an unaccepted draft, the drawer.

(b) If an item is dishonored, a customer or collecting bank transferring the item and receiving settlement or other consideration is obliged to pay the amount due on the item (i) according to the terms of the item at the time it was transferred, or (ii) if the transfer was of an incomplete item, according to its terms when completed as stated in Sections 3–115 and 3–407. The obligation of a transferor is owed to the transferee and to any subsequent collecting bank that takes the item in good faith. A transferor cannot disclaim its obligation under this subsection by an indorsement stating that it is made "without recourse" or otherwise disclaiming liability.

(c) A person to whom the warranties under subsection (a) are made and who took the item in good faith may recover from the warrantor as damages for breach of warranty an amount equal to the loss suffered as a result of the breach, but not more than the amount of the item plus expenses and loss of interest incurred as a result of the breach.

(d) The warranties stated in subsection (a) cannot be disclaimed with respect to checks. Unless notice of a claim for breach of warranty is given to the warrantor within 30 days after the claimant has reason to know of the breach and the identity of the warrantor, the warrantor is discharged to the extent of any loss caused by the delay in giving notice of the claim.

(e) A cause of action for breach of warranty under this section accrues when the claimant has reason to know of the breach.

§ 4–208 Presentment Warranties.

(a) If an unaccepted draft is presented to the drawee for payment or acceptance and the drawee pays or accepts the draft, (i) the person obtaining payment or acceptance, at the time of presentment, and (ii) a previous transferor of the draft, at the time of transfer, warrant to the drawee that pays or accepts the draft in good faith that:

(1) the warrantor is, or was, at the time the warrantor transferred the draft, a person entitled to enforce the draft or authorized to obtain payment or acceptance of the draft on behalf of a person entitled to enforce the draft;

(2) the draft has not been altered; and

(3) the warrantor has no knowledge that the signature of the purported drawer of the draft is unauthorized.

(b) A drawee making payment may recover from a warrantor damages for

assures that "all signatures are authentic and authorized." But the warranty to a drawee (4–208) assures only "no knowledge that the signature of the purported drawer * * * is unauthorized." If the drawer's signature is forged, but the transferee has no knowledge of the forgery, the warranty to the payor has not been broken even though the larger warranty to a collecting bank would have been broken.[5]

Section 4–208(a) adds clarity in yet another way. The pre–1990 Code's section 4–207 contained a warranty that the transferor "had good title." But section 4–208(a) now says that the warrantor is "a person entitled to enforce the draft or authorized to obtain payment or acceptance of the draft on behalf of a person entitled to enforce the draft." We believe this latter language will be easier to understand, at least once one understands the identity of a "person entitled to enforce". In most cases, this warranty really boils down to the statement "no forged indorsements here." There are other changes as well. We discuss 4–208(c) in 19–7. The Code now provides explicit authority to recover expenses and loss of interest under section 4–208(b). The pre–1990 language that required one to

breach of warranty equal to the amount paid by the drawee less the amount the drawee received or is entitled to receive from the drawer because of the payment. In addition, the drawee is entitled to compensation for expenses and loss of interest resulting from the breach. The right of the drawee to recover damages under this subsection is not affected by any failure of the drawee to exercise ordinary care in making payment. If the drawee accepts the draft (i) breach of warranty is a defense to the obligation of the acceptor, and (ii) if the acceptor makes payment with respect to the draft, the acceptor is entitled to recover from a warrantor for breach of warranty the amounts stated in this subsection.

(c) If a drawee asserts a claim for breach of warranty under subsection (a) based on an unauthorized indorsement of the draft or an alteration of the draft, the warrantor may defend by proving that the indorsement is effective under Section 3–404 or 3–405 or the drawer is precluded under Section 3–406 or 4–406 from asserting against the drawee the unauthorized indorsement or alteration.

(d) If (i) a dishonored draft is presented for payment to the drawer or an indorser or (ii) any other item is presented for payment to a party obliged to pay the item, and the item is paid, the person obtaining payment and a prior transferor of the item warrant to the person making payment in good faith that the warrantor is, or was, at the time the warrantor transferred the item, a person entitled to enforce the item or authorized to obtain payment on behalf of a person entitled to enforce the item. The person making payment may recover from any warrantor for breach of warranty an amount equal to the amount paid plus expenses and loss of interest resulting from the breach.

(e) The warranties stated in subsections (a) and (d) cannot be disclaimed with respect to checks. Unless notice of a claim for breach of warranty is given to the warrantor within 30 days after the claimant has reason to know of the breach and the identity of the warrantor, the warrantor is discharged to the extent of any loss caused by the delay in giving notice of the claim.

(f) A cause of action for breach of warranty under this section accrues when the claimant has reason to know of the breach.

5. Warranties made by a transferor of a check do not go beyond the drawee. Thus, the depositary bank that presents a check for payment makes no warranty to the drawer.

raise a warranty defense within a "reasonable time" is gone[6].

How do the warranties apply in the "double forgery" case? An embezzler who forges the drawer's name is a fool if she enters her own name on the payee line of the forged check. Accordingly she is likely to adopt a pseudonym and then to indorse in the name of that pseudonym. When that happens the payor bank will inevitably argue the check on which it has paid should be treated as one bearing a forged indorsement, not merely a forged drawer's signature. The legal significance of that argument is that it would enable the payor to recover from the depositary bank for breach of the warranty of good title. In general the courts have rejected this argument, and correctly so. Most courts have interpreted checks of the kind described as forged drawer checks and have concluded that none of the presentment warranties are broken when such a check is presented for payment by one who took it in good faith. For an elaborate discussion of that issue, see Perini Corp. v. First National Bank of Habersham.[7] For example, under the pre–1990 Code one could have concluded that the thief had adopted the name put on the payee's line as her name and thus that any signature in that name was a valid indorsement and therefore not a breach of the warranty. Alternatively, one might simply read the general theory of loss allocation under *Price v. Neal* and under the warranty scheme to demand that outcome. Reaching the opposite conclusion would seriously undermine the rule of *Price v. Neal*—at least if one concludes that most forged checks also bear indorsements in the name of persons other than the true name of thief who is indorsing.

Most difficulties of this kind have been resolved by the 1990 revised Code, particularly by section 3–404 and 3–110. Consider 3–404(b):

> (b) If (i) a person whose intent determines to whom an instrument is payable (Section 3–110(a) or (b)) does not intend the person identified as payee to have any interest in the instrument, or (ii) the person identified as payee of an instrument is a fictitious person, the following rules apply until the instrument is negotiated by special indorsement:
>
> (1) Any person in possession of the instrument is its holder.
>
> (2) An indorsement by any person in the name of the payee stated in the instrument is effective as the indorsement of the payee in favor of a person who, in good faith, pays the instrument or takes it for value or for collection.

---

6. Note that under 207(d) and 208(e) notice of a claim of breach must still be given within 30 days or the damages will be reduced to the extent of loss caused by the delay.

7. 553 F.2d 398, 21 UCC 929 (5th Cir.1977), reh'g denied, 557 F.2d 823 (5th Cir.1977). For a discussion of *Perini* see 4–4.

Under 3–110 "the person whose intent determines" is the embezzler who forges the name of the drawer. Since that person either does not intend the person identified as the payee to have an interest or the person identified is fictitious, anyone holding the instrument is a holder and any indorsement is effective. The consequence of these rules is that the warranties in 3–417(a) and 4–208(a) are not broken. Because the thief herself is now a holder, she can make the depositary bank a holder in due course and because it is a holder in due course, the depositary bank will be "a person entitled to enforce the draft." Thus, the depositary bank that makes the warranty of entitlement in 3–417(a)(1) and 4–208(a)(1) will not break it in the "double forgery" case.

Some depositary banks attempt to raise the impostor defense in 3–404. However, this is seldom appropriate as that provision requires that the impostor impersonate another in order to induce the drawer to issue a check to him.[8] Merely accepting a check from someone who claims to be the named payee does not fall within the scope of this defense.

Warranties apply to alterations in much the same way they apply to forged indorsement cases. After the payor bank recredits the account of its customer, it may sue banks up the collection stream (presenting, collecting, depositary) on the warranty embodied in 4–208(a)(2) and the party sued may sue even farther up the stream under 4–207(a)(3) if there are other defendants.

§ 3–8 Remotely Created Checks

A drawer may make a payment from his checking account, not by physically writing out a check, but by giving out information such as the name of his bank, his account number, and the MICR numbers on his check. A typical example may be a transaction between a debtor and a debt collection agency. The debt collector may call the debtor and ask for payment on the debt he owes to the collector's client. By giving the name of his bank, his account number, and the MICR numbers on his check, the debtor can make his debt payment with a remotely created check.[1] The debt collector then uses that data to fill out an instrument that looks like a check and signs "Authorized by [Debtor]" in the drawer's line. Another common example is a transaction by a credit card holder making payment to the credit card company with a telephone call. The remote nature of these checks naturally creates a need for warran-

---

8. See 4–4 for a more extended discussion of this issue.

1. See subsection (fff) of 12 C.F.R. § 229.2 for definition of remotely creat-

ed checks and (FFF) of 12 C.F.R. Pt. 229, App. E for commentary to the definition.

ties, without which the parties to these transactions would not readily take such checks.

Amendments to Regulation CC have created new warranties for remotely created checks.[2] The old Reg. CC and the 1990 Code essentially preserve the finality principle in *Price v. Neal*, placing the loss on the drawee bank absent negligence of the customer. Under Reg. CC and the 2002 Code, the rule of *Price v. Neal* does not apply to remotely created checks that have been forged or materially altered. The drawee bank can put the loss back upstream and ultimately to the bank of first deposit. The new federal warranty and the 2002 Code's section 3–417 represent a step back from *Price v. Neal* and are consistent with the policy goal of placing the burden on the party that is in the best position to avoid the loss. Note that the bank of first deposit cannot sue the depositor, e.g., a telemarketer, because the warranty does not run from a depositor to a depositary bank. However, the bank of first deposit can, by contract, protect itself against the risk of bearing all the loss. The Federal Rule will hopefully help the 2002 Code gain acceptance.

We discuss the encoding warranties in 4–209 in Section 5–6, *infra*. Usually, but not always, an error in the encoding warranty does not involve a theft or fraud. Thus, we think it better to think of those as part of the non-embezzlement, day-to-day operation of the banking system.[3]

2. 12 C.F.R. § 229.34 (2006).

Regulation CC is the Federal Reserve regulation that implements the Expected Funds Availability Act (EFAA) enacted in 1987 by the U.S. Congress. The relevant provisions of the revised Reg. CC are as follows:

(d) Transfer and presentment warranties with respect to a remotely created check.

(1) A bank that transfers or presents a remotely created check and receives a settlement or other consideration warrants to the transferee bank, any subsequent collecting bank, and the paying bank that the person on whose account the remotely created check is drawn authorized the issuance of the check in the amount stated on the check and to the payee stated on the check. For purposes of this paragraph (d)(1), "account" includes an account as defined in § 229.2(a) as well as a credit or other arrangement that allows a person to draw checks that are payable by, through, or at a bank.

(2) If a paying bank asserts a claim for breach of warranty under paragraph

(d)(1) of this section, the warranting bank may defend by proving that the customer of the paying bank is precluded under U.C.C. 4–406, as applicable, from asserting against the paying bank the unauthorized issuance of the check.

3. One might wonder why have both 3–416 and 3–417, and 4–207 and 4–208. § 3–416 is virtually identical to § 4–207, and § 3–417 is virtually identical to § 4–208, with three notable exceptions. First, the Article 4 sections apply to all "items," while the Article 3 sections apply to "instruments." Second, while 3–417(a)(3) provides that "the warrantor has no knowledge that the signature of the drawer of the draft is unauthorized," § 4–208(a)(3) provides that "the warrantor has no knowledge that the signature of the *purported* drawer of the draft is unauthorized." No explanation for this difference is given in the comments (and its significance escapes us). Finally, 4–207 contains the following subsection, which does not appear in 3–416:

(b) If an item is dishonored, a customer or collecting bank transferring the

§ 3–9   Warranty Damages

The Code frowns on those who take their warranty obligations casually. A person who breaches a warranty may have to repay the value of the instrument and could face additional burdens, including the opposing party's attorney's fees.[1] As with conversion, actual damage should be required.

A transferee who took an instrument for consideration and in good faith "may recover from the warrantor as damages for breach of warranty an amount equal to the loss suffered as a result of the breach, but not more than the amount of the instrument plus expenses and loss of interest incurred as a result of the breach."[2] This language opens the door to attorney's fees, as Comment 6 explains.

> There is no express provision for attorney's fees, but attorney's fees are not meant to be necessarily excluded. They could be granted because they fit within the phrase "expenses * * * incurred as a result of the breach." The intention is to leave to other state law the issue as to when attorney's fees are recoverable.

The transfer warranty of Article 4 (4–207) concerning bank deposits and collections contains language virtually identical to that quoted from 3–416. This "other state law" that Comment 6 refers to will generally incorporate the "American Rule" that prohibits attorneys' fees in the absence of contract or a special statute. For example, in E.S.P., Inc. v. Midway National Bank,[3] the payee of a

item and receiving settlement or other consideration is obliged to pay the amount due on the item (i) according to the terms of the item at the time it was transferred, or (ii) if the transfer was of an incomplete item, according to its terms when completed as stated in Sections 3–115 and 3–407. The obligation of a transferor is owed to the transferee and to any subsequent collecting bank that takes the item in good faith. A transferor cannot disclaim its obligation under this subsection by an indorsement stating that it is made "without recourse" or otherwise disclaiming liability.

This subsection places liability on a transferor as if the transferor had indorsed the item, whether or not the transferor *actually* indorsed the item.

§ 3–9

1. In addition to the sections discussed here, the lawyer should also consider 4–103(e), which defines the meas-

ure of damages for negligent handling of an item as "the amount of the item reduced by an amount that could not have been realized by the exercise of ordinary care. If there is also bad faith it includes any other damages the part suffered as a proximate consequence." As Comment 6 to that section points out, a party may recover at most the value of the item, unless there was bad faith. Typically such liability would not arise out of theft, the topic of this chapter, without a delay or other mishandling in which funds were not received by the payee because the check was presented too late.

2. § 3–416(b). See County of Pierce v. Suburban Bank, 815 F.Supp. 1124, 21 UCC2d 75 (N.D.Ill. 1993) for a case where the warrantor was not held liable because the loss suffered was not a result of the breach of warranty, but of the misconduct of one of the payees.

3. 466 N.W.2d 417, 14 UCC2d 824 (Minn.App. 1991).

check that had been paid with a forged indorsement sued the drawee bank for conversion. The drawee bank in turn sued the depositary bank upstream on a breach of warranty theory under 4–207. The drawee bank attempted to recover all of its attorneys' fees from the collecting bank. The court allowed the drawee bank's attorneys' fees for defending the conversion action brought by the payee, because it found statutory authority for that under 4–207. It disallowed the drawee bank's attorneys' fees for its indemnification action against the collecting bank. When the cause of action directly benefits the plaintiff under Minnesota law, the plaintiff is only entitled to attorneys' fees if they are authorized by a specific statute or contract, and there was no express statutory authority for awarding the drawee bank these fees.

The person obtaining payment for a draft, and previous transferors of the draft, also make presentment warranties to the drawee under 3–417. The drawee, under 3–417(b), may:

> recover from any warrantor damages for breach of warranty equal to the amount paid by the drawee less the amount the drawee received or is entitled to receive from the drawer because of the payment. In addition, the drawee is entitled to compensation for expenses and loss of interest resulting from the breach.

As in the case of 3–416, Comment 5 to section 3–417 says the rule opens the door for attorney's fees. Furthermore, the drawee can recover under the warranty even if the drawee was negligent in making payment.[4]

PROBLEM

As Doris became more experienced at embezzling, she began forging the President's signature (as drawer) on Agency checks. She made these checks payable to real and fictitious suppliers of Agency and after forging the indorsement, deposited them in her account through ATMs. When the checks were returned at the end of the month, Doris destroyed them (she of course sent a second check to the real suppliers).

1. Agency sues depositary bank for conversion under 3–420.

    As an "issuer," Agency loses, 3–420(a).

2. Agency sues its own (payor) bank for improper payment under 4–401.

---

4. See 3–417(b): "The right of the drawee to recover damages under this section is not affected by any failure of the drawee to exercise ordinary care in making payment."

Agency has a good cause of action. (It may lose for reasons shown in the next chapter.)

3. Payor bank in turn joins depositary bank in a suit for breach of warranty under 4–207 and 4–208.

Payor loses. Since the 4–207 warranties run only to "transferees" and not to "drawees," payor does not get this warranty. Since 4–208 grants a warranty only that the transferring bank has no *knowledge* that the drawer's signature is forged, the depositary bank, which is surely without actual "knowledge" of the forgery, does not break the warranty. (For reasons disclosed in the next chapter, depositary bank does not breach 4–208(a)(1)—trust us—this will be treated as a forged drawer check not as a forged indorsement check even though both are forged on this check.)

Chapter 4

REALLOCATION OF LOSS
BECAUSE OF FAULT

Analysis

§ 4–1 Introduction

The modern check collection system is complex, impersonal and highly automated. It is at the mercy not only of human error but also of clever manipulation. When manipulation happens, the parties involved may confess their own responsibility, but more often they claim that somebody else's negligence caused the loss. A customer may point to sloppy bank procedures: the bank negligently paid over a forged signature, so the bank should bear the loss and recredit the account from which money was improperly drawn. The bank may point instead to the customer's sloppy management of its own finances: the customer negligently let an embezzler get hold of the rubber stamp used to sign checks, and the customer should bear the loss.

In general the Uniform Commercial Code responds to this finger pointing by holding each negligent party liable for its substantial contribution to the loss. This allocation of liability based on comparative negligence was incorporated into the Code as part of the 1990 amendments to Article 3 and 4.[1] Before the 1990 amendments, "preclusion" cases were standard contributory negligence cases. A bank might argue that the customer was negligent, and the customer would respond that the bank was contributorily negligent. If both claims were proven, negligence would disappear from the case and the bank would be barred from asserting the customer's negligence.

One consequence of adopting a comparative negligence standard is that there will have to be wider recognition of negligence as a basis not merely for a defense (preclusion), but also as a basis for asserting an affirmative claim. For example, in section 3–406(a), a depositor may be precluded from asserting alteration if the depositor's failure to exercise ordinary care substantially contributed to the alteration. Under 3–406(b), the "loss is allocated" between the two parties if the bank also failed to exercise ordinary care. Although it does not say so in terms, the "loss allocated" language in 3–406(b) must be interpreted to grant an affirmative cause of action to one of the parties as a means of recovering for that part of the loss which the bank should bear. As the statute is written, the bank's negligence no longer merely lifts the preclusion of 3–406(a), as it did before 1990. Rather, the bank's negligence sometimes gives other parties a cause of action to recover an appropriate share under 3–406(b). In that respect, the 1990 revisions state a subtle

---

§ 4–1

1. § 3–406 provides in part:

(a) A person whose failure to exercise ordinary care substantially contributes to an alteration of an instrument or to the making of a forged signature on an instrument is precluded from asserting the alteration or forgery against a person who, in good faith, pays the instrument or takes it for value or for collection.

(b) Under subsection (a), if the person asserting the preclusion fails to exercise ordinary care in paying or taking the instrument and that failure substantially contributes to loss, the loss is allocated between the person precluded and the person asserting the preclusion according to the extent to which the failure of each to exercise ordinary care contributed to the loss.

modification of the theories of recovery, and not merely a readjustment of the identities of those who bear losses.

§ 4–2   Overview of the Basic Rules

The 1990 Code expanded the liability of the employer in embezzlement cases. Also, the Code allocated some new losses to the employer of an embezzler. This was accomplished by expanding 3–405 to cover new cases and also by the definition of negligence now found in 3–103(a)(9).[1]

In addition, the time allowed to a customer to discover and report unauthorized signatures or alterations under 4–406 was modified in 1990.

Section 3–406, discussed above, lays out the rule regarding negligence that contributes to forged signatures or alterations. Section 4–406 imposes a duty on the customer to report unauthorized signatures or alterations. All four of these sections (3–404, 3–405, 3–406, and 4–406) incorporate comparative negligence. We discuss these sections immediately below.

§ 4–3   Negligence Contributing to a Forgery or Alteration, Section 3–406

Section 3–406 reads in full as follows:

(a) A person whose failure to exercise ordinary care substantially contributes to an alteration of an instrument or to the making of a forged signature on an instrument is precluded from asserting the alteration or the forgery against a person who, in good faith, pays the instrument or takes it for value or for collection.

(b) Under subsection (a), if the person asserting the preclusion fails to exercise ordinary care in paying or taking the instrument and that failure substantially contributes to loss, the loss is allocated between the person precluded and the person asserting the preclusion according to the extent to which the failure of each to exercise ordinary care contributed to the loss.

(c) Under subsection (a), the burden of proving failure to exercise ordinary care is on the person asserting the preclusion.

---

§ 4–2

1. § 3–103(a)(9): "Ordinary care" in the case of a person engaged in business means observance of reasonable commercial standards, prevailing in the area in which the person is located, with respect to the business in which the person is engaged. In the case of a bank that takes an instrument for processing for collection or payment by automated means, reasonable commercial standards do not require the bank to examine the instrument if the failure to examine does not violate the bank's prescribed procedures and the bank's procedures do not vary unreasonably from general banking usage not disapproved by this Article or Article 4.

Under subsection (b), the burden of proving failure to exercise ordinary care is on the person precluded.

Note first that the protection of 3–406 is available to any person who pays in good faith or takes an instrument for value or collection in good faith. Prior to 1990, only a "holder in due course, drawee," or "other payor," could assert the rights in 3–406. The former section 3–406 read in full as follows:

> Any person who by his negligence substantially contributes to a material alteration of the instrument or to the making of an unauthorized signature is precluded from asserting the alteration or lack of authority against a holder in due course or against a drawee or other payor who pays the instrument in good faith and in accordance with the reasonable commercial standards of the drawee's or payor's business.

The pre–1990 law was too narrow. Persons who took an instrument in good faith, but who were not drawees, payors, or holders in due course should also have been entitled to the protection of 3–406. Assume that a depositary bank in good faith took a check bearing a forged indorsement. The bank would not be a holder in due course, drawer or other payor. Technically the bank would not have been entitled to 3–406's protection (at least until the section itself had been applied to make the indorsement effective). Today, that depositary bank can invoke the protection of 3–406, even if it is not a holder in due course.

Subsection (c) to 3–406 explicitly allocates the burden of proof, giving part to one party and part to the other.

a. *Forged Signature or Alteration*

The 1990 redraft of section 3–406 has another subtle but important difference from the old 3–406. The new section covers only negligence that results in alteration or the making of a "forged signature." Formerly section 3–406 also covered "unauthorized signatures." In the words of Comment 2 to revised 3–406:

> Unauthorized signature is a broader concept that includes not only forgery but also the signature of an agent which does not bind the principal under the law of agency.

Similarly the term "fraudulent indorsement" that is the basis for a claim under section 3–405 means a "forged indorsement," not one that is merely unauthorized.

To understand the significance of this change, consider one of our favorite cases, Gresham State Bank v. O & K Construction Co.[1]

§ 4–3

1. 231 Or. 106, 370 P.2d 726 (1962), opinion clarified on denial of rehearing,

231 Or. 106, 372 P.2d 187 (1962).

In that case Justice O'Connell of the Oregon Supreme Court applied Article 3 by analogy; the case arose prior to the effective date of the UCC in Oregon. Theft occurred when McKenna, an embezzler, who had "neither express or implied authority to indorse the checks other than for deposit" indorsed a number of checks (that were payable to his employer, O & K Construction) and cashed them at Zimmerman's store. He pocketed the proceeds and his employer sued Zimmerman and Zimmerman's bank, Gresham. Despite the quoted statement which shows Justice O'Connell's conclusion that McKenna did have authority to indorse for deposit, the court analyzed the case as a 3–406 negligence case and concluded that Zimmerman was liable since Zimmerman's contributory negligence negated O & K's negligence.

One might regard O & K as a prototypical 3–406 case and conclude that the loss would be allocated on a comparative fault basis between O & K and Zimmerman's store under revised 3–406 and 3–405. But if McKenna had authority to sign and if, therefore, his signature was not a "forged" signature, but merely an "unauthorized" signature, neither section 3–406 nor the 3–405 applies to the case. The comments state the drafters' intention to limit those sections to forgeries and to exclude unauthorized signatures that are not forgeries.

Where does that leave one? Perhaps sections 3–420 and 3–307(b) apply. If Zimmerman knows of McKenna's fiduciary status, as it does, and further knows that the money is to be taken for personal use, as it might, presumably Zimmerman is the proper defendant in a 3–420 action and bears 100 percent of the loss notwithstanding any negligent behavior by O & K, the employer.

If section 3–307 does not apply (because, for example, Zimmerman is not on notice that McKenna is using the money for his personal use), is 100 percent of the loss on O & K because there is neither forgery nor violation of 3–307? Perhaps one returns to section 3–402 (signature by representative) for the answer to that question. If O & K would have been bound by McKenna's signature on a simple contract, they are bound by his indorsement under 3–402. That makes the check properly payable and there is no conversion by the payor bank or by Zimmerman's.

But what if the local law coming in via 3–402 says that O & K is not bound by McKenna's signature—because it is unauthorized? Is there then a conversion action under 3–420? That seems possible, but note the irony. By acknowledging that it has granted McKenna authority to indorse, O & K opens this avenue of argument: even though our signature was not forged, it was nevertheless unauthorized and thus did not bind us under the common law of Oregon brought in by 3–402. Therefore, we are not bound and can recover the entire loss from the payor, Zimmerman or the depositary bank. By showing themselves to have granted greater authority to McKenna, they put 100 percent of the loss under 3–420 on Zimmerman or the payor and protected themselves from a comparative negligence counterclaim under 3–405 or 3–406. That is crazy.

b. Substantially Contributes

Section 3–406 precludes one who "substantially contributes" to an alteration or the making of a forged signature from asserting a claim arising from such an alteration or signature against other parties. The acts sufficient to "substantially contribute" to a material alteration or to the making of an unauthorized signature are limited only by man's capacity for slovenly business transactions. We cannot hope to catalog all those mistakes here, nor even to divide them into useful categories; we only pass on notions from decided cases as guides to lawyer ruminations about what is and what is not negligence in dealing with checks. One source of guidance is the nonexclusive list in Comment 3 to 3–406. The comment contains three hypothetical cases to illustrate the kind of conduct that can be the basis of a preclusion. One example suggests that keeping a rubber stamp for an employer's signature in an unlocked desk drawer might substantially contribute to forgery by an embezzling employee. A second example shows that sending a check to a person bearing the right name but in the wrong state could be a substantial contribution to that person's forgery. The last case tells that leaving a large blank space at a critical spot on a check would be failure to exercise ordinary care substantially contributing to an alteration. None of these examples is surprising. They only reiterate the substance of Comment 2: while the principal cause of the alteration may be the act of a thief, things that make the thief's job easier may preclude the customer's claim.

One can extract some ideas from the cases that have addressed this issue, but even the most generous would not call them principles. First, it may be negligent not to have one's books audited. Second, it may be negligence not to follow general business practices of organizations of similar size and sophistication. One might suppose it is always a bad business practice in an organization with more than a few employees to have disbursements made by the same employee who also reconciles cancelled checks with the bank statement. In some cases, courts have said that an employer who fails to inquire into an employee's references has been negligent. Not surprisingly, signing blank checks is negligent. Additionally, a party who sets up procedural safeguards and then fails to follow them may be in hotter water than one who has no procedures at all. Of course, what is good for the goose is not necessarily good for the duck. We suspect that the two employee nonprofit corporation that runs the local Red Cross and is governed by a busy volunteer board of directors can safely use more slovenly procedures without being negligent than can a more sizeable for-profit corporation.

Comment 2 to 3–406 explains why the drafters retained "substantial contribution" to a loss in 1990: in order to preclude one from asserting a forgery or alteration, that person need not prove that the person's behavior was a "direct and proximate cause" of the forgery or alteration, but only that it "substantially contributed" thereto. Thus, where there are multiple causes of loss (not the least of which may be a deficiency in the thief's morality), one person's act could be a substantial cause even though other events might be more direct and powerful causes. This is made clear by the concluding paragraph in Comment 2 that reads in full as follows:

> The "substantially contributes" test of former Section 3–406 is continued in this section in preference to a "direct and proximate cause" test. The "substantially contributes" test is meant to be less stringent than a "direct and proximate cause" test. Under the less stringent test the preclusion should be easier to establish. Conduct "substantially contributes" to a material alteration or forged signature if it is a contributing cause of the alteration or signature and a substantial factor in bringing it about. The analysis of "substantially contributes" in former Section 3–406 by the court in Thompson Maple Products v. Citizens National Bank of Corry, 211 Pa.Super. 42, 234 A.2d 32, 4 UCC 624 (1967), states what is intended by the use of the same words in revised Section 3–406(b). Since Section 3–404(d) and Section 3–405(b) also use the words "substantially contributes" the analysis of these words also applies to those provisions.

c. Good Faith

Section 3–406 permits one to assert preclusion only by a person that acts "in good faith." In Article 3 good faith means "honesty in fact and the observance of reasonable commercial standards of fair dealing." Because the drafters of the 1990 amendments changed the definition of good faith in Article 3,[2] section 3–406 arguably has a different meaning than its predecessor even though the words are the same.

Although 3–406(b) contemplates splitting a loss between two negligent parties, there is no splitting with a person who does not act in good faith. If the customer is negligent but the bank acts in bad faith, the bank will likely bear the loss. To see how little the

---

2. Under the pre–1990 Code, Article 3 relied on the definition of "good faith" contained in § 1–201(19): " 'Good faith' means honesty in fact in the conduct or transaction concerned."

new good faith rules will do, assume that a corporate customer asked the payor to recredit its account where there was a payment over a forged signature. The bank responds that the customer is precluded by its own negligence. The depositor may then respond that the bank cannot assert preclusion because its payment was not "in good faith." That argument was almost always a loser for the depositor under the old Code, where good faith meant merely honesty in fact. But because good faith now additionally requires observance of "reasonable commercial standards of fair dealing," one might conclude (incorrectly) that the customer could avoid the preclusion entirely. The customer might argue as follows: "While it may be true that I did not supervise my employee effectively, the check that caused the theft was made payable to the order of the corporation. Your teller failed to follow reasonable commercial standards in allowing the embezzler to deposit the check in a personal account." If the depositary bank failed to follow reasonable commercial standards, does this mean that the bank is not in good faith and therefore, bears the entire loss so that we never get to the comparative negligence question in revised 3–406(b)? We do not think so.

We think that the case posed does not show a lack of good faith. Note that under the Article 3 definition, good faith means "honesty in fact and the observance of reasonable commercial standards *of fair dealing*." The bank may well have failed to follow reasonable commercial standards "of care," but those standards had nothing to do with "fair dealing."[3] One could fail to follow reasonable commercial standards if those standards did not have to do with "fair dealing" and yet be in good faith. The drafters incorporated reasonable commercial standards of fair dealing into the good faith idea to be sure that one be as "fair" as commercial standards require, not necessarily that one be as "careful" as they require. What the depositor will be arguing in the hypothetical case posed is not that the bank failed to "deal fairly," but that it was negligent in its handling of the check. That dispute should be resolved by 3–406(b)—comparative negligence. This is not a case in which the depositor is able to cast the entire loss on the bank because the bank failed to act in "good faith."

d. Comparative Negligence

Subsection 3–406(b) is an invitation for a plaintiff to roll the dice with the jury. Exactly how a judge or jury is to decide the

---

3. See Wachovia Bank, N.A. v. Federal Reserve Bank of Richmond, 338 F.3d 318, 51 UCC2d 26 (4th Cir. 2003) (A failure to comply with reasonable commercial standards of fair dealing requires a showing of actions in an unfair or dishonest manner, not mere negligence).

"extent to which the failure of each * * * contributed to the loss" is not defined in the Code, nor could it be.

When no prior preclusion?

In the typical embezzlement case not explicitly covered by 3–404 or 3–405, the bank will argue that the employer hired, supervised, and dealt day-to-day with the thief. The bank, on the other hand, may not have ever had face-to-face dealings with the thief and may have seen only pieces of paper. The employer will respond that one of the purposes for having a checking account is to protect against theft, and that that protection is what the bank was selling. In the case posed (where the teller allowed the thief to deposit a check in a personal account), the depositor may even point to the bank's own teller's manual which is likely to prohibit such deposits of corporate checks.

The arguments about what constitutes negligent behavior and what does not was little changed by the 1990 revision. What has changed are the consequences of proving that the bank was negligent. Before 1990, proof that the bank was negligent generally meant that the entire loss fell on the bank, not the depositor, regardless of the depositor's negligence. After 1990, the depositor will seldom be able to cast the entire loss on the bank; the loss will be shared.

As we have indicated above, 3–406 and the accompanying sections carry with them something that did not exist before 1990, namely, a new cause of action. In our hypothetical case, assume that the bank paid the check over the forged indorsement of the embezzling employee. Assume also that the employer-depositor acknowledges that it substantially contributed to the forgeries, yet asserts that some part of the loss should be borne by the bank. How does the employer-depositor recover that portion from the bank? Because it has admitted that it is precluded under 3–406(a), the depositor does not have a claim against its bank for wrongful payment under 4–401. Yet there must be some mechanism by which a portion of the loss is cast on the bank. This mechanism is an affirmative cause of action for negligence under 3–406(b) (and similar causes of action under 3–404, 3–405 and 4–406) where the depositor-employer recovers a part of its loss by affirmative proof that the negligent behavior of the defendant bank caused a portion of it. Because 3–404(d) and 3–405(b) state that the party bearing the loss "may recover" from the other negligent party, those sections create the affirmative cause of action more clearly than 3–406(b) which states only that the loss "is allocated" among the negligent parties.

A section 3–406(b) cause of action is governed by 3–118(g) as an action "to enforce * * * [a] duty or right arising under this

Article * * * '' that must be commenced within three years after the cause of action accrues. As we indicate below, arguments will arise over when this cause of action accrues. Is it upon the improper payment by the bank or upon the depositor's learning the facts from which it should have concluded that the loss occurred?

How the losses are to be allocated by the law is not a simple question. At the most simplistic level, one can argue that comparative negligence is more desirable because it does not leave the slightly negligent plaintiff empty handed, as does a contributory negligence regime. However, prior to 1990, the party injured by the contributory negligence scheme was not the classic pitiful plaintiff; the party was likely to be a payor or depositary bank. So analyzed the change from a contributory to a comparative negligence standard benefits payor and depositary banks.

However, one learned in the dynamics of judge and jury decision-making might predict a different outcome. That person might predict that a jury, not sympathetic to the banks' interests and invited explicitly by 3–406(b) to compare the relative fault of poor depositor with that of rich bank, would not favor the bank. Moreover, judges who would have awarded summary judgment in a contributory negligence regime to a bank that was only slightly negligent might now feel compelled to give those cases to the jury under a comparative negligence scheme. (Those judges would be wrong. Now as under the old law, the bank's negligence becomes relevant only if it "substantially" contributes to the loss. If it did not substantially contribute, the bank has exactly the same rights to a summary judgment as before.)

Of course, life is yet more complicated than we have described. The outcomes in these cases are often governed not by what a jury or even a judge does, but by what the lawyers for the parties believe a judge or jury will do if faced with the case. If the bank lawyers are convinced that most judges will not grant summary judgment and believe that juries will favor the depositor in comparing the fault, and if, furthermore, banks and bank lawyers are congenitally risk averse, the ultimate effect of the comparative negligence standard could allocate yet a greater share of the loss to the banks.

Of course, all of the foregoing is mischievous speculation about the minds and souls of lawyers, judges, and jurors. But it invites deeper study than we have time or interest for on the question, just how do courts and juries go about allocating loss between a favored party (the consumer-depositor) and a disfavored one (the bank).

e. Reasonable Commercial Standards

Note that 3–406(b) gives an affirmative cause of action to a plaintiff against a person who "fails to exercise ordinary care in paying or taking the instrument * * *." The definition of "ordinary care" incorporates the observance of reasonable commercial standards.[4] Pre 1990s 3–406 was more explicit, permitting estoppel as a defense by payors and drawees only if payment was made "in accordance with reasonable commercial standards" of the drawee's or payor's business. Because the expanded definition of ordinary care incorporates reasonable commercial standards, it is no longer necessary for the Code to refer explicitly to those standards in 3–406. Thus, the drafters deleted the reference, but that change will not alter the result of disputes arising under 3–406.

f. Bank's Failure to Exercise Ordinary Care

The ways in which a bank might be guilty of negligence are familiar. One way is the way discussed above, namely, for a teller to take a check payable to the order of a corporation when the teller should know that the check would not normally be deposited in the account of an individual employee of the corporation. Many other claims can be made about the appearances of the person who stands at the teller's window, about the form and style of the indorsement, and about indications of irregularity on the face of the instrument itself.

Most of the familiar questions about bank negligence are untouched by the 1990 elaborations in Section 3–103(a)(9) of the definition of ordinary care:

> "Ordinary care" in the case of a person engaged in business means observance of reasonable commercial standards, prevailing in the area in which the person is located, with respect to the business in which the person is engaged. In the case of a bank that takes an instrument for processing for collection or payment by automated means, reasonable commercial standards do not require the bank to examine the instrument if the failure to examine does not violate the bank's prescribed procedures and the bank's procedures do not vary unreasonably from general banking usage not disapproved by this Article or Article 4.

The first sentence incorporates the familiar "reasonable commercial standards." Reasonable commercial standards are limited in two ways. The sentence itself confines the standards to those "prevailing in the area" where the bank is located, and "with respect to the business in which the person is engaged." A bank in New York might have to behave differently from a bank in Evansville, and a liquor store in Manhattan might be held to different

---

4. § 3–103(a)(9) reads in part as follows:

"Ordinary care" in the case of a person engaged in business means observance of reasonable commercial standards, prevailing in the area in which the person is located, with respect to the business in which the person is engaged.
* * *

standards than Chase Manhattan. Within a particular trade and within a particular geographic area there might be different standards, depending upon the size of the bank and the modus operandi of a bank of that size. Also, the responsibilities of a particular bank do not necessarily rise in linear relationship with its size. A large bank that processes almost all of its checks electronically might fail to observe a defect on the face of a check without being negligent even though that defect would put a smaller bank on notice.

The last sentence of the definition is aimed squarely at cases such as Wilder Binding Co. v. Oak Park Trust and Savings Bank,[5] Rhode Island Hospital Trust National Bank v. Zapata Corp.,[6] and Medford Irrigation District v. Western Bank.[7] In *Medford*, the court held that the bank's practice of not reviewing signatures on checks under $5,000 constituted a lack of ordinary care as a matter of law—despite the prevalence of this practice throughout the banking industry. *Wilder* and *Zapata* disagree with that reasoning and outcome. In *Wilder*, the court held that ordinary care is an issue for the trier of fact, and depended on whether the bank's practice constituted "general banking usage." Likewise, the court in *Zapata* held that the bank had made out a prima facie case that it used ordinary care where its practice coincided with normal industry practice.

It is now commonplace for payor banks to process checks electronically and without human intervention. Some banks verify randomly to see whether there are signatures on some checks, but most banks examine only checks above a certain dollar amount.[8] Even when each check is examined there may or may not be an actual comparison of the signature on the check with a signature on file.

The last sentence in 3–103(a)(9) immunizes a bank that follows such automated procedures (does not examine checks to see if there is a signature, or compare the signature with a specimen) from claims that it is *per se* guilty of negligence. In fact, we believe that 3–103(a)(9) goes further and indorses those acts, at least if the bank has no internal procedures that require such examination and if other banks generally have similar procedures. Others need not

---

5. 135 Ill.2d 121, 142 Ill.Dec. 192, 552 N.E.2d 783, 10 UCC2d 916 (1990).

6. 848 F.2d 291, 6 UCC2d 1 (1st Cir.1988).

7. 66 Or.App. 589, 676 P.2d 329, 38 UCC 411 (1984).

8. A theory that supports random examination of checks with lower dollar amounts is that forgery and embezzlements are more likely to involve checks in the medium range than checks with large dollar amounts. Thus, one with a limited budget to examine checks could logically conclude that it would be better to examine the signatures on a random number of checks with the dollar amounts between $500 and $5,000 than to examine the signatures on all checks over a large dollar amount. This would be rational if one concluded that the embezzler was much more likely to strike in the $500 to $5,000 range and not in the over $20,000 range.

do exactly the same thing; it is enough to relieve a bank of responsibility if that particular bank's procedures do not "vary unreasonably" from the practice of other banks. However, at least one court has declined to apply the section to an analogous situation. In Govoni & Sons Const. Co., Inc. v. Mechanics Bank,[9] a fraudulent accountant duped his employer into providing him with 132 unnecessary checks which were payable to the Commonwealth by falsely overstating the company's tax returns. The accountant would then deposit the unauthorized checks alongside multiple other checks at a local bank during busy hours. The bank's practice on multi-item deposits was for its tellers to flip through the checks and scan the backside for missing indorsements. However, since the accountant was a regular customer at the bank and his deposits were during busy hours, the judge inferred that the tellers did not fan the checks for indorsements. Furthermore, the bank had a policy of processing State tax checks despite a missing indorsement in order to prevent the State from assessing penalties for late tax payments from the bank's customers. Although "comparable" banks within the area followed identical procedures, the court stated that the bank's procedures were unreasonable; customary practice, by itself, is insufficient to make the procedures reasonable since "[a]n entire industry may behave unreasonably." Of course, the statutory formulation was not precisely applicable to this case since the bank did not take the checks by "automated means."

Before one becomes apoplectic at the thought that the banks have quietly escaped from all liability for forged signatures, a person should understand how 3–103(a)(9) works. Assume a thief steals a consumer's check, forges the drawer's signature and succeeds in getting final payment on it. Unless the consumer is precluded by 3–406, the payor bank has paid improperly and the loss will rest with it. This is true not because the bank was negligent but because the bank violated its contractual and statutory obligation to its customer (4–401). Section 3–103(a)(9)'s definition of ordinary care becomes relevant only if the bank is able to establish that the customer's negligence substantially contributed to the forgery and if the customer then asserts that the bank's failure to examine the signature was negligence that contributed to the loss. When the bank is not able to establish its customer's negligence, it will bear the loss. In those cases, the bank gains no relief from 3–103(a)(9).

To understand instances in which 3–103(a)(9) will apply, consider a typical business case. Assume that Wilson's Machine Shop hired Hillary as a bookkeeper without examining her employment history, and that an examination would have shown her to have a record of check fraud. Assume, further, that Wilson did not follow

9. 51 Mass.App.Ct. 35, 742 N.E.2d 1094, 43 UCC2d 1058 (2001).

any of the normal security practices concerning its checking account, on examining its statement, or in maintaining controls against embezzlement. Over a period of three years, Hillary stole $70,000 from Wilson by forging the drawer's signature, forging indorsements, and causing checks to be made payable to fictitious payees. Wilson's behavior will be examined under 3–406, 3–404, 3–405, and 4–406. Clearly Wilson's negligence has "substantially contributed" and under 3–406 or other sections, Wilson will be at least partially liable for the loss.

Wilson will argue that the payor failed to observe reasonable commercial standards because it failed to discover that many of the signatures were forgeries. In that case, the payor bank might be victorious because of 3–103(a)(9). As we know, and as Wilson should appreciate, the payor bank is processing checks mechanically without human examination and at a very low charge. Additionally, it is likely never to have contact with Hillary, and no datum gleaned electronically from the check will put it on notice that anything is amiss. In that circumstance, Wilson is most at fault and is likely to be the least-cost risk avoider. That is to say, Wilson is the one who could most cheaply prevent the loss. By doing a background check of the people it hires and by using normal protections against embezzlement, Wilson could have prevented the loss.

Note that the last sentence of 3–103(a)(9) will almost always protect intermediary banks, will usually protect payor banks, but will less frequently protect depositary banks. In many cases the claim against the depositary bank will have to do with information that should have been collected by the teller in dealing with the embezzler, who, in many of these schemes, brings corporate checks to the bank and deposits them in a personal account. In effect, the last sentence of 3–103(a)(9) addresses electronic and mechanical dealing with checks and with data from checks, but it does nothing to protect a bank that deals face-to-face with the embezzler.

All of this is consistent with the migration of the check from paper to the electronic medium. In the early 20th Century the check was a paper transaction and only a paper transaction. All the data on the check were written and were picked off and used by human examination and manual recording. With the addition of the MICR line at the bottom of the check and with the further addition of the MICR encoding of the dollar amount, the check is no more than a carrier of an electronic message to be deciphered and recorded by a machine. Currently, a check often travels as the carrier of the electronic message or in some cases, travels in tandem with an electronic tape that is already bearing the check's electronic message.

With truncation (i.e., the seizure and destruction of the paper check before it gets to the payor), the check will be photographed and destroyed and the electronic message will go alone—perhaps all the way from the depositary bank to the payor. Presumably the electronic version will have the capacity to produce a true copy of the check for the payor so the payor will be able to verify the signature even though it will never actually receive the check. When truncation becomes the norm, the distinction between check transactions and electronic funds transactions will become even more fuzzy than it is now. Then the need for a rule such as that set out in 3–103(a)(9) will become even greater.

Of course, this migration from paper to an electronic medium is not without its difficulties for the banks. Nowhere in bank advertisements or disclosures does one see prominent assertions: "WE EXAMINE NO SIGNATURES", or "SAVE SOME TIME, OMIT THE SIGNATURE LINE." In truth, today the signature does not play the same part that it played at its inception. Even though a payor must recredit a nonnegligent depositor's account when it pays a check without a proper signature, the signature is no longer a symbol used by the payor to distinguish between items that are properly payable and those that are not. But the banks have not been eager to disclose this to their customers.

The banks face a dilemma. Most banks would be quite willing to have their honest depositors understand that the depositor's signature is not used to distinguish between checks that should be paid and those that should not be paid. On the other hand, the banks would like to keep this knowledge out of the hands of thieves who are already busy. Banks might legitimately fear that disclosures to put honest depositors on notice would put thieves and dishonest depositors on notice as well. All of this leaves the bank in the uncomfortable position of having to assert loudly in court something that it merely whispers outside of court, namely, payor banks check few signatures. Banks wishing fully to reap the benefits offered by 3–103(a)(9) may have to reveal to their depositors how insignificant the signature and how infrequent their examination of the signature line.

In summary, the 1990 changes in 3–406, and the analogous changes having to do with comparative negligence in the other sections, together with the definition of ordinary care in 3–103(a)(9), have probably caused a significant but subtle change in the allocation of civil liability arising out of check forgeries. The changes call for careful examination of existing bank disclosure and contracting practices and perhaps for developing different practices.

PROBLEM

Thief gains entry to Manufacturer's office and steals five large checks payable to Manufacturer that were temporarily held with hundreds of other checks in Manufacturer's office. Manufacturer does not miss the checks until weeks later when it inquires about the payments that it has no record of receiving from its customers. It develops that the five checks, totaling $500,000, were deposited in an account that Thief maintained under a fictitious name at Depositary Bank. The checks were paid by the payors. Manufacturer sues Depositary in conversion under 3–420 and Depositary argues that Manufacturer is precluded from asserting its claim because its negligence substantially contributed to the loss.

1. Assume that the court finds that Manufacturer's negligence, if any, did not substantially contribute. Depositary then argues that the $500,000 loss should be allocated between it and Manufacturer according to each person's negligence even if Manufacturer's negligence was not a "substantial" cause. Depositary loses. There is no free standing right to assert negligence and the allocation here arises under 3–406 only if the substantiality test is met. Depositary bears the entire loss as a converter.

Thief also stole five blank checks of Manufacturer. Thief uses Manufacturer's facsimile signature machine, which is sitting on a desk next to the check file, to sign each of them and those clear two weeks later in a sum of $1,000,000. Manufacturer sues payor bank for improper payment.

1. Payor argues that the $1,000,000 was authorized because of the use of the machine and because of a term in the deposit agreement that specified that any signature done with the machine was deemed authorized. Payor wins and can debit the account.

2. Assume that there is no term in the deposit agreement about the use of the machine, but Payor argues that Manufacturer was negligent in leaving the machine in an unprotected place and that negligence substantially contributed to the loss. Payor is right and the suit for conversion is "precluded."

3. Next Manufacturer responds that the loss must be allocated under 3–406(b) according to the parties' negligence. Manufacturer is right, but how was Payor negligent? Manufacturer argues as follows:

    a. Payor failed to examine the checks before it paid. Manufacturer loses this argument. First the signatures were perfect and second it is not negligent to fail to look at the checks that it pays via an automated process 3–103(a)(9).

    b. Payor was in bad faith for not examining the checks manually since other banks in the community do so. If it was in bad faith, it may not assert the preclusion under 3–

406(a). Manufacturer loses this argument. Good faith requires the observance of reasonable commercial standards of "fair dealing" not of "due care." At most the alleged failure amounts to negligence not to lack of good faith.

4. Manufacturer sues Depositary Bank in negligence as to the $1,000,000 worth of checks. Manufacturer loses. There is no free standing cause of action in negligence and this action is not authorized by 3–406 nor by any other section of Article 3.

§ 4–4   Impostors, Fictitious Payees, Section 3–404; Employers' Responsibility, Section 3–405

Sections 3–404 and 3–405 deal with the common forms of embezzlement involving checks, namely embezzlement by an impostor and embezzlement by an employee who tampers with a check, pads a payroll or conducts some other such scam. Readers familiar with the old Code will notice that the 1990 amendments have shifted responsibility in some cases from banks to employers, on the theory that employers are best able to halt embezzlement and ought to bear the burden of failing to do so. We deal below with the different forms, one at a time.

a.   Impostors

Section 3–404(a) reads in full as follows:

(a) If an impostor, by use of the mails or otherwise, induces the issuer of an instrument to issue the instrument to the impostor, or to a person acting in concert with the impostor, by impersonating the payee of the instrument or a person authorized to act for the payee, an indorsement of the instrument by any person in the name of the payee is effective as the indorsement of the payee in favor of a person who, in good faith, pays the instrument or takes it for value or for collection.

Cases dealing with impostors are infrequent and are likely to remain so. Note that section 3–404(a) covers cases in which the impostor impersonates a payee and also cases in which the impostor poses as the agent of a legitimate business and makes off with a check payable to the order of the principal. This is a change from the old Code, where the false agent was not regarded as an impostor.[1] Before 1990, the indorsement by the impostor-agent was not effective and, assuming 3–406 and 4–406 did not apply, the duped drawer (who made the check payable to the legitimate

---

§ 4–4

1. Thus the 1990 Code would overturn results like that of Valley Bank v. Monarch Inv. Co., 118 Idaho 747, 800 P.2d 634, 13 UCC2d 1161 (1990), rev'd, 120 Idaho 733, 819 P.2d 1133, 15 UCC2d 953 (1991). There, a thief named Palmer represented himself as an agent

principal and not the false agent) could force the bank to recredit the account. This rule was sometimes justified by arguing that the drawer had taken care to draw the check to the order of the principal, and so deserved the protection of the law. In the 1990 Code the loss falls on the drawer, who will be precluded under 3–404(a). This point is made explicit in Comment 1 to 3–404.[2]

b. Acts by Authorized Parties

When a treasurer draws a check to a payee who is either fictitious or is not intended to have any rights in the check, the treasurer is made the "holder" by 3–404(b)(1); 3–404(b)(2) makes an indorsement by any person effective. There is a distinction here between the case in which a treasurer forms the intention to steal before he or she has pen in hand and the case in which he or she decides on the spur of the moment to steal a check after having written it with an honest intent. The latter case is not covered by 3–404(b) because the treasurer's "intent"—determined at the time of signing—was for the named payee to have the funds. Even in that case, the treasurer's status within the company combined with his or her later indorsement will usually bind the company under 3–405(b). In that case our treasurer is somebody "entrusted with responsibility" and 3–405(b) makes his or her signature effective. Under the pre–1990 Code, the latter case would have been handled under 3–406 on negligence; it was not covered by 3–405.

c. Acts by Unauthorized Parties

Under 3–404(b), whether an indorsement is effective turns on the aim of the "person whose intent determines to whom an

---

of Monarch Investment and sold a stolen backhoe to the Neibaurs. The Neibaurs wrote Palmer a check made out to Monarch Investment, which Palmer was able to receive a cashier's check for at the Neibaurs' bank. The Neibaurs were able to force their bank to recredit their account, because they were entitled to have the indorsement of Monarch Investment. Under new 3–404, the Neibaurs would have to share the Bank's loss. This case was vacated on rehearing and the court held that on remand the bank could assert that drawer's negligence precluded an assertion that the indorsement was unauthorized.

2. The relevant part of Comment 1 reads as follows:

Subsection (a) changes the former law in a case in which the impostor is impersonating an agent. Under former Section 3–405(1)(a), if Impostor impersonated Smith and induced the drawer to draw a check to the order of Smith, Impostor could negotiate the check. If Impostor impersonated Smith, the president of Smith Corporation, and the check was payable to the order of Smith Corporation, the section did not apply. See the last paragraph of Comment 2 to former Section 3–405. In revised Article 3, Section 3–404(a) gives Impostor the power to negotiate the check in both cases.

But see Lewis v. Telephone Employees Credit Union, 87 F.3d 1537, 29 UCC2d 1121 (9th Cir. 1996) (bank bears loss in cases where an imposter "represents that he or she is an agent of an actual existing principal and the check is issued in the name of that principal" on the theory that the bank was in a better position to detect a fraudulent indorsement since the drawer was only duped about the "true powers of the agent").

instrument is payable." Subsections 3–110(a) and (b) define the "person whose intent determines to whom an instrument is payable," and make clear that it is the person signing as the issuer of the instrument or supplying the name of the payee to a check-writing machine, *whether or not such person is authorized to do so*. Imagine Thief who is not an employee or agent of Corporation. Thief steals a blank check from Corporation and makes the check payable to a real person whom Thief does not intend to have any interest in the check, or Thief obtains access to Corporation's check-writing machine and causes it to produce a check payable to a non-existent company. Subsection 3–404(b) still applies to make Thief the holder of the check because it is in its possession. Therefore, Thief's indorsement would be effective, and the drawee bank is entitled to pay the check and debit Corporation's account.

d. Padded Payroll

Where a clerical embezzler steals from his or her employer by issuing checks payable to the order of people not on the payroll or who claim to be suppliers but are not, the cases sometimes fall under 3–404 and sometimes under 3–405. Irrespective of which section is applicable, the outcomes will usually be the same, but they could be different.

Consider first the classic padded payroll. A New York payroll clerk, Sara Pall, prepares a check payable to the order of Charles de Gaulle, a fictitious person in New York. She procures the signature of the treasurer (an authorized signer), forges Charles de Gaulle's signature and gets the money. The case is covered by 3–404. That section refers us to 3–110(a) and (b) to determine whose "intent" is important.[3] In this case, it is the treasurer's, the authorized signer. However, section 3–404(b)(i) does not apply because the treasurer in his or her ignorance does intend Charles de Gaulle to have an interest in the instrument. Section 3–404(b)(ii) does apply because Charles de Gaulle is a fictitious person. Accordingly our thief, the payroll clerk, is a holder and any indorsement is effective. Thus, as in all of these cases, when the bank debits the employer's account, it is making proper payment and need not recredit the account since the indorsement is effective and each party downstream will become a holder.

---

3. § 3–110 says in part:

(a) The person to whom an instrument is initially payable is determined by the intent of the person, whether or not authorized, signing as, or in the name or behalf of, the issuer of the instrument. * * *

(b) If the signature of the issuer of an instrument is made by automated means, such as a check-writing machine, the payee of the instrument is determined by the intent of the person who supplied the name or identification of the payee, whether or not authorized to do so.

Now assume that Sara knows that Dorothy Summers has worked for the company but has recently resigned. Sara causes a check to be issued in the name of Dorothy Summers, not a fictitious person, steals the check, forges Dorothy's indorsement and gets the money. Where are we now? Again we look to the intention of the treasurer, who intended that Dorothy have the instrument, therefore 3–404(b)(i) does not apply. Since the person identified is not fictitious, 3–404(b)(ii) also does not apply. We must therefore consult 3–405, where 3–405(b) will probably produce the same result as 3–404, i.e., an "effective" indorsement.

In the above hypothetical, when we consult 3–405, the indorsement is effective only if it is made by an employee "with responsibility with respect to the instrument," or by "a person acting in concert." In other words, these cases are treated as ones in which there is a legitimate check payable to the order of a third party. Unlike the 3–404 cases where an indorsement by anyone is effective, here the indorsement must be by a particular person identified in 3–405(a)(3). Because most embezzlers fit within 3–405(a)(3)'s description of indorsers with "responsibility," we suspect the distinction between 3–404 and 3–405 will not generally be important.

To reiterate, in padded payroll cases where a clerical employee fools the authorized signer, some cases will fit under section 3–404 (e.g., where the person payable is a fictitious person), while others will fit under 3–405 (e.g., payee is a real person and honest signer intends payment to that person). Presumably the drafters regarded the employer as somewhat less culpable when the check is made payable to Dorothy Summers, a real person on the payroll, as opposed to checks made payable to the order of Charles de Gaulle. In the former, reasonable cross-checks might not disclose the theft, but in the latter, an examination of the vendor and employee list (or even a passing knowledge of modern French history) should show that Charles de Gaulle was never employed by nor deals with the company. In the latter case, the company is conceivably more culpable.

Some padded payroll cases might not fit under either 3–404 or 3–405. For instance, what of the case where the thieves set up a real or near real corporation? In Prudential–Bache Securities, Inc. v. Citibank, N.A.,[4] John Efler was employed by Prudential–Bache and had authority to issue checks. He and his partner, Lawrence Artese, set up two fictitious companies, M.N. Corporation and Harvard Corporation. The corporations set up checking accounts at Citibank without proper corporate resolutions and with fictitious corporate officers with the help of two bribed Citibank employees. Efler then caused the issuance of Prudential–Bache checks made payable to the fictitious companies, and Artese deposited the checks

4.   73 N.Y.2d 263, 536 N.E.2d 1118, 539 N.Y.S.2d 699, 7 UCC2d 1345 (1989).

in the companies' accounts at Citibank and withdrew funds when the checks cleared. Efler and Artese embezzled more than $18 million over two years. Prudential–Bache sued Citibank for conversion and other claims based on Citibank's facilitation of the scheme. Reserving the possibility of liability on some other theory, the Court of Appeals concluded that Prudential–Bache's basic claim under Article 3 should be dismissed because old section 3–405(1)(c)[5] made the indorsements effective and did not provide for contributory negligence.

Under the 1990 Code, how would the $18 million loss have been allocated? Under 3–404(b)(ii), Citibank could claim that the persons identified, M.N. Corporation and Harvard Corporation, are fictitious persons because of the failure to comply with the necessary formalities for forming a corporation, so that an indorsement by any person in the name of the payee would be effective. The loss would then be split between Prudential–Bache and Citibank according to their comparative negligence, per 3–404(d). But what if, rather than setting up phony corporations, Efler and Artese had formed genuine corporations and properly opened accounts at Citibank? Then Prudential–Bache's checks would not fit within 3–404(b)(ii), because the corporations were not fictitious. Nor would they fit within 3–404(b)(i), because the signer, Efler, would intend the corporations to have an interest in the instrument. Section 3–405 would not apply, because no employee of Prudential–Bache would have made a fraudulent indorsement. Artese, as a genuine corporate officer of M.N. or Harvard, would have the authority to indorse the checks.

How about 3–406? That section applies only to alterations and forged signatures, and Efler was authorized to issue checks in the name of Prudential–Bache. Is it conceivable that these checks are properly payable under section 4–401, that no warranties have been broken, and that loss allocation rules under 3–404 through 3–406 do not apply? That is conceivable, but it seems unfortunate to us. Efler could just as well have used the name of a person whom he did not intend to have an interest. If he had done so, section 3–404(b) would apply to the transaction and Prudential–Bache would bear a major part of the liability but would be able to shift some of it to Citicorp, who in this case, was itself at fault. Presumably one solution to the dilemma is to bend and twist 3–404 to cover this case by concluding that even if an actual corporation owned by the signer is the intended beneficiary, the signer really does not "intend" that person to have any interest, but is in fact using the

---

5. (1) An indorsement by any person in the name of a named payee is effective if

(c) an agent or employee of the maker or drawer has supplied him with the name of the payee intending the latter to have no such interest.

corporation as a shell for checks in which he and he alone has an interest. Unfortunately, *Prudential–Bache* does not reveal the only crack in the structure of 3–404 et seq.

e. Checks With Forged Signatures and Forged Indorsements

One of the best known "dual forgery" cases[6] arose not at Citibank or Manufacturers Hanover, but at the small First National Bank of Habersham County, Georgia, where an embezzler successfully made off with more than $1 million that was never recovered. Perini Corp. maintained checking accounts with two New York banks, and drew against these accounts using preprinted checks signed by a facsimile signature machine. Seventeen preprinted checks were stolen, run through the machine and made out to the order of Quisenberry Contracting Co. and Southern Contracting Co., both fictitious firms. A man calling himself Jesse D. Quisenberry opened accounts in the names of these payees at First National Bank, deposited the stolen checks in the accounts and later withdrew almost all of the credit in both accounts.

When Perini discovered the fraud, Quisenberry was long gone. Worse still, Perini had filed a facsimile specimen with its two banks and agreed to hold them harmless if checks purporting to bear the facsimile signature were honored. Perini was left with recourse against First National Bank only. First National Bank found itself in a bind, because Quisenberry had indorsed the checks to the fictitious companies in his *personal* capacity, yet First National Bank offered no resistance to this practice. The checks therefore presented an unusual combination of circumstances: they bore undoubtedly the forged drawer's signatures, but also bore indorsements that could also be characterized as forged.

Under the pre–1990 Code, the Fifth Circuit treated the checks as forged signature cases. The Court cites earlier cases and concludes that the majority of jurisdictions treated double forgery cases as if they involved forged drawer's signatures alone. Moreover, under old 3–405(1)(b), any indorsement by any person in the name of a named payee was effective if the person signing as the drawer intended the payee to have no interest in the instrument. Although Quisenberry did not indorse the checks in the name of the payees, it was assumed that he did not intend these fictitious companies to have any interest in the proceeds of the checks—providing further reason to treat them as forged checks only. Accordingly, First National Bank did not breach its warranty of title. The case was remanded so Perini could challenge First National's good faith in handling these checks.

---

6. Perini Corp. v. First Nat. Bank,   1977), reh'g denied, 557 F.2d 823 (5th 553 F.2d 398, 21 UCC 929 (5th Cir.   Cir.1977).

Under revised 3–404, *Perini* is clearly a forged check, not a forged indorsement, case. Section 3–404(b)(1) provides that if the signer does not intend the payee to have any interest in the instrument, or if the payee is a fictitious person, any person in possession of the instrument is its holder. Therefore any person in possession is a person entitled to enforce (3–301), is capable of passing title by indorsement, and the depositary bank does not breach a warranty under 3–417 or 4–208 by passing those checks. Case #5 in Comment 2 to 3–404 explicitly states that the loss will rest with the drawee bank unless 3–406 or 4–406 applies, whether the thief indorses the check in a name other than the payee's, or does not indorse the check at all.

f. Employer's Responsibility for Fraudulent Indorsement by Employee

Almost all the cases now falling under 3–405 would have been outside the reach of the pre–1990 Code's section 3–405; they would have been argued under 3–406. Undoubtedly the drafters are correct in concluding that people in commerce should and do regard an embezzler's behavior as the same whether the embezzler is forging an indorsement on a check payable to the employer or is causing a check of the employer to be issued to a fictitious payee. The effect of revised 3–405 is to put certain losses arising from forgeries of indorsements on the back of the embezzler's employer. Section 3–405 does not include all forged indorsements. For example, in Universal Premium Acceptance Corp. v. York Bank & Trust,[7] the payee's indorsements on drafts were forged and deposited into an account named "Small Businessman's Service Corporation" albeit the drafts contained the provision "PAY AND DEPOSIT ONLY TO THE CREDIT OF: Great American Insurance Company." Unlike cases where an employee writes a check out to a fictitious individual and cashes it, the court distinguished the present case, stating that the explicit language on the drafts precluded transfer and made them non-negotiable. Declining the opportunity to expand the scope of the fictitious payee exception, the court held that 3–405 was inapplicable to non-negotiable instruments.

In 1990, the drafters concluded that the employer should bear the responsibility for the forgery of certain embezzlers—those who have "responsibility with respect to instruments," i.e., treasurers, payroll clerks, programmers of sensitive computer programs, and the like. These people are known by the employer to have the keys to the bank. In some cases they will be bonded. All employers should have procedures that encourage these people to be trustworthy and that expose them when they are not.

7. 69 F.3d 695, 28 UCC 2d 1(3d Cir. 1995).

In general, therefore, section 3–405 applies only when the embezzler has a particular status in the company. This status is defined in 3–405(a)(3):

"Responsibility" with respect to instruments means authority (i) to sign or indorse instruments on behalf of the employer, (ii) to process instruments received by the employer for bookkeeping purposes, for deposit to an account, or for other disposition, (iii) to prepare or process instruments for issue in the name of the employer, (iv) to supply information determining the names or addresses of payees of instruments to be issued in the name of the employer, (v) to control the disposition of instruments to be issued in the name of the employer, or (vi) to act otherwise with respect to instruments in a responsible capacity. "Responsibility" does not include authority that merely allows an employee to have access to instruments or blank or incomplete instrument forms that are being stored or transported or are part of incoming or outgoing mail, or similar access.

The consequences of an indorsement by such a person are described in 3–405(b):

For the purpose of determining the rights and liabilities of a person who, in good faith, pays an instrument or takes it for value or for collection, if an employer entrusted an employee with responsibility with respect to the instrument and the employee or a person acting in concert with the employee makes a fraudulent indorsement of the instrument, the indorsement is effective as the indorsement of the person to whom the instrument is payable if it is made in the name of that person. * * *

Note, however, that 3–405(b) requires that the employee be entrusted with responsibility with respect to *"the* instrument" at issue in a particular case, not instruments in general. Therefore, it would not be sufficient that an employee in the personnel department meets the requirements of 3–405(a)(3) with respect to payroll checks, if she forged the indorsement of a check from the accounting department intended for a supplier. She would not have been entrusted with responsibility with respect to the supplier's check, and section 3–405 would not apply. The drawee bank would have to assert 3–406 or possibly 4–406 against the employer in lieu of 3–405.

Section 3–405's application is illustrated by the cases in Comment 3:

Case #1. Janitor, an employee of Employer, steals a check for a very large amount payable to Employer after finding it on a desk in one of Employer's offices. Janitor forges Employer's indorsement on the check and obtains payment. Since Janitor was not entrusted with "responsibility" with respect to the check, Section 3–405 does not apply. Section 3–406 might apply to this case. The issue would be whether Employer was negligent in safeguarding the check. If not, Employer could assert that the indorsement was forged and bring an action for conversion against the depositary or payor bank under Section 3–420.

* * *

Case #3. The duties of Employee, a bookkeeper, include posting the amounts of checks payable to Employer to the accounts of the drawers of the checks. Employee steals a check payable to Employer which was entrusted to Employee and forges Employer's indorsement. The check is deposited by Employee to an account in Depositary Bank which Employee opened in the same name as Employer, and the check is honored by the drawee bank. The indorsement is effective as Employer's indorsement because Employee's duties include processing checks for bookkeeping purposes. Thus, Employee is entrusted with "responsibility" with respect to the check. Neither Depositary Bank nor the drawee bank is liable to Employer for conversion of the check. The same result follows if Employee deposited the check in the account in Depositary Bank without indorsement. Section 4–205(a). Under subsection (c) deposit in a depositary bank in an account in a name substantially similar to that of Employer is the equivalent of an indorsement in the name of Employer.

* * *

Case #5. The computer that controls Employer's check-writing machine was programmed to cause a check to be issued to Supplier Co. to which money was owed by Employer. The address of Supplier Co. was included in the information in the computer. Employee is an accounts payable clerk whose duties include entering information into the computer. Employee fraudulently changed the address of Supplier Co. in the computer data bank to an address of Employee. The check was subsequently produced by the check-writing machine and mailed to the address that Employee had entered into the computer. Employee obtained possession of the check, indorsed it in the name of Supplier Co., and deposited it to an account in Depositary Bank which Employee opened in the name "Supplier Co." The check was honored by the drawee bank. The indorsement is effective under Section 3–405(b) because Employee's duties allowed Employee to supply information determining the address of the payee of the check. An employee that is entrusted with duties that enable the employee to determine the address to which a check is to be sent controls the disposition of the check and facilitates forgery of the indorsement. The employer is held responsible. The drawee may debit the account of Employer for the amount of the check. There is no breach of warranty by Depositary Bank under Section 3–417(a)(1) or 4–208(a)(1).

The reference to computers requires one to think beyond the conventional payroll clerk.[8] As we have indicated above, the definition in section 3–405(a)(3) of the "person with responsibility" for instruments is so broad that it is likely to include all major league and most minor league embezzlers. The janitor or the mail clerk may score occasionally, but they are unlikely to have continuing access both to checks and the records needed to cover their tracks in the way most successful embezzlers do. In most long-term embezzlements, many of the losses will be covered by section 3–404 and so allocated to the employer; in those cases most losses from forgeries on third party checks will also be allocated to the employer under section 3–405. We doubt that there will be many cases where the employer eats the padded payroll losses under 3–404, but escapes responsibility for the forged indorsement of third party checks under 3–405.

Note, too, that the indorsement under section 3–405 need not be by the employee, but can be by a "person acting in concert." The fact that a husband co-conspirator signs the checks stolen by his wife, the employee, will not relieve the employer from liability.

g. Substantially Similar Indorsement; Deposit Accounts in Similar Names

Section 3–404 and 3–405 earn an expanded universe of covered indorsements in 1990; each also now deals with "same or similar name" accounts.[9] Contrary to some cases decided prior to 1990, these sections hold that an indorsement which is "in a name substantially similar" is an indorsement covered by these sections. Likewise the law of 3–404 and 3–405 applies to cases where there is no indorsement, but merely an account opened in a name similar to that of the named payee—whether that name is the name of the employer or the name of a third party supplier.

Although cases involving an "account in the name of the payee" surely merit the same law as is applied to the padded payroll cases, how the old 3–405 dealt with such cases was not clear. We know a case where an employee of the "Girl Scout

---

8. Note that 3–110(b) recognizes that it is the intention of the person who controls the machine producing the check that is relevant in determining the applicability of 3–404(b).

9. See 3–405(c) and 3–404(c).

Council of X" opened an account in the name of "Girl Scouts of X," and signed a signature card giving herself power to draw. She stole and periodically deposited legitimate checks that came to the "Girl Scout Council of X" into her own "Girl Scouts of X" account. Eventually she withdrew the money. With the 1990 amendments, these cases will now be treated under 3–404 and 3–405 as though the embezzler had forged the Girl Scouts' name or had the checks drawn on the employer's account.

h. *Negligence Defense in 3–404 and 3–405 Cases*

Although 3–406 and 4–406 have always had a provision that diminished (even to zero) a bank's rights if it was negligent, that was not true of 3–405 until 1990. In the absence of a stated contributory negligence standard in former 3–405 (and despite our arguments to the contrary), courts mostly held that the depositary bank's negligence was not relevant in a case under former 3–405. This was so even though negligence contributing to the loss could easily be committed by a bank that cashed or took a padded payroll check for deposit. The 1990 revision changed that. The preclusions in 3–404 and 3–405 are both subject to a comparative negligence standard similar to that described above with respect to 3–406.

Comment 4 to section 3–405 deals with a specific type of embezzlement that has only rarely appeared in the cases. It addresses a bank's responsibility when an embezzler opens an account in a name not his or her own, for example, in the name of a corporation that the embezzler claims to represent. Some banks require proof of the existence of a corporate entity or verification of a person's identity before they will open an account in that name. Many require some proof of the authority of the one opening the account. Comment 4 deals with cases in which the prevailing standard is to investigate or at least to get some evidence from the person seeking to open the account that the principal exists and that the person opening the account is an authorized agent. If the bank fails to comply with the prevailing standard, failure to collect the necessary information may itself be held to be negligence that contributes to the loss. The drafters make this point as follows:

> [T]he depositary bank may have failed to exercise ordinary care when it allowed the employee to open an account in the name "Supplier Co.," to deposit checks payable to "Supplier Co." in that account, or to withdraw funds from that account that were proceeds of checks payable to Supplier Co. Failure to exercise ordinary care is to be determined in the context of all the facts relating to the bank's conduct with respect to the bank's collection of the check. If the trier of fact finds that there was such a failure and that the failure substantially contributed to loss, it could find the depositary bank liable to the extent the

failure contributed to the loss. The last sentence of subsection (b) can be illustrated by an example. Suppose in Case #5 that the check is not payable to an obscure "Supplier Co." but rather to a well-known national corporation. In addition, the check is for a very large amount of money. Before depositing the check, Employee opens an account in Depositary Bank in the name of the corporation and states to the person conducting the transaction for the bank that Employee is manager of a new office being opened by the corporation. Depositary Bank opens the account without requiring Employee to produce any resolutions of the corporation's board of directors or other evidence of authorization of Employee to act for the corporation. A few days later, the check is deposited, the account is credited, and the check is presented for payment. After Depositary Bank receives payment, it allows Employee to withdraw the credit by a wire transfer to an account in a bank in a foreign country. The trier of fact could find that Depositary Bank did not exercise ordinary care and that the failure to exercise ordinary care contributed to the loss suffered by Employer. The trier of fact could allow recovery by Employer from Depositary Bank for all or part of the loss suffered by Employer.[10]

Obviously, what procedures are expected of a bank in opening an account may vary from place to place, and time to time. A lawyer who is challenging a bank's practices should dig deeply into this question. In order to avoid not just fraud of the kind discussed here, but more likely other kinds of fraud, some banks are quite careful to determine the actual identity of the person opening an account. New accounts opened by unknown persons offer a variety of risks that banks will seek to minimize. For example, a bank may be fearful that an account opened with a large check will be the beginning of a kite or the commencement of a one-event theft where a large check is deposited and the funds withdrawn before the depositary bank learns that the deposited check is bad. One challenging a bank's procedures for opening new accounts should depose the person in charge of security and examine any bank manuals or internal documents that explain the questions to be asked, the information to be collected and the certificates of incorporation, board resolutions, or other indicia of bona fides to be provided on the opening of new accounts.

In summary, the 1990 amendments in sections 3–404 and 3–405 shifted some burden of embezzlement from the payor and depositary banks back to the employer. In general we applaud that outcome and find it to be a sensible reallocation of risk.

---

10. § 3–405, Comment 4.

PROBLEM

Employee, without authority to draw and using a blank check of Employer, draws a $50,000 check to the order of Ronald McDonald, indorses in that name and deposits the check. The check is paid and Employer's account is debited. Which of the following statements are accurate?

1. Depositary bank is a holder of the check despite the forged indorsement and once it has given value, a holder in due course.

   True, 3–404(b). The Section cements the judicial conclusion that this should be treated like a forged check not as a proper check bearing a forged indorsement.

2. Since Drawee took from a holder in due course, it may debit Employer's account.

   False. Unless Employer is precluded from challenging the forged drawer's signature by 3–406, the check is still not properly payable and Drawee must recredit, 4–401. (This outcome could be changed by an agreement concerning a check writing machine for example.)

3. If Drawee pays it may recover from the Depositary bank under 4–208.

   False. Since the holder is one entitled to enforce the instrument, the Depositary bank breaks no warranties as long as it does not know that the drawer's signature is forged.

4. If Drawee pays it may recover from Depositary bank under 3–404(d), if Depositary's negligence substantially contributed to the loss.

   True (we think). The text of 3–404 seems clearly to give this right, but arguably this outcome conflicts with the intent and effect of the warranties that give Drawee no recourse. (There is no claim against Employer under (d) because Employer did not take for value or pay. But Employer's negligence can be asserted through 3–406 if Drawee declines to pay.)

§ 4–5 Notice of Breach of Fiduciary Duty, Section 3–307

Sleeping quietly in Part 3 of Article 3, section 3–307 may awaken to a large role in allocating embezzlement losses. This section comes from old 3–304 and from state laws on fiduciaries' rights and responsibilities. It reads:

§ 3–307. Notice of Breach of Fiduciary Duty.

(a) In this section:

    (1) "Fiduciary" means an agent, trustee, partner, corporate officer or director, or other representative owing a fiduciary duty with respect to an instrument.

    (2) "Represented person" means the principal, beneficiary, partnership, corporation, or other person to whom the duty stated in paragraph (1) is owed.

(b) If (i) an instrument is taken from a fiduciary for payment or collection or for value, (ii) the taker has knowledge of the fiduciary status of the fiduciary, and (iii) the represented person makes a claim to the instrument or its proceeds on the basis that the transaction of the fiduciary is a breach of fiduciary duty, the following rules apply:

    (1) Notice of breach of fiduciary duty by the fiduciary is notice of the claim of the represented person.

    (2) In the case of an instrument payable to the represented person or the fiduciary as such, the taker has notice of the breach of fiduciary duty if the instrument is (i) taken in payment of or as security for a debt known by the taker to be the personal debt of the fiduciary, (ii) taken in a transaction known by the taker to be for the personal benefit of the fiduciary, or (iii) deposited to an account other than an account of the fiduciary, as such, or an account of the represented person.

    (3) If an instrument is issued by the represented person or the fiduciary as such, and made payable to the fiduciary personally, the taker does not have notice of the breach of fiduciary duty unless the taker knows of the breach of fiduciary duty.

    (4) If an instrument is issued by the represented person or the fiduciary as such, to the taker as payee, the taker has notice of the breach of fiduciary duty if the instrument is (i) taken in payment of or as security for a debt known by the taker to be the personal debt of the fiduciary, (ii) taken in a transaction known by the taker to be for the personal benefit of the fiduciary, or (iii) deposited to an account other than an account of the fiduciary, as such, or an account of the represented person.

The section applies most obviously and directly to cases where a trustee embezzles money from a trust by use of checks. Because the section applies not merely to those formally titled "trustees," but also to agents, partners, corporate officers, "or other representative[s] owing a fiduciary duty", the section reaches far beyond embezzlements from trusts. In ways that are not entirely clear to us, the section will interact with sections 3–404, 3–405 and 3–406. That interaction is particularly tangled where the embezzling person is a corporate employee.

Section 4 of the Uniform Fiduciary Act makes the taker of an instrument from a fiduciary liable "if * * * such instrument is transferred by the fiduciary in payment of or as security for a personal debt of the fiduciary to the actual knowledge of the creditor, or is transferred in any transaction known by the transferee to be for the personal benefit of the fiduciary. * * * In those circumstances the transferee is liable to the principal * * *." See also sections 5 and 6 to the same effect.

First we identify cases covered by section 3–307 and not covered by 3–404, 3–405, or 3–406; then we identify the cases that *might* be covered by 3–307 and 3–404, 3–405, or 3–406 as well.

For 3–307(b) to come into play, one must take the instrument from a fiduciary and have "knowledge of the fiduciary status of the fiduciary," and the "represented person" (i.e., the trust, corporation or other principal) must make a claim to the instrument or its proceeds. If those conditions are met, the substantive sections (b)(2), (3), and (4) may deny holder in due course status to the taker. Below we consider the probable legal consequence of that denial.

For the first case, assume that John Jones, a trustee with power to draw on the trust checking account, draws a check payable to the order of "John Jones, as trustee." Alternatively, assume that an agent authorized to draw on the account of General Appliance Corp. draws a check on the corporate account payable to the order of "John Jones, as agent of General Appliance Corp." Assume further that both the trustee and the agent in the examples intend to embezzle funds. If the embezzler in either case passes the check by indorsement to a third party, that party's right to the instrument or its proceeds may be affected by 3–307(b)(2). Because the check in each case was made payable to the order of the thief, and the thief's indorsement is not forged, neither 3–404 nor 3–405 applies.[1] If the thief uses the check to pay a personal debt or to purchase an asset known by the taker of the check to be for the thief's personal use, or if the thief deposits the check in an account of John Jones personally (as opposed to "John Jones, trustee" or "John Jones, agent of General Appliance Corp."), then the taker would be held under 3–307(b)(2) to be on notice of breach of the fiduciary duty and of the claim of the represented person. Accord-

§ 4–5

1. See § 3–405, Comment 3, Case #2.

ingly, the taker fails to be a holder in due course—at least if these or other facts also give the taker knowledge that Jones is a fiduciary.

A second case that may fall under 3–307(b)(2) but not under 3–404 or 3–405 arises when a bona fide check drawn by a third party and payable to the trust is indorsed by the trustee for deposit in the trustee's own account personally, or in payment of a personal debt, or for use in a transaction known by the taker to be for the personal benefit of the trustee. Here too the taker would be on notice of the claim of the represented person and would fail to qualify as a holder in due course. This case would probably fall outside of section 3–405 for two reasons. First, if the trustee has authority to indorse as well as to sign checks of the trust, the trustee's signature would not constitute a fraudulent indorsement under 3–405(a)(2). Second, the trustee might be regarded as only a "trustee" and therefore not an "employee" as that term is defined in 3–405(a)(1). If the trustee is not an employee, the transaction is outside 3–405 for that reason as well.

Note that if this latter case arises in the corporate context (the payee is not a trust but is General Appliance Corp.), then 3–405 may apply as well as 3–307. In this case there will be an indorsement by an "employee." If the employee has authority to draw but no authority to indorse, then the employee's indorsement in the corporate name would itself be a fraudulent indorsement under 3–405(a)(2). Because there would be a fraudulent indorsement by an "employee," the fraud would fall within 3–405, as well as 3–307(b)(2).

To see the difficulties this could cause in practice, examine the case of Gresham State Bank v. O & K Construction Co.[2] O & K employed Francis McKenna as an office manager and bookkeeper. McKenna had the authority to deposit checks in the company's bank account, but no authority to indorse checks other than for deposit. McKenna received checks payable to the construction company. He indorsed them by stamping the company's name on the back, followed by his signature with the designation "Office Manager." McKenna then took the checks to the local Zimmerman Twelve Mile Store and cashed them. Zimmerman's employees knew McKenna was the office manager of O & K, and relied on that fact in cashing the checks for him. O & K sued the drawee banks in conversion, who in turn sued upstream to Zimmerman.

The 1962 court relied on the old section 3–406 and held that although O & K was negligent in its supervision of McKenna, it was not precluded from asserting McKenna's lack of authority to in-

2. 231 Or. 106, 370 P.2d 726, 1 UCC 276 (1962), reh'g denied, 231 Or. 106, 372 P.2d 187 (1962).

dorse against Zimmerman because Zimmerman had failed to act in accordance with reasonable commercial standards.

But see the two very different results the case could have today. If O & K claims the checks were not properly payable and sues in conversion, Zimmerman can respond that McKenna's indorsement in the company name is a fraudulent indorsement under 3–405(a)(2) and is effective by virtue of 3–405(b). O & K can respond that Zimmerman failed to exercise ordinary care, and the loss would be shared by the two according to their respective negligence.

But what if O & K brings suit under the auspices of 3–307?[3] O & K can assert that Zimmerman is subject to 3–307(b)(2), for it knew McKenna was a fiduciary and by cashing checks payable to O & K for him, Zimmerman was on notice of a breach of fiduciary duty. Now Zimmerman cannot respond with an assertion of O & K's negligence, because 3–307 contains no comparative negligence provision similar to 3–405(b). Zimmerman cannot assert O & K's negligence under 3–406 either, because that section only deals with negligence that contributes to an alteration or a forged indorsement. McKenna's indorsement was unauthorized, but it was not forged. It appears Zimmerman must bear the entire loss.

Should plaintiffs like O & K be allowed to make such an end run around 3–405(b)'s contemplated comparative negligence provision? It won't take long for smart plaintiff's attorneys to realize that 3–307 is the better route and 3–405's comparative negligence scheme will be nullified in this situation. Perhaps the solution is to include a comparative negligence provision in 3–307, if for no other reason than consistency with the scheme set up in 3–405 and 3–406.

In any case it seems doubtful to us that cases like *O & K* where an embezzler arguably has authority to deposit should be removed from the reach of 3–404, 3–405, and 3–406. If the drafters intended to do so (as suggested by Case 4 in Comment 3 to section 3–405), we believe they have made a mistake. As a practical matter, everybody at General Motors down to the lowest messenger has authority to put a check payable to General Motors into a General Motors bank account. Its bank will accept that check without indorsement and *a fortiori* will accept it with the indorsement of the lowest messenger to the highest executive. To attempt then to distinguish between cases by removing those with "authority to deposit" from 3–404 through 3–406 and by including those where there is no such authority within the allocation scheme in 3–404 through 3–406 makes no sense to us. In real life the acts of the

3. See *infra* for a discussion of what types of suits are available to a payee or represented party under 3–307.

embezzler with authority to deposit and of the embezzler without authority to deposit are the same and the allocation of loss should be the same. If the comparative negligence theories apply to the former case, they should apply to the latter. Accordingly, in our view, it is a mistake to transfer some undetermined number of these cases into 3–307 and there to have the loss allocated apparently without regard to comparative negligence and by a scheme that is not clear from 3–307 or other provisions of Article 3.

A third case covered only by 3–307 and not by 3–404, 3–405 or 3–406 arises when the embezzling trustee or agent with authority to draw makes a check payable to the trustee or agent personally. Because this check is made payable to the "fiduciary personally" it is covered by (b)(3), not by (b)(2) (where it would have to be payable to the represented person or "fiduciary as such"). This case is not covered by 3–404 or 3–405 because John Jones is the payee, signs his own name and does not forge the indorsement.[4]

Here section 3–307(b)(3) will normally protect the taker unless the taker is in cahoots with the embezzling fiduciary. That is fair because the instrument itself gives no real indication to the taker that it is part of a fraudulent transaction. For example, if a trustee were to be paid by the trust for his services, one would expect him to receive a trust check payable to his order personally, not "as trustee." Likewise, an employee of General Appliance Corp. might be expected to receive a check payable to his order for services rendered. This case is unlike those covered by 3–307(b)(2), for here the check simply shows the payee to be Jones "personally" and not the fiduciary "as trustee" or "as agent".

A fourth case covered by 3–307(b) and not covered by any of the other sections is a common and ancient fraud. This occurs when the embezzler causes a trust or corporate employer to draw a check payable to the order of a bank (or other "taker"). The thief then takes the check to the bank and causes the bank to deposit it in his own personal account and to give him a cashier's check or cash. This fraud often works because tellers frequently confuse this transaction with the legitimate transaction in which a depositor withdraws his or her own funds from the bank by drawing a check to the order of the bank. The teller is unlikely to distinguish

---

4. § 3–405, Comment 3, Case #2 states:

X is Treasurer of Corporation and is authorized to write checks on behalf of Corporation by signing X's name as Treasurer. X draws a check in the name of Corporation and signs X's name as Treasurer. The check is made payable to X. X then indorses the check and obtains payment. Assume that Corporation did not owe any money to X and did not

authorize X to write the check. Although the writing of the check was not authorized, Corporation is bound as drawer of the check because X had authority to sign checks on behalf of Corporation. This result follows from agency law and Section 3–402(a). Section 3–405 does not apply in this case because there is no forged indorsement. X was payee of the check so the indorsement is valid. Section 3–110(a).

between the case in which the person on the other side of the counter is the owner of the account and the case discussed here where that person is not the owner but merely an agent who has no right to this money. In theory the teller should respond to the embezzler: "Why should I give you this money? By this draft *your* employer has ordered me to pay $50,000 to *my* employer, the bank. Why should the money go into your account? Or why a cashier's check to your order?" Where the teller or other person at the bank is bamboozled and deposits the amount into the personal account of the trustee or agent, section 3–307(b)(4) states that the bank or other taker is held to be on notice and presumably therefore takes subject to the claim of the represented party.[5]

Consider now three analogous cases where 3–404, 3–405 or 3–406 come in to play and where 3–307(b) may or may not be applicable. Assume first that John Jones, an embezzling employee or trustee, makes a check payable to the order of Charles de Gaulle, a fictitious payee. Jones indorses de Gaulle's name and his own and deposits it in his personal account. As we have indicated above, this case will be covered by 3–404. Is it also covered by 3–307? We think not. Subsection (b)(2) by definition applies only to checks payable to the represented person or the fiduciary as such—not to a fictitious payee. Subsection (b)(3) applies only to checks payable to "the fiduciary personally" and (b)(4) deals only with checks payable to "the taker as payee." Even if the fraud is committed by a trustee, this fraud is entirely outside of 3–307.

But should these facts put the bank on notice of a breach of fiduciary duty? Isn't it unlikely that a corporation or trust would draw a check to a third party, who would turn around and negotiate the check back to a fiduciary of that corporation or trust? It seems to us that such a situation is at least as suspicious as the case where the fiduciary deposits a check made out to the represented person into his own account.

To see the uncertain borders between 3–307 and 3–404 or 3–405, compare a second and third case. Assume for the purpose of the two following hypotheticals that Jones has authority to draw but not to indorse on behalf of the trust or corporation. In one, John Jones as agent for General Appliance Corp. makes a check payable to the order of General Appliance Corp., forges its indorsement and receives the proceeds. Alternatively assume that John Jones as trustee makes the check payable to the "trust," forges the trust's indorsement and gets the funds. Subsection 3–307(b)(2) is potentially applicable to both of these cases because in each of them the instrument is made payable to "the represented person." If the

5. This may depend on the cause of action asserted by the defrauded party. See the discussion of this issue, *infra*, in the subsection entitled "Legal Consequence of Application of Section 3–307."

embezzler formed the intent to steal the check before it was written, section 3–404 will apply to both cases.[6] If, on the other hand, the embezzler formed the intention to steal the checks only after they had been properly written, then 3–405 might apply. Section 3–406 might apply to either.

If John Jones is a corporate employee "with responsibility with respect to the instrument," then section 3–405 would clearly apply. If he is merely a trustee and not "an employee," 3–405 would not apply because the embezzler would not have the right status. To summarize, if the trustee or agent makes a check payable to the order of the represented person (the corporation or the trust) and steals the money by fraudulent indorsement, the case will potentially be covered by section 3–307, possibly by 3–404 and conceivably by 3–405. Below we discuss the probable legal consequences of the violation of 3–307. Arguably it sidesteps all of the comparative negligence rules of 3–404, 3–405 and 3–406 and pushes the loss downstream on to the banks.

All of this is complicated and we appreciate the difficulty one might have in swallowing it in one bite. To assist, we make all of the same points about coverage in a chart below.

| Drawer | Payee | Indorsement | | Applicable |
		Name	Status	Sections
John Jones as trustee	John Jones as trustee	"Jones"	Not forged	3–307(b)(2)
John Jones as agent of GAC	John Jones as agent of GAC	"Jones"	Not forged	3–307(b)(2)
Third party	Trust	"Trust"	Forged	3–307(b)(2) & 3–405 only if trustee is "employee" within meaning of 3–405; 3–406
Third party	GAC	"GAC"	Forged	3–307(b)(2); 3–405; 3–406
Jones as trustee or agent	Jones	"Jones"	Not forged	3–307(b)(3)
Jones as trustee or agent	Bank	"Bank"	Not forged	3–307(b)(4)
Jones as trustee or agent	Charles de Gaulle		Forged	3–404; 3–405; 3–406
Jones as agent	GAC	"GAC"	Forged	3–307(b)(2);

6. § 3–404(b)(ii).

| Drawer | Payee | Indorsement | | Applicable |
		Name	Status	Sections
of GAC				3–404; 3–405; 3–406
Jones as trustee	Trust	"Trust"	Forged	3–307(b)(2); 3–404; possible but unlikely: 3–405; 3–406
Third party	GAC	"GAC"	Unauthorized but not forged	3–307(b)(2)

a. Requirements for Satisfaction of Section 3–307

Because they are important and complicated, we reiterate the requirements for coverage under section 3–307. For 3–307(b) to apply, the taker of the instrument must have two kinds of knowledge. First, under the preamble in (b), the taker must know of the fiduciary status of the transferor. Second, under the various subsections of 3–307(b), the taker must either know facts that put it on notice of the embezzler's theft or have knowledge of that misappropriation. Put another way: the taker must know (1) that the person is a fiduciary and (2) that the fiduciary is doing a bad thing. In addition, of course, the instrument must be taken from the fiduciary, the represented person must make a claim against the taker and the transaction must fall within the particular coverage of 3–307(b)(2), (3), or (4). It is important to scrutinize the transaction carefully because some transactions that are generically similar are treated in different subsections or, in some cases, omitted entirely from 3–307.

Comment 2 to 3–307 elaborates on the requirement of knowledge of fiduciary status:

> Section 3–307(b) applies only if the person dealing with the fiduciary "has knowledge of the fiduciary status of the fiduciary." Notice which does not amount to knowledge is not enough to cause Section 3–307 to apply. "Knowledge" is defined in Section 1–201(25). In most cases, the "taker" referred to in Section 3–307 will be a bank or other organization. Knowledge of an organization is determined by the rules stated in Section 1–201(27). In many cases, the individual who receives and processes an instrument on behalf of the organization that is the taker of the instrument "for payment or collection or for value" is a clerk who has no knowledge of any fiduciary status of the person from whom the instrument is received. In such cases, Section 3–307 doesn't apply because, under Section 1–207(27), knowledge of the organization is determined by the

knowledge of the "individual conducting that transaction," i.e., the clerk who receives and processes the instrument. Furthermore, paragraphs (2) and (4) each require that the person acting for the organization have knowledge of facts that indicate a breach of fiduciary duty. In the case of an instrument taken for deposit to an account, the knowledge is found in the fact that the deposit is made to an account other than that of the represented person or a fiduciary account for benefit of that person. In other cases the person acting for the organization must know that the instrument is taken in payment or as security for a personal debt of the fiduciary or for the personal benefit of the fiduciary. For example, if the instrument is being used to buy goods or services, the person acting for the organization must know that the goods or services are for the personal benefit of the fiduciary. The requirement that the taker have knowledge rather than notice is meant to limit Section 3–307 to relatively uncommon cases in which the person who deals with the fiduciary knows all the relevant facts: the fiduciary status and that the proceeds of the instrument are being used for the personal debt or benefit of the fiduciary or are being paid to an account that is not an account of the represented person or of the fiduciary, as such. Mere notice of these facts is not enough to put the taker on notice of the breach of fiduciary duty and does not give rise to any duty of investigation by the taker.

Presumably there are easy cases, but we are unlikely to see those in the courts. For example, the trustee of a trust might come to the teller's window with a $50,000 check drawn on the trust payable to the order of the trust, indorse it, and ask for cash. A brazen thief might brag to the teller that he or she intends to use the cash to buy a new pleasure boat or for a trip to Atlantic City for a little gambling.

Most likely the fact that the check is drawn by the trustee on an account clearly marked on the face of the check as a trust account gives the teller "knowledge" of the fiduciary status of the fiduciary. But to comply with 3–307(b) the teller must also have knowledge that the transaction is "for the personal benefit of the fiduciary" and for that it will be necessary that the money either be put in the trustee's personal account and thus qualify under 3–307(b)(2)(iii), be used to pay a personal debt of the trustee, 3–307(b)(2)(i), or be accompanied by the kind of comment about Atlantic City or the pleasure boat that we have described above. Almost any deviation from that routine will make it impossible to prove the taker's knowledge of the trustee's malevolent intentions.

What if the embezzler did not work for a trust, but was an employee of General Appliance Corp., drew a check payable to

General Appliance Corp., forged an indorsement (no authority to indorse) and deposited that check in his or her own account by putting it in a night depositary together with a deposit slip? The conditions of 3–307(b)(2)(iii) have been met because the money has been deposited in an account "other than an account of the fiduciary, as such, or an account of the represented person." But does the taker, a depositary bank, "have knowledge of fiduciary status of the fiduciary"? Assume that the only person who sees the check is a machine operator who MICR encodes the dollar amount at the bottom right hand corner and causes that amount to be deposited in the account identified by number on the deposit slip. Is the knowledge of that person enough? If it is not, the conditions in the preamble to 3–307(b) have not been met and the terms of 3–307(b)(2)(iii) (which have been met) will never come into play. However, if we conclude that any teller who would have seen this instrument is considered to have the knowledge that the instrument reveals (i.e., knowledge that Jones is an agent for General Appliance), then it seems to us, the bank should be considered to have knowledge when the check passes through the machine operator's hands during the night in the night depositary case. Having said that, we are certain that many cases await the courts on the question when the taker does "have knowledge."

b. *Legal Consequence of Application of Section 3–307*

Section 3–307 is designed to interact with 3–302 and 3–306. That is to say, one who has the knowledge specified in 3–307(b) has notice of a "claim," and fails to be a holder in due course (3–302). Such a person will then be "subject to" that and other "claims" (3–306).

Section 3–307 seems to be inviting the owner of the account (the corporate employer or trust) or the owner of valid third party checks to sue in conversion. Typically a conversion suit is the way one would pursue a "possessory or property claim" to which the taker is "subject." Under 3–420, when an embezzler steals a third party check made payable to the order of the corporation or the trust, there is clearly a conversion cause of action.

But when an embezzler draws on the account of a corporation or trust, there is a difficulty. Section 3–420 states that an action for conversion of an instrument may not be brought by "the issuer or acceptor of the instrument. * * * " Comments to 3–420 tell us that the drafters were adopting the position of the *Stone and Webster* case.[7] The section as amended in 1990 denies the drawer a conversion cause of action where the drawer's signature has been forged.

---

7. Stone & Webster Eng'r Corp. v. First Nat. Bank & Trust Co., 345 Mass. 1, 184 N.E.2d 358, 1 UCC 195 (1962).

Would our hypothetical trust and corporation then be foreclosed from pursuing a conversion suit under 3–420 because they are the "issuers"? We hope not. The statute plainly says that drawers (issuers) have no conversion cause of action, perhaps there is still room for some action where embezzlement has occurred not as a result of a forged drawer's signature, but as a result of theft conducted by one with authority to draw on the account. If the bank is not guilty of conversion in these cases, the corporation or trust drawer will have to assert an affirmative cause of action in negligence (or breach of fiduciary duty?). In some cases the represented person could demand a recredit under 4–401 because the instrument would not be "properly payable." The explicit reference to section 3–306 in the comments of section 3–307, and the characterization in the comments of the represented person's interest as a "claim" (as opposed to a "defense") all suggest that the drafters conceived of the plaintiff as asserting a property interest, i.e., a conversion claim.

In Travelers Casualty and Surety Co. v. Northwestern Mutual Life Insurance,[8] the Court decided that the insurer for the embezzler's employer cannot recover from Merrill Lynch because the statute of limitations has passed. In dictum the court notes that Travelers "might well have a good claim" under section 3–307. However, because the statement is merely dictum and because the opinion contains no discussion of the issues raised above about the confusion over the proper cause of action, the case is not strong authority for the proposition that there is a cause of action buried somewhere in section 3–307. As the only case that has ever come close to this issue, and because it was decided by Judge Posner, it deserves some consideration.

Whether the cause of action is considered to be in conversion, common law negligence, or something else might make a difference. First, a suit under 3–420 in conversion would be subject to the three-year statute of limitation in section 3–118. Second, the recovery in the conversion cause of action, but not in the negligence cause of action, would be limited by 3–420(b). Third, the array of affirmative defenses—depending upon the corporation's own negligence and liability under 3–404, 3–405, and 3–406—might be different in a conversion cause of action than in a common law negligence cause of action. Moreover, even if the cause of action is in conversion, the cause of action contemplated in 3–307 may not depend upon the presence of an unauthorized signature and may, as we suggest below, be completely untouched by sections 3–404, 3–405, and 3–406.

Finally, one must also consider the possibility of the payor bank as the defendant. In this case, the cause of action by the

---

8.   480 F.3d 499, 62 UCC2d 500 (7th Cir. 2007).

corporation or trust drawer would be under 4–401—"the check is not properly payable." But is this a "claim of a property or possessory right in the instrument or its proceeds"? A demand to recredit an account certainly seems to be a claim of a possessory right in the proceeds. If the depositary bank was not a holder in due course the payor could not use 4–407 to hide behind the depositary bank's skirts.

c. *Which Sections Govern?*

As we discussed, in at least two of the hypothetical cases described above, section 3–307(b) could apply as well as 3–404, 3–405, 3–406, or some combination of these. First, when an embezzler authorized to draw on a corporate account draws a check payable to the order of the corporation and passes that check, the case may fit within 3–307(b)(2) and will almost certainly fit within 3–404. Second, when a person responsible for handling the checks (but with no authority to indorse) steals a third party's check payable to the order of a corporation, section 3–307(b)(2) as well as 3–405 and 3–406 will apply.

In sections 4–3 and 4–4 *supra*, we deal at length with liability under 3–404, 3–405 and 3–406. Under the new comparative negligence standards, those cases end with an apportionment of the comparative fault of the parties. Do those rules also apply to 3–307(b) cases?

Initially we thought that sections 3–404 through 3–406 should be stretched to reach 3–307 cases and that these cases too should be included within the comparative negligence regime. Because 3–307 merely denies holder in due course status to the taker and does not confer an affirmative cause of action, it would not be hard to pull 3–404, 3–405, and 3–406 into the action. In fact, many of the cases in which these sections are involved deal with conversion and fall under 3–420.

On reflection we are doubtful about the application of the comparative negligence rules from sections 3–404 et seq. to a conversion cause of action based upon the behavior described in 3–307. Note first that sections 3–404, 3–405, and 3–406 deal almost exclusively with forged signatures. Their principal effect is to preclude one party—often the owner of the account or check—from proving the forgery of a signature. Yet in many of the cases contemplated in section 3–307 there will be no forged signature or alteration. As we have illustrated above, 3–307(b) can be violated in many ways by a trustee or corporate employee with some authority to sign (so no forgery), or who signs only his own name and commits no forgery but makes an "unauthorized" signature. This is particularly true of cases falling under 3–307(b)(3) and (b)(4).

If one concludes that a conversion cause of action lies in any case in which the terms of section 3–307(b) have been met and that that cause of action is not dependent upon proof of a forged drawer's signature or forged indorsement or alteration, then the use of 3–404 through 3–406 to validate a signature that happens to be forged would be no defense because there might be no forgery. To put it another way, the depositary bank or other taker has committed conversion (presumably common law conversion invited into the Code by 3–420) even in circumstances in which the owner of the deposit may be precluded from showing lack of authority of one of the drawers or indorsers. If one comes to that conclusion, the use of sections 3–404 through 3–406 will protect the bank or other taker from liability on one conversion theory (payment or taking over a forged indorsement), but not necessarily on another (payment or taking with knowledge of fiduciary violation).

To understand this, return now to the case in which the embezzler, with authority to draw, draws a check payable to the order of the corporation, forges the corporate indorsement (he or she has no authority to indorse) and passes the check to a depositary bank. The corporate owner of the account upon discovery of the embezzlement sues the depositary and drawee banks in conversion. Those banks defend on the ground that the forged indorsement is "effective" under 3–404(b)(2) and therefore they have no liability under 3–420 or 4–401 for taking or paying a check bearing a forged indorsement. The owner of the account then responds that his or her conversion cause of action does not depend upon the presence of a forged indorsement, but that, as invited by 3–420, he or she is using the "law applicable to conversion of personal property" in the common law and that this claim to the instrument is implicitly recognized by 3–307(b). The owner of the account might strengthen this case by noting that he or she has carried the substantial burden by proving the conditions required under 3–307(b), has shown not only that the person who received payment was known to be a fiduciary by the taker, but also that the taker made the money available to the fiduciary personally by putting it in his or her account or otherwise in a transaction known to be for the embezzler's personal use. Having met such a high standard of proof and having proved such substantial fault on the part of the bank—so the argument goes—the bank (taker) should have liability and should be foreclosed from passing any part of it back on a comparative negligence standard. Do you now see how this line of analysis takes the case completely away from sections 3–404, 3–405, and 3–406? Of course, the depositary bank might rummage around in the common law of the state to find a negligence counterclaim of some sort.

Ultimately we are uneasy about all of this. As we have indicated elsewhere, we believe that most embezzlement losses should fall on the corporate employer and not on the banks downstream. In accordance with that policy judgment, our initial inclination was to stretch sections 3–404, 3–405, and 3–406 to cover most of the cases covered by 3–307. However, the policy argument of the account owner to the effect that "I have proved that the bank has done a lot of stupid things and so should have liability," together with the technical arguments made above, leave us uncertain. While we think courts should be hesitant to allow wholesale migration of embezzlement cases from 3–405 and 3–406, we are ultimately sympathetic to the argument that cases clearly covered by 3–307(b) do not depend upon proof of forgery or alteration and therefore cannot be defeated by preclusion (validation of forged signatures) under 3–404 et seq. Whether counterclaims in negligence can and should be found in the common law of the state to put part of the loss on the corporate employers of embezzlers is another question. We leave that to the courts.

This confusion all results from the omission in 3–307 of a comparative negligence provision similar to that found in 3–404, 3–405, 3–406 and 4–406. Given that the drafters' intent in substituting comparative negligence for the old contributory negligence scheme was more accurately to reflect the reality that usually several parties' fault contributes to embezzlement, why didn't the drafters choose to recognize that same truism in the case of a fiduciary's breach of duty? The negligence of an employer in entrusting an embezzling employee with responsibility with respect to checks will often be similar to the level of negligence of a represented party in supervising a fiduciary that ultimately breaches his duty. In the former case, 3–405 provides that the employer must bear the portion of the loss that is commensurate with its negligence. Yet in the latter case, for all of its similar negligence, 3–307 allows the represented party to escape liability for its failure to keep a tight rein on its fiduciary.

d. Drawee Liability for Section 3–307 Violations

Above we have described our difficulty in determining the cause of action that the drafters intended to give to the "represented person" whose account has been depleted in a way that offends section 3–307(b). If one agrees with the position we have taken there, namely that there is a conversion cause of action, that cause of action should lie against the "taker" (often a depositary bank). But what of the drawee? The data on the offending checks might not alert even the most diligent drawee that the funds had been put into the hands of an embezzler. For example, if a check were deposited at the depositary bank without indorsement of the thief and payable to the order of the trust or represented corporation, the payor would not necessarily know where the money came to rest.

Assume the check is signed by an authorized drawer and made payable to the order of depositary bank, but because it is part of an intricate theft, there are neither forged indorsements nor unauthorized drawer's signatures on the check. It seems to us that such checks are properly payable and in paying them the drawee does not commit conversion. On the other hand, sometimes the embezzler will have forged the indorsement of the represented person; if the owner of the account is not precluded from challenging that indorsement by 3–404, 3–405 or 3–406, such checks are not properly payable and the drawee bank is obliged to recredit the drawer's account. In other cases the signature will be unauthorized but not forged, and so not properly payable (We think).

We conclude therefore that the drawee will have liability either in conversion under 3–420 or in contract under 4–401 in some but not all of these cases. If courts conclude that the cause of action available for 3–307 is common law negligence, the range of cases in which the drawee could be found liable would be even smaller, for, by hypothesis, even if certain checks are not properly payable, the payor bank would not be on notice and could not be said to be negligent in making payment.

e. Drawee Versus Depositary Bank, Warranty and Restitution

Assuming *arguendo* that the drawee sometimes has liability to the represented person in conversion or under section 4–401, does the drawee also have a warranty cause of action back upstream against the depositary bank under 4–208(a)? That subsection says:

> If an unaccepted draft is presented to the drawee for payment or acceptance and the drawee pays or accepts the draft, (i) the person obtaining payment or acceptance, at the time of presentment, and (ii) a previous transferor of the draft, at the time of transfer, warrant to the drawee that pays or accepts the draft in good faith that:
>
> > (1) the warrantor is, or was, at the time the warrantor transferred the draft, a person entitled to enforce the draft or authorized to obtain payment or acceptance of the draft on behalf of a person entitled to enforce the draft;
> >
> > (2) the draft has not been altered; and
> >
> > (3) the warrantor has no knowledge that the signature of the purported drawer of the draft is unauthorized.

Neither 4–208(a)(2) nor 4–208(a)(3) has been violated because the draft has not been altered and the *signature* of the drawer is authorized (even though used in an unauthorized transaction).

Has the depository bank violated its warranty in 4–208(a)(1) that it is "a person entitled to enforce the draft or authorized to obtain payment or acceptance of the draft on behalf of a person entitled to enforce the draft"? We are uncertain. Section 3–301 defines a "person entitled to enforce" as the holder of an instrument or a non-holder who has the rights of the holder. In some of the cases we pose (e.g., where the instrument is drawn directly to the order of the depository bank), the bank will clearly be a holder. Yet if the signature is unauthorized and that is known to the depository bank, it will not be a holder in due course. Arguably it is therefore not entitled to enforce. In other cases, the embezzler will have authority to indorse the check payable to the order of trustee, ("John Jones, as trustee"), and thus will have made the taker a holder. The 4–208(a)(1) warranties will not have been broken in some of the cases and will probably have been broken in others.[9]

When all else fails, a drawee bank that has paid but has no warranty cause of action can turn to restitution. The drawee bank could argue that it paid such a check in the mistaken belief that the transaction was authorized when it was not. The depository bank will likely counter that it is not a proper defendant in restitution under 3–418(c) because it took the instrument in good faith and for value. But the depository bank's knowledge of the fiduciary status and of breach of the fiduciary duty deprives it of good faith. One not in good faith cannot claim the protection of 3–418(c).

To us the trip upstream from the drawee to the depository bank or other "taker" can best be traveled along the restitution tributary, but we foresee trouble whether one goes by restitution or by warranty. On one thing we are unequivocal. In almost all of these cases the loss should rightfully fall on the one who took the instrument from the thief, usually the depository bank (but possibly a liquor store or other "taker"), or on the corporate drawer (employer) and not on the drawee. Recall that it is the depository bank or other taker who actually confronts the embezzler, who has "knowledge" and who should act on that knowledge. Even in circumstances where it would be perfectly obvious to anyone with a very small brain at the depository bank that theft was happening, that fact may be completely obscured from a drawee bank who sees

---

9. There is a possibility that the warranty in subsection 4–205(2) will have been violated in the case in which there is no indorsement, but the money is put into the trustee's account, not in the "account of the customer." See 4– 205(2): "the depository bank warrants to collecting banks, the payor bank or other payor, and the drawer that the amount of the item was paid to the customer or deposited to the customer's account."

only the check itself and who normally views the check exclusively through the medium of a machine.

PROBLEM

Office manager (Leo) has President, an authorized signer, sign checks prepared by Leo to the order of Employer's bank (Bank). On the memo line of each check Leo puts his personal account number, 88887. When these checks are deposited in the night depository without any instructions, Bank employees, not knowing what else to do, put the funds in account number 88887. After several years and several millions, Employer discovers the embezzlement and demands that Bank recredit its account. Contending that the funds were properly payable and that it was without notice of any problem, Bank refuses.

1. Employer sues Bank for conversion and for breach of fiduciary duty. Employer wins, 3–307. Bank has notice of breach of fiduciary duty under 3–307(b)(4) since it knew that Leo was the agent of Employer and knew that 88887 was Leo's account. Because 3–420 says that an issuer may not sue in conversion, the court may have some trouble finding a cause of action, but if the state has the Uniform Fiduciaries Act, that should do and a court might even interpret the 3–420 limit to be inapplicable here.

2. Bank counters with 3–406 and 4–406 and contends that Employer's manifest negligence should cause it to bear the lion's share of the liability. Bank loses. There is no "alteration" or "forgery" nor any "unauthorized signature" on the checks thus no risk sharing under either 3–406 or 4–406.

---

§ 4–6   Customer's Duty to Discover and Report Unauthorized Signature or Alteration, Section 4–406

Like the other negligence sections, section 4–406 now bears a comparative negligence rather than a contributory negligence standard. The basic obligation is stated in 4–406(c).

In its second sentence ("The statement of account provides sufficient information if the item is described by item number, amount, and date of payment."), section 4–406(a) facilitates the truncation of checks. It is now common in credit unions for the depositor to receive merely a listing of monthly checks without identification of the payee by name and with identification of individual checks only by item number, amount, and date of payment. If the depositor has maintained a decent ledger of checks drawn during the month, this limited information will be enough to identify most unauthorized payments. Presumably the banks favored the inclusion of the quoted statement from 4–406(a) to insure that a court would not find them to have violated some unstated obligation by failing to return checks to the depositor, or by not giving a more detailed statement of account.

Section 4–406(b) obliges the person retaining the checks to maintain either the checks themselves or the capacity to make copies available for seven years after receipt of the items. Presumably this section cannot be waived in the normal deposit agreement.

In certain places, section 4–406 refers to "an unauthorized signature" and could therefore be interpreted to apply to forged indorsements as well as to alterations or forgeries of a customer's signature. However, by adding the modifier "the customer's" unauthorized signature, 4–406(d)(2) makes it clear that a depositor's claim because of payment over a forged indorsement—as opposed to a forged drawer's signature—is not cut off for failure to complain. Put another way, a depositor's examination of his or her statement is to discover forged checks, not forged indorsements on valid checks. Another change from the pre–1990 Code is that the fourteen day reasonable period in 4–406(d)(2) has now been extended to a time not exceeding 30 days.

Subsection 4–406(f) provides a one-year limit on the customer's right to the recredit of a debit arising from the customer's unauthorized signature or an alteration. It requires a customer to notify banks of any unauthorized signature or alteration within one year of receiving a statement; otherwise the claim is precluded, even when plaintiff would have an otherwise valid common law claim. The customer must give the bank clear notice of unauthorized signatures. In cases involving multiple items over a period of time, most courts treat each item as a separate transaction with a separate one-year limit. There is some disagreement among the courts about whether the limit applies in cases where the bank acted in bad faith and even (despite the language of 406(f)) in cases where the bank did not act with ordinary care. Courts have not limited 4–406(f) to payor banks, but have applied it to other institutions as well. The one-year time limit can be altered by agreement between the parties.

Section 4–111 imposes a general three-year statute of limitation, which will probably create a three-year limitation on discovering and reporting unauthorized indorsements. Section 4–406 formerly had an explicit three-year limitation on reporting such indorsements, but the drafters deleted it in 1990. Because of new 4–111, the omission may not be significant. We say "probably" because the three-year limitation period under 4–111 runs from the time of "accrual" of the cause of action whereas the three year period under former 4–406(4) ran from the time the items or statements were "made available" to the depositor. If (contrary to our inclination) courts find that the cause of action did not "accrue" until a customer discovered or should have discovered the embezzlement, the clock might have started to tick well after the statement was made available to customer.

Note that the underlying cause of action against the bank—where 4–406 becomes relevant—arises under 4–401. Essentially the depositor argues that an item was not properly payable and that the bank has a contractual or statutory obligation to recredit the account. Even so, the question remains under 4–401 whether three years commences to run when the offending item was improperly charged to the account by the bank or when the depositor discovered or should have discovered that it was improperly charged to the account. Comment 5 to 4–406 suggests that the three-year statute runs from the time the account is improperly charged:

> Section 4–111 sets out a statute of limitations allowing a customer a three-year period to seek a credit to an account *improperly charged* by payment of an item bearing an unauthorized indorsement. (Emphasis added.)

§ 4–7   Allocation of Liability for Fraud Among Multiple Parties

When Article 4 was originally drafted, the drafters recognized the possibility that not only the drawer (often an embezzler's employer) but also the drawee and the depositary bank could have had a hand in contributing to a loss arising from the forgery or alteration of a check. Having granted the drawee a warranty claim against the depositary bank in the event that there were forged indorsements or alterations, the drafters evidently feared that the drawee might favor its customer by recrediting the customer's account and making a warranty claim against the depositary bank—even when the drawer was the one principally at fault. In the most common embezzlements the one who deals most closely and continuously with the embezzler is the embezzler's employer, the drawer. Therefore, in many circumstances the greatest share of the loss should fall at the feet of the employer, not on the depositary or the drawee bank. To avoid the drawee's distortion of that liability, the original drafters included 4–406(5) which read:

> If under this section a payor bank has a valid defense against a claim of a customer upon or resulting from payment of an item and waives or fails upon request to assert the defense the bank may not assert against any collecting bank or other prior party presenting or transferring the item a claim based upon the

unauthorized signature or alteration giving rise to the customer's claim.

The quoted section gave an incentive to the drawee properly to assert its defenses against its own customer, the embezzler's employer.

Experience under the Code has shown that 4–406(5) was not a complete solution to the problem. Since the subsection dealt only with the customer's negligence in failing to examine its statement, it did not reach cases in which the customer may have been negligent in hiring and supervising the employee and thus a proper candidate for "preclusion," not under the old Code's 4–406, but under former 3–406 or 3–405. Although the policy appears to be the same, courts had difficulty in concluding that the drawee bank was obliged to assert *former* 3–406 and 3–405 against its own customer as a condition to recovering in warranty against the depositary bank. For example, the court in Girard Bank v. Mount Holly State Bank,[1] dealt with that problem by allowing the depositary bank a direct cause of action in negligence against the drawer. The effect of *Mt. Holly* is the same as though the drawee had asserted the negligence, but it comes by a different avenue. Because of the absence of a provision comparable to 4–406(5) in pre–1990 Code's sections 3–405 and 3–406, other courts found that the drawee did not have to raise those defenses and declined to find a separate cause of action in the depositary bank.

Knowing what the original drafters knew and informed by the experience under the Code, the drafters of the 1990 revision determined to put the loss on the drawer. This is to occur not merely in the case where there is a failure of the drawer to examine its statement, but also in other cases where the drawer should bear that loss because of 3–404, 3–405, and 3–406. Revised 4–208(c)—a limitation on the drawee's right to recover in warranty—accomplishes that purpose:

> (c) If a drawee asserts a claim for breach of warranty under subsection (a) based on an unauthorized indorsement of the draft or an alteration of the draft, the warrantor may defend by proving that the indorsement is effective under Section 3–404 or 3–405 or the drawer is precluded under Section 3–406 or 4–406 from asserting against the drawee the unauthorized indorsement or alteration.

Only under peril of losing its warranty claim can the drawee ignore its 3–404, 3–405, 3–406, and 4–406 claims against its customer. Because 4–208(c) refers not only to 4–406, but also to all of the

1. 474 F.Supp. 1225, 26 UCC 1210

other relevant sections in Article 3, the drawee has the same responsibility with respect to those as with respect to negligence in examining statements of account. So far, so good. Under the revisions, a court faced with the *Mt. Holly* situation need not construct a separate cause of action by the depositary bank against the drawer. Instead, the depositary bank can simply defend against the warranty suit by asserting 4–208(c) and thus avoid liability. The drafters have solved the basic problem that presented itself under the existing Code.

Unfortunately, the combination of the new language in 4–208(c) with the provisions of 3–404, 3–405, 3–406 and 4–406, and with the idea of sharing fault in a comparative negligence regime, add new complexities and uncertainties.

To understand how courts dealt with these problems before 1990, consider a 1988 Missouri case, Garnac Grain Co. v. Boatmen's Bank & Trust Co.[2] In that case, Mrs. Millison, an employee of Garnac, had embezzled more than $2 million by forging and altering checks. Garnac was negligent under the old Code's 3–406 in hiring and supervising Mrs. Millison, for she was hired from a halfway house where she was serving time for her third offense involving check fraud. When she was hired, she had told Garnac she was in prison for marijuana possession. Garnac's negligence in checking on her background was compounded by inadequate supervision; that negligence doubtless substantially contributed to the losses, per 3–406. Likewise Garnac was probably negligent in its failure to examine the returned items and statements under 4–406.

State Bank of Oskaloosa, one of the depositary banks where Mrs. Millison deposited the forged and altered checks, was also negligent. Mrs. Millison altered outgoing checks payable to actual suppliers of Garnac by typing "or L.R. Millison" (the name of her husband) beneath the name of the rightful payee. She indorsed her husband's signature and deposited the checks in a joint account bearing her and her husband's name. Without questioning her, Oskaloosa accepted these strangely altered checks for large amounts of money despite the fact that L.R. Millison had no contact with the bank, Garnac or the rightful corporate co-payee. After Mrs. Millison's scheme was uncovered, Boatmen's Bank, the drawee, settled with Garnac for almost $1 million.[3]

---

2. 694 F.Supp. 1389, 7 UCC2d 505 (W.D. Mo. 1988).

3. One of the lawyers in the case reports that, far from being repentant, Mrs. Millison was scornful of the banks for their ignorance in dealing with her. One marvels at the coolness and confidence of Mrs. Millison. Apart from their lack of moral fiber, we suspect that the principal quality that ties embezzlers together consists of steely nerves and a unique ability to inspire confidence in others. If they were only a little more honest, most would be successful lawyers or business people.

More pertinent to proving Oskaloosa's negligence, that lawyer tells of another depositary bank whose employees cut

Boatmen's then sued Oskaloosa for breach of its warranty. Oskaloosa argued unsuccessfully that Boatmen's settlement with Garnac constituted a waiver or failure to assert defenses under 4–406(5) and that this failure foreclosed Boatmen's right to recover for breach of warranty. In the earlier action, Boatmen's had asserted a 4–406 defense against its depositor, Garnac, but had not raised 3–406. The court held that section 4–406(5) did not require a drawee to raise 3–406 defenses against its depositor and that 4–406(5) required only that Boatmen raise the defenses, not that it actually litigate to the bitter end. The court distinguished between 3–406 and 4–406 on the ground that 4–406 was based on a stronger policy, the policy of encouraging customers promptly to examine their bank statements. Ironically, Boatmen's success turned in part on its ability to show that *it* was negligent—and thus had only a weak claim under 4–406 against its drawer. In the end Garnac bore part of the loss and Oskaloosa, most of the rest.

Now, consider how the *Garnac* case would come out today, under the post–1990 Code. Assume first that Garnac sues Boatmen's, the drawee, to demand that its account be recredited. Boatmen's will have to respond not only with the 4–406 defense, but with defenses that might arise out of 3–404, 3–405, and 3–406. If it does not assert those defenses, it will not be able to pass the loss back upstream on the warranties to Oskaloosa. That much has been solved.

Assume that the comparative negligence causing the $2 million loss among the three can be apportioned at 50 percent to Garnac, 40 percent to Oskaloosa, and 10 percent to Boatmen's. If that is true, presumably Boatmen's could safely settle with Garnac for $1 million, could it not? Assume that it does so. Boatmen's then sues Oskaloosa on the warranties under 4–208.

Now the statutory troubles begin. The depositary bank's response to the complaint will be that the drawee, Boatmen's, has no warranty cause of action against Oskaloosa because the instrument was effective under 3–404 or 3–405 or the drawer was "precluded" under 3–406 or 4–406. Where there is preclusion or an effective signature, 4–208(c) allows the depositary bank to "defend" by showing that preclusion. This—according to Oskaloosa—would be a complete defense for it to Boatmen's warranty claim, not a set off or a pro rata reduction of liability.

Boatmen's will respond that it acted responsibly in settling with Garnac because of the threat under 3–406(b) that Garnac would put 50 percent of the loss on it on a comparative negligence

Mrs. Millison off after she passed a few checks because they knew "something   was wrong. That wasn't her money."

theory. Oskaloosa will reiterate that 4–208(c) forecloses all warranty claims if there is "preclusion."

Note that 3–406(a) causes the preclusion but 3–406(b) does not lift *the preclusion.*[4] Subsection (a) states that one whose negligence substantially contributes is "precluded" (or that indorsements are effective). That language is repeated in 4–208(c). The precluded party escapes from 3–406(a) by asserting a comparative negligence claim under 3–406(b), but the comparative negligence leavening to 3–406(a)'s preclusion is nowhere built into or contemplated by the unequivocal language of 4–208(c). To put it another way, the preclusion in 3–406 or effective indorsement in 3–404 or 3–405, ipso facto gives a defense irrespective of the fact that the legal consequence of this "preclusion" or "effective indorsement" is substantially altered by an offsetting comparative negligence claim. Read literally, therefore, the 1990 Code would put half the loss on Garnac, and the other half on the drawee, with Oskaloosa escaping unscathed. If 4–208(c) is so read, the drawee will not be able to pass any of the loss upstream to the depositary bank.

Of course, the drawee will challenge the depositary bank's interpretation of 4–208(c). First, Boatmen's might point to 4–208(b), which explicitly states "[t]he right of the drawee to recover damages under this subsection is not affected by any failure of the drawee to exercise ordinary care in making payment." The inference of the quoted statement is that even a negligent drawee can recover in warranty from a depositary bank. With some justification, Boatmen's will argue that Oskaloosa's interpretation of 4–208(c) conflicts with the idea that a negligent drawee should be able to cast that loss back upstream in warranty. Virtually every embezzlement claim contains a potential preclusion under 3–404, 3–405, and 3–406; had the drafters intended 4–208(c) to cut off any warranty claim in all cases where there was an initial preclusion, they have given the drawee an empty right in the statement quoted from 4–208(b) about a drawee's negligence.

We find the drawee's argument persuasive, but how would one arrive at the correct conclusion under the law as it stands? One possibility is to find a common law cause of action in the drawee against the depositary bank for a proper share of the loss (for the moment we have put aside the question "what is a proper share"). This is a crude way to arrive at a fair result. It is somewhat distasteful, however, to contemplate that we already have to start engrafting common law causes of action onto a newly drafted statute in order to arrive at fair results. While 3–406(b) gives the drawer an implied cause of action in negligence (to allocate the

---

4. In similar fashion part of 3–404 and 3–405 make certain indorsements "effective," but the negligence of the other party does not reverse that effectiveness, it merely allows a suit for negligence.

losses between the drawer and the depositary or drawee bank), there is no suggestion that it also confers an implied cause of action in negligence on the drawee against either of the other parties.

A second way to arrive at a more palatable conclusion is to interpret 4–208(c) more narrowly than it is drawn. Could section 4–208(c) be interpreted to operate as a "defense" against a warranty action only *to the extent that* the drawee did not assert its claims vigorously enough against the drawer? In the context of our hypothetical, assume first that Boatmen's, the drawee, settled so that Garnac would only have to bear $250,000 of the loss, not $1 million. Assume that a vigorous assertion of the claims would have caused the drawer, Garnac, to bear $1 million of the $2 million loss. When the drawee, Boatmen's, asserts a warranty claim against the depositary bank, Oskaloosa, for the remaining $1,750,000, this interpretation of 4–208(c) would give the depositary bank, Oskaloosa, not a complete defense but only a defense "to the extent," i.e., a defense against $750,000 of liability. In addition to the $250,000, the drawer should bear $750,000. So interpreting 4–208(c) has the salutary effect of putting a proper share on the drawer and the rest on the depositary bank. If this result was intended by the drafters, why did they not say so explicitly? Interpreting 4–208(c) in this way is a bit of a stretch.

Another way to read 4–208 is as follows. We use 4–208(a) to determine if Depositary breached a warranty. We use (b) to determine the measure of damages. Section 4–208(c) refers to a "defense" against the claim in subsection (a), not a defense against the *amount* of damages in (b): "If a drawee asserts a claim for breach of warranty under subsection (a) * * * the warrantor may defend * * *." Read this way, 4–208(b)'s statement about the irrelevance of Drawee's negligence does not apply to cases falling under (c), since a successful defense against a breach of warranty claim under (a) would take the case entirely outside of 4–208.

While we are engaging in such speculation, let us consider yet another interpretation. All of the negligence and preclusion sections now incorporate comparative negligence theories. If comparative negligence is good for adjustment of the liability between the drawer and other parties, why is it not good for the adjustment of the liabilities between the drawee and the depositary bank? Perhaps $1 million should go on the drawer in our hypothetical case, and the warranty claim of the drawee bank should be limited to $800,000 (the remaining share, less the 10 percent, which by hypothesis was caused by drawee). What do you think? Does the sentence in 4–208(b) (that gives the drawee a warranty cause of action despite its own negligence) conflict with that conclusion? That sentence suggests that comparative negligence does not reign in a regime where one party gives a warranty to another.

Returning to *Garnac*, let us consider another possibility under the 1990 Code. In a single lawsuit, Garnac could sue the drawee for recredit of its account under 4–401 and simultaneously sue the depositary bank under 3–406(b), could it not? Courts have usually held that a drawer whose signature was forged does not have a conversion or any other cause of action against the depositary bank, but only a cause of action against the drawee bank, who in turn can sue upstream on the warranties. As we have previously argued, however, 3–406(b) contains an implied cause of action. This cause of action applies not merely to drawee payors, for the section speaks of persons "paying or taking." The choice of the two verbs must mean that persons other than payors (i.e., depositary banks, who are not "paying" but are "taking") may have liability under 3–406(b).

If this interpretation of 3–406 is correct (and still assuming fault of 50% Garnac, 40% Oskaloosa and 10% Boatmen's), Garnac could join both parties, could recover 40 percent of the $2 million loss directly from Oskaloosa, $200,000 from Boatmen's and would itself bear $1 million of the loss. If Boatmen's paid $200,000 and if Oskaloosa had already paid $800,000, the only damages remaining to be recovered on the breach of warranty suit by Boatmen's against Oskaloosa would be $200,000 that the drawee had to put in the pot. On the hypothetical given, there is no reason why Garnac should not recover the entire $1,000,000 directly from the depositary bank, Oskaloosa, and so avoid the necessity of joining the drawee Boatmen's and having Boatmen's assert a separate cause of action against the depositary bank, Oskaloosa, true?

If we correctly read the drafters (that the sentence quoted above in 4–208(b) means that no part of this loss should fall on the drawee, even though the drawee is negligent),[5] we are confident that the outcome described above ($1 million on Garnac, $1 million on Oskaloosa) is the correct allocation. If we have read too much into the statement in 4–208(b), then all bets are off and the allocations would be different than we have described above.

The skeptic might ask: would the drafters impose a comparative negligence scheme in all of the various sections from 3–404 through 4–406—and even apply that against the drawee, where

---

5. See the drafters' elaboration in Comment 6 to 3–417, which reads in full:

Subsection (c) applies to checks and other unaccepted drafts. It gives to the warrantor the benefit of rights that the drawee has against the drawer under Section 3–404, 3–405, 3–406, or 4–406. If the drawer's conduct contributed to a loss from forgery or alteration, the drawee should not be allowed to shift the loss from the *drawer* to the *warrantor*. (Emphasis added).

This comment seems to support our interpretation, that the purpose of 4–208(c) is to clarify allocation of the loss between the negligent drawer and warrantor, not to dump some of the loss onto the drawee.

there is no depositary bank involved—but deviate from that allocation where there is a depositary bank or other warrantor? We are not sure. The statement in 4–208(b) and 3–417(b) that "[t]he right of the drawee to recover damages under this subsection is not affected by any failure of the drawee to exercise ordinary care in making payment" fits uncomfortably with the statement at the end of 3–405 which gives "the persons bearing the loss" a right to "recover from the person failing to exercise ordinary care * * * " and with similar provisions in 3–404, 3–406, and 4–406. If one assumes that drawees can be negligent and assumes further that the loss should be allocated based on that negligence in a suit between the drawer and the drawee, why does the drawee's negligence become irrelevant once there are three parties and it has become a beneficiary of a warranty? By hypothesis, if we apply the Learned Hand definition of negligence, the warranty rule will allocate a greater share of the loss to the depositary bank than it should bear under the least cost-risk avoider analysis.

Perhaps the drafters are telling us that the facts we have assumed here and that the courts have sometimes found really can not be facts, and that the courts' conclusions are erroneous. The drafters might be saying that a drawee who fails to discover an alteration or a forged indorsement is *never* negligent in that failure, no matter how obvious the alteration or indorsement, and that it is always operating both in good faith and with ordinary care when it relies upon the warranty that is given it by the depositary bank. As check collections become even more mechanical, particularly as checks are truncated and only the electronic information about the check itself goes to the payor, there will be fewer and fewer possibilities for the payor to commit negligence, or to be accused of negligence, based upon defects on the face of the check. If that is true, a regime that puts the loss back upstream on the depositary bank or other party is sensible and doubtless puts the loss at the right place. Perhaps, therefore, commerce will grow into the law that the drafters have given us. We hope so.

Chapter 5

NSF CHECKS, DOCUMENTARY DRAFTS, AND FORGED CHECKS: LIABILITY OF PAYORS AND OF COLLECTING BANKS, FINAL PAYMENT, DELAY

Analysis

---

§ 5–1 Introduction

The transaction at the center of this chapter is quite straight-forward. It might happen as follows: A check is presented to a payor bank that holds it for two or three days and then sends it back to the collecting bank and ultimately to the payee. Drawer has no funds in its account and bank holds the check by mistake or in the hope that the drawer will soon put money in the account.

We will see that the payor's liability arises because of its delay—its failure to act by its midnight deadline (usually midnight of the next banking day after it receives the check). In rare cases the payor may be able to pass the loss back upstream to a collecting or depositary bank, or even to the payee, but that will be the exception. Of course the payor can recover from its depositor under 4–401, but because we start with the hypothesis of insufficient funds, the depositor is likely to be a dry hole.

In addition to making final payment by delay, the payor bank can make final payment in several other ways. For example, it might pay the check over the counter in cash or it might give its own cashier's check in return for the depositor's check presented for payment. The consequences are the same whether the bank has missed the midnight deadline or made final payment in any of the other ways outlined in 4–215.

In this chapter we will deal with the related provisions of Article 3, Article 4, and with the federal regulations. Final payment is defined primarily by 4–215, but we will defer a detailed discussion of it until after we have considered the legal consequences of final payment, defined partly by 4–213, but also by 3–418 and by common law rules of restitution.

Federal law, in Regulations J and CC, 12 CFR 210 and 12 CFR 229, supplement the UCC rules discussed above. Regulation J governs the collection of checks through the Federal Reserve system; Regulation CC applies to check collections generally. In general, the federal regulations coexist peacefully with the UCC,[1] but it is important to understand how the state and federal regulatory schemes fit together—something that is not always obvious. The federal regulations sometimes impose liability on a payor bank in situations when the UCC would not, and vice versa.

§ 5–1

1. 12 CFR § 229.41.

Collecting banks can also be liable for delay or for other negligent behavior in the handling of items for collection. Although uncommon, this liability can arise on an ordinary domestic check and is governed primarily by sections 4–104, 4–202, and 4–214. Collecting banks are liable more often when a documentary draft is sent to a bank for collection and the bank fails to make the collection until many moons have passed. Documentary drafts are governed partly by 4–302, but more extensively by 4–501 and the other sections in part 5 of Article 4. We deal separately with documentary drafts, for special rules apply to them, both as to the collecting parties and as to the payors. They raise some questions that do not appear in check transactions.

Because a payor's liability to upstream claimants for paying a forged check is similar to its liability when it pays an NSF check, we also consider the forged check in this chapter.

One type of final payment not considered here arises from electronic funds transactions. We consider the liability of banks and other parties to a wire transfer in Chapter 7.

§ 5–2 Legal Consequences of Final Payment of the Check

In general, a payor bank that has never accepted nor made final payment on a customer's check has no liability on that check. If it dishonors, neither the payee nor any subsequent taker typically can sue the bank. This dishonor, of course, might be wrongful dishonor for which the bank would have liability to its depositor under 4–402, but that is another story.[1] Checks that are presented through clearing houses, over the counter, or by any other method—but never paid—are simply sent back. Credits and debits are routinely and automatically reversed; for the most part, the payor is free of liability.

On the other hand, a payor bank's liability for having made final payment is heavy, so heavy that the bank can seldom cast it off. With limited exceptions, a payor bank that makes final payment cannot recover from the party paid. Exceptions to that rule are cases where there is a broken warranty (e.g., payment over a forged indorsement) or where restitution is permitted under the applicable common law or section 3–418 and not barred by other provisions of 3–418.

Before examining these rules in detail, we consider the general policies behind the final payment rules. When the drawer's signature is forged, Comment 1 to 3–418 explains that the Code clings to

1. See 21–4 discussing a bank's liability to its customer.

the doctrine expounded in the famous English case, Price v. Neal.[2] Section 3–418(c) preserves the rule that a drawee who accepts or pays an instrument with a forged drawer's or maker's signature, is bound by its payment or acceptance.

A variety of policies purportedly justify the rule in *Price v. Neal*, but none is entirely satisfactory. The traditional justification, recited in the comments to former 3–418, but dropped from the 1990 version, is "that the drawee is in a superior position to detect a forgery because he has the maker's signature and is expected to know and compare it."[3] Another justification is that it is better to end the transaction on an instrument when it is paid rather than reopen and upset a series of commercial transactions at a later date.

The problem with both of these rationales is that neither is consistent with the rules for forged indorsement cases. If *Price v. Neal* is founded on the theory that any drawee who fails to discover a forged drawer's signature is negligent and thus is not entitled to recover payment, there should be an exception to that doctrine for those cases in which the signature is so cleverly forged that a banking employee using due care could not discover the forgery. Alternatively, if the rule is premised on the desirability of ending and not reopening commercial transactions, then the same rule should apply to forged indorsement cases as well as forged drawer cases. We see no adequate rationale to explain the difference between the liability of the drawee bank on checks bearing forged indorsements and its liability on those bearing forged drawer's signatures.

Similar and perhaps stronger policies are at work when the alleged defect is not a forged signature but insufficient funds in the drawer's account with the bank. If every payee who took a personal check from a customer faced the prospect that he would be at risk to return funds received from a payor against NSF checks until a three or six-year statute of limitations had run, commerce would be stultified. Without the heavy liability that attends even modest delay, a payor bank might adopt a much more leisurely payment procedure. Absent incentive for quickness, the payor's interest is to hold (and use) the drawer's money as long as possible. Faced with those possibilities, merchants would not treat checks as the equivalent of cash and might instead insist upon cash or some other mode of payment that would not carry threats of delay or reversal.

Surely the rule is justified by the expectations of the payees and other parties, expectations supported by the rules in Articles 3 and 4 that any deficiency in the depositor's funds will be communi-

---

2. 3 Burr. 1354 (1762).

3. Comment 1 to 3–418 (pre–1990 version).

cated promptly to the payee. Not only does this limit the payee's exposure to a relatively short time, but it enables the payee to protect itself, for example, by holding goods that are the consideration for the check for a short period or pursuing the drawer while the trail is hot. Therefore it seems clear—at least as checks are currently used in our society—that prompt response in the case of NSF checks is an integral and critical part of the bank's performance.

If one seeks merely to minimize NSF losses by placing the loss on one who can best prevent it, that rule also points to the payor, not to the payee. Except in rare cases, the payee will not know the exact status of the drawer's account, but the payor should know it. The payor should know whether there are sufficient funds, and whether the funds are "good" or "uncollected." Moreover, the payor may have a better knowledge of the reliability and current prosperity of the drawer than the payee has. At least in the case of NSF checks, placing the loss on the payor who makes final payment will facilitate the use of the check as a medium of exchange, and will force the one who can most cheaply avoid the loss (by bouncing the check) to do so.

In the simple case where a payor bank misses its midnight deadline, 4–302(a) creates strict liability that holds the payor accountable for the amount of the item. What the bank may or may not know is mostly irrelevant.[4] Citizens Fidelity Bank & Trust Co. v. Southwest Bank & Trust Co.[5] illustrates the usual consequences of delay. There, Greenwade deposited a check for $138,427 in his account at Citizens Bank in Kentucky. The check bore the proper facsimile signature of the drawer, County Wide. Citizens properly forwarded the check to the payor, Southwest, where it arrived on July 3. Early on July 7, the depositary bank, Citizens, released $20,000 in cash and $50,000 in "certified funds" to Greenwade. Only minutes after releasing the funds, Citizens got wind of the fact that Greenwade had been passing counterfeit checks, and called Southwest Bank. Because it was told that the check had already cleared, Citizens felt no need to warn Southwest of the forgery. The court properly affirmed a judgment for Citizens (the depositary bank) against Southwest (the payor) on the ground that Southwest had finally paid and was strictly liable for the amount of the check under 4–302.

But there are also cases in which the courts have allowed banks that missed the midnight deadline to escape liability on the ground that the plaintiffs were guilty of fraud. In Lombardo v.

---

4. Schwegmann Bank & Trust Co. v. Bank of Louisiana, 595 So.2d 1185, 17 UCC2d 827 (La.App. 1992), writ denied, 598 So.2d 360 (La. 1992) (banks' knowledge about kiting scheme irrelevant to liability for final payment).

5. 238 Neb. 677, 472 N.W.2d 198, 15 UCC2d 548 (1991).

Mellon Bank,[6] the court holds even though the bank is strictly liable for missing the 4–302 midnight deadline, it has the right to raise certain defenses, such as mistake of fact or unjust enrichment. Also, consider the facts of In re Spring Grove Livestock Exchange, Inc.[7] The plaintiffs were trustees of the bankruptcy estates of individual and corporate debtors that engaged in a check-kiting scheme. They brought claim against the debtors' banks, which reversed provisional credits to the debtors' accounts in an attempt to minimize their losses in connection with the kiting scheme. The court held that the debtors' fraud, in connection with the check-kiting scheme, relieved the banks of any liability to trustees of the debtors' estates for allegedly failing to return kited checks prior to the expiration of the midnight deadline.

§ 5–3   Restitution

Consider now the unusual case—where the payor bank can recover its payment from someone upstream. What is its cause of action? One possibility is for the payor to assert a breach of warranty by someone upstream. Examination of 3–417 and 4–208 shows a warranty suit to be fruitless in the case of an NSF check and of marginal value in the case of a forged drawer's signature. The warranty of title does not include a warranty that the drawer's signature is valid. Moreover, there is no warranty whatsoever that would cover the NSF check (and rightly so, for it is the payor bank, not the payee or the depositary bank, who knows the status of the drawer's account).

The payor is left with an action for restitution but this claim is rarely available, and when available, can be asserted against a limited number of defendants. Under the pre–1990 Code the issue was complicated by ambiguous language in former 4–213(1)(d): "upon final payment * * * the payor bank shall be *accountable* for the amount of the item." Some (including us, in our youthful ignorance) interpreted the word "accountable" to mean that final payment cut off the payor bank's right to restitution. That argument was eventually rejected by most courts and commentators, and the 1990 Code puts the matter to rest. The offending language has been removed from 4–215 (the statutory successor to 4–213) and revised 3–418 clarifies the payor bank's right to restitution.

Almost all of the cases arising under 3–418 will be NSF cases in which the payor bank allowed its midnight deadline to pass or otherwise made final payment. When that happens, the payor bank often looks to the presenter of the check, i.e., the party it has paid,

---

6.   454 Pa.Super. 403, 685 A.2d 595, 33 UCC2d 154 (1996).

7.   205 B.R. 149, 33 UCC2d 160 (Bankr. D. Minn. 1997).

as a potential defendant in a restitution cause of action. Section 3–418 makes a recovery possible, but unlikely.

Section 3–418(a) states two statutory bases for restitution. First is the case in which the payor paid in the "mistaken belief" that there was no stop payment order. Second is payment on the mistaken belief that the signature of the drawer was authorized, despite the drawer's claim of forgery or lack of authority in the signing agent.

Section 3–418(b) incorporates other (non UCC) state laws of restitution and permits the payor bank who has paid by mistake to recover the money from the party paid—where state common law allows. This means, of course, that the payor bank's right to restitution will depend in part on law that will vary from state to state.

Subsection 3–418(c) significantly restricts the payor bank's ability to recover under both the statutory restitution rights in (a) and the common law rights in (b). Restitution is barred if the potential defendant qualifies as "a person who took the instrument in good faith and for value," or who "in good faith changed position in reliance on the payment or acceptance." As the comments concede, the payor bank on an NSF check will usually not have a cause of action under subsection (a) or (b) because the potential defendant will likely qualify under the language of (c).

In Crossland Savings v. Foxwood & Southern Co.,[1] the court finds that the defendants who took two checks as a down payment were holders in due course and denies recovery and restitution claims; but on a third check which was held in escrow, the defendants failed to demonstrate as a matter of law that they were holders or that they gave value or changed their position in reliance on the payment, thus the plaintiff bank has a cause of action with respect to that check. Also, in Gotham Apparel Corp. v. Manufacturers Hanover Trust Co.,[2] defendant bank refused to honor two checks payable to plaintiff that it previously certified. Plaintiff's motion for summary judgment was denied because a triable issue of fact existed as to whether the plaintiff was a holder in due course under 3–302 and whether the plaintiff in good faith changed its position in reliance on the check under 3–418.

To enjoy the protection of 3–418(c) one need not be a holder in due course, but only a person who took the instrument in good faith and for value. Thus one technically not a holder (for example, because of the absence of an indorsement) can nevertheless be a

§ 5–3

1. 202 A.D.2d 544, 609 N.Y.S.2d 282, 25 UCC2d 446 (1994).

2. 1995 WL 326630, 26 UCC2d 172 (N.Y. 1995).

person who took in good faith and for value, and thus would have a good defense against a payor bank seeking restitution.

Section 3–418(d) gives "rights on the instrument" to one who is forced to return a payment in a restitution suit. In the words of that section, the instrument is "treated as dishonored." In effect the instrument is resurrected so that the defendant in the restitution action who has had to repay the drawee can recover from any drawers or indorsers upstream. Under the pre–1990 Code a right to sue would have been doubtful since most believed that an instrument that had been finally paid could never be dishonored and, therefore, claims on the drawer or indorser's contracts (which are conditioned upon prior dishonor) could not be proven. As revised in 1990, 3–418(d) reverses that conclusion.

To clarify all of this, consider the facts of First National City Bank v. Altman.[3] In that case, Altman, a diamond dealer, was twice visited by a diamond purchaser who turned out to be a thief. In each case the thief presented a forged check and in each case City Bank made final payment. In the first transaction Altman held the diamonds until the check had cleared, but he did not do so after the thief's second visit. If the suit arose under the revised Code, Altman would seek protection under 3–418(c) as one who has changed his position in reliance upon final payment; he had done so by giving up the diamonds. With respect to the first check, Altman's argument is strong. He refused to release the diamonds until the first check had "cleared."

With respect to the second check, Altman's reliance is less certain. Because he gave up the diamonds before the check had cleared, he may not have "changed position in reliance on the *payment* or *acceptance*" (emphasis added). Under former 3–418 one who did not change his position in reliance on "payment or acceptance" could nevertheless recover if he were a holder in due course. Under the revised 3–418(c), one who cannot show reliance on payment or acceptance need only prove that he "took the instrument in good faith and for value" in order to protect himself against restitution. Even though Altman might not have been a holder in due course, presumably he took the check in good faith and for value, and thus could defeat a restitution claim under the revised Code.

But what is "mistake" under (b) and "mistaken belief" under (a)? Subsections 3–418(a) and (b) permit restitution only when there is *payment or acceptance* on a "mistaken belief" or "by mistake." Stated more generally: when does the payor bank have a right to restitution?

3. 1966 WL 8964, 3 UCC 815 706, 277 N.Y.S.2d 813 (1967). (N.Y.Sup. 1966), aff'd mem., 27 A.D.2d

The general right to restitution for a mistaken payment rests on common law unjust enrichment principles set forth in sections 1, 6, and 15–38 of the Restatement of Restitution. The basic elements of the payor's prima facie case are (1) that the payment must have been made on the basis of a mistake of fact existing at the time of payment, and (2) the payment would not have been made had the true facts been known to the payor. Section 59 of the Restatement also recites the rule that negligence of the payor does not, as such, bar it from a restitution recovery.[4]

Even with these general principles in mind, some cases are not clear. There is no mistake when a bank knowingly pays an instrument against uncollected funds or against an overdrawn account. Here the bank makes a conscious judgment to lend money to its customer in the belief the customer will repay. If the bank is mistaken about its customer's creditworthiness, that is not a *payment* mistake, but a *credit* mistake and the bank has no right to restitution. Consider, for example, Demos v. Lyons,[5] where Somerset Trust paid a check drawn on Demos' account even though the payment created a $9600 overdraft. Demos never covered the overdraft, and the bank sued the payee to recover the money. The court correctly concluded that the bank was barred from restitution because there was a conscious decision to "pay." The bank could not prove the *sine qua non* of restitution recovery, payment by *mistake*.

Alternatively, consider the facts of National Savings and Trust Co. v. Park Corporation.[6] Here the payee of a check telephoned the drawee to determine the status of the drawer's account. Although the payee was informed that the drawer had insufficient funds, it submitted the check for payment. The payor bank had put a hold on the account, but when the $75,000 check arrived it was paid (even though there was only $236.75 in the account) because the employee supervising the account was not at work and the employees on duty were confused. That was a payment by mistake.

In establishing *Demos* and *Park* as the outer boundaries, we have done nothing to resolve the difficult cases that lie between. Consider some cases that might help in determining when restitution is appropriate and when not. First are the classic kiting cases. In these cases, one bank ends the kite by dishonoring a large number of checks. After the dust has settled may one bank sue the other on checks previously paid? It will argue, of course, that it

---

4. The Restatement also contains various special doctrines. For example, Section 33 provides that there is no right to restitution after payment on an NSF check. That rule is probably undone by the 1990 revision of 3–418.

5. 151 N.J.Super. 489, 376 A.2d 1352, 22 UCC 754 (1977).

6. 722 F.2d 1303, 37 UCC 817 (6th Cir.1983), cert. denied, 466 U.S. 939, 104 S.Ct. 1916, 80 L.Ed.2d 464 (1984).

made payment in the mistaken belief that there were or would be sufficient funds.

For several reasons, we are unsympathetic to banks that are left holding the bag at the end of a kite. By hypothesis, all banks in a kite are paying against uncollected funds (allowing draws against balances that themselves represent funds on which final payment has not been made). In our judgment, most banks paying against uncollected funds know what they are doing, and in any event should not be deemed to have made "mistaken payments." Moreover, in a typical kite, it is difficult to maintain that one of the banks is more at fault than the other. All are culpable. The court in First Nat. Bank in Harvey v. Colonial Bank[7] takes a similar stand. It holds that a party to a kite that waited beyond its midnight deadline to return the checks is absolutely liable to the other party under 4–302. In this case, Plaintiff bank, suspecting a kite scheme, decided to dishonor a set of checks and return them to defendant bank. Defendant argued that plaintiff lacked good faith in giving notice of the return because it used Fedwire instead of a telephone, a practice that is rarely used and less desirable than telephone notices because a wire notice may not come to the attention of an employee for some time. Also, plaintiff bank changed the reason for the return from "uncollected funds" to "refer to maker." The court rejects this argument. After giving an elaborate analysis of the cases that deal with the obligations of one bank to the other at the end of a kite, the court sides with the majority of cases that find that "a bank has no good faith obligation to disclose a suspected kite or to refrain from attempting to shift the kite loss."

But in Murray v. Bank of America, N.A.,[8] plaintiff was arrested and served with warrants for 15 fraudulent checks as a result of an identity theft. Plaintiff had never had a checking account with defendant bank, but prior to her arrest, she discovered that an impostor had opened a new account in her name at the bank using her stolen driver's license. Plaintiff requested that the bank close the account immediately and inform the merchants to which the bank had returned the NSF checks about the situation. The bank did not close the account until almost a month later. Plaintiff sued under a common law negligence theory. She did not have a claim for wrongful dishonor under 4–402 since she was not a customer of the bank. The South Carolina appellate court held that the bank failed to respond promptly upon request, thus it violated its common law duty of care to plaintiff. The ruling conflicts with the general rule that banks do not owe a common law duty of care to a non-customer. The court did not address the fact that even if the bank had acted promptly to close the account, the checks would still

---

7. 898 F.Supp. 1220, 28 UCC2d 290 (N.D.Ill. 1995).   **8.** 354 S.C. 337, 580 S.E.2d 194 (App. 2003).

have bounced, thus it is unclear how the bank's failure to act harmed the plaintiff.[9]

An early draft of the 1990 revised 3–418 would have given the bank an argument for recovery. Prior to 1991, the proposed revision to section 3–418(a) had three subsections. Two of those remain; the third, which arguably would have dealt with kite cases reads as follows:

> [The drawee may recover where it acted on the mistaken belief that] (iii) the balance in the drawer's account with the drawee represented available funds. * * *[10]

In response to critics who suggested that this section might allow one bank in a kite to recover from another, the drafters withdrew 3–418(a)(iii) and replaced it with an equivocal statement at the end of Comment 3 concerning kites:

> In some cases, however, it may not be clear whether a drawee bank should have a right of restitution. For example, a check kiting scheme may involve a large number of checks drawn on a number of different banks in which the drawer's credit balances are based on uncollected funds represented by fraudulently drawn checks. No attempt is made in Section 3–418 to state rules for determining the conflicting claims of the various banks that may be victimized by such a scheme. Rather, such cases are better resolved on the basis of general principles of law and the particular facts presented in the litigation.

The situation is further clouded by Comment 3 to 4–302 (1990) which states in part:

> Decisions that hold an accountable bank's liability to be "absolute" are rejected. A payor bank that makes a late return of an item should not be liable to a defrauder operating a check kiting scheme. In Bank Leumi Trust Co. v. Bally's Park Place, Inc., 528 F.Supp. 349 (S.D.N.Y. 1981), and American National Bank v. Foodbasket, 497 P.2d 546 (Wyo. 1972), banks that were accountable under Section 4–302 for missing their midnight deadline were successful in defending against parties who initiated collection knowing that the check would not be paid.

Quaere, are the drafters here retreating from the position that was apparently taken in 3–418, namely, to deny the kiter the right to recover? *Bank Leumi* was not a kiting case, but a case where the payee knew that the drawer was dead when the payee presented the check for payment.[11] But, in GMAC v. Bank of Richmondville,[12]

9. Barkley Clark, Clark's Bank Deposits and Payments Monthly, vol. 12, No.2, (2003).

10. Proposed Final Draft, April 12, 1990 § 3–418(a)(iii).

11. In *Bank Leumi*, a casino sought to receive payment on a $60,000 check,

the court rejects the argument that the Plaintiff should be estopped from asserting its claim because it knew that the checks would not be paid when it deposited them. The court here does not explicitly decline to follow *Bank Leumi*; it finds no clear evidence of the payee's knowledge. The case shows the uneasiness that some courts feel toward *Bank Leumi*. *Foodbasket* is a more doubtful precedent for the proposition that a presenter with knowledge of insufficiency of the account cannot keep the payment.[13] We hope that the quoted comment, inviting a recovery from a "defrauder," does not include a bank in a kiting scheme that has some suspicion of the scheme, but is not committing fraud itself.

We still believe it should be rare that one bank in a kiting scheme gets restitution from another. Although it can be argued that no bank in a kite scheme has acted in good faith (because each had some knowledge of the scheme), we do not think such payments should be regarded as "mistaken." Enticing defrauded banks into a big lawsuit after a kite to show that one bank was more culpable than another has about the same social value as cock

---

where the drawer's executor had informed Bank Leumi that the drawer had died insolvent. Bank Leumi deposited the $60,000 check anyway, hoping that either the bank would mistakenly fail to return the check by the midnight deadline, or, that the information received from the executor was incorrect.

Sure enough, errors by both the collecting bank (failing to magnetically encode the maker's account number) and the drawee bank (failing to manually process and dishonor the check by the midnight deadline) caused the drawee bank to miss the deadline. In fact, Bank Leumi failed to return the check until seven months later.

In ordering the casino to repay the amount of the check to Bank Leumi, the court stressed three factors: (1) that the check was not in computer-readable form, it being a blank check issued by Bally's casino for the convenience of its customers who stupidly (or wisely) failed to bring their bank-issued checkbook to the casino; (2) that the casino had been reliably informed that the maker was dead and his estate was unable to pay; and (3) that the casino had not suffered any loss through the mistake of Bank Leumi. (The opinion also noted that the dead maker's executor "found it surprising that Bally's extended Brinker [the maker] $60,000 in credit because Brinker had been adjudicated as bankrupt two

years earlier and was generally unable to obtain credit. He had only one credit card, from Avis Rent–A–Car.")

12. 203 A.D.2d 851, 611 N.Y.S.2d 338, 24 UCC2d 160 (1994).

13. In *Foodbasket*, an employee bookkeeper (Pat McPherson) wrote two checks to her employer (Foodbasket) totalling $8,400. She also indorsed and deposited the checks as an agent of Foodbasket. When she wrote her checks, she knew that she had insufficient funds in her account to cover the checks. She requested a loan from her bank to cover the checks. The bank denied her request and informed her that it would dishonor the checks, but it failed to meet the midnight deadline.

The drawee bank "points out" to the court that "under [4–302], if [the bank] did not give notice until after the midnight deadline, it is accountable for the amounts of the checks *only* in the absence of a valid defense." The main issue in this case seems to be one of agency: as a defense to accountability, can the bank maintain that Pat McPherson, as Foodbasket's agent, had no reason to expect the bank to honor the checks? The court said yes, and rejected Foodbasket's argument that McPherson's knowledge should not be imputed to her employer since she was acting in her own interest.

fighting. It may be fun for the handlers (the lawyers) but it is hard on the cocks (the banks).

Other claimed "mistakes" arise from the nature of the check processing system itself. Consider the case in which a check is presented, run through the bank's machinery and paid by the passage of the midnight deadline without any conscious decision. This might be done because the drawer was a good customer and thus no attention was paid to the fact that the apparent balance in his account rose because of uncollected funds, or because the bank's computer was not programmed to distinguish between collected and uncollected funds, or because the bank routinely allowed many customers to draw against uncollected funds even though the daily computer printout correctly showed the status of their accounts as lacking sufficient collected funds to support the payments. For reasons like those discussed above concerning kites, we do not believe that payments made in these circumstances are "mistaken." In all of these cases, the payor bank has the capacity to determine which checks are drawn against funds that are probably uncollected and to return them. Having chosen for its own business reasons (arising out of the status of the particular customer or based upon past averages) not to do so, we see little merit in allowing restitution to such a bank when the averages go against them or when its erstwhile good customer turns bad.

There is a final technical issue on liability under the new final payment rules. Assume, for example, that a payor bank receives a check through the Federal Reserve and takes no action until its midnight deadline has passed. Under 4–215(a)(3) and 4–301, the bank has made final payment. But assume that the bank "reverses" the transaction at the Federal Reserve by sending the check back on the third day after presentment and the payee or depositary bank now seeks the fruit of this "final payment" by suing the payor bank. Where is its cause of action? Under the former Code the payee could sue under 4–213 because the payor was "accountable." This language is gone from 4–215. Under the revised Code, one might argue that the payee has a cause of action under 4–302. That section makes the payor "accountable," but a close reading of 4–302(a)(1) shows that the payor is accountable only if the bank "does not pay or return the item." In our case, the bank has paid (at least in the sense that the midnight deadline has passed) so the 4–302 language does not work. Surely there must be a cause of action and certainly the drafters intended the payor bank to be liable—even though they removed the accountability language.

One way to find a cause of action is to read the verb "pay" in 4–302(a)(1) to have a different meaning than the term "final payment" in 4–215(a). That is, one might read the verb pay in 4–302(a)(1) to mean a more generic "payment" in which not merely the technical events in 4–215 have occurred, but also money has been transmitted to the depositary bank and payee. Another place to find a cause of action would be to infer it from 4–301, which states that the payor "may revoke" if it did not wait beyond its midnight deadline. One might draw the inference from 4–301 that it "may not revoke" in other cases and thus has liability under 4–301 itself. We are quite certain that the drafters intended the payor to have liability here and we are equally certain that the courts will find a basis for that liability, but at this writing the source of this liability is not clear.

§ 5–4   Final Payment Defined

The time of payment of a check is crucial in determining the liabilities discussed in Sections 5–2 and 5–3. Until the drawee pays, it is not liable on the check itself.[1] Thus if a bank discovers before it makes final payment that the drawer's signature is forged, or that there are insufficient funds in the customer's account, the drawee can dishonor the check, and the presenter will have no power to make the drawee pay. In that case the presenter may seek to throw the loss back upstream. If the drawee has made final payment, we have seen that it will usually bear the loss. The crucial cutoff point—the point at which the drawee becomes bound under 3–418 and the doctrine of *Price v. Neal*—occurs when the drawee makes final payment under 4–215.[2]

At the outset one should distinguish between NSF and forged drawer cases on the one hand, and priority conflicts over the account on the other. Conflicts of the latter kind arise when one party presents a check at or near the same time another party issues a stop order or garnishes the account or the drawee learns of the drawer's death or petition in bankruptcy. The priority cases are essentially conflicts between two claimants to the proceeds in the account. On the one hand, the check holder demands payment; on the other, the depositor's creditor demands the funds by garnishment. Some courts have erroneously analyzed these cases under the predecessor to 4–215 on the theory that the check wins if final payment is made before the other event (for example, garnishment) occurs, but loses if the other event occurs first. The correct analysis for priority cases is to go to 4–303, a provision similar to, but significantly different from 4–215.

§ 5–4

1. "A check or other draft does not of itself operate as an assignment of funds in the hands of the drawee available for its payment, and the drawee is not liable on the instrument until the drawee accepts it." § 3–408.

2. On that rare occasion when the payor receives an item without settling for it, § 4–302(a)(1) imposes accountability on the payor for the item regardless of whether it is properly payable or not, if the payor fails to "pay or return the item or send notice of dishonor until after its midnight deadline."

Turning to the final payment issues and 4–215, consider the following hypothetical case: Payee, Repeunzel receives two checks, each in the amount of $3,000. Since she is worried about the solvency of one of drawers, she takes the check to the drawee bank and procures cash for it over the counter. She deposits the other check in her own account at depositary bank, and the next morning it is delivered to the drawee bank. The drawee takes no action with respect to the second check for three days. Ultimately it develops that both checks were drawn against insufficient funds. The drawee bank asks its lawyer whether it can now dishonor the checks or send them back to the presenter. The answer, as we have seen, is that the drawee probably cannot send them back if it has made final payment. On the facts given, the drawee made final payment on the first check when it paid cash across the counter. The drawee made final payment on the second check by failing to return it to the one who presented it or to send notice of dishonor to that person before its midnight deadline (or before such longer period as an agreement or clearing house rule might give it).

Final payment on the first check occurred under 4–215(a)(1); final payment on the second occurred because of the operation of 4–215(a)(3). Section 4–215(a) reads in full as follows:

> An item is finally paid by a payor bank when the bank has first done any of the following:
>
> (1) paid the item in cash;
>
> (2) settled for the item without having a right to revoke the settlement under statute, clearing-house rule, or agreement; or
>
> (3) made a provisional settlement for the item and failed to revoke the settlement in the time and manner permitted by statute, clearing-house rule or agreement.

The 1990 revision of section 4–215(a) did away with the nettlesome provision of former 4–213(1)(c) which provided that an item was finally paid when the payor "completed the process of posting." The term "process of posting," actually meant something before machine processing and digital accounts. Posting was actually done by a clerk wearing a green eyeshade, holding a pencil in one hand and a check in the other. The clerk compared the check to the ledger showing the account of the drawer and determined if there were sufficient funds to cover the draft. If there were funds available, the clerk subtracted the amount of the check (so "posting" it to the account) and marked the check paid. In modern-day practice no such events occur. Checks enter payor banks in large sacks with many other checks, are run through the payor bank's processing equipment and are charged to various accounts without human intervention. These technological developments made "posting" a dead metaphor. Recognizing former 4–213(1)(c) as an anachronism, the drafters of the revisions to Article 4 removed it.

a. Payment in Cash

In the usual case, section 4–215(a)(1) should cause no difficulty. The payee presents the check across the counter at the drawer's bank and walks out of the lobby with cash in hand. The item has been "paid in cash;" final payment has occurred.

Consider two variations on that transaction. In the first variation, drawee bank has many branches and the payee takes the check not to the branch where the drawer maintains its account, but to another. The payee receives cash and leaves the lobby. Are we to treat this branch of the drawee as the drawee itself or as a collecting bank? Many cases now address that issue in another context that we discuss later in this section. Section 4–107 says that for certain purposes separate branches should be treated as separate banks. If the bank where the money is paid over the counter is treated as a separate bank under 4–107, there has been no final payment. That is so because a collecting bank, not the "payor bank" identified in 4–215 has made the payment. The court in Kirby v. First and Merchants National Bank,[3] may have made the mistake of not recognizing that two branches of the same bank were involved. It is not certain from the facts in Kirby that two branches were involved, but it seems likely. Below we will consider when separate branches should be regarded as separate banks.

In determining whether a multi-branch bank should be treated as one or many banks, one might consider the form of communication among the branches. If every teller station in a system has an on-line computer that allows the teller instantaneous access to a customer's balance maintained in a central computer memory, it is more logical to hold each branch to be part of one bank and to treat the payment as final. If, on the other hand, the teller at one branch has no ready means of determining the balance of any account at another branch, it is unfair to the bank to say that it has made final payment when one branch has paid cash on a check drawn on another branch. In the latter case the bank should have the right to charge back against its customer who received cash for a check which proves to be drawn against insufficient funds.

The second interpretive difficulty in section 4–215(a)(1) is also demonstrated by Kirby. In that case the payee presented a $2500 check and asked that $2300 be deposited in her account and that she be given $200 in cash. Should that transaction be characterized as the bank's payment of an entire $2500 to the payee and the subsequent deposit of $2300 in cash, or should it be treated as the

---

3.   210 Va. 88, 168 S.E.2d 273, 6 UCC
694 (1969).

deposit of $2500 in the payee's account followed by a withdrawal of $200?

If the former, the item has been paid in cash. If the latter, there has been no final payment but merely the deposit of a check to be collected from funds owing to the drawer. Although it seems unfortunate, we suppose there is no way to escape a detailed examination of the transaction done at the teller's station. If the teller is careful to require a deposit slip for the full $2500 and then to insist that the payee take out her own check and withdraw the $200, presumably we have a transaction that is different in form and therefore in substance from the one in which cash is given directly for a portion of the $2500 check. Still, we are uncomfortable with legal distinctions that rest on such formalistic differences because we suspect that the parties to the transaction do not appreciate their significance and would, in fact, regard each transaction as identical.

b. *Settling Without Reservation*

Settling for an item without reserving a right to revoke under subsection (2) is quite unusual. The usual settlement among banks is covered by subsection (3), in which there is a provisional settlement for an item with the payor bank having the right, either under 4–301, clearing-house rules, or the federal regulations to examine its own accounts and to return the check and undo the "provisional settlement" within a limited time.

What cases fit here under subsection (2)? The definition of "settle" in 4–104(a)(11) tells little. It indicates that settlement may be "in cash, by clearing-house settlement, in a charge or credit or by remittance, or otherwise as agreed." Thus, presumably, giving a check in return or authorizing a debit in an account at the Federal Reserve would all be modes of settlement. In the only cases that have arisen under 4–213(1)(b), the predecessor to 4–215(a)(2), payee presenting a check has received a cashier's check. That payee then argues that the payor's giving of its own cashier's check was a settlement and was done without reserving a right to revoke. Clearly, under 4–104, giving the cashier's check was a settlement and if one regards the cashier's check for this purpose as equivalent of cash, it is done without reserving a right to revoke. Surely there would be no right once the check got into the hands of a holder in due course.[4]

---

4. One case has demonstrated that a party who has received final payment does not necessarily yet have the money and may never receive it. In Farmers & Merchants State Bank v. Western Bank, 841 F.2d 1433, 5 UCC2d 372 (9th Cir. 1987), two parties had been running a kite between a rural bank in Oregon and a rural bank in Idaho. Concluding that there was a kite and that it wished to end the transaction, a representative of the Idaho bank personally presented for

To see the confusion that might arise here, assume a payee presents a $100,000 check at the payor bank's counter and takes away a teller's check in payment. Alternatively assume the check is presented through the banking system and a teller's check is sent back in settlement for the check presented. In the first case final payment has occurred at the bank's counter under 4–215(a). The payor bank and the drawer are off the hook on the original check and the payee has to look to the liability on the teller's check for payment. (In this case the payor would be the drawer of the teller's check and so would have liability on that check.) In any event, there would have been final payment on the underlying check; liability on that check would have been discharged. That conclusion is stated explicitly in Comment 8 to 4–215: "However, if presentment of the item was over the counter for immediate payment, final payment has occurred under 4–215(a)(2)." That comment then goes on to note that there is no final payment if there has been only provisional settlement which is withdrawn before it becomes final.

In the other presentation—through the banking system and not over the counter—settlement occurs when the teller's check is sent (under 4–213(a)(2)), but "final settlement" does not occur under 4–213(c) until 1) final payment on *that* check if it is sent for collection, or 2) if not sent for collection, at the midnight deadline of the person receiving the settlement. We are uncertain of the reasons for this distinction between settlements over the counter and other settlements—but there they are.

c. *Midnight Deadline*

The more common settlement case—where the payor has such a right to revoke—is governed by subsection 4–215(a)(3). Under that subsection the payor makes final payment when its provisional settlement (for example, with the Chicago Federal Reserve) becomes final because of the passage of time. Section 4–301(a) gives the payor bank until its "midnight deadline" to return the item or to send notice of dishonor.[5] If it fails to do either before its

---

payment $700,000 of checks drawn on the Oregon bank. To what must have been the recipient's great amazement, the Oregon bank gave a $700,000 cashier's check in return for the checks drawn upon it. Before the cashier's check was finally paid, the Oregon bank awakened and refused to make payment on that check.

5. § 4–301(a) reads:

If a payor bank settles for a demand item other than a documentary draft presented otherwise than for immediate payment over the counter before midnight of the banking day of receipt, the payor bank may revoke the settlement and recover the settlement if, before it has made final payment and before its midnight deadline, it

(1) returns the item; or

(2) sends written notice of dishonor or nonpayment if the item is unavailable for return.

midnight deadline or before any later time under an agreement, it will make final payment under 4–215(a)(3).[6]

In Hanna v. First National Bank of Rochester,[7] the New York Court of Appeals found that Fleet Bank, the payor had made final payment on a series of checks even though the bank had returned the checks by its midnight deadline. The court also found that the depositary bank was obliged to re-credit its customer's account under section 4–212 because the payor bank had made final payment. While the language of the opinion is not felicitous, the interesting issue is an apparently straightforward application of the rules in 4–302. That section gives a payor bank until its midnight deadline to return checks but it does so only if the payor has "settled" for the checks on the day they are received. Since Fleet Bank did not settle, it had no right to wait beyond midnight the day of receipt and its return of the checks before the midnight deadline on the next day was fruitless. All of that is quite straightforward and understandable.

What is not understandable is how Fleet could have received the 18 bad checks through a "clearing house" without having settled with the presenting bank as part of the clearing house process. As we understand it, banks that trade checks at a manual clearing house (as opposed to an automated clearing house) physically exchange checks with one another and somehow arrange, through a credit at the federal reserve or through a remittance instrument, for the one who owes the larger dollar amount to pay that amount to the other bank. In footnote 1 the court rejects Fleet's argument that it made a "clearing house settlement". The Court states that the plaintiffs established that Fleet "had not done anything more than internally process the checks * * *." It states that Fleet presented "no admissible evidence" of its "settling" as part of the clearing house process.

Under 4–104(a)(10) the midnight deadline is "midnight on its next banking day following the banking day on which it receives the relevant item." Thus if a bank receives a check on Wednesday morning and makes a provisional settlement for it (e.g., a credit to the presenter's account in the Federal Reserve), it would have until Thursday midnight to return that item or give notice. If it fails to do so before Thursday midnight it will have made final payment under 4–215(a)(3).

Note, however, that it may have additional time because of a clearing house rule or other agreement. If, for example, it settles with a local bank under a clearing house rule which allows three

---

6. See § 5–5 through 5–7 *infra* for collecting Bank's obligation on "payable through" items under Article 4 and Regulation CC.

7. 87 N.Y.2d 107, 637 N.Y.S.2d 953, 661 N.E.2d 683, 28 UCC2d 417 (1995).

days,[8] it would have that additional time to return the item or give notice before its payment is deemed final under (a)(3). The lawyer who argues that a payor bank has made final payment because it failed to revoke a provisional settlement must first determine when the midnight deadline occurred and then must examine the clearing house rule, the Federal Reserve rules, and any other pertinent agreements to determine whether the midnight deadline is extended in such cases.

Computing the midnight deadline is not always easy. Superficially, section 4–104(a)(10) is simple enough. It means that items received on Monday have a midnight deadline of Tuesday midnight. If action is required before that time and not taken, there is final payment.

The first complication is posed by 4–108,[9] which states that certain items received at 2:00 p.m. or later may, at the bank's election, be treated as though they were received on the next day. Thus, in our example, if an item comes in at 3:00 p.m. on Monday, or with a group of other checks on Monday evening, these items will be treated as though they were received on Tuesday and their midnight deadline will be Wednesday. When a bank exercises the 4–108 option, the burden is on the bank to show that checks were received after the cutoff hour or the checks will not be considered timely dishonored.[10]

Note that 4–108(b) refers to the "banking day." Section 4–104(a)(3) defines banking day as "the part of a day on which a bank is open to the public for carrying on substantially all of its banking functions * * *."[11] Sunday, when no part of the bank is open, is not a banking day; but what about Saturday, when certain teller windows are open and when occasionally a loan is written? Some state legislatures have dealt with that question by amending the 4–104(a)(3) definition of a "banking day" to make it more explicit, but in other cases there will be uncertainty.[12] If Saturday is a

---

8. For a case including such rules see, e.g., West Side Bank v. Marine Nat. Exch. Bank, 37 Wis.2d 661, 155 N.W.2d 587, 4 UCC 1003 (1968).

9. § 4–108 reads:

(a) For the purpose of allowing time to process items, prove balances, and make the necessary entries on its books to determine its position for the day, a bank may fix an afternoon hour of 2 P.M. or later as a cutoff hour for the handling of money and items and the making of entries on its books.

(b) An item or deposit of money received on any day after a cutoff hour so fixed or after the close of the banking day may be treated as being received at the opening of the next banking day.

10. Third Century Recycling, Inc. v. Bank of Baroda, 704 F.Supp. 417, 8 UCC2d 105 (S.D.N.Y. 1989).

11. The definition in Regulation CC is virtually identical:

"Banking day" means that part of any business day on which an office of a bank is open to the public for carrying on substantially all of its banking functions.

12 CFR 229.2(f).

12. For a discussion of "banking" day as compared with "business" day

banking day, checks received late on Friday will have a midnight Monday deadline. If Saturday is not a banking day, the late Friday arrivals might be treated as received on Monday morning and thus have a Tuesday night deadline. These concerns may seem picayune, but consider a kiting transaction in which several banks are involved and in which each bank processes tens of thousands of dollars every day. The extension or restriction of the midnight deadline by one day in that setting can cause swings of hundreds of thousands of dollars among various banks in the kiting scheme.

The most significant difficulty in measuring the midnight deadline is the determination in a multi-branch payor when the clock starts to tick and when it stops. Free-standing, single office banks are now the exception. As multi-state banking increases and branching within a state becomes more prevalent, the norm will be a bank with many branches and one or more regional data processing centers where all checks for a region are processed. To understand the difficulty that a multi-branch system poses for determining when final payment has been made, consider the differing results reached in an Idaho case and an Alabama case.

The check involved in Idah–Best, Inc. v. First Security Bank[13] was drawn by Wesley Prouty on the Hailey branch of First Security Bank of Idaho and was issued to Idah–Best. Idah–Best deposited the check in its account at Twin Falls (Idaho) Bank and Trust Company on October 31, a Friday. On Monday, Twin Falls, acting as a collecting bank, mailed the check to the Boise branch of First Security for deposit in Twin Falls' commercial account there. The check arrived on Tuesday, November 4, at the data processing center in the basement of the Boise branch, where it was indorsed, encoded with MICR information, and provisionally entered on the books of the Hailey branch. Information about the check was transmitted to First Security's central computer in Salt Lake City during the night of November 4. The central computer posted all First Security checks to the proper accounts and printed out a list of NSF checks, including the Idah–Best check. On the morning of November 5, the Idah–Best check was physically sent to Hailey via bankers' dispatch. At the Hailey branch, the check was proofed to determine the validity of the signature and was given to the branch manager for his decision to pay or dishonor. On Thursday, November 6, the day after receiving it, the branch manager decided not to pay the Idah–Best check. The check was then stamped and returned to the Boise branch, which received it on Friday, November

and how the question might be governed by clearing house rules see Texas American Bank/Farmers Branch v. Abrams Centre Nat. Bank, 780 S.W.2d 814, 10 UCC2d 927 (Tex.App. 1989). For a discussion of the words "banking day" and "substantially all of its banking functions" see United Bank of Crete–Steger v. Gainer Bank, N.A., 874 F.2d 475, 8 UCC2d 337 (7th Cir.1989).

13. 99 Idaho 517, 584 P.2d 1242, 25 UCC 209 (1978).

7. On Monday, November 10, the Boise branch reversed its provisional credit to Twin Falls' account for the Idah–Best check and sent the check back to Twin Falls. Since November 11 was a legal holiday, Twin Falls Bank did not receive the check until November 12. The depositary bank notified Idah–Best of the dishonor on November 13; one can imagine the company's surprise in discovering, two weeks after deposit, that the check was not good.

Idah–Best argued that First Security was but a single bank, and therefore the midnight deadline clock began to run on November 3, when the check arrived at the Boise branch. Citing former 4–106 (now 4–107),[14] the Idaho court concluded that each of the branches of the First Security system was a separate bank and that the data processing center itself, being part of a branch, should be treated as a separate bank. Thus each had a midnight deadline and when all the deadlines were tacked together, none was violated.

In a line of cases that started with Farmers & Merchants Bank v. Bank of America[15] and predated *Idah-Best*, other courts have come to the opposite conclusion of the Idaho court. In *Farmers and Merchants* the California courts found receipt of a check at the Bank of America's Montibello computer center should be treated as received at the branch and thus to cause the clock to begin to tick. The majority of the courts that have faced the question since *Idah-Best* have distinguished it on the facts or have rejected its reasoning. The tendency now is to regard the computer center for a multi-branch system as a part of the branches that the computer center serves. Illustrative of these cases is Central Bank v. Peoples National Bank.[16] There Mrs. White made out a check payable to her son drawn on her account at the Florence branch of Central Bank. She cashed the check herself (after apparently forging her son's signature) on September 18 at a branch of Peoples Bank. The check was sent by Peoples to the local Federal Reserve which served as a local clearing house. The Fed sent the check to the Decatur data processing center of Central Bank on September 20. The Decatur computer center did basic bookkeeping for all Central Bank branches and "substantially all the accounting functions" for the Florence branch. On September 21, the Decatur center sent the check to the

---

14. Revised § 4–107 reads:

A branch or separate office of a bank is a separate bank for the purpose of computing the time within which and determining the place at or to which action may be taken or notices or orders shall be given under this Article and under Article 3.

The statutory predecessor to 4–107, former 4–106 offered the following bracketed language, "[maintaining its own deposit ledgers]", which could be inserted following the first use of the word "bank" in the quoted section. At least 37 states chose to omit the bracketed language. The comment to revised 4–107 explains that it was removed because it had little relevance to a system where account records are stored electronically and widely accessible.

15. 20 Cal.App.3d 939, 98 Cal.Rptr. 381 (1971).

16. 401 So.2d 14, 31 UCC 1428 (Ala. 1981).

Florence branch, where it was checked for forgeries and a final decision about payment was made. The Florence branch manager decided not to pay the check, and attempted to return it by courier directly to Peoples National on September 22. Peoples National refused to accept the check from the courier, whereupon Central Bank unsuccessfully attempted to return it through the Fed.

In the resulting lawsuit, defendant Central Bank argued that Alabama had not adopted the optional language of 4–106, so that the Florence branch should be considered a separate bank even if it did not maintain its own ledgers. Holding that the Decatur computer center, the designated place of presentment, was part of the Florence branch for purposes of 4–104, 4–301 and 4–302, the court disagreed. Therefore, the midnight deadline clock began ticking when the check arrived at the computer center on September 20, giving Central Bank only until midnight on September 21 to pay or dishonor.

The court distinguished *Idah-Best* on the ground that in the Idaho case the computer center was not the designated place of presentment, and that Idaho, unlike Alabama, by statute requires that the face of bank checks designate the place of presentment.

The Alabama court's technical basis for distinguishing *Idah-Best* cannot disguise the fact that it came to the opposite conclusion in a strikingly similar case. The functions performed by the Boise processing center with the help of the Salt Lake City computer seem to be the same as those performed by the Decatur computer center in Alabama. In each case, all that was left for the branch to do was to look at the check for forgeries and make the final payment decision. The Alabama court, however, emphasized how many functions were performed by the computer center before the check arrived at the branch, and dismissed the importance of the location of the final payment decision. In contrast, the Idaho court discounted the functions performed at the computer center and focused on the significance of the fact that only the branch had the authority to make the final payment decision, and that that decision could only be made after the branch had received the check.

Although it is not a complete solution, we suspect that Regulation CC will resolve many of the data center cases. Regulation CC codifies the *Farmers & Merchants Bank* line of cases and rejects *Idah-Best*. Section 229.36(b) reads in full as follows:

(b) *Receipt at bank office or processing center.* A check is considered received by the paying bank when it is received:

(1) At a location to which delivery is requested by the paying bank;

(2) At an address of the bank associated with the routing number on the check, whether in magnetic ink or in fractional form;

(3) At any branch or head office, if the bank is identified on the check by name without address; or

(4) At a branch, head office, or other location consistent with the name and address of the bank on the check if the bank is identified on the check by name and address.

Normally a check would be sent to a processing center at the "request" of the paying bank and would be considered "received" at that place under (b)(1). The commentary to 229.36 states that the bank "must accept presentment" at any one of the four locations identified in (b). Moreover, it states that subsection (1) adopts the common law rule of a number of legal decisions that the processing center acts as the agent of the paying bank "to accept presentment and to begin the time for the processing of the check."

Section 229.36 may also override 4–107 in the cash payment case. Assume a situation like *Kirby*.[17] In that case a payee procured payment of a check at one branch of a bank that may have been drawn on another branch. If the two branches are treated as separate banks under 4–107, there would be no final payment even though the check had been "cashed" because it would have been cashed by a collecting bank not by the payor and so not paid.

Although sections 229.36(b)(3) and (4) are mostly designed for cases in which a check is presented for credit and not for cash payment, some courts might use them to determine whether one branch must be treated as a separate bank or is merely part of the same bank on which the check was drawn. One could certainly argue that a check which identifies a multi-branch bank by name only and "without address" is payable at any branch and thus that payment over the counter at any branch constitutes final payment. It seems unlikely that the drafters of Regulation CC had that in mind, but they might have.

One could bolster that argument by showing that the definition of paying bank under 229.2(z) pulls all branches into a "single paying bank" whether the branch is identified on the check or not. We believe that reads too much into the definition; we doubt the drafters intended that.

One difficulty with all this is that it is not certain that Regulation CC states a federal rule intended to override contrary state law in all situations. The Supremacy Clause of the Constitution does not become relevant until one has determined that the

17. Kirby v. First and Merchants   UCC 694 (1969).
Nat. Bank, 210 Va. 88, 168 S.E.2d 273, 6

federal government's agents intended federal law to override contrary state law. Indeed, it is not clear that the Federal Reserve
intended that these provisions of Regulation CC would govern the
issue of timing for the purpose of determining final payment. In
some places in Regulation CC the Federal Reserve explicitly de-
clares its intent to modify contrary state law.[18]

Because Regulation CC does not claim exclusively to control
the issue of separate branches, and the UCC does not explicitly bow
to Regulation CC, it is possible that 4–107 allows separate branches
to be treated like separate banks, at least in certain situations.
Comment 4 to 4–107 states that "if a branch functions as a
separate bank, it should have the time limits available to a separate
bank." That language seems to refer to the timing of the midnight
deadline and it may be that the drafters wish to permit banks that
require presentment at a particular branch the right to insist upon
that before the midnight deadline commences to run. That possibility is strengthened by the confession in Comment 1 that the
drafters could not find a "single rule that is logically correct, fair in
all situations and workable under all different types of practices."
However, the comment's explicit reference to 229.36(b) as setting
the "time when a check is received by a payor bank" suggests
either that the drafters changed their minds by the time they got to
Part 2 of Article 4 or that the drafters of the comments to 4–107
never talked to drafters of the comments to 4–204. The comment to
4–204 adopts the federal rule and applies it to presentment questions under Article 4. The last sentence in the comment to 4–204
reads in full as follows: "The time when a check is received by a
payor bank for presentment is governed by Regulation CC Section
229.36(b)."[19]

d.   The Mechanics of Return

Knowing only when the clock starts is never enough. One must
also know whether the bank has taken the necessary steps to
"return" the item before the midnight deadline. Under 4–301 and
similar clearing-house rules and regulations, the payor must take
some act prior to the midnight deadline or prior to some other time,
such as a 4:00 p.m. clearing house exchange. Section 4–301(a)
specifies that the payor must either "return" the item or, if the
item is unavailable for return, send written notice of dishonor or
nonpayment.

But what acts are sufficient for the payor to "return" an item
by the midnight deadline? Section 4–301(d) defines "return" as
follows:

18. See Reg. CC 229.30(c) (extending
midnight deadline of the UCC in specific
circumstances).

19. For more on Reg. CC see 5–5
infra.

An item is returned:

(1) as to an item presented through a clearing house, when it is delivered to the presenting or last collecting bank or to the clearing house or is sent or delivered in accordance with clearing-house rules; or

(2) in all other cases, when it is sent or delivered to the bank's customer or transferor or pursuant to instructions.

This definition draws a clear distinction between items presented through a clearing house and items presented through the federal reserve or otherwise.

The acts necessary to return an item are relatively straight forward for items which are not presented through a clearing house; an item is considered returned when it is "sent" or "delivered." Since sending is a prerequisite to delivery we can conclude that an item not presented through a clearing house is returned when it is sent by the payor bank. We will call this a "send system," and under Section 1–201(38), the item is considered returned at the time the payor deposits it in the mail or starts its return by other usual means. The outbound check will not necessarily retrace the steps of the inbound checks. Often the paying branch will skip the computer center and send the item directly to the depositary bank or to the presenting bank. It will send only a debit notice back through its computer center. If that is the case, the item is "sent" if it is in the mailbox outside the walls of the bank by the midnight deadline. But consider First Bank of Immokalee v. Farm Worker's Check Cashing, Inc.,[20] which was decided under Florida's 4–302(a) and 4–201. Customer notified bank that its new address would be effective on March 31, and the bank attempted to return checks to customer at that address on March 3. Florida's 4–201(38) states: " 'Send' in connection with any writing or notice means to deposit in the mail ... to an address specified thereon or otherwise agreed...." It goes on to state that the "receipt of any writing or notice within the time at which it would have arrived if properly sent has the effect of a proper sending."[21] The jury found that sending notice to the wrong address did not satisfy the midnight deadline.

But there are many other variations here and it is not always obvious how the rules should apply to them. The trial court in *Farmers & Merchants Bank* held that the clock started ticking on the arrival of the check at the computer center when the check was inbound to the branch. The court then found that the bank satisfied its obligation to return the instrument if it left the branch itself by the midnight deadline. Apparently the court reasoned that

---

20. 745 So.2d 994, 39 UCC2d 663 (Fla.App. 1999).   **21.** F.S.A. § 671.201(38).

if putting the check in the mailbox would constitute "sending" then commencing its journey back through the computer center (by an even more expeditious route) should itself be regarded as "sending."[22]

Section 4–301(d)(1) has separate rules for items presented through a clearing house. Under that provision, return must be made in accordance with "clearing house rules" or it can be "delivered to the presenting or last collecting bank." If one concludes that 4–301(d)(1) is the exclusive method of returning an item through a clearing house, the "send" option is not available as to such items.

To understand the problem, consider the following hypothetical. Assume that a payor bank receives an item through a clearing house at a 4:00 p.m. clearing on Wednesday. The clearing house rules provide that items presented on Day 1 shall be returned no later than the last clearing on the next day. Accordingly the items must be returned no later than the 4:00 p.m. clearing on Thursday. What if the payor does not discover that this is an NSF item in time to make the 4:00 p.m. clearing on Thursday? It might try to return the item in two ways. First, it could simply mail the item before Thursday night midnight and argue that it had returned the item by "sending it" as provided in (d)(2). Since the alternative to compliance with clearing house rules is the "delivery" to the sending or last collecting bank, we do not believe such a "sending" is an effective return.

Alternatively the payor could have a bank messenger actually deliver the check to the presenting bank before midnight Thursday or even sometime before Friday midnight. In those cases, the payor bank could argue that it was returning the check before its midnight deadline (in this case midnight of Friday, since the item was presented after 2:00 p.m.) and in accordance with the rules set out in (d)(1) because it was actually delivered and not merely sent to the depositary or presenting bank.

There are several difficulties with this argument. First, the presenting bank will argue that returning through the clearing house is the only method of return and that—notwithstanding the provisions in (d)(1)—the bank who has received something through a clearing house and who has signed onto clearing house rules that require a return by 4:00 p.m. the next day may not deviate from those rules. If that is what the rules say, we think that would be a correct interpretation and that the payor would have given up the

---

22. In the appendix of *Farmers & Merchants* one can see that the court found that the Bank of America had returned some of the checks by the midnight deadline, but not others. One then must read the trial court records to find that the trial court concluded the checks that had been returned had, in fact, not yet gone all the way back through the computer center.

right apparently granted by (d)(1) physically to deliver the check directly to the presenting or last collecting bank. If, on the other hand, the clearing house rule merely said that any return to the clearing house had to be by 4:00 p.m., that rule in and of itself would not eliminate the right to do a direct return of the item.

The second issue is whether the clearing house rule should be construed to cut down the midnight deadline so that the deadline is midnight Wednesday as opposed to midnight Thursday in circumstances where a post–2:00 p.m. presentment on Tuesday would make Thursday midnight the midnight deadline. Again, one would have to read section 4–108 together with the terms of the clearing house agreement and with the cut off time set by the payor bank. It is possible that the payor bank's own rules or the clearing house rules would render 4–108 inapplicable to an instrument presented through the clearing house. If that were true, so be it. If that were not true, we are uncertain what the outcome would be. We can imagine circumstances where it would be unclear whether the clearing house rules and the bank's internal procedure caused the bank to give up the right to the additional day that it would otherwise have under 4–108.

To summarize, the presentment of an item through a clearing house will in some circumstances limit the rights the payor bank would otherwise have to return the check by alternative means and not through the clearing house. Almost certainly presentment through a clearing house will foreclose the right the bank would otherwise have to stop the clock by "sending." At a minimum, the bank who receives a check through a clearing house will likely have to deliver it to the presenting bank before the midnight deadline or get it back to the appropriate clearing under the clearing house rules.

What the clearing house regulations portend, Regulation CC makes explicit in another context, namely, that we are moving from a regime in which the payor bank's responsibility was to "send" to a regime in which its responsibility will be to "deliver." Already the analogous obligations in Regulation CC for the return of items are dependent upon normal time of receipt, not upon the time of sending.[23] Although Regulation CC does not require that the payor bank deliver a particular item at a specified time, it requires the sending of items in such a way that they would "normally" be received at a particular time. Thus, it is a modified delivery system.

Once the sending and returning of checks down and up stream becomes entirely electronic, we imagine that payor banks will be bound to deliver these messages and will not be able to escape final payment liability merely by sending a message.

23. See Regulation CC §§ 229.30(a), 229.31(a) and Section 5–5, *infra*.

Note finally that the rules in Regulation CC do not, for the most part, directly modify part 3 of Article 4—even though they establish analogous obligations. When there has been a late return of an item, one must typically examine not only Regulation CC but also the UCC. The penalties for violation of these provisions differ. Generally the penalties are more severe for failing to comply with 4–302 (namely, responsibility for the full amount of the check under 4–302) than for violation of Regulation CC. Regulation CC, 229.38, punishes failure only by imposing damages "proximately caused"—a number that often is zero even where liability under 4–302 is for the full amount.[24]

e. *Agreements Varying the Midnight Deadline Rules*

There are at least three ways in which parties to a clearing house or other collection agreement might change the rules that would otherwise apply under Regulation CC, J, or Article 4 of the UCC. The first is exemplified by Bon Bon Productions, Ltd. v. Xanadu Productions, Inc.[25] There the Federal Reserve Bank of Boston, First National Bank of Boston and Old Colony Trust had made an agreement which provided that the Federal Reserve would deliver checks to First National Bank of Boston that were drawn on Old Colony Trust. First National Bank of Boston would do Old Colony's data processing. It was agreed among the three that checks should not be deemed to be presented until they were physically received at Old Colony Trust. In effect, the parties by agreement sought to change the rule that would otherwise apply under cases like *Farmers & Merchants* in California. Despite the fact that it had the effect of delaying the midnight deadline by one day, the agreement was accepted by the court in Massachusetts as binding not only on those parties, but also on the payee on the check who later asserted that the bank had held it beyond its midnight deadline.

In similar fashion some clearing house rules provide that a check is considered returned when it leaves the branch not when it leaves the computer or data processing center on the return trip after it has been dishonored. This, too, in effect changes the rule that might otherwise apply in some cases (though not under *Farmers & Merchants*) if one treated the data processing center as part of the branch on both the inbound and outbound legs. It too will have the effect of extending the period the bank has to act by a day,

---

24. For a case where Regulation CC explicitly overruled the UCC, see Reg. CC § 229.30(c) (extending the midnight deadline of the UCC in specific circumstances); for an example of the UCC bowing to Regulation CC, see § 4–204,

Comment 4 (recognizing Regulation CC § 229.36(b) as governing the time of receipt by a payor bank).

25. 1981 WL 138017, 32 UCC 253 (D.Mass. 1981).

but it does so by adjusting the back end instead of the front end of the transaction.

We believe that all such reasonable rules adopted by groups of banks are valid and should be upheld. They are explicitly affirmed by 4–103(c). Because banks are on all sides of these transactions there is little likelihood that they will conspire to favor their own interests and injure those of the consumer. Because presenting banks wish to get payment as soon as possible, they can be expected to oppose rules that include unreasonably long extensions of the midnight deadline.

If an agreement of this type takes the form of an explicit extension of the midnight deadline, it may not be binding on the Federal Reserve because of Regulation J. In keeping with the Federal Reserve's interest in reducing the float and stimulating the fastest possible payment of checks, Regulation J[26] invalidates explicit extensions of the midnight deadline. The Federal Reserve itself has entered into indirect extension agreements such as that in the *Bon Bon* case; presumably therefore Regulation J is aimed merely at agreements that would explicitly extend the time, not at those which accomplish the same result by specifying the time for beginning or ending of the payor bank's time to pay. To the extent items not presented through the Federal Reserve are not subject to Regulation J, we believe that the party should have the right to extend the midnight deadline either explicitly with respect to particular checks or as a matter of agreement. Apparently that was done in the *West Side Bank* case.[27] We see no reason why such agreement should not be recognized under 4–103 in exactly the same way similar agreements are recognized in the *Bon Bon* and *Catalina Yachts* cases.

§ 5–5   The Effect of Regulations J and CC

In this section we consider how the rules described above have been modified by two important federal regulations. Regulation J, 12 CFR 210, governs the rights of parties in the collection process through the Federal Reserve banks. Originally Regulation J prescribed rules similar to Article 4; a number of the rules, however, have been changed by Regulation CC. Regulation CC, 12 CFR 229, was adopted by the Board of the Federal Reserve System to implement the Expedited Funds Availability Act.

---

26. See 12 CFR 210.12(a) which provides in part as follows:

The rules or practices of a clearinghouse through which the item was presented, * * * may not extend these return times, but may provide for a shorter return time.

27. West Side Bank v. Marine Nat. Exch. Bank, 37 Wis.2d 661, 155 N.W.2d 587, 4 UCC 1003 (1968).

Regulation CC is divided into three parts. Subpart A includes definitions and the means for administrative enforcement. Subpart B requires banks and other depositary institutions to make funds available according to specific time schedules, to accrue interest on interest-bearing accounts upon receipt of credit for the funds, and to disclose funds availability schedules to their customers. Subpart C establishes rules to expedite the collection and return of checks by payor and returning banks to help depositary banks meet the availability standards set out in Subpart B.

To appreciate the significance of Regulation CC, one must understand something about banking practices. Since World War II the collection of checks in the United States has become highly automated. Every bank has mechanical readers that read the MICR line at the bottom of the check and so determine what account is to be charged and the amount of that charge. Moreover MICR lines enable depositary banks automatically to route checks to the payors; the payor bank's location and identification is encoded on the bottom of the check. The practice has made collection of checks, their transmission from depositary to payor bank and passage of the money back upstream, highly efficient and speedy.

The same is not true of the return of checks that are dishonored. Because the depositary bank's code is not included on the MICR line and because machines are incapable of reading scrawled or stamped indorsements on the rear of the check, dishonored checks have traditionally been returned by a slow, laborious hand process. As part of that process, a payor bank might send a check back to the bank from which the payor received it, who in turn would send the check to the bank from which the check was received, and so on. If the indorsements were illegible or if there was a mistake by a clerk, the process is slowed yet further. Because of the sluggishness of this process, it has not been uncommon for a depositary bank to receive notice of dishonor (on a check that it had sent for payment) many days and occasionally weeks after the depositary bank had sent the check downstream toward the payor bank. The possibility of such tardy returns made depositary banks hesitant to grant withdrawal rights to their customers. A common response to this problem by the depositary banks was not merely to single out the suspect large checks, but to put "blanket holds" on all consumer deposits. Banks defended their action by pointing to section 4–213(4)(a), predecessor to 4–215(e)(1), which stated that the funds need not be made available until "the bank has had a reasonable time to learn that the settlement is final."

Organizations representing bank customers sought both federal and state legislation to require banks to grant earlier credit. These attempts bore fruit in California and New York and, in 1988, in the Congress. With the passage of the Expedited Funds Availability Act in 1988, all banks are required to make funds available according to a schedule that we discuss below. This requirement, of course, gives the bank a stimulus to mechanize and speed up the return of dishonored checks. Subpart C, titled Collection of Checks (229.30 et seq.), contains a set of rules that will require banks who are returning checks to speed up that process. The requirements concerning the placement of indorsements on the check, and how they are to read, are results of this process. In various places the regulation holds out small bits of candy (in the form of the extension of the midnight deadline, for example) to those who facilitate the expedited return of checks by MICR encoding the return information and by the use of particularly expeditious means of return.

Regulation CC is extensive and complicated. For the novice, we include a general description of its provisions, however, we deal in detail only with those sections that will either change the state law on liability for late return of an item or will add potential liability under the federal law for one who fails to act in a timely fashion. The detailed and complicated provisions on the timing of funds availability in specific circumstances are beyond the scope of this book. One who would advise a bank as to its responsibility *as a depositary bank* to its customers who deposit checks should study the details of the Regulation closely, and might also consult the Clarks' work or another treatise that considers the issues in greater detail.[1]

a. *Structure of Regulation CC*

The rules in Subpart B on availability supplant the reasonable time standard of section 4–215.[2] The timetables are based on a variety of factors such as distance of the payor bank from the depositary bank, the risk associated with the sum (large versus small checks), and the probability of dishonor (new accounts versus seasoned accounts). Needless to say, liability for violating these rules concerning availability cannot be disclaimed by the depositary bank.

Look first at the definitions in Subpart A. Note that "banking day" is not the same as "business day," that local checks may differ from non-local checks in mysterious ways, and that there are a variety of other definitions such as "qualified return checks," "returning bank," and "non-proprietary ATM." To interpret the schedules correctly, one must study the definitions carefully.

§ 5–5

1. B. Clark & B. Clark, Regulation CC, Funds Availability and Check Collection (1988).

2. See Regulation CC § 229.1 for authority and purpose, § 229.2 for definitions and § 229.3 for administrative enforcement.

To understand the basic rules, consider the responsibility of a depositary bank first with respect to a local check, then with respect to a non-local check. Under section 229.12(b) local checks must be made available not later than "the second business day following the banking day" on which they are deposited. Thus, if the depositor deposited a local check on Monday morning, the depositary bank would have to make the funds available for local withdrawal on Wednesday.

To taste the complexity, note that if the deposit were made at a night depository on Monday when the depositary bank was not open for business, then the deposit would not have been made during the "banking day" Monday and would be treated as though it had been deposited on Tuesday, so to be available on Thursday.

Nonlocal checks must be available not later than the fifth business day following the banking day of deposit. This means that the depositary bank may bar withdrawal of deposits from nonlocal checks until nearly one and one-half weeks have passed. Saturday and Sunday are not business days and thus do not count in the five. Local and nonlocal personal checks are but two of the instruments that could be deposited. Below we summarize the rules with respect to many other forms of deposit.

The Regulation provides for next day availability[3] for cash deposited in person to an employee of the depositary bank and other low risk deposits including (1) electronic payments which have been received by the depositary bank; (2) checks drawn on the Treasury of the United States; (3) United States Postal Service money orders; (4) checks drawn by a State or a unit of local government; (5) cashier's checks, certified checks or teller's checks; (6) checks drawn on the same or another branch of the same bank; and (7) the lesser of $100 or the aggregate amount deposited not subject to next day availability.[4]

In addition to modifying the "reasonable time" standard of the UCC, Regulation CC alters the availability of funds for "on us" checks and cash deposits. Under section 4–215(e)(2) where the bank is both the depositary and the payor bank, the deposited funds would otherwise become available for withdrawal as of right "at the opening of the bank's second banking day following receipt of the item." For the most part, Regulation CC calls for shorter availability (one day) under 229.10(c)(vi) if both branches of the bank are

3. Next day availability is defined as the "business day" after the "banking day" on which the cash is deposited under § 229.10. "Business day" and "banking day" are defined terms under § 229.2(f) and (g).

4. See § 229.10(a)-(c). Specific presentation restrictions (i.e., in person, to an employee of the depositary bank, with a special deposit slip, etc.) and content restrictions (i.e., deposited in an account held by payee, deposited in same state as government drawer, etc.) apply to each form of deposit mentioned. In the event that these requirements are not met, check holds will be extended.

located in the same state or check processing region. However, an "on us" check deposited into a *new account* would fall under one of the recognized exceptions to the funds availability schedule thereby allowing the bank to impose a longer hold.[5]

There are some important exceptions to the funds availability schedule, most notably: for new accounts, 229.13(a); large deposits (in excess of $5,000), 229.13(b); and cases where there is reasonable cause to doubt collectibility, 229.13(e). If an exception applies, the depository bank may extend the temporary and permanent schedules for a "reasonable time," but must provide the depositor with written notice.[6]

b. *Payment of Interest*

The "anti-float" provisions of Regulation CC provide for the payment of interest on interest bearing accounts "not later than the business day on which the depositary bank receives credit for the funds."[7] Given the variability as to when the depositary bank has "actually" received credit on any individual check, the bank may rely on the funds availability schedule of the Federal Reserve Bank or the Federal Home Loan Bank to establish the time when interest will start to accrue.[8]

c. *Disclosure Requirements*

Four sections deal with disclosure: (1) the general ground rules under 229.15, (2) specific availability policy disclosure under 229.16,

---

5. § 229.13(a)(1)(iii) provides that a deposit into a "new account," is "not subject to the availability requirements of   229.10(c)(1)(vi)   * * *." § 229.10(c)(1)(vi) calls for next day availability for "on us" checks. An account is considered a "new account" during the first 30 calendar days after the account is established under 229.13(a)(2).

Cash deposit availability has been *extended* by Regulation CC in some circumstances but for the most part remains the same as under the UCC—next day availability. Whereas the UCC calls for the availability of funds for withdrawal "as of right at the opening of the bank's next banking day," Regulation CC will only provide such availability if the deposit is made "in person to an employee of the depositary bank." Generally see § 4–215(f) and § 229.10(a)(1). If the cash deposit is not made in person to an employee of the bank, Regulation

CC mandates availability not later than the second business day after the banking day on which the cash is deposited. See § 229.10(a)(2). Given that Regulation CC availability standards must yield to state laws providing for quicker availability under 229.20(a)(1), banks should follow the UCC standard of next day availability regarding cash deposits.

6. See § 229.13(h). A reasonable time is presumed to be an extension of up to one "business day" for "on us" checks and checks drawn on a branch of the same bank located in same state or processing region; five business days for local checks; and six business days for nonlocal checks. See § 229.13(h)(4). A longer extension than those provided here may be reasonable, but the bank will bear the burden of so establishing. § 229.13(h)(4). The notice requirements are outlined in § 229.13(g).

7. See § 229.14(a).

8. See § 229.14(a)(1).

(3) initial disclosure under 229.17 and, (4) additional disclosure requirements under 229.18.

The general ground rules section identifies the necessary *form of disclosure* as "clearly and conspicuously in writing" in a form that the "customer may keep."[9] The commentary suggests that a bank should publish "plain English" booklets that state the terms of the deposit agreement and highlight the funds availability policy. The uniform reference to day of availability as "the _____ business day after the day of deposit," is intended to provide a common denominator by which customers can compare bank fund availability policies. Use of such a word formula is similar to the uniform reference to "annual percentage rate" under the Truth in Lending Act. Other rules state bank obligations regarding disclosure to multiple account customers and to holders of dormant and inactive accounts.[10]

An "initial" detailed disclosure of the bank's specific availability policy must be made to holders of new and existing accounts.[11] Among the many additional required disclosures are notices of any adverse changes in policy 30 days before the policy is implemented.[12]

The specific availability policy disclosure contains five elements: (1) a summary of the bank's availability policy; (2) a description of categories of deposits not available on a next day basis and how these categories are determined; (3) a description of any Reg. CC 229.13 exceptions that may be invoked by the bank and a statement regarding notification under such circumstances; (4) a description of any case-by-case policy which would extend holds; (5) how to differentiate between proprietary and non-proprietary ATMs if there is a relevant distinction to be made regarding availability policies.[13]

Some banks will claim the largest amount of time permissible under the rule of Regulation CC. Other banks have decided to grant next day availability on all items with exceptions for case by case situations. For example, a bank might take the position that it will normally grant next day availability, but that it will place a hold on deposits of particularly large items. Section 229.16(c) provides for the specific notice that must be given that there will be a hold on a particular check. Of course, complications can arise in that case from the fact that the check may be deposited at an ATM and not over the counter. In those cases the notice must be mailed to the depositor.

---

9. See § 229.15(a).
10. See § 229.15(c) and (d).
11. See § 229.17(a) and (b).
12. See § 229.18(a) through (e).
13. See § 229.16(b).

The complex set of rules and the detailed form of disclosures that are required raise the specter of the early days of the Truth in Lending law when large amounts of paper were put in the hands of hundreds of thousands of consumer debtors who discarded the disclosures unread. We see no way to avoid a similar expenditure of resources under Regulation CC. Because of the civil liability provisions discussed below, and particularly because of the provisions that contemplate class action recovery of as much as $500,000, no bank can afford to ignore these rules nor dare any lawyer read them in a casual and cavalier way.

d. Civil Liability

Under 229.21 the bank is liable not only for "actual damages" but also for "such additional amount as the court may allow," but not more than $1,000 nor less than $100 in an individual action, or more than the "lesser of $500,000 or 1 percent of the net worth of the bank" in a class action. The rule contains provisions to guide the court in the case of class action awards and specifies that the bank is not liable "if the bank demonstrates by a preponderance of the evidence that the violation was not intentional and resulted from a bona fide error, notwithstanding the maintenance of procedures reasonably adapted to avoid any such error."[14] There is a one year statute of limitation.[15]

e. Subpart C

Subpart C deals with the payor and collecting banks' responsibility for return of dishonored checks. Subpart C does three separate but interrelated things. First it obliges payor and the returning (collecting) banks to return dishonored checks in an "expeditious manner." Except to the extent that it might supersede the weaker obligation of ordinary care under the Code, this rule is new, imposed by federal law and unrelated to any state-law obligation. If the bank fails to comply with the duty of expeditious return, liability arises exclusively from section 229.38 of Regulation CC; there are no state-law consequences.

The second element of Subpart C modifies and expands the requirement formerly found in Regulation J that a payor bank give electronic notice of certain dishonors. To understand a payor bank's responsibility, one must now read not only Regulation J, but also section 229.33 on Notice of Non–Payment.

Finally, Subpart C modifies state-law rules on final payment in certain circumstances. In some cases a payor bank that would have liability for the full amount of a check, because it has failed to meet

---

14. See § 229.21 (c)(1).   **15.** See § 229.21(d).

its midnight deadline under sections 4–301 and 4–302, will be freed from liability by Regulation CC.

f. Duty of Expeditious Return of "Returned Checks"

Sections 229.30 and 229.31 impose a duty of "expeditious return." Paying and returning banks[16] satisfy the duty of "expeditious return" by meeting either of two tests, one called the two-day/four-day test, and the other the forward collection test. This duty complements the requirements in Subpart B for the depositary bank to make proceeds promptly available to the customer. By requiring that dishonored checks be returned in an expeditious manner, the rule minimizes the exposure of the depositary bank who must answer B's commands to make funds available.

The two-day rule requires the bank to send the returned check in a manner so that such check would normally be received by the depositary bank not later than 4:00 p.m. (local time of the depositary bank) of the second business day following the banking day on which the check was presented to the local paying bank. The four-day test applies the same rule on a four day cycle with respect to nonlocal checks. For example, a check presented on Monday to a local paying bank must be returned to the depositary bank by 4:00 p.m. on Wednesday. Likewise, a check presented to a nonlocal paying bank on Monday must be returned to the depositary bank by 4:00 p.m. on Friday.

Because the payor or collecting bank must only return the check so that it would "normally" be received within the two or four-day period, it is not necessary that any particular check actually arrive within this period in order for the payor or returning bank to have complied with the test. It is enough to show that in normal circumstances the check would have arrived within the deadline.[17] If a particular dishonored check does not arrive within that time because of abnormal delays in communication or transportation, the test is nevertheless satisfied if under normal circumstances it would have arrived.

---

16. A paying bank is specifically defined in Regulation CC § 229.2(z). The general definition is the bank by which a check is payable, unless the check is payable at or through another bank and is sent to the other bank for payment or collection. A returning bank is defined under Regulation CC § 229.2(cc) as a bank other than the paying or depositary bank handling the returned check or notice in lieu of return. A returning bank is also a collecting bank for the purpose of § 4–202(a) and (b).

17. See generally § 229.30(a)(1) and § 229.31(a)(1). Both sections define ex-peditious return as sending "the returned check in a manner such that the check would *normally* be received by the depositary bank not later than * * *" (emphasis added). The commentary to § 229.30 (a)(1) confirms that the "two-day/four-day test does not necessarily require actual receipt of the check by the depositary bank within these times. Rather, the paying bank must send the check so that the check would normally be received by the depositary bank within the specified time."

Doubtless there will be reasonable differences of opinion about what is normal and about the extent to which the payor or returning bank must take account in a particular case of the circumstances that then exist in determining what the "normal arrival" would be in such a case. Assume, for example, transmission through a particular correspondent would normally cause the check to be returned within the two-day period, but that the payor bank knows that on particularly busy days around Christmas that bank would not meet the two-day schedule. Can the payor bank continue to use that method and defend it on the ground that what happens on 350 days out of the year is "normal" even though one might expect the check would not arrive by two days in five out of the ten days preceding the Christmas holidays? Because we are always suspicious of depositors who claim they have suffered substantial losses because they did not receive timely notice of dishonor, we would be quite liberal in reading this test.

Note that the two or four business day test commences to run on "the banking day on which the check was presented to the paying bank * * *."[18] That is true whether one is testing the compliance of the paying bank or of a downstream returning bank. In other words, if the check was presented to the payor on Monday, it and any returning bank would have the duty of sending the check by a method under which it would "normally" be received not later than 4:00 p.m. on Wednesday, in the case of a local check, or on Friday, in the case of an out of town check. To make the point another way, the time when the *returning* bank receives the check has no bearing on the end of the two or four-day period.

The alternative to the two-day/four-day rule is the forward collection test. It provides that the payor or returning bank has made an expeditious return if it returns the check as expeditiously as a similarly situated bank would normally send a check for *collection*. As we have seen above, the check collection system is highly automated and efficient. Because it relies upon the MICR encoding that appears on nearly every check currently used in the United States, collection entails speedy transfer of checks without manual intervention. By adopting the speed of collection time as a test to measure expeditious *return*, the Board has essentially used a case in which it is in the banks' interest to procure speedy transfer to measure the case where the bank is indifferent. That test is set out in full as follows in Section 229.30(a)(2):

> *Forward collection test.* A paying bank also returns a check in an expeditious manner if it sends the returned check in a manner that a similarly situated bank would normally handle a check—

18. §§ 229.30 and 229.31.

(i) Of similar amount as the returned check;

(ii) Drawn on the depositary bank; and

(iii) Deposited for forward collection in the similarly situated bank by noon on the banking day following the banking day on which the check was presented to the paying bank. Subject to the requirement for expeditious return, a paying bank may send a returned check to the depositary bank or to any other bank agreeing to handle the returned check expeditiously under § 229.31(a). A paying bank may convert a check to a qualified returned check. A qualified returned check must be encoded in magnetic ink with the routing number of the depositary bank, the amount of the returned check, and a "2" in position 44 of the MICR line as a return identifier, in accordance with the American National Standard Specifications for Placement and Location of MICR Printing, X9.13 (Sept. 1983). This paragraph does not affect a paying bank's responsibility to return a check within the deadlines required by the UCC, Regulation J [12 CFR Part 210], or § 229.30(c).

Note that this test, like the two-day/four-day test, requires only that the bank handle the check in a way that a "similarly situated bank would *normally*" handle a check for collection.

If the returning bank converts the dishonored check into a "qualified return check," the time for expeditious return under the forward collection test (but not the two-day/four-day test) is extended by one business day. To make a check a "qualified return check," one magnetically encodes the check in such a way that it can be sent back to the depositary bank automatically by use of a MICR reader. Specifically, section 229.31(a) requires:

[a] qualified returned check must be encoded in magnetic ink with the routing number of the depositary bank, the amount of the return check, and a "2" in position 44 of the MICR line as a return identifier * * *.

Note that the extension granted to qualified return checks does not apply when a returning bank is returning the check directly to the depositary bank. This restriction recognizes that the processing time advantages associated with a qualified return check can only be recognized when the return check is sent to the depositary bank via another returning bank.

The additional day for return is an incentive to the returning bank to encourage MICR encoding. Why a similar incentive is not granted to the paying bank and why it does not apply to the two-day/four-day test is not clear. As we note below, making a check a qualified return check also grants the returning bank an additional day under the Uniform Commercial Code final payment rules.

g. Notice of Nonpayment

Prior to its amendment by Regulation CC, Regulation J required wire notice of dishonor by "midnight of the second banking day of the paying bank following the deadline for return of the item. * * * " Regulation J required such notice of dishonor only with respect to checks of $2500 or more that were collected through the Federal Reserve system.

Regulation CC changed Regulation J in two important ways. First, it broadened the rule to require wire notice, not just with respect to checks collected through the Federal Reserve, but with respect to all checks in the amount of $2500 or more. Second, Regulation CC shortened the time by one day. Under section 229.33(a) notice must now be given so that it is "received by the depositary bank by 4:00 p.m. (local time) on the second business day following the banking day on which the check was presented to the paying bank." At first reading it may not be apparent that the time was actually shortened. A careful reading of the quotes from old Regulation J and from new Regulation CC shows that Regulation CC cuts off one day by starting the clock ticking on the banking day of presentment. Regulation J started the clock only at the "deadline for return." Thus, if the check were presented on Monday morning, its deadline for return under the UCC would be Tuesday night. Ticking two days from that date, Regulation J formerly would have given until midnight Thursday. The Regulation CC clock, on the other hand, commences ticking at the time of presentment, Monday, and requires that the notice be received by 4:00 p.m. on Wednesday, the second business day after Monday.

The contents of the notice under Regulation CC are comparable to those in former Regulation J. They include the name and routing number of the paying bank, the name of the payee, amount, date of the indorsement, account number, branch name of the depositary bank, trace number of the depositary bank, and the reason for nonpayment. In addition Regulation CC requires that the depositary bank give notice to its customer of the check's return "by midnight of the banking day following the banking day on which it received the returned check or notice, or within a longer reasonable time."[19]

When a payor loses a check that it has dishonored, it may satisfy its duty of expeditious return by sending written notice of nonpayment, together with the information specified in section 229.33(b). According to the final version of the Regulation, electron-

19. Compare § 4–214 with
§ 229.33(d).

ic notice itself is not sufficient to satisfy the payor bank's duty of expeditious return. Earlier versions of the Regulation permitted electronic notice in lieu of the return of a hard copy where the check was unavailable. The final version requires that the paying bank must also send a written notice.[20]

h. Presentment

Section 229.36 describes the places where a check can be presented and is deemed to be "payable" (i.e., whether at the processing center or one of the branches of the headquarters). An unanswered question is whether 229.36 governs not only the rules under Regulation CC, but also determines when the clock starts ticking under Article 4 of the Uniform Commercial Code and so determines when the midnight deadline has run. The section merely says: "[a] check is considered received by the paying bank when it is received: (1) at a location to which delivery is requested by the paying bank; * * * [or one of three other alternatives]." Parts of Regulation CC clearly override Article 4, and it is possible that the Federal Reserve intended to do that here, i.e., that it intended to start the clock for the midnight deadline at delivery to the central processing center and to overrule contrary cases interpreting Article 4.[21] The Clarks so interpret section 229.36.[22]

The last sentence in Comment 4 to 4–204 reads as follows: "The time when a check is received by a payor bank for presentment is governed by Regulation CC Section 229.36(b)." At least if one takes that comment to be authoritative, that sentence settles the issue, Regulation CC controls.[23] If 229.36 is read as setting not only the rules under Regulation CC, but also the rules under Article 4, a check "directed to be delivered" at a processing center would be considered received by the payor both for the purposes of Regulation CC and for the purpose of the timing under Article 4 when the check is received at that processing center. For a more extensive discussion of Regulation CC's impact on the place of presentment under Article 4, see Section 5–4 *supra*.

20. See the "Section by Section Analysis" of Regulation CC § 229.30(f) and comments 229.30(f) for a discussion of the latter comments received regarding notice and the revised regulation.

21. The Board printed the following comment to 229.36(b) later in the section by section analysis: "Three commentators suggested that it be clearly stated that the regulation will override provisions of the UCC which deal with the receipt of presentment."

22. B. Clark & B. Clark, Regulation CC, Funds Availability and Check Collection § 3.21(2) (1988).

23. See § 229.30, where the duties established do not affect a paying bank's responsibility under the UCC; § 229.31, which explicitly modifies UCC midnight deadline requirements; and § 229.41, which states "[t]he provisions of this subpart *supersede* any inconsistent provisions of the UCC as adopted in any state * * * but only to the extent of the inconsistency" (emphasis added).

i. *Extending the Midnight Deadline*

Under the Uniform Commercial Code, a payor bank must normally dishonor a check by its midnight deadline or be liable for the face amount.[24] A collecting bank is responsible only to use ordinary care and it is presumed to have complied with its duty of ordinary care if it acts by its midnight deadline.

Clearly Regulation CC modifies these deadlines in certain respects. Exactly how extensive is that modification remains to be seen. The basic extension of the deadline is set out in 229.30(c). It reads in full as follows:

> *Extension of deadline.* The deadline for return or notice of nonpayment under the UCC or Regulation J [12 CFR Part 210] or § 229.36(f)(2) of this part is extended:
>
> (1) If a paying bank, in an effort to expedite delivery of a returned check to a bank, uses a means of delivery that would ordinarily result in the returned check being received by the bank to which it is sent on or before the receiving bank's next banking day following the otherwise applicable deadline; this deadline is extended further if a paying bank uses a highly expeditious means of transportation, even if this means of transportation would ordinarily result in delivery after the receiving bank's next banking day; or
>
> (2) If the deadline falls on a Saturday that is a banking day, as defined in the applicable UCC, for the paying bank, and the paying bank uses a means of delivery that would ordinarily result in the returned check being received by the bank to which it is sent prior to the cut-off hour for the next processing cycle, in the case of a returning bank, or on the next banking day, in the case of a depositary bank, after midnight Saturday night.

In a related provision in section 229.31(a)(2)(iii), the UCC time limit is extended when the returning bank converts the check into a "qualified return check":

> [T]he deadline for return under the UCC and Regulation J [12 CFR Part 210], are extended by one business day if the returning bank converts a return check to a qualified return check.

Return now to the first quoted section to see how it might extend the midnight deadline by one day. Assume that the payor bank receives a $100,000 check on Monday morning and that it discovers on Wednesday morning that it failed to send the check back by Tuesday midnight (the midnight deadline), but it now wishes to dishonor the check. Under the UCC the midnight dead-

---

24. See §§ 4–215 et seq., § 4–301 and § 4–302.

line would have passed, and unless it had an unusual defense, payor would be liable for the $100,000. Regulation CC may change that. If the bank can somehow get the check back to the depositary bank before that bank's close of business on Wednesday, it escapes its liability under the UCC. That appears to be the meaning of the first sentence of 229.30(c) quoted above.

But there is a bit of ambiguity in section 229.30(c). First it extends the deadline only if the payor uses this means of delivery "in an effort to expedite delivery." Quaere whether a one-time use (as opposed to a regularly practiced procedure) qualifies as an "effort to expedite delivery"? We believe it does, but we can imagine a court reading the language otherwise. One doubting our interpretation might suggest that the Federal Reserve had a specific case in mind when it extended the deadline and a doubter might claim that that case did not encompass a one-time transaction. A case clearly contemplated by the Federal Reserve arises when a payor bank returns checks by a courier but after midnight. Under the courier procedure, the courier might leave the bank after midnight (so missing the deadline), but arrive at a local depositary bank in the early morning hours of the same night. In theory that would be a late return under Article 4 because the check would not have left the payor bank until after the midnight deadline; yet the check would have arrived at the depositary bank long before it might have arrived had it been sent at 10 p.m. through the U.S. Postal Service. Wishing to bless such courier deliveries that started later but arrived sooner than other permissible modes, the Federal Reserve granted the additional day. Some read section 229.30(c)[25] as applying only to the courier and not to our one-time return of a large number of checks in the closure of a kite.

We read the language more broadly. Surely the banker hastening to return kited checks seeks to "expedite delivery" (when is that more necessary than when a kite is being closed?), but more to the point, we are not sure why a third party who has not been injured by a two-hour delay in the start of the trip should be protected by the midnight deadline when the checks are delivered much earlier than they would be had they been sent prior to midnight. If the drafters of the regulations had intended to limit the regulation to the routine courier case, they could have said so but they did not. In First National Bank of Chicago v. Standard Bank & Trust,[26] the bank officers discovered a check kiting scheme and then drove the checks over to the other bank the day after the midnight deadline had passed. The court ruled that the returning bank was entitled to Regulation CC's extension of the deadline,

---

25. B. Clark & B. Clark, Regulation CC, Funds Availability and Check Collection § 3.15(4)(1988).

26. 172 F.3d 472, 38 UCC2d 1 (7th Cir.1999).

notwithstanding the fact that it was a one-time use of that means of delivery. We think this is a sensible decision; not only is it consistent with the Regulation's goal of expediting the check return process, it also rewards the bank officers' diligence in discovering and preventing a kite scheme.

Secondly, it is not entirely clear from the quoted sentence whether the payor bank must actually get the check into the hands of the depositary bank or whether it must merely get it into the hands of the bank to which it would normally return the check by that time. The quoted sentence in 229.30(c) speaks of the return of a check "to a bank" and requires that the check be received "by the bank to which it is sent." Because we originally envisioned a case in which a bank would return a check by ground courier to a nearby depositary bank, we thought that the bank referred to in Regulation CC was the depositary bank. In view of the implicit conclusion otherwise in the Northern Trust case cited below and, in view of regulation CC's explicit authorization to return a check not merely to the depositary bank to "any other bank" that agrees to handle a check, we have changed our minds. We now believe that the reference to "a bank" refers to any bank–whether the bank is the depositary bank or some intermediary that is a proper recipient for the check when it leaves the payor bank after dishonor. Moreover, we read banking day (defined in 229.2(f)) to end when the banking office closes.[27]

In Oak Brook Bank v. Northern Trust Co.,[28] a check kiter with accounts at both banks deposited large checks (none for less than $2500 and totaling $450,000) into his Oak Brook account. The checks were drawn on his Northern account, which only had a small balance. The checks were presented to Northern for payment on February 11, 1998. On February 13, Northern decided to dishonor them and it informed Oak Brook of that decision by phone shortly before 4 p.m. By that time, however, Oak Brook had credited the kiter's account and he had withdrawn all but about $7000 of the money in the account. At 4:30 p.m., Northern sent the dishonored checks by courier to the Federal Reserve Bank, which received them sixteen minutes later. Northern did not contest that it missed the midnight deadline on the next banking day under UCC 4–302(a)(1), but it argued that it should be qualified for the one-day extension under Regulation CC 229.30(c)(1) because the checks arrived at the Federal Reserve Bank on the "next banking day following the otherwise applicable deadline." The Regulation CC definition of a "banking day" is "that part of any business day

---

27. § 229.2(f) reads in full as follows: " 'Banking day' means that part of any business day on which an office of a bank is open to the public for carrying on substantially all of its banking functions."

28. 256 F.3d 638, 44 UCC2d 1082 (7th Cir.2001).

on which an office of a bank is open to the public for carrying on *substantially all of its banking functions"* (emphasis added). The case thus turned on the question whether at 4:46 p.m. on February 13, 1998, the Federal Reserve Bank was still carrying on substantially all of its banking functions.

The court observed that, for purposes of Regulation CC, all of a bank's banking functions means "check processing." The court held that 4:46 p.m. was part of the banking day because the Federal Reserve Bank of Chicago was open for the receipt of checks 24 hours a day. The Court also pointed out that Oak Brook was negligent in allowing the kiter to withdraw the money too fast.

The court implies that the duty under Regulation CC is merely to get the checks to the presenting bank by the end of the next banking day, not all the way to the depositary bank.

Consider now the second sentence of 229.30(c). It authorizes a "further" extension if the payor uses a "highly expeditious" means of transportation. Assume our hypothetical case in which the check is presented on Monday and the payor bank's error is not discovered until Thursday. Assume further that the payor is in Los Angeles and the depositary bank is in New York. If the payor puts the check on an airplane and flies it to New York on Thursday, two days after the Tuesday midnight deadline when the check should have left the California bank, has it complied with the second sentence so it is free of liability for passage of the midnight deadline?

This second sentence, specifying only "further" time and requiring "highly expeditious means of transportation," is unusually sloppy. Does it cover a case in which the check lay under a counter at the payor bank for 60 days, then was flown supersonically to New York? We assume not.[29] Only science fiction knows a mode of transportation that is so fast that it makes the past into the future. We believe there must be some outer limit on the "further" which cannot be made up by use of extraordinarily speedy transportation.

We believe that the courts should read these sections with common sense and focus on the time of receipt instead of the time of dispatch. Under the UCC the time when the clock stops ticking for the payor is the time when the check leaves the bank, never mind that it fails to arrive at the depositary for days or a week later. In effect, Regulation CC (229.30(c)) is moving from that "time of dispatch" by the payor toward a "time of receipt" by the depositary bank. A way to test the "further" time is to ask whether the check arrived at the depositary bank because of the highly expeditious mode of transportation before it otherwise would have

---

29. One may interpret "further" as modifying "day." Under this reading, delivery extends the deadline to the next banking day (which means before the close of business), while highly expeditious delivery may "further" extend the deadline until the end of the day (midnight of the next banking day).

arrived, had it left the payor bank before the midnight deadline and been transmitted only by ordinary means. Presumably this would put an outer limit of a few days on the second sentence.

Turn now to the time extension that is contained in 229.31 for checks that are made into "qualified return checks." Only a returning, not payor, bank gains a one day extension under (1) the forward collection test, (2) the deadline for return under the UCC and (3) the deadline for return under Regulation J (12 CFR §§ 210) by converting a check into a qualified return check according 229.31. Does that mean that the additional business day applies only to the returning bank's time under the UCC or does it also apply to the payor's time under the UCC?

Assume our same case in which the payor bank's midnight deadline is Tuesday midnight and in which it misses that deadline and returns the check only on Wednesday to its collecting bank for upstream processing. However, the returning bank now MICR encodes it to make it a qualified check and sends it on to the depositary bank via an additional returning bank. In the meantime the depositary bank has permitted the customer to withdraw the money and sues the payor for missing its midnight deadline. The payor, of course, will argue that it (the payor) received one additional business day, not because of anything it did, but because of the act of its returning bank in making the check into a qualified return check. However, the comments to 229.30 indicate that payor banks, unlike returning banks, are not allowed a one-day extension when converting checks to qualified return checks.[30] The Board stated:

> [a]lthough paying banks may wish to prepare qualified return checks * * * the extension is not available to paying banks because a paying bank has more time available to dispatch the check.

Since the drafters were unwilling to grant the payor bank a one day extension for its own actions (converting a check to a qualified return check), it is unlikely that a court should allow the payor bank to benefit from the identical action of others (the returning bank's conversion to a qualified return check).

With the enactment of Regulation CC, few final payment cases will be completely resolved by examination of Article 4 of the UCC. In nearly all cases the lawyer will have to examine not only Regulation J, but also Regulation CC to see whether the payor bank earned an additional day by its act or by the act of its returning bank.

---

30. It is unclear whether the "extension" referred to by the Board Commentators applies to the Regulation CC duty of expeditious return, the UCC midnight deadline, and Regulation J, or only to a subset of these provisions.

j. Liability

Section 229.38 on liability under Subpart C has eight subparts. It is quite complex and its provisions must be read together with those under the UCC. The critical sections read in part as follows:

(a) *Standard of care; liability, measure of damages.* A bank shall exercise ordinary care and act in good faith in complying with the requirements of this subpart. A bank that fails to exercise ordinary care or act in good faith under this subpart may be liable to the depositary bank, the depositary bank's customer, the owner of a check, or another party to the check. The measure of damages for failure to exercise ordinary care is the amount of the loss incurred, up to the amount of the check, reduced by the amount of the loss that party would have incurred even if the bank had exercised ordinary care. A bank that fails to act in good faith under this subpart may be liable for other damages, if any, suffered by the party as a proximate consequence. Subject to a bank's duty to exercise ordinary care or act in good faith in choosing the means of return or notice of nonpayment, the bank is not liable for the insolvency, neglect, misconduct, mistake, or default of another bank or person, or for loss or destruction of a check or notice of nonpayment in transit or in the possession of others. This section does not affect a paying bank's liability to its customer under the UCC or other law.

(b) *Paying bank's failure to make timely return.* If a paying bank fails both to comply with § 229.30(a) and to comply with the deadline for return under the U.C.C., Regulation J [12 CFR Part 210], or § 229.30(c) in connection with a single nonpayment of a check, the paying bank shall be liable under either § 229.30(a) or such other provision, but not both.

(c) *Comparative negligence.* If a person, including a bank, fails to exercise ordinary care or act in good faith under this subpart in indorsing a check [§ 229.35], accepting a returned check or notice of nonpayment [§§ 229.32(a) and 229.33(c)], or otherwise, the damages incurred by that person under § 229.38(a) shall be diminished in proportion to the amount of negligence or bad faith attributable to that person.[31]

31. Section 229.38 (d), (e), (f), (g), and (h):

(d) *Responsibility for certain aspects of check.* (1) A paying bank, or in the case of a check payable through the paying bank and payable by another bank, the bank by which the check is payable, is responsible for damages under paragraph (a) of this section to the extent that the condition of the check when issued by it or its customer adversely affects the ability of a bank to indorse the check legibly in accordance with § 229.35. A depositary bank is responsible for damages under paragraph (a) of this section to the extent that the condition of the back of a check arising after the issuance of the check and prior to

Note first that the basic standard of liability is negligence, not strict liability. Moreover, the basic measure of damages provided in (a) is the same as that found in Regulation J and in section 4–103(e), namely, the amount of the check "reduced by the amount of the loss that party would have incurred even if the bank had exercised ordinary care." Thus, if a bank fails to make an expeditious return and the depositary bank had allowed customer to withdraw the funds prior to the time it would have received notice had there been an expeditious return, in most cases there will be no damage, because the amount of the check is "reduced" by the amount of the loss that party would have incurred if the bank had exercised ordinary care. ($100,000 loss – $100,000 loss even if timely return = 0.)

Note that 229.38 allows additional damage if the bank failed to act "in good faith" and the other party suffered damages as a "proximate consequence." This language will send shivers up the spine of the banker who has learned that many things thought to be normal behavior in days past are now bad faith.

Compare the two sentences at the end of (a) and (b): "This section does not affect a paying bank's liability to its customer

acceptance of the check by it adversely affects the ability of a bank to indorse the check legibly in accordance with § 229.35. Responsibility under this paragraph shall be treated as negligence of the paying or depositary bank for purposes of paragraph (c) of this section.

(2) Responsibility for payable through checks. In the case of a check that is payable by a bank and payable through a paying bank located in a different check processing region than the bank by which the check is payable, the bank by which the check is payable is responsible for damages under paragraph (a) of this section, to the extent that the check is not returned to the depositary bank through the payable through bank as quickly as the check would have been required to be returned under § 229.30(a) had the bank by which the check is payable—

(i) Received the check as paying bank on the day the payable through bank received the check; and

(ii) Returned the check as paying bank in accordance with § 229.30(a)(1). Responsibility under this paragraph shall be treated as negligence of the bank by which the check is payable for purposes of paragraph (c) of this section.

(e) *Timeliness of action*. If a bank is delayed in acting beyond the time limits

set forth in this subpart because of interruption of communication or computer facilities, suspension of payments by a bank, war, emergency conditions, failure of equipment, or other circumstances beyond its control, its time for acting is extended for the time necessary to complete the action, if it exercises such diligence as the circumstances require.

(f) *Exclusion*. Section 229.21 of this part and § 611(a), (b), and (c) of the Act [12 U.S.C. 4010(a),(b), and (c)], do not apply to this subpart.

(g) *Jurisdiction*. Any action under this subpart may be brought in any United States district court, or in any other court of competent jurisdiction, and shall be brought within one year after the date of the occurrence of the violation involved.

(h) *Reliance on Board rulings*. No provision of this subpart imposing any liability shall apply to any act done or omitted in good faith in conformity with any rule, regulation, or interpretation thereof by the Board, regardless of whether the rule, regulation, or interpretation is amended, rescinded, or determined by judicial or other authority to be invalid for any reason after the act or omission has occurred.

under the UCC or other law" and "[T]he paying bank shall be liable under either 229.30(a) or such other provision, but not both * * *" discussing a payor's liability for failure to make a timely return. The latter statement is clear, namely the plaintiff can sue for the full amount of the check if that is payor bank's liability for failure of timely return under the UCC or accept a different amount (that would always seem to be less) under 229.38. The impact of the former sentence, which states that the section does not affect payor bank's liability under the UCC, is less clear. Is that section merely saying that when a bank acts in bad faith, plaintiff can recover that bad faith amount as well as the amount of the check in case of late return? We do not know.

Note finally the comparative negligence standard in (c). Application of the comparative negligence standard occurs in very limited circumstances. It requires (1) that damages be established under 229.38(a) (failure to exercise ordinary care or bad faith) and (2) that the negligence of plaintiff alleged by the defendant as comparative negligence be the failure of plaintiff to meet a duty imposed by Subpart C of Regulation CC and not negligence unrelated to Regulation CC Subpart C duties. The comparative negligence standard can perhaps best be interpreted as modifying the ordinary care and good faith requirements of 229.38(a): the measure of damages equals the loss (up to the amount of the check) minus loss if bank had exercised ordinary care minus comparative negligence of plaintiff for failure to satisfy duties imposed under Subpart C.

To illustrate the first point, assume the case posed above in which the depositary bank allows the customer to withdraw the money on the day after the check is deposited and well before it could have received notice of a dishonor even if the notice had been sent expeditiously. We suggested that the damages would be zero under 229.38(a) because the claim would be fully reduced "by the amount of the loss the party would have incurred even if the bank had exercised ordinary care."

If a court found the depositary bank negligent as well as the payor bank, should it find that section 229.38(c) requires a sharing of the loss? The answer is no; section 229.38(c) (comparative negligence standard) directs only that damages under 229.38(a) be *diminished* in proportion to the negligence. If the payor bank incurs no liability under 229.38(a) (ordinary care and good faith standard), the comparative negligence standard cannot establish liability since it only *diminishes* liability incurred under 229.38(a). Applying (c) would be incorrect for another reason. The hypothetical negligence of the depositary bank related to funds availability and not to the breach of any duty imposed under Subpart C, yet (c) applies only breach of Subpart C duties.

Regarding the second point, some may argue that the comparative negligence standard only applies to the duties specifically outlined (indorsement, acceptance of returned check, and notice of nonpayment). The "or otherwise" in the middle of the sentence indicates to us it applies to all parts of Subpart C. Even if the "or otherwise" is read expansively, the "under this Subpart" language limits the application of comparative negligence to breach of duties established under Subpart C—collection of checks (§§ 229.30 through 229.42).

The most obvious candidate for the application of these sections is one in which the depositary bank smudges the indorsements, puts them in the wrong place, or otherwise puts them on in such a way as to make it difficult or impossible for the payor to identify the depositary bank and send the check back expeditiously. One must assume that the payor is also negligent in sending the check back or in sending notice, and finally that payment is made by the depositary bank after the time when it would have received notice had it been sent promptly. Under that scenario, section 229.38(a) would put liability on the payor bank because of its negligence. That liability would not be reduced under (a) because there would be a direct causal relation between the payor's negligence and the depositary bank's loss. On the other hand, section 229.38(c) would reduce the depositary bank's (plaintiff) recovery because of its own negligence in smudging the original indorsement. In USAA Investment Management Co. v. Federal Reserve Bank of Boston,[32] plaintiff USAA indorsed in the wrong place on the back of a check and so made it difficult to discover the identity of the depositary bank. After dishonor by the payor bank, the check was bounced back and forth between the New York Federal Reserve and the Boston Federal Reserve several times before it was lost. A year later, someone finally discovered that the check had been lost and sent a request for a charge back against USAA. USAA sued the Boston Federal Reserve Bank, the New York Federal Reserve Bank and the payor bank. The court holds that comparative negligence rules in Regulation CC 229.38 apply, that USAA was 40% at fault and the New York Federal Reserve was 60% at fault.

Having studied the two subsections, and having considered the hypotheticals that might arise under them, it is much easier to pose hypotheticals not governed by 229.38(c) than to pose those covered by it. In fact, the section is so narrow that even a mouse would have trouble squeezing through.

Finally, one should note that there are a variety of other sections that have relevance to damage recoveries. Specifically, 229.34(c) has its own provision concerning damage arising from the warranties in that section. Section 229.37 reduces (almost to noth-

---

32.   906 F.Supp. 770, 28 UCC2d 959
(D.Conn. 1995).

ing) the power of a bank to disclaim its liability or limit its damages, and 229.38(d) has an explicit set of rules concerning responsibility for the form of the back of the check and for illegible indorsements.

k. Miscellaneous

Section 229.34 puts certain implied warranties into the mouths of payor and returning banks who return checks back upstream. These are analogous to the warranties found in Regulation J and in Article 4 of the UCC. Among other things, they include a warranty that the payor has returned its check within its deadline under the UCC. These warranties run to the depositary bank and to the owner of the check. The owner of the check—who would normally sue the payor on nonpayment—can sue the returning bank (but not the depositary bank) because that bank will itself be warranting that payor bank returned the check within its deadline. We suspect that the principal effect of 229.34 (which has other rules on damages and tender of defenses) will be procedural, namely, to offer an injured plaintiff potential defendants that are not currently available.

Damages for breach of warranty outlined in 229.34(d) parallel former section 4–207(3) (predecessor to 4–207 and 4–208): "Damages for breach of these warranties shall not exceed the consideration received by the bank that presents or transfers a check or returned check, plus interest compensation and expenses related to the check or returned check, if any."[33] The phrase "expenses related to the [returned check]," as interpreted by former Comment 5 to section 4–207, may "be ordinary collecting expenses and in appropriate cases could also include such expenses as attorneys fees."[34] Therefore, failure to meet the midnight deadline results in a breach of warranty under Regulation CC and may allow plaintiff to recover attorneys' fees, a recovery previously not available on an action for a late return.

Section 229.35 and its attached Appendix D set out an explicit and rigid set of rules concerning indorsements. These rules ease the burden of a payor bank or another returning bank who needs to get the check back to the depositary bank in short order. They facilitate the identification of the depositary bank and ultimately will enable the process to be done automatically. Consider for a moment the difficulty one might face in the basement of a payor bank looking at the back side of a dishonored check. The check, at that point, might include a variety of stamps, manual signatures, and

---

33. Reg. CC § 229.34(c).

34. Although 4–208(b) alters the language of former 4–207(3), the comments continue to recognize that attorneys' fees may be recoverable as "expenses" resulting from the breach. See Comment 5 to 3–417 as applicable to 4–208.

perforations. Some of the indorsements might be illegible and it would not necessarily be obvious which of the indorsements was that of the depositary bank and which were those of intervening collecting banks. The rules in Appendix D should make the job of that clerk easier and ultimately allow the clerk to be replaced by a machine.

l. Payable Through

Under the Uniform Commercial Code, checks payable "through" a bank are not drawn on that bank; the Code recognizes that bank as a collecting bank. Typically such instruments are drawn on third parties such as insurance companies. Nevertheless, Regulation CC Section 229.36 will give such collecting banks the obligations of return and notice as if they were payors:

> (a) *Payable through and payable at checks*. A check payable at or through a paying bank is considered to be drawn on that bank for purposes of the expeditious return and notice of nonpayment requirements of this subpart.

The payable through bank will have liability under Regulation CC if it fails to make expeditious return or to send notice of nonpayment. We do not read the quoted section to change the bank's (quite limited) liability under Article 4.

m. Check Clearing for the 21st Century Act (Check 21 Act)

As checks have become merely the physical carriers for electronic messages, the practice of transmitting paper checks from the drawer to the payee's bank and back to the payor bank has become more and more inefficient by comparison with the available alternatives. Once the dollar amount of the check has been entered on the MICR line, the data can be transmitted to the payor bank electronically and if the payor has the right equipment, it can debit the right account and so complete the transaction without ever having had possession of the physical check. This process of destroying or holding the check and of sending the electronic information downstream to the payor is known as truncating.

The current version of the Uniform Commercial Code permits electronic presentment in section 4–110, but it does so only when a clearing house rule, a Federal Reserve regulation or an agreement between the parties permits electronic presentment. At least since the Funds Availability Act was passed in 1987,[35] Congress has had an interest in facilitating electronic presentment. Despite the presence of section 4–110 and the presence of the Congressional encouragement in the Funds Availability Act, electronic presentment has

---

35.   12 U.S.C.§§ 5001–5002(18).

been slow in coming. Today, like five years ago and like ten years ago, dozens of airplanes leave dozens of airports late at night with cargoes of checks to be carried across the country and presented for payment. The cost of this physical presentment is enormous and the benefits, when compared with electronic presentment, are minimal.

One might have thought that Congress would command the American banking system to adopt electronic presentment and so, in one fell swoop, to ground the airplanes and the needless carriage of paper checks across the night skies. In the Check Clearing For The 21st Century Act (enacted in 2004),[36] Congress merely provided for "substitute checks." Under section 5001,[37] a "substitute check" is a "paper reproduction of the original check" that has an image of the front and back of the original check and contains, on a MICR line, all of the information that was on the MICR line of the original check.

Section 5003 of the Act does not authorize one to do an electronic presentment but only to present a "substitute check."[38] Since the substitute check itself must be in paper form, it might appear that Congress has done nothing by enacting these rules on check clearing. That is not true; Congress anticipates that many payor banks will accept electronic presentment. The rule concerning substitute checks should facilitate electronic presentment for the shrinking minority of payor banks who refuse to accept electronic presentment. The Act contemplates sending the check information electronically to a correspondent bank in the geographic area of the balking payor and then contemplates the correspondent bank's presenting a substitute check that it has produced from the information received electronically from the depositary bank.

So if things ultimately work out the way Congress apparently intended,[39] we should soon have extensive electronic presentment and the number of airplanes carting checks around the night skies should be considerably reduced.[40]

In addition to the provisions on substitute checks, the Act imposes certain warranties on banks that transfer, prepare, or present substitute checks. The Act also provides for indemnity and for expedited recredit for consumers and banks.[41] Exactly how these warranties and indemnities will work is not spelled out by the Act or by the Regulations, and there is considerable, theoretical room for mischief. Since the Act contemplates actual checks and substitute checks, it leaves open the possibility that two paper documents

---

36. 12 U.S.C. § 5014 (2004).

37. Id.

38. Id.

39. 149 Cong. Rec. S12, 632 (2003).

40. 9 N.C. Banking Inst. 179, 183 (2005).

41. Regulation CC: Availability of Funds and Collection of Checks, 12 C.F.R. § 229.53 (2004).

representing the same liability could be simultaneously outstanding. If both checks are paid and a drawer's liability is so twice paid, someone must eat a loss and normally it should not be the drawer. How that loss is to be distributed is but one of several theoretical problems with the Act and Regulations. The next five to ten years should show whether these fears will be realized or whether these new parts of Regulation CC will enjoy the same benign circumstances (little controversy and less litigation) that other parts of Regulation CC have enjoyed. We are skeptical that the practice will deliver much of the mischief that has been forewarned.

PROBLEM

Customer draws a $30,000 check on her account in a New York bank and gives the check to a Fort Wayne seller.

1. If seller deposits the check in Fort Wayne National on the morning of Tuesday, May 2, when does Fort Wayne have to make the full $30,000 available under Reg CC?

   a. Tuesday the 9th (229.12(c)(1))

   b. Wednesday the 17th (229.13(b), (h)(4))

   c. Thursday the 4th (229.12(b))

   d. Monday the 8th (229.12(c))

   The answer is "b." Since it is a non local check in Fort Wayne and it is a large amount, it earns five business days under .12(c) and six days more under .13(h)(4). Saturday and Sunday are not business days.

2. If the check is presented early on Friday, May 5 for payment in New York, what must the drawee do and by when to avoid becoming "accountable" for the $30,000?

   a. Get the check to Fort Wayne no later than May 8th.

   b. Meet the 2 day 4 day test.

   c. Send the check to Fort Wayne by midnight Tues the 9th.

   d. None of the above.

   The answer is "d." Under Article 4 the bank must only "return" as that term is used in 4–301, i.e., "send." And it has to do that by midnight Monday, its midnight deadline.

3. If payor makes its midnight deadline but the check floats slowly back to Fort Wayne and misses the 2 day 4 day test, New York Bank is accountable for $30,000.

   False. Liability under Reg CC is as stated there and in no case does it directly impose liability automatically for the full amount of a late returned check. Usually there will be no liability because the late return will not cause a loss, only disappointment.

4. If New York Bank misses its midnight deadline it can recover its loss from Fort Wayne or the payee in restitution or warranty.

False. But if it can find the drawer and he is solvent, bank can recover from him.

§ 5-6 Collecting Bank's Liability for Delay or Other Negligence in the Collection of Checks and Other Drafts

Almost always the collecting bank is the Pontius Pilate of a final payment suit; it can disclaim all responsibility. In rare cases the collecting bank's misbehavior causes another to lose money on a draft which the drawee never paid, or on a forged instrument. Section 4–202 states the basic responsibility of the collecting bank; it must use ordinary care and, having done so, it does not have liability. Action taken by the midnight deadline is presumed to be timely and "[t]aking proper action within a reasonably longer time may constitute the exercise of ordinary care, but the bank has the burden of establishing timeliness" (section 4–202(b)). If the collecting bank is not paid and there is no final payment, the collecting bank may chargeback its customer's account under 4–214, and it may do so even though it ultimately is liable and has to recredit the account. In effect 4–214 permits the collecting bank to hold the funds while it is determined whether it, or its customer, must bear the liability.

Reminiscent of the liability rule in Regulation J, section 4–103(e) limits the collecting bank's liability for negligence to "the amount of the item, reduced by an amount that could not have been realized by the exercise of ordinary care * * *." Except for the liabilities of banks as collecting banks on documentary drafts, there have been few cases. Occasionally a court concludes that a bank, as an apparent collecting bank, is in fact a payor and has a payor's liability, but collecting banks usually escape liability for delay.

New technologies have brought additional burdens to collecting banks. In several cases, collecting banks have been caught in the middle of fraud in which thieves procured money from depositary bank by using checks with altered MICR encoding lines. We discuss one of those, United States Fidelity & Guaranty Co. v. Federal Reserve Bank,[1] at length *infra*. These banks have also faced claims

1. 590 F.Supp. 486, 39 UCC 944   (S.D.N.Y. 1984), and 620 F.Supp. 361, 41 UCC 1153 (S.D.N.Y. 1985), both

that the depositary banks have caused losses by improperly encoding the dollar amount on the bottom of the check. With the 1990 revision of Article 4, most of these cases are covered by a new warranty in 4–209. While the responsibility of the depositary bank is rising, the liability of the collecting bank that is not a depositary remains insignificant. Below we deal with the cases involving negligence and then with MICR encoding warranties.

a. Negligence: Frauds Exploiting the Check Collection System

The highly automated check collection process has created an opportunity for clever criminals to exploit the system. When thieves manage to make checks drift around in the system long enough for the depositary bank to conclude that the check has been paid and so to release the funds, collecting banks may be sued by the depositary bank that was holding the bag after a successful fraudulent check scheme.

United States Fidelity and Guaranty Co. v. Federal Reserve Bank[2] is a nice example of a fraud based on exploitation of the MICR process. On May 6, 1980, Marvin Goldstein deposited a check for $880,000 in Union Trust Maryland Bank. On the face of the check were printed the words, First Pennsylvania Bank of Philadelphia, as payor. The routing numbers printed in the upper right hand corner of the check identified the State Bank of Albany as the payor. The MICR number along the bottom of the check had a number for the payor that identified no bank at all. On May 6 Union Trust forwarded the check for collection to Philadelphia National Bank, who apparently selected Albany State as the correct payor bank because of the routing number and sent it to the New York Federal Reserve on May 7. The New York Federal Reserve sent it to Albany State who returned it May 9 "Sent in Error." The New York Federal Reserve then sent it back on May 12 to the Federal Reserve Bank in Philadelphia who in turn sent it to First Pennsylvania on May 14. On May 16 First Pennsylvania notified Philadelphia National Bank that it dishonored the check and Philadelphia National passed the word on to Union Trust. Unfortunately, on the 13th Goldstein had withdrawn all but $1,000 from his account. Union Trust allowed him to withdraw the money because, two weeks having passed, it concluded the check had been paid. Union Trust and its insurer then sued various parties on a number of theories.

aff'd, 786 F.2d 77, 42 UCC 1715 (2d Cir.1986).

2. 590 F.Supp. 486, 39 UCC 944 (S.D.N.Y. 1984), and 620 F.Supp. 361,

41 UCC 1153 (S.D.N.Y. 1985), both aff'd, 786 F.2d 77, 42 UCC 1715 (2d Cir.1986).

The court ultimately held that a depositary bank which was the victim of "MICR fraud" may be precluded from recovering damages from collecting banks under 4–202(1) (now 4–202(a)) if these banks can demonstrate that negligence of the depositary bank played a substantial role in the success of the fraud. In this case, Union Trust had repeatedly violated its own procedures in its handling of the Goldstein account, thus aiding Goldstein in getting his hands on the cash. First, Goldstein opened the account with only one ID, an out-of-state driver's license. Next, Goldstein's bank reference was not transferred to his signature card as required. Third, the teller who accepted the $880,000 check for deposit violated procedures in failing to present it to a branch manager.

Assistant branch manager Clement, who had been involved with the account from the beginning, and branch manager Gemmill, both inquired with credit bureaus about Goldstein's business record. No record on Goldstein was found. Gemmill then asked Clement to look at the account information card on Goldstein, but it contained no bank references because Clement had forgotten to transfer them onto the card. So Gemmill told Clement to look into the account on which the $880,000 check was drawn. Clement instructed an employee to call First Pennsylvania; that employee was told that no such account existed. The employee informed Clement, who in turn informed Gemmill. All of this took place within four days of the check's deposit, in plenty of time to prevent Goldstein from withdrawing the cash. Gemmill then went on vacation, apparently leaving Clement in charge. It was also Clement who carried out the wire transfer a few days later. According to the court, Clement concluded that the report that First Penn did not know of the account was "incorrect." He did not inquire again before okaying the release of the funds.

The court declined to make a choice as to which bank (payor, depositary, collecting) should be assigned liability in all circumstances; it took the admirable position that a determination who is in the best position to prevent loss is a legislative task, not a judicial one. However, the court did observe that a depositary bank has an opportunity to examine a check free of time pressures and is in the unique position of being able to examine both the depositor and the check. Therefore, the court stated, the depositary bank has a duty to examine and an initial burden of care.

Despite the fact that First Pennsylvania, the apparent payor, held the check beyond its midnight deadline, Judge Haight declined to find it liable. While his conclusion seems fair, it is not obvious how one rationalizes that conclusion under the rules of Article 4.

In Regulation CC a paying bank is "[t]he bank whose routing number appears on the check in magnetic ink or in fractional form and to which the check is sent for payment or collection * * * " (subsection 229.2(z) contains different definitions of "paying bank"). Arguably in a future case like *United States Fidelity*, Albany (the bank identified by the fraction) and not First Pennsylvania (the bank identified in words) would be the payor and might face liability for final payment.

Where one seeks to recover from a Federal Reserve Bank as a collecting bank, he has an additional hurdle to leap. In Greater Buffalo Press, Inc. v. Federal Reserve Bank,[3] the payee on some checks issued by a bankrupt drawer attempted unsuccessfully to recover from the Federal Reserve, which had delayed several days between the time it received the checks and when it presented them to the payor. The court concluded that there was no proof that the action by the Federal Reserve was negligent and therefore in violation of 4–202. More importantly, the court read Regulation J as effective, even under the UCC, to cut off the agency relationship between the payee and the Federal Reserve Bank and thus presumably to deprive it of the duty that would otherwise be imposed under 4–202 between principal and agent. To one concerned with the interplay between Regulation J and the UCC, this case is important reading.

b. *Charge Back*

In the normal course of events, a collecting bank is free to charge back a customer's account and wait until the dust settles to determine whether it, or the customer, must bear the loss.[4] There are, however, a few exceptions to this general rule.

In Smallman v. Home Federal Savings Bank,[5] the court denied a bank's right to charge back against its customer's account under former 4–212 (now 4–214). In April, the Smallmans deposited a check payable to their order for $703.87. Home Federal submitted the check for processing and collection through First American National Bank, through the Federal Reserve Bank of Atlanta and then to AmSouth for final payment. AmSouth apparently did a timely dishonor but the check was lost in the mail on the return

---

3. 866 F.2d 38, 7 UCC2d 956 (2d Cir.1989), cert. denied, 490 U.S. 1107, 109 S.Ct. 3159, 104 L.Ed.2d 1022 (1989).

4. See, e.g. Chitty v. Bank One, N.A., 42 UCC2d 799 (Ohio App. 2000) (Plaintiff got a provisional credit of $22,000 and drew on it before the cashier's check that had been deposited bounced; the bank then set off the $8000 in the Plaintiff's account. The court rejected the Plaintiff's argument that the bank had lost the right to charge back because the orginal cashier's check had been finally paid, instead it held that there was nev-

er a settlement and the bank was thus not foreclosed from a charge back by 4–214); Mahopac National Bank v. Gelardi, 299 A.D.2d 460, 750 N.Y.S.2d 115, 49 UCC2d 573 (2002) (Although bank had provisionally credited customer's account in the amount of a third-party check, when the check was returned unpaid, the bank can charge back the amount which the customer drew on the provisional credit).

5. 786 S.W.2d 954, 11 UCC2d 1202 (Tenn.App. 1989).

trip. On July 30th, more than three months after the check was first deposited, Home Federal received a photocopy of the check and a notice saying it was being returned for non-payment. There was no explanation for the delay. The agent of the bank did not notify the Smallmans but, believing he was doing the right thing, again attempted to collect the check. After these attempts failed, and after being instructed that there had been a timely dishonor, Home Federal notified the Smallmans in early September that there had been a charge back to their account in the amount of the check.

As a result of the charge back, fourteen of the Smallmans' checks bounced. However, all but two of these checks had been written after the Smallmans received actual notice that the original check had been returned and charged back. The Smallmans offered no proof that the check could have been collected had they received timely notice of dishonor.

Since the depositary bank did not act within its midnight deadline or a further reasonable time, even after it had received final notice of non-payment in September, the court held that the bank had no right to charge back under former 4–212 (revised 4–214). The case follows one line that holds that meeting the midnight deadline or a further reasonable time is a condition precedent for charging back.

As revised in 1990, section 4–214(a) rejects the holding in the Smallman case and explicitly adopts the position of Appliance Buyers Credit Corp. v. Prospect National Bank.[6] That change was brought about by the addition of the following sentence to 4–214(a):

> If the return or notice is delayed beyond the bank's midnight deadline or a longer reasonable time after it learns the facts, the bank may revoke the settlement, charge back the credit, or obtain a refund from its customer, but it is liable for any loss resulting from the delay.

The implication from the sentence is that the bank is not liable if no loss is caused by the delay.

Consider, too, Tropin v. Chase Manhattan Bank.[7] There, the depositary bank failed to send notice of a charge back or return the item for 18 days after the check that had been deposited at Chase had been returned to it. In the meantime the plaintiff customer of Chase withdrew funds from her account in the belief she had a sufficient balance. When the deposited checks bounced, the bank deducted the amount of the plaintiff's withdrawal from her "credit balance." The court held that Chase, the depositary bank, did not have a right to debit the account under former 4–212 and that its liability for doing so was the full amount of the checks. The court

---

6. 708 F.2d 290, 36 UCC 231 (7th Cir.1983).

7. 1991 WL 337541, 16 UCC2d 1113 (N.Y. City Civ.Ct. 1991).

rejected Chase's defense based on 4–103(5) (revised 4–103(e)) (no damage caused) and found that the bank was not accused of negligence, a cause of action to which former 4–103(5) applies, but of violating its obligation under former 4–212 (revised 4–214). Revised 4–214(a) reverses the holding in *Tropin* also.

Golden Gulf, Inc. v. AmSouth Bank, N.A.[8] shows the charge back rules in a slightly different setting. AmSouth, the depositary bank, had received a $250,000 check from its depositor. After the deposit the customer called to find out whether the check had been collected and whether the funds were "available." AmSouth told the depositor that the funds were "available for use." At the request of the depositor, AmSouth then wired the funds; only later AmSouth discovered that the check had been dishonored. AmSouth promptly notified the depositor of the dishonor and revoked the credit it had given. AmSouth claimed that the credit was only provisional. Revocation of the credit resulted in an overdraft of $248,965.69. Amsouth sued for recovery under former 4–207 and former 4–212. Finding that AmSouth gave the depositor notice by the midnight deadline, the court affirmed summary judgment on behalf of the bank for the amount of the overdraft. Along the way, the court made clear that neither the payor, nor Amsouth took any action that would constitute final payment or would otherwise bind the collecting bank under former 4–213(3) or former 4–212.

Does 4–214 (former 4–212) give the depositary bank an affirmative cause of action against its customer? The dispute in Bank of New York v. Asati, Inc.,[9] arose after the Bank allowed Asati to draw against uncollected funds and the check representing those funds was dishonored by the payor, First Union National Bank. The deposit agreement between the Bank of New York and Asati authorized the bank to charge back all items "for which we are not paid."

Bank of New York sued Asati and apparently relied upon 4–212 to give it an affirmative cause of action. The majority upheld the bank's suit, even though it did not give notice of dishonor for approximately four days after it learned of the dishonor of the deposited check. Assuming arguendo that 4–212 (4–214) does give an affirmative cause of action, we agree with the majority that the strict midnight deadline should not apply and that a substantially longer time might be a "reasonable" period particularly where the customer cannot show any injury. The language in the statute that authorizes the bank not only to "charge back" but also to "obtain refund" from its customer seems to grant a cause of action.

8. 565 So.2d 114, 12 UCC2d 780 (Ala. 1990).

9. 184 A.D.2d 443, 585 N.Y.S.2d 411, 18 UCC2d 535 (1992).

c. Encoding Warranties

At least one warranty in 1990 Article 4 will occasionally favor a payor bank even where there is no fraud. This is the encoding warranty in section 4–209 that reads in full as follows:

(a) A person who encodes information on or with respect to an item after issue warrants to any subsequent collecting bank and to the payor bank or other payor that the information is correctly encoded. If the customer of a depositary bank encodes, that bank also makes the warranty.

(b) A person who undertakes to retain an item pursuant to an agreement for electronic presentment warrants to any subsequent collecting bank and to the payor bank or other payor that retention and presentment of the item comply with the agreement. If a customer of a depositary bank undertakes to retain an item, that bank also makes this warranty.

(c) A person to whom warranties are made under this section and who took the item in good faith may recover from the warrantor as damages for breach of warranty an amount equal to the loss suffered as a result of the breach, plus expenses and loss of interest incurred as a result of the breach.

Typically, the depositary bank encodes the amount of the check in magnetic (machine readable) ink at the bottom right-hand corner before it passes the check on. After that encoding has been done, the depositary bank, all the collecting banks, and the payor can read that MICR encoding line by machine, and most treat the check as though it is no more than an electronic message. Because this encoding is done manually, error occurs. The encoded amount may be greater or less than the true amount of the check. Since the check is thereafter handled without human intervention, the incorrect encoding will almost certainly result in a debit to the drawer's account of the amount encoded, not of the correct amount listed on the face of the check. In those circumstances, revised 4–209—like most cases decided under the existing Code, gives a claim against the "person who encodes." The same warranty is made with respect to electronic presentment under revised 4–209(b) in case of retention (in the trade, "truncation"). In those cases, the depositary bank retains the paper and sends forward the electronic message for presentment.

Revised section 4–209(c) allows the party to whom the encoding and retention warranties are made to recover damages for breach of warranty. Thus, if the payor bank debits the drawer's account for an *overencoded* $10,000 (not for $1,000 as the check provides) and later has to recredit the account, it would have a claim for $9,000 against the encoding party.

Of course, the plaintiff has to show actual damage. In NBT Bank v. First National Community Bank,[10] defendant bank FNCB, intending to dishonor an overdrawn check, mistakenly encoded the check with the wrong depositary bank but still presented it to the Federal Reserve by midnight. NBT, the depositary bank, instituted an action against FNCB claiming that FNCB's encoding error meant FNCB had failed to return the disputed check prior to the midnight deadline as required by the UCC, and that FNCB was therefore accountable to NBT for the full amount of the disputed check. The court ruled that NBT could not recover against payor bank because the depository bank did not suffer actual damages, inasmuch as NBT had received written and oral notice from FNCB before the deadline that the disputed check had been dishonored. The court rejected NBT's claim for strict liability under UCC 4–302 and held that Regulation CC 229.38(a) should apply.

Proving the loss where there is *underencoding* will be more tricky. Consider the case given in Comment 2 to section 4–209. A check for $25,000 is improperly encoded as $2,500. Since the depositor's balance exceeded $25,000, there would be no loss, because as the comment points out, the payor bank could simply debit the account for the additional amount when it was discovered that the original debit was too small. If the account had less than $25,000 at discovery, the payor needs a defense when it is sued by the payee or depositary bank for having "finally paid" a $25,000 check without settling for the full amount. The payor need not go beyond the drawer's account. The presenting party will claim that the payor is "accountable" for the full amount, namely, $25,000, because of its final payment. The payor can then assert a counterclaim against the depositary bank for breach of warranty. The payor will be able to show warranty damages if the account balance covered the true amount at presentment but was thereafter depleted. The comment states: "There is no requirement that the payor bank pursue collection against the drawer beyond the amount in the drawer's account as a condition to the payor bank's action against the depositary bank for breach of warranty."

The comment and the section seem to adopt the proposition that a payor who pays an underencoded amount has made final payment on the check or has liability for the full face amount to other parties. However, the payor can recover or set off any difference that it cannot get from its customer from the encoding depositary bank. Thus, the payor would first have to attempt to charge its depositor's account for the amount of the check and if it could not—either because the account had been closed or there was

10. 287 F.Supp. 2d 564, 51 UCC2d 909 (M.D.Pa. 2003), aff'd, 393 F.3d 404 (3d Cir. 2004).

a stop payment—it would have a warranty claim against the depositary bank.

A question buried in section 4–209 is illustrated by the facts of Azalea City Motels, Inc. v. First Alabama Bank.[11] In that case, William Hannah issued a check payable to Azalea City Motels for $100,000 drawn on an account at First National Bank of Livingston, Tennessee (FNBL). Azalea City deposited the check in First Alabama, where it was incorrectly encoded $10,000 instead of $100,000. Consequently, the Azalea City account was provisionally credited $10,000 instead of $100,000. First Alabama sent the check for collection and both the Federal Reserve branch and FNBL processed the check as a $10,000 item. FNBL paid the item as if it were a $10,000 draft and deducted a corresponding $10,000 from Hannah's account.

Approximately two weeks after the initial deposit, Azalea City learned that First Alabama had miscredited its account and complained. First Alabama provisionally credited the Azalea City account for $90,000, the difference between the original check and the misencoded item. First Alabama then presented a $90,000 adjustment and a photocopy of the check to the Federal Reserve, which, after a month's delay, forwarded it to FNBL. When FNBL finally received the item it dishonored, but in the meantime First Alabama had allowed Azalea City to withdraw virtually all of the $90,000 provisional credit.

First Alabama obtained a default judgment against Hannah, but was unable to enforce it because Hannah had disappeared, so the bank turned its attention to its customer, Azalea City, and the principals behind Azalea City. First Alabama argued alternatively that those parties had indorsement liability to the bank or that the bank had a restitution claim against them. The court rejected both arguments. Because indorsement claims are conditioned upon dishonor, the plaintiff depositary bank had to prove the check had been dishonored. Since the underencoded check had been presented and the underencoded portion had been paid, the court concluded there was no dishonor, and consequently no indorsement liability. Analyzing all the facts and circumstances to determine whether there was "unjust" enrichment, the court concluded that there was not.

The *Azalea City* case was decided under the pre–1990 Code, but even applying the revised 4–209, there are difficulties. Assume that Hannah has only $11,000 in his account when he cuts a $100,000 check which is then encoded as $10,000 at the depositary bank. When the check is presented to the payor, Hannah's account would be debited $10,000, leaving a positive balance of $1000. Assume

11. 551 So.2d 967, 9 UCC2d 1009 (Ala. 1989).

further that that $1000 represents Hannah's entire net worth and that he files bankruptcy 30 days after the check has drawn.

Applying the 4–209 warranties, it is clear that as between the payor bank and the depositary bank that the depositary bank would bear any loss. But can the depositary bank who has credited an additional $90,000 to its customer turn to its payee customer and recover either on the indorsement or in restitution? Taking the indorsement issue first, if one follows the Azalea City case, and the apparent effect of 4–209, the payee would not be liable on the indorsement because there had been no dishonor.[12]

The restitution issue is less clear, but we think the solution should turn on what the payee has done between the time it deposited the check and when the depositary bank finally learned that the check would not be paid. If Azalea City had no other claim on Hannah's assets and had not otherwise acted in reliance upon the apparent payment, it would receive an $89,000 windfall. In such circumstances, we believe that the depositary bank should be allowed to recover in restitution from the payee.

§ 5–7 Liability for Delay in Handling Documentary Drafts

The process by which banks handle and pay checks may be a mystery to the student or the lawyer, but at least each recognizes a check, is familiar with their use, and has a basic understanding of their operation outside the banking system. The same cannot be said for documentary drafts. Documentary drafts live in a faintly roguish world far removed from large commercial banks. Typically they are transferred between buyers and sellers of cattle, hogs, used cars and the like. Although banks often transfer them and act as collecting agents on them, neither the banks nor practice dictates a specific and invariable form of the kind one finds with domestic checks. For that reason these drafts differ in form from industry to industry, from place to place, and from transaction to transaction.

In common practice such a draft might be drawn by the seller of cattle on the buyer. The draft might provide that it is "payable through" the buyer's bank. In that case the draft might be attached to a bill of sale ("the document") and it is likely to be collected through the banking system. The drawer will have deposited the draft for collection in his own bank, who in return will have transferred it for collection to buyer's bank.

---

12. Consider Sonenberg v. Marine Midland Bank, 201 A.D.2d 329, 607 N.Y.S.2d 635, 23 UCC2d 499 (1994). Marine Midland, the depository bank, mistakenly encoded a check of $20,000 as $2,000, but the account was overdrawn even for $2,000. The court granted a summary judgment for the defendant bank, reasoning that there was no damage under 4–103(5) since the check would have been dishonored whether properly encoded or not. The bank charged back within a reasonable time and had a right to do so under 4–212(1).

To understand the setting in which these cases arise, consider Memphis Aero Corp. v. First American National Bank.[1] In that case a customer of First American Bank, a local Piper dealer, Midsouth Aviation, purchased an aircraft from the regional Piper dealer, Memphis Aero. Initially the sale was financed by Piper Finance Corporation who held a security interest in the aircraft. The local dealer instructed Memphis Aero or Piper to present a draft to First American for payment of the aircraft. The draft, instructing First American to pay $30,664 to Piper Finance and containing the ambiguous instruction "value received and charge to the account of Midsouth Aviation Inc." arrived on November 14 at First American. It was presented by Trust Company of Georgia, Piper's bank. Mr. Cohen, a First American official whose name actually appeared on the draft, contacted Midsouth on several occasions, but Midsouth was never able to produce sufficient funds to pay the draft. On November 26, Mr. Cohen informed Piper and Memphis Aero that Midsouth did not have sufficient funds to pay the draft. On December 20, First American returned the draft to Trust Company of Georgia. Although it is unclear from the facts of the case, it seems likely that Midsouth improperly resold the airplane to a buyer in the ordinary course who took free of Piper's security interest. If that were true, it meant the $30,000 loss would fall either on the bank or on Piper Finance. Presumably Midsouth had insufficient assets to satisfy its liability.

The initial question, and one determined by the lower court, was the identity of the payor. Despite the fact that the document in the lower left-hand corner stated that it was "to" First American, First American argued that the words "value received" and "charge to the account of Midsouth Aviation Inc." meant that Midsouth was the payor and First American Bank was merely a collecting agent. It seems likely that banks and those knowledgeable in the trade never expect banks to be payors on such documents, but the courts in a number of circumstances, including Memphis Aero, have held them to be payors.

A recent example of such a decision, and its consequences, is Bank South, N.A. v. Roswell Jeep Eagle, Inc.[2] There, the payee sued on several documentary drafts given to pay for a used car. It sued the bank to whom the drafts had been forwarded for payment but which had returned them unpaid. The court concluded that the bank was the payor, not a collecting bank, and followed *Memphis Aero* in concluding, therefore, that former 4–302(b) (revised 4–302(a)(2)) applied and that the bank did not have to act by its midnight deadline only but "within the time allowed."

§ 5–7

1. 647 S.W.2d 219, 35 UCC 910 (Tenn. 1983).

2. 204 Ga.App. 432, 419 S.E.2d 522, 18 UCC2d 1210 (1992).

An example of the timing elasticity allowed a collecting bank with a documentary draft is seen in Southern Cotton Oil Co. v. Merchants National Bank.[3] There Merchants National acted as a collecting bank on sight drafts drawn on a buyer to the order of seller Southern Cotton Oil. The bank held the drafts for fifty-two days before South Cotton received notice of dishonor. The appeals court upheld the district court's finding that Merchants National had acted reasonably in delaying notice of dishonor. Citing 1–205 and 3–503, the appeals court stated that a course of dealing may establish the seasonableness of an action. In this case the bank had delayed notice in seven prior transactions for periods of nine to forty-five days. In none of those cases had Southern Cotton Oil complained. Therefore, holding the drafts for fifty-two days on this occasion was not unreasonable.

When the court decides that the bank is not a collecting bank, but rather a payor, one returns to the more rigid rules of 4–302. We have seen that 4–302(a)(1) imposes strict liability on the bank if it fails to pay by its midnight deadline, or in some cases by a shorter time. Generally that is not the case with respect to documentary drafts. Such drafts fall under 4–302(a)(2) as "other properly payable items" and as to those, the payor has until the expiration of "the time allowed." Presumably the time allowed could be specified, but more likely it is to be found in the practice and behavior of the parties to the transaction or the persons in the trade.

There are two significant differences between 4–302(a)(1) and 4–302(a)(2). In the first place the payor has liability under (a)(2) only for items "properly payable." An item is not properly payable unless there are sufficient funds in the account to pay it. In *Memphis Aero* the court held that the bank was not liable for holding the item more than a month because at no time did Midsouth have enough funds in its account to pay the item. Thus, it was never "properly payable" and the bank never became accountable under 4–302. By hypothesis in such cases, the person ultimately liable on the instrument is in financial distress or, at minimum, is having cash flow problems. Thus, in many cases, the bank who is held to be a payor will be saved by the "properly payable" language. Section 4–104(1)(i) formerly defined "properly payable" as requiring "availability of funds for payment."[4] That definition was removed in the 1990 revision in order to "give meaning to properly payable" in section 4–401(1). Comment 1 to 4–401 now makes it clear that a check drawn against insufficient funds may nevertheless be "properly payable" and that a payor who chooses to charge such a check to an overdrawn account has a right to recover that

---

3. 670 F.2d 548, 33 UCC 632 (5th Cir.1982).

4. " 'Properly payable' includes the availability of funds for payment at the time of decision to pay or dishonor."

amount from the drawer.[5] We see no intention, however, to change the meaning of "properly payable" as it is used in 4–302(a)(2) and as interpreted by *Memphis Aero* and other cases. Comment 1 to 4–401 says only that such an item *may* be properly payable. Thus, we think those cases still come out the same way, namely, that a documentary draft drawn against insufficient funds is not "properly payable" under 4–302(a)(2) and thus imposes no liability even on a bank who is found to be a payor and who holds the draft for a considerable period.

The second difference between (a)(1) and (a)(2) and one to which we referred above is the fact that payor bank may hold the item for "the time allowed." That time may be quite long.

§ 5–8   Miscellaneous Factors Relating to Bank Liability for Delay in Handling and Paying Checks

Here we consider odds and ends in the check collection system. We begin with the question of multiple presentment and continue with the problems that arise when banks give special but often ambiguous instructions regarding particular items.

a.   *Multiple Presentment of Checks*

Once a check has been dishonored, the payee often presents it again in the hope that it will be paid. This common practice creates a question not explicitly answered by either the former or the revised Articles 3 and 4: is a payor bank obligated to handle all checks presented for collection in the same manner, or is it permitted to treat a once-dishonored check differently? More importantly, if the payor decides to dishonor a second presentment of a check, must it do so within the 4–302 midnight deadline?

Although there is some authority to the contrary, the answer seems to be that checks are checks and the rules are the same whether an item is arriving for the first, second, or even third time. In David Graubart, Inc. v. Bank Leumi Trust Company,[1] Graubart was issued a check for $13,000 drawn by the Prins Diamond Company on the latter's account with the payor, Bank Leumi. Graubart deposited the check in its account at National Bank of North America, which forwarded it through the normal collection channels to Bank Leumi. When Bank Leumi learned that the drawer's account was overdrawn, it marked the item "insufficient

---

5.   Comment 1 to 4–401 can be read to conflict with our interpretation: "An item drawn for more than the amount of a customer's account may be properly payable. Thus, under subsection (a) a bank may charge the customer's account for an item even though payment results in an overdraft." We think and hope this sentence is directed exclusively at 4–401 and 4–402 and not at 4–302.

§ 5–8

1.   48 N.Y.2d 554, 423 N.Y.S.2d 899, 399 N.E.2d 930, 27 UCC 1184 (1979).

funds" and returned it before the midnight deadline. Graubart then redeposited the check with National Bank. The check was again forwarded to Bank Leumi, which this time held it for more than a week before dishonoring.

Bank Leumi argued that it was not liable for holding the check beyond its midnight deadline the second time it was presented. Bank Leumi relied on former 3–511(4), which provided:

> Where a draft has been dishonored by nonacceptance a later presentment for payment and any notice of dishonor and protest for nonpayment are excused unless in the meantime the instrument has been accepted.

Bank Leumi argued that "nonacceptance" of a "draft" was equivalent to "nonpayment" of a "check." The court rejected that argument. The court pointed to former 3–410 (current 3–409) and explained that nonpayment and nonacceptance "are distinctly different concepts." In short, the court concluded that former 3–511(4) had nothing whatsoever to do with demand items.[2] It concluded, therefore, that a redeposited check should be afforded "the full panoply of Article 4 protection."[3]

The 1990 revisions do not deal specifically with the redeposited check problem. The language in former 3–511(4) has been changed somewhat, and is now found in 3–502(f), which states:

> If a draft is dishonored because timely acceptance of the draft was not made and the person entitled to demand acceptance consents to a late acceptance, from the time of acceptance the draft is treated as never having been dishonored.

We believe that the changes do not change the result in *Graubart*. It is still true that nonacceptance means something different from nonpayment, so the section simply does not apply to redeposited check problems. This means that unless there is some agreement to the contrary, a bank which handles a represented check must meet the midnight deadline. Given the reality of the modern check processing system we think that is the correct result, but we are sympathetic to the complaints of banks like Leumi. It seems unfair to allow a payee to stand beyond gun range and lob check after check into the fort in the hope he will eventually get a hit.

---

2. A student note points out that the historical forerunners of 3–511(4) "dealt only with fixing the liabilities of drawers and indorsers on time items" and that "[i]it was not designed for demand items, nor was it meant to be used in connection with any notice required of payor banks." Note, Uniform Commercial Code—Nonapplicability of Payor Bank's "Midnight deadline" to Re-presented Checks, 18 Kan.L.Rev. 679, 683 (1970).

3. Huntmix, Inc. v. Bank of America Nat. Trust & Sav. Ass'n, 134 Cal.App.3d 347, 184 Cal.Rptr. 551, 34 UCC 617 (1982) contains a useful discussion of the issues and cases in this area.

b. *Instructions to Hold*

Even though the *Graubart* court held that Bank Leumi could not hide behind former 3–511(4), Bank Leumi escaped on other grounds. When the check was presented the third time it was accompanied by an "advice to customer" slip (a copy of which had been given to Graubart) indicating that credit would be given only when the depositary bank received payment. In addition, in a space bearing the legend "Special Instruction: (Return immediately if not paid unless otherwise instructed)," the slip contained a typed direction that the payor bank (Bank Leumi) was to "remit cashier's check when paid." The court concluded that those were instructions to hold the check to seek payment and therefore waived return by the midnight deadline.

The possibility that instructions by the presenting party may modify the payor's duties presents two questions. First, who may give such instructions and who is bound by them? Second, what constitutes appropriate instructions? Assume, for example, that upon a first dishonor, a collecting bank takes it on itself to instruct the payor to "hold for collection." Is the payee on the check who is ignorant of those instructions bound by them? The only Code section that is relevant does not apply directly. Section 4–203 states when a collecting bank follows instructions from its transferor it "is not liable to prior parties for any action taken pursuant to the instructions or in accordance with any agreement with its transferor." This section does not apply directly because it deals with collecting banks and says nothing about payors.

One might argue that all parties, including the payee, must consent to the agreement. On the other hand, if trade practice calls for such instructions, and if the collecting bank is the customer's agent, the customer has authorized its agent to give such instructions and should be bound. As long as the depositary bank acts in good faith and in the apparent best interest of its customer, we believe the customer should be bound by any such instructions. Section 4–201 makes the depositary bank "an agent or sub-agent of the owner of the item." We read that agency relationship as broad enough to authorize the bank to give instructions that bind the owner-payee.

A second question remains: what language or what act constitutes instructions to hold a check beyond the midnight deadline? In certain contexts mere words "for collection" or the mode of presentation of the check (not as a "cash item") may themselves be enough to instruct the payor to hold the item beyond the midnight deadline. In *Graubart*, for instance, the court found that the instructions "for collection" and "please remit cashier's check when paid," together with a custom of holding such checks past the midnight deadline, constituted an agreement that the Graubart check was a collection item, not a demand item. Since non-demand items that are properly payable fall under 4–302(a)(2), which requires only action within the "time allowed," Bank Leumi was not liable for holding the check. Many cases have followed *Graubart* and most seem correctly decided.

When they are considering cases involving ambiguous instructions, we hope courts will look to the practice among banks. Bankers should be bound by bankers' messages even if those messages are not clear to a layman.

Consider Wolverton Farmers Elevator v. First American Bank.[4] Wolverton, a farm cooperative, received a series of checks from sales of corn to Dakota Crackin' Inc. Dakota Crackin's checks were sent for payment to First American in the normal course. An officer of First American called the depository bank, First National, to inquire how First American should treat the checks. First American ultimately treated the checks as "collection items," namely items transferred out of the normal banking channels and accompanied by an advice form that allows the payor to hold them for a period of time while the account is checked for adequate funds. At the request of the payee's attorney, the checks were returned to First National on January 23, 1986; in February Dakota Crackin' declared bankruptcy.

After the various bankers testified at trial, the court concluded that the payee Wolverton did not have an intention to make a present demand for payment. The court found that the advice forms attached to the checks contained ambiguous language which, when construed against the drafter, allowed the items to be treated as collection items.

This case occurs repeatedly: the parties have an understanding, often inadequately spelled out and almost never written down, that the payor will hold the checks for a time in an attempt to collect them. The fact that the payor had to go all the way to the court of appeals to win suggests that the payors should insist on written, explicit, instructions.

---

4. 851 F.2d 223, 6 UCC2d 1203 (8th Cir.1988).

Chapter 6

THE PAYOR BANK AND ITS CUSTOMER

Analysis

307

§ 6–1 Introduction

The foundation of the relationship between bank and customer is the bank's agreement to pay out the customer's money according to the customer's order. Although one might think of the bank as the bailee of the depositor's money, that would be wrong. The bank has no obligation to keep one depositor's money segregated from another's; rather the law regards the bank's relation to its depositor as a debtor-creditor relation, with the customer as the creditor and the bank as the debtor.[1] That is, in the eyes of the law, the customer has "lent" the amount in the account to the bank and the bank is obliged to pay it out on order. Generally, the bank must obey the customer's order not only to pay but also *not* to pay funds on deposit. Most controversies between the customer and the bank arise either when the bank pays a check it ought not to have paid or when the bank fails to pay a check it ought to have paid. Of course "ought" and "ought not" are only legal conclusions which follow when one has answered the questions we discuss in the following pages. In this chapter we will examine when an item is properly payable, what constitutes wrongful dishonor and the extent of liability for a wrongful dishonor. We will also explore uncertainties that revolve around customer stop-payment orders and the like. In addition, we will survey the bank's defenses when it has paid an item that it should not have paid. Finally, we will consider the Code provision on priority of a check holder *vis-a-vis* persons who wish to prevent payment and seize the account in satisfaction of their own claims. Since we have already treated the legal effects of the customer's negligence in contributing to and failing to discover forgeries and alterations, here we only refer the reader to Chapter 4 *supra*.

Most of the relevant law on the depositor-bank relationship is in Part 4 of Article 4 of the Code entitled "Relationship Between Payor Bank and Its Customer." It would not stretch the truth much to assert that bankers wrote Part 4 of Article 4 for bankers. Protection of payor banks is the dominant theme of Part 4; relatively little in Part 4 spells out rights of the customer on the bank's default. Two definitions control the scope of Part 4. Section 1–201(b)(4) contains the threshold definition:

"Bank" means any person engaged in the business of banking.[2]

§ 6–1

1. The pre-Code cases which describe the customer-bank relationship as one of debtor-creditor are legion. See 5A A. Michie, Banks & Banking ch. 9, § 1 at 1–8 (1950). Cases decided under the Code take the same position. See, e.g., Stone

& Webster Eng'g Corp. v. First Nat. Bank & Trust Co., 345 Mass. 1, 5, 184 N.E.2d 358, 360–61, 1 UCC 195, 199 (1962).

2. Presumably this functional definition encompasses savings and loan associations and credit unions. Conceivably

Subsection 4–104(a)(5) defines a "customer" as:

> * * * a person having an account with a bank or for whom a bank has agreed to collect items, including a bank that maintains an account at another bank.

"Customer" may include corporations, partnerships, associations and even other banks.[3] In any litigated dispute our "customer" will also be a "drawer" of a check, a "maker" of a note, or perhaps a "payee" or "indorsee," but these terms suggest liabilities[4] of only tangential concern in this chapter. Here we will call our entity "customer" or alternatively "depositor" because those terms express the deposit relationship with the bank which is our focus here. Last is "[i]tem," another important defined term. Subsection 4–104(a)(9) defines an "item" as:

> * * * an instrument or a promise or order to pay money handled by a bank for collection or payment. The term does not include a payment order governed by Article 4A or a credit or debit card slip.[5]

Personal checks are the most common "items," but the term also includes bank checks, cashier's and teller's checks, notes and non-negotiable instruments payable at a bank.

§ 6–2   The Deposit Contract and Permissible Variation of Code Provisions, Section 4–103

We have copied a typical bank-customer deposit agreement in the footnote.[1] For accounts that raise additional legal problems (for

---

it also covers a variety of other organizations in certain of their activities such as stock brokers, mutual funds and the like.

3. § 1–201(b)(27) provides that " 'Person' includes an individual or an organization."

4. We discuss the liability incurred by a maker or drawer under 3–414 in Section 1–6 *supra*.

5. Thus, the 1990 revision reverses cases like Broadway Nat. Bank v. Progressive Casualty Ins. Co., 775 F.Supp. 123 (S.D.N.Y. 1991), aff'd, 963 F.2d 1522 (2d Cir.1992), which held that credit card sales slips were "items of deposit" within the meaning of a financial institution bond's uncollected funds exclusion.

§ 6–2

1. The signature card reads as follows:

It is mutually agreed by and between the BANK and the depositor as follows:

All transactions under the account hereby opened shall be subject to the following:

(1) The Bank is hereby authorized to recognize the signature executed herewith in payment of funds.

(2) Credits for all items are subject to final payment in cash or solvent credits.

(3) The depositor waives protest for and notice of the dishonor and/or nonpayment of any items deposited. The liability of the depositor, as endorser, shall not be released by the Bank procuring certification of any check deposited.

(4) This Bank shall have a lien on all items handled by it, and on the proceeds thereof, and upon any goods and securities for which such items are drawn, for any advances made by it or other indebtedness, and for any expenses incurred, including court costs and attorneys' fees.

example, joint,[2] partnership[3] or corporate[4] accounts), the deposit contract will include additional terms. Some of the clauses of the

(5) Stop payment requests and renewals and revocations thereof must be in writing on a form satisfactory to and served on this Bank. This Bank shall not be liable for unintentional payment through oversight or accident only of a check on which payment has been stopped.

(6) The amounts entered on receipts or in the passbook are taken from the depositor's deposit ticket without verification. This Bank reserves the right, after examination, to correct any mistakes and change any entries which are in error.

(7) All items transmitted for collection to any Federal Reserve Bank shall be governed by the rules and regulations of such bank and of the Federal Reserve Board.

(8) Any item drawn on or payable at this Bank may be charged back to the depositor at or before the end of the second business day following the day of deposit in the event that the item is found not good or not payable for any reason.

(9) This account shall be subject to service charges in effect from time to time at the Bank.

(10) Statements of account together with paid and canceled checks shall be available to the depositor either by mail or delivery at regular monthly intervals, and all objections to any item thereof for any cause or reason whatsoever, whether then known or unknown, not made on or before 15 days after available date for delivery or mailing shall be absolutely barred and waived.

2. A typical joint account agreement would include these terms:

When signed below, this account becomes a Joint Account payable to either during the lifetime of both or to the survivor. The bank may make payments from this account upon the orders or receipts of both or either and the bank's records for any payment so made shall be a sufficient acquittance therefor. Each of the undersigned appoints the other attorney with power to endorse (by rubber stamp or otherwise) for deposit to this account checks, drafts, notes, orders and receipts for the payment of all money belonging or payable to either or both of the undersigned.

3. A partnership or association account would include the following:

The following represent that they are partners or members of _____ and hereby agree (1) the Bank is designated as its depository for monies, checks or other instruments which may come into the possession of the Partnership/Association. Endorsement may be by any person authorized to sign checks in writing or by stamp without designation of person so endorsing; and (2) until written revocation is received by the Bank, any _____ of the above persons are authorized on behalf of the Partnership/Association to: a) sign checks or other payment orders against the account, b) withdraw or release its property held by the Bank, c) accept instruments of payments at the Bank and d) endorse, negotiate and receive payment of proceeds of any instrument payable to or belonging to the Partnership/Association.

4. A corporate account requires terms such as these:

This certifies that on _____ 19__, a meeting of the Directors of _____ adopted a resolution (1) designating the bank as a depository of its funds subject to the standard rules and regulations of the Bank; and (2) authorizing the Bank to accept for credit to the account of the corporation and/or collection, any and all checks, drafts, notes and other negotiable instruments when endorsed in the name of the corporation in writing, by rubber stamp or otherwise with or without designation of the party making the endorsement; and (3) authorizing the Bank to pay out funds standing to the credit of the corporation upon checks, drafts, notes or other instruments when signed in the name of the corporation and by ____ of the above. Provided further that the Bank may honor and pay any such instrument without inquiring as to the circumstances of issue of the disposition of proceeds including those drawn to the individual order of officers of the corporation, any authorized signers or otherwise. This resolution shall remain in full force and effect until written notice to the contrary is received by the Bank.

deposit contract merely restate Code law.[5] Other clauses modify Code provisions only slightly to emphasize points of particular interest to the bank.[6] Since a comparatively unfettered and perhaps zealous bank lawyer usually drafts the deposit agreement, it may overreach a bit and whether it includes impermissible departures from the Code provisions may be the only important lawyer question that the deposit agreement poses. For example, we question the validity of clauses (5) and (10) in the quoted deposit agreement. Section 4–103(a) prohibits a bank's disclaimer of its "responsibility for its lack of good faith or failure to exercise ordinary care." It explicitly authorizes the parties to agree on the standards by which the bank's responsibility should be measured "if those standards are not manifestly unreasonable." The bank drafter there must pay attention to the relevant definitions of "ordinary care" and to insure that it is authorizing only acts "in good faith" (i.e., those that involve honesty in fact and "the observance of reasonable commercial standards of fair dealing"). Within those broad limits there is a great deal of discretion but, particularly in consumer deposit agreements, it is possible to cross the boundaries of good faith and ordinary care. For example a few courts have invalidated exculpatory clauses in night depository agreements. In Hy–Grade Oil Co. v. New Jersey Bank[7] the parties had signed an agreement containing the following clause:

> 3(a) The bank shall not be responsible for the loss or destruction of the pouch or its contents, in whole or in part, either before or after its being placed in the night depository, resulting directly or indirectly from (1) defects in the pouch or its lock; (2) defects in or failure of the night depository entrance chute or safe; (3) theft, burglary or embezzlement. The finding of the bank as to the presence or absence of the pouch in the night depository, and as to the contents thereof shall be conclusive and binding upon the undersigned.

> (b) It is hereby expressly understood and agreed that the use of the night depository facilities is a gratuitous privilege extended by the bank to the undersigned for the convenience of

---

5. Clause (2) restates § 4–215(c) and (d). Clause (7) restates § 4–103(b). Clause (8) restates § 4–214(a).

6. Clause (3) implements the waiver of notice of dishonor authorized by 3–504(a)(iv) and thus reduces the bank's duty under 3–503 and 3–505. The second sentence of the clause alters the rules of discharge on certification stated in 3–415(d) in the instance where the bank, as holder, procures certification. Clause (4) states the bank's common law lien on items handled, a principle incorporated in large part by 4–210(a) and extended there to include the entire bank collection process. This particular contract goes beyond 4–210(a) in attaching "goods and securities" for which such items are drawn.

7. 138 N.J.Super. 112, 350 A.2d 279, 18 UCC 729 (1975), cert. denied, 70 N.J. 518, 361 A.2d 532 (1976).

the undersigned, and the use of the night depository facilities shall be at the sole risk of the undersigned.

The plaintiff claimed to have deposited $1,585.00 in the night depository box; the bank asserted that it found part of the plaintiff's bag but none of the money the following morning. The trial judge granted the bank's motion to dismiss based in part on the agreement and "the legal relationship established therein." The Court of Appeals found the agreement to be invalid in view of the fact that a bank is "affected with a public interest" and sent the case back for a new trial.

This is the classic case in which a bank argues that its only protection against fraudulent claims of nonexistent deposits lies in the agreement of the kind quoted. The customer responds that the bank should not be so exculpated from what may be its own negligence in allowing an employee to steal the contents of the bag. The courts have split on the question.

Why do we think clauses (5) and (10) of the deposit agreement set out in the footnote may be invalid? The clauses deprive the customer of substantial rights he would otherwise have under the Code. Clause (5) reads in full as follows:

> Stop payment requests and renewals and revocations thereof must be in writing on a form satisfactory to and served on this Bank. This Bank shall not be liable for unintentional payment through oversight or accident only of a check on which payment has been stopped.

First, the payor bank is seeking through Clause (5) to deprive the customer of the right to give oral stop orders, a right the customer would have under Part 4 of Article 4 if the contract were silent. Second, the payor bank is exculpating itself for failure to follow a stop order where that failure is the result of its "oversight or accident." Is "oversight" not a synonym for negligence?

Clause (10) reads in full as follows:

> Statements of account together with paid and canceled checks shall be available to the depositor either by mail or delivery at regular monthly intervals, and all objections to any item thereof for any cause or reason whatsoever, whether then known or unknown, not made on or before 15 days after available date for delivery or mailing shall be absolutely barred and waived.

This clause imposes a 15–day statute of limitations in circumstances in which the customer might have as long as one year to make a complaint under 4–406(f). Like Clause (5), Clause (10) would deprive the customer of substantial rights he would otherwise have under Part 4 of Article 4.

Can the payor bank enforce such clauses against the customer? Several Code sections grant considerable leeway for the parties to work out their own bargain.[8] Section 4–103(a)[9] provides:

> The effect of the provisions of this Article may be varied by agreement, but the parties to the agreement cannot disclaim a bank's responsibility for its lack of good faith or failure to exercise ordinary care or limit the measure of damages for the lack or failure. However, the parties may determine by agreement the standards by which the bank's responsibility is to be measured if those standards are not manifestly unreasonable.

Is 4–103 the only restriction on the power of the parties to vary the Code by agreement? For example, could a court hold an agreement at variance with the Code invalid because it was contrary to a public policy? Unconscionable under 2–302? We conclude that other general principles beside those embodied in 4–103 limit the bank's power to alter Part 4's provisions. For example, 4–103 would not itself prohibit a customer and a bank from agreeing that the customer had no right whatsoever to stop payment. Yet we read Comment 1 to 4–403 as a statement of public policy that the customer should have such right:

> The position taken by this section is that stopping payment or closing an account is a service which depositors expect and are entitled to receive from banks notwithstanding its difficulty, inconvenience and expense. The inevitable occasional losses through failure to stop or close should be borne by the banks as a cost of the business of banking.

We believe that 4–103 incorporates the standard principle that parties may not depart from legislative statements of public policy, that 4–403(a) is a statement of such a public policy and that the foregoing Comment is an indication that the Code drafters did not

---

8. § 1–302 provides a general rule for all Articles of the Code. It reads as follows:

(a) Except as otherwise provided in subsection (b) or elsewhere in [the Uniform Commercial Code], the effect of provisions of [the Uniform Commercial Code] may be varied by agreement.

(b) The obligations of good faith, diligence, reasonableness and care prescribed by [the Uniform Commercial Code] may not be disclaimed by agreement. The parties, by agreement, may determine the standards by which the performance of those obligations is to be measured if those standards are not manifestly unreasonable. Whenever [the Uniform Commercial Code] requires an action to be taken within a reasonable time, a time that is not manifestly unreasonable may be fixed by agreement.

(c) The presence in certain provisions of [the Uniform Commercial Code] of the phrase "unless otherwise agreed," or words of similar import, does not imply that the effect of other provisions may not be varied by agreement under this section.

9. Note that the customer might find itself bound by agreements to which it is not a party. § 4–103(b) provides:

Federal Reserve regulations and operating circulars, clearing-house rules, and the like, have the effect of agreements under subsection (a), whether or not specifically assented to by all parties interested in items handled.

intend that banks should have the right to eliminate the practice of stopping payment.

Whether the customer can invoke section 2–302 on unconscionability is more doubtful. That section is part of Article 2 on sales of goods. Admittedly, courts have frequently applied 2–302 to security transactions but most of those cases also involved sales of goods. It may stretch the section too far to apply it to a bank-customer relationship. We conclude that 2–302 can be applied to Article 4 transactions only by analogy.

Returning to the two clauses in our deposit agreement, how should a court come out? The first clause (Clause (5)) would deprive the customer of its right to give oral stop orders and would free the bank from liability for payments made "through oversight or accident." One may attack the bank's attempt to free itself of liability for oversight or accident as an effort to evade its responsibility under 4–103 for "failure to exercise ordinary care."[10] Although "accident or oversight" are not identical to negligence, they so closely overlap that we cannot think of a realistic hypothetical case in which the bank would be guilty of oversight or accident but not negligence. We conclude that Clause (5) is invalid under 4–103 (or alternatively, that it would, to be valid, have to be construed so narrowly as to be of no practical effect). We have more difficulty with the question whether Clause (5) can change the rule of 4–403(b) (an oral order is effective for six months, or for fourteen days if not confirmed in writing within that period), but because of the public policy recognized by the comment to give customers stop-payment rights,[11] we doubt the validity of that part of Clause (5).

---

10. See Opinion of Attorney General of Utah, 1966 WL 8829, 3 UCC 115 (1966) (clause which exculpates bank for payment through "inadvertence or accident only" is invalid). § 4–103(c) provides guidelines for determining what is "ordinary care."

11. In remarks before the New York Law Revision Commission, Mr. Malcolm, an Article 4 Draftsman, said:

However, that particular issue [requiring written stop orders] was battled in many forums and on many occasions, in the smaller groups and in the larger groups of the sponsoring organizations, and in September 1951 when the final form of Article 4 was approved, the specific issue was considered by the joint houses of the Institute and the Commissioners and the vote was not to shift to the California rule [requiring written stop orders], and there is the voice of authority so far as I am concerned. That was the policy decision that was made.

1 N.Y. State Law Revision Comm'n, 1954 Report 467 (1954).

The drafters responded to criticisms of the 1952 Official Draft of section 4–403(b) as follows:

The provision that an oral stop order is binding upon the bank only "until a customer has had reasonable opportunity to send the bank a written confirmation if the bank requests such a confirmation" has been criticized on several grounds, particularly that this language either requires banks to print on signature cards or similar forms standard requests for confirmations of all stop payment orders, or there is likely to be a disputed issue of fact as to whether a written confirmation was requested. The change prescribes a flat fourteen day period in which the customer must confirm in writing an oral stop payment order. *This preserves the right of the customer to give an oral stop payment*

Clause (10) imposes a fifteen-day statute of limitations on certain customer claims. That is, the customer must inspect its canceled checks and make any complaints about them (e.g., that there are forgeries) within fifteen days or lose all its rights. Clause (10) comes close to the line. Although it is not in form a "disclaimer," in substance it disclaims the bank's " * * * responsibility for its lack of good faith or failure to exercise ordinary care * * *." As a practical matter a short statute of limitations can serve as effectively to enable the bank to escape liability as an outright disclaimer. The bank may argue that Clause (10) only sets a standard by which its responsibility is to be measured and that 4–103 therefore validates the clause. Of course one can respond that Clause (10) is "manifestly unreasonable" and that 4–103(a) therefore cannot validate it.

Some courts have considered these questions and they have been quite generous to the banks. In two cases the Appellate Division of the New York courts has upheld terms in deposit agreements that limit the payor bank's liability. In the first, Retail Shoe Health Commission v. Manufacturers Hanover Trust Co.,[12] the payor bank successfully defended against its customer's claims arising out of an embezzlement by relying upon two terms in the deposit agreement. One of these required the depositor to give notice of any error in the statement within six months of receipt of that statement or the statement should be "considered correct" for all purposes. A second term in the agreement required the customer to commence suit within 18 months. Citing both of these provisions with approval the court upheld the argument of the bank that it had no liability to the customer whose funds had been embezzled. In a similar and more striking case, Qassemzadeh v. IBM Poughkeepsie Employees Federal Credit Union,[13] the court relied upon a term in the deposit agreement that required the depositor to notify the Credit Union of error within 30 days after it received the statement of account. In this case the customer did not notify them of an error (a check for approximately $10 had been raised to approximately $10,000) until one year after the occurrence.

To the extent these cases put the risk on the one best able to protect against it, namely the employer from whom the embezzlement is made and the deposit holder who can discover the faults by

order but gives some protection to the bank against the uncertainties of oral orders by terminating the binding effect of an oral order unless it is confirmed in writing within fourteen days.

Uniform Commercial Code, 1952 Official Draft of Text and Comments 36–37 (Supp. No. 1, 1955) (emphasis added).

12. 160 A.D.2d 47, 558 N.Y.S.2d 949, 13 UCC2d 476 (1990).

13. 167 A.D.2d 378, 561 N.Y.S.2d 795, 13 UCC2d 833 (1990).

examining the account statement, we generally agree with them. Because we recognize that many deposit agreements, particularly in the consumer context, are signed by depositors who do not carefully examine them, we have a twinge of discomfort, but only a slight one. After all, how does one explain the fact that a Credit Union depositor does not discover a $10,000 error in his account? There is, of course, a small irony in these two cases. Namely, that a large and powerful urban bank gives its customers six months to give notice, but the small community bank—a credit union dedicated to the interests of its members—gives those members only 30 days notice. Perhaps even the consumers appreciate the virtues of promptness.

In Borowski v. Firstar Bank Milwaukee, N.A.,[14] the Wisconsin Court of Appeals holds that the bank agreement that shortens the time period under 4–406 from one year to 14 days is not "manifestly unreasonable" under 4–103. The court observes that there is very limited authority on this issue, but citing one case from another jurisdiction and a commentary on that case,[15] the court ruled for the bank. In Stowell v. Cloquet Co-op Credit Union,[16] the Minnesota Supreme Court held that the 20–day limit in the Draft Withdrawal Agreement was not "manifestly unreasonable" under 4–103. In support of its holding, the court cited a precedent with a similar factual pattern in which a 15–day limit was upheld. The court also held that under 4–406, "once account statements are mailed to the account holder's proper address, the risk of nonreceipt falls on the account holder and interception of the statements by a wrongdoer does not relieve the account holder of the duty to examine the statements and report unauthorized items to the bank." Observing that banks do not have a good way to verify the receipt of the monthly statements, the court declined to put that burden on them. Given the fact that the client made repeated efforts to contact the bank about the missing monthly statements and each time the bank did nothing more than resend the statements, we wonder if the bank is not at least comparatively negligent in this case.

In American Airlines Employees Federal Credit Union v. Martin,[17] the Texas Supreme Court came to a similar decision. The court held that defendant bank's notification to depositors of its adoption of a deposit agreement shortening the notice period for identifying and reporting unauthorized transactions to 60 days, together with depositor's agreement to be bound by polices of the

---

14. 217 Wis.2d 565, 579 N.W.2d 247, 35 UCC2d 221 (App. 1998).

15. Barkley Clark & Barbara Clark, The Law of Bank Deposits, Collections and Credit Cards ¶ 3.01[3][c] at 3–28 (rev. ed. 1995) ("The reduction in notice from one year to 14 days does not seem out of line, although a bank would be pushing it by attempting to reduce the period further.")

16. 557 N.W.2d 567, 31 UCC2d 623 (Minn. 1997).

17. 29 S.W.3d 86 (Tex. 2000).

bank at the time the account was opened and his decision to continue his account at the bank after the change in notice period, were sufficient as a matter of law to demonstrate that the parties agreed to be bound by a shorter notice period.

Together these cases show the courts' consistent willingness to allow banks to restrict the customer's time to give notice of errors in the monthly statement based on the theory of freedom of contract under 4–103(a).[18]

In Halifax Corp. v. First Union National Bank,[19] the Supreme Court of Virginia declined to use the doctrine of good faith to cut the customers some slack. Plaintiff, who failed to inform the bank within the one-year period about embezzlements by its employee, argued that the bank acted in bad faith and, as a result, should not be able to assert the 4–406(f) defense. Plaintiff cited 1–203: "Every contract or duty within [the UCC] imposes an obligation of good faith in its performance or enforcement," and argued that this provision should govern, even though 4–406(f) itself does not have a good faith requirement. The court rejected this argument. Invoking the "plain meaning" and negative implication principle of statutory interpretation, the court observed that revised 4–406 makes reference to a bank's duty of good faith in subsections (d) and (e), but not in (f). Also the phrase "good faith" in former 4–406(1) was omitted from revised 4–406(c).

a. Disclaimers of Duty to Examine Signatures

It is commonplace and proper for banks to disclaim any obligation to find a forgery of a drawer's signature that is done by machine. After all, a facsimile machine that produces the signature will produce the same signature at the direction of the forger as at the direction of an authorized person. It is easy to justify a term in the deposit agreement that places this risk on the drawer. More problematic are terms that occasionally appear in deposit agreements and put all responsibility on the drawer for forged signatures—or sometimes for first class forgeries that cannot be easily distinguished from authorized signatures.

A bank that processes checks mechanically and electronically and makes its customers aware of the fact that it does not check signatures but pays on the basis of the electronic information on the MICR line might avoid liability. But banks have a dilemma; they are hesitant to tell depositors how infrequent their examina-

---

18. But See American Airlines Employees Federal Credit Union v. Martin, 991 S.W.2d 887, 40 UCC2d 17 (Tex. App. 1999), where the Texas court refused to enforce the bank's amendment to its deposit agreement that shorten the one-year check fraud reporting period to 60 days, on the ground that the 60–day notice provision was vague and ambiguous and the customer did not knowingly consent to the amendment.

19. 262 Va. 91, 546 S.E.2d 696, 44 UCC2d 661 (2001).

tion of signatures. Having failed to make those facts known to the depositor, we question whether a clause exculpating a drawee bank from liability for paying over forged signatures should be recognized. We discuss that issue more fully in section 6–3, *infra*.

b. Check Holding (Delayed Funds Availability)

Some customers assume that when they deposit a check into their account, the check is "good" immediately and can be drawn against at once. That is wrong. Banks usually put a hold (commonly known as Delayed Funds Availability, or DFA) on uncollected funds represented by a deposited check. A bank's hold regulations are usually included in the deposit agreement (either explicitly or by reference), printed on the back of deposit slips, or both.

One may suspect banks of ulterior motives in imposing check holds,[20] but, in fact, the holds are justifiable and necessary protection for depositary banks. When a depositary bank allows the customer to draw on uncollected funds, the bank is making a loan to its customer in reliance on the check's ultimate payment (so "collected fund"). A bank seldom learns directly that a check has been honored. Instead, "no news is good news." If after the hold period has elapsed, the deposited check has not been returned by the drawee bank to the depositary bank, the latter assumes that the check was good and permits withdrawal. The percentage of checks returned by drawee banks is tiny; only 2/3 of 1 percent of all checks are returned.[21] However, the number of returned checks is significant; every year, approximately 300 million checks are returned and the annual loss sustained by banks on returned checks may exceed that lost in robberies.

However justified the DFA policy may be, consumer disgruntlement over check "holds" first prompted state legislatures to deal with the problem and then caused Congress to authorize Regulation CC.[22] That regulation provides "availability requirements" for

---

20. For example, there are claims that the banks profit enormously by having use of the customers' money from the day the bank receives provisional credit for checks until the day checks are finally paid. Although we have no hard figures, we are certain that banks are not losing money on this "float."

21. If the check is returned after the depositary bank has given final and irrevocable credit to the customer's account, the bank cannot charge back customer's account. § 4–214(a). The bank can proceed against the drawer of the check under 3–414(b), or, if the customer has endorsed the check, against the custom-

er under 3–415(a). Because this is expensive, bankers like long holds.

22. 12 C.F.R. Part 229. Subsections 4–215(e) and (f) specifically provide that they are subject to "applicable law stating the time for availability of funds * * *." These are invitations to look at Regulation CC and in effect are explicit incorporations of the terms of Regulation CC. Even if one could somehow make an argument that this is properly a matter of state law—notwithstanding the supremacy clause of the U.S. Constitution—that argument is now undermined by these explicit references in 4–215.

various methods and types of deposits. For a complete description of Regulation CC's availability requirements, see Section 20–5.

Some states have also set actual limits on the number of days checks may be held.[23] Regulation CC provides that where these laws require funds be made available for withdrawal in a shorter time than Regulation CC, state law governs. Otherwise, the federal regulation overrides inconsistent state law.[24]

c. The Bank's Right to Charge Fees to Its Customer on Non-sufficient Funds (NSF) Checks

It is standard practice for banks to impose fees on checks written on insufficient funds (NSF checks). Both the drawer and payee are usually charged by their respective banks (payor and depositary) for NSF checks. With the decline in bank profits during the 1980s, banks looked for ways to increase their earnings. One of the most fruitful was to charge fees to customers for the return of NSF checks (drawn by customers), for handling stop orders, and for recrediting depositors' accounts when the NSF checks of third parties (deposited by customers) were returned by payors. Banks typically maintain that they have a right to negotiate whatever fee the customers are willing to pay.

NSF fees have become a living thing for banks. In 2000 an estimated 251 million checks were returned by drawee banks for insufficient funds[25] and a large number—in the tens or hundreds of millions—were paid even though there were not sufficient funds in the account on which they were drawn. In nearly every case, whether the check was returned or was paid despite insufficient funds, the bank charged a fee. Today the median fee for an NSF check, paid or not,[26] is in the neighborhood of $25[27] and some New York banks charge as much as $33.[28] By one estimate banks earned more than $33 billion on NSF and Overdraft fees in 2003. These fees make up more than half of banks' earnings on consumer checking accounts.

---

23. See, e.g., N.Y. Banking Law Sec. 14(d)(1) (McKinney, 1987 Supp.); Cal. Codes Annot., Financial Code, Sec. 866.3 (West, 1986 Supp.).

24. 12 C.F.R. § 229.20.

25. See Geoffrey R. Gerdes and Jack K. Walton II, *The Use of Checks and Other Noncash Payment Instruments in the United States*, at page 6, article from the Federal Reserve Bulletin, 2002, *available at* http://www.federalreserve. gov/pubs/bulletin/2002/0802_2nd.pdf.

26. When we refer to "NSF fees," in general we mean to include fees charged for any check drawn against insufficient funds whether the check is paid or returned.

27. http://www.bankrate.com/brm/ news/chk/20050511d1.asp?prodtype= bank.

28. See Dilyara Bareeva and Katherine Wyatt, *NSF and Overdraft Fees in New York State: The Impact of Bank Characteristics and Changes in Retail Payments*, Feb. 2002, *available at* https://www.banking.state.ny.us/rp0502. pdf.

The problem with NSF fees is that the amounts banks earn on them are large in comparison with their costs (a dollar or less to return a check) and risk (none when the check is returned and slight when it is not).

The two most prominent cases dealing with banks' rights to charge NSF fees are Perdue v. Crocker National Bank,[29] a 1985 decision of the California Supreme Court, and Best v. United States National Bank of Oregon,[30] a 1987 decision of the Oregon Supreme Court. Both were class actions.

In *Perdue* the California court reversed the trial court's grant of a demurrer and allowed several causes of action to go ahead (whether charges set in good faith, whether the charges were unconscionable, whether the bank engaged in deceptive practices). In a holding that has been followed in all the later decisions,[31] the Court notes that there is no promise by the depositor not to draw checks on insufficient funds. And if there is no promise to be broken, then the $6 NSF fee cannot be a valid penalty for breaking the contract. In response to plaintiff's claim of unconscionability, the Court states that the 2000 percent difference between the NSF charge of $6 and the claimed cost of 30 cents did not prove plaintiff's case, particularly since the 30 cent cost was contested. But, with apparent approval, it cites several cases that find price to be unconscionable, and it explicitly rejects the defendant's best argument—that a price equal to the market price cannot be unconscionable. The Court concludes by drawing attention to the small print of the deposit agreement and to the fact that under the agreement, the "bank has all the rights and the depositor all the duties."[32]

In *Best* the court reversed the trial court's grant of summary judgment for defendant on the issue whether the defendant had set its NSF fees in good faith. Disagreeing with the California Supreme Court at every turn, the Oregon Court rejected plaintiffs' claim of unconscionability. The Court noted that the plaintiffs had agreed to charges "existing at any time." It noted that the costs were relatively small[33] ($5 NSF fee) and were similar to those charged by others (so moving toward the rejected market defense?). The plaintiffs could close their accounts at any time and apparently had at least "ordinary intelligence and experience." So unconscionability might be ok for the funny people in California, but not for Oregonians. The Court did find that the defendant had to use good faith in setting the NSF fees. The Court concluded that there was a genuine

---

29. 38 Cal.3d 913, 216 Cal.Rptr. 345, 702 P.2d 503 (1985).

30. 303 Or. 557, 739 P.2d 554 (1987).

31. *See, e.g.,* Howard v. Babcock, 6 Cal.4th 409, 25 Cal.Rptr.2d 80, 863 P.2d 150 (1993).

32. 702 P.2d at 513.

33. 739 P.2d at 556.

issue of material fact whether the bank set its fees in "accordance with the reasonable expectations of the parties," and if the fees were not in accordance with those expectations, they would be in bad faith.

Perdue and *Best* were the high water marks. No plaintiff ever won again—at least there are no reported opinions to document any plaintiff victories after 1987. In Tolbert v. First National Bank of Oregon,[34] the Oregon Supreme Court cut the legs out from under *Best*. In *Tolbert* the Bank argued that a bank could act in bad faith only if it set the NSF fees in a way that conflicted with the "reasonable contractual expectations" of the plaintiffs. Noting that its employees and its documents made the initial fees clear, that the agreement plainly gave the bank "discretion" to set new fees, and that new fees were announced to the customers by mail at or near the time they were instituted, the Bank argued that, as a matter of law, the customers could not challenge the fees as set in bad faith because every customer had agreed to the fees under First National's scheme. The Court found that the plaintiffs' "reasonable expectations" were irrelevant where the plaintiffs had agreed to the fees charged by the Bank. Alternatively, the Court held that the forms of notice and the terms and kinds of agreement proved that the plaintiffs' reasonable expectations had been met.

After *Tolbert* little is left of *Best*. If a bank is careful to make written disclosures of its current charges, to state how it uses broad discretion to set new charges and to send notice of changes, the bank cannot be attacked for having failed to use good faith in setting its NSF fees. Any bank that pays the least attention to its agreements and disclosure can meet the Tolbert test.

Banks sometimes post multiple checks on the same account in a largest-first order. There have been a few class actions challenging that practice, under the theory that the primary reason for banks to do so is to maximize NSF fees and that it constitutes "bad faith" and "unfair dealing." None of these challenges have been successful. In Fetter v. Wells Fargo Bank Texas, N.A.,[35] the Texas appellate court affirmed summary judgment for the bank. The court pointed to 4–303(b), which expressly provides that "items may be accepted, paid, certified, or charged to the indicated account of a bank's customer *in any order* * * *." [emphasis added] The court also rejected the plaintiff's argument that the bank breached its duty of good faith under 1–203, observing that unless the bank had violated its own deposit agreement or the statute, there is no independent cause of action for breach of the good faith duty. The

---

34. 312 Or. 485, 823 P.2d 965 (1991), *accord Wallace v. National Bank of Commerce*, 938 S.W.2d 684 (Tenn. 1997).

35. 110 S.W.3d 683 (Tex. App. 2003).

court ended its opinion by pointing out that case law is unanimous in rejecting good-faith challenges to banks' high-to-low posting method.

As this is written in 2007, the Ninth Circuit has reversed a lower court's decision that denied certification of a class against Washington Mutual Bank.[36] The case appears to raise many of the familiar challenges to NSF fees: failure to make truth in lending disclosures, violation of usury law, and violation of state deceptive practice laws. According to the claims in this case, the bank's advertising material assured customers that "we will cover you" and that the customers would enjoy "Automatic Protection." The class plaintiffs argued that the overdraft fees were "financial charges" in violation of the truth in lending law and were "interest" in violation of The Homeowners Loan Act. The lower court threw out all of the claims; on appeal the Ninth Circuit reinstated the truth in lending claim regarding unsolicited credit cards but accepted the lower court's decision that there was no usury claim. It is too soon to tell whether this case foretells renewed vigor in plaintiffs' attempts to challenge NSF fees in court.

From the beginning the Comptroller of the Currency has played a role in the dispute between depositors and their banks. In 2005 the federal financial agencies collectively proposed practices concerning overdraft fees. Since 1971 the Comptroller has had a regulation that urges banks to set their fees "on a competitive basis and not on the basis of agreement * * *."[37] The function of the 1971 regulation seems only to warn banks away from anti-trust violations. In 1983 the Comptroller issued a revision that was plainly aimed at NSF fees, among others. Subsection (c) of the revision asserted federal preemption in the setting of fees: "[State laws setting or restricting fees] impair the efficiency of national banks and conflict with the regulatory scheme governing the national banking system and are preempted by federal law."[38] The irony here is that the Comptroller is a federal official whose duty is to seek the common good, not merely to help banks skin their customers. Under subsection (b)(1) of 12 CFR 7.8000, the bank

---

36. See, In Re Washington Mutual Overdraft Protection Litigation, 2006 WL 2570957 (9th Cir. 2006).

37. 12 C.F.R. § 7.8000 (1971): All charges to customers should be arrived at by each bank on a competitive basis and not on the basis of any agreement, arrangement, undertaking, understanding or even discussion among banks or their officers.

38. 12 C.F.R. § 7.8000 (1983) (c), quoted in fn 40 supra.

In *Perdue* the Court noted that Article 4 of the UCC governs many aspects of

the relationship between the depositor and his bank. In general no state statutes limit banks' NSF fees, so the preemption issue has not been pushed by the banks. But the issue arose in 1999 when two California municipalities (Santa Monica and San Francisco) set limits on ATM fees; *see also* article by Stateline.org, *available at* http://www.stateline.org/live/ViewPage.action?site NodeId=136 & languageId=1 & contentId=13856.

should consider its costs and a proper "profit margin" in setting its fees. Here is a case where the banks' costs are trivial and the profit margin grandly in excess of that earned on any other loan in the bank. How does subsection (b)(1) justify a fee of $25 or $30? The second subsection indorses banks' deterrence of misuse; presumably this means keeping depositors from overdrawing their accounts, but drawing an NSF check is a "misuse" only if one regards an NSF check from the perspective of the payee. NSF fees are a "profit center" for the drawee, and bouncing checks is a valued use, not a misuse of one's account. The third and fourth subsections of (b) concern only the bank's wealth, its "competitive position" and its "safety and soundness." Stated as baldly as they are, these justifications sound like the Comptroller is urging "do what you need to do to make money, even if you take advantage of your most stupid and weak customers." The Comptroller has issued revisions in 1984, 1988, 1996, and 2001. All of the revisions maintain the four rules with little change. The preemption rule has been softened, and the language of the regulation has been modified to make clear the Comptroller's opinion that NSF fees are not interest charges.

In February 2005 the four federal agencies that govern financial institutions[39] issued a document called "Joint Guidance on Overdraft Protection Programs"[40] ("Guidance"). The Guidance does not deal with fees for checks that are returned; it deals with the growing alternative of paying and charging for overdrafts. The Guidance shows the federal agencies either to be in denial about banks' practices or to be engaging in a splendid hypocrisy. On the one hand, the Guidance seems to deny that overdraft fees are charged as loans. On the other, the Guidance urges the banks not to market these plans as loans. Yet the Guidance insists that these transactions (discretionary overdrafts) be treated as loans in banks' reports to the federal agencies, but the Guidance directs that they be made in such a way that they will not be regarded as loans for the Truth in Lending Act, insuring that no APR needs to be revealed to the depositor/debtor. So, the Guidance recognizes and encourages behavior that makes the transaction appear to be something other than a loan for the purposes of consumer credit disclosures, and insists that the transaction be treated as a loan for reporting to the agency and for the bank's own underwriting. Put more harshly, the Guidance condones misrepresentation to the depositor.

---

39. The Office of the Comptroller of the Currency (OCC), Board of Governors of the Federal Reserve System (Board), Federal Deposit Insurance Corporation (FDIC), and National Credit Union Administration (NCUA).

40. *See* Federal Register Vol. 70, No. 33, February 18, 2005, pp. 8428—31, *available at* http://www.ots.treas.gov/docs/7/73252.pdf.

d. The Bank's Right to Charge Check-cashing Fees

In the last decade, a series of cases has challenged a bank's right to charge check-cashing fees.[41]

The most prominent case is Wells Fargo Bank of Texas, N.A. v. James.[42] In that case the Fifth Circuit upheld a federal district court decision to strike down a Texas "par value" statute, which expressly prohibited check-cashing fees by banks against non-customers. Plaintiff and other national banks argued that the Texas statute was preempted by federal banking law, particularly 12 CFR § 7.4002, promulgated by OCC, which expressly permits a national bank to "charge its customers non-interest charges and fees." Although on its face the OCC regulation only refers to a bank's right to charge its customers, the OCC has interpreted the word "customer" to mean anyone who presents a check for payment. The court held that although many of the non-banking policy considerations, such as the negotiability of checks, consumer protection or labor compensation implicated in the Texas statute, were not within OCC's regulatory authority, the express language of OCC should still preempt any conflicting state regulation.

Other plaintiffs that challenge a bank's right to charge check-cashing fees have been equally unsuccessful. In Hayes v. First Commerce Corp.,[43] the plaintiff filed a class action against defendant bank, challenging the $2 check-cashing fee charged against non-customers. The plaintiff argued that the placing of such a condition on the cashing of paychecks violated the principle of negotiability of checks under UCC 3–104. The court rejected this contention, finding no private cause of action in the UCC rule. In Sexton v. PNC Bank, N.A.,[44] the plaintiff challenged a $3 check-cashing fee in a class action based on a slightly different theory. The plaintiff argued that the drawee bank had a duty to pay properly indorsed checks drawn against good funds. The court disagreed, holding that the $3 was not assessed on negotiation of the check, it was instead a service charge. The court pointed out that the fee "neither alters the payable-on-demand character of checks presented for cashing, nor constitutes an undertaking or instruction by the drawer over and above the promise to pay, the fee does not impair the negotiability of those checks," and its imposition does not violate UCC 3–104.

At this writing in 2008, banks' right to charge check-cashing fees, both to customers and non-customers, seems settled.

41. Barkley Clark, Clarks' Bank Deposits and Payments Monthly, Vol. 15, No. 5 (2006).

42. 321 F.3d 488 (5th Cir. 2003).

43. 763 So.2d 733, 43 UCC2d 335 (La. Ct. App. 2000).

44. 2002 WL 33281441, 43 UCC2d 341 (Pa. Com. Pl. 2000).

§ 6–3 When Banks May Charge Customer's Account, Sections 4–401, 4–404, 4–405

Section 4–401(a) contains the two most important rules in Part 4 of Article 4. First, the section states that a bank may charge the customer's account for items "properly payable." Equally important, the section implies that the bank may not charge the customer's account on items not "properly payable." Section 4–401(a) reads in full:

> A bank may charge against the account of a customer an item that is properly payable from that account even though the charge creates an overdraft. An item is properly payable if it is authorized by the customer and is in accordance with any agreement between the customer and bank.

Whether an item is properly payable is the crucial question in a variety of conflicts between customer and bank. Translated into practical terms, if a court finds that an item is properly payable, the bank is entitled to charge the depositor's account; conversely, if a court finds that an item is not properly payable, the bank may not charge the customer's account, and if it has done so, it must recredit the account. Here we will consider the most common "properly payable" issues:

(1) Are checks bearing alterations, forged indorsements or forged drawer's signatures properly payable?

(2) Are bearer checks that have been stolen properly payable?

(3) Are checks dated later than the time of payment properly payable before the stated date?

(4) Are checks that will create an overdraft properly payable?

(5) Are stale checks (generally checks presented six months or more after the date of issue) properly payable?

(6) Can a non-customer recover damages for improper payment?

a. Checks Lacking Necessary Signatures and Altered Checks

Are checks without the customer's signature "properly payable"? A check may not bear any signature or may bear an unauthorized or forged signature. Absent customer's ratification or negligence, pre-Code and post-Code cases hold that these checks are not "properly payable" and that the bank must recredit the customer's account when it pays these checks. By analogy section 3–401(a) supports this result, for it states that a person is not liable on an instrument unless the person signed the instrument or the person is represented by an agent who signed the instrument and the signature is binding on the represented person.[1]

Because of changes in the check process, the "no signature" cases are not as easy as they once were. To accommodate the explosive growth of checks, banks have automated almost all of the payment process. Except for random examination, most banks look at signatures only on checks above a fixed dollar amount. In truncation systems, the payor bank never receives the depositor's checks and, *a fortiori*, never sees the signature on the original check.

Despite this electronic evaluation, we hesitate to say that checks completely omitting the drawer's authenticating mark can be properly payable. Yet clearly the practice is changing and clearly the law must follow.

As an interim step we would indorse certain agreements that explicitly place the risk of no signature or of the wrong signature on the depositor. We foresee a time when the market presents the customer with various alternatives. Some banks will return checks and will accept responsibility for determining whether the customer's signature is proper. Other banks will truncate, will so reject such responsibility, and will charge a smaller fee for their services. We believe the law should not stand in the way of such a market or inhibit knowing and free allocation of the risk between banks and their customers.

More common than checks without signatures are those bearing defective drawer's signatures. For example, the check may display fewer than the requisite number of authorized signatures. Some courts have decided that the absence of a required signature does not amount to an "unauthorized signature" within 1–201(43) or 4–406. The same reasoning has led some courts to refuse to apply the 4–406(f) time limits to "incomplete" indorsements. But others disagree. In Harvey v. First Nat. Bank of Powell,[2] the court considers the question of whether a missing signature on a two-signature check falls within the meaning of an "unauthorized signature." The court follows the majority of cases that hold that a missing signature does fall within the meaning of an "unauthorized signature." As a result 4–406, which requires the reporting of the "unauthorized signature" within the one-year time limit, cuts off a drawer's claim.

The court in Knight Communications, Inc. v. Boatmen's National Bank[3] surveys various jurisdictions and concludes that a missing signature in most courts means an unauthorized signature.

§ 6–3

1. For a discussion of 3–401(a), see 1–3 through 1–5 *supra*.

2. 924 P.2d 83, 32 UCC2d 214 (Wyo. 1996).

3. 805 S.W.2d 199, 14 UCC2d 1146 (Mo.App. 1991).

Boatmen's paid checks missing one of the two signatures required under the signature card agreement for the checking account of Knight Communications. Boatmen's appealed from the trial court's denial of its motions for a directed verdict and judgment n.o.v. on grounds that Knight's failure to notify the bank of the checks with unauthorized signatures within the one year limit precluded recovery. Considering the question for the first time in Missouri, the appellate court agreed with Boatmen's that a missing signature is an unauthorized signature under 4–406. The court reasoned that the contract between Knight and Boatmen's authorized payment of a check containing two signatures and that defining a missing signature as an unauthorized signature implements the public policy of 4–406.

Is a check bearing a forged indorsement "properly payable"? Comment 1 to 4–401 now says it is not. That is consistent with common sense and with Article 3. In the case of an order[4] instrument, forgery precludes negotiation, so that no subsequent transferee can be a "person entitled to enforce the instrument" under Article 3;[5] accordingly, no payment can be proper since only a person entitled to enforce can make proper presentment and receive payment.[6]

In a backhanded way 4–401(d) tells us that altered items are properly payable only to the extent of their "original tenor" but not beyond.[7] Subsection (d)(1) implies as much in stating that the bank may charge the account of its customer according to "the original terms of the altered item."[8] Thus, if the payor pays out $1,000 on

---

4. Since anyone (even a thief or his transferee) in possession of bearer paper qualifies as a holder, his presentment is valid, and payment discharges the drawer's obligation on the check and the underlying obligation. (§§ 1–201(20); 3–602; 3–310). As a result the loss is thrown back upon the person who lost the check. He can most likely prevent its recurrence. See White, Some Petty Complaints About Article Three, 65 Mich. L.Rev. 1315 (1967).

5. See § 3–201. Note that indorsement is not necessary to negotiate bearer paper.

6. See § 3–501(a).

7. Thus a check altering the name of the payee is not properly payable to anyone beside the payee. See Biltmore Assocs. Ltd. v. Marine Midland Bank, N.A., 178 A.D.2d 930, 578 N.Y.S.2d 798, 17 UCC2d 179 (1991).

8. § 4–401(d) protects the payor bank as 3–407(c) does a holder in due

course against alteration or unauthorized completion of an item. It reads in full as follows:

A bank that in good faith makes payment to a holder may charge the indicated account of its customer according to

(a) the original terms of the altered item; or

(b) the terms of the completed item, even though the bank knows the item has been completed unless the bank has notice that the completion was improper.

The significance of the provision is apparent once one recalls that on such items the customer would otherwise be discharged (§ 3–407(b)). § 4–401(d) is consistent in policy with 3–407 and is a necessary corollary to 3–407.

§ 4–401(d) affects not only the customer's liability but the liability of holders and collecting banks as well. In Franklin Nat. Bank v. Bank of Westbury

what was originally a $100 check, $100 is properly payable and the remaining $900 is not. The payor must recredit the $900 to the customer's account. Of course, even the $100 payment might not be properly payable for other reasons (for example, the check might bear a forged indorsement). Note too that the check may be payable to the full $1,000 if the depositor's negligence substantially contributes to the alterations (see 3–406 and 4–406).

b. Postdated Checks

Section 4–401(c) deals with the awkward interaction of postdated checks and modern electronic payment. Although bankers blanch at the process, parties have long used checks as notes. To do this a drawer gives a check to a payee and postdates the check. The understanding between the two is that the payee will not present the check for payment until the date of the check. But sometimes the payee gets antsy and submits the check prior to its date. Because the payor bank's electronic equipment cannot read the date (it is not encoded on the electronic MICR line at the bottom of the check) and because human eyes rarely alight upon the face of a check at the payor bank, the bank is unlikely to discover the postdating unless the check is somehow flagged electronically. Accordingly, the payors are likely to pay these checks. Although there have been few appellate cases on postdated checks, both pre-Code,[9] and post-Code pre–1990 Article 3 cases held that a check is not "properly payable" until the date on its face. The legal rule so collides with electronic payment.

Revised section 4–401(c) accommodates both the interests of customers and of banks. It puts the burden on the customer to give the bank notice of the postdating by "describing the check with reasonable certainty." When the bank receives notice, it must pick out that check and be sure it does not charge it to the account of the customer prior to the date stated. If it charges the account prior to that date, it is liable for any damages it causes. Moreover,

Trust Co., 65 Misc.2d 604, 318 N.Y.S.2d 656, 8 UCC 1299 (Dist. Ct. 1971), collecting bank received an item altered to read $313, presented it to payor bank, and was paid. After the payor bank's customer notified it of the alteration, the payor bank successfully sued the collecting bank on its 4–207 warranty. But since the customer was liable to payor bank for the original tenor of the item ($13), the collecting bank was only liable for the $300 difference caused by the alteration.

9. See, e.g., Montano v. Springfield Gardens Nat. Bank, 207 Misc. 840, 140 N.Y.S.2d 63 (Sup. App. Term 1955) (pre-mature payment and stop order before stated date); Wilson v. McEachern, 9 Ga.App. 584, 71 S.E. 946 (1911) (bank's refusal to pay check before stated date not a dishonor) (dictum); Smith v. Maddox–Rucker Banking Co., 8 Ga.App. 288, 68 S.E. 1092 (1910). See generally Annot., 76 A.L.R.2d 1301 (1961). The analyst for the New York Law Revision Commission viewed pre-revision § 3–114(2)'s statement that postdated checks are not properly payable until the date stated on the check as a new statutory formulation of the existing case law. 2 N.Y. State Law Revision Comm'n, 1955 Report 824 (1955).

subsection (c) makes it clear that the loss may include "damages for dishonor of subsequent items. * * * "[10] If the customer gives no notice to the bank, the bank is free to pay the check when it is presented even if that is before the date on the check.

c. Overdrafts

Subsection 4–401(a) states that overdrafts may be properly payable, but 4–402(a) makes it clear that the bank is not required to pay a check that would create an overdraft unless it has agreed to do so. Thus, "adequacy of funds" is still necessary for an item to be "properly payable." Some customers may expect the bank to cover certain overdrafts and may be indignant if the bank refuses, but the bank's option to pay or not pay overdrafts is a business decision that turns on factors such as the size of the overdraft, and the bank's opinion of its customer. The only limit on the bank's authority to honor an overdraft is that it must be otherwise properly payable.

Section 4–401(b) deals with an overdraft problem unique to joint accounts.[11] Assume a case in which husband and wife are in the process of divorce, but are still maintaining a joint account. Assume further that the husband overdraws the account and that the bank goes after the wife to satisfy the overdraft. There is a certain equity to her argument that she should not be liable for her deadbeat husband's overdraft, particularly in circumstances where the money was spent in ways in which she did not approve and

---

10. Even in this type of case, however, the customer often will not have an effective complaint against the bank. In the first place the bank will claim under 4–407 that it is subrogated to the rights of the party it paid. See Siegel v. New England Merchants Nat. Bank, 386 Mass. 672, 437 N.E.2d 218, 33 UCC 1601 (1982). If this party was a holder in due course (as for example a depositary bank) the payor as subrogee under 4–407 to the presenter's rights will have a valid defense to its customer's complaint. At least one court has gone even further and (in our judgment incorrectly) stated that the payor bank was itself a holder in due course of post-dated checks. See Roland v. Republic Nat. Bank, 463 S.W.2d 747, 8 UCC 1076 (Tex. Civ. App. 1971).

11. For a sampling of the various problems created by joint accounts, see Pacenta v. American Sav. Bank, 195 Ill. App.3d 808, 142 Ill.Dec. 535, 552 N.E.2d 1276, 11 UCC2d 912 (1990) (cosigner of joint account was liable for overdrafts even though she personally did not present the check which was dishonored creating the overdraft, and bank could collect by charging a separate individual account she held at the bank); First Tennessee Bank, N.A. v. Mungan, 779 S.W.2d 798, 10 UCC2d 1318 (Tenn.App. 1989) (non-drawing cosigner is not liable for joint checking account overdraft); Williams v. Cullen Center Bank & Trust, 685 S.W.2d 311, 40 UCC 337 (Tex. 1985) (joint account signer who had never signed a check nor made a withdrawal was not liable for an overdraft in the absence of evidence that she had derived any benefit or participated in any way in the withdrawal); United States Trust Co. v. McSweeney, 91 A.D.2d 7, 457 N.Y.S.2d 276, 35 UCC 205 (1982) (wife held liable for overdrafts she drew on account despite claims that she received no benefit and was simply following the instructions of her husband); Cambridge Trust Co. v. Carney, 115 N.H. 94, 333 A.2d 442, 16 UCC 1078 (1975) (bank could not collect from joint account holder on an overdraft created by her husband who had left town).

from which she did not benefit. Section 4–401(b) protects her interests:

> A customer is not liable for the amount of an overdraft if the customer neither signed the item nor benefited from the proceeds of the item.

Of course cases will arise where the husband and wife pretend to be estranged and where in fact one benefited from the overdrafts of the other. Whether there is a "benefit" is a problem familiar to those dealing with accommodation parties. One can fruitfully turn to accommodation cases for analogy.

A case that serves as a good illustration of this principle is First Interstate Bank of Oregon v. Wilkerson.[12] Defendant and Sanderson opened a joint business checking account at plaintiff bank. The agreement provided that either defendant or Sanderson had authority to write checks on the account. A check written by Sanderson, which would create a $95,000 overdraft, was presented to plaintiff bank. After defendant promised to get sufficient funds to pay the check within a few days, the bank paid the check. Defendant never did, and the bank sued. The Court of Appeals affirmed summary judgment for plaintiff, holding that the check was properly payable. The court reasoned that even though defendant did not personally sign the check, she should nonetheless be held liable for the overdraft either because she benefited from the payment or because she ratified the transaction.

Defendant also argued that the bank breached a common-law duty of good faith when it paid the check that caused the overdraft. The defendant relied on a state statute ORS 71.1030, which provides that "the specific content of a good faith standard is not limited to the [UCC's] four corners." The court rejected this argument and pointed out, correctly we think, that the state statute is a gap-filler, and since the UCC has specifically defined "good faith," the UCC definition rules. To rule otherwise is to punish a good deed.

d. Stale Checks

A payor bank has the option to pay or not to pay a stale check. Section 4–404 states in full:

> A bank is under no obligation to a customer having a checking account to pay a check, other than a certified check, which is presented more than six months after its date, but it may charge its customer's account for a payment made thereafter in good faith.

12. 128 Or.App. 328, 876 P.2d 326, 26 UCC2d 407 (1994).

The rule reflects general distrust of checks,[13] too long outstanding, yet recognizes that many stale checks ought to be honored in the ordinary course of business even though payees do not present them within six months. The bank is free of liability to its customer if it dishonors a stale check or pays it without consulting the drawer, so long as it acts in good faith. A drawer who wants its bank to dishonor a stale check may issue a stop order.

The bank has a right to charge its customer's account on payment of a stale check only if it pays "in good faith."[14] Good faith is among the most slippery concepts in the Code.[15] Does it mean that the bank must examine each check to determine if it is stale? For example, does a bank violate 4–404 if it pays a stale check in the normal computer run under circumstances in which no bank employee knew it to be stale? We think not; this bank lacks the requisite dishonesty.

The few relevant cases are neither very helpful nor, one suspects, very forthright. In Charles Ragusa & Son,[16] the Louisiana Court of Appeal held that a bank which had paid a stale check, apparently in ignorance of its staleness, could not debit the depositor's account. The court so held by concluding first that the payor bank had the obligation to use ordinary care as well as good faith. It stated that the bank had produced no evidence to prove that it acted without negligence and in good faith and secondly "that the payment of such an obviously stale check, three years old, demonstrates the bank's lack of due care and prevents it from claiming a defense of good faith * * *." In a similar case a New York court has held open the prospect that the depositor can cause its bank to recredit if it shows the bank's lack of ordinary care.[17] To the extent that these cases mean that a bank has the duty of inquiry to examine the date on every check, we believe that they are incorrect. In IBP, Inc. v. Mercantile Bank of Topeka,[18] seller cashed a nine-year old check, and the drawer sued the depositary bank, the payor bank and the payee. The court found for the banks. The court held that without a business relationship, the depositary bank had no duty to drawer to examine checks manually to determine whether they were over six months old. As for the payor bank, the court

---

13. Note that § 4–404 applies only to checks.

14. Nevada has varied § 4–404 by omitting the words "in good faith." The District of Columbia also varies the provision by stating that a bank may at its option pay a stale check in the absence of an effective stop payment order. Nev. Rev.Stat. § 104.4404 (1973); D.C.Code § 28:4–404 (1981).

15. See Summers, "Good Faith" in General Contract Law and the Sales

Provisions of the Uniform Commercial Code, 54 Va.L.Rev. 195 (1968).

16. Charles Ragusa & Son v. Community State Bank, 360 So.2d 231, 24 UCC 725 (La.App. 1978).

17. Advanced Alloys, Inc. v. Sergeant Steel Corp., 79 Misc.2d 149, 360 N.Y.S.2d 142, 12 UCC 1173 (1973).

18. 6 F.Supp.2d 1258, 36 UCC2d 270 (D.Kan. 1998).

held that the bank's use of an automated processing system shows it exercised ordinary care and paid the check in good faith, because the magnetic ink character recognition (MICR) encoding system provided no basis for detecting a check's date.

But what if the bank discovers the check is stale and yet pays? As a general proposition we believe that the bank so paying has not acted in good faith and that the depositor should be permitted to have its account recredited either on the basis that the payment was not made in good faith or, as in the New York court's analysis, it was made without due care. A 1974 New York case illustrates how a bank might discover that a check was stale and how a depositor might be able to prove as much:

> Here the check was not merely stale; it was ten years stale. It was written on paper of a different color than currently used for plaintiff's checks. It was written on paper imprinted with an address from which plaintiff had moved almost seven years prior to payment. And finally it was written on an account which plaintiff had closed almost seven years prior to payment. Nor was the check paid inadvertently as suggested by defendant in its opposing papers. That defendant was aware of at least the staleness and the closing of the account is demonstrable from the face of the check.[19]

One sentence in the Comment to 4–404 suggests that at least some payments may be made in good faith despite the fact that the bank has knowledge of the staleness: "[The bank] is therefore not required to do so, but is given the option to pay because it may be in a position to know, as in the case of dividend checks, that the drawer wants payment made." This cryptic comment does not explain why a payor bank will be in a position to know that a drawer of dividend checks, more than a drawer of any other check, will wish payment made. Presumably, at the time any drawer draws a check, he wishes it to be paid. Perhaps stale dividend checks differ from mine-run checks in that they are commonly presented more than six months after the date of issuance. That is, one might keep a $20 dividend check in his dresser drawer for several months without cashing it whereas he can rarely afford to squirrel away his payroll check in that fashion. If that is not the factor that sets dividend checks apart from others and permits the bank to infer that the drawer still wants payment made six months after issuance, then the comment is completely mysterious to us. Except with respect to types of checks that are routinely presented more than six months after issuance, we conclude that a bank may

19. New York Flameproofing Co. v. Chemical Bank, 1974 WL 21730, 15   UCC 1104 (N.Y. City Civ.Ct. 1974).

not assume that the drawer "wants payment made" and that a bank which knowingly pays such checks will not be in good faith.

One may argue that a stop order which expires at the end of six months still leaves the bank on notice, and that any payment of that check cannot be in good faith. This interpretation is not consistent with the section on stop orders which limits their effective duration to six months. If any payment after six months is in bad faith, then the written stop order is good in perpetuity and not for just six months. We reject any interpretation that reads the six month limitation out of 4–403.

Notwithstanding the *Ragusa* case and the New York court's reservations, we interpret the good faith limitation in 4–404 as follows: We think payments in accordance with the bank's normal custom and in ignorance of the staleness of the check are in good faith. We think 4–404 does not require a bank employee to examine the date of each check, and of course the computer cannot read the date on the check for that number is not printed in magnetic type. If an employee does discover that a check is stale (perhaps because the computer kicks the check out as NSF or as a large item), we think that except in rare cases the bank acts in bad faith if it thereafter pays without first contacting its depositor. The rare cases would be those involving dividend checks and other cases in which payees commonly hold checks for more than six months before cashing them.

There is a special rule for certified checks. The bank must pay these even though they are presented more than six months after issuance. Certified checks represent the bank's obligation, and banks typically charge the customer's account when the check is certified.

e. Checks Presented After Customer's Death or Adjudication of Incompetence, Section 4–405

Under 4–405(a) a bank's authority to handle items on its customer's account terminates when the bank learns that the customer has died or been adjudged incompetent. Section 4–405(a) reads in full as follows:

> A payor or collecting bank's authority to accept, pay, or collect an item or to account for proceeds of its collection, if otherwise effective, is not rendered ineffective by incompetence of a customer of either bank existing at the time the item is issued or its collection is undertaken if the bank does not know of an adjudication of incompetence. Neither death nor incompetence of a customer revokes the authority to accept, pay, collect or account until the bank knows of the fact of death or of an adjudication of incompetence and has reasonable opportunity to act on it.

Note that the subsection applies to the relationship between the customer-holder and the collecting bank as well as that of the customer-drawer and payor. Two interesting questions arise. When does the bank have knowledge and what constitutes a reasonable opportunity for the bank to act on that knowledge? With respect to the first question, subsection 1–202(f) states:

> Notice, knowledge or a notice or notification received by an organization is effective for a particular transaction from the time when it is brought to the attention of the individual conducting that transaction, and in any event from the time when it would have been brought to his attention if the organization had exercised due diligence.

It is not sufficient that the janitor have notice or reason to know of the customer's death or adjudication of incompetence. In typical bank procedure, the head cashier, a branch manager or a head of the accounts department likely supervises the two places in a bank where payment commonly occurs—teller's windows where items are cashed or the accounts department where items are deposited.[20] We think the bank is charged with knowledge only when the information reaches (or, but for bank negligence, would have reached) such persons of responsibility to the bank.

Judicial opinions provide little guidance as to what constitutes a reasonable opportunity for the bank to act. In one case the court said that a bank's authority to deal with the proceeds of checks terminated when the bank learned of the payee's death at the beginning of the banking day on which it processed the checks. Perhaps even less time suffices where notice of death comes to the branch manager at the branch in which the deceased kept his account.[21] With regard to the bank's obligation to notify the payee of a drawer's death or incompetence, at least one court has held

20. Doubtless there is a variety of ways in which a bank can arrest the payment process on a check presented through banking channels. For example, it could instruct the computer to throw out all checks drawn on certain accounts. Or it could assign a clerk to collect data on the death or bankruptcy of its depositors and to intercept checks (after the computer run) drawn on the accounts of dead or bankrupt depositors. If the bank has established any such procedure and the information reaches the person whose responsibility it is to instruct the computer or to intercept such checks, but that person fails to act, clearly the bank has "knowledge." Moreover, if the information reaches any bank employee but fails to reach the crucial employee only because of the bank's negligence, the bank also has "knowledge" under 1–201(27). We assume, for example, that information reaching the branch manager of the relevant branch would always give the bank "knowledge" and that information reaching a variety of responsible employees in the central headquarters would also constitute knowledge. Because the titles and responsibilities of such parties vary from bank to bank, we hesitate to identify by name those whose knowledge should be attributed to the bank.

21. See Comment 4 to 4–107 which says that for the purpose of receiving knowledge each branch is a separate entity. See also the discussion in 20–4.

that the drawee bank is entitled to dishonor checks without written notice to the payee under 4–405 upon learning of the drawer's death.

Subsection (b) of 4–405 states a special rule for checks when a customer dies:

> Even with knowledge, a bank may for 10 days after the date of death pay or certify checks drawn on or before that date unless ordered to stop payment by a person claiming an interest in the account.

This section provides a way of paying deceased's recent and usually valid obligations; it so avoids running the claims through probate. Note that the last clause of 4–405(b) gives a person claiming an interest in the account an implicit right to stop payment. Comments indicate that the bank is under no duty "to determine the validity of the claim or even whether it is 'colorable.' "[22] As a result, once the bank learns of its customer's death, it is likely to obey any stop order without inquiry. In some cases unsecured creditors may want to stop payment of all outstanding checks immediately on the debtor's death; otherwise, their competitors may gain priority by promptly cashing decedent's checks.

Finally, where the name on an account is not a legal entity, a variety of facts must be examined by the bank upon the death of a person associated with the account. One New Mexico court has enumerated such factors, including the name on the account, the authorized signatories, the circumstances surrounding the opening of the account, what persons control the account, and the beneficial interests of persons so associated with the account.

f. Duty to Non–customer for Improper Payment

In the usual case there is no doubt about the status of the party to whom the bank owes the duty to pay checks that are properly payable and not to pay checks that are not properly payable. Parties who are somehow associated with the depositor as a principal or an investor or in some other way sometimes claim damages from the bank as a result of improper payment.

In two cases the bank successfully argued that its duty ran to the depositor, not to any individual party that has the power to sign or who is somehow one of the principals of or related to the depositor itself.[23]

Note that these cases are not the same as the cases dealing with the question who is the "customer" for purposes of wrongful

---

22. § 4–405, Comment 3.

23. See Dodd v. Citizens Bank, 222 Cal.App.3d 1624, 272 Cal.Rptr. 623, 12 UCC2d 465 (1990); Schoenfelder v. Arizona Bank, 165 Ariz. 79, 796 P.2d 881, 12 UCC2d 469 (1990).

dishonor. We discuss those cases in Section 6–4. In wrongful dishonor the question is whether a slander that occurs because of the dishonor has injured the party non-depositor and whether therefore that person should be included in the definition of "customer." In the cases discussed here the real issue is not whether a tortious injury has occurred to a plaintiff, but rather who owns the cause of action against the bank for improper payment (usually at the behest of a forger).

PROBLEM

A check might be claimed to be improperly payable by the payor bank because it was stolen and bore forged signatures or because it was presented too late ("stale") or because at the time of presentment, the drawer had died. Consider the following possibilities:

1. Employee steals from employer by two methods. She forges the signature of the authorized drawer and she forges the indorsement of the authorized indorser on checks of third parties. Are these checks properly payable?

    The payor might argue that it could not tell that the signature of the drawer was forged because it was so cleverly done. That argument loses. Both kinds of checks are not properly payable and the payor may not charge the drawer's account in either case absent estoppel caused by the drawer's negligence under the rules discussed in earlier chapters.

2. Bank pays a post-dated check before its date and pays a second check one year after its issue. Clearly the drawer did not intend that the first be paid when it was and the second is "stale" under 4–404.

    No matter. The bank is within its rights to pay both. Everyone now knows that checks are processed electronically and that the process relies on the information on the MICR line not on other things on the check. While that might not protect a bank that pays over a forged signature that the machine cannot detect, it will protect the bank from liability in paying a stale check or one bearing a date later than the time of payment.

3. Husband and Wife are in the process of divorce. Wife draws a $50,000 check when there is only $10,000 in the parties' joint account. Bank pays because the depositors are valued customers. Can Bank recover the $40,000 overdraft from Husband if Wife does not deposit funds to cover?

    Probably yes. In general, payment against overdrafts is okay (even hoped for and expected by many depositors) so the only question here is whether Bank can recover from the other

> party. We think it can, but we can imagine a court finding
> otherwise on some equitable ground in egregious cases.

§ 6–4 The Bank's Liability to Its Customer for Wrongful Dishonor, Section 4–402

Thankfully, section 4–402 was much rewritten during the 1990 amendments. It now reads in part:

(a) Except as otherwise provided in this Article, a payor bank wrongfully dishonors an item if it dishonors an item that is properly payable, but a bank may dishonor an item that would create an overdraft unless it has agreed to pay the overdraft.

(b) A payor bank is liable to its customer for damages proximately caused by the wrongful dishonor of an item. Liability is limited to actual damages proved and may include damages for an arrest or prosecution of the customer or other consequential damages. Whether any consequential damages are proximately caused by the wrongful dishonor is a question of fact to be determined in each case.

In an opinion that reads like a Tale of the Old West (Loucks v. Albuquerque National Bank),[1] the New Mexico Supreme Court passed on the real and imagined effects of a bank's dishonor of a series of checks. Martinez, who owned an auto body shop, borrowed $500 from the bank. Soon afterwards he joined Loucks in partnership, closed his proprietorship account and opened a partnership account. Martinez later fell delinquent on the note. Over his partner's protests, the bank set off the $402 that Martinez owed on his proprietorship note against the partnership account which left a balance of $3.66 in that account. The partners closed the account and thereafter the bank dishonored ten outstanding checks. Because their checks bounced all over town, Loucks and Martinez allegedly encountered these difficulties: their supplier would deal only in cash; people who had previously accepted their checks now refused to do so; credit previously granted was denied; and a salesman who had sold them a map for one of the rubber checks ripped the map off their wall because they had given him "a bad check for it." The parties also alleged other less tangible injuries, and Loucks complained of an ulcer and was absent from work for awhile. Both believed that the bank had damaged their personal reputations.

Loucks and Martinez sued the bank for:

§ 6–4

1. 76 N.M. 735, 418 P.2d 191, 3 UCC 709 (1966).

(1) recovery of the amount set off against the account ($402);

(2) compensatory damages to the partnership for injury to partnership credit and business reputation ($5,000) and for lost profits due to Loucks' absence caused by his ulcer ($1,800);

(3) punitive damages for injury to the partnership ($14,404);

(4) compensatory damages to each partner individually for injury to personal credit and business reputation ($5,000 each);

(5) punitive damages for injury to Loucks and Martinez individually ($60,000 and $10,000 respectively);

(6) compensatory damages for injury to Loucks for an ulcer allegedly caused by the dishonor ($25,000).

At trial plaintiffs recovered the amount set off by the bank, but the court dismissed all other claims. On appeal the New Mexico Supreme Court disallowed all claims for injury to Loucks and Martinez in their individual capacities (that is, compensatory and punitive damages for injury to plaintiffs' personal reputations and Loucks' ulcer). The court held that the protection of section 4–402 ran only to customers and that individual partners had no cause of action on a partnership account. The court said that the question of compensatory damages for injury to the partnership was one for the jury. On the issue of punitive damages the court ruled that proof of malice or willfulness was necessary to sustain the claim, and concluded that evidence of intemperate remarks by a bank officer when plaintiffs closed the account was not sufficient to warrant submitting that issue to the jury.

The bank's liability for wrongful dishonor is the converse of the bank's liability for paying checks not properly payable. Typically, wrongful dishonor occurs as the result of bookkeeping errors, a computer error, a charge to the wrong account or the like. It may also occur, as in Loucks, when the bank improperly exercises a setoff against the customer's account.[2] An improper hold or freeze on an account can also result in wrongful dishonor. The cases suggest that a bank should deal gingerly with setoffs, freezes, and third party claims. Courts do not recognize purity of heart as a defense when a bank acts erroneously with respect to its customer's account. Even when the bank dishonors an item for legitimate cause, it must act consistently with 4–303 priorities.[3]

Before we concern ourselves with the extent of the bank's liability under 4–402, we would first ask to whom the liability runs. The section states that a bank is liable to "its customer." "Custom-

---

2. Raymer v. Bay State Nat. Bank, 384 Mass. 310, 424 N.E.2d 515, 31 UCC 1537 (1981); Elizarraras v. Bank of El Paso, 631 F.2d 366, 30 UCC 627 (5th Cir.1980).

3. For a discussion of § 4–303, see 6–7, infra.

er" may include corporations, partnerships, associations and even other banks. The determination who can sue under 4–402 is not always as easy as checking the name of the account or the name on the signature card. In order to determine who the customer really is a few courts have been willing to inquire into the circumstances surrounding the account. In First National Bank v. Hobbs,[4] plaintiff had set up the account referred to as "Holiday Inn–Operating Account." Plaintiff had authorized the lessee of the Holiday Inn to deposit funds in and to draw checks on the account, so long as the checks were countersigned by plaintiff or his son-in-law. The court held that since plaintiff was instrumental in opening the account and since he had signed the signature card, he qualified as a "customer." A contrary result was ultimately reached in Sinwellan Corp. v. Farmers Bank.[5] The lower court in that case held that the individual plaintiff who set up the bank account of a corporation of which he was president and designated those who were to have authority to sign the corporation's checks qualified as a "customer" of the bank. The decision was reversed on appeal on the grounds that the statutory definition requires a literal reading (i.e., the person having the account was the corporation, not the individual plaintiff) and that there was no record support for the lower court's finding that the bank regarded plaintiff as its customer. A variation on that theme occurred in a 1975 California case[6] in which the court admitted that shareholders and officers of a corporation may not generally recover for wrongful dishonor of a corporation check. In this case, however, the individuals were "customers" within the contemplation of the statute because the corporation was undercapitalized and "nothing but a transparent shell." In addition, defendant bank looked to the individual plaintiffs to satisfy the obligations of the corporation and required them to execute a personal guarantee of the loan.

The statute gives a cause of action to none other than a "customer." In Knauf v. Bank of LaPlace[7] the payee sued the payor bank for wrongful dishonor. The first time the checks in question were presented, they were dishonored for lack of a proper indorsement even though the payee had put his account number on the reverse and signed them for "deposit only." The court found these

---

4. 248 Ark. 76, 450 S.W.2d 298, 7 UCC 323 (1970).

5. 345 A.2d 430, 18 UCC 178 (Del. Super. 1975), rev'd, 367 A.2d 180, 20 UCC 1267 (Del. 1976).

6. Kendall Yacht Corp. v. United California Bank, 50 Cal.App.3d 949, 123 Cal.Rptr. 848, 17 UCC 1270 (1975). Accord, Parrett v. Platte Valley State Bank & Trust Co., 236 Neb. 139, 459 N.W.2d

371, 12 UCC2d 598 (1990); Murdaugh Volkswagen, Inc. v. First Nat. Bank, 801 F.2d 719, 2 UCC2d 25 (4th Cir.1986); Karsh v. American City Bank, 113 Cal. App.3d 419, 169 Cal.Rptr. 851, 30 UCC 624 (1980).

7. 567 So.2d 182, 13 UCC2d 467 (La. App. 1990), writ denied, 572 So.2d 71 (La. 1991).

to be an effective indorsement. The second time the checks were deposited they were dishonored as NSF.

The court held that the payee had no cause of action for wrongful dishonor against the payor bank, but that he had properly stated a cause of action in tort. In effect, the payee was maintaining that the check could and should have been paid on the first presentment and that he suffered damages equal to the amount he would have received on the first presentment. These injuries were suffered because the account had no funds on the second presentment. The case is a dangerous precedent. Making wrongful dishonor a tort actionable by a payee is not substantively different from giving the payee a cause of action for wrongful dishonor, yet the Code clearly rejects that cause of action.[8]

In Hecker v. Ravenna Bank,[9] the Nebraska Supreme Court considered whether the payees of a cashier's check were "customers" within the meaning of 4–402. The Heckers, who owed money to Ravenna Bank, were payees of a cashier's check issued by Ravenna. Ravenna Bank dishonored the check and applied the proceeds to the Heckers' outstanding loan balance without their consent. Concluding that the Heckers were not customers (they only alleged that they were payees) and that they could not bring an action against Ravenna for wrongful dishonor, the court approved a cause of action for "wrongful refusal to honor." This occurs, according to the court, when a payee of a cashier's check delivers or negotiates the check for payment, and the issuing bank refuses to honor the check. The Heckers also had a cause of action for conversion. We have doubts about these cases. Whether framed as "wrongful refusal to honor" or negligence, they look like end runs around the Code's prohibition on suits by the payee for wrongful dishonor. Hecker perhaps can be distinguished because the bank was both the drawer and drawee with liability on the drawer's contract under 3–414. The courts should be careful about extending liability to the payee every time a payor dishonors. In general the payor of an unaccepted check has no contract with and owes no clearly defined duty to the payee of a check.

Two clauses were deleted from pre-revision 4–402 in its 1990 reincarnation as 4–402(b). These clauses referred to a dishonor that occurs "through mistake" and to "damages proximately caused and

---

8. Other courts have upheld negligence actions by payees though denying them a 4–402 action. See Ha v. Dominion Bank, 1991 WL 165755, 14 UCC2d 806 (Va. Cir. Ct. 1991) (payee as owner of item is owed a duty of ordinary care); Cardenuto v. Dominion Bank, 1991 WL 165767, 14 UCC2d 811 (Va. Cir. Ct. 1991); Agostino v. Monticello Greenhouses, Inc., 166 A.D.2d 471, 560 N.Y.S.2d 690, 13 UCC2d 472 (1990) (UCC does not prohibit a cause of action in negligence arising out of wrongful dishonor of check). These too are dangerous precedents.

9. 237 Neb. 810, 468 N.W.2d 88, 14 UCC2d 815 (1991).

proved." In an earlier edition, we argued that the now deleted phrases left the implication that "willful dishonor," as opposed to "mistaken dishonor" might make the payor bank liable for damages under the "trader rule," even in circumstances where no actual damages could be proved. Even though the Code comments said that the "trader rule" was abolished, the inartful drafting of 4–402 left that in doubt.[10] The deletions from 4–402(b) now put the trader rule in its grave and the comments to 4–402 state clearly that that is the drafters' intention.[11]

Almost all of the interesting lawyer questions under 4–402 have to do with the nature, amount and proof of damages. In 4–402 the drafters have given the plaintiffs something valuable. The third sentence of 4–402(a) reads as follows: "Whether any consequential damages are proximately caused by the wrongful dishonor is a question of fact to be determined in each case." Comment 3 tells us that this sentence rejects "decisions holding that as a matter of law the dishonor of a check is not the 'proximate cause' of the arrest and prosecution of the customer* * *.'' Presumably a customer whose check bounces is now entitled to recover any damages that it can convince the court or jury were proximately caused by wrongful dishonor of its checks. But what are the outer limits of actual damages? May one recover for mental distress, etc.?

Certainly courts might take a sympathetic view of customers' claims of financial injury due to wrongful dishonor. For example, in Skov v. Chase Manhattan Bank,[12] the customer contended that the bank's dishonor caused his supplier to stop doing business with him. The trial court awarded the customer three years of lost profits and the Third Circuit affirmed.

The saga of a failing car dealership inspired the Fourth Circuit Court of Appeals to be even more generous than the *Skov* court in its estimation of damages proximately caused by the wrongful

---

10. The confusion resulted from the wording of the section. The second sentence of 4–402 read as follows: "When the dishonor occurs *through mistake* liability is limited to actual damages proved." (Emphasis added.) The negative implication is that when wrongful dishonor occurs not "through mistake" but willfully, the court may impose damages greater than "actual damages." That the drafters may have intended to perpetuate the per se liability rule in "willful" cases was also supported by the Code history embodied in a pre-Code statute and decisions under it. That statute and those cases made just the distinction we suggested; namely, that a

bank that dishonors a check through inadvertence or mistake is not liable for per se defamation of a merchant or trader, and is so liable only if its dishonor is willful or malicious. If the drafters wished to abolish the trader rule altogether, they should have chosen stronger language originally in the face of this pre-Code statutory and case law history. Certainly the reference to "mistake" in the second sentence of 4–402 invited a court to adopt the relevant pre-Code distinction.

11. See § 4–402, Comment 1.

12. 407 F.2d 1318, 6 UCC 170 (3d Cir.1969).

dishonor. In Murdaugh Volkswagen, Inc. v. First National Bank,[13] a car dealership had an agreement with the bank allowing it to draw immediately against funds deposited in its corporate account. Apparently without notice to the customer, the bank reneged on the agreement. Several of the dealership's checks bounced, and the car dealership, already in trouble, quickly went bankrupt. Mrs. Murdaugh, the dealership's president and sole stockholder, brought suit for wrongful dishonor and won damages in the amount of the dealership's assets at the time it filed for bankruptcy, a sum totalling $250,000. This amount included compensation for the loss of Mrs. Murdaugh's home, which had been mortgaged for the company's benefit. These damages were upheld on appeal, even though the mortgage had been foreclosed by *another* bank after the Murdaughs had ceased dealing with the defendant bank. The appeals court also affirmed the grant to Mrs. Murdaugh of $175,000 in damages for personal defamation, thereby recognizing her as a customer for 4–402 purposes.[14] It is safe to say that such generosity will be the exception rather than the rule. However, the trend does seem to be towards a more expansive view of damages proximately caused by a wrongful dishonor.

In recent years, courts have also become more sympathetic to claims for mental distress and suffering caused by dishonored checks. In Twin City Bank v. Isaacs,[15] plaintiffs discovered on a Sunday morning that they had lost their checkbook. They reported the loss to the bank on Monday morning, but by that time two forged checks totalling $2000 had been presented to and honored by the bank. Shortly thereafter, the bank chose to freeze the Isaacs' checking account, which had a balance of $2000. All checks presented after the freeze were dishonored. Although the individual responsible for the forgeries was quickly caught, the bank apparently feared that Mr. Isaacs, a convicted burglar, had something to do with the crime. Even after being assured twice by the police that Mr. Isaacs was merely an innocent victim, the bank refused to release the funds in the account. Four years later, the parties ended up in court, the account still frozen, and the Isaacs angry. The Arkansas Supreme Court upheld the jury's award of $18,500 in compensatory damages, which included an award for mental anguish. The Arkansas court cited other decisions upholding recovery for mental suffering under the Code[16] and stated that it was not necessary to prove such damages with exactness.

---

13. 801 F.2d 719, 2 UCC2d 25 (4th Cir. 1986).

14. See the discussion of who is a customer, *supra.*

15. 283 Ark. 127, 672 S.W.2d 651, 39 UCC 35 (1984).

16. The court cited Morse v. Mutual Federal Sav. & Loan Ass'n, 536 F.Supp. 1271, 34 UCC 230 (D.Mass. 1982) (damages for mental suffering awarded only in non-mistaken dishonor cases); Farmers & Merchants State Bank v. Ferguson, 605 S.W.2d 320, 30 UCC 300 (Tex.

We think that "actual damages" does not exclude recovery for mental distress. The drafters went to great efforts to assure that customers can recover for arrest and prosecution. Moreover, cases under the predecessor to 4–402, the American Banking Association statute, held that "actual damages" includes damages for mental distress.

Mindful of the excesses of the American tort system, and of the role that damage awards for "pain and suffering" have played in producing those excesses, we would go slow in awarding damages for mental distress in check cases. Some injuries must be borne by the one who has suffered them. That is particularly true in cases in which the injuries are hard to express in money terms and are easy to simulate. It is easy to say there should be recovery when there has been a false arrest, but the court should be more hesitant to authorize a jury to speculate—in the absence of such an overt act as arrest that obviously causes substantial anguish. After all, banks are classic "target" defendants, and we fear that juries unfettered by judicial restrictions may grant large awards to plaintiffs who do not deserve them without giving appropriate consideration to the costs of those awards and to the fact that they ultimately will be borne by other bank customers.

Because subsection (b) limits the plaintiff to "actual" damages, arguably punitive damages may not be recovered under 4–402. But the adjective "actual" probably is not intended to bar punitive damages. If the dishonor is found to be intentional, or worse, "malicious" or "reckless," the customer may be able to recover punitive damages. Comment 1 states that a bank may be liable for punitive damages if other law, through section 1–103, allows it. In effect the comment bows to applicable non-code law. A Texas case[17] gives one the flavor of the facts on which a jury will award punitive damages and a court will affirm:

> A forger had secured a number of printed checks of one Marvel Fikes and proceeded to include Palmer as one of his victims. A person showed up at the Bank seeking to cash the $275 check payable to Palmer. The teller ascertained that Palmer had an account with the Bank and paid out the money. She could not testify as to whether this person was or was not Palmer. Some four or five days later, the check was returned by the bank on which it was drawn because the signature was not like the signature of Fikes which it had on file. The checks written by Palmer, which are in question here, had already been paid by

---

Civ. App. 1980), aff'd, 617 S.W.2d 918, 31 UCC 198 (Tex. 1981) (damages for mental distress awarded only if there is a showing of an intentional tort); Northshore Bank v. Palmer, 525 S.W.2d 718, 17 UCC 488 (Tex. Civ. App. 1975).

17. Northshore Bank v. Palmer, 525 S.W.2d 718, 17 UCC 488, 491 (Tex. Civ. App. 1975).

the Bank, when the situation with respect to the forgery became known to it. The officer in charge immediately charged Palmer's account with the forged check despite his protestations that his endorsement was a forgery. When he went to see the Bank officer to deny endorsement and receipt of the proceeds of the forged check, the officer called over a uniformed guard. Even though the checks had been cleared for payment and were covered by sufficient funds when presented, the Bank recalled them and returned them marked "paid in error" or "account closed." Palmer immediately reported the forgery to the police, contacted the bank on which the forged Fikes check was drawn, and contacted Mr. and Mrs. Fikes. He then underwent the embarrassment of calling on each of the payees of the dishonored checks. The Bank never relented. They charged appellee $5 for each check they considered drawn on "insufficient funds." Additionally, after all of the claims of Palmer were known to the Bank officer having charge of the matter, the Bank placed the claimed balance due in the hands of a collection agency, where it rests today. The Bank never has paid Palmer the $275 which under the jury's findings is wrongfully charged to his account. Under the Bank's own evidence, each step it took was deliberate and intentional and done with a knowledge of Palmer's claim of right. The exemplary damages found by the jury are reasonably related to the amount of actual damages found and are fully justified under the evidence. We overrule appellant's points attacking special issue number five and the answer of the jury thereto.[18]

In summary, the mine run consumer whose check is wrongfully dishonored is not likely to receive a windfall. Of course, if the customer is arrested and put in jail for bounced checks, the customer has the same right to recovery as any other party. Likewise the customer may recover for any additional loss suffered because of a fallen credit rating, and presumably for mental distress in states that permit it. We suspect that the customer will have difficulty showing any damages at all in the usual case, and that courts will not sympathetically receive arguments that plaintiffs suffered compensable loss because they had to look at a twelve inch screen rather than the twenty-four inch TV they could have afforded with an untarnished credit rating.

a. *Electronic Dishonor*

Section 4–402(c)[19] now accommodates electronic handling of checks within the modern bank. It makes clear that a payor bank

---

18. Id at ____.

19. 4–402(c) reads as follows:

A payor bank's determination of the customer's account balance on which a

that examines the customer's balance—usually electronically—and finds there are not sufficient funds may dishonor a check even in circumstances in which sufficient funds come into the account after that examination and before the relevant check leaves the bank. If, on the other hand, the payor goes back for a second look and finds enough funds, it is bound by the second look under the last sentence of 4–402(c).

To understand all of this, consider the following example. Drawer's account stands at $10,000 of collected funds on the night of Day 1. At that time a $12,000 check is presented. A computer makes a comparison of the amount drawn and the amount of the account and determines that payment of the check will overdraw the account. In the morning of the following day, an additional $10,000 are deposited in the account (or alternatively, $10,000 of formerly uncollected funds become collected). Now there are sufficient funds in the account to pay the $12,000 check. Nevertheless, the bank is not required to examine the account a second time with respect to its decision to dishonor the $12,000 check. Having decided during the night of Day 1 that there are insufficient funds, it may return the check. If, however, it decides to make a second check at noon on Day 2, before it returns the $12,000 item, and then discovers there are $20,000 of good funds, it must pay the check. None of this seems surprising; all of it is sensible.

b. *Right to Draw on Uncollected Funds*

Banks routinely allow certain customers to draw on uncollected funds. Sometimes draws of that sort are permitted by explicit agreement, but more commonly bankers simply allow their good customers to draw against uncollected funds secure in the knowledge that the checks creating those balances will be paid (far more than 95 percent of all checks are ultimately paid). Trouble comes when these good customers stumble. Can the bank change its practice? Can it stop honoring checks against insufficient funds or against uncollected funds? In some cases the banks give notice; in some cases they do not. Sometimes the depositor suffers serious loss because the bank changes its practice. The resulting suits take many forms but all are variations of the argument that there was an obligation on the bank to continue to do what it had been doing: to pay on uncollected funds or to cover certain overdrafts. The

decision to dishonor for insufficiency of available funds is based may be made at any time between the time the item is received by the payor bank and the time that the payor bank returns the item or gives notice in lieu of return, and no more than one determination need be made. If, at the election of the payor bank, a subsequent balance determination is made for the purpose of reevaluating the bank's decision to dishonor the item, the account balance at that time is determinative of whether a dishonor for insufficiency of available funds is wrongful.

bank's failure is claimed to be a wrongful dishonor or, more broadly, defamation or some other tort.

This problem probably could be resolved by an agreement between the depositor and bank. For example, in Thiele v. Security State Bank,[20] the deposit agreement stated that the bank was not obliged to pay overdrafts "regardless of the frequency" with which bank may do so as a "matter of practice." Presumably an agreement of that sort—particularly one that refers also to uncollected funds—tells the depositor not to rely and would render any reliance unreasonable.

In most cases there is no agreement and the question is whether there is an oral or written agreement, or, failing that a course of dealing, that would require the bank to continue to honor against uncollected funds. These arguments are fully discussed in Schaller v. Marine National Bank.[21] The court found that a practice of honoring checks drawn against uncollected funds or of allowing overdrafts, did not require the bank to continue that practice. The court notes that the course of performance language in 2–208 is applicable only to contracts of sale and that the course of dealing described in 1–205 is principally for the interpretation of existing contracts. Since it decided there was no existing contract that obliged the bank to continue to pay overdrafts, the court found that 1–205 did not apply. The court distinguishes *KMC v. Irving Trust* by noting that Marine Bank, unlike Irving, had no agreement to extend credit. It describes the act of the bank (paying overdrafts) as "bookkeeping courtesies."

In Murdaugh Volkswagen, Inc. v. First National Bank,[22] the court comes to the opposite conclusion of that in the *Schaller* case. There the court affirms a jury verdict on behalf of Murdaugh whose bounced checks were drawn on uncollected funds in accordance with a long practice of drawing against such funds. Since the holding is merely a conclusion that there was evidence from which the jury could have found wrongful dishonor, the opinion is not as persuasive as it might have been, yet the thrust of the case is directly contrary to *Schaller*.

For a number of reasons we think *Schaller*, not *Murdaugh,* is the correct outcome. *Murdaugh* is merely a variation of the argument routinely thrown up to all Good Samaritans: if you pick the Philistine out of the ditch, you are obliged to carry him to Jericho. If *Murdaugh* were the law, banks would exercise sensible discretion in the interest of—or at the explicit request of—their customers

20.   396 N.W.2d 295, 3 UCC2d 686 (N.D. 1986).

21.   131 Wis.2d 389, 388 N.W.2d 645, 1 UCC2d 1283 (App. 1986), rev. den'd, 131 Wis.2d 594, 393 N.W.2d 297 (1986).

22.   801 F.2d 719, 2 UCC2d 25 (4th Cir.1986).

only at their peril. Having behaved in a generous way toward a customer on several occasions, the bank would be obliged to continue that generous behavior, or at least to give notice to and an opportunity for the customer to change his ways. We doubt banks should be made to do that and we are skeptical of depositors' claims of reliance and unfair surprise. In the most common cases the bank stops paying against uncollected funds only in the face of worsening financial circumstances. Many dishonors are stimulated by an increase in the number and amount of drawings against uncollected funds or of overdrafts. In almost all of these cases the bank has spoken with the depositor about its concerns, sometimes about which checks to pay and which to bounce. Almost always the depositor understands the bank's concern and better than the bank, appreciates the downward spiral of his financial circumstances. So we greet the depositor's argument of the reasonable reliance with skepticism. When the bank is faced with rising overdrafts or growing draws against uncollected funds and particularly when those uncollected funds may be part of a kite, the bank is understandably concerned. Without any agreement to do so, the bank, generously but foolishly, has extended a line of credit to the customer. We do not believe that a customer who has lucked upon an unagreed line of credit is entitled to the kind of notice that the court required in *KMC*. In most of these cases we suspect that it is no surprise to the depositor when the line of credit is abruptly cancelled.

Of course, the bank who changes its hold rules will have an obligation to comply with Regulation CC. Regulation CC supports our conclusion; it requires only *ex post facto* notice of new and longer check holds.[23]

PROBLEM

Customer draws a $50,000 check as a deposit on the purchase of a $1 million piece of property. Because the Payor had incorrectly charged a $200,000 check of another customer to Customer's account, the account appeared overdrawn and the Payor dishonored Customer's check. Because the check was dishonored, the seller refused to close the deal with Customer and the property was sold to another person. A year after that sale the buyer resold the property for $3 million. Customer sued payor for $2 million, for an additional $1 million for injury to his reputation and an additional million as punitive damages. What is Customer's most likely recovery? $4 million, $3 million, $2 million, $1 million, or nothing?

---

23. 12 CFR 229.13(g).

1. Customer is unlikely to recover punitive damages. Comment 1 to 4–402 opens the door a little to punitive damages but only when some "other rule of law" would allow.

   Here there is no showing of malice or willfulness that might justify punitive damages under the common law. So no punitive damages.

2. Can Customer recover for injury to his reputation?

   Probably not. He can do so only if he can show "actual damage" to his reputation and that the dishonor was the "proximate" cause. All of that seems a stretch in most cases and this case is no different. So nothing for damage to his reputation.

3. Can Customer recover the $2 million gain that he lost out on? Section 4–402 specifically mentions "consequential damages" and so infers that they are recoverable but only if they are "proximately caused."

   So we would need to know more about why the deal did not go through and to hear evidence that Customer would have held the property for two years and would have found a buyer for $3 million. All of that is quite speculative right now. Customer would have to explain why the seller would not accept his and the bank's explanation for the bounced check and why the seller refused to deal with him if their deal contemplated a closing at which customer would pay the price by cashier's check. So the most likely outcome here on the evidence currently available is also zero.

§ 6–5   The Customer's Right to Stop Payment, Section 4–403

A customer may stop payment on "any item drawn on the customer's account."[1] Since stop-payment orders are common only for checks, we consider the relevant rules only in reference to checks. A stop-payment order poses a variety of problems. Here we examine: (1) Who may issue a binding stop-payment order? (2) What form must a stop-payment order take? May it be oral? (3) How are the usual stop-payment order rules altered because a personal check is certified or because the check in question is a cashier's or bank check? (4) What is the bank's liability for failure to follow a binding stop-payment order? (We deal with this last question mostly in the following section for it inevitably turns on

§ 4–403, Comment 3.

1. § 4–403(a). By analogy the rule extends to drawees other than banks.

the question of subrogation of the bank to the presenter's rights under 4–407.)

A drawer promises to pay the holder (3–414), and orders its bank to pay from its account. The drawer's stop-payment order does not rescind the promise to pay the holder and does not impair the holder's suit on that promise. The drawer's stop-payment order is addressed only to the bank and affects only the relationship with it. Subsection (a) of 4–403 states:

> A customer or any person authorized to draw on the account if there is more than one person may stop payment of any item drawn on the customer's account or close the account by an order to the bank describing the item or account with reasonable certainty received at a time and in a manner that affords the bank a reasonable opportunity to act on it before any action by the bank with respect to the item described in Section 4–303. If the signature of more than one person is required to draw on an account, any of these persons may stop payment or close the account.

The right to stop payment is consistent with the concept that "[a] check * * * does not of itself operate as an assignment of funds in the hands of the drawee [bank] available for its payment, and [that] the drawee is not liable on the instrument until the drawee accepts it."[2] Although some post-Code decisions have blurred the point, a drawer's stop-payment order is not only effective against holders but also against holders in due course.[3] The presenter's status as a holder in due course can have practical impact where the bank pays over a binding stop-payment order,[4] but it does not impair the validity of the drawer's stop-payment order.

a.　Who May Issue Effective Stop–Payment Orders?

Ordinarily only a customer-drawer has the right to stop payment. A payee or indorsee does not have this right.[5] Although some cases have held otherwise (erroneously we think), a bank drawing a check on its account with another bank is a customer and has the right to stop payment.[6] On the death or incompetence of the

---

2. § 3–408.

3. Comment 7 to 4–403 explains:

It has sometimes been said that payment cannot be stopped against a holder in due course, but the statement is inaccurate. The payment can be stopped but the drawer remains liable on the instrument to the holder in due course (Sections 3–305, 3–414) and the drawee, if it pays, becomes subrogated to the rights of the holder in due course against the drawer.

4. For a discussion of the bank's subrogation rights upon payment over a stop-payment order, see 6–6 *infra.*

5. § 4–403, Comment 2.

6. See § 4–104(a)(5); Citizens Nat. Bank v. Fort Lee Sav. & Loan Ass'n, 89 N.J.Super. 43, 213 A.2d 315, 2 UCC 1029 (1965) (drawer bank could stop payment but holder in due course entitled to enforce rights on check).

customer, "a person claiming an interest in the account" may also stop payment.[7]

Section 4–403(a) deals with another problem unique to joint accounts. Assume that husband and wife have a joint account but that things are not going well between them. The husband discovers that the wife has drawn a large check from the joint account payable to the lawyer she intends to retain for her divorce. The husband issues a stop-payment order. Must the bank follow the stop-payment order? Under 4–403(a), the answer is yes. A party entitled to draw on an account has a unilateral right to veto the payments of the other party on the account.

Indeed, 4–403(a) goes farther. It permits an authorized signer to stop payment or close the account even where it would take two signatories to draw on the account.[8]

b. Form of Stop–Payment Orders

Section 4–403(a) specifies that the stop-payment order must describe the item "with reasonable certainty," and the comments make clear that this requires the customer, in the absence of a contrary agreement, to give sufficient information to allow the bank to identify the item under current "technology."[9] The reference in the current Comment to "existing technology" may be an attempt to bend the law slightly in favor of a bank that searches electronically and not manually for checks that are to be stopped. As we indicate below, a series of disputes has arisen between customers and banks when the customer has provided information (e.g., a dollar amount one digit off) that would allow a manual searcher to find the check, but did not allow an electronic searcher (at least with unsophisticated software) find it. The reference in the comment to existing technology may be a direction to a court to be more generous to banks who insist upon a customer's providing the right data for an electronic search. The statute continues the obligation of the customer to identify the check "with reasonable certainty" and neither the statute nor the comment specifically overrules earlier cases generally defining what is and what is not reasonable certainty. In the banker's Utopia, stop-payment orders accurately identify the drawer, the payee, the account number, the

---

7. See § 4–405(b), discussed in 6–4, *supra.* Comment 3 to 4–405 reads:

Any surviving relative, creditor or other person who claims an interest in the account may give a direction to the bank * * * not to pay a particular check. * * * The bank has no responsibility to determine the validity of the claim or even whether it is "colorable." But obviously anyone who has an interest in the estate, including the * * * executor * * * is entitled to claim an interest in the account.

8. This precludes the result of cases like Brown v. Eastman Nat. Bank, 291 P.2d 828 (Okla. 1955), a pre-Code case holding that a wife lacked power to stop payment on a check drawn by her husband against an account held by the husband and wife as joint tenants.

9. § 4–403, Comment 5.

date and, particularly, the amount of the check.[10] Printed forms that banks supply also commonly ask the customer to state its reason for stopping payment.[11] Absent contrary agreement, we think any stop-payment order is sufficient that reasonably identifies the account by the drawer's name or account number and that reasonably identifies the check by number, by name of the payee or by that information combined with the date and amount of the check. If, for example, the customer had drawn only one check to a given payee and the customer had given the bank his account number and the name of the payee, we think the order should be valid (absent a customer agreement to give more information).

By giving additional but erroneous information a customer may render an otherwise valid stop-payment order invalid. This is particularly true in the computer age. Even the smallest banks search electronically for particular information on the check. Banks sometimes search by comparing the amount of the check with the amount written on the stop-payment order. When the check is presented for payment, another bank has already encoded the amount on the check in computer-readable form. If the amount of the check varies by as little as one cent from the amount on the stop-payment order, the stop-payment order may be in vain. As one court noted, computers are finicky creatures.[12]

Nevertheless, in cases decided prior to the 1990 amendment, drawers usually prevailed against banks in suits for payment over stop-payment orders containing erroneous information. Why should banks be liable for a payment made due to a customer's mistake? The majority of courts rationalized the bank's liability on the grounds that the customer, although mistaken in one essential piece of information, still provided sufficient correct information to afford the bank a reasonable opportunity to act. The case of Parr v.

---

10. The cases provide no guidance on the question of the minimum amount of information the customer must supply. The use of stop payment forms may explain the dearth of case law on this point.

The effect of erroneous information is another matter. The stop-payment order was held effective despite erroneous information in the following cases: Elsie Rodriguez Fashions, Inc. v. Chase Manhattan Bank, 1978 WL 23503, 23 UCC 133 (N.Y. Sup. 1978); Kentucky–Farmers Bank v. Staton, 314 Ky. 313, 235 S.W.2d 767 (1951) (customer supplied wrong amount but gave correct date, number, and name of payee); Shude v. American State Bank, 263 Mich. 519, 248 N.W. 886 (1933) (incorrect date not

significant when bank erroneously placed hold on wrong account). The stop-payment order was held ineffective because the customer supplied erroneous information in the following cases: John H. Mahon Co. v. Huntington Nat. Bank, 62 Ohio App. 261, 23 N.E.2d 638 (1939) (erroneous check number); Mitchell v. Security Bank, 85 Misc. 360, 147 N.Y.S. 470 (1914) (wrong date and misdescribed payee).

11. See 4 R. Henson & W. Davenport, Uniform Laws Annotated 314–20 (1968).

12. Poullier v. Nacua Motors, Inc., 108 Misc.2d 913, 439 N.Y.S.2d 85, 32 UCC 258 (1981).

Security National Bank[13] is typical. There Parr correctly supplied her bank with the account number, the check number, the date and the payee. She incorrectly gave the amount as $972.46; the correct amount was $972.96. This fifty-cent error stumped the bank's computer. The bank argued that whether or not it had a reasonable opportunity to act on Parr's information should be determined in reference to the bank's own procedures. An Oklahoma Appeals Court rejected the bank's reasoning and found for Parr. According to the Oklahoma court, it seemed reasonable to require banks to accept reasonable information. Once the customer has provided such information, the Parr court stated, any loss because of the bank's particular system should be on the bank. This objective standard, which ignores a particular bank's procedures in determining whether or not a customer provided sufficient correct information on a stop-payment order form has been applied by other courts too. However, Comment 5 now supports the bank's argument for gauging the reasonableness of the supplied information in reference to "the technology then existing."

Although the courts often take the side of the drawer, this result is not inevitable. The courts seemed to share the opinion that everybody is entitled to one mistake—but only one. The more mistakes a customer makes on the stop-payment order form, the more likely that the court will find that the information was not reasonably certain. In a computer search, the number of mistakes does not necessarily affect the success or failure of the search. Only the *type* of mistake is significant. If the information the computer needs is wrong, the accuracy of all other information is immaterial. The courts, however, still think in human terms.

Several courts have stated that banks may not be liable for payment over stop-payment orders if they give the customer notice that absolute accuracy is necessary. But in New Jersey even spelling out the need for precision may not be enough. In Staff Service Associates, Inc. v. Midlantic National Bank,[14] a clause in the stop-payment order warned the customer that all information must be correct, including check amount "to the penny." The customer made a one digit error in the amount of the check and sued when the check was paid over the timely stop-payment order. In finding for the drawer, the court said the bank's explicit warning was not enough. In order for a warning to be effective, the court said, a bank must tell the customer *why* this is so. The court also found indications of bad faith in the fact that the bank's warning stated that all information must be accurate, when in fact only the check amount had to be correct. The court concluded that it was "manifestly unreasonable" for the bank to have failed to focus the

---

13. 680 P.2d 648, 38 UCC 275 (Okla. App. 1984).

14. 207 N.J.Super. 327, 504 A.2d 148, 42 UCC 968 (1985).

customer's attention on the one truly essential piece of information in the stop-payment order, thereby denying the customer the opportunity to give the bank a reasonable opportunity to act. The *Staff Service* decision is an example of the lengths to which a court will go to protect bank customers. The plain English of "to the penny" was a pretty clear warning of the need for accuracy.

The decisions in stop-payment order cases raise the question how a bank can avoid liability for paying over a stop-payment order containing erroneous information. The *Parr* court suggested that to avoid liability banks should either seek an amendment to 4–403 that would require exact information in a stop-payment order, or notify the customer of the need for accuracy at the time the stop-payment order is given. The first alternative, legislation, has now occurred with the revisions of 4–403. While the section does not require exact information in a stop-payment order, it does require a description of the item with reasonable certainty, and it also demands that this standard be judged in accordance with currently existing technology. In a case brought under a similarly amended version of 4–403, a Florida court[15] relieved the bank of liability where the plaintiff had misstated the check amount.[16]

As for the Oklahoma court's second method for preventing a bank's liability—notice—the *Staff Service* case suggests that simply giving notice may not protect a bank. To be really safe, a bank would be wise to provide customers with a comprehensive explanation of the check catching system the bank uses, and the stop-payment order form should have all essential information highlighted in the most conspicuous manner possible. Note too that asking for additional information may decrease the quality of the bank's notice. (If the dollar amount or check number is everything, why did they ask for the date and payee's name?)

The real difficulty is that customers (and judges) think of computers in anthropomorphic terms. They assume that the computer, like a human, will assign less weight to the digits to the right of the decimal point than it will to those on the left. Seldom will a customer make mistakes about the numbers of thousands or tens of thousands on her check, but the customer may well be unconcerned with whether her check showed 25 cents or 24 cents on the right-hand end of the digits. Absent sophisticated programming each numeral is the same to the computer; it accords no greater weight to thousands or tens of thousands than to cents or tens of cents. It is unclear what notice could bring this fact home to the customer.

---

15. Capital Bank v. Schuler, 421 So.2d 633, 34 UCC 1287 (Fla. App. 1982).

16. Even without the amendment, the bank might have prevailed; the Flor-

ida court also took into account the needs of defendant bank's check search procedures in determining the sufficiency of the information plaintiff had provided.

Perhaps something like the following would do. NOTE WELL: A COMPUTER WILL SEARCH FOR YOUR CHECK. THE COMPUTER WILL SEARCH EXCLUSIVELY BY THE DOLLAR AMOUNT. IT CAN READ NOTHING ELSE ON THE CHECK. IF THE DOLLARS ARE CORRECT BUT THE PENNIES VARY BY EVEN ONE CENT (e.g., $7565.55 vs. $7565.56), THE COMPUTER WILL NOT FIND YOUR CHECK AND NO STOP WILL BE MADE.

Banks that wish completely to avoid the cases described above have at least two alternatives. The first is to devise more flexible software that throws out checks for human inspection that are close but not identical to the one identified by the customer. Moreover, the computer could cross-check the number of the check and could throw out every check that corresponded with either the number shown on the stop-payment order or the dollar amount. Doubtless there are other things that can be done; when and if more information is MICR encoded on the check, the computer can be programmed to consider that as well.

Secondly the bank might offer two modes of check service. For $40.00 the bank might agree to do a manual search of the account and to be liable if it fails to stop a check that any reasonable human should have found. Alternatively and for a lower price, it might agree to search by computer and with respect to the second mode of search to insist upon absolute accuracy. If the dollar amount for the first is reasonably equivalent to the cost of conducting a human search and if a customer rejects it in favor of a cheaper but less effective search, the courts should be more inclined to the bank's side and should reject the customer's complaint in the case in which the customer fails to identify the check accurately after selecting the less expensive mode of search.

Subsection 4–403(b) entitles the customer to stop payment orally.[17] Although this provision caused unhappiness in the banking community, the Code drafters decided that banks should honor oral as well as written stop-payment orders. As we indicated in Section 6–2, we read 4–403(b) and comments as a statement of public policy and believe that a bank may not by contract deprive a customer of his right to stop payment orally. For the same reasons, we think courts should invalidate stop-payment order forms that completely exculpate banks for failure to follow stop-payment orders.[18]

---

17. However, several states have enacted a version of 4–403 which requires written stop-payment orders. See, e.g., Tex.Bus. & Com.Code § 4.403(b) (1968).

18. If the stop-payment order has expired, the bank has no liability. See M.G. Sales, Inc. v. Chemical Bank, 161 A.D.2d 148, 554 N.Y.S.2d 863, 12 UCC2d 177 (1990).

c. Certified, Cashier, and Bank Checks

As we have seen, when the customer draws a check she can order payment stopped. However, when the customer uses a certified check, a cashier's check, or a bank check, the matter becomes more complicated.[19] (From a customer's viewpoint, the three checks are functionally identical. One will serve the purpose of the other, and in most cases the customer will procure a certified, a bank, or a cashier's check to satisfy someone who insists upon a more solid promise than the customer's personal promise.) Complications arise because these checks, unlike ordinary personal checks, carry the promise of the bank to the holder. Recall that 3–408 says a drawee is not liable to the holder of a check unless the check is certified.[20] Accordingly, two related questions arise in relation to certified, cashier's, or bank checks: (1) What right does the customer have to compel the bank to stop payment? (2) What are the legal consequences if the bank stops payment?

A bank can incur direct liability to the customer's payee several ways. First, it can certify the customer's check.[21] Second, it can issue a cashier's check (that is, a check on which it is both the drawer and the drawee). Third, it can issue a bank check (that is, a check on which it is the drawer and the drawee is a second bank). In all three cases the bank incurs direct liability to the payee, either as an acceptor on the check or as a drawer. If the customer orders the bank not to pay the certified check or the cashier's check or asks it to order payment stopped on a bank check, that customer is asking the bank to break the bank's own contract under 3–412, 3–414 or 3–409. In none of these cases does the customer have a right to insist that its bank dishonor[22] or, in the case of the bank check, insist that it order payment stopped. In Weldon v. Trust Co. Bank of Columbus, N.A.,[23] the court held that purchaser of a cashier's check had no cause of action when bank honored check after she issued a stop-payment order. Under 4–303 a stop-payment order is too late if it is received after the bank has accepted the item, and the court found that a cashier's check is "accepted" by the act of its issuance. The court also observed that if bank had voluntarily

---

19. Although many might lump personal money orders into this category, most courts equate personal money orders with personal checks. The prevailing and correct view is that personal money orders can be stopped by the customer prior to acceptance, certification or payment.

20. § 3–408 reads as follows:

A check or other draft does not of itself operate as an assignment of funds in the hands of the drawee available for its payment, and the drawee is not liable

on the instrument until the drawee accepts it.

21. See §§ 3–409, 3–411, 3–412, 3–413. For a discussion of certification and the bank's liability, see 1–6 *supra*.

22. § 4–303(a) explicitly states that a stop-payment order "comes too late" if the payor has certified the check. For a discussion of 4–303, see 21–7 *infra*.

23. 231 Ga.App. 458, 499 S.E.2d 393, 35 UCC2d 1291 (1998).

honored the stop-payment order, the payee would have had a cause of action against the bank, i.e., the customer was asking the bank to break its contract. Nevertheless, in deference to a good customer, a bank may voluntarily dishonor a certified check, or a cashier's check, and may voluntarily order payment stopped on the bank check. If the bank chooses to dishonor the certified or cashier's check or to order its bank to stop payment on the bank check, the holder will have a cause of action against the bank.[24] If the holder chooses to sue just the bank on its acceptor's or drawer's liability, generally the bank may not raise defenses available to its customer against the holder.[25] Before the bank accedes to its customer's request, it would be well advised to obtain the customer's agreement to defend any lawsuit that might result.

Two New York lower courts have disagreed with our analysis with respect to bank checks. In those cases the courts held that one bank that had drawn a check on another bank could not stop payment. In Malphrus v. Home Savings Bank,[26] payee sued the drawer of a bank check that had stopped payment at the request of its depositor. In granting plaintiff's motion for summary judgment the court said that the drawer of a bank check had no right to stop payment because business people treat bank checks like cash and the issuance of the bank check discharges the buyer from the underlying obligation under 3–310 (at the time of the case, the relevant section was 3–802). We think the case was wrongly decided. In the first place the drawer of a bank check qualifies as a "customer" under 4–104(a)(5) and that status entitled the bank to issue a stop-payment order under 4–403. Secondly, even if the drawer-bank stops payment, it remains liable to the payee under 3–414. Thus even if the buyer-depositor is discharged from the underlying obligation the payee has a solvent bank to sue. More-

---

24. Section 3–310(a) provides:

Unless otherwise agreed, if a certified check, cashier's check, or teller's check is taken for an obligation, the obligation is discharged to the same extent discharge would result if an amount of money equal to the amount of the instrument were taken in payment of the obligation. Discharge of the obligation does not affect any liability that the obligor may have as an indorser of the instrument.

Accordingly, if the person taking a cashier's check or a bank check wishes to preserve his rights against the customer, he should secure his indorsement.

25. Subsection 3–305(c) prohibits a bank from raising certain defenses of its customer against the holder. The subsection reads as follows:

* * * in an action to enforce the obligation of a party to pay the instrument, the obligor may not assert against the person entitled to enforce the instrument a defense, claim in recoupment, or claim to the instrument (Section 3–306) of another person, but the other person's claim to the instrument may be asserted by the obligor if the other person is joined in the action and personally asserts the claim against the person entitled to enforce the instrument.

26. 44 Misc.2d 705, 254 N.Y.S.2d 980, 2 UCC 373 (Co. Ct. 1965).

over, a seller who wishes to retain its rights against the buyer can protect itself by obtaining the buyer's indorsement.

The *Malphrus* case and others questioning a bank's right to stop payment on a bank or to refuse to pay its own check are better analyzed as cases dealing with the question whether a bank that has issued such a check can assert its customer's defenses. We analyze those cases at 2–11 *supra*.

§ 6–6   Payor Bank's Liability for Its Failure to Follow a Legitimate Stop Order, Section 4–403(c); Its Right to Subrogation on Improper Payment, Section 4–407; Drawer's Burden of Proof, Section 4–403(c)

The payor bank's liability to its customer for improper payment under section 4–403 is entwined with its 4–407 rights to subrogation. Consider the following illustration: Repeunzel gives her personal check for $30,000 to Cicero for a painting. Subsequently, Repeunzel has second thoughts about the purchase and orders payment stopped. The bank fails to follow the stop-payment order. Repeunzel will argue that the bank is liable under 4–403(c) for failing to follow the stop-payment order. Repeunzel's bank will argue that it is subrogated to the rights of either Cicero or Cicero's depositary bank under 4–407. To establish the basis for these arguments, we review sections 4–403 and 4–407.

a.   Payor Bank's Liability and Subrogation Rights

Section 4–403(a) and (b) appear to give the drawer considerable flexibility in issuing stop orders. These sections allow for "oral" stop-payment orders by "a customer or any person authorized to draw on the account." While flexibility for the drawer is the rule in sections (a) and (b), obtaining damages for the bank's failure to follow a stop-payment order is made quite difficult by 4–403(c) and 4–407. Section 4–403(c) reads:

> The burden of establishing the fact and amount of loss resulting from the payment of an item contrary to a stop-payment order or order to close an account is on the customer. The loss from payment of an item contrary to a stop-payment order may include damages for dishonor of subsequent items under Section 4–402.

The customer's first hurdle will be in proving "the fact and amount of loss" resulting from the bank's payment. We discuss the customer's burden of proof in more detail below. The drawer's second hurdle arises from 4–403(c)'s relationship with 4–407.[1] Un-

---

1. § 4–403, Comment 7 reads in part:

A payment in violation of an effective direction to stop payment is an improper payment, even though it is made by mis-

der 4–407 the bank that improperly paid over a valid stop-payment order is subrogated to the rights of certain named parties. Section 4–407 states:

If a payor bank has paid an item over the order of the drawer or maker to stop payment, or after an account has been closed, or otherwise under circumstances giving a basis for objection by the drawer or maker, to prevent unjust enrichment and only to the extent necessary to prevent loss to the bank by reason of its payment of the item, the payor bank is subrogated to the rights

(1) of any holder in due course on the item against the drawer or maker;

(2) of the payee or any other holder of the item against the drawer or maker either on the item or under the transaction out of which the item arose; and

(3) of the drawer or maker against the payee or any other holder of the item with respect to the transaction out of which the item arose.

Returning to the Repeunzel hypothetical, the drawee bank will argue that 4–407 subrogates it to the rights of Cicero as the payee of the item. Repeunzel agreed in the underlying transaction to pay $30,000 for a painting and a draft was exchanged in consideration for the painting. The payor bank will be subrogated to Cicero's claim on the draft[2] as well as Cicero's rights on the underlying transaction.[3] If Repeunzel sues the bank for paying over the stop-payment order, the payor bank can defend by showing either that Repeunzel was liable on the draft or the underlying transaction to Cicero. The payor bank will win unless Repeunzel has a valid defense against Cicero's claim to the $30,000 payment. For example, if Cicero claims to have sold Repeunzel an original Monet when

take or inadvertence. * * * The drawee is, however, entitled to subrogation to prevent unjust enrichment (Section 4–407).

2. Recall that a stop-payment order under § 4–403 does not alter the drawer's liability to a holder. Thus Cicero could enforce the drawer's contract (§ 3–314) in a suit against Repeunzel. This assumes, of course, that Repeunzel has no good defense (§ 3–305).

3. § 4–407 Comment 2 reads as follows:

Paragraph (2) also subrogates the bank to the rights of the payee or other holder against the drawer or maker either on the item or under the transaction out of which it arose. It may well be that the payee is not a holder in due course but still has good rights against the drawer. These may be on the check but also may not be as, for example, where the drawer buys goods from the payee and the goods are partially defective so that the payee is not entitled to the full price, but the goods are still worth a portion of the contract price. If the drawer retains the goods it is obligated to pay a part of the agreed price. If the bank has paid the check it should be subrogated to this claim of the payee against the drawer.

it was actually a copy, Repeunzel's fraud defense will defeat the payor bank's subrogated rights on the underlying transaction and the draft. Repeunzel will not fare so well, however, if the payor bank can claim subrogation to the rights of a holder in due course.

Assume that Cicero deposited the check in its depositary bank and immediately withdrew the funds. The depositary bank qualifies as a holder in due course to the extent that it satisfies 3–302 and allowed Cicero to draw on the funds represented by Repeunzel's check.[4] Because the payor bank will be subrogated to the rights of a holder in due course, Repeunzel's defenses are limited to those available in section 3–305(a)(1). Therefore, in this case, Repeunzel's fraud defense would be useless against the payor bank.

In the case of the fake "Monet," Repeunzel might be able to persuade her bank to recredit her account. Comment 3 to 4–407 explains that if the bank reimburses its customer, 4–407(3) authorizes the bank's recovery of that money from the payee or any other holder by asserting the drawer's rights. Under 3–418 final payment does not bar the bank's recovery of payment mistakenly made over a stop-payment order.[5]

Section 4–407 sometimes goes beyond subrogated rights. In Scott Stainless Steel v. NBD Chicago Bank,[6] defendant bank agreed to disregard the drawer's stop-payment order in return for the payee's indemnity against loss. Payee argued that its indemnification agreement with the bank was invalid because the bank acted in bad faith by not following a customer's stop-payment order. (Some chutzpah, to attack a co-conspirator's act in furtherance of the conspiracy!) The court held the indemnification agreement to be valid under 4–103, and allowed the bank's affirmative defense under 4–407.

Finally consider a case in which bank pays in disregard of a valid stop-payment order to one who is a holder in due course or a holder with a good cause of action against the drawer but who would not have sued the drawer had payment been stopped. Assume for example that the payee (who has received the proceeds of the check) lives in a distant state and would have sold the goods to a third party and forgotten the transaction if payment had been stopped. In that a case, the bank can use its subrogation rights

---

4. See §§ 4–211; 4–210(a)(1).

5. § 3–418(a) provides in part:

Except as provided in subsection (c), if the drawee of a draft pays or accepts the draft and the drawee acted on the mistaken belief that (i) payment of the draft had not been stopped pursuant to Section 4–403 * * * the drawee may recover the amount of the draft from the person to whom or for whose benefit payment was made or, in the case of acceptance, may revoke the acceptance. * * *

6. 253 Ill.App.3d 256, 192 Ill.Dec. 333, 625 N.E.2d 293, 24 UCC2d 609 (1993).

regardless of the inclination of the person presenting the check.[7] However, if the theory behind section 4–407 is that the customer recovers to the extent that the bank's wrongful payment causes injury, the bank should not have the protection of 4–407 where its action is the cause of the injury. Customer argues "if you had followed my stop-payment order, my money would never have come into the hands of seller, and seller would have dropped the whole matter. Because you failed to follow my stop-payment order, seller now has the money, and I cannot get it back. Since seller would not have come after me for the money you in fact 'caused' my loss." Although the customer's argument has considerable appeal, we find no place for it in 4–407. Rather 4–407 flatly grants the bank the right to assert the payee-seller's action for the price in this circumstance and so to free itself from any liability to its customer. Those who feel compassion for the customer here should recall that the customer is trying to weasel out of a valid obligation to the seller.

The preamble to 4–407 states that the section comes into play only where the bank has paid over the customer's stop-payment order or after an account has been closed or where the customer otherwise has a "basis for objection." Presumably the bank can invoke 4–407 every time the customer complains about payment of an item that was not "properly payable."[8] The bank can take advantage of 4–407 subrogation rights "to prevent unjust enrichment"[9] and "only to the extent necessary to prevent loss to the

---

7. Although the drafters clearly intended that the bank could resurrect the transaction and assert the payee's or holder's rights against the drawer, the Code does not provide a mechanism for that miracle. §§ 3–602 and 3–310 discharge the drawer from his liability on the instrument and the underlying obligation when the bank pays the check. One commentator suggests that the bank's improper payment does not discharge the drawer because it is not "his payment or satisfaction." See Clarke, Bailey & Young, Bank Deposits and Collections 159 (3d ed. 1963).

8. For a discussion of 4–401 and the meaning of "properly payable," see 6–3 *supra.*

9. The meaning of the phrase "to prevent unjust enrichment" is not clear. One might construe the preamble as requiring unjust enrichment as a prerequisite to the bank's assertion of its subrogation rights. See Commercial Ins. Co. v. Scalamandre, 56 Misc.2d 628, 289 N.Y.S.2d 489, 4 UCC 956 (City Civ.Ct. 1967) (payee-defendant's motion for

summary judgment granted when plaintiff failed to allege unjust enrichment or that drawer had right to refuse payment). However, under that construction, 4–407 begins to sound like "Catch 22": "The bank must show unjust enrichment before it can assert subrogation rights. The bank can show unjust enrichment only by asserting its subrogation rights." If the drafters did not mean that unjust enrichment was a prerequisite to subrogation, then what did they mean?

The genealogy of 4–407 reveals that the unjust enrichment language first appears in a comment to the May, 1949 Draft of the Code. Comment 8 to § 3–415 (May 1949 Draft) read in part:

A payment in violation of an effective direction to stop payment is an improper payment, even though it is made by mistake or inadvertence, and it may not be charged to the drawer's account. Any agreement to the contrary is invalid under Subsection (4). The drawee is, however, entitled to subrogation to prevent unjust enrichment.

bank." Comment 4 explains that the quoted language is intended to prevent the bank from obtaining a double recovery. If, for example, the bank refused to recredit its customer's account (and therefore was out no money), it would not be subrogated to its customer's claim against the payee. That a bank would seek recovery in those circumstances seems improbable.

The plaintiff in Sunshine v. Bankers Trust Co.[10] argued that a bank which had not debited a customer's account had no claim under 4–407 because the customer suffered no loss to which the bank could be subrogated. While that argument has a superficial appeal, the court rightly concluded that accepting it would have produced unintended and undesirable results. If the argument were accepted the bank would be compelled to debit the account of its customer who had issued the stop-payment order in order to have a right of subrogation. It would add insult to injury to make the innocent customer, who has already been once wronged by the bank's failure to follow a stop-payment order, await the outcome of the long law suit without the use of the funds. The court rejected the argument and concluded that 4–407 conferred "the substantive rights of subrogation even if the technical mechanical requirements of common law subrogation have not been met."

The phrase "unjust enrichment" first appears in the statutory text in 4–402(4) of the Spring, 1950 Draft which read:

To prevent unjust enrichment a payor bank which has paid an item drawn or made by a customer and which it may not charge to his account may in an action

(a) against the holder who has received payment recover any part of the payment due its customer or any prior party in respect of the transaction in which the customer of the depositary bank acquired the item; and

(b) against its customer recover any amount which would have been due from him on the item if payment had been refused.

The bank has no right to charge the customer's account in respect of such cause of action. The bank may bring either or both such actions but may have only one satisfaction and any right to consequential or punitive damages remains with the customer or holder.

The section quoted above makes it clear that 4–407 was originally drafted on the premise that a bank which had paid an item over a stop-payment order could not debit its customer's account.

As originally drafted, the section contemplated that the bank would sue the drawer, payee, or holder to recover such payment. In the words of Mr. Leary, the original draftsman of Article 4, "[T]he obvious justification is the prevention of unjust enrichment at the expense of the payor bank who may be deemed to have paid out its own funds." Leary, Check Handling Under Article Four of the UCC, 49 Marq.L.Rev. 331 (1965).

It appears that the draftsmen's viewpoint changed considerably between the Spring, 1951 Draft and the Official Draft promulgated in 1952. The present version of 4–407 repeats the 1952 version. The section contemplates that the bank will use its subrogation rights primarily to defend against a suit by the customer to recover payment. This approach reflects the assumption that a bank who pays over a stop-payment order can legitimately charge its customer's account.

Despite this change in approach, the unjust enrichment language remains. We conclude the phrase at best states the purpose of the section, and at worst it adds meaningless confusion.

10.   34 N.Y.2d 404, 358 N.Y.S.2d 113, 314 N.E.2d 860, 14 UCC 1416 (1974).

But the 4–407 right to subrogate is not always available to a bank that inadvertently makes an unauthorized payment. In Roosevelt Bank v. Moore,[11] husband opened a "pay on death saving account" and identified his wife as the beneficiary. When the couple separated, wife withdrew $5,500 from the account. Husband found out and demanded the bank reimburse him. The bank did, and subsequently sued wife claiming it was subrogated to the rights of the husband to recover any unauthorized withdrawals under 4–407. The court rejected this claim, holding that aside from being the account owner, husband had nothing to do with the transaction. Instead, wife was the drawer, maker and payee. Thus there is no right to subrogate.

In Guaranty Bank & Trust v. Smith,[12] drawer wrote a check for $18,198 to defendant and issued a stop-payment order when he found only $18,171 was due. He wrote another check for the correct amount. Defendant presented both checks for payment and the bank, failing to follow the stop-payment order, paid both. Bank sued payee under the common law remedies of unjust enrichment and restitution. The trial court granted summary judgment to plaintiff bank. On appeal, defendant claimed drawer owed him more than $18,000 so he was entitled to the second check as well. He argued the bank failed to prove that the drawer had a defense to the payment of the second check, and as a result the bank could not be subrogated to the right of the drawer under 4–407. The court held that restitution is available to bank only to the extent that drawer is not liable. The appellate court reversed and remanded.

Sections 4–407 and 4–403(c) leave us with several questions concerning the liability of a payor bank to its customer for payment over an effective stop-payment order. If 4–403(c) means that for the customer to have a cause of action against the bank, the bank's failure to follow a valid stop-payment order must be the cause of the customer's loss, then 4–407 adds little for it seems simply to restate that rule. If the holder who received payment would have had a good cause of action against the customer had payment been stopped, the bank's failure to follow the stop-payment order would not be the cause of the customer's ultimate loss and the customer would lose its action against the bank under 4–403(c). Section 4–407 subrogates[13] the bank to the holder's cause of action against the customer-drawer and thus yields the same result in the same

---

11. 944 S.W.2d 261, 32 UCC2d 895 (Mo.App. 1997).

12. 952 S.W.2d 787, 33 UCC2d 1181 (Mo.App. 1997).

13. Comment 5 to § 4–407 makes it clear that the section does not preempt the bank's right to raise the defense of ratification against the customer or to

seek restitution. See Woodmere Cedar-hurst Corp. v. National City Bank, 157 Misc. 660, 284 N.Y.S. 238 (1935) (retention of full consideration for check with knowledge of payment constitutes ratification) (dictum); 1 N.Y. State Law Revision Comm'n, 1954 report 364–68 (1954).

circumstances. We are not certain how 4–407 and 4–403(c) fit together.

b. Customer's Burden of Proof

The customer has the "burden of establishing the fact and amount of loss" due to the bank's payment over a valid stop-payment order. Mr. Malcolm, an Article 4 draftsman, tells us that subsection 4–403(c) was inserted as a trade-off for the banks when the drafters decided to allow customers to give oral stop-payment orders.[14] We can readily understand the requirement that the customer show that it gave a valid stop-payment order. However, the requirement that the customer establish the fact and amount of loss before recovery from bank is more controversial and has a controversial history. One aspect of that controversy revolved around the explanatory Comment 9 which appeared in the 1952 version of the Code. The comment reads as follows:

> When a bank pays an item over a stop payment order, such payment automatically involves a charge to the customer's account. Subsection (3) [now (c)] imposes upon the customer the burden of establishing the fact and amount of loss resulting from the payment. Consequently until such burden is maintained either in a court action or to the satisfaction of the bank, the bank is not obligated to recredit the amount of the item to the customer's account and therefore, is not liable for the dishonor of other items due to insufficient funds caused by the payment contrary to the stop payment order.

Comment 9 was deleted from the 1958 Official Text. However, the ghost of Comment 9 may still haunt us.

The 1990 revision solved one important damage issue—the last sentence of 4–403(c) explicitly authorizes the customer to recover damages "for dishonor of subsequent items under Section 4–402" where the bank has failed to follow a stop-payment order and thus caused dishonor of other items. The provision anticipates a common pattern: customer issues a stop-payment order on a large check

14. Testifying before the New York Law Revision Commission, Mr. Malcolm, in an explanation of the decision to permit oral stop-payment orders, said:

However, one interesting thing developed in that particular debate and argument which touches on another criticism that has been made, and that was that after the two houses voted down the bank concept on those two issues, then somebody said from the floor would it not be fair if at least in this situation the burden of proof was placed upon the depositor to establish that there was a stop payment order and the extent of his damages.

Again, without any participation on my part, the actual draftsmen of the Code responded very quickly that they thought that would be a fair proposition, and it was acquiesced in. The policy decision was made, and subsection (3) [now (c)] was subsequently drafted to meet that policy decision.

1 N.Y. State Law Revision Comm'n, 1954 Report 467–68 (1954).

and, believing that the check has been stopped, draws other checks. If the bank fails to follow the stop-payment order, it will then regard the subsequent checks as NSF and will dishonor them. When this happens, it is now clear that the bank will suffer the potentially large liability for wrongful dishonor under 4–402, even though that dishonor was caused by breach of the bank's duty under 4–403.

Dunnigan v. First Bank[15] addresses the meaning and scope of 4–403(3) [now revised as 4–403(c)]. The Connecticut Supreme Court restricted a customer's proof of loss resulting from wrongful payment of a check over a valid stop-payment order. Cohn Precious Metals, Inc., a customer of First Bank, purchased coins from Lamphere Coin, Inc. Due to a bookkeeping error, Cohn overpaid Lamphere by $19,606 in a wire transfer. Two days later, Cohn discovered its bookkeeper's error and directed First Bank to stop payment on two checks that had been given to Lamphere in other valid transactions. First Bank complied to one of the checks for $9,000, but inadvertently honored the second check for $12,175. Cohn never recovered its overpayment from Lamphere.

When Cohn brought an action for wrongful payment over a valid stop-payment order against First Bank, the bank argued that Cohn could not establish a loss under 4–403 by relying on prior unrelated transactions. It argued that as long as there was good consideration for the particular ($12,175) check, as here, a bank paying over a valid stop-payment order is not liable to its customer because no loss results from payment. The Connecticut Supreme Court agreed; it held that Cohn was not entitled to resort to the credits from its prior transaction with Lamphere to establish "the fact and amount of loss" under 4–403. Cohn suffered no loss within the meaning of 4–403(3), because there was valid consideration and no defenses arising out of the particular transaction for which the check was given. The dissent argued that the majority's view was too narrow in that it restricted a bank's liability to situations where there is failure of consideration arising from the particular transaction in which the check was issued.

The dissent may have the better argument. Section 4–403(c) seems to affirm the dissent's position, at least with respect to subsequent items. The last sentence in revised 4–403(c) tells that damages can arise from other events. Although *Dunnigan* dealt with damages arising because of a prior, not a subsequent, transaction, 4–403(c) indicates that proof of loss is not as narrow as the Connecticut majority seemed to say.

One cannot overstate the importance to the customer of the bank's decision to recredit or not recredit after paying over a stop-

---

15. 217 Conn. 205, 585 A.2d 659, 13 UCC2d 1196 (1991).

payment order. The first job for the customer's lawyer is to convince the bank to recredit. If the bank agrees to recredit, the customer will have the use of the funds during the ensuing negotiation and litigation with the payee and the customer may even convince the bank to litigate the issue at the bank's expense.

If one finds under 4–403(c) that a bank must recredit the customer's account pending the outcome of litigation, what is the significance of 4–403(c)? In Cicci v. Lincoln National Bank & Trust Co.,[16] a New York lower court considered the effect of subsection 4–403(3) [now (c)]. A customer sued the bank for payment over a stop-payment order. Lincoln defended on the ground that plaintiff suffered no loss as the result of payment. Citing 4–403(3) the court denied plaintiff's motion for summary judgment. Section 4–403(3) altered the pre-Code law that allowed a plaintiff to recover without alleging damage. Under that section, plaintiff must allege as part of his *prima facie* case that he suffered injury as the result of payment over the stop-payment order. It is not sufficient merely to show that the customer's bank account was reduced by the amount of the check. As we read the *Cicci* case, if the customer-drawer cannot allege damages from subsequent dishonor of other checks, he must at least allege that if the bank had followed the stop-payment order, the drawer would have had a good defense against a suit by holder. We confess that our reading of 4–403(c) and of the *Cicci* case leaves very little if any scope for 4–403(c).

One lower court New York case leaves even less substance to 4–403(c). In Thomas v. Marine Midland Tinkers National Bank,[17] defendant bank "virtually rested on plaintiff's case" which had consisted of proof of the valid stop-payment order and of defendant's payment over it. The court rejected defendant bank's argument that plaintiff had failed to present a prima facie case because it failed to introduce evidence to negate the payee's right to the proceeds of the stopped check. The court reasoned that once plaintiff had shown payment over a valid stop-payment order, the burden shifted to defendant bank to come forward with evidence which would show an absence of actual loss to the customer. Had defendant gone forward with the evidence, the ultimate burden of proof would have been on plaintiff. Although the court points out that this case differs from the *Cicci* ruling on summary judgment in that here all the evidence on both sides had been heard, it admits its comes "to a different conclusion" than that reached by the *Cicci* court. The *Thomas* interpretation does some violence to the drafters' intent under 4–403. While we do not think a court's disregard of rather clear statutory directions is appropriate, we suspect that the banks who had a large hand in the drafting of Article 4 here

16. 46 Misc.2d 465, 260 N.Y.S.2d 100, 2 UCC 1093 (City Ct. 1965).

17. 86 Misc.2d 284, 381 N.Y.S.2d 797, 18 UCC 1273 (City Civ.Ct. 1976).

suffer the consequences of being a bit too greedy in the drafting process.

PROBLEM

Payor banks often pay despite their customers' orders to dishonor. Then there is first a question about the validity of the stop order and then a question about the injury to the customer from the bank's failure. Consider some of these:

1. Customer orders bank to stop payment on check number 4150. Bank encodes the request as check number 4151 and fails to stop the correct check. Customer incorrectly listed the amount of the check as $989 when it was actually $978. On the ground that the customer gave it the wrong amount, bank argues that it did not violate its duty.

    If the check number is in the MICR line and the search was done electronically, bank loses. The wrong amount would be irrelevant in such a search. Formerly banks searched for checks by the amount of the check (that would have been encoded in the MICR line at the depositary bank). More recently banks have put the check number in that line and, where so, could, and presumably will, search by number.

2. Customer procures a cashier's check payable to car dealer for $55,000. On the day he is to pick up the car, Customer chooses not to go through with the deal and asks bank to dishonor the cashier's check. Bank refuses and Customer sues.

    Customer loses. Bank has a drawer's liability on the cashier's check and Customer has asked it to break its contract. Bank has no duty to dishonor a cashier's check–and in fact the availability of such a right would considerably diminish the utility of cashier's checks.

3. Customer gives a check for $35,000 to car dealer for a new car and discovers before the check clears that the car is a different model than he ordered. Bank fails to follow customer's proper stop order and customer demands that bank recredit his account. If Bank does that it may pursue customer's claim against dealer, 4–407.

    But what if Bank believes that customer is not telling the truth? Then Bank can refuse and when sued by customer assert dealer's defense that it (dealer) complied with the contract. Better, if there was a depositary bank, which took for value and without notice, between dealer and payor bank, payor can assert depositary bank's rights as an HIDC who took free of any defense of the customer.

§ 6–7　Priorities in the Customer's Bank Account, Section 4–303

Since a check is not an assignment of customer's funds but merely represents the customer's order to its bank to pay a certain sum to the order of a certain person or bearer, the holder is not legally entitled to have the drawee honor the check upon presentment.[1] Of course, the drawee will normally honor. But between the time a check is issued and the time it is presented for payment, a variety of things might interfere with the normal payment procedure. For instance, the customer may change its mind and countermand the order (stop payment). Alternatively the drawee may dishonor the check because the customer's creditors have seized the funds in the account to satisfy debts owed them. Section 4–303 provides a rule to settle the rights of the holder of a check demanding payment when certain events intervene to prevent payment from the drawer's account. These events, known to *cognoscenti* as the "four legals," include: (1) knowledge or notice of the customer's death, incompetency or bankruptcy; (2) the customer's stop-payment order; (3) legal process (for example, garnishment); and (4) setoff by the payor bank.

The effect of each of the "four legals" is to draw off customer's funds and so prevent normal payment of checks drawn on the customer's account. Elsewhere we have discussed the Code provisions governing the customer's stop-payment orders[2] and the effect of the customer's death or adjudication of incompetency.[3] Setoff and garnishment against an account are actions by the customer's creditors to take the funds on deposit to satisfy the customer's debts. In the case of setoff the bank is the creditor. Suppose, for example, that a checking account customer also has a loan from the bank to purchase a new car. If the customer defaults on the loan, the bank can repossess the car or it might choose to apply any funds in the account against the customer's debt. The bank sets off its debt to the customer (the amount of the account) against the debt owed by the customer (the promissory note). In most cases the bank's right to set off will arise from the common law. That right might be acknowledged or elaborated upon in the deposit agreement.

Creditors other than the bank reach funds in the customer's account by garnishment. Typically the garnishee process is issued upon the creditor's affidavit and service is made by the sheriff or a similar person upon the bank.[4] The writ orders the garnishee

---

§ 6–7

1. See § 3–408.

2. See 6–6 *supra.*

3. See 6–3 *supra.*

4. For example, Michigan Court Rule 3.101(D) states the grounds for issuance of a writ of garnishment. The rule reads as follows:

(bank) to disclose any assets of the debtor in its possession and compels it to hold those assets on pain of personal liability to the creditor.

A customer's bankruptcy disrupts payment of checks because under section 542(b) of the Bankruptcy Reform Act[5] the bank must pay any accounts to the order of the trustee or the debtor acting as the trustee. Thus a trustee might argue that bankruptcy freezes the customer's account and that—regardless of notice—the payor is accountable for checks paid after that time.

At this point it should be apparent that each situation involving one of the four legals presents a potential priority dispute between the holder of a check who demands payment and the third party who claims funds in the account. Like the priority provisions of Article 9, section 4–303 repeats the ancient rule of first in time, first in right. If the legal arrives at the payor bank *after* the bank has performed one of the steps ("milestones") in the payment process of a check, then the legal cannot interfere with payment of that check. Section 4–303(a) reads as follows:

> Any knowledge, notice, or stop-payment order received by, legal process served upon, or setoff exercised by a payor bank comes too late to terminate, suspend, or modify the bank's right or duty to pay an item or to charge its customer's account for the item, if the knowledge, notice, stop-payment order, or legal process is received or served and a reasonable time for the bank to act thereon expires or the setoff is exercised after the earliest of the following:
>
> (1) the bank accepts or certifies the item;
>
> (2) the bank pays the item in cash;
>
> (3) the bank settles for the item without having a right to revoke the settlement under statute, clearing-house rule, or agreement;
>
> (4) the bank becomes accountable for the amount of the item under Section 4–302 dealing with the payor bank's responsibility for late return or items; or

The clerk of the court that entered the judgment shall issue a writ of garnishment if the plaintiff, or someone on the plaintiff's behalf, makes and files an affidavit stating:

(1) that a judgment has been entered against the principal defendant and remains unsatisfied;

(2) the amount of the judgment and the amount remaining unpaid;

(3) that the affiant knows or has good reason to believe that

(a) a named person has control of property belonging to the defendant, or

(b) a named person is indebted to the principal defendant.

5. Bankruptcy Reform Act of 1978, Pub.L. No. 95–598, 92 Stat. 2594–5, 11 U.S.C.A. § 542(b)(2) (1979); see also § 541.

(5) with respect to checks, a cutoff hour no earlier than one hour after the opening of the next banking day after the banking day on which the bank received the check and no later than the close of that next banking day or, if no cutoff hour is fixed, the close of the next banking day after the banking day on which the bank received the check.

Stated briefly, as between one of the four legals and a specific check, the one to get to the bank first is entitled to the funds in the account. Note that the quoted section bears a strong similarity to 4–215. Note too, as we will point out below, it differs significantly from 4–215.

To determine priority in the bank account as between the owner of a check and the conflicting legal, the lawyer must first pinpoint the two relevant events. If any of the events ("milestones") listed in 4–303 has occurred with respect to the check before the effective time of the conflicting legal, the check wins. If, on the other hand, the legal becomes effective before any of the events in 4–303 occur, the legal wins. Thus the lawyer must ask two questions: (1) What was the effective time of the legal; for example, when did garnishment occur? When did bank get notice of bankruptcy? and (2) As of that time had any of the events in 4–303 occurred?

a. Timing of the Legals

In the case of stop-payment orders and notice of customer's bankruptcy or assignment for the benefit of creditors, the Code supplies the criteria for determining the effective time of the legal. Section 1–201(25) defines "notice" and "knowledge" and section 1–201(27) provides, in part:

> Notice, knowledge or a notice or notification received by an organization is effective for a particular transaction from the time when it is brought to the attention of the individual conducting that transaction, and in any event from the time when it would have been brought to his attention if the organization had exercised due diligence * * *.

Where the bank designates a particular person to handle stop-payment orders the legal is effective (at the latest) a reasonable time after it is communicated to that person. Note too that the time begins to run when that person should have known about the facts in question and one could certainly argue that knowledge on behalf of certain other responsible but undesignated parties (for example, a branch manager) should also start the clock.

Garnishment is a statutory remedy and one must consult local statutes to determine when the garnishment is effective. Some states have statutes specifying the proper procedure for garnishing a bank account,[6] while other state statutes merely provide that garnishment is governed by the same rules that govern service of process.[7] Typically, the latter statutes require only that the party serve a corporate officer.

Sections 542(b) and 541(a) of the Bankruptcy Reform Act[8] vest control in a petitioning debtor's account in the trustee. Payment of checks drawn before a bankruptcy petition but presented for payment after the petition present the "Bank of Marin" problem. In *Marin*, the question was whether the bank (who had paid debtor's prepetition check) had violated its obligation to hand over the property of the estate to the trustee in bankruptcy (or to pay it according to the order only of the trustee in bankruptcy) and thus must pay again to the bankruptcy trustee, or whether the bank, having paid in good faith, is freed from its obligation. In *Marin*, Justice Douglas held in favor of the payor bank and found that it satisfied its obligation by paying the checks.[9] That result has been codified in section 542(c) of the Bankruptcy Reform Act of 1978. Under that section a bank that pays in good faith without "actual notice" or "actual knowledge" of the commencement of the bankruptcy case is treated as though the payment had occurred prior to the filing of the petition. If one interprets "actual notice" and "actual knowledge" to be the equivalent of notice under 4–303, one arrives at similar results under the Bankruptcy Act and under 4–303 at least as to the payor bank.

Note, however, that the Bankruptcy Act apparently overturns the rules that would apply under 4–303 with respect to the payee's right to keep the proceeds of such a check. Specifically, 542 frees only "the entity making such transfer," i.e., the payor bank, from liability to the trustee. Under 549(a) the trustee would have the power to avoid the transfer to the payee and under 550(a) the trustee could reach the value of the property at least from the "initial transferee." Thus to the extent that 4–303 purports to the leave the transaction at rest and to give the payee priority over the trustee in bankruptcy, it may be overturned by the Bankruptcy Act.

Note that the "legals" discussed above (notice, stop-payment order or legal process) do not become effective upon bank's receipt of notice but only after the passage of "a reasonable time for the bank to act" on the notice. In other words, if customer telephones a

---

6. See, e.g., Cal.Civ.Pro.Code § 488.455 (Supp. 1994).

7. For example, Michigan Court Rule 3.101(F)(1) provides as follows:

The writ of garnishment and the disclosure form, and a copy of the writ for each principal defendant, must be served on the garnishee defendant in the man-

ner provided for the service of a summons and complaint in MCR 2.105.

8. Bankruptcy Reform Act of 1978, Pub.L.No. 95–598, 92 Stat. 2594–5, 11 U.S.C.A. §§ 541(a), 542(b) (1979).

9. Bank of Marin v. England, 385 U.S. 99, 87 S.Ct. 274, 17 L.Ed.2d 197 (1966).

stop-payment order at 9:00 a.m. and holder cashes a check over the counter at 9:15 a.m., the check would win because it was cashed before the bank had a reasonable time to act upon the stop-payment order. Just what constitutes a reasonable time is an open question. For example, in Harbor Bank of Maryland v. Hanlon Park Condominium Association, Inc.,[10] bank was served with a writ of garnishment and 2.5 hours later paid a check for $15,000 out of the account. The circuit court granted a summary judgment to creditor. The Court of Special Appeal vacated the judgment and remanded, holding that the circuit court erred in not determining whether 2.5 hours to respond to the writ of garnishment was a "reasonable time" under 4–303. Presumably the answer turns not only on banking practices in the particular community, but also on a particular bank's situation. Our examination of one bank's practices showed that a bank with five to ten branches serving a community of 100,000 expected to be able to notify all tellers and all bookkeeping departments of a stop-payment order in less than four hours. Where the stop-payment order indicated that the check had been given to a local payee and was apt to be presented immediately, one bank had a special procedure for notifying its tellers within one hour.

A bank has two ways of exercising its setoff right. It may make a bookkeeping entry or require customer to draw a check payable to bank against the account in the amount of the setoff. In either case the setoff is effective when the bank makes the entry or in the case of checks does one of the acts listed in 4–303(a)(1)-(5). Where the bank takes customer's checks, subsection 4–303(b) permits the bank to charge those checks in "any order." Presumably this language authorizes bank to pay setoff checks to itself ahead of those payable to others. The general rule is that a deposit not made specifically applicable to some other purpose is general in nature and may be setoff by the bank against indebtedness of the depositor. For example, in Bank One, Akron, N.A. v. National City Bank,[11] Bank One improperly encoded a check deposited by its customer for $5,000 rather than the written amount of $50,000. The drawee bank paid $5,000, and before it was notified of Bank One's error, exercised its setoff rights and closed the drawer's account. The court disagreed with Bank One's argument that $45,000 in the drawer's account was earmarked for payment of the underencoded check prior to the setoff.

Similarly, in Four Circle Co-op v. Kansas State Bank & Trust Co.,[12] the court held that in the absence of proof by payees of a

---

10. 153 Md.App. 54, 834 A.2d 993, 51 UCC2d 903 (Ct. Spec. App. 2003).

11. 66 Ohio App.3d 91, 583 N.E.2d 439, 16 UCC2d 725 (1990).

12. 771 F.Supp. 1144, 16 UCC2d 460 (D.Kan. 1991).

property interest in the drawer's funds, setoff is proper. Fleming Grain Company, Inc. was a middleman in the sale of grain that maintained an account and line of credit at Kansas State Bank and Trust. After Fleming had been experiencing financial difficulties for several months and was in default on several notes, KSBT was advised that Fleming's principals had lost over one million dollars of Fleming's assets by speculating in the commodity futures market. KSBT immediately seized all of the funds in the Fleming account and applied the money to Fleming's indebtedness to the bank. As a result of the setoff, checks which Fleming had written to the plaintiffs, who were grain farmers and suppliers, were returned unpaid. At the time of setoff, 84 percent of all deposits to Fleming's account at KSBT were proceeds of grain sales.

The plaintiffs argued that they had an ownership interest in Fleming's account that made setoff improper. Citing Iola State Bank v. Bolan[13] as dispositive, the plaintiffs claimed that KSBT's setoff was prohibited because KSBT had actual knowledge that the funds in the Fleming account were generated by grain sales and belonged to the plaintiffs. The court disagreed, reading *Bolan* to require ownership in the funds; it is not enough that the plaintiffs presented checks.

Although the grain farmers' case is sympathetic, it is not clear how the plaintiffs could have met their burden of proof to demonstrate a property interest in the drawer's funds. The Fleming account, into which sales proceeds were deposited, was a general account. And money—as the court recognized in a footnote—is fungible.

b. Section 4–303 Milestones

After establishing the effective time of the legal, the next and more difficult task is to determine whether the competing check has passed one of the milestones in the payment process listed in 4–303. If any of the enumerated events occurs before the legal arrives (or in an appropriate case before the bank has a reasonable opportunity to act upon the legal), the check wins. Some will find the following discussion not up to our usual high standards of clarity and wit; we suggest that those unfamiliar with the general mechanics of the check collection process grit their teeth and hold on.

The events listed in subsection 4–303(a)(1) (certification) and 4–303(a)(2) (cash payment) are everyday events. If the bank has paid the check in cash out of the teller's window, no one would suggest that a subsequent legal could have any effect upon that check. For example, Reston Hospital Center v. Querry[14] shows one situation in which a garnishment summons is ineffective because it

---

13. 235 Kan. 175, 679 P.2d 720, 38 UCC 755 (1984).

14. 1992 WL 396350, 18 UCC2d 831 (Va.Cir.Ct. 1992).

arrives too late. At 2:00 p.m. on 12 December 1991, Mr. Querry, who had a balance of $453.19, cashed a $375 check drawn on his account at Farmers & Merchants National Bank. After Mr. Querry received $375 in cash, a computer entry reduced his "available balance" by $375. However, because the transaction occurred after 2 p.m., the check still had not been debited on the actual balance of the account in the bookkeeping department when, at 12:12 p.m. on 13 December 1991, the garnishment summons was served on an officer of F & M. Showing an actual balance of $453.19, F & M debited this amount from the account and paid it to the court. When Mr. Querry's $375 check was finally processed, it was debited from the account creating an overdraft. The court found that F & M had finally paid the check on 12 December 1991 when it gave Mr. Querry $375 in cash, and that under 4–303, any legal process served upon a payor bank comes too late after the bank has finally paid the item in cash. As a result, the garnishment summons was only effective as to $79.18. Similarly, if the drawee bank has certified the check by signing it or stamping it, the bank has become liable for payment[15] and a subsequent legal directed at the customer's account cannot interfere with the bank's discharge of its obligation.

Two of the criteria listed in 4–303 focus on the payor bank's settlement for the check. Subsection 4–303(a)(3) covers settlement without the right to revoke and subsection 4–303(a)(4) covers cases in which the payor bank makes provisional settlement but fails to revoke it within a specified time. Subsection 4–104(a)(11)[16] defines the term "settle" and Comment 10 to that section explains that one may settle for an item in a variety of ways:

> Examples of the various types of settlement contemplated by the term include payments in cash; the efficient but somewhat complicated process of payment through the adjustment and offsetting of balances through clearing houses; debit or credit entries in accounts between banks; the forwarding of various types of remittance instruments, sometimes to cover a particular item but more frequently to cover an entire group of items received on a particular day.

Subsection 4–303(a)(3) provides that a milestone has been passed if the bank "settles for the item without having a right to revoke the settlement under statute, clearing-house rule, or agreement." When the bank has such right to revoke either under the

---

15. See §§ 3–411, 3–413, 3–415.

16. Section 4–104(a) reads as follows:

In this Article, unless the context otherwise requires * * *

(11) "Settle" means to pay in cash, by clearing-house settlement, in a charge or credit or by remittance, or otherwise as agreed. A settlement may be either provisional or final. * * *

Code, under a clearing-house rule or under an agreement with the presenter, the check does not win the priority race unless one of the events discussed in 4–303(a)(4) has preceded the legal. Section 4–303(a)(4) provides that the legal comes too late if "the bank becomes accountable for the amount of the item under Section 4–302 dealing with the payor bank's responsibility for late return of items."

To maintain at least a perilous grip on the real-life transactions that underlay the operations of 4–303(a)(3) and (4), consider the following hypothetical: On Tuesday morning depositary bank sends a check to payor bank through the Chicago Federal Reserve. Each maintains an account at the Chicago Federal Reserve, and the Reserve credits the depositary bank with the amount of the check and debits the account of the payor bank in a corresponding amount. Thus payor provisionally settles with the depositary bank. Since the payor has a right to revoke that settlement under 4–301[17] until its midnight deadline (that is, midnight of the next business day after it receives the item), and may have a right to revoke under a Federal Reserve rule[18] as well, payor will not have passed any of the milestones under 4–303(a)(3) because there is still a right to revoke; payor has not yet "become accountable" under 4–303(a)(4) until its midnight deadline passes, causing the provisional settlement at the Chicago Federal Reserve to become final. When payor's 4–301 right to revoke with the Federal Reserve runs out on Wednesday at midnight (and assuming no Federal Reserve rule gives it a longer time to revoke) the bank becomes accountable and thus passes the 4–303(a)(4) milestone. Thus any garnishment notice, etc., presented to the payor bank after midnight Wednesday will lose to the check for the check now fits 4–303(a)(4).

---

17. § 4–301(a) provides:

(a) If a payor bank settles for a demand item other than a documentary draft presented otherwise than for immediate payment over the counter before midnight of the banking day of receipt, the payor bank may revoke the settlement and recover the settlement if, before it has made final payment and before its midnight deadline, it

(1) returns the item; or

(2) sends written notice of dishonor or nonpayment if the item is unavailable for return.

Note that 4–301 is unavailable to a payor bank which is not also a depositary bank (§ 4–105) unless the payor settles for the item by midnight of the day of receipt.

§ 4–104(a)(10) defines midnight deadline as follows:

"Midnight deadline" with respect to a bank is midnight on its next banking day following the banking day on which it receives the relevant item or notice or from which the time for taking action commences to run, whichever is later.

However, a local clearing-house rule might extend the time for return of a check. See West Side Bank v. Marine Nat. Exch. Bank, 37 Wis.2d 661, 155 N.W.2d 587, 4 UCC 1003 (1968) (bank returned check after midnight deadline but within clearing house deadline and before completing process of posting).

18. See, e.g., Regulation J, "Return of Cash Items," 12 C.F.R. § 210.12 (1979).

We can play out a similar scenario with respect to a settlement made in a local clearing house. In such case presenter and payor will trade checks; each in effect credits the other with the amount of the checks so presented. Under the clearing-house rules the parties will only be settling provisionally, and each will have the right to return the checks one or two days later if it develops that they are NSF, subject to stop-payment orders or otherwise not properly payable. In such case the checks will not comply with any of the provisions under 4–303(a) until the time has passed when the payor could no longer return them and undo the credit (assuming the time limit of 4–303(a)(5) has not run).

If the payor has the right to revoke, either under the Code (for example, 4–301) or clearing-house rule or through an agreement with the presenter, the lawyer's job is to cross-examine his client to find the facts with respect to the check in question, examine all pertinent agreements and the Code, and thus determine the last time at which the bank could revoke the settlement it made. That time is the milestone under 4–303(a)(4) against which the lawyer must measure garnishments, notices, etc.

The latest criterion added by the 1990 Amendments to 4–303 is stated in 4–303(a)(5).[19] Under that section, a bank must recognize a legal that arrives at the proper place for action within the bank on the same day a check received for normal payment is received. The bank may have to recognize the legal even if it arrives on the second day. Section 4–303(a)(5) states that a legal comes too late if it comes after:

> * * * a cutoff hour no earlier than one hour after the opening of the next banking day after the banking day on which the

---

19. That subsection replaces former subsection 4–303(1)(d), which provided that a legal came too late if the bank had completed "the process of posting" or had otherwise "evidenced by examination of such indicated account and by action its decision to pay the item." The "process of posting" was defined by Section 4–109 as the usual procedure followed by a payor bank in determining to pay an item, with the requirement that one of several recording steps had been taken.

Whether a bank had completed the process of posting requirement was open to interpretation. In an earlier edition, we concluded that a bank had always completed the process of posting when it had examined the computer printout showing the status of the account, found it to be in order, examined the check and found it to be in order, and taken some other action such as stamping the check "paid." This interpretation was at odds with that of the Wisconsin Supreme Court in West Side Bank v. Marine Nat. Exchange Bank, 37 Wis.2d 661, 155 N.W.2d 587, 4 UCC 1003 (1968). There the court found that the process of posting was not completed until the opportunity for the bank's decision to correct or reverse any entry, whether correct or erroneous, had passed.

Fortunately, the drafters recognized, as stated in Comment 5 to Section 4–215, that "[d]ifficulties in determining when the events described in former Section 4–109 take place make the process-of-posting test unsuitable for a system of automated check collection or electronic presentment," and accordingly have eliminated this test as a criterion under 4–303.

bank received the check and no later than the close of that next banking day or, if no cutoff hour is fixed, the close of the next banking day after the banking day on which the bank received the check.

The quoted section allows a bank to set a cutoff hour in the morning of Day 2 and to disregard legals received after that hour as to checks presented on Day 1. The quoted section also imposes an implicit duty on the bank to follow legals that are received before the cutoff. This could mean, for example, that if a check arrived at 1:00 a.m. on Day 1, and a stop-payment order was given at 3:30 p.m. on Day 1, the bank would have to honor the stop-payment order, even though the computer had processed the check and had made an electronic decision to pay. It could also mean that a stop-payment order received during business hours on Day 2 could be disregarded (if there was a cutoff) or would have to be followed (if no cutoff). (We assume for the purpose of this example that the bank has neither accepted or certified, nor paid an item in cash, nor settled without having a right to revoke.)

In conclusion, the student and lawyer should not let 4–303 intimidate them. When the holder of a check, on the one hand, and a third party, on the other (for example, a trustee in bankruptcy, a garnishor or the like), make conflicting claims to funds in a bank account, the lawyer should turn to 4–303. If one bears in mind that the section is simply a priority statute and that one need only check out the facts, he will often find that 4–303 yields a certain and precise answer to priority conflict. Sometimes the lawyer will have to determine when notice to the bank became effective (because of the passage of a reasonable time), but aside from that difficulty he will usually be able to narrow the area of factual dispute to manageable proportions. Of course if the client is not the payor bank and if the bank's interests are in conflict with those of the client, the lawyer may have a mean task of digging the appropriate facts out of the bank employees on deposition, but that is a routine, if difficult, problem that lawyers must often face anyway.

Chapter 7

ELECTRONIC FUNDS TRANSFERS

Analysis

----

§ 7–1   Types of Electronic Payments and Applicable Law

Electronic funds transfers (EFTs) governed by Article 4A are merely one of a number of different electronic payments that exist in today's financial world. This section is a broad overview of the types of transactions that may arise in this area of commercial law practice.

In general, all types of EFTs share one common theme—they consist of an order by one person, typically to a bank or other financial institution, either to credit or charge the bank account of another person. The transaction is usually conducted between the banks by way of a system that is set up to handle such interbank transfers, although intrabank transfers that do not use such systems are also possible. Exactly which law, or, increasingly, which *laws* apply to a particular situation will depend on several factors: (1) whether the person making the payment is a consumer or a commercial party, (2) whether the payment is conducted as a traditional Article 4A funds transfer involving originating and beneficiary banks over Fedwire or another large wire transfer system, (3) whether the payment is classified as a "credit payment" or "debit payment,"[1] and (4) which one of the available funds

§ 7–1   types of transactions.

1. See *infra*, § 7–3(b) for a discussion of the distinction between these

transfer systems is used to complete the transaction.

Consumers have different rights in certain EFT transactions as a result of federal legislation enacted as Subchapter VI of the Federal Consumer Credit Protection Act (15 U.S.C. §§ 1693 et seq.), more commonly called the Electronic Fund Transfer Act (EFTA). Passed in 1978, this federal law deals with the legal problems arising out of consumer use of debit cards and similar consumer EFT transactions such as automated clearing house (ACH) transactions. A consumer is defined in section 903 (15 U.S.C. § 1693a) of the EFTA as a natural person. Among other things, the Act regulates liability when a consumer's negligence facilitates a thief's use of the consumer's card. It also establishes rules about the resolution of errors when there is a dispute between the consumer and the consumer's bank.

"Electronic funds transfer" defined in 15 U.S.C. § 1693a(6)[2] excludes virtually all of the transactions that are the subject matter of Article 4A, however. For example, the EFTA does not deal with a transfer if the transfer is "made by a financial institution on behalf of a consumer by means of a service that transfers funds held at either Federal Reserve Banks or other depositary institutions and which is not designed primarily to transfer funds on behalf of a consumer. * * * " Thus, almost every electronic transfer that involves both an originator's bank and a beneficiary's bank would be outside of the Federal Consumer Protection Act. The separation of the Federal Consumer Law from Article 4A is made explicit by

---

2. "[T]he term 'electronic funds transfer' means any transfer of funds, other than a transaction originated by check, draft, or similar paper instrument, which is initiated through an electronic terminal, telephonic instrument, or computer or magnetic tape so as to order, instruct, or authorize a financial institution to debit or credit an account. Such term includes, but is not limited to, point-of-sale transfers, automated teller machine transactions, direct deposits or withdrawals of funds, and transfers initiated by telephone. Such term does not include—

(A) any check guarantee or authorization service which does not directly result in a debit or credit to a consumer's account;

(B) any transfer of funds, other than those processed by automated clearinghouse, made by a financial institution on behalf of a consumer by means of a service that transfers funds held at either Federal Reserve banks or other depository institutions and which is not

designed primarily to transfer funds on behalf of a consumer;

(C) any transaction the primary purpose of which is the purchase or sale of securities or commodities through a broker-dealer registered with or regulated by the Securities and Exchange Commission;

(D) any automatic transfer from a savings account to a demand deposit account pursuant to an agreement between a consumer and a financial institution for the purpose of covering an overdraft or maintaining an agreed upon minimum balance in the consumer's demand deposit account; or

(E) any transfer of funds which is initiated by a telephone conversation between a consumer and an officer or employee of a financial institution which is not pursuant to a prearranged plan and under which periodic or recurring transfers are not contemplated;

as determined under regulations of the Board[.]"

section 4A–108: "This Article does not apply to a funds transfer any part of which is governed by the Electronic Fund Transfer Act of 1978 * * * as amended from time to time." If any "part" of the transaction, no matter how small, is covered by EFTA of 1978, no part is covered by 4A. Of course it is possible that a consumer transaction exempt from the EFTA may fall within Article 4A if all of the other conditions are met.[3]

Another important source of law related to consumer EFTs is Regulation E, drafted by the Board of Governors of the Federal Reserve System under authority granted to it under the EFTA. Regulation E appears in 12 CFR Part 205, and has its own scope provision (12 CFR § 205.3) that is quite similar to that in the EFTA. Regulation E is designed to cover consumer credit and debit card transactions, ATM transfers and payments via ACH networks, among others. As with the EFTA, traditional Article 4A funds transfers conducted "through Fedwire or through a similar wire transfer system that is used primarily ... between financial institutions or between businesses" are exempt from coverage under Regulation E.

If the EFT at issue is similar to the one discussed in § 7–2, *infra* (e.g., an instruction from one entity to its bank to make a wire transfer payment to another entity's bank account that is conducted through the Federal Reserve), the transaction initially falls squarely under Article 4A. This is the case regardless of whether the originator is a consumer or a commercial entity, due to the express language excluding these types of transactions from the EFTA and Regulation E.

Thus far, we have briefly covered the first two distinctions between different types of EFT transactions listed above—those dealing with consumers vs. commercial entities, and EFTs conducted over large wire transfer systems.

The third distinction, that between credit and debit transactions, arises from the words of 4A–103(a)(1)(ii), which exclude all debit transactions from the coverage of Article 4A. In general, a credit transaction is an order by an account holder for its bank to credit the account of a beneficiary. In a sense, the account holder "pushes" the money to the beneficiary. Conversely, a debit transaction is one where the account holder authorizes a beneficiary to issue an instruction to the account holder's bank to make a payment to the beneficiary. Here, the beneficiary "pulls" money

---

3. *See generally* Tomme Jeanne Fent, Note, Commercial Law: Electronic Funds Transfers: How New U.C.C. Article 4A May Affect Consumers, 43 Okla. L.Rev. 339 (1990); Fry, Basic Concepts in Article 4A: Scope and Definitions, 45 Bus.Law. 1401, 1405 (1990); Miller, The Emerged and Emerging New Uniform Commercial Code: An Overview of Article 4A, C664 ALI–ABA 1 (Sep. 12, 1991), pg. 9 of 19 from Westlaw.

from the account holder. Most originators of credit transactions are debtors and most originators of debit transactions are creditors.

Once outside of Article 4A's coverage, such debit transactions will be covered by the EFTA and Regulation E (for consumer debit EFTs) and the particular clearing house association rules described below (for commercial debit EFTs). For a further explanation of the distinction between credit and debit transactions, see § 7–3b, *infra.*

There are a number of funds transfer systems that different transactions might use: (1) Fedwire, which is operated by the Federal Reserve Banks and is usually used to transmit traditional Article 4A funds transfers between banks, (2) the Clearing House Interbank Payment System (CHIPS)[4] or the Society for Worldwide Interbank Financial Telecommunications (SWIFT), both private associations of financial institutions that deal with international EFTs, and (3) the Automated Clearing House (ACH) Network, another nationwide network of banks designed to handle batches of smaller payments.

In an EFT conducted through Fedwire, The Federal Reserve Board's Regulation J supercedes Article 4A pursuant to 12 CFR 210.25 et seq., titled "Funds Transfer Through Fedwire." EFTs covered under Regulation J will involve transfers through Fedwire among Federal Reserve Banks and between Federal Reserve Banks and private banks. Most transfers governed by 4A are accomplished by Fedwire, so Regulation J will apply to the majority of funds transfers. Note that 4A–107 makes an explicit bow to the Federal Reserve Regulations and acknowledges the Federal Reserve Bank's power to "supersede any inconsistent provision of this Article to the extent of the inconsistency." Even without 4A–107, the supremacy clause of the Constitution gives the federal government overriding power to govern these transactions.

Subpart (B) of Regulation J (§§ 210.25 through 210.32) was redrafted coincidentally with the drafting of Article 4A, and it now "incorporates [certain] provisions of Article 4A" as gap fillers. Since Regulation J is less comprehensive than Article 4A, the latter is implicated in nearly all funds transfer cases involving Fedwire. Because each body of law was drafted with an eye to the other, in its present form Regulation J rarely conflicts with 4A. Of course, there are exceptions.[5] Even though Regulation J specifically incor-

---

4. The CHIPS Rules are *available* at: http://www.chips.org/reference/docs_rules/docs_reference_rules.php.

5. It is worth highlighting the major differences between Regulation J and Article 4A: (1) the "reasonable time" in which a customer must give notification of a fraudulent or erroneous payment order to its bank under 4A–204(a) or 4A–304 is deemed to be within 30 days for payment orders conducted through Fedwire (12 CFR § 210.28(c)), (2) Article 4A permits postdated payment orders to be sent, but such payment orders are not permitted to be sent to Federal Reserve Banks (12 CFR § 210.30(c)), (3) the time that a payment is deemed to be received in a payment order involving

porates provisions of Article 4A, whenever a Federal Reserve Bank sends or receives an electronic funds transfer, the rights of the other bank may be governed by Regulation J, and one will have to examine 12 CFR 210.25 et seq.

Another source of federal law relating to Fedwire transactions is the operating circulars issued by the Federal Reserve Bank.[6] In addition to credit transfers within 4A, these circulars deal with debit transfers outside 4A.[7]

EFTs conducted over private networks and clearing houses outside of Fedwire, such as CHIPS and ACH, are subject to private agreements beyond the provisions of Article 4A; 4A–501(a) allows the parties to a funds transfer to vary most of Article 4A's terms by agreement. Therefore, when a particular transaction uses one of these private networks, the parties are likely to be bound by the more specific terms of agreements issued by these organized groups. The primary source of private law regarding ACH transactions are the Operating Rules of the National Automated Clearing House Association (NACHA). There are some private ACH networks that are composed of local banks which may apply their own local rules, but NACHA is the national "gold standard" in this area. Transfers conducted via ACH networks can be of either the credit or debit variety, so the rules of these networks will apply to any transaction conducted over the network in question.

A final bedrock source of law is contract. Aside from the rules of the funds transfer system among the system's members, there will be many other relevant contracts as, for example, those between an originator and the originator's bank, or between two banks involved in a funds transfer.

§ 7–2 Introduction to Article 4A "Funds Transfers" and Definitions

Assume that General Motors owes $10 million to a principal supplier, Goodyear. Goodyear has an account at National City Bank in Cleveland. General Motors has an account at JP Morgan Chase in Detroit. In order to pay Goodyear, General Motors instructs JP

Fedwire is usually once the receiving or beneficiary bank's Fed account is credited (12 CFR § 210.31), compared to a variety of later events under 4A–403 (when the sender is deemed to have paid the receiving bank) and 4A–405 (when the beneficiary bank is deemed to have paid the beneficiary), and (4) parties to a Fedwire transaction cannot agree to hold a Federal Reserve Bank liable for damages beyond those listed in Article 4A and a Federal Reserve Bank cannot agree to be liable for consequential damages under 4A–305(d) (12 CFR § 210.32(a)).

6. Before the late 1990s, individual Federal Reserve branches around the country issued their own operating circulars. These are now consolidated into one set of Operating Circulars issued by the Federal Reserve Bank and are available at: http://www.frbservices.org/OperatingCirculars/index.html.

7. See § 7–3(b), *infra*, for a discussion of electronic debit transfers.

Morgan Chase to transfer $10 million from General Motors' account to the Goodyear account at National City. JP Morgan Chase carries out the order by issuing an instruction to the Federal Reserve to cause National City to credit the account of Goodyear for $10 million. National City then credits the account of Goodyear, and General Motors' debt is paid.

The entire process by which General Motors thus pays Goodyear, beginning with the initial instruction General Motors gave to JP Morgan Chase and ending with the credit by National City to the account of Goodyear, is defined in Article 4A as a "funds transfer."[1] Article 4A applies only to "funds transfers." A "funds transfer" is the process by which a party, the "originator," and a "sender," instructs its bank, the "receiving bank," to transfer funds through the banking system, typically from its account to the account of another party, defined by 4A-103(a)(2) as the "beneficiary." For most purposes the funds transfer is completed when the beneficiary's bank "accepts" a payment order directing payment to the beneficiary.

The instructions given to pay Goodyear, first by General Motors to JP Morgan Chase, and then by JP Morgan Chase to the Federal Reserve in Chicago, and then by the Federal Reserve in Chicago to National City, are each defined by Article 4A as "payment orders."[2] A payment order is an instruction to a bank to pay, or cause another bank to pay, the beneficiary. The typical funds transfer is accomplished through a series of payment orders.

To understand how Article 4A operates, one must first understand the definitions. In a typical Article 4A funds transfer, the participants include the "originator" of the funds transfer (General Motors), the "originator's bank" (JP Morgan Chase), the "senders" of payment orders (General Motors, JP Morgan Chase and the Federal Reserve), the "receiving banks" of payment orders (JP Morgan Chase, the Federal Reserve, and National City Bank), the "intermediary banks" (Federal Reserve), the "funds transfer system" (Fedwire) and the "beneficiary" (Goodyear) of the funds transfer.

The "sender" of a payment order is "the person giving the instruction to the receiving bank."[3] The "receiving bank" is the "bank to which the sender's instruction is addressed."[4] In the hypothetical example, when General Motors gave an instruction to JP Morgan Chase to pay Goodyear, General Motors was the "sender" of the payment order, and JP Morgan Chase was the "receiving

§ 7-2

1. § 4A-104(a). Article 4A has been adopted in all fifty U.S. states, the district of Columbia, Puerto Rico and the U.S. Virgin Islands.

2. § 4A-103(a)(1).

3. § 4A-103(a)(5).

4. § 4A-103(a)(4).

bank" of the payment order. Likewise, when JP Morgan Chase gave an instruction to the Federal Reserve to cause National City Bank to pay Goodyear, JP Morgan Chase became the "sender" of the payment order, and the Federal Reserve the "receiving bank" of that payment order. Finally, when the Federal Reserve gave an instruction to National City Bank to pay Goodyear, the Federal Reserve in Chicago became the "sender" of the payment order, and National City the "receiving bank" of the Federal Reserve's payment order. In other words:

General Motors —> JP Morgan Chase —> Fed. Res. —> National City —> Goodyear
        #1   #2   #3

1) General Motors is the sender of payment order #1.

2) JP Morgan Chase is the receiving bank of payment order #1; JP Morgan Chase is sender of payment order #2.

3) Federal Reserve is the receiving bank of payment order #2; Federal Reserve is the sender of payment order #3.

4) National City is the receiving bank of payment order #3.

The "originator" of the funds transfer is also the "sender of the first payment order in a funds transfer."[5] In our hypothetical example, General Motors is the "originator."

The "originator's bank" is either the "receiving bank to which the payment order of the originator is issued if the originator is not a bank, or * * * the originator if the originator is a bank."[6] Thus, in our example, General Motors' bank, JP Morgan Chase would be the "originator's bank." If, however, General Motors were a bank, General Motors would be considered the originator of the funds transfer *and* the originator's bank.

The "beneficiary" of a funds transfer is the "person to be paid by the beneficiary's bank."[7] This is the person that the "originator" of the funds transfer has instructed to be paid. In our example, Goodyear is the beneficiary of the funds transfer.

The "beneficiary's bank" is the "bank identified in the payment order in which an account of the beneficiary is to be credited pursuant to the order or which otherwise is to make payment to the beneficiary if the order does not provide for payment to an account."[8] In our example, National City is the beneficiary's bank. In the vast majority of funds transfer transactions, the beneficiary bank will be different than the originator's bank. It is important to note, however, that intrabank transactions have occasionally been held to be Article 4A "funds transfers."[9]

5. § 4A–104(c).

6. § 4A–104(d).

7. § 4A–103(a)(2).

8. § 4A–103(a)(3).

9. *See* Fitts v. AmSouth Bank, 917 So.2d 818 (Ala. 2005) (holding that a transfer between two accounts at the

The "intermediary bank" is a "receiving bank other than the originator's bank or the beneficiary's bank."[10] In our example, the Federal Reserve is neither the originator's bank nor the beneficiary's bank. Thus, the Federal Reserve in Chicago is an intermediary bank.

Finally, a "funds transfer system" is a "wire transfer network, automated clearing house, or other communication system of a clearing house or other association of banks through which a payment order by a bank may be transmitted to the bank to which the order is addressed."[11] A payment order need not pass through a funds transfer system to be an Article 4A transfer. It need not even be a wire transfer. An Article 4A funds transfer may be by any means. If a funds transfer does pass through a funds transfer system, some of the rights and obligations of the sender and receiving bank of the payment order will be defined by the rules of the funds transfer system. In most cases, the rules of Article 4A will defer to the applicable rules of a funds transfer system.

§ 7–3   Scope of Article 4A

In Article 4A questions of scope provide their usual sport. Prior to the enactment of Article 4A, electronic funds transfers were governed by a mish mash of common law, contracts, Federal Reserve rules, Federal Reserve operating letters, rules of automated clearing houses, rules of organizations such as CHIPS, and Section VI of the Federal Consumer Credit Protection Act. Even after the adoption of Article 4A, as indicated in § 7–2, *supra*, electronic funds transactions are governed not only by Article 4A, but also by common law, contract, Federal Reserve rules, Federal Reserve operating letters, rules of automated clearing houses, CHIPS and Section VI of the Federal Consumer Credit Protection Act and are still a mish mash. Article 4A is comprehensive, but not completely so.

Generally, even in the transactions nominally governed by Article 4A, there will be a substantial intrusion of rules from contract, from organizations such as the National Automated Clearing House Association (NACHA) and CHIPS, and from the Federal Reserve. In addition to scope issues arising because the law governing a transaction comes partly from one source and partly from

same bank was a funds transfer governed by Article 4A); Brooks v. First Fed. Sav. and Loan, 726 So.2d 640 (Ala. 1998) (holding that a customer's intra-bank transfer between a trust account and his personal account was an Article 4A funds transfer); European Am. Bank v. Bank of Nova Scotia, 12 A.D.3d 189, 784 N.Y.S.2d 99; 12 A.D.3d 189, 784 N.Y.S.2d 99, 55 UCC2d 200 (N.Y. App. Div. 2004) (holding that account debits and credits on the books of several affiliated banks constituted Article 4A payment orders).

10. § 4A–104(b).

11. § 4A–105(a)(5).

another, there are less serious scope questions about transactions entirely beyond Article 4A's coverage. These are governed, for example, by the EFTA in certain consumer transactions, or by Articles 3 and 4 having to do with checks, or by automated clearing house rules having to do with debit transfers.

Thus scope questions come in two basic forms. First—as to transactions partly covered by Article 4A, but also partly covered by contract, by CHIPS' rules or by Fedwire rules, or other law—which part is covered by 4A and which by the other rules? Second—as to transactions completely beyond Article 4A—which are these and what are their characteristics?

As a brief illustration of how one transaction requires knowledge of a variety of different laws, consider 4A–403 (Payment By Sender to Receiving Bank). That section states that payment of the sender's obligation can occur "when the receiving bank receives final settlement of the obligation through a Federal Reserve Bank or through a funds transfer system." "Final settlement" occurs at the time specified by the rules of the Federal Reserve or by those of the funds transfer system. Thus to know when payment occurs under 4A–403, one must look not only at 4A but also at the rules of the funds transfer system used and at the Federal Reserve rules.

a. Transactions Covered, Transactions Not Covered

To get a grip on the transactions covered by Article 4A, return to our hypothetical case. Assume that General Motors, the debtor, owes Goodyear, the creditor, $10 million in payment for tires that have been delivered by Goodyear to General Motors for installation on new cars. General Motors decides to pay Goodyear by issuing a payment order to JP Morgan Chase (General Motors' bank) in Detroit. The order directs JP Morgan Chase to make a payment of $10 million to the Goodyear Tire & Rubber Company. The order will identify the bank in which Goodyear keeps its account and may instruct the payment to be made through that bank. Assume that Goodyear maintains the account in which these funds are to be paid at National City Bank in Cleveland. To fulfill its instructions, JP Morgan Chase instructs the Chicago Federal Reserve branch in Detroit to make payment to Goodyear of $10 million at National City Bank. The Federal Reserve either sends the order directly to National City, or more likely, to the Federal Reserve Bank in Cleveland. The Federal Reserve Bank in Cleveland then sends an instruction to National City to credit Goodyear's account for $10 million.

Assume for the purpose of discussion that General Motors gives its order in writing to JP Morgan Chase at 3:00 p.m. on Monday afternoon. At 3:15 p.m. JP Morgan Chase sends its order to the Federal Reserve in Detroit, who at 3:20 in turn sends its order to the Federal Reserve in Cleveland, who at 3:25 sends the order to pay Goodyear to National City Bank. Whether Goodyear finds out about the order to transfer immediately or at a later time will depend upon the agreement between Goodyear and its bank. Since the transfer is through the Federal Reserve system and by "Fedwire," payment of this order and its "settlement" under Federal Reserve rules will occur almost simultaneously with the transfer order through Fedwire. Moreover, the special event that has so much legal significance under Article 4A, "acceptance," will also happen concurrently with, or perhaps slightly before, payment. In our case "acceptance," "settlement," and "payment" are all likely to happen before 4:00 p.m. on Monday. (Trust us; we explain below.)

Article 4A aims squarely at transactions like that involving General Motors, its bank, the Federal Reserve, and Goodyear. Several things distinguish this paradigm transaction from those not covered by Article 4A. First, General Motors' instruction goes directly to *its* bank, not to Goodyear and then back to General Motors' bank as with a check. Second, the debtor, General Motors, not the creditor, Goodyear, initiates the transaction. Third, the transfer is for big dollars between business professionals; it is not for $24 at a point of sale terminal between a consumer and a merchant. Fourth, the transfer involves banks. Regrettably, the best known "wirer" of funds, Western Union, is outside of 4A because it is not a bank.

General Motors, the debtor, uses neither a check nor a credit card. But it is not the absence of paper that makes this transaction into a 4A transfer or the presence of paper that excludes checks and credit cards from Article 4A's coverage. In fact, General Motors' instruction to its own bank to make the payment could and often will be in writing, but that would not keep this from being a funds transfer covered by 4A. It is for other reasons that the credit card and the check transaction fail to fall under Article 4A. The drafters of 4A intended to exclude from 4A check transactions, credit card transactions, most consumer point of sale and ATM transactions, and transactions outside of the banking system (e.g., Western Union). Article 4A is law designed to deal with known, widely practiced types of transactions. It is not law designed to show the way to a new mode of business now unknown.

The principal provision defining the scope of Article 4A is the definition of "payment order" found in 4A–103(a)(1). To understand that, we must consider the other scope provisions. Section 4A–102 states: "this Article applies to funds transfers defined in 4A–104." Section 4A–104 in turn defines funds transfer as "the series of transactions, beginning with the originator's payment order, made for the purpose of making payment to the beneficiary of the order." The definition includes any payment order issued by the originator's bank or an intermediary bank intended to carry out the originator's payment instruction. Section 4A–104(a) repeats the words "order" or "payment order" six times.

So we arrive at 4A–103 through section 4A–102 (on "subject matter") and via section 4A–104 (on funds transfer). In truth the scope provision in Article 4A *is* the definition of payment order, set out in 4A–103(a)(1). It reads in full as follows:

(a) In this Article:

(1) "Payment order" means an instruction of a sender to a receiving bank, transmitted orally, electronically, or in writing, to pay, or to cause another bank to pay, a fixed or determinable amount of money to a beneficiary if:

(i) the instruction does not state a condition to payment to the beneficiary other than time of payment,

(ii) the receiving bank is to be reimbursed by debiting an account of, or otherwise receiving payment from, the sender, and

(iii) the instruction is transmitted by the sender directly to the receiving bank or to an agent, funds-transfer system, or communication system for transmittal to the receiving bank.

To understand the definition fully, one needs to know who a sender is, who a receiving bank is, who the beneficiary is, and some other things. For the time being we will ignore those difficulties, and simply look at 4A–103(a)(1) to see what Article 4A eliminates because the event is not a "payment order" and what it includes when the event is a "payment order." Note first how frequently the words "payment order" appear within a sampling of Article 4A's sections. Under 4A–201 security procedures are those for the purpose of verifying a "payment order." Section 4A–202 tells what are "authorized" and "verified" payment orders; section 4A–203 deals with the enforceability of certain verified payment orders; 4A–205 deals with erroneous payment orders. The list goes on endlessly and, in effect, the idea of payment order is the thread that runs throughout many of the sections of 4A and ties many of them together.

Returning to the definition of payment order, consider why certain common transactions are not payment orders. First, what about a check? Assume in our hypothetical case that General Motors had drawn a check on JP Morgan Chase payable to the order of Goodyear. Would that be a payment order? The fact that it is in writing and not electronic would not eliminate it because "payment order" includes instructions transmitted "orally, electronically, or in writing." The check would not be a payment order because it fails 4A–103(a)(1)(iii).[1] The "check" instruction would not have been transmitted by the "sender directly to the receiving bank;" it (the check) would have been transmitted by mail or by other physical delivery directly to the merchant payee, Goodyear, not to the receiving bank. Thus, it would not be a direct transmission "to the receiving bank."

If one views General Motors' bank, JP Morgan Chase, as the receiving bank, as one might under 4A–103(a)(4), the check otherwise would meet the definition of payment order because JP Morgan Chase would be reimbursed by debiting a General Motors' account under (a)(1)(ii). The instruction would not state conditions to payment, and it would constitute an instruction of the sender (General Motors) to the receiving bank (JP Morgan Chase) to pay a fixed or determined amount of money. Therefore the check transaction is not a 4A–103(a)(1) payment order only because the instruction is transmitted by the sender to the payee and not "directly to the receiving bank or to an agent, funds transfer system, or communication system for transmittal to the receiving bank."

It is, however, still possible for a check to be the *means of payment* in an Article 4A funds transfer, even though the check itself is outside the coverage of Article 4A. Consider the following example taken from the comments to 4A–104:

> Assume that Originator instructs Originator's Bank to pay $10,000 to the account of Beneficiary in Beneficiary's Bank. Since the amount of Originator's payment order is small, if Originator's Bank and Beneficiary's Bank do not have an account relationship, Originator's Bank may execute Originator's order by issuing a teller's check payable to Beneficiary's Bank for $10,000 *along with instructions* to credit Beneficiary's account in that amount. The instruction to Beneficiary's Bank to credit Beneficiary's account is a payment order. The check is the means by which Originator's Bank pays its obligation as sender of the payment order. The instruction of Originator's Bank to Beneficiary's Bank might be given in a letter accompanying the check or it may be written on the check itself. In either case, the instruction to Beneficiary's Bank is a payment

§ 7–3

1. Comment 5 to 4A–104 makes the point as follows: The principal effect of subparagraph (iii) of subsection (a) of Section 4A–103 is to exclude from Article 4A payments made by check or credit card. In those cases the instruction of the debtor to the bank on which the check is drawn or to which the credit card slip is to be presented is contained in the check or credit card slip signed by the debtor. The instruction is not transmitted by the debtor directly to the debtor's bank. Rather, the instruction is delivered or otherwise transmitted by the debtor to the creditor who then presents it to the bank either directly or through bank collection channels. These payments are governed by Articles 3 and 4 and federal law.

order but the check itself (which is an order to pay addressed to the drawee rather than to the Beneficiary's Bank) is an instrument under Article 3 and is not a payment order. The check can be both the means by which Originator's Bank pays its obligation under § 4A–402(b) to Beneficiary's Bank and the means by which the instruction to Beneficiary's Bank is transmitted.[2] (Italics supplied.)

Now, let us consider a credit card transaction. The credit card is not within the payment order definition for the same reason as the check. It is an instruction given initially in the form of the credit card and a signed slip to the merchant, Goodyear. It is not transmitted under (a)(1)(iii) "directly to the receiving bank."[3]

Consider another type of consumer transaction, one that seems to fit within Article 4A. Assume a consumer is standing at the checkout counter at Meijer Thrifty Acres using her debit card. By allowing her debit card to be run through the point of sale terminal, she sends an electronic message to her bank (the receiving bank) and instructs them to pay Meijer's bank (the beneficiary's bank). Unless one concludes that the use of Meijer's point of sale terminal does not constitute a direct transmission to the receiving bank, this transaction appears to meet all of the tests of a payment order under 4A–103(a)(1). To say the transaction is not "direct" seems a quibble, for the point of sale terminal is merely an electronic terminal that happens to be located at the checkout counter and is not otherwise under the control of the beneficiary. What then excludes our consumer transaction from Article 4A? Nothing in 4A–103 or 4A–104. Rather section 4A–108 states flatly that this Article "does not apply to a funds transfer any part of which is governed by the Electronic Fund Transfer Act of 1978," i.e., 15 U.S.C. 1693 et seq. "Part" of this consumer point of sale transaction *is* covered by the Federal Electronic Fund Transfer Act,

---

2. § 4A–104, Comment 5.

3. Under a strained reading of 4A–103(a)(1)(ii), credit card and check transactions might also flunk the test of (ii). Under (ii) the receiving bank is to be reimbursed by debiting an account of or otherwise receiving payment from the sender. If that contemplates only debit transactions and not transactions in which the sender has arranged for a line of credit at the receiving bank, then the credit card transaction could fail (a)(1)(ii) as well. If one concluded that the payee of a check or a merchant payee of a credit card slip was the sender in those transactions, then they would fail 4A 103(a)(1)(ii) as well as (iii). In those cases the receiving bank (the

drawee's bank) would not be reimbursed by debiting the account of the sender. That is to say, if the payee and not the drawer were deemed to be the "sender", these would become debit and not credit transfers, because the receiving bank would be debiting the account of the drawer not the account of the payee sender.

As we indicate in the body, we think this is a strained reading of check and credit card transactions and that in fact they fall outside of Article 4A not because of (a)(1)(ii), but because of (a)(1)(iii), ("the instruction is [not] transmitted by the sender directly to the receiving bank. * * * ")

and is therefore not covered by Article 4A. As we will see in the next subsection, such debit transactions are also excluded from Article 4A by 4A–103(a)(1)(ii) and comment 4 to 4A–103.

Another common type of transaction not covered by Article 4A consists of Western Union transfers. Because Western Union is not a bank, instructions to it to pay money to a third party do not constitute a payment order under 4A–103(a)(1), for every instruction that qualifies as a payment order must be to a "receiving bank."

PROBLEM

Customer made several payments to its creditor by credit card and one by check. Customer argues that all of the transfers were "erroneous" and would be recoverable under Section 4A–205 or other provisions of Article 4A. Are these "payment orders" covered by Article 4A and so subject to Customer's arguments?

1. Is a credit card payment a payment order?

   No. 4A–103(a)(1)(iii) excludes "instructions" that are not transmitted directly to the "receiving bank." Here the receiving bank is the issuer of Customer's card but the instruction goes first to the merchant and then to the merchant's bank and only then to the "receiving bank." (Note if the merchant's bank were considered the receiving bank, then subsection (ii) would not be satisfied.)

2. The check?

   No, for the same reason as above.

3. What about the same argument with respect to a debit card?

   Still no. Here the debit card's message to Customer's bank probably is a payment order, but because the transaction is likely governed at least in part by the EFTA of 1978, 4A–108 excludes the transaction from 4A.

---

b. *Debit Transfers*

1. Distinction between debit and credit transfers

Debit transfers are excluded from Article 4A under section 4A–103(a)(1)(ii). Comment 4 to section 4A–104 says:

> In a credit transfer the instruction to pay is given by the person making payment. In a debit transfer the instruction to pay is given by the person receiving payment. The purpose of subparagraph (ii) of subsection (a)(1) of Section 4A–103 is to

include credit transfers in Article 4A and to exclude debit transfers.

Now, assume General Motors gives a general authorization to its bank, JP Morgan Chase, and to its creditor, Goodyear, to allow Goodyear to draw in certain specified ways on General Motors' bank account at JP Morgan Chase. Pursuant thereto, Goodyear's instruction to pay could be electronic, but because of 4A–103(a)(1)(ii) it is not a payment order and is therefore not covered by Article 4A. It is a debit transfer because the instruction to pay is given by the party receiving payment. It is therefore not a "payment order" because the receiving bank is to be reimbursed by debiting the account of General Motors, not the account of Goodyear, the "sender." An order is a payment order only if the "receiving bank is to be reimbursed by debiting an account of, or otherwise receiving payment from, the sender * * *." Since Goodyear, not General Motors, is the "sender," the transaction is not a payment order. It has become a "debit" and not a "credit" transaction. It is unfortunate that the Code identifies one set of transactions as "credit" and another as "debit" transactions. These labels do little to distinguish transactions, at least in the dim bulb minds of your authors.

A common form of debit transaction is a pre-authorized draw of the kind that consumers arrange to pay recurring monthly obligations such as those to insurance companies and mortgagees. In those cases the transactions are initiated by the creditor (the insurance company or mortgagee) by sending a written or electronic request for reimbursement to the debtor's bank.

All of the foregoing is stated as follows in Comment 4 to 4A–104:

> In a debit transfer, a creditor, pursuant to authority from the debtor, is enabled to draw on the debtor's bank account by issuing an instruction to pay to the debtor's bank. If the debtor's bank pays, it will be reimbursed by the debtor rather than by the person giving the instruction. For example, the holder of an insurance policy may pay premiums by authorizing the insurance company to order the policyholder's bank to pay the insurance company. The order to pay may be in the form of a draft covered by Article 3, or it might be an instruction to pay that is not an instrument under that Article. The bank receives reimbursement by debiting the policyholder's account. Or, a subsidiary corporation may make payments to its parent by authorizing the parent to order the subsidiary's bank to pay the parent from the subsidiary's account. These transactions are not covered by Article 4A because subparagraph (2) is not satisfied. Article 4A is limited to transactions

in which the account to be debited by the receiving bank is that of the person in whose name the instruction is given.

Exactly why debit transfers are not covered by Article 4A is unclear. They remain in the limbo occupied by both debit and credit transfers before Article 4A. Most will be governed by automatic clearing house rules, by Federal Reserve operating letters, and, to a limited extent, by Article 4.

Are there any transactions that lie on the border between debit and credit that might or might not be included in 4A? We can think of at least one. Assume in our General Motors–Goodyear transaction that a clever lawyer wished to bring a transaction within Article 4A even though General Motors had authorized Goodyear to draw on its bank account—a classic debit transfer. Could that lawyer argue persuasively that for this limited purpose General Motors' authorization to draw had made Goodyear into its agent, so that the instruction was in fact made directly to the receiving bank (by General Motors through its agent Goodyear), and thus that General Motors, not Goodyear, was the "sender" and the receiving bank, JP Morgan Chase, was to be reimbursed under (a)(1)(ii) by debiting an account of the "sender"? We believe that in this hypothetical case, that argument should be rejected. Here the proof of agency is not strong enough; granting authorization to draw is not the same as making the drawer "my agent" for any draw. It is clear that the drafters intended to exclude debit transactions from 4A, yet if one is willing to stretch the idea of agency as much as this example would stretch it, there would be no boundary whatsoever between debit and credit transactions.

On the other hand, the drafters of Article 4A explicitly envisioned certain situations involving agency where what appear to be preauthorized debit transfers will be considered credit transfers covered by Article 4A. The comments to Article 4A give the following example:

> A authorizes Bank B to draw on A's account in Bank A to transfer funds to its account in Bank B. A also makes an agreement with Bank A under which Bank A is authorized to follow the instructions of Bank B, as agent of A. Bank B instructs Bank A to debit A's account in Bank A and cause a credit to occur in A's account in Bank B. Here, Bank A is reimbursed by A, and A is also considered the sender of the payment order. Bank B is merely the "agent" of the sender. This is a credit transfer covered under Article 4A.[4]

---

4. § 4A–104, Comment 4. See also Fry, Basic Concepts in Article 4A: Scope and Definitions, 45 Bus. Law. 1401, 1411, n.49 (1990); Leary and Pitcairn, The Uniform New Payments Code: The Essential Identity of "Pay" Orders and "Draw" Orders, 12 Hofstra L.Rev. 913 (1984).

In this example, the beneficiary's bank is the "agent." But if agency is extended to include every beneficiary of the funds transfer as an agent, nothing will be left of the debit/credit distinction. In the example given in the comments, we do not know why the beneficiary's bank is transferring funds to the beneficiary's account. The beneficiary's bank may be transferring funds in order to set off a debt owed to it. If the parties explicitly and clearly make the beneficiary an agent of the originator, we suppose that courts should recognize the relationship.

Suppose Ace Corporation pays its employees by having its Treasurer, as agent of the corporation, instruct Ace's Bank to debit Ace's account and transfer money into its employees' respective bank accounts. This is clearly a credit transfer covered by Article 4A. The transfer should not become a debit transfer just because Treasurer instructs Ace's Bank to transfer the appropriate funds into Treasurer's account.

Beware the debit transaction. We are confident only that we do not understand all of the ways in which a debit and a credit transaction can be confused. One thing is certain—the number of debit and credit transactions are growing at a significant rate and represent roughly equivalent numbers of transactions. In the 3rd Quarter of 2003, the Automated Clearing House Network processed 874 million debit transactions and just over 1 billion credit transactions. Each category represented roughly half of the total $5.4 trillion in total funds transferred during the quarter. When compared to the 3rd Quarter of 2002, the raw number of transfers represent increases of 21.9% for debit transactions and 7.0% for credit transactions.[5] If debit transactions continue to grow in number and size, perhaps it will be the work of the 21st century to include them in Article 4A.

Most commercial electronic debit transfers[6] occur through automated clearing houses (ACHs) and settlement occurs in the

5. ACH Network Volume Grows by 13% in 3rd Quarter 2003, NACHA—The Electronic Payments Association, October 7, 2003, *available at* http://www. nacha.org/news/Stats/stats3Q2003/index. htm.

6. Generally speaking, consumer electronic debit transfers are covered by, and purely commercial electronic debit transfers are excluded from, the Electronic Fund Transfers Act, Title IX of the Consumer Credit Protection Act. 15 U.S.C.A. § 1693 et seq. The Act defines "electronic fund transfer" in section 903(6) (15 U.S.C.A. § 1693a(6)):

(6) the term "electronic fund transfer" means any transfer of funds, other than a transaction originated by check, draft, or similar paper instrument, which is initiated through an electronic terminal, telephonic instrument, or computer or magnetic tape so as to order, instruct, or authorize a financial institution *to debit or credit an account.* Such term includes, but is not limited to, point-of-sale transfers, automated teller machine transactions, direct deposits or withdrawals of funds, and transfers initiated by telephone. (Emphasis added.)

While this section alone does not seem to limit the Act to transfers involving consumers, the Act limits its definition of "account" to "accounts established

Federal Reserve System. Electronic credit transfers also use ACH systems, so do not be fooled into thinking that an ACH transaction is automatically a debit transfer. Returning to our hypothetical case, the originator, Goodyear, would instruct its bank, National City, to transmit a "debit entry" (request for the payment of money), through an ACH operated by the local Federal Reserve Bank in Cleveland, to the receiving bank, JP Morgan Chase. The ACH in Cleveland would instruct the Federal Reserve Bank system to credit $10 million to National City's account, and to debit $10 million from JP Morgan Chase's account.

The rules governing these transactions originate from three sources: (1) the "operating circulars" of the Federal Reserve Bank that govern the clearing and settlement of ACH credit and debit items by the individual Federal Reserve Bank branches and that incorporate ACH rules; (2) the Operating Rules of the National Automated Clearing House Association (NACHA), a private organization and of local ACHs, both incorporated into the operating circulars; and (3) Article 4 of the Uniform Commercial Code that is incorporated as a fallback in certain cases by section 14.1.26 of the Operating Rules of NACHA. Only the operating circulars could be characterized as federal law; they are issued pursuant to 12 U.S.C. § 248–1 (approved Sept. 21, 1994) and other sections of the Federal Reserve Act.

Of all these potential sources, the real "law" governing debit transfers is in a document containing fourteen articles and 39 pages without appendices entitled *Operating Rules of The National Automated Clearing House Association* (hereinafter "NACHA Operating

---

primarily for personal, family, or household purposes * * *."

Consumer debit transfers are covered by section 907 (15 U.S.C.A. 1693e), Preauthorized transfers. Preauthorized transfers from a consumer's account for a determined amount are governed by section 907(a), which reads in full as follows:

(a) A preauthorized electronic fund transfer from a consumer's account may be authorized by the consumer only in writing, and a copy of such authorization shall be provided to the consumer when made. A consumer may stop payment of a preauthorized electronic fund transfer by notifying the financial institution orally or in writing at any time up to three business days preceding the scheduled date of such transfer. The financial institution may require written confirmation to be provided to it within fourteen days of an oral notification if, when the oral notification is made, the consumer is advised of such requirement and the address to which such confirmation should be sent.

Section 907(b) covers transfers from a consumer's account which may vary in amount:

(b) In the case of preauthorized transfers from a consumer's account to the same person which may vary in amount, the financial institution or designated payee shall, prior to each transfer, provide reasonable advance notice to the consumer, in accordance with regulations of the Board, of the amount to be transferred and the scheduled date of the transfer.

In light of these restrictions, such transfers seem to hover at the outer boundaries of the definition of "debit transfers."

Rules").[7] These rules derive their authority from two sources. First, by contract, they bind the banks and others who are members of NACHA and others who deal through those members. The Association Operating Rules comprise a multiparty contract and derive most of their necessary legal force from that alone. Second, the Federal Reserve Operating Circulars in effect elevate the rules of NACHA, and in some cases, the rules of regional or local associations, to the level of federal law. For example, Operating Circular No. 4 of the Federal Reserve Bank provides as follows:

> 1.1 This operating circular ... govern[s] the clearing and settlement of commercial automated clearing house (ACH) credit and debit items ... by the Federal Reserve Banks, sending banks, and receiving banks.

* * *

> 1.4 The following rules and agreements, as amended from time to time, are incorporated in this Circular as applicable ACH rules with respect to items, regardless of whether the sending bank or receiving bank is a member of an ACH association:
>
> > (a) The Operating Rules of the National Automated Clearing House Association (NACHA), unless other rules apply under subparagraph(b).
>
> > (b) The Operating Rules of regional ACH Associations that are members of NACHA, to the extent such rules (i) bind both the sending bank and the receiving bank or (ii) in the case of a transaction involving a nonmember(s) of an ACH association, generally apply to transactions within the region where the sending bank and receiving bank are located.[8]

The NACHA Operating Rules then bring Article 4 into the game:

> For all entries except RCK entries [re-presented checks that were initially returned NSF], each debit entry shall be deemed an "item" within the meaning of Revised Article 4 of the Uniform Commercial Code (1990 Official Text) and that Article shall apply to such entries except where the application is inconsistent with these rules, in which case these rules shall control.[9]

---

7. Printed by the National Automated Clearing House Association, whose address is 13665 Dulles Technology Drive, Suite 300, Herndon, VA 20171, Phone (703)561–1100, www.nacha.org.

8. Operating Circular No. 4, "Automated Clearing House Items" effective Aug. 1, 2004, at 3. *Available at:* http:// www.frbservices.org/OperatingCirculars/ pdf/Oc4.pdf.

9. NACHA Operating Rules, § 14.1.26 (2006).

These rules and regulations thus establish a pecking order of supremacy: the operating circulars can peck the NACHA Operating Rules, which can peck Article 4 of the Uniform Commercial Code, which can peck no one.

Some commercial electronic debit transactions may fall under only part of these rules or under none of them. If settlement occurs outside of the Federal Reserve System and in an ACH not operated by the Federal Reserve, the participating banks may be subject only to the NACHA Operating Rules. Even more extreme, the participating banks may have agreed on a funds transfer which excludes NACHA entirely. What if National City maintained an account at JP Morgan Chase and sent messages directly to it? Presumably most local ACH association rules will conform to the NACHA Operating Rules, but that will not always be true. Where not, and where both participants to a debit transfer are members of the local association, it is possible that local rules, in some ways different from the national rules, will govern. Thus, there is at least a theoretical possibility that the same transaction between two banks in New York City will be subject to different rules than would be the case in the same transaction between two banks in Des Moines. Therefore, it is imperative that a competent attorney dealing with a debit transaction case determine exactly which particular agreements govern the transaction between their client and the other bank.

2.   The NACHA Operating Rules as interpreted by the courts

The NACHA Operating Rules are the dominant source of debit transaction law because most debit transfers are conducted through the ACH network or via Federal Reserve Banks where Operating Circulars will direct users to the NACHA Operating Rules. Therefore, a further explanation of some specific NACHA rules is necessary for dealing with these types of cases.

A slight twist upon our running hypothetical involving General Motors and Goodyear will serve to illustrate the key terms in an EFT transaction implicating the NACHA Operating Rules. Assume once again that General Motors owes $10 million to Goodyear and that payments will be made in a debit transaction. Using NACHA Operating Rules definitions, Goodyear is the "Originator" of the "debit entry" (a request for the payment of funds), National City is the "Originating Depositary Financial Institution" (ODFI), JP Morgan Chase is the "Receiving Depositary Financial Institution" (RDFI), and General Motors is the "Receiver." Goodyear initiates the debit transfer by instructing its bank, National City, to transmit a "debit entry" to General Motors's bank, JP Morgan Chase. National City complies by relaying the necessary information—the identity of the receiving bank, the creditor's account number, and the amount—to National City's automated clearing house, located at (and probably operated by) the Federal Reserve Bank in Cleveland. National City is almost certain to transmit this information electronically, but can still do so by magnetic tape.[10] The ACH Operator in Cleveland will total the debit and credit activity received from and transmitted to other ACHs and participating "DFIs" (Depository Financial Institutions) during each banking day.[11] The ACH Operator will then calculate the settlement amounts and communicate the information to the local Federal Reserve Bank in Cleveland. Settlement occurs through the Federal Reserve System by debiting and crediting the accounts of JP Morgan Chase and National City with the Federal Reserve Banks.[12] On the settlement date, the Federal Reserve Bank in Cleveland will credit $10 million to National City's account, and the Federal Reserve Bank in Chicago will debit $10 million from JP Morgan Chase's account.[13] Unless JP Morgan Chase "returns" (rejects) the debit entry, JP Morgan Chase will debit $10 million from General Motors's account with JP Morgan Chase.[14]

Despite the significant number of transactions that occur daily over ACH networks or through Federal Reserve Banks where the NACHA Operating Rules are implicated, a minimal number of reported cases exist dealing with specific terms of the Rules. Those that are out there, however, deal with items of great interest to banks and other parties involved.

Consider, for example, the question whether the Originator in an ACH debit transaction can gain the benefit of the NACHA Operating Rules, which provide a shorter return notification dead-

---

10. Since late 1997, the NACHA Board of Directors has "strongly urge[d] Originators and * * * ODFI's" to "interface with each other via a secured telecommunications link for all ACH related activity." Non-electronic means of transmission are further discouraged because the use of magnetic tape is "subject to approval by an ACH Operator." See Appendix One to the NACHA Operating Rules, Section 1.2.

11. NACHA Operating Rules, §§ 9.1(5), 9.1(6).

12. NACHA Operating Rules, § 7.2.

13. A Federal Reserve Bank may refuse to grant the credit to National City until the Bank receives final and irrevocable payment from JP Morgan Chase. Paragraph 11.1 of Operating Circular No. 4 reads in full as follows:

11.1 DEBIT ITEMS The Reserve Bank may refuse to permit the use of credit given for a debit item if it judges

that there may not be sufficient funds in the sending bank's settlement account to cover chargeback or return of the item. If a Reserve Bank does not receive actually and finally collected funds in settlement of a debit item at or before 8:30 a.m. ET on the banking day following the settlement date, the Reserve Banks that hold the sending and receiving banks' settlement accounts may reverse the debit and credit previously made in settlement of the item by 8:30 a.m. ET, and will notify the sending and receiving banks (or a correspondent bank whose account a bank uses for settlement) as soon as possible.

14. NACHA Operating Rules § 4.4.2 reads in full: *Time of Debiting of Entries*—An RDFI must not debit the amount of any entry to a Receiver's account prior to the Settlement Date of the entry, even if the effective entry date of the entry is different from the Settlement Date of the entry.

line than the "midnight deadline" for check returns under Article 4.[15] Sinclair Oil Corp. v. Sylvan State Bank[16] is important to note for two reasons. First, the case demonstrates the shorter time period that an RDFI has to return an ACH entry compared to a standard check under Article 4. Secondly, *Sinclair* illustrates that Originators can have a difficult time bringing suit to enforce the Rules, unless they are actually party to an agreement that incorporates the Rules, because the Rules themselves do not expressly grant a benefit to Originators.

In *Sinclair*, Plaintiff Sinclair Oil originated four debits via ACH against the account of one of its customers, Home Oil, at Defendant Sylvan State Bank where Home Oil maintained an account. Sylvan returned all of the entries because Home Oil's account was NSF. Sinclair claimed that Sylvan only met the Article 4 "midnight deadline," with its ACH returns and not the earlier deadline imposed by an applicable Federal Reserve Operating Letter, which pointed to the NACHA Operating Rules, including Rule § 6.1.2. On a certified question from the U.S. District Court, the Supreme Court of Kansas determined that Article 4 did not apply to ACH transactions, so any available remedy for Sinclair would have to arise via the Operating Letter and NACHA Operating Rules.

Sylvan argued that bank customers are not automatically party to those agreements and cannot take advantage of the associated benefits. The court found no language in the NACHA Operating Rules indicating that they were adopted for the benefit of bank customers, and also denied Sinclair's third party beneficiary claim. The court did hold that bank customers may become bound by the Rules, but that this requires the customer to actually agree to become so bound.

Next, recall the discussion from § 7–3(b)(i), *supra*, that NACHA Operating Rule § 14.1.26 specifically states that the provisions of Article 4 are incorporated within the Rules, so long as Article 4 is not inconsistent. Security First Network Bank v. C.A.P.S., Inc.[17] provides a good discussion of this provision in light of a Receiver's claim for contract warranty damages under NACHA Operating Rule § 2.2.1.1 and statutory warranty damages under the Illinois equivalents of 4–207 and 4–208. The facts of this case

---

15. *See* NACHA Operating Rule § 6.1.2 (requiring that the ODFI actually receive notification of the returned entry "no later than the opening of business on the second banking day following the settlement date of the original entry.").

16. 894 F.Supp. 1470 (D. Kan. 1995), but note that the numbering of this particular NACHA Operating Rule was § 5.1.2 at the time of the *Sinclair* court's decision.

17. *Id*. Again, note that the NACHA Operating Rules have been renumbered since this case arose, so the court's discussion of § 13.1.20 corresponds to today's § 14.1.26.

are complicated and not necessary to understand the court's discussion regarding the applicability of Article 4.

The Receiver in the ACH transaction at issue in *Security First* had an agreement with its bank (the RDFI) that implicated the NACHA Operating Rules, so the court held that the Receiver's warranty claims under the Rules were valid, getting beyond the hurdle that the plaintiff in *Sinclair* had to surmount. As for the Receiver's Article 4 claims under 4–207 and 4–208's transfer and presentment warranties, the court held that these warranties could apply as a result of Rule § 14.1.26. While not inconsistent with the warranties provided by the NACHA Operating Rules, the court held that to allow Article 4 warranties in this case would be unnecessarily duplicative because the Receiver had a valid NACHA warranty claim. Therefore, the court denied the Receiver's Article 4 claims.

Section 7.3, involving settlement and returned entries, is an important NACHA rule. As noted in the *Sinclair* case above, Rule § 6.1.2 requires that notification of a returned entry be given to the ODFI by the opening of business on the second banking day following settlement. Section 7.3 significantly reduces a bank's potential liability in certain settlement cases where the bank may have other common law rights with regards to the entry.

In the bankruptcy case In re Ocean Petroleum, Inc.,[18] the court interpreted this provision to allow the RDFI's common law defense of mistake in allowing it to return an ACH entry beyond the time listed in Rule § 6.1.2. Fleet Bank was the RDFI in a number of transactions with the same ODFI, an institution called BACC. Fleet returned an ACH entry due to insufficient funds, but an internal computer glitch at Fleet resulted in this return not getting communicated to BACC even though the return was credited to the debtor's account. As a result, that transfer became final under Rule § 6.1.2 and Fleet's clearing house account was charged for the amount of the entry. BACC then proceeded to initiate two ACH entries after the debtor filed for bankruptcy, which Fleet paid thinking that there were sufficient funds in the account. The court agreed with Fleet's argument that Rule § 7.3 allowed a common law claim of mistaken payment under these circumstances.

3. Electronic check conversion, a new form of debit transfer

A relatively recent development in the debit transaction arena that has yet to spawn litigation is the process of creditors' using a customer's paper check to originate an ACH debit that is processed electronically. The procedure is called electronic check conversion, and is being used by retailers at the point of sale, as well as by

---

18. 252 B.R. 25 (Bankr. E.D. N.Y. 2000). The NACHA Operating Rules have been amended since this case, such that current Rule § 7.3 corresponds to old Rule § 6.3 as discussed by the court.

many large creditors when customers send in paper checks as payment. Electronic check conversion has grown significantly in recent years, and the trend is expected to continue due to the benefits to creditors from using this method of payment.[19] These benefits include reduced float times, quicker notification of returned items and fewer NSF returns (because most banks post electronic debits before they post regular check transactions).[20]

Electronic check conversion is used two different ways: (1) by a retail cashier at the cash register (known as a "Point of Purchase Entry" (POP) in the unique vernacular of the NACHA Operating Rules, or "point of sale ECC" in Professor Budnitz's article), or (2) by a creditor processing check payments sent in by customers (an "Account Receivable Conversion Entry" (ARC) under NACHA's terminology, or "lockbox ECC").[21] A POP Entry involves the customer handing a paper check to the cashier, who then scans the check for its MICR information on the account number, bank routing number and check number. The cashier also keys in the amount of the sale to complete the information necessary for an ACH debit to be processed.[22] Effective September 15, 2006, the NACHA Operating Rules require that the cashier void the check and return it to the customer at the point of sale.[23] Lastly, the customer must be given a receipt with specific information about the transaction.[24]

ARC Entries, on the other hand, occur much more seamlessly from the customer's perspective. In those transactions the customer sends his payment to the creditor by U.S. Mail or drops the payment off at a dropbox. Instead of processing the payment through the regular check processing system, however, the creditor uses the check as authorization to originate an ACH debit against the customer's account for the amount of the payment. As with POP Entries, the creditor must initially scan the customer's account number, bank routing number and check number from the

---

19. NACHA reported that total electronic check conversion transactions in the 3rd Quarter of 2003 increased to over 82 million transactions. This represented a 141% jump over the same quarter of 2002. See ACH Network Volume Grows by 13% in 3rd Quarter 2003, NACHA—The Electronic Payments Association, October 7, 2003, *available at* http://www.nacha.org/news/Stats/stats3 Q2003/index.htm.

20. Barkley Clark & Barbara Clark, 14 Clarks' Bank Deposits and Payments Monthly, November 2005 at 6.

21. Mark E. Budnitz, *Payment Systems Update 2005: Substitute Checks,* *Remotely–Created Items, Payroll Cards and Other New–Fangled Products*, 59 Consumer Finance Law Quarterly Report 3 at 4 (2005); Barkley Clark & Barbara Clark, 14 Clarks' Bank Deposits and Payments Monthly, October 2005 at 3–4.

22. It is important to note that the Rules only allow the cashier to key in the payment amount—the account number, bank routing number and check number must be scanned electronically. See NACHA Operating Rules § 3.8.2.

23. *Id.,* § 3.8.1.

24. *Id.,* § 3.8.3.

MICR line on the check.[25] With ARC Entries, however, the creditor is allowed to manually key in numbers to correct errors from the initial information scan.

An ODFI who processes payments via ARC Entries also makes several specific warranties that do not arise in POP Entry cases. These include warranting the information transferred from the check itself, affirming that the ODFI will keep a copy of the source document for two years, and destroying the actual source document within fourteen days of the Settlement Date of the entry.[26]

Despite the fact that these transactions begin with a paper check, the check collection provisions contained in Articles 3 and 4 do not apply here. Since the payments are actually processed electronically, the applicable sources of law are the Electronic Funds Transfer Act and Regulation E (for consumer transactions), and the NACHA Operating Rules or other clearinghouse rules (since most electronic check conversion transactions are conducted via ACH networks).

A modification to the NACHA Rules that went into effect on September 15, 2006 enlarged the scope of electronic check conversion to cover non-consumer transactions for the first time. Still, not all commercial transactions will be covered because the modification only applies to businesses that use the smaller six-inch check size typically used by individuals. Most businesses use the larger nine-inch check size, and any business that does not want to be subject to its paper checks being converted into an electronic check conversion transaction can simply switch to the larger check size.

In any ARC Entry, the customer does not receive his cancelled check back or see a copy of the check on the monthly statement. Still, the customer must receive some type of notice under both Regulation E and the NACHA Operating Rules for all types of electronic check conversions, including ARC Entries. Currently, Regulation E requires that customers authorize each individual payment that will be conducted by electronic check conversion.[27] Still, this is not as onerous as it may seem at first glance, since a customer "authorizes a one-time electronic funds transfer ... when the consumer receives notice and goes forward with the transaction." Regulation E does not actually require that the consumer sign an authorization form before each use of electronic check conversion.

In point of sale transactions, merchants must give notice by posting a sign at the point of sale and provide written notification to the consumer at the time of each transaction. Although the Regulation E provision is not completely clear, it appears that ARC

---

25. *Id.*, § 2.9.2.
26. *Id.*, §§ 2.9.3–2.9.3.4.

27. 12 CFR § 205.3(b)(2).

Entry transactions also only require one-time notice.[28] Most creditors seeking to use ARC Entry presumably place this notice in the customer's monthly bill along with other disclosures.

The NACHA Operating Rules contain similar notice requirements, except that POP Entries require a signed written authorization by the customer that clearly and conspicuously states the terms of the POP Entry.[29] For ARC Entries, the creditor must give clear and conspicuous notice that sending in a check will authorize an ACH debit "before the receipt of each source document,"[30] but does not have to obtain a signed authorization.[31] The fact that the debtor sends in the check after receiving notice is sufficient here. We would expect creditors seeking to use ARC Entries simply to include the required notice in the fine print contained with each month's billing statement.

As noted above, one of the factors of electronic check conversion that might make it less attractive to payors is the reduced ability to issue a stop payment order, due to the greater speed of the transaction relative to one conducted with a paper check. The NACHA Operating Rules are actually more generous to receivers in this area than Regulation E, as Regulation E does not contain any provisions covering a consumer's ability to issue a stop payment. Under NACHA Operating Rules §§ 8.4 and 8.5, a receiver may order a stop payment on an electronic check conversion entry "at such time and in such manner as to allow the RDFI a reasonable opportunity to act upon the stop payment order prior to acting on the debit entry." Exactly how much time is "reasonable?" We are not sure, but given the speed with which electronic debit transactions are conducted, we are certain that the receiver would have to act quickly.

One final area of distinction between electronic check conversion cases and paper checks is a customer's duty to notify their bank regarding any unauthorized or fraudulent debits against the account. Recall that in paper check cases falling under 4–406, a customer has a reasonable time to notify its bank, not to exceed thirty days after a statement becomes available. For electronic check conversions that are subject to Regulation E, the customer is not liable for any fraudulent transactions so long as it notifies the bank "within 60 days of the . . . transmittal of the statement."[32] The period under the NACHA Operating Rules is potentially even

---

28. *Id.*
29. NACHA Operating Rules § 2.1.2.
30. *Id.*, § 2.1.4.
31. "The authorization for ARC Entries consists of a notice meeting the

requirements of subsection 2.1.4." *Id.*, § 2.1.2.

32. 12 CFR § 205.6(b)(3).

shorter than Article 4, however, as the receiver only has fifteen calendar days to deliver a written statement to the RDFI.[33]

At the present time, the application of the NACHA Operating Rules in electronic check conversion transactions is not a significant threat to consumers, as the NACHA Operating Rules contain some provisions that are actually more favorable to consumers than those in the UCC and Regulation E.[34] These include the ability to opt out of electronic check conversion, required destruction of the check in ARC Entry cases, and specific rights to issue stop payments and receive refunds.[35] That said, the rules of NACHA and other local clearinghouses present a potential risk to consumer welfare due to the fact that they can be changed at the discretion of the particular association or clearinghouse at any time without any input from the political process.[36] If the use of electronic check conversion continues to expand, this is an area where we expect to see additional statutory attention in future years. As with the general scope questions surrounding funds transfer transactions that we saw earlier in this section, electronic check conversions are governed by a complex web of varying sources of law. Especially given the relatively short time that electronic check conversions have been in existence, one advising clients in these areas must pay close attention to which law applies to the particular transaction at issue.

c. Scope Leftovers

In summary, the scope question comes in two forms under Article 4A. In the first, Article 4A has nothing whatever to do with the transaction that is covered completely by other law. Consumer point of sale transactions are illustrative. Even the usual excluded debit transfer is easy to distinguish, for there the instruction to pay is given by the person receiving payment.

The difficult scope questions arise in the second class of cases when a single transaction clearly governed by Article 4A gets its tail caught in CHIPS, Fedwire, or the Federal Reserve Regulations. Consider just one example. Section 4A–403(a) states that payment of the sender's obligation under 4A–402 occurs, among other things, if the receiving bank "receives final settlement of the obligation through a Federal Reserve Bank or through a funds transfer system." Presumably the rule so stated requires one to understand when final settlement has occurred not according to Article 4A, but according to the rules of the Federal Reserve Bank

---

33. NACHA Operating Rules §§ 8.6.2, 8.6.4.

34. See Mark E. Budnitz, *Consumer Payment Products and Systems: the Need for Uniformity and the Risk of Political Defeat,* 24 Annual Review of Banking and Financial Law 247, 263 (2005).

35. *Id.,* at n.72.

36. *Id.* at 264.

or the funds transfer system. Thus, that section leads one beyond 4A into the non–4A law governing the transfer. Here we see trouble and opportunity for error.

Lastly, recall the definition of "Payment Order" contained in 4A–103(a)(1) and the requirements that section imposes for a particular transaction to fall under Article 4A. A payment order must instruct the payment of a "fixed or determinable amount of money to a beneficiary," 4A–103(a)(1). "Fixed or determinable" is not defined in Article 4A, but it probably has the same meaning as similar terms in negotiable instruments law. Thus, any order that required payment of a specific amount of money plus interest for a specified amount of time at a rate to be computed by a formula would constitute a fixed or determinable amount of money.[37] Cases instructing such transfers are certain to be rare; most orders will state fixed amounts.

A payment order must not "state a condition to payment of the beneficiary other than time of payment," section 4A–103(a)(1)(i). Few transactions will include such conditions.[38] The exception for "time of payment" means that a payment order need not order immediate payment, though most do. For example, a payment order may specify that a certain amount of money must be paid on a certain date to a particular beneficiary. To understand why the drafters did not wish to involve banks in inquiries into whether other conditions have occurred, let us return to the transactions that are contemplated by Article 4A:

> The function of banks in a funds transfer under Article 4A is comparable to the role of banks in the collection and payment of checks in that it is essentially mechanical in nature. The low price and high speed that characterize funds transfers reflect this fact. Conditions to payment * * * other than time of payment impose responsibilities on * * * [the] bank that go beyond those in Article 4A funds transfers.[39]

§ 7–4 Preemption of Common Law Claims

The unifying themes behind the drafting of Article 4A are illustrated in the comment to 4A–102, and include a desire by the drafters to create unique rules for funds transfers in an attempt to

---

37. §§ 3–104(a), 3–112(b).

38. For an example with unique facts, see Trustmark Insurance Co. v. Bank One, Arizona, N.A., 202 Ariz. 535, 48 P.3d 485 (App. 2002) Defendant Bank One agreed to transfer funds out of Trustmark's account once the balance exceeded $110,000. The transfers stopped after an internal restructuring of Bank One's wire department opera-

tions, and the account reached a value of over $19 million by the time the parties discovered the discrepancy. The court dismissed Trustmark's Article 4A claim because these were conditional instructions, so the letter agreement was not an Article 4A payment order under 4A–103(a)(1)(ii).

39. § 4A–104, Comment 3.

create a high degree of specificity when determining the responsibilities and resulting liabilities of the parties involved in these transactions.[1] This is especially important in allowing funds transfer participants accurately to predict the risk of conducting these large dollar value transactions before they happen.

To that end, the drafters provided that Article 4A is designed to be the "exclusive means of determining the rights, duties and liabilities of the affected parties in any situation *covered by particular provisions of the Article*" (emphasis added). Article 4A preempts any common law claim that would "create rights, duties and liabilities *inconsistent with those stated in* [Article 4]" (emphasis added). One item from these excerpts bears repeating—this is not a blanket preemption of all common law claims once a transaction implicates Article 4A. Only issues covered by the provisions of Article 4A or claims that would create inconsistent rights, duties or liabilities are preempted.

The drafters appear to have succeeded in the effort toward standardization in funds transfer law, for few cases have arisen under Article 4A over the past decade despite the massive number of funds transfers that are executed on a daily basis. The preemption question, however, has received considerable attention from the courts. We believe the drafters were too optimistic in thinking that it would be easy to determine which claims were "consistent" with the specific provisions of Article 4A and which not.

The claims that appear to have the greatest chance of being preempted are negligence and conversion. This result is in accord

§ 7–4

1. [A]ttempts to define rights and obligations in funds transfers by general principles, or by analogy to rights and obligations in negotiable instrument law or the law of check collection have been unsatisfactory.

In the drafting of Article 4A, a deliberate decision was made to write on a clean slate and to treat a funds transfer as a unique method of payment to be governed by unique rules that address the particular issues raised by this method of payment. A deliberate decision was also made to use precise and detailed rules to assign responsibility, define behavioral norms, allocate risks and establish limits on liability, rather than to rely on broadly stated, flexible principles. In the drafting of these rules, a critical consideration was that the various parties to funds transfers need to be able to predict risk with certainty, to insure against risk, to adjust operational

and security procedures, and to price funds transfer services appropriately. This consideration is particularly important given the very large amounts of money that are involved in funds transfers.

Funds transfers involve competing interests—those of the banks that provide funds transfer services, and the commercial and financial organizations that use the services, as well as the public interest. These competing interests were represented in the drafting process and were thoroughly considered. The rules that emerged represent a careful and delicate balancing of those interests and are intended to be the exclusive means of determining the rights, duties and liabilities of the affected parties in any situation covered by particular provisions of the Article. Consequently, resort to principles of law and equity outside of Article 4A is not appropriate to create rights, duties and liabilities inconsistent with those stated in this Article.

with the general absence of negligence-based rules in Article 4A compared to sections in Articles 3 and 4, such as 3–406 and 4–406, which contain detailed loss-allocation rules depending on the individual actions of each party to a bank transaction gone wrong. Defendant banks have also successfully used 4A–502 to defeat claims of conversion and unjust enrichment arising out of cases where the bank setoff against the beneficiary's funds or allowed the beneficiary to withdraw the funds. The theory is that 4A–502 specifically allows the beneficiary bank to take such actions, so any common law claims covering the bank's behavior would be inconsistent with the specific provisions of Article 4A.

An illustration of the reasoning that courts have typically employed to decide Article 4A preemption cases is given by the contrasting decisions in Grain Traders, Inc. v. Citibank, N.A.[2] and Sheerbonnet, Ltd. v. American Express Bank, Ltd.[3] In *Sheerbonnet*, plaintiff Sheerbonnet, Ltd. claimed that American Express wrongfully setoff proceeds of a payment order that it received as an intermediary bank rather than continuing to send the amounts on to the beneficiary. The funds transfer instructed Citibank to credit its account for Bank of Credit and Commerce, S.A. ("BCCI") and then issue a payment order for BCCI to credit Sheerbonnet's account at BCCI. On the date of the transfer, regulators suspended BCCI's European and American operations, which included freezing BCCI's account at American Express. Even though it knew the account had been frozen, American Express accepted the payment order and subsequently set off that amount against its outstanding debts owing from BCCI.

The Southern District of New York noted that Article 4A should be a party's primary source of a remedy for problems with a funds transfer, but held that Sheerbonnet's common law claims of conversion, tortious interference and unjust enrichment were not preempted because Article 4A did not address the act of crediting an account known to be frozen.

Subsequently, in *Grain Traders*, plaintiff Grain Traders, Inc. originated a funds transfer with instructions to route the various payment orders through defendant Citibank to an intermediary bank, Banque du Credit et Investissement Ltd. ("BCIL"), who held an account with Citibank, and on to the end beneficiary bank. After Citibank received the payment order and credited BCIL's account, BCIL became insolvent and the funds never reached Grain Traders' stated beneficiary because Citibank setoff the funds against its existing debt from BCIL.

The Second Circuit dismissed Grain Traders' common law claims for conversion and money had and received, saying that any

---

2.   160 F.3d 97 (2nd Cir. 1998).   **3.**   951 F.Supp. 403 (S.D.N.Y. 1996).

actions for improper handling of the payment order had to be brought under Article 4A. The court distinguished *Sheerbonnet* by noting that there was no allegation that Citibank actually knew BCIL was insolvent at the time it accepted Grain Traders' payment order.

Unfortunately for plaintiffs in these cases, the Second Circuit precedent in *Grain Traders* is likely to give defendant banks significant ammunition from which to argue in future cases involving conversion claims under similar factual circumstances. Yet one is left with a lingering feeling of unfairness, towards the Grain Traders outcome even acknowledging that Citibank was ignorant of BCIL's insolvency. The funds transfer process rests upon a number of assumptions that are designed to ensure that these large transactions will be done cheaply and quickly with a minimal degree of unknown risk to the parties involved. It seems to us that plaintiffs in cases such as *Grain Traders* and *Sheerbonnet* make a valid argument when they claim that defendant banks like American Express and Citibank should not be permitted to take opportunistic advantage of their position as a mere intermediary bank in a funds transfer transaction.[4] If anything, allowing such behavior creates additional risk and uncertainty for originators in transactions where the funds transfer cannot be completed directly with the beneficiary's bank, which necessitates the use of beneficiary bank accounts at third party intermediary banks.

Another example of a case where a state law claim survived preemption is Regions Bank v. The Provident Bank, Inc.,[5] which involved alleged fraud by one of the persons involved in a funds transfer. The case arose out of Provident Bank's setoff of amounts in a mutual customer's account, where those funds originally came from a warehouse line of credit funded by Plaintiff Regions Bank. Regions brought state law claims, including accepting funds that were fraudulently obtained. The Eleventh Circuit allowed the state law claim because fraud is not covered in Article 4A, so such a claim would not be inconsistent with any of Article 4A's provisions. The court also reasoned that Article 4A cannot serve as a "shield for fraudulent activity." This case arguably interprets the comment to 4A–102 correctly in limiting preemption to those items actually covered by Article 4A's provisions. As a side point, however, we think that such cases should *not* turn on how the potentially liable bank receives the funds at issue. The rule should be the same

---

4. Compare comment 2 to 1–103, however, where the drafters indicate that the *Sheerbonnet* decision "was inconsistent with the underlying purposes and policies reflected in the relevant provisions of the Code." Nevertheless, we would still argue that Article 4A should not support intermediary banks taking advantage of their status as a mere conduit in a funds transfer transaction for personal gain at the expense of a payment order's sender.

5. 345 F.3d 1267 (11th Cir. 2003).

whether the bank receives the funds in cash over the counter or via an Article 4A funds transfer.

Several courts have also distinguished between separate actions taken by the defendant bank that occurred prior to the funds transfer at issue in the subject litigation in determining whether Article 4A preempts particular claims. Eisenberg v. Wachovia Bank[6] involved plaintiff Eric Eisenberg, who lost $1 million when Wachovia customer Douglas Reid convinced him to wire money into a Wachovia account titled "Douglas Walter Reid dba Bear Stearns," under the guise that Reid worked for Bear Stearns and would invest the money on Eisenberg's behalf. Eisnenberg claimed that Wachovia was negligent in allowing Reid to set up an account in that name without proper verification. The Fourth Circuit allowed the negligence claim to proceed because it involved the bank's actions in setting up the account, not in handling the incoming funds transfer from Eisenberg to Reid's account, and was therefore not preempted by Article 4A.

Another Fourth Circuit case, Donmar Enterprises, Inc. v. Southern National Bank of North Carolina,[7] provides a good example of a claim that the court found was directly addressed by Article 4A's provisions and warranted preemption. Plaintiff Donmar claimed that a funds transfer it sent was for joint beneficiaries (Donmar and another company it was doing business with) and that Southern National violated Article 4A by crediting the entire amount of the funds transfer solely to the other beneficiary. The court upheld a dismissal of Donmar's state law claims for negligence and wrongful payment because 4A–404(a) explicitly covers a beneficiary bank's damages liability in the event that it pays an improper beneficiary, so Article 4A preempted the common law negligence claim.

In sum, we feel that most, if not all, of these cases were decided correctly, with the possible exception of *Eisenberg* and *Grain Traders*. First, reconsider those cases we consider to be properly decided. When there is some sort of additional act that occurred outside of the funds transfer itself, such as the alleged fraud in *Regions Bank*, there is no reason to preclude a state law fraud claim. As noted by the court in that case, Article 4A–102 should not serve as a shield for those who would commit fraud in a funds transfer transaction. Similarly, American Express's additional actions in *Sheerbonnet*—of crediting an account known to be frozen so it could effectuate a setoff—went beyond what Article 4A expects of intermediary banks. As such, that court properly permitted the sender's conversion, tortious interference and unjust enrichment claims. *Donmar* presented a case where the court properly precluded a sender's claim

<hr>

6. 301 F.3d 220 (4th Cir. 2002).   **7.** 64 F.3d 944 (4th Cir. 1995).

for negligence, as the defendant's allegedly tortuous conduct was covered by express duties contained in Article 4A.

Now, recall *Eisenberg* and *Grain Traders*. We have some doubt that each of these cases was decided correctly, but they certainly rest closer to the preemption dividing line than *Regions* and *Sheerbonnet* due to the absence of secondary acts by the defendants that were patently wrongful.

Surely the sender in *Eisenberg* may have had a viable claim of negligence against Wachovia for allowing the fraudster to open an account under the name Bear Stearns without requiring proper documentation. We believe that Wachovia had an equally strong claim that this was not an Article 3 or 4 transaction incorporating comparative negligence. Article 4A was designed with a precisely defined system of rights and obligations, and to disregard a 4A–102 preemption in favor of allowing what is essentially a comparative negligence claim is inconsistent with the provisions of Article 4A. Under these facts, it seems to us that the court should have preempted the sender's negligence claim and left him to litigate exclusively under Article 4A, since the only relationship between the plaintiff Eisenberg and Wachovia involved a funds transfer transaction.

As noted previously, our main bone of contention with the Second Circuit over *Grain Traders* is the way that this holding permitted Citibank to take advantage of its position as an intermediary in the funds transfer transaction for its own personal gain. Citibank's actions are not as egregious in our minds as American Express's were in *Sheerbonnet*, but courts must protect the integrity of the funds transfer system against potential abuses by intermediary banks that could discourage senders from issuing payment orders. A potential counterargument is that finality is also an important consideration in commercial transactions, and clearly the *Grain Traders* holding would support that goal. Needless to say, this is an exceedingly close case with competing policy arguments that fall on either side of what is inconsistent with Article 4A. Perhaps the best we can hope to do at this point is lay out the arguments along with our general feeling that this case came out the wrong way.

Whether Article 4A preemptions will continue to be the leading source of funds transfer litigation remains to be seen. Plaintiffs need to be aware of distinctions they can draw to avoid preemption, such as temporally separating the alleged wrongful act from the funds transfer itself and focusing on events that are not covered by the provisions of Article 4A. On the other hand, defendant banks seeking dismissal of claims will focus on cases such as *Grain Traders* and *Donmar* in arguing that the particular claims at issue are already covered by Article 4A.

§ 7–5   Variation by Agreement

In an electronic funds transfer case an agreement between the parties may be the most significant source of law in the entire transaction. That is because many participants will be parties to multi-party agreements such as CHIPS, S.W.I.F.T., or to two-party agreements between banks and their customers. Section 1–102(3) states the basic rule regarding variation of the UCC's provisions by agreement:

> The effect of provisions of this Act may be varied by agreement, except as otherwise provided in this Act and except that the obligations of good faith, diligence, reasonableness and care prescribed by this Act may not be disclaimed by agreement but the parties may by agreement determine the standards by which the performance of such obligations is to be measured if such standards are not manifestly unreasonable.

Within Article 4A itself, Section 4A–501 specifically embraces variation by agreement or by funds transfer system rules. Section 4A–501(b) goes farther than other provisions of the Uniform Commercial Code:

> * * * Except as otherwise provided in this Article, a funds transfer system rule governing rights and obligations between participating banks using the system may be effective even if the rule conflicts with this Article and indirectly affects another party to the funds transfer who does not consent to the rule. A funds transfer system rule may also govern the rights and obligations of parties other than participating banks using the system to the extent stated in Sections 4A–404(c), 4A–405(d), and 4A–507(c).

A common restriction on the power of a party to establish rules by agreement is that such an agreement cannot affect the rights of non-signers. Here the drafters of Article 4A have endorsed the contrary notion, namely, that the rights of non-parties can be determined by funds transfer rules to which they have not agreed. This strengthens the argument that the rules of CHIPS, NACHA, and similar associations can and should govern the rights not only of the banks who sign such agreements, but also their customers.

We reiterate: funds transfer agreements are critical. A lawyer who advises a client on electronic funds transfers in ignorance of relevant agreements such as those of CHIPS, NACHA, and other such associations flirts with malpractice. In the following sections we critique a sample funds transfer agreement between a bank and its customer. Section 4A–501's broad allowance of variation by agreement is not carte blanche. Without claiming that the list is exhaustive, we identify several subsections that, explicitly or implicitly, prohibit variation by agreement.

§ 7–6 Bank–Customer EFT Agreement

The following is a sample bank-customer agreement and our critique of some of its provisions.

AGREEMENT

1. *Applicable Law*. All funds transfers to or from the Customer's accounts at the Bank, and all payment orders which the Customer sends to the Bank to originate any funds transfers shall be governed by the laws of the State of _____, including the _____ Uniform Commercial Code, and applicable Federal laws.

2. *Payment for Transfers and Services*. The Customer shall pay to the Bank the amount of each payment order instructing the Bank to make payment from the Customer's account(s) at the Bank, and the Bank's standard funds transfer fees and charges in accordance with the Bank's fee schedule as from time to time in effect, and the Bank may charge the Customer's accounts therefor. Such payment to the Bank for funds transfers originated by the Bank for the Customer's account shall be made on or before the date of transmission by the Bank.

3. *Notice of Receipt of Funds Transfers*. The periodic statements provided to the Customer by the Bank will notify the Customer of funds transfer payments received by the Bank for credit to the Customer's accounts at the Bank. The Customer is hereby notified and agrees that the Bank shall not be required to provide any other notice to the Customer of such receipt of payments.

[Compare the estoppel for errors revealed in paragraph 10.]

4. *Credits from Funds Transfers are Provisional*. All credits to the Customer's accounts for funds transfers which the Bank receives are provisional until the Bank receives final settlement for the funds. If the Bank does not receive such final settlement, the Customer is hereby notified and agrees that the Bank is entitled to a refund of the amount credited to the Customer's account for that transfer. In that situation, the person who originated the transfer to the Customer's account will not be deemed to have paid the amount of that transfer and, accordingly, the Customer's right to expect that payment from that third party would be preserved.

5. *Security Procedures*. Various security procedures apply to the payment orders that the Customer transmits to the Bank. Such security procedures vary depending on whether the transfer is to be by Automated Clearing House (ACH) or by wire

transfer. The full scope of security procedures which the Bank offers and strongly recommends for wire transfers is available only if the Customer's payment orders for wire transfers are transmitted by the Customer directly to the Bank's wire room either by phone, personal computer, or other electronic means. Those security procedures are designed to assure both the authenticity and the correctness of the payment orders, and any amendments of payment orders, which are transmitted to the Bank. Some or all of those security procedures, such as recorded telephone lines, codes, passwords, personal identification numbers, algorithms and encryptions are available only if the Customer's payment orders and amendments are transmitted directly to the Bank's wire room.

If the Customer instead chooses to transmit such payment orders by telephone to a Bank representative outside the wire room (such as the Customer's relationship manager or his or her assistant), the security procedures are limited to possible voice recognition. Voice recognition can provide only limited assurance of authenticity, and of course voice recognition is not always possible. Furthermore, it provides little assurance, if any, of the correctness of the payment orders that we believe have been transmitted to the Bank. Accordingly, if the Customer transmits any payment order or amendment to a Bank representative outside the wire room, the Customer will be deemed to have refused the security procedures that the Bank is offering and recommending as "commercially reasonable," and the Customer will be deemed to have agreed to be bound by any such payment order, whether or not authorized, which is issued in the Customer's name and accepted by the Bank in good faith.

[Section 4A–202(f) generally bans redefinition of the terms "authorized and verified payment orders." A bank can neither bind its customer to a particular form of security procedure that is not, by an objective standard, commercially reasonable, nor conclusively define what is "commercially reasonable." This prohibition protects a customer's right to a security procedure and the attendant right to reject a transaction that is not authorized and not appropriately verified. Section 4A–202(f) might therefore be interpreted to preclude paragraph 5 of the sample agreement to the extent the paragraph purports to bind the Customer to any payment—whether or not authorized—that is transmitted to a Bank representative outside the wire room. A security procedure that does not even guarantee voice recognition may not constitute a "commercially reasonable" procedure.

Also, section 4A–204 obliges a receiving bank to refund a payment received from a customer where the payment order was not authorized and was not effective as the order of the customer. Subsection 4A–204(b) prohibits the bank from evading this obligation by agreement. The prohibition also casts doubt on paragraph 5 of the sample agreement.

The paragraph might also stumble over 4A–402(f). Section 4A–402(f) bars an agreement that denies the sender of a payment order the right to an excuse from the obligation to pay when there is otherwise such a right, or a right to a refund from the sender's receiving bank.]

6. *Inconsistent Name and Account Number Appearing In A Payment Order.* If a payment order describes the intended recipient of funds inconsistently by name and account number, then the Customer acknowledges that payment by the receiving bank (which may be the Bank) may be made on the basis of the account number even if that account is not owned by the person named in the payment order. If the Customer is the originator of a payment order containing an inconsistent name and account number, the Customer acknowledges and agrees that its obligation to pay to the Bank the amount of that payment order shall not be excused in such circumstances.

7. *Cut-Off Times.* Payment orders shall be transmitted to the Bank in compliance with the format requirements and cut-off hours established by the Bank from time to time. Payment orders received by the Bank after such cut-off hours established by the Bank may be treated by the Bank as received on the following Bank business day.

8. *Rejection of Entries.* Except as otherwise expressly provided in a written agreement signed by the Bank, the Bank shall have the right to reject any payment order for any reason, including without limitation the Customer's failure to maintain a sufficient account balance. If the Bank rejects any payment order, the Bank shall endeavor to notify the Customer by phone, electronic transmission, or other reasonable means no later than the business day that such payment order would otherwise have been executed by the Bank. The Bank shall have no liability to the Customer by reason of the rejection of any such payment order, or the fact that such notice was not given at an earlier time.

9. *Cancellation or Amendment of Payment Orders.* The Customer shall have no right to cancel or amend a payment order after it has been received by the Bank. However, the Bank shall make a reasonable effort to act on the Customer's request for cancellation or amendment or a payment order prior to the time that the Bank executes such payment order, but shall

have no liability if such cancellation or amendment is not effected.

[A customer's lawyer might argue that 4A–211 bars the rule contained in paragraph 9 (Customer has no right to cancel or amend a payment order after it has been received by the Bank). Paragraph 9 does not require that the Bank has accepted the order, an event which generally occurs only when the Bank has executed the order (4A–209(a)). Until the Bank has executed the order, 4A–211(b) states that a communication by the sender canceling or amending the order is effective if received in time to afford the Bank a reasonable opportunity to act before it accepts. Comment 3 to 4A–211 makes this point even clearer: "If the receiving bank has not yet accepted the order, there is no reason why the sender should not be able to cancel or amend the order unilaterally so long as the requirements of subsections (a) and (b) are met." Since nothing in 4A states that 4A–211 is not variable by agreement and since it does not state a rule of good faith or ordinary care, paragraph 9 probably trumps 4A–211.]

10. *Account Reconciliation.* Funds transfers to or from the Customer's accounts will be reflected on the periodic statements issued by the Bank with respect to each account. The Customer agrees to notify the Bank promptly of any discrepancy between the Customer's records and the information shown on any such periodic statement. If the Customer fails to notify the Bank of any discrepancy within 30 days of receipt of a periodic statement containing such information, the Customer agrees that the Bank shall not be liable for any other losses resulting from the Customer's failure to give such notice or any loss of interest with respect to such funds transfers. If the Customer fails to notify the Bank of any such discrepancy within sixty days of receipt of such periodic statement, the Customer shall be precluded from asserting such discrepancy against the Bank.

[Does Paragraph 10 run afoul of Section 4A–505? That section requires that the Customer complain within "one year" to correct an improper debit. Section 4A–505 says nothing of the right of the parties to vary the one-year term. By comparison, section 2–725 of Article 2 establishes a four-year statute of limitations and explicitly prohibits reduction to less than one year.

Can the parties shorten the one-year provision of 4A–505, as in Section 10 to sixty days? At least one court has held that any modification of the one-year period is entirely unenforceable. See Regatos v. North Fork Bank, 257 F.Supp.2d 632 (S.D.N.Y. 2003) discussed, *infra*, § 7–26, although we are not fully persuaded by its reasoning on this point.

Regatos notwithstanding, if the parties were to do this by agreement and so reduce the right of the customer to recover an improper payment to sixty days after notice was received by the customer reasonably identifying the order, would this be a modification of the sender's right to a refund and thus violate 4A–402(f)? Or possibly a modification of 4A–204 and thus violate 4A–204(b)?

Put another way, 4A–505 operates after one year to preclude a request by the customer to recredit its account for an inappropriate charge because the order itself was not authorized or verified. The Comment to 4A–505 refers to the invariability of 4A–204 and 4A–402. Section 4A–505 should not be interpreted to allow what cannot be done by agreement under 4A–204 and 4A–402. Surely a one day cutoff would violate 4A–402(f) and 4A–204(b). What about six months or sixty days? We are sure that a one day period would fail; where the line should be drawn we are not sure, but we are skeptical of the sixty day rule in the quoted agreement. Again, the only case to directly address this issue is *Regatos*. In supporting its holding, that court also indicated that the fifteen-day period at issue in that case would have been unreasonable, even if it had not held that any modification of 4A–505 is barred.]

11.   *Limitations on Liability; Indemnity.*

(a) The Bank shall be liable only for its negligence in performing the services which it has agreed to perform in respect to funds transfers. The Bank shall not be responsible for the Customer's acts or omissions or for those of any other person, including without limitation any Federal Reserve Bank or transmission or communications facility or any intermediary or receiving financial institution, and no such person shall be deemed an agent of the Bank. The Customer agrees to indemnify the Bank against any loss, liability, or expense (including attorneys' fees and expenses) resulting from or arising out of any claim of any person that the Bank is responsible for any act or omission by the Customer or any other person described in this Section 11(a).

(b) In no event shall the Bank be liable for any consequential, special, punitive, or indirect loss or damage which the Customer may incur or suffer in connection with the Bank's funds transfer services (even if the Bank has been informed of the possibility of such damages), including without limitation loss or damage from subsequent wrongful dishonor of any checks or drafts resulting from the Bank's acts or omissions in handling any funds transfers to the Customer's accounts or any payment order requesting such transfers.

(c) Without limiting the generality of the foregoing provisions, the Bank shall be excused from any failure or delay which is caused by legal constraint, interruption of transmission or communication facilities, equipment failure, war, emergency conditions, or other circumstances beyond the Bank's reasonable control. In addition, the Bank shall be excused from any failure or delay in transmitting a payment order or executing a funds transfer if such transmittal or execution would result in the Bank's violating any applicable state or federal law, rule, regulation, or guideline.

[Section 4A–305(f) limits the power of a receiving bank by agreement to escape liability for late or improper execution, and for failure to execute a payment order. Because 4A–305 grants consequential damages only against a bank that agrees in writing to be liable for consequential damages, the exclusion of those damages in Paragraph 11 is clearly valid and does not offend 4A–305. On the other hand, to the extent that other terms in Paragraph 11 might be construed to free the bank from liability it would have for other forms of damages under 4A–305(a) and (b), the paragraph is invalid because of 4A–305(f) "the liability of a receiving bank under subsections (a) and (b) may not be varied by agreement."]

12. *Amendments.* From time to time, the Bank may amend any of the terms and conditions contained in this Agreement. Such amendments shall become effective upon notice to the Customer or such later date as may be stated in the Bank's notice.

———————

Other sections of Article 4A prohibit variations by agreement that may not affect the validity of the Sample Agreement. For instance, section 4A–211(h) states that a funds transfer rule is "not effective" to the extent that it conflicts with 4A–211(c)(2). Section 4A–211(c)(2) limits a beneficiary's bank's right to escape an effective payment order to three cases in which the beneficiary has no right to the funds and no equitable claim to them (as where the beneficiary has received duplicate payment). Subsection (h) provides that a funds transfer rule may not expand the rights of a beneficiary's bank to cancel or amend an order it has accepted beyond the three sets of circumstances.

As a final note on permissible variations by agreement, the lawyer should observe that Section 4A–203(a)(1) provides a means by which the customer can escape liability for an unauthorized but effective payment order. That section provides that a receiving bank may limit the extent to which it is entitled to enforce or retain payment of such an unauthorized but effective payment order by express written agreement. Generally, if a payment order is unauthorized but nonetheless effective by virtue of having passed through a commercially reasonable security procedure, the customer is liable for the payment order, and the receiving bank is entitled to enforce it. However, a particularly important customer might be able to persuade its bank to share liability with it, by means of a clause such as the following in their funds transfer agreement:

> *Liability for Unauthorized Payment Orders.* If an accepted payment order is not under Section 4A–202(a) of Article 4A of the _____ Uniform Commercial Code an authorized order of Customer but is effective as an order of Customer pursuant to Section 4A–202(b) thereof, Bank, notwithstanding that it might otherwise be entitled to enforce or retain payment of the order, expressly agrees to assume liability for one-half of any loss sustained by Customer (not to exceed one-half of the payment order), provided that: (i) it cannot be determined who caused the payment order notwithstanding detailed investigations by Customer or the Federal Bureau of Investigation or other governmental authorities; (ii) Bank cannot prove that the order was caused by a person referred to in Section 4A–203(a)(2) of Article 4A; and (iii) Customer shall at all times relevant to the causing of the payment order have exercised reasonable care in safeguarding the security procedures entrusted to it by Bank for the purpose of verifying the authenticity of payment orders issued to Bank in the name of Customer and in protecting its payment order transmitting facilities. Bank and Customer shall cooperate with one another in the investigation of the payment order.

§ 7–7 Finality and the Completion of a Funds Transfer: Introduction

Knowing when a funds transfer is completed can be important for several reasons. First, the originator's bank may have sent the payment order in the mistaken belief that the originator had funds on deposit when in fact the originator's account was overdrawn. This parallels a payor bank's final payment on an NSF check and may leave the bank holding the bag. Second, the originator (General Motors) may wish to stop payment, in order to cancel the transaction. Third, the originator may need to know when it has discharged its underlying obligation to the beneficiary. When is General Motors free of its obligation, and when, therefore, must Goodyear depend exclusively upon a claim against its own bank for satisfaction?

Finally, and least likely of all, is the question of liability of the various participants where one of the banks within the system becomes insolvent and closes in the midst of a set of EFT transactions. The last of these calamities—the bank equivalent of a nuclear holocaust—would arise if one of the members of CHIPS or a large

New York bank such as Citicorp were unable to fulfill its commitment to others in the CHIPS system at the end of the day. If the Federal Reserve failed to step into the gap, there would be nice questions and interesting possibilities about how the shortfall in the system should be divided among the various banks, beneficiaries, originators, and other senders. Dare we even whisper about that possibility?

§ 7–8   Finality—Payments by Originator's Bank on NSF Accounts

In thousands or perhaps tens of thousands of cases every year, payor banks fail to return NSF checks by their midnight deadlines and thus become liable on them to payees even though their customers' accounts do not have sufficient funds, and the checks are therefore "NSF." The wire transfer analogy to that final payment scenario arises when General Motors issues its payment order to JP Morgan Chase, so instructing JP Morgan Chase to make payment to Goodyear, the beneficiary of a payment order (not the payee of a check). Just as JP Morgan Chase might make a mistake in holding a check drawn on it beyond its midnight deadline, in this case it might make a mistake in issuing the payment order to the Federal Reserve in the incorrect belief that General Motors had sufficient money in its account to cover the payment order. A lawyer for JP Morgan Chase is then faced with a question similar to that in the check situation, i.e., when will JP Morgan Chase be bound on its obligation to some third party payee? Or to put the question another way, what is the Article 4A analog to Article 4's final payment rules?

Assume in our case that General Motors instructs JP Morgan Chase to deliver $10 million to a numbered account of Goodyear at National City Bank in Cleveland. Assume further that the order is given at 3:00 p.m. on Monday and that it is to be carried out at once. (There would be additional complications if the order was given on Monday, but was not to be executed until Thursday or a week from Tuesday. We avoid those for the time being.) Let us assume that a clerk at JP Morgan Chase prepares a payment order at 3:15 p.m. and at 3:16 p.m. sends the payment order to the Detroit branch of the Federal Reserve Bank of Chicago. Assume that the Federal Reserve transfers that order to the Cleveland Federal Reserve at 3:20 p.m. who at 3:30 p.m. sends it on to National City Bank.

At 5:00 p.m. an executive of JP Morgan Chase discovers that there are insufficient funds in General Motors' account, and hearing ominous rumors about General Motors' financial instability, decides to cancel the payment order. Is it too late?

The legal event that usually establishes liability of the originating bank under Article 4A is "acceptance." Acceptance in 4A has nothing to do with the term of the same name in Article 2. Also involved will be a series of events including payments or settlements that in one way or another feed into the definition of acceptance in Article 4A. One could start at the JP Morgan Chase end of the transaction and work toward the beneficiary, but it makes more sense to start at the other end.

We can safely predict that the law will not leave the beneficiary bank, National City Bank, with a binding obligation to Goodyear for $10 million, but without a claim against its upstream senders, JP Morgan Chase or the Federal Reserve Bank. The obligation of National City to Goodyear is set out in Article 4A–404, "Obligation of Beneficiary's Bank to Pay and Give Notice to Beneficiary." With exceptions that are not relevant, section 4A–404 states that National City is obliged "to pay the amount of the order" to Goodyear once it "accepts." If any act of National City or other event qualifies as a 4A "acceptance" by National City, then there is a duty to pay, and Goodyear has a good claim against National City for payment.

Has National City accepted? Turn to 4A–209(b). This section outlines several ways that acceptance by National City could have occurred before 5:00 p.m. on Monday. First, generally the beneficiary's bank accepts under 4A–209(b) if it "notifies the beneficiary of receipt of the order or that the account of the beneficiary has been credited with respect to the order * * *." Under UCC 1–201(26) the bank would have "notified" by taking the steps necessary to inform Goodyear, even though Goodyear had not yet been informed. If an electronic message of receipt had been sent to Goodyear or if a paper message had been deposited in the mail for Goodyear, that would constitute acceptance under 4A–209(b)(1)(ii). Or the beneficiary's bank might have accepted under 4A–209(b)(1)(i) (cross-referencing to 4A–405(a) and (b)) by using the funds received to set off against a Goodyear overdraft, or against another obligation that Goodyear owed to the bank, or even by "making available" the funds to Goodyear.

If the beneficiary's bank, here National City, has received "payment" from the Federal Reserve, it has also accepted. Under 4A–403(a)(1) payment happens when there is "final settlement" through the Federal Reserve Bank or through a funds transfer system. Since the sender of the payment order to National City is itself the Federal Reserve, the transaction was undoubtedly done through Fedwire. Under 12 C.F.R. 210.31 payment occurs under Fedwire to a receiving bank at the earlier of the time "when the amount of the payment order is credited to the receiving bank's account or when the payment order is sent to the receiving bank."

At least the second and probably the first of those events will have occurred at the Federal Reserve in Cleveland before 5:00 p.m. National City will thus have accepted, and will be obliged to pay Goodyear. At least as far as National City is concerned, the deal is complete before 5:00 p.m. on Monday.

If the Federal Reserve were not involved and if National City did not give Goodyear notice of the receipt of the credit, you might think that acceptance by National City might not occur until the beginning of the next "funds transfer business day" of National City. But even then National City will generally have accepted as of the "opening of the next funds transfer business day" under the terms of 4A–209(b)(3) if the amount of the sender's order (JP Morgan Chase's) is fully covered by a withdrawable credit balance in JP Morgan Chase's name at a third bank, or the bank has otherwise received full payment from the sender.

To summarize, a combination of sections 4A–209, 4A–404, 4A–403(a)(1), and 12 CFR § 210.31 are likely to cause instantaneous settlement of transfers done through Fedwire, which in turn means there has been payment to National City under 4A–403(a)(1). This in turn means that National City has accepted because of 4A–209(b). Furthermore, in such instances, National City owes an obligation to pay Goodyear under 4A–404. If the transaction did not occur through Fedwire, it is possible that acceptance and therefore the obligation to pay on the part of National City would not occur until the next funds transfer business day.

Turn now to the obligation of the intermediary bank, the Federal Reserve, to National City and the obligation of JP Morgan Chase, the originating bank, to the Federal Reserve. Common sense should tell us that the drafters would not leave National City hung out to dry. Surely any properly drafted statute should give the beneficiary's bank a right against upstream banks once it is obliged to pay its beneficiary—assuming always that it has behaved reasonably.

We think that this is true here, but follow along. The obligation of the Federal Reserve to National City (to the extent not preempted in the future by federal regulations) is governed by 4A–402, a section that describes the "Obligation of Sender to Pay Receiving Bank." Under 4A–402(b) acceptance by the beneficiary's bank of an order directed to the beneficiary's bank "obliges the sender to pay the bank the amount of the order * * *." Thus, the same event, namely acceptance by National City, that gave rise to its obligation to Goodyear, also generates a corresponding obligation of the Federal Reserve to it.

Finally what is the obligation of JP Morgan Chase, the originator's bank, to its receiving bank, the Federal Reserve? Again we return to 4A–402, but in this case to 4A–402(c). Here it is "acceptance of the order by the receiving bank" that obliges the sender to pay the bank the amount of the sender's order. If, therefore, the receiving bank (the Federal Reserve) has accepted, then JP Morgan Chase is obliged under 4A–402(c) to pay the Federal Reserve. Returning to the definition of acceptance under 4A–209, we find that the Federal Reserve as a receiving bank accepts under 4A–209(a) when it "executes the order." Section 4A–301 states that an order is executed by a receiving bank when it "issues a payment order intended to carry out the payment order received by the bank." Thus, the Federal Reserve accepted the order and earned a right to payment against JP Morgan Chase at 3:20 p.m. when it sent its payment order to National City.

There is one more step in our analysis. We have assumed for the purpose of the hypothetical case that JP Morgan Chase or any other person who sends a payment order has the power in certain circumstances to cancel that order. That assumption is confirmed by section 4A–211. It gives the sender the unilateral right to cancel an order if it gives notice to the receiving bank with a "reasonable opportunity to act on the communication before the bank accepts the payment order." After acceptance, 4A–211(c) authorizes cancellation only with the agreement of the receiving bank, or if the funds transfer system allows cancellation or amendment without agreement.

Even if National City were willing to agree to a cancellation—an unlikely event since it would certainly face a lawsuit by Goodyear—section 4A–211(c)(2) prohibits such a cancellation. The beneficiary's bank may not enter into a binding agreement to cancel an accepted payment order unless the payment is an unauthorized payment or is issued by a mistake of a particular kind. We do not believe that the mistake which JP Morgan Chase will assert ("we thought there was money in General Motors's account") fits within (c)(2). The restriction on the beneficiary's bank's rights to agree to a cancellation of an acceptance appears to protect the beneficiary against a doublecross by its own bank.

The upshot of 4A–211 is that the beneficiary's bank, National City, dare not agree to reject and has no right to do so. Since that is true, neither the Federal Reserve nor any other intermediary bank is likely to agree to cancel, for it will be bound to National City. Comment 5 to 4A–211 illustrates the precarious position of the beneficiary's bank.

> If the receiving bank has incurred liability as a result of its acceptance of the sender's order, there are substantial risks in agreeing to cancellation or amendment. This is particularly true for a beneficiary's bank. Cancellation or amendment after acceptance by the beneficiary's bank can be made only in the four cases stated and the beneficiary's bank may not have any

way of knowing whether the requirements of subsection (c) have been met or whether it will be able to recover payment from the beneficiary that received payment. Even with indemnity the beneficiary's bank may be reluctant to alienate its customer, the beneficiary, by denying the customer the funds.[1]

§ 7–9 Acceptance of Payment Order by an Intermediary Bank

To reiterate, an intermediary bank is a receiving bank that is not also the originator's bank or the beneficiary's bank. An intermediary bank accepts the payment order it has received when it "executes the order."[1] A payment order is "executed" by the intermediary bank when it "issues a payment order intended to carry out the payment order received by the bank."[2] So long as the intermediary bank issues a payment order *intending* to carry out the payment order it received, acceptance by the intermediary bank has occurred, even if the order issued by the intermediary bank does not carry out the order received by the intermediary bank.[3]

Consider the following examples.

1) At 9:00 A.M., JP Morgan Chase, originator's bank, sends a payment order to the Federal Reserve in Chicago, instructing it to cause a $1 million credit to Goodyear's account at National City. At 9:01 A.M., the Federal Reserve in Chicago receives the order. At 1:00 P.M., the Federal Reserve in Chicago issues its own payment order to National City, instructing National City to cause a $1 million credit to occur in Goodyear's account. At 1:01 P.M. National City receives the order.

2) Assume the same facts as in example (1), but instead of issuing a payment order for $1 million to National City at 1:00 P.M., the Federal Reserve in Chicago mistakenly issues a $500 thousand payment order to National City. Realizing its mistake, at 4:00 P.M., it issues a second $500 thousand payment order to National City.

<hr/>

§ 7–8

1. Quaere whether a funds transfer system rule that allows cancellation without a beneficiary's bank's agreement overrides the rule in 4A–211(c)(2) which limits the effect of a cancellation. A sentence in Comment 5 could be so read: Subsection (c) leaves the decision to the beneficiary's bank unless the consent of the beneficiary's bank is not required under a funds transfer system rule or other interbank agreement. However, we read 4A–211(h) to invalidate any such funds transfer rule unless it were in a federal system and therefore trumped Article 4A.

§ 7–9

1. § 4A–209(a).

2. § 4A–301(a).

3. See § 4A–301, Comment 1.

3) Assume the same facts as in example (1), but instead of issuing a payment order for $1 million to National City, the Federal Reserve in Chicago mistakenly issues a $1 million payment order to Continental Bank at 1:00 P.M.

In each of these examples, acceptance by the intermediary bank, Federal Reserve in Chicago, occurred at 1:00 P.M. This is the time that the Federal Reserve in Chicago executed an order that was intended to carry out the payment order it received. The latter two examples are cases of erroneous execution, i.e., execution has occurred, but the execution is erroneous. Erroneous execution of payment orders by receiving banks is covered in 4A–303, and discussed later in this chapter.

§ 7–10   Acceptance by Beneficiary's Bank

According to 4A–209(b), the beneficiary's bank can accept a payment order in one of four ways:

1) by paying the beneficiary,

2) by notifying the beneficiary of receipt of the order or notifying the beneficiary that its account was credited,

3) by receiving full payment from the sender, or

4) by passage of time, i.e., "the opening of the next funds transfer business day of the bank following the payment date of the order * * *."

A beneficiary's bank is considered to have accepted a payment order when the earliest of the four means of acceptance occurs.[1]

a.   Paying the Beneficiary; Obligating Itself to Pay the Beneficiary

One common way for a beneficiary's bank to accept a payment order is simply by paying a beneficiary. This requirement makes sense. After all, the payment order sent by the sender to the beneficiary's bank instructs the beneficiary's bank to pay the beneficiary. When the beneficiary's bank follows the instructions by paying the beneficiary, acceptance by the beneficiary's bank should logically occur.

But what constitutes "paying"? Does the beneficiary's bank have to pay the beneficiary in cash? Is crediting the beneficiary's account sufficient? Section 4A–209(b)(1) provides that a bank accepts a payment order by paying the beneficiary pursuant to 4A–405(a) or (b). Section 4A–405(a) applies if the bank credits the account of the beneficiary; section 4A–405(b) applies if the bank does not credit the account of the beneficiary. Crediting the account

§ 7–10

1.   § 4A–209(b).

of the beneficiary constitutes payment under 4A–405(a) when and to the extent:

(i) the beneficiary is notified of the right to withdraw the credit, (ii) the bank lawfully applies the credit to a debt of the beneficiary, or (iii) funds with respect to the order are otherwise made available to the beneficiary by the bank.

If the beneficiary's bank does not credit the account of the beneficiary of the payment order, 4A–405(b) provides that:

when payment * * * occurs is governed by principles of law that determine when an obligation is satisfied.

Some "paying events" will be clear (beneficiary withdraws money) and some not so clear (other principles govern).

A beneficiary's bank may accept a payment order under 4A–209(b)(1) if instead of paying the beneficiary under 4A–405(a) or (b), the beneficiary's bank notifies the beneficiary of receipt of the payment order or that the account of the beneficiary has been credited with respect to the order. A beneficiary's bank usually credits the account of the beneficiary upon receipt of a payment order. As indicated above, crediting the account of the beneficiary constitutes payment under 4A–405(a) when the beneficiary's bank notifies the beneficiary of its right to withdraw the credit, or applies the credit to a debt of the beneficiary, or makes funds available to the beneficiary. Funds are typically "made available" to a beneficiary by allowing the beneficiary the right to withdraw. In some situations, the beneficiary's bank will allow the beneficiary to withdraw the funds, but will attempt to condition the right of the beneficiary to use the funds upon the beneficiary bank's receipt of full payment from the sender of its payment order.

We do not know exactly what the drafters had in mind with the "otherwise made available" language of 4A–405(a)(iii). Official comment 5 to 4A–209 describes a somewhat strange situation involving the beneficiary's bank granting the beneficiary a loan, and indicates that this would fall under 4A–405(a)(iii). There must be other circumstances that would qualify besides this particular one, but we have a hard time believing that the act of crediting the beneficiary's account alone constitutes "making funds available." If that action would suffice, then the requirement of 4A–405(a)(i) that the beneficiary's bank notify the beneficiary of the right to withdraw the credit would appear to be superfluous.

But, in First Security Bank of New Mexico v. Pan American Bank,[2] the only known case directly on point, the Tenth Circuit said otherwise, holding that crediting the beneficiary's account constituted acceptance under 4A–405(a)(iii). That case involved a fraudu-

---

2.   215 F.3d 1147 (10th Cir. 2000).

lent scheme instituted by Beatrice Stonebanks whereby she convinced other banks to originate funds transfers to an account that she owned at First Security under the guise that the banks were purchasing certificates of deposit from First Security. First Security followed 4A–207 and credited each payment to the account listed on the payment order, which resulted in the money going to Stonebanks' account even though the originating bank was actually listed as the named beneficiary on each payment order. As part of its internal procedures, a First Security employee would contact each beneficiary of a payment order to advise of the funds' arrival. Instead of contacting the individual banks, however, First Security called Stonebanks, since she was the actual owner of the account that was credited.

The *First Security* court argued that 4A–205(a)(iii) could not simply be limited to the unique situation listed in the comment involving a loan to the beneficiary,[3] and noted that it could not "ascertain from the plain statutory language why funds are not 'otherwise made available' to a beneficiary * * * when a beneficiary's bank credits a beneficiary's account and immediately makes the funds available to the beneficiary."[4] As such, the court held that First Security "accepted" the payment order immediately upon crediting Stonebanks' account, and the originating banks were liable to pay First Security in the amount of the order.

We disagree with this court's conclusion regarding 4A–405(a)(iii)'s coverage, as it essentially makes subsection (a)(i) superfluous. In addition, it is unclear why this issue even arose in the first place, because the court did not discuss whether First Security actually gave notice in this situation, and the earlier district court case went unreported. Perhaps the originators argued that First Security did not give notice to the actual named beneficiaries. Remember, First Security credited Stonebanks' account based on number alone in accordance with 4A–207, so it did not actually "accept" the payment order under 4A–209(b)(1), and the beneficiary would not have reimbursed First Security. Beyond First Security's potential defense that it notified the proper party in accordance with 4A–207, they could also easily defend under 4A–209(b)(3) and argue that acceptance occurred by passage of time (which we will discuss *infra*).

Article 4A mandates acceptance even in the face of some conditions. The obligation of the sender to pay the beneficiary's bank is separate from the obligation of the beneficiary's bank to pay the beneficiary. The drafters considered each of the payment orders to be separate "mini-transactions" that are connected only insofar as they are part of an entire funds transfer. If the receiving

---

3. *Id.* at 1158.   **4.** *Id.* at 1156–57.

bank fears that the sender's insolvency would prevent payment to the receiving bank, the receiving bank should not accept the order. In the drafters' view, once the receiving bank accepts, it should not be able to pass the credit risk on to the beneficiary. As stated by Thomas C. Baxter, Jr.:

> By making credit to the beneficiary "provisional," and subject to the sender discharging the sender's obligation to settle with the beneficiary's bank, the beneficiary's bank could transfer this form of credit risk to the beneficiary. What was disturbing about such provisional credit was the inability of the beneficiary to control or limit its credit risk. Because of a lack of privity between the beneficiary's bank's sender and the beneficiary, the beneficiary was ill-suited to reject payment orders from those who were considered unworthy of credit. The beneficiary's bank was the party best positioned to prevent that kind of loss because it was in privity with this sender. Because it is a fundamental principle of commercial law to place risk of loss on the party best positioned to control it, 4A–405(c) provides that any agreement rendering provisional the credit to the beneficiary's account is not enforceable.[5]

Thus, the beneficiary's bank generally makes funds available to the beneficiary, and so pays and accepts, even if the beneficiary's bank conditions the right to keep the funds upon the beneficiary's bank receiving payment from the sender of the payment order to the beneficiary's bank, and the beneficiary agrees to this condition of payment.[6] That is, making the credit "provisional" will not prevent payment and acceptance.

By contrast, if the beneficiary's bank credits the account, but unequivocally informs the beneficiary that it cannot withdraw or use the funds until the beneficiary's bank gets paid, the beneficiary's bank does not make funds available to the beneficiary. We are certain that crediting the account but with a stern and clear prohibition on use of the funds, on the one hand, and treating the credit as "provisional," on the other, does not exhaust the possible agreements between the beneficiary and the beneficiary's bank. Undoubtedly, imaginative lawyers will draft other forms of agreement between the beneficiary and its bank. Doubtless there is a gray area between provisional settlement (acceptance) and crediting the account with no right to draw (nonacceptance).

---

5. Baxter, Commercial Law and Practice Course Handbook Series, Basic UCC Skills 1990: Article 4A Payment, 542 PLI/Comm 93 (1990), pg. 27 of 253 from Westlaw.

6. There are two exceptions to this rule, one concerning automated clearing house rules, and another concerning the failure of a loss-sharing agreement of a funds transfer system.

When an upstream bank fails, it will be in the interest of the beneficiary's bank to argue that the credit was not useable or withdrawable so that payment and acceptance did not occur, and it will be in the interest of the beneficiary to argue that their agreement was merely an ineffective attempt to make the credit provisional. At this point we are hesitant to predict the outcome of such conflicts, but we are confident that they will ultimately arise. We suspect that close cases will go against the beneficiary's bank.

Finally, if a beneficiary's bank does not credit the beneficiary's account, payment occurs when the beneficiary's bank notifies the beneficiary of the receipt of the order and the beneficiary's right to the use of funds, or if the beneficiary's bank does not so receive and notify, payment occurs according to non Article 4A rules on satisfaction of obligations.

PROBLEM

Better to understand when a beneficiary's bank accepts a payment order by paying the beneficiary, consider the following examples:

1. i. 9:00 A.M., Beneficiary's bank receives payment order directing Beneficiary's bank to credit Beneficiary's account for $1M.

    ii. 9:10 A.M., Beneficiary's bank credits Beneficiary's account.

    iii. 9:15 A.M., Beneficiary's bank notifies Beneficiary of right to withdraw credit.

    Barring a deposit contract which states otherwise (see example 5 below), acceptance occurs at 9:15 A.M.

2. Same facts as in example (1)(i) and (ii), but at 9:15 A.M., Beneficiary's bank notifies Beneficiary of its right to withdraw the credited funds but conditions any withdrawal on the right of Beneficiary's bank to debit beneficiary's account for the amount of the credit if Beneficiary's bank is never paid. Beneficiary agrees.

    Acceptance occurs at 9:15 A.M. That the settlement is claimed to be provisional does not foreclose acceptance.

3. Same facts as in example (1)(i) and (ii), but Beneficiary's bank takes no further action.

    No acceptance yet, because Beneficiary has not been notified, see 4A–209(b)(1).

4. Same facts as in example (1)(i) and (ii), but at 9:15 A.M., Beneficiary's bank notifies Beneficiary of credit. Beneficiary's bank informs Beneficiary that funds may not be withdrawn

until Beneficiary's bank receives payment from the sender of its payment order.

No acceptance yet. Beneficiary's bank has not made funds available for beneficiary's use.[7] Note the difference here from example 2. Here the agreement is not conditional, Beneficiary is prohibited from withdrawal.

5. The same facts as example (1)(i) and (ii), but at 9:15 A.M., Beneficiary's bank notifies Beneficiary of the credit but says nothing about its right to withdraw or about any limitation on withdrawal.

If the deposit agreement is silent on the right to withdraw the funds, the outcome is probably the same as Example 1 and acceptance occurs at 9:15 A.M. But if the deposit agreement says that there is no right to withdraw the funds, we are in trouble. Depending upon the clarity of the deposit contract (and practice?) between the beneficiary and its bank there may or may not be a right to withdraw. Subsection 4A–209(b)(1)(ii) provides that acceptance occurs "unless the notice indicates" that funds may not be withdrawn. We suspect that a prohibition on withdrawal in the deposit contract and not "in the notice" will suffice, at least if the prohibition has not been violated by the bank's prior practice. We suspect that the drafters would interpret an ambiguous prohibition as allowing acceptance.

Note that 4A–404 obliges the bank "to pay the amount of the order to the beneficiary" once it has accepted the order. So acceptance seals National City's fate; it must hand the funds over to its customer and look elsewhere for payment.

b. Receiving Payment of Entire Amount of Sender's Order

A further basic way a beneficiary's bank accepts a payment order is by receiving payment of the entire amount of the sender's order. A well-advised beneficiary's bank should not accept a payment order if it fears that it will not receive payment from the sender. Yet if the beneficiary's bank has received payment of the entire amount of the sender's order, there is no risk of loss and the bank should be obligated to pass the payment on to the beneficiary. Accordingly, 4A–209(b)(2) states that the beneficiary's bank accepts when:

the bank receives payment of the entire amount of the sender's order pursuant to 4A–403(a)(1) or 4A–403(a)(2).

Under 4A–403(a)(1), a beneficiary's bank receives payment of the entire amount of the sender's order when:

7. See § 4A–209(b)(1)(ii).

the [beneficiary's] bank receives final settlement of the obligation through a Federal Reserve Bank or through a funds-transfer system.

Under 4A–403(a)(2), a beneficiary's bank receives payment of the entire amount of the sender's order if:

the sender (i) credited an account of the [beneficiary's] bank with the sender, or (ii) caused an account of the [beneficiary's] bank in another bank to be credited, [and] * * * the credit is withdrawn, or if not withdrawn, at midnight of the day on which the credit is withdrawable and the [beneficiary's] bank learns of that fact.

In order for acceptance by a beneficiary's bank to occur under 4A–209(b)(2), the sender of the payment order must be a bank.[8] Because a funds transfer must be executed through the banking system, all senders of payment orders, except for the originator of the funds transfer, must be banks. Thus, this requirement that the bank must be the sender of the payment order precludes acceptance by a beneficiary's bank only where the originator of the funds transfer, a non-bank sender, transfers a payment order to the originator's bank, and the originator's bank is also the beneficiary's bank.

Under 4A–209(b)(2), a beneficiary's bank most frequently accepts by receiving final settlement of the obligation through the Federal Reserve Bank or through a funds transfer system. To settle through the Federal Reserve, both the sender of the payment order and the receiving bank (or their representatives) must maintain accounts at the Federal Reserve. To settle through a funds transfer system, both the sender and the receiving bank must be participants in the funds transfer system.

If a payment order is sent from the sender to the receiving bank through a Federal Reserve Bank, the payment order will normally be sent by a Fedwire transmission. For each payment order that a Federal Reserve Bank receives over Fedwire, the Federal Reserve Bank immediately debits the account of the sender and credits the account of the receiving bank.[9] Payment occurs under Regulation J (12 CFR § 210.31) at the time the receiving bank's account is credited. But even though the receiving bank's account has been credited, acceptance of a payment order cannot occur until the receiving bank also receives the payment order.[10] Thus, in a Fedwire transmission through a Federal Reserve Bank, because the beneficiary's bank account has already been credited, final settlement may occur at once but acceptance cannot occur

8. See § 4A–403(a)(1) & (a)(2).

9. § 4A–403, Comment 1.

10. § 4A–209(c).

under 4A–209(c) until the receiving bank (beneficiary's bank) also receives the payment order.

By contrast, in a funds transfer through CHIPS, final settlement occurs at the end of the day. Sometimes CHIPS participants will be senders of payment orders; sometimes they will be recipients of payment orders. In other words, sometimes they will owe funds; sometimes they will be owed funds. Rather than settling each payment order as it is received, CHIPS participants simply send each other payment messages during the day. A central computer records these messages, and at the end of the day, it determines the net debit or net credit positions of all the participants. Each member of CHIPS that is a net debtor is then required to transfer funds via Fedwire into a special CHIPS settlement account maintained at the New York Federal Reserve Bank. After all of the net debtors have funded the special settlement account, the New York Federal Reserve Bank will be instructed to credit the accounts of the net creditors via Fedwire. When all of the funds have been disbursed by outgoing Fedwires, final settlement occurs.[11]

In summary, if a Federal Reserve Bank receives a payment order over Fedwire, the Federal Reserve Bank will immediately debit the account of the sender and credit the account of the receiving bank. Payment occurs under Regulation J (12 CFR § 210.31) at the time the receiving bank's account is credited, but acceptance may occur only after it receives the payment order. By contrast, if a payment order is sent through a funds transfer system, like CHIPS, final settlement occurs not on credit of the account or on receipt of the order, but when net creditors are paid. In our example, this occurs at the end of the day.

If the sender and receiving bank do not settle an obligation through a Federal Reserve Bank or through a funds transfer system, payment is usually made when the sender credits an account of the receiving bank, or causes a credit to occur in the account of the receiving bank, and the receiving bank withdraws the credit. If the receiving bank does not withdraw the credit, payment occurs on midnight of the day on which the receiving bank learns that the credit is withdrawable.

11. See § 4A–403, Comments 1 and 4; Lawrence, Expansion of the Uniform Commercial Code: Kansas Enacts Article 4A, 59, SEP J.Kan.B.A. 27 (Sept. 1990); Baxter, Commercial Law and Practice Course Handbook Series, Basic UCC Skills 1990: Article 4A Payment, 542 PLI/Comm 93 (1990), pg. 14 of 253 from Westlaw.

PROBLEM

1. At 9:00 A.M., JP Morgan Chase issues a payment order through the Federal Reserve Bank via Fedwire for National City to credit the account of Goodyear for $1 million. At 9:01 A.M., the Federal Reserve debits JP Morgan Chase's account, and credits National City's account. At 9:10 A.M., Federal Reserve Bank sends JP Morgan Chase's payment order to National City who receives it at 9:11 A.M. When does payment occur?

   Payment by Sender to the Receiving Bank occurred at 9:01, 4A–403(a)(1). At 9:01 National City, "accepted" the order, 4A–209(b)(2) and National City is so obliged to pay Goodyear, 4A–404.

2. At 9:00 A.M., Citibank issues a payment order through CHIPS to National City instructing National City to credit the account of Goodyear for $1 million. At 9:01 A.M., National City receives the payment order. At 5:00 P.M., net creditors of transfers through CHIPS are paid.

   Because the order is sent through CHIPS, acceptance occurs at the end of the day when net creditors are paid by the New York Federal Reserve Bank via Fedwire. Therefore, National City Bank accepted at 5:00 P.M.

3. At 9:00 A.M., General Motors, a non-bank, sends a payment order to its bank, JP Morgan Chase, instructing it to transfer funds to Bridgestone Tire, who also maintains an account with JP Morgan Chase. At 9:02 A.M., JP Morgan Chase receives the order. At 9:15 A.M., JP Morgan Chase credits Bridgestone Tire's account. At 9:20 A.M. JP Morgan Chase notifies Bridgestone Tire of its right to withdraw credit.

   Because the order is sent by a non-bank sender to the Beneficiary's Bank, acceptance cannot occur under 4A–209(b)(2). Acceptance occurs under 4A–209(b)(1) at 9:20 A.M. when Bridgestone Tire is notified of its right to withdraw the credit.

4. At 9:00 A.M., JP Morgan Chase issues a payment order directly to National City to credit the account of Goodyear for $1 million. At 9:10 A.M., JP Morgan Chase credits the account of National City at JP Morgan Chase for $1M. At 9:15 A.M., JP Morgan Chase notifies National City of the credit. At 9:20 A.M. National City withdraws (debits) the credit and makes the funds available for Goodyear to withdraw.

   Acceptance occurs at 9:20 A.M. when National City "receives payment" under 4A–209(b)(2), 4A–403(a)(3).

c. Passage of Time, Inaction

Finally, a beneficiary's bank can accept a payment order by passage of time, without any action on its part. In order for acceptance to occur by inaction, the beneficiary's bank must have received full payment from the sender in a way that did not constitute acceptance under 4A–209(b)(2). Section 4A–209(b)(3) provides for that acceptance as follows:

> [Acceptance occurs at the] opening of the next funds transfer business day of the bank following the payment date of the order if, at that time, the amount of the sender's order is fully covered by a withdrawable credit balance in an authorized account of the sender or the bank has otherwise received full payment from the sender, unless the order was rejected before that time or is rejected within (i) one hour after that time, or (ii) one hour after the opening of the next business day of the sender following the payment date if that time is later.

This provision applies whether or not the sender is a bank. It applies in two situations. First is the rare case where the sender has paid the receiving bank by a method other than causing a credit to occur in the bank account of the beneficiary's bank. Second is the case where the transfer is fully covered by a withdrawable credit balance in a bank account of the *sender* maintained at the beneficiary's bank.

Section 4A–209(b)(3) provides that when one of these cases arises, the beneficiary's bank accepts the order at the opening of the next funds transfer day after the payment date of the order. The beneficiary's bank can avoid such acceptance only by successfully rejecting the payment order before the opening of the next transfer day, or within one hour of that time.[12]

---

12. Comment 7 to 4A–209 reads in full as follows:

Subsection (b)(3) covers cases of inaction by the beneficiary's bank. It applies whether or not the sender is a bank and covers a case in which the sender and the beneficiary both have accounts with the receiving bank and payment will be made by debiting the account of the sender and crediting the account of the beneficiary. Subsection (b)(3) is similar to subsection (b)(2) in that it bases acceptance by the beneficiary's bank on payment by the sender. Payment by the sender is effected by a debit to the sender's account if the account balance is sufficient to cover the amount of the order. On the payment date (Section 4A–401) of the order the beneficiary's bank will normally credit the beneficiary's account and notify the beneficiary of receipt of the order if it is satisfied that the sender's account balance covers the order or is willing to give credit to the sender. In some cases, however, the

bank may not be willing to give credit to the sender and it may not be possible for the bank to determine until the end of the day on the payment date whether there are sufficient good funds in the sender's account. There may be various transactions during the day involving funds going into and out of the account. Some of these transactions may occur late in the day or after the close of the banking day. To accommodate this situation, subsection (b)(3) provides that the status of the account is determined at the opening of the next funds transfer business day of the beneficiary's bank after the payment date of the order. If the sender's account balance is sufficient to cover the order, the beneficiary's bank has a source of payment and the result in almost all cases is that the bank accepts the order at that time if it did not previously accept under subsection (b)(1). In rare cases, a bank may want to avoid acceptance under subsec-

In order to determine when a beneficiary's bank accepts under 4A–209(b)(3), one must first determine the "payment date" of the order. The "payment date" is the day that the beneficiary is to be paid by the beneficiary's bank. This day will be either the date specified on the payment order if the beneficiary's bank receives the order before the date specified, or the day the order is received by the beneficiary's bank if no payment date is specified or if the beneficiary's bank receives the order after the date specified.[13] To illustrate the latter possibility, suppose that National City, the beneficiary's bank, receives a payment order on Day 2 with a specified payment date of Day 1. Because a payment date cannot be before the beneficiary's bank receives the payment order, the payment date will be considered to be Day 2. If Sender has paid National City by means other than a credit or has sufficient funds in an authorized account to cover the balance, acceptance by the beneficiary's bank will occur under 4A–209(b)(3) at the opening of the next funds transfer business day, here Day 3 if Day 3 is a business day.[14]

§ 7–11 Acceptance by Originator's Bank

If the originator's bank is also the beneficiary's bank, acceptance generally occurs when it pays the beneficiary. If the originator's bank is not also the beneficiary's bank, the originator's bank is treated like an intermediary bank, and acceptance by an originator's bank generally occurs when the originator's bank "executes the order."[1]

tion (b)(3) by rejecting the order as discussed in Comment 8.

13. § 4A–401.

14. One should note that the day the order is physically received by the receiving bank, whether it is the originator's bank, beneficiary's bank, neither, or both, may not be the day the payment order is legally received for purposes of Article 4A. First of all, the payment order may be received by the receiving bank outside the "funds transfer business day", i.e., the "part of a day during which the receiving bank is open for the receipt, processing, and transmittal of payment orders and cancellations and amendments of payment orders" (§ 4A–105(4)). Furthermore, the receiving bank may establish "cut-off" times for the receipt and processing of payment orders. These cutoff times do not have to be uniform. Section 4A–106(a) provides that:

Different cut-off times may apply to payment orders, cancellations, or amendments, or to different categories of payment orders, cancellations, or amendments. A cut-off time may apply to senders generally or different cut-off times may apply to different senders or categories of payment orders. § 4A–106(a).

If a payment order is received after the close of the "funds transfer business day" or after the "cut-off" time, the order is deemed to be received at the opening of the next funds transfer business day (§ 4A–106(a)); See, Baxter, Commercial Law and Practice Course Handbook Series, Basic UCC Skills 1990: Article 4A Payment, 542 PLI/Comm 93 (1990), pgs. 205 of 253 from Westlaw; Fry, Basic Concepts in Article 4A: Scope and Definitions, 45 Bus. Law. 1401, 1423 (1990).

§ 7–11

1. § 4A–209(a). Acceptance by the originator's bank cannot occur before the payment date, if the originator's

One should note that only the originator's bank is precluded from accepting an order before the execution date, or payment date, whichever is applicable. Regardless of the execution date specified, a receiving bank that is not the originator's bank (or the beneficiary's bank) accepts an order by executing it. While the receiving bank may be liable for early or late execution, its execution constitutes acceptance. A beneficiary's bank can accept an order, regardless of the payment date, either by paying the beneficiary or by receiving full payment from its immediate sender.

PROBLEM

Assume that General Motors sends a payment order to its bank, JP Morgan Chase, instructing that JP Morgan Chase transfer funds from its account and cause a credit to occur in the account of Goodyear at National City. General Motors specifies an execution date and payment date of Day 5. JP Morgan Chase receives the order at 1:00 P.M. on Day 1. At 4:45 P.M. on Day 1, JP Morgan Chase executes the order by issuing its own payment order to National City, instructing National City to credit Goodyear's account. At 10:00 A.M. on Day 2, National City credits Goodyear's account and notifies Goodyear of its right to withdraw the credit. On Day 3, Goodyear files for Chapter 11. Later on Day 3, General Motors decides to cancel its payment order to Goodyear. Can General Motors cancel the order and get its account with Chase recredited?

It can. Even though JP Morgan Chase executed its payment order on Day 2, JP Morgan Chase (originator's bank) cannot accept the payment order until the execution date on Day 5,

---

bank is also the beneficiary's bank, or the execution date, if the originator's bank is not the beneficiary's bank (§ 4A–209(d)).

As previously stated, the "payment date" is the day that the beneficiary is to be paid by the beneficiary's bank. This day will be specified on the payment order by the sender, or will be the day the order is received by the beneficiary's bank, if receipt occurs later than the date specified. If no date is specified on the payment order, the "payment date" is the day the order is received by the beneficiary's bank (§ 4A–401).

The "execution date" of the payment order is the day on which the receiving bank may properly issue a payment order in execution of the sender's order (§ 4A–301). The "execution date" refers to the time a receiving bank should execute a payment order, rather than the day the receiving bank actually executes a payment order (§ 4A–301 Comment 2).

The "execution date" will be:

1) the day the order is received if no instruction or payment date is given; or

2) the day specified by instruction of the sender of the payment order, but not before the day the order is received; or

3) if only a payment date is given, the execution date is the payment date, or an earlier date on which execution is reasonably necessary to allow payment to the beneficiary on the payment date, but the execution date cannot be before the day the order is received (4A–301(b)).

4A–209(d). A sender of a payment order is not obligated to pay the receiving bank until the receiving bank accepts the payment order. Furthermore, the sender may cancel or amend a payment order at any time before a receiving bank accepts the order. Because JP Morgan Chase is deemed to have accepted only on Day 5, General Motors successfully canceled its payment order, and therefore, is not obligated to pay JP Morgan Chase for the amount of the payment order. However, JP Morgan Chase cannot cancel its payment order to National City because National City accepted the payment order on Day 2 when it credited the account of Goodyear and notified Goodyear of its right to withdraw the credit (4A–209(b)(1)). JP Morgan Chase is left to fight with Goodyear's trustee in bankruptcy (or with General Motors for restitution if General Motors gets its tires).[2]

§ 7–12   Exceptions to the General 4A–209 Rules of Acceptance

In certain circumstances, specifically those listed in 4A–209(c) and (d), acceptance of a payment order does not occur despite the potential occurrence of events that would otherwise constitute acceptance under earlier provisions of 4A–209. The result of such situations is that the sender of the payment order at issue retains title to the funds involved, as the receiving bank did not take title by properly accepting the payment order.[1]

Several of these restrictions on acceptance are temporal and apply to all manners of acceptance listed in 4A–209. "Acceptance of a payment order cannot occur before the order is received by the receiving bank."[2] Furthermore, as noted in § 23–5, "payment order[s] issued to the originator's bank cannot be accepted until the payment date if the bank is the beneficiary's bank, or the execution date if the bank is not the beneficiary's bank."[3]

PROBLEM

1. An employee in General Motors' Treasury Department calls her contact in JP Morgan Chase's Wire Transfer Department

---

2. Note that a restitution claim would not be preempted by Article 4A on these facts, given the express allowance for such a claim in 4A–209(d).

2. § 4A–209(c).

3. § 4A–209(d).

§ 7–12

1. *See* U.S. v. BCCI Holdings (Luxembourg), S.A., 980 F.Supp. 21 (D.D.C. 1997).

at 9:05 A.M. to advise of the particulars regarding an important payment order to Goodyear that she will be sending later that day. Unfortunately, the JP Morgan Chase employee misunderstands the instructions, and sends a payment order to National City Bank at 9:15 A.M. National City then credits Goodyear's account at 9:35 A.M. Just before sending the payment order to JP Morgan Chase at 11:00 A.M., the General Motors employee discovers that the payment was not due until the following week, so she files the payment order away without contacting JP Morgan Chase. In the interim, Goodyear files for bankruptcy, and JP Morgan Chase sues General Motors seeking reimbursement for the payment order. Who wins?

Section 4A–103(a)(1) does allow payment orders to be sent orally, but if General Motors can prove that its agreement with JP Morgan Chase required an electronic or hard copy of the order, acceptance would not have occurred under 4A–207(c) because JP Morgan Chase never actually received its copy of the order. In that case, JP Morgan Chase would take the loss and would not be entitled to reimbursement from General Motors.

2. General Motors sends two payment orders to JP Morgan Chase on Day 1. The first instructs JP Morgan Chase to credit another one of its customer's accounts for $5 million, with an execution date of Day 4. The second order instructs JP Morgan Chase to issue a payment order to Citibank to pay $10 million to a New York-based consulting firm with a payment date of Day 2. On Day 3, General Motors contacts JP Morgan Chase and seeks to cancel both payment orders. Can General Motors cancel?

Yes and no. Section 4A–209(d) will allow them to cancel the first order (because the execution date has not yet been reached), but the second order cannot be cancelled (as the payment date has passed, and JP Morgan Chase already "accepted" the order).

The remaining exceptions are limited to acceptances listed in 4A–209(b)(2) and (3) (acceptance occurs on receipt of full payment of the sender's payment order or on the opening of the next business day). Here, acceptance does not occur if "the beneficiary of the payment order does not have an account with the receiving bank, the account has been closed, or the receiving bank is not permitted by law to receive credits for the beneficiary's account."[4]

§ 7–13 Rejection of Payment Orders

What if JP Morgan Chase receives the instruction to pay from General Motors, but does not wish to follow the instructions? JP

---

4. § 4A–209(c).

Morgan Chase may wish to reject the payment order for a number of reasons: General Motors's account may be overdrawn and JP Morgan Chase may not be willing to bear the risk of General Motors's insolvency; JP Morgan Chase may find the payment instructions ambiguous or inconsistent; or JP Morgan Chase may not be able to carry out the instructions because of equipment failure, credit limitations or some other factor which makes proper execution of the order technically impossible.[1]

In the absence of an agreement to the contrary, and unless the receiving bank is a participant in a funds transfer system that requires acceptance of payment orders, a receiving bank has no duty to accept a payment order.[2] The payment order is merely a request to the receiving bank to accept the order.[3] A receiving bank may send notice of rejection orally, electronically, or in writing.[4] If notice is given by reasonable means, rejection of the payment order is effective when the notice is sent. If the means is not reasonable, rejection is effective only when the notice is received.[5] However, because the receiving bank and the sender will be in electronic contact with each other, the notice of rejection will normally be received milliseconds after it is sent.[6] If the parties have specified a means of rejecting payment orders, reasonableness will be defined by those means.[7]

a. Rejection by Receiving Bank That Is Not Beneficiary's Bank

Absent an express agreement or a funds transfer system rule, a receiving bank that is not a beneficiary's bank can accept a payment order only by executing its own payment order. That is, such a receiving bank cannot accept a payment order by remaining silent. Therefore, a receiving bank that is not the beneficiary's bank need not send notice of rejection of the payment order to the sender in order to reject the payment order. It can reject by inaction.

While the receiving bank generally has no obligation to accept a payment order or to give notice of rejection, at least one court has suggested that the receiving bank has a limited duty to not reject the payment order in bad faith or as an abuse of discretion.[8] In any

---

§ 7–13

1. See § 4A–210, Comment 1.

2. § 4A–212 and Comment.

3. However, the receiving bank is bound by its first act of acceptance or rejection. Acceptance of a payment order precludes later rejection of the payment order; rejection of the payment order precludes later acceptance (§ 4A–210(d)).

4. § 4A–210(a).

5. § 4A–210(a).

6. § 4A–210, Comment 2.

7. See § 4A–210(a).

8. See Banco de la Provincia de Buenos Aires v. BayBank Boston, N.A., 985 F.Supp. 364 (S.D.N.Y. 1997) (holding that BPBA did not act in bad faith or abuse its discretion when it refused to execute a payment order from its customer, Banco Faigan, another Argentinean bank that had its operations

event, the receiving bank may still be liable to pay interest to the sender under certain situations. For example, if the receiving bank fails to execute a payment order after its execution date and the sender had a withdrawable credit balance in an authorized account sufficient to cover the payment order, the receiving bank should be liable for any delay.[9] The sender will be entitled to interest on the amount of the order, if the funds were placed in a non-interest bearing account, for the number of days elapsing after the execution date of the payment order to the earlier of (1) the close of the fifth funds transfer day after the execution date[10] or (2) the day the sender receives notice or learns that the order was not executed (counting the final day of the period as an elapsed day).[11]

b. Rejection by Beneficiary's Bank

A beneficiary's bank can accept payment orders either by inaction or through receipt of payment without any other act on its part.[12] Acceptance by passage of time under 4A–209(b)(3) occurs at "the opening of the next funds-transfer business day of the [beneficiary's] bank following the payment date of the order if, at that time, the amount of the sender's order is fully covered by a withdrawable credit balance in an authorized account of the sender or the bank has otherwise received full payment from the sender," provided that the beneficiary's bank does not reject the order before that time (or within one hour of that time, or one hour after the opening of the next business day of the sender following the payment date if that time is later). Article 4A gives the bank overnight to ensure that the sender has sufficient funds to pay:

> In some cases * * * it may not be possible for the bank to determine until the end of the day on the payment date whether there are sufficient good funds in the sender's account. There may be various transactions during the day involving funds going into and out of the account. Some of these transactions may occur late in the day or after the close of the banking day. To accommodate this situation, subsection (b)(3) provides that the status of the account is determined at the opening of the next funds transfer business day of the beneficiary's bank after the payment date of the order.[13]

Even if the beneficiary's bank successfully rejects a payment order, the beneficiary's bank may be obligated to pay interest to the

suspended by Argentinean banking authorities, and instead set off proceeds in the subject account to satisfy a debt owed by Banco Faigan to BPBA.)

9. See § 4A–210(b) and Comment 3.

10. Under § 4A–211(d), unaccepted payment orders are deemed canceled by operation of law "at the close of the fifth

funds transfer business day of the receiving bank after the execution date or payment date of the order."

11. §§ 4A–210(b), 4A–211(d).

12. See § 4A–209(b)(2)–(3).

13. § 4A–209, Comment 7.

sender. If notice of rejection is received by the sender after the payment date, and the sender had sufficient funds placed in a non-interest bearing account to cover the payment order, the beneficiary's bank is obliged to pay interest to the sender as provided in the last two sentences of 4A–209(b)(3).[14] By paying interest the beneficiary's bank is compensating the sender for being deprived of the use of funds reasonably expected to be used to pay the beneficiary's bank.[15]

§ 7–14   Cancellation and Amendment of Payment Orders

a.   Originator's Power to Stop Payment

What if the originator, not the originator's bank (General Motors, not JP Morgan Chase), has second thoughts and wants to stop payment? Assume that General Motors discovers at 4:30 on Monday afternoon that Goodyear has filed bankruptcy, but has not yet delivered the tires for which payment is being made. Frantic, it calls JP Morgan Chase and asks JP Morgan Chase to cancel the $10 million payment order. Can the order be canceled?

In the case posed there will be no unilateral right to cancel under 4A–211. This is so because of the reasons stated above in the discussion of JP Morgan Chase's attempt to cancel the payment order. As there, the receiving bank, JP Morgan Chase, has accepted by executing the order under 4A–209(a). The order was executed by sending it on to the Federal Reserve, 4A–301(a). Because JP Morgan Chase has accepted, it has no obligation under 4A–211 to recognize General Motors's cancellation. Nevertheless it could agree to cancel the order, but it would be foolish to do so unless it could confirm that there had been no acceptance at the Federal Reserve or at National City in Cleveland. If either downstream bank has accepted, JP Morgan Chase may be liable to them.

The effect of all of this is that the customer (the person who would be the drawer on a check) has essentially the same right to cancel a payment order as the originator's bank (the payor in a check transaction). But because of the speed of an electronic funds transfer, the opportunity routinely available in a common check transaction for the drawer to issue a stop payment order to its payor in a leisurely manner a few days after the check has been drawn is *not* available to the originator of a funds transfer. Also, the payor is at the beginning of the transaction in an electronic funds transfer (not at the end as in a check transaction). Thus, the rights of the two parties, the originator and the originator's bank,

---

14. *See*   §§ 4A–209(b)(3),   4A–209   **15.** *See* § 4A–209, Comment 8.
Comment 8.

to cancel are likely to be cut off at about the same time by acceptance and payment downstream.

To see how these rules in Article 4A apply, consider the facts of the *Delbrueck* case. Although Delbrueck & Co. v. Manufacturers Hanover Trust Co.[1] is a pre-Article 4A case, its facts remain instructive for illustrating the mechanics of canceling payment orders. Delbrueck was buying and selling large quantities of foreign currency. Delbrueck entered into three foreign exchange contracts with Herstatt. Two contracts called for payment on June 26; one contract called for payment on June 27. Delbrueck agreed in the contracts to pay by transferring U.S. funds to Herstatt's bank account at Chase Manhattan in New York. Herstatt agreed in return to transfer equivalent deutschemarks to Delbrueck's bank account in Hamburg, Germany at Landeszentralbank. On June 25, Delbrueck instructed its bank, Manufacturers, to transfer funds due on June 26 to Herstatt's bank account at Chase. Early on June 26, Delbrueck instructed Manufacturers to transfer further funds due on June 27 to Herstatt's bank account. Herstatt had transferred deutschemarks to Delbrueck's bank account in Germany late on June 26, and the funds were credited to Delbrueck around 6:00 A.M. (New York time). At 10:45 A.M., Delbrueck learned that the German banking authorities had closed Herstatt because it was insolvent.

At 11:30 A.M. and before Manufacturers had executed any of Delbrueck's three payment orders, Delbrueck instructed Manufacturers to cancel the June 27 payment order. At 11:36 A.M. and 11:37 A.M., respectively, Manufacturers transferred through CHIPS to Chase the two payment orders due to Herstatt on June 26. At noon, Delbrueck instructed Manufactures to cancel the two June 26 payment orders, but Manufacturers had already executed the orders. By oral communication during the afternoon, Manufacturers tried to cancel the payment order to Chase, but Chase refused; it credited Herstatt's account at 9:00 P.M.

Delbrueck sued Manufacturers. It argued that the transfers were revocable until 9:00 P.M., that Manufacturers was negligent and that Manufacturers breached its implied creditor-depositor contract with Delbrueck by failing to revoke the transfers. Specifically, Delbrueck argued that if Manufacturers had delivered to Chase a written revocation of the transfer before 9:00 P.M., Chase would have been obligated under common law to return the funds.

In ruling against Delbrueck, the court found that common law and the understanding of banks using the CHIPS system at the time supported the conclusion that the transfers were irrevocable.

§ 7–14
1. 609 F.2d 1047 (2d Cir.1979).

How would Article 4A apply if it had been in force? Because Manufacturers had already "accepted" Delbrueck's order by "executing" it before noon on the 26th, Delbrueck, as the originator would have had no unilateral right to cancellation under section 4A–211. On the other hand, it is possible that Manufacturers would have agreed to attempt to cancel its order to Chase and it is quite possible that its order had not yet been accepted by Chase at the time Delbrueck attempted cancellation on the morning of the 26th. Under section 4A–209(b) Chase probably had not yet accepted the order from Manufacturers to pay Herstatt. To have accepted the order Chase would have had to have paid Herstatt (and to have done that under 4A–405, it would have had to have credited Herstatt's account and notified Herstatt that the funds were available, or ""'otherwise'"" have made them available). These events probably did not happen by noon on the 26th.

Alternatively, Chase would have accepted under 4A–209(b)(2) if it had "received payment" under 4A–403(a)(1) or (a)(2), but since the payment was through CHIPS where settlement was not to occur until the evening of the 26th, Chase would not yet have "received payment." The other acceptance possibility, 4A–209(b)(3) ("the opening of the next funds transfer business day") does not contemplate acceptance until the morning of the 27th.

Thus, under Article 4A (and ignoring the current version of CHIPS Rule 2 discussed *infra* in subsection b) it is likely that the *Delbrueck* case would have come out differently than it did under the common law. Contrary to the common law conclusion in the *Delbrueck* opinion, payment orders under 4A are normally cancelable until the time of their acceptance and, in this case, it is likely that acceptance of the second order (to Chase) would not have occurred until late on the 26th or the morning of the 27th.[2]

b.   Cancellation of an Unaccepted Payment Order

Under Article 4A, a sender who wishes to cancel or amend a payment order may transmit a request to do so orally, electronically, or in writing.[3] The sender, however, must transmit this request at a time and in a manner that gives the receiving bank a reasonable opportunity to act on the communication before it accepts the original payment order.[4] Furthermore, if a security procedure is in effect between the sender and the receiving bank, the receiving bank is not bound by the communication canceling or amending the

---

2. For a post-Article 4A case dealing with similar facts, see Aleo International Ltd. v. Citibank, N.A., 160 Misc.2d 950, 612 N.Y.S.2d 540, 24 UCC2d 164 (N.Y.Sup.Ct. 1994).

3. § 4A–211(a). Under Article 4A, an amendment of a payment order is treat-

ed as a cancellation of the original payment order at the time of amendment and the issuance of a new payment order in the amended form at the same time. § 4A–211(e).

4. § 4A–211(b).

order unless the communication is verified by the security procedure or the receiving bank agrees to cancel or amend the payment
order.[5]

Assuming the receiving bank has not yet accepted the payment
order, and has a reasonable opportunity to act on the communication before acceptance, the sender may unilaterally cancel or amend
the order. Section 4A–211 so provides. A receiving bank cannot
accept an effectively canceled order.[6] For instance, in *Delbrueck*, if
Delbrueck had telexed Manufacturers at 11:30 A.M. to cancel all of
its payment orders to Herstatt, this instruction would have been
effective to cancel all of the payment orders to Herstatt. As of this
time, Manufacturers had not begun executing any of Delbrueck's
payment orders to Herstatt.

Under the current CHIPS Rules,[7] even a cancellation transmitted prior to acceptance under Article 4A may not be effective to
countermand a payment order that has already been transmitted.
This is not because of any rule in Article 4A, but because of a
sentence in CHIPS Rule 2(d). The sentence states:

> Release of a payment message by CHIPS to the Receiving
> Participant creates an obligation of the Sending Participant to
> pay the Receiving Participant the amount of the payment
> message, and ... this obligation is netted to the extent provid-
> ed for in Rule 13 and settled in accordance with Rule 13.

The most obvious reading of that sentence would bind both Chase
and Manufacturers Hanover as early as 11:37, once CHIPS had
"released" the "payment message" to Chase. Manufacturers Hanover, therefore, could no longer "cancel" or "amend" it.

Lastly, 4A–211(d) provides that "[a]n unaccepted payment
order is canceled by operation of law" five business days after the
"execution date or payment date of the order." Given the speed
with which most funds transfer transactions are processed, this
situation should not arise often. However, *Impulse Trading, Inc. v.
Norwest Bank Minnesota, N.A.*[8] illustrates one such case where the
court applied this provision in holding that the subject payment
order could not have been accepted because it was "canceled by
operation of law."

c. *Cancellation of an Accepted Payment Order*

Under the circumstances there provided, section 4A–211 generally allows unilateral cancellation of unaccepted orders. It also

---

5. See §§ 4A–211(a), 4A–211, Comment 2.

6. See §§ 4A–211(b), 4A–211(e), 4A–
211, Comment 3.

7. Available at: http://www.chips.org/
reference/docs_rules/docs_reference_
rules.php.

8. 907 F.Supp. 1284 (D. Minn. 1995).

permits cancellation of accepted orders if the receiving party agrees to the cancellation. And it permits cancellation of some accepted orders without the agreement of the receiving bank if a funds transfer system rule allows cancellation. All of this is set out in section 4A–211(c) that reads in full as follows:

> (c) After a payment order has been accepted, cancellation or amendment of the order is not effective unless the receiving bank agrees or a funds transfer system rule allows cancellation or amendment without agreement of the bank.
>
> > (1) With respect to a payment order accepted by a receiving bank other than the beneficiary's bank, cancellation or amendment is not effective unless a conforming cancellation or amendment of the payment order issued by the receiving bank is also made.
> >
> > (2) With respect to a payment order accepted by the beneficiary's bank, cancellation or amendment is not effective unless the order was issued in execution of an unauthorized payment order, or because of a mistake by a sender in the funds transfer which resulted in the issuance of a payment order (i) that is a duplicate of a payment order previously issued by the sender, (ii) that orders payment to a beneficiary not entitled to receive payment from the originator, or (iii) that orders payment in an amount greater than the amount the beneficiary was entitled to receive from the originator. If the payment order is canceled or amended, the beneficiary's bank is entitled to recover from the beneficiary any amount paid to the beneficiary to the extent allowed by the law governing mistake and restitution.[9]

We have difficulty understanding the relationship between subparts (1) and (2) of the subsection. To understand our difficulty, consider two hypothetical cases. Assume first that a funds transfer rule allows cancellation even though the receiving bank does not agree and even though the order has been accepted. And assume further that the order to be canceled is a conventional order that does not exhibit any of the three conditions outlined in 4A–211(c)(2). Does the sender have a unilateral right to cancel because of the funds transfer system rule? Or does the funds transfer rule govern only if the transfer meets the conditions having to do with

---

9. See Community Bank v. Stevens Fin. Corp., 966 F.Supp. 775 (N.D. Ind. 1997) (interpreting 4A–211(c)(2)(i) in a situation involving an originator's bank that sent an initial payment order to the wrong beneficiary bank but then sent a second payment order to the proper beneficiary bank without first securing return of the funds from the initial payment order. The court held that the initial payment order did not qualify as a "duplicate" under 4A–211(c)(2)(i) because that section only contemplates the second payment order to be a duplicate).

mistake, duplication, and the like in (c)(2)?[10] The Comments, and specifically the cross reference in Comment 3 of 4A–211 to section 4A–501 (contrary rule by agreement), might suggest that even accepted orders that do not meet the conditions in (c)(2) may be unilaterally canceled by the sender if they were transmitted through a funds transfer system that so permits. But 4A–211(h) specifically overrules that inference and makes the funds transfer rule not effective to the extent it conflicts with subsection (c)(2). The same is not necessarily true for (c)(1). The Comments suggest that the conditions in (c)(1) are not conditions on the operation of a funds transfer rule that would provide for the opposite and allow for a cancellation.

Since the people who have drafted the NACHA rules, the CHIPS rules, and the federal regulations all had a hand in drafting Article 4A or in advising the drafters, those other regulations and association rules are not likely to deviate far from the rules in Article 4A. For example, rule 7.1 of the NACHA operating rules bars "a right to recall, require the return of or adjustment to, or stop the payment or posting of any entry" after the automated entry has been "received" by the ACH operator. Exceptions to rule 7.1 permit some limited reversals where there have been duplicate entries or where erroneous data was transmitted. These exceptions to the bar are generally analogous to the rule in 4A–211(c)(2).[11]

d. Beneficiary's Bank's Limited Right to Agree to a Cancellation

Section 4A–211(c)(2) also limits the right of the receiving bank (the beneficiary's bank) to "agree" to a cancellation in certain circumstances where there is no rule that gives a unilateral right to cancel. That these limit a beneficiary's bank's right to agree to a cancellation is supported, for example, by Comment 4 to 4A–211 that reads in part as follows:

> Since acceptance affects the rights of the originator and the beneficiary it is not appropriate to allow the beneficiary's bank to agree to cancellation or amendment except in unusual cases. Except as provided in subsection (c)(2), cancellation or amend-

10. Of course, if there is no funds transfer system anywhere that purports to allow such cancellation the question is moot for the time being at least.

11. Rule 7.1 *Recall by ODFI or Originator*—Except as allowed by sections 2.4 (Reversing Files), 2.5 (Reversing Entries), and 2.6 (Reclamation Entries), neither an Originator nor an ODFI has the right to recall an entry or file, to require the return of or adjustment to an entry, or to stop the payment or posting of an entry, once the entry or file has been received by the Originating ACH Operator.

Section 2.4 provides for reversal of some entries after acceptance.

Regulation J currently has no provision that would allow reversal long after acceptance, nor are we aware of any other communication system that does.

ment after acceptance by the beneficiary's bank is not possible unless all parties affected by the order agree. Under subsection (c)(2), cancellation or amendment is possible only in the four cases stated.

If, therefore, one reads (c)(2) to say that a beneficiary's bank that has accepted an order may agree to cancellation of that order only if one of four sets of circumstances exist, what are those circumstances? First, the beneficiary's bank may agree to cancel (or amend) where the order was issued in execution of an unauthorized payment order. Second, the beneficiary's bank may agree to cancel (or amend) where, because of a mistake by a sender in the funds transfer, the payment order is a duplicate of a payment order previously issued by the sender. Third, the beneficiary's bank may agree to cancel (or amend) where, because of a mistake by a sender in the funds transfer, the payment order requires payment to a beneficiary not entitled to receive payment from the originator. Fourth, the beneficiary's bank may agree to cancel (or amend) where, because of a mistake by a sender in the funds transfer, the payment order calls for payment in an amount greater than the amount the beneficiary was entitled to receive from the originator. In none of these is the beneficiary entitled to receive all of the money in the payment order and in many of the cases the beneficiary would be entitled to none of the money under the payment order.

Note that the beneficiary's bank is not obligated to agree to such a cancellation[12] and as Comment 5 points out:

> [T]he beneficiary's bank may not have any way of knowing whether the requirements of subsection (c) have been met or whether it will be able to recover payment from the beneficiary that received payment.

Even though agreement to a cancellation automatically entitles the bank to indemnification from the sender under subsection (f), the bank that enters into such an agreement is certain to anger its customer and likely to involve itself in a lawsuit. Indemnification may not be a complete protection. We expect to see few agreements by beneficiaries' banks to cancel (or amend) accepted orders. This is particularly true since the beneficiary's bank will not know whether one of the four sets of circumstances in (c)(2) has been met and may be understandably hesitant to accept the sender's word.

---

12. The only case on point is Cumis Ins. Society, Inc. v. Citibank, N.A., 921 F.Supp. 1100 (S.D.N.Y. 1996), where the court held that the beneficiary's bank was within its rights under 4A–211(c) when it allowed the beneficiary to withdraw the funds transfer's proceeds, even though Citibank previously told the originator's bank that it would put a hold on the beneficiary's account.

e. *Cancellation of Payment Orders, Some Examples*

To understand that a *sender* will rarely be able to cancel or amend an accepted payment order, consider the following problems and solutions:

PROBLEM

9:00 A.M., General Motors issues a payment order to its bank, JP Morgan Chase, to cause a credit of $10 million to occur in the account of Goodyear at National City.

9:30 A.M., General Motors, because of Goodyear's bankruptcy, changes its mind and wishes to cancel the payment order.

9:31 A.M., General Motors instructs National City to cancel the payment order when National City receives the payment order from JP Morgan Chase.

9:40 A.M., JP Morgan Chase executes the payment order by issuing its own payment order to National City. The payment order is executed through CHIPS and instructs National City to credit Goodyear's account for $10 million.

9:45 A.M., General Motors instructs JP Morgan Chase to cancel its payment order.

9:47 A.M., National City notifies Goodyear of receipt of order.

9:50 A.M., JP Morgan Chase instructs National City to cancel its payment order.

9:51 A.M., National City refuses.

10:00 A.M., National City credits Goodyear's account, but then sets off, i.e., applies credit to debt of the beneficiary, Goodyear owed to National City.

9:00 P.M., Settlement of JP Morgan Chase and National City's account through CHIPS.

1. Did General Motors effectively cancel its payment order to JP Morgan Chase?

    No. JP Morgan Chase executed General Motors' payment order at 9:40 A.M., thus accepting the payment order. General Motors did not instruct JP Morgan Chase to cancel its payment order until 9:45 A.M.

2. Did General Motors effectively cancel its payment order to National City?

    Probably not. General Motors is not the sender of the payment order to National City. JP Morgan Chase is the sender. Thus, only JP Morgan Chase has the right to cancel the payment order to National City. (Technically the immediately preceding statement is correct under 4A–211(b) which authorizes a cancellation as "effective" only when sent by "the sender." However, in the case posed we would not be surprised to see a court stretch 4A–211 to give a non-sender, General Motors, the power to cancel an unaccepted payment order.)

3.   Did JP Morgan Chase effectively cancel the payment order to National City?

No. JP Morgan Chase instructed National City to cancel at 9:50 A.M. Thus, the cancellation was ineffective if National City had accepted before 9:50 A.M. 4A–209(b) states that National City accepts at the earliest of the following times:

(1) when the bank pays the beneficiary or notifies the beneficiary of receipt of the order or that the account has been credited.

(a) National City notified Goodyear of receipt of the order at 9:47 A.M.

(b) National City paid Goodyear under 4A–405(a) at 10:00 A.M. by applying the credit to a debt that Goodyear owed National City.

(2) when beneficiary's bank receives payment of the entire amount of sender's order.

(a) National City received payment of the entire amount of JP Morgan Chase's payment order at 9:00 P.M, when accounts were settled through CHIPS.

(3) opening of the next funds transfer business day unless rejection before that time or within one hour of that time.

(a) National City could not accept at the opening of the next funds transfer business day because JP Morgan Chase canceled the payment order beforehand. Generally a receiving bank cannot accept a canceled payment order.

National City accepted at the earliest of the possible times, which was 9:47 A.M. This acceptance occurred before the instruction by JP Morgan Chase to cancel at 9:50 A.M. under (1) above. Therefore, cancellation was ineffective.

4.   What if National City had agreed to cancel the payment order at 9:50 A.M. after it had accepted at 9:47 A.M.? Would this cancellation be effective?

No. Problem 1 stated that General Motors "changed its mind" and then decided to cancel. Under 4A–211(c)(2), cancellation by a beneficiary's bank after it accepts is effective only if the payment order issued was an unauthorized payment order, or the payment order was issued because of certain mistakes by the sender in the funds transfer. Learning belatedly about Goodyear's bankruptcy is not one of circumstances specified in 4A–211(c)(2).

5. Assume the same facts as in Problem 1, except that Goodyear was never notified by National City of the receipt of the payment order. Would attempted cancellation by JP Morgan Chase at 9:50 A.M. be effective?

Yes. JP Morgan Chase agreed to cancel General Motors' payment order and a conforming cancellation of JP Morgan Chase's payment order to National City was also made. Chase effectively canceled its payment order because National City received notice of cancellation before it accepted, i.e., before Goodyear was notified.

§ 7–15   Discharge of the Originator's Underlying Obligation to the Beneficiary, § 4A–406

When has the originator (the debtor, or General Motors) discharged its underlying obligation to the beneficiary (the creditor, or Goodyear)? Recall that the underlying obligation of General Motors in our example to Goodyear arose out of a sales transaction in which General Motors agreed to pay Goodyear $10 million for tires. Section 4A–406(b) says that this obligation is discharged upon "payment" by the originator to the beneficiary. Section 4A–406(a) tells us that payment generally occurs at the time the payment order for the benefit of the beneficiary is accepted by the "beneficiary's bank."[1] In our hypothetical case this would have occurred under 4A–209(c)(2) and 4A–403(a)(1) at the time of the Fedwire transmission and settlement. Section 4A–406 discharges the originator at the same time the beneficiary's bank becomes obliged to pay the beneficiary. None of this should be surprising.

§ 7–15

1. The originator of the funds transfer does not pay the beneficiary, even though the beneficiary's bank has accepted if one of the following occur:

1) the sender of the payment order to the beneficiary's bank successfully cancels the payment order after acceptance by beneficiary's bank [4A–211(c)];

2) a funds transfer system makes acceptance by the beneficiary's bank provisional on receipt of payment by beneficiary's bank [4A–405(d)];

3) a funds transfer system, which has a loss-sharing agreement fails to settle for the sender of the payment order to the beneficiary's bank after the sender fails to pay the beneficiary's bank ("doomsday" exception) [4A–405(e)].

In each of these three situations, acceptance by the beneficiary's bank is nullified. Thus, the beneficiary's bank is deemed not to have accepted the payment order, and the originator is deemed not to have paid the beneficiary. Inasmuch as the funds transfer was not completed because the acceptance of the beneficiary's bank was nullified, however, the originator should be entitled to a refund from the originator bank under the "money back guarantee" rule.

Note that the originator of the funds transfer is generally deemed to pay the beneficiary the amount of the order accepted by the beneficiary's bank, but limited to the amount of the originator's payment order. See 4A–406(a).

Section 4A–406 contains one exception to the basic rule of discharge. This exception in subsection (b) provides that there is no discharge if (1) the payment was made by a "means prohibited by the contract of the beneficiary with respect to the obligation," (2) "the beneficiary, within a reasonable time after receiving notice of receipt of the order by the beneficiary's bank, notified the originator of the beneficiary's refusal of payment," (3) the funds were "not withdrawn by the beneficiary or applied to a debt of the beneficiary," and (4) the beneficiary would "suffer a loss that could reasonably have been avoided if payment had been made by a means complying with the contract."

In these exceptional circumstances, the underlying obligation of the originator to the beneficiary is not discharged. Because the funds transfer had been completed, however, the "money back" guarantee rule does not apply, and the originator will have to pay twice. The originator will have to pay the originator's bank under the funds transfer, and will still have to pay the beneficiary on the underlying obligation. The originator will then be subrogated to the rights of the beneficiary to receive payment of the order from the beneficiary's bank, in order to recover the funds expended in the additional payment.[2]

What does the exception to the basic discharge rule signify? In substance it signifies that if the bank to which the transfer is made on behalf of the beneficiary fails, and accordingly the beneficiary is unable to withdraw its funds, the beneficiary (creditor) may have a continuing and undischarged claim against the debtor.

Note the requirements that make it most unlikely—even where the beneficiary's bank fails—that the beneficiary's bank will have accepted without discharge of the originator's debt having already occurred. The requirements of the exception to the basic discharge rule are first that the contract (between General Motors and Goodyear) prohibit—note "prohibit"—a funds transfer to this particular bank. Second, the beneficiary, Goodyear, cannot allow the funds to remain in the prohibited bank, but must refuse the transfer promptly. Third, Goodyear cannot withdraw the funds or allow them to be applied against its debt by way of setoff. Finally, Goodyear must show that the loss suffered because of the bank's failure could have been avoided if the payment had been made in accordance with the contract.

The reasons for the rule and illustrations of it are given as follows in the comments:

> The rationale is that the Originator cannot impose the risk of Bank B's insolvency on Beneficiary if Beneficiary had specified

---

2. § 4A–406(b).

another means of payment that did not entail that risk.[3]

What is the probability that all these requirements of the exception to the basic discharge rule will be satisfied in a situation in which there is also a bank failure? Small or none.

Assume a contract that called for the debtor to give the beneficiary a cashier's check drawn on Bank A. Instead the debtor sends a funds transfer to the benefit of the beneficiary at Bank B and Bank B fails. If the beneficiary is required to accept the originator's payment, the beneficiary would suffer a loss that would not have occurred if payment had been made by a cashier's check on Bank A. In such a case the originator would and should have to pay twice.[4]

Comment 4 illustrates the possibility that the beneficiary's instructions have been ignored but that the originator's liability is discharged:

> Suppose Beneficiary's contract called for payment by a Fedwire transfer to Bank B, but the payment order accepted by Bank B was not a Fedwire transfer. Before the funds were withdrawn by Beneficiary, Bank B suspended payments. The sender of the payment order to Bank B paid the amount of the order to Bank B. In this case the payment by Originator did not comply with Beneficiary's contract, but the noncompliance did not result in a loss to Beneficiary as required by subsection (b)(iv). A Fedwire transfer avoids the risk of insolvency of the sender of the payment order to Bank B, but it does not affect the risk that Bank B will suspend payments before withdrawal of the funds by Beneficiary. Thus, the unless clause of subsection (b) is not

---

3. § 4A–406, Comment 3. Comment 3 reads in full as follows:

Suppose Beneficiary's contract stated that payment of an obligation owed by Originator was to be made by a cashier's check of Bank A. Instead, Originator paid by a funds transfer to Beneficiary's account in Bank B. Bank B accepted a payment order for the benefit of Beneficiary by immediately notifying Beneficiary that the funds were available for withdrawal. Before Beneficiary had a reasonable opportunity to withdraw the funds Bank B suspended payments. Under the unless clause of subsection (b) Beneficiary is not required to accept the payment as discharging the obligation owed by Originator to Beneficiary if Beneficiary's contract means that Beneficiary was not required to accept payment by wire transfer. Beneficiary could refuse the funds transfer as payment of the obligation and could resort to rights

under the underlying contract to enforce the obligation. *The rationale is that Originator cannot impose the risk of Bank B's insolvency on Beneficiary if Beneficiary had specified another means of payment that did not entail that risk.* If Beneficiary is required to accept Originator's payment, Beneficiary would suffer a loss that would not have occurred if payment had been made by a cashier's check on Bank A, and Bank A has not suspended payments. In this case Originator will have to pay twice. It is obliged to pay the amount of its payment order to the bank that accepted it and has to pay the obligation it owes to Beneficiary which has not been discharged. Under the last sentence of subsection (b) Originator is subrogated to Beneficiary's right to receive payment from Bank B under Section 4A–404(a). (Emphasis added.)

4. § 4A–406, Comment 3.

applicable and the obligation owed to Beneficiary is discharged.[5]

5. § 4A–406, Comment 4. The rules in 4A contemplate a variety of cases where banks fail in the middle of a funds transfer. We think these problems are so remote that they deserve only a footnote.

Assume that General Motors instructs its bank, JP Morgan Chase, to transfer $5 million to Goodyear's account at National City. JP Morgan Chase accepts the order by instructing Comerica to cause a credit to occur in Goodyear's account at National City. Comerica accepts by instructing National City to credit Goodyear's account for $5 million. Before National City accepts or has received payment from Comerica, Comerica becomes insolvent and suspends payments. Who should bear the risk of Comerica's insolvency? Under Article 4A, the answer will turn on two factors: 1) whether the funds transfer was completed; and 2) whether a participant in the funds transfer process requested routing through the insolvent bank.

Article 4A operates under the assumption that each payment order is a separate mini-transaction, and, most of the time, the obligations of the participants in the funds transfer will not extend beyond the sender-receiving bank relationship. Operating on this assumption, upon the successful completion of a funds transfer, each sender is obligated to pay its receiving bank. Thus, the receiving bank who accepts bears the risk of the sender's insolvency, and if the sender cannot make payment to its receiving bank, the receiving bank suffers the loss. In this case, if National City accepts, thus completing the funds transfer, National City will bear the loss. National City will be obligated to pay Goodyear $5 million because it accepted the order, but will not receive full payment from Comerica because of Comerica's insolvency. The fact of Comerica's insolvency will not affect the obligation of JP Morgan Chase to pay Comerica because Comerica accepted the order. JP Morgan Chase will not suffer a loss, however, because General Motors is obligated to pay JP Morgan Chase. Furthermore, General Motors will not suffer a loss by paying JP Morgan Chase because its obligation to the beneficiary, Goodyear, was discharged upon the acceptance of the payment order by National City.

If a funds transfer is not completed, for example if National City was aware of Comerica's insolvency and rejected the payment order, the money back guarantee rule provides that no sender is obligated to pay its receiving bank, and the sender is entitled to a refund of any amount paid to the receiving bank on account of the payment order. If JP Morgan Chase has already paid Comerica, JP Morgan Chase would suffer the loss because its receiving bank, Comerica, would be unable to refund the amount owed to JP Morgan Chase. However, under the money back guarantee rule, JP Morgan Chase would be obligated to refund any payments made by General Motors to JP Morgan Chase. If JP Morgan Chase has not paid Comerica, no bank would suffer a loss.

Would the result change if General Motors requested routing through the insolvent bank, Comerica? (Customers will rarely pick out intermediary banks, but it may happen.) Common sense tells us that if a funds transfer is not completed due to the insolvency of a bank picked by the customer, the customer, and not the sender of the payment order to the receiving bank, should bear this risk of loss. Under Article 4A, a sender does not bear the risk of insolvency of a receiving bank if another sender required routing through that receiving bank and the insolvency of that receiving bank caused the funds transfer not to be completed. In this situation, each receiving bank who complied with instruction for routing through the intermediary bank is entitled to receive or retain payment from the sender of the order it accepted. Thus, the original sender who requested routing through an intermediary bank bears the risk of insolvency and is required to make payment to its receiving bank who complied with the instructions, and if not the originator of the funds transfer, by also refunding to the sender of the payment order it accepted which did not request routing through the insolvent intermediary bank. The sender who originally requested routing through the insolvent bank will be subrogated to the rights of the bank that paid the failed intermediary bank. (See, 4A–402(e); Baxter, Jr.,

Finally, nothing in Article 4A provides that the sender of a payment order instructing payment through an intermediary bank bears the risk of that intermediary bank's insolvency in a successfully completed funds transfer.[6] The text and comments of Article 4A provide only that such a sender bears the risk in an uncompleted or an erroneously completed, funds transfer. Thus, unless a court is influenced by the original sender's picking the insolvent bank, the receiving bank of the insolvent's bank's payment order bears the risk of the intermediary bank's insolvency.[7]

The originator and beneficiary may agree to vary the rights of the originator and the beneficiary as to payment and discharge

Commercial Law and Practice Course Handbook Series, Basic UCC Skills 1990: Article 4A Payment, 542 PLI/Comm 93 (June 1, 1990), pg. 8–10 of 253 from Westlaw.) To see more clearly how this operates, follow a more comprehensive example:

(1) A issues payment order to Bank A instructing a credit to occur in the bank account of G, at Bank E. Bank A issues a payment order to Bank B, requesting routing through Bank D. After receiving a payment order from Bank B, Bank C issues a payment order to Bank D. Bank D accepts the payment order. Bank C pays Bank D. Bank D suspends payments before Bank E accepts the payment order. Thus, Bank E timely rejects the payment order because of Bank D's insolvency.

A—>BA—>BB—>BC—>BD—>BE

At this point, the funds transfer has not been completed, and each sender in the funds transfer chain is entitled to its "money back" if it has made payment to a receiving bank, or is excused from making payment to receiving bank, if it has not made payment. In this situation, however, 4A–402(e) provides that Bank A should bear the risk of loss for the insolvency of Bank D because Bank A originally requested routing through Bank D, the insolvent bank, and Bank D's insolvency caused the non-completion of the funds transfer. Bank A is required to refund A's payment order and pay the amount of its payment order to Bank B. B is then required to pay the amount of its payment order to C. C is required to pay the amount of its order to D. Bank A is subrogated to the rights of C to obtain a refund of payment from D.

If the funds transfer is not completed for reasons other than the insolvency of

the intermediary bank (for example, because the beneficiary's bank received the payment order from the intermediary bank and rejected the payment order because of an equipment failure before it learned of the insolvency of the intermediary bank), it is unclear whether the original sender who instructed routing through the insolvent intermediary bank is still obliged to bear the loss due to the intermediary bank's insolvency. The text appears to mandate that the original sender who instructed routing through the insolvent intermediary bank bear the loss, but the comments limit the application to situations where the insolvency of the intermediary bank caused the loss. (See §§ 4A–402(c); 4A–402, Comment 2.)

6. If the funds transfer is erroneously completed, by payment to the wrong beneficiary, or in an amount greater than the amount of the original payment order, or by issuing a duplicate payment order, senders may be released from their obligation to pay the erroneous amount under §§ 4A–205, 4A–207, or 4A–303 governing erroneous payment orders. If such a sender has already paid the order, the sender may recover the erroneously paid amount from the receiving bank under § 4A–402(d). In this case, the sender bears the risk of an intermediary bank's insolvency even after the completion of the funds transfer. We discuss erroneous payment orders below. See, Baxter, Commercial Law and Practice Course Handbook Series, Basic UCC Skills 1990: Article 4A Payment, 542 PLI/Comm 93 (1990), pg. 9–10 of 253 from Westlaw.

7. See Nelson, Settlement Obligations and Bank Insolvency, 45 Bus. L. 1473, 1476–77 (1990).

under this section. A funds transfer system rule, however, cannot vary the rights of the originator or beneficiary.

Completing the Funds Transfer: Making Payment

SENDER'S OBLIGATION TO PAY RECEIVING BANK

Acceptance of the sender's payment order by the receiving bank creates an obligation of the sender to pay the receiving bank the amount of the order.[8] The sender has no other obligation to the receiving bank, and no other person has any rights against the sender with respect to the sender's order. Payment is not due until the execution date if the receiving bank is not also the beneficiary's bank. However, if the receiving bank is also the beneficiary's bank, payment is due on the payment date (4A–402(c)).

The sender discharges its obligation by paying the receiving bank. Under § 4A–403(a), payment can occur in one of three ways:

1) by final settlement through a funds transfer system;

2) the sender's crediting an account of the receiving bank, if the credit is withdrawn or withdrawable and the receiving bank learns of that fact; or

3) the receiving bank debits the account of the sender with the receiving bank, to the extent the debit is covered by a withdrawable credit balance in the account.

If payment does not occur in one of these three ways (for example, when sender does not have an account relationship with the receiving bank and does not settle through a Federal Reserve bank), the time when payment occurs is determined by law outside of Article 4A that determines when an obligation is satisfied.[9]

In many situations, a bank will be both the sender and the receiving bank of various payment orders. Section 4A–403(c) does not require that payment occur separately with respect to each payment order. Section 4A–403(c) specifically upholds private agreements between two banks to net bilaterally their payment orders. Section 4A–403(b) specifically authorizes multilateral netting among members of a funds transfer system and provides that settlement occurs in accordance with the rules of the funds transfer system.

PROBLEM

1. BILATERAL NETTING: A and B agree to settle their payment orders at the end of each day and provide that amounts

---

8. See § 4A–402, Comment 3.   **9.** See § 4A–403(d) and Comment 5.

set off shall constitute payment to each other. At 9:00 A.M., A sends a $10 million payment order to B. At 10:00 A.M., B sends a $5 million payment order to A. At 1:00 P.M., B sends a $2 million payment order to A.

At the end of the day, B credits the account of A for $3 million. The $3 million is considered payment to A. The $7 million set off is considered payment by each bank to each other. Settlement and payment has occurred at the end of the day.

2. MULTILATERAL NETTING: At 9:00 A.M., A sends a $10 million payment order to B. At 10:00 A.M., B sends a $5 million payment order to C. At 1:00 P.M., C sends a $2 million payment order to A. All transfers are done through CHIPS.

At the end of the day, A is a net-debtor for $8 million; B is a net-creditor for $5 million; C is a net-creditor for $3 million. A would transfer $8 million to a special settlement account at the New York Federal Reserve. When all net-debtors have "paid up," the New York Federal Reserve will issue credits to the net-creditors, including a $5 million credit to B, and a $3 million credit to C. Settlement and payment occurs at the time the "net-credits" are sent by Fedwire.

If the transfers in the foregoing problem were not done over a funds transfer system, the participants in the funds transfer could not agree to engage in multilateral netting. Article 4A only authorizes bilateral netting by private agreement between two banks; Article 4A does not authorize multilateral netting by private agreement by more than two banks. Thus, if these payment orders were effectuated outside of a funds transfer system, none of these three payment orders could be netted, and A, B, and C would each have to make separate payment on their individual payment orders.

Article 4A does not provide a remedy for the receiving bank if the sender does not pay the receiving bank. The common law of debt and contract would govern the transaction.

BENEFICIARY BANK'S OBLIGATION TO PAY BENEFICIARY

Upon the acceptance of a payment order by the beneficiary's bank, the beneficiary's bank becomes obligated to pay the beneficiary (§ 4A–404(a)). Because a beneficiary's bank can accept a payment order by paying the beneficiary, acceptance and payment may occur simultaneously. Under § 4A–405:

1) If the beneficiary's bank credits an account of the beneficiary, payment occurs when and to the extent that:

a) the beneficiary is notified of the right to withdraw the credit,

b) the beneficiary lawfully applies the credit to a debt of the beneficiary, or

c) funds with respect to the order are otherwise made available to the beneficiary by the bank (§ 4A–405(a));

2) If the beneficiary's bank does not credit an account of the beneficiary, (for example, when the payment order directs beneficiary's bank to pay currency to the beneficiary who is not an account holder at the beneficiary's bank) payment occurs according to principles of law that determine when an obligation is satisfied (§ 4A–405(b)).

Once the beneficiary's bank pays the beneficiary, the beneficiary's bank generally has no right to recover the payment from the beneficiary. If the beneficiary's bank releases funds to the beneficiary before it receives payment from the sender, it assumes the risk that the sender of the payment order may not pay its order. Furthermore, private agreements (that the right to withdraw the credit is conditional on the beneficiary's bank receiving payment of the order) are generally unenforceable.[10]

§ 7–16   Excusing a Sender's Obligation to Pay

Recall that a "funds transfer" is a series of payment orders which begins with the payment order initiated by the originator and ends with the final payment order being received by the beneficiary's bank. In some cases, although a payment order has been issued, the funds transfer is not completed. Yet some acceptances will have occurred, and some tentative obligations will have arisen. In those circumstances, there must be machinery for undoing the upstream payment orders that have now become surplusage because the ultimate transaction, the funds transfer, is not to be completed. This problem is analogous to the problem with checks in which the depositor might receive a provisional credit from the depositary bank and the depositary bank in turn receive a provisional credit from an intermediary bank, all on a check that is ultimately dishonored. When dishonor occurs, those provisional credits must be undone.

The issue here is different from but analogous to the provisional credit case. When the funds transfer is not completed because the beneficiary's bank rejects the payment order of an intermediary bank that had accepted the order of the originator's bank that had accepted the order of the originator, the earlier payment orders need to be undone. When the beneficiary's bank rejects or other-

---

10.   § 4A–405(c) and Comment 2.

wise does not accept the payment order, all senders are excused from their obligations to pay the respective receiving banks and are entitled to refunds for any amounts paid on the excused payment orders. These rights are specified in 4A–402(c) and (d):

> (c) * * * The obligation of that sender to pay its payment order is excused if the funds transfer is not completed by acceptance by the beneficiary's bank of a payment order instructing payment to the beneficiary of that sender's payment order.

> (d) If the sender of a payment order pays the order and was not obliged to pay all or part of the amount paid, the bank receiving payment is obliged to refund payment to the extent the sender was not obliged to pay. * * *

This process by which a sender is excused from the obligation to pay the order and becomes entitled to a refund if the sender paid and the funds transfer is not completed enforces what is known in the banking community as the "money back guarantee." This "money back guarantee" may not be varied by agreement.[1] Consider the following examples:

PROBLEM

1. General Motors instructs its bank, JP Morgan Chase, to cause a $5 million credit to occur in Goodyear's account at National City. JP Morgan Chase accepts the order by instructing the Federal Reserve in Chicago to cause a $5 million credit to occur in Goodyear's account at National City. The Federal Reserve in Chicago accepts the order by instructing National City to cause a $5 million credit to occur in Goodyear's account. National City accepts the order by crediting Goodyear's account for $5 million and notifying it of its right to withdraw the funds.

General Motors—>   JP Morgan Chase—>   Fed.Res.—>   Nat'l City—>   Goodyear
                          $5M $5M $5M $5M

In this example, the funds transfer was completed upon acceptance by beneficiary's bank, National City. The payment order accepted by National City mirrored the payment orders sent by each sender to its receiving bank in the funds transfer chain. Each sender must pay its respective receiving bank.

2. Assume the same facts, but assume that National City rejected the payment order.

---

§ **7–16**
1. § 4A–402(f).

General Motors—>   JP Morgan Chase—>   Fed.Res.—>   Nat'l City
                            $5M $5M $5M

> Because National City rejected the payment order, the funds transfer was not completed. The obligation of each sender to pay its receiving bank is excused, and each sender is entitled to a refund for any amount paid to its receiving bank on the payment order (4A–402(c) and (d)), thereby implementing the money back guarantee. In seeking a refund, however, a sender is limited to a claim against the receiving bank immediately below the sender in the chain of transactions.

Consider the case of Grain Traders, Inc. v. Citibank, N.A.[2] where the plaintiff, Grain Traders, originated a funds transfer through its bank, Banco de Credito Nacional ("BCN"), with instructions to route the various payment orders through defendant Citibank to an intermediary bank, Banque du Credit et Investissement Ltd. ("BCIL"), and on to the end beneficiary bank. After Citibank received the payment order and credited BCIL's account, BCIL became insolvent and the funds never reached Grain Traders' stated beneficiary because Citibank setoff the funds against its existing debt from BCIL. The court dismissed Grain Traders' claims against Citibank on jurisdictional grounds because 4A–402(d)'s "money back rule" only operates between the sender and its receiving bank that is immediately downstream in the funds transfer transaction. As such, Grain Traders would only have this right against BCN, not Citibank, and they were left to pleading common law claims in the suit against Citibank.

§ 7–17 Return of Payments Made to a Beneficiary

In sections 4A–405(d) and (e), Article 4A deals explicitly with circumstances where payments actually made to a beneficiary should be returned. The question is also dealt with in 4A–205(a) and lurks just below the surface elsewhere.[1] Under section 4A–405, a beneficiary's bank that has made a provisional payment under a funds transfer rule that allows such provisional payment, can, in certain circumstances, recover the money from the beneficiary if it (the beneficiary's bank) is not paid. The rule has several conditions including one concerning notice to the beneficiary about the provisional nature of such settlements and the agreement of the parties to be bound by the rule. These agreements will appear in the deposit agreement signed by the beneficiary and perhaps in the agreement signed by the beneficiary's bank when it joins a system

---

2. See Grain Traders, Inc. v. Citibank, N.A., 160 F.3d 97, 101 (2nd Cir. 1998).

§ 7–17

1. For a general discussion of Restitution in 4A, see § 7–29.

or agrees to operate under a set of funds transfer rules. Whether attempts to make settlements provisional will become widespread is unclear. If they do become commonplace, one will have to examine those rules with care to determine when the provisional nature will end and to reconsider almost all the rules concerning finality that have been discussed above. Section 4A–405(d) reads in full as follows:

> (d) A funds-transfer system rule may provide that payments made to beneficiaries of funds transfers made through the system are provisional until receipt of payment by the beneficiary's bank of the payment order it accepted. A beneficiary's bank that makes a payment that is provisional under the rule is entitled to refund from the beneficiary if (i) the rule requires that both the beneficiary and the originator be given notice of the provisional nature of the payment before the funds transfer is initiated, (ii) the beneficiary, the beneficiary's bank and the originator's bank agreed to be bound by the rule, and (iii) the beneficiary's bank did not receive payment of the payment order that it accepted. If the beneficiary is obliged to refund payment to the beneficiary's bank, acceptance of the payment order by the beneficiary's bank is nullified and no payment by the originator of the funds transfer to the beneficiary occurs under Section 4A–406.

In two exceptional sets of circumstances, a beneficiary's bank that has made "payment" to the beneficiary can recover that payment if it does not itself receive payment from its immediate sender of the order it accepted. One set involves credit transfers through a funds transfer system where:

> 1) the funds transfer system provides for provisional payment to the beneficiary;

> 2) the beneficiary and originator of the funds transfer have notice of this provision;

> 3) the beneficiary, originator's bank, and beneficiary's bank agreed to be bound by the rule; and

> 4) the beneficiary's bank did not receive payment of the order.[2]

In these circumstances, the beneficiary's bank's acceptance of the payment order can be "nullified." The beneficiary's bank is treated as if it had rejected the payment order and can recover its payment from the beneficiary. Because the beneficiary's bank is deemed to have rejected the order, the funds transfer is not completed. Thus, the beneficiary is not paid, the originator's obligation to the beneficiary is not discharged, and the "money back guarantee" rule of section 4A–402(c) and (d) kicks in.

---

2. § 4A–405(d).

The Article 4A drafters intended this exception to apply to automated clearing house (ACH) transfers. CHIPS does not have a provisional payment transfer system rule; many ACHs do.[3] ACH transfers are made in batches.

> A beneficiary's bank will normally accept, at the same time and as part a single batch, payment orders with respect to many different originator banks. The custom in ACH transfers is to release funds to the beneficiary early on the payment date even though settlement to the beneficiary's bank does not occur until later in the day. The understanding is that payments to beneficiaries are provisional until the beneficiary's bank receives settlement.[4]

To meet the second condition above, notice need not be given with respect to each particular funds transfer. Once the participants in a funds transfer have notice of the provisional payment provision and have agreed to be bound by the rule, the notice and agreement are effective for all subsequent payments to or from the participants in the funds transfer.[5]

A second exceptional set of circumstances where a beneficiary's bank might escape payment of an accepted order involves "doomsday." Doomsday might occur, for example, if a giant such as Citicorp proved unable to meet its obligations at the end of the day as a member of the CHIPS system. This is a highly unlikely event and would make the various financial panics of the 19th century seem small by comparison. (One suspects that settlement among banks might be the least of one's worries if this happened.) Doomsday is covered by section 4A–405(e) that reads in full as follows:

> (e) This subsection applies to a funds transfer that includes a payment order transmitted over a funds-transfer system that (i) nets obligations multilaterally among participants, and (ii) has in effect a loss-sharing agreement among participants for the purpose of providing funds necessary to complete settlement of the obligations of one or more participants that do not meet their settlement obligations. If the beneficiary's bank in the funds transfer accepts a payment order and the system

---

3. Operating Rules of The National Automated Clearing House Association (hereinafter "NACHA Operating Rules," § 4.4.7), www.nacha.org. "For a credit entry subject to Article 4A, credit given to the Receiver by the RDFI as provided in subsection 4.4.1 (Availability of Credit Entries to Receivers) is provisional until the RDFI has received final settlement through a Federal Reserve Bank or has otherwise received payment as provided in Section 4A–403(a) of Article 4A. If such settlement or payment is not re-ceived, the RDFI is entitled to a refund from the Receiver of the amount credited, and the Originator is considered not to have paid the Receiver the amount of the entry. This subsection applies only if the Receiver has agreed to be bound by the rules contained in this subsection 4.4.7."

4. § 4A–405, Comment 3.

5. See § 4A–405, Comment 3.

fails to complete settlement pursuant to its rules with respect to any payment order in the funds transfer, (i) the acceptance by the beneficiary's bank is nullified and no person has any right or obligation based on the acceptance, (ii) the beneficiary's bank is entitled to recover payment from the beneficiary, (iii) no payment by the originator to the beneficiary occurs under Section 4A–406, and (iv) subject to Section 4A–402(e), each sender in the funds transfer is excused from its obligation to pay its payment order under Section 4A–402(c) because the funds transfer has not been completed.

The drafters intended this exception to apply to funds transfer systems with loss sharing agreements, such as CHIPS.[6] Under the CHIPS loss sharing rules, participants in CHIPS agree to contribute funds to allow the system to settle for payment orders sent over the system during the day in the event that a participating bank is unable to meet its settlement obligations. For instance, if National City accepts a payment order over CHIPS from JP Morgan Chase, National City would receive payment from the funds in the CHIPS loss sharing agreement if JP Morgan Chase could not pay National City on the amount of the accepted payment order because JP Morgan Chase suspended payments. In the unlikely event that CHIPS fails to settle the obligation of JP Morgan Chase despite the loss sharing agreement, 4A–405(e) provides that the acceptance by National City is revoked.[7] Because the beneficiary's bank's acceptance is revoked, the beneficiary's bank is deemed to have rejected the order, and the funds transfer is not completed. Thus, the beneficiary is not paid, the originator's obligation to the beneficiary is not discharged, and the "money back guarantee" rule of 4A–402(c) and (d) kicks in.[8]

§ 7–18   Finality in Debit Transfers

Finality in debit transfers is quite similar to finality for checks in Article 4. Under subsection 6.1.2 of the NACHA Operating Rules, a returned entry to be sent back by a receiving bank "must be received by the RDFI's ACH operator by its deposit deadline for the return entry to be made available to the ODFI no later than the opening of business on the second banking day following the settlement date of the original entry." To put this in words of one syllable, if the receiver wants to bounce a debit that it receives on Day 1, it must do it in such a way that the reversal gets back to the

6. § 4A–405(e). See, Baxter, Commercial Law and Practice Course Handbook Series, Basic UCC Skills 1990: Article 4A Payment, 542 PLI/Comm 93 (1990), pg. 28–29 of 253 from Westlaw.

7. See § 4A–405, Comment 4.

8. See 4A–405(e); 4A–405, Comment 4. See also, Baxter, Jr., Commercial Law and Practice Course Handbook Series, Basic UCC Skills 1990: Article 4A Payment, 542 PLI/Comm 93 (June 1, 1990), pg. 28–29 of 253 from Westlaw.

originating financial institution no later than the opening of business on Day 3—assuming days 1, 2, and 3 are banking days.

Although the quoted rules address only the receiving bank's right to return an entry and not the receiver's right to stop payment, we anticipate that the receiver's rights would be governed by its contract with its bank and that the bank would see to it that it received notice in time for it to act within the deadline set by the quoted provisions in Return of Entries in 5.1. Receivers do have a right to issue stop payment orders under the NACHA Operating Rules, but these "must be provided to the RDFI at such time and in such manner as to allow the RDFI a reasonable opportunity to act upon the stop payment order prior to acting on the debit entry"— certainly not giving the receiver much time to do so given the speed at which these transactions settle. For recurring debit entries, notification must be made "at least three banking days before the scheduled date of the transfer."[1]

As in Article 4 (see 4–302) the RDFI becomes "accountable for the amount of all debit entries received that are not returned in accordance with these rules" as set out in 7.4. Thus, if the receiving bank (JP Morgan Chase in our case) misses its deadline in 6.1.2, the bank itself has liability on the item and is obliged to pay even if its customer cannot. To reiterate, the rules here are like those in Article 4. The RDFI, like the payor bank, has a period of one day (or possibly a little longer) to decide to return and, as in Article 4, if it fails to do so it will incur strict liability for that amount.

One reading of the remainder of section 6 of the NACHA rules (6.2 Dishonor of Returned Entries[2]) contradicts the assertions about finality that we made in the preceding paragraph. For example, subsection 6.2.1 states that an ODFI may dishonor a returned entry (i.e., refuse to accept the RDFI's return) if it can prove that the RDFI did not return it in a timely way *and* if the Originator or the Originator's bank suffers a loss as a result. Is the implication of 6.2.1 that the ODFI *must* take back even an untimely return unless it or the Originator has suffered a loss? It is not. So read, section 6.2.1 would directly conflict with the rules described above and the ideas about payor banks' liabilities under Article 4.

Section 6.2 and specifically 6.2.1 are not intended to permit untimely items by receiving banks. Section 6.2 is a procedure that may be followed for adjustment of entries within the ACH. The ACH contains other provisions limiting the number of times an item can be bounced back and forth and instructing the parties that they must seek redress elsewhere if they cannot resolve their differences within the limited number of bounces permitted. Thus,

§ 7–18   **2.** See Section 6.2.

1. NACHA Operating Rules §§ 8.4, 8.5.

what appears to require an ODFI to take even an untimely return unless it can prove a loss is only a limitation upon its rights within the system, and not a limitation upon its rights to sue and so impose liability on a late returning RDFI under sections 6.1 and 7.4.

To make this clear, the National Association added a sentence to subsection 7.4. The sentence reads as follows: "The RDFI's accountability under this section is not affected by the failure of the ODFI to comply with any of the provisions of section 6.2 (Dishonor of Return Entries)."[3] The added sentence makes it clear that the ODFI need not even complain or attempt to "dishonor" a returned entry within the 15 days allowed by 6.2.1. Under the quoted language, the ODFI could simply stonewall the RDFI, allow its account to be debited by the returned entry, and then commence suit against the RDFI to recover under the provisions of section 7.4.

We have found only one reported opinion involving the responsibility of an RDFI for a late return. In American National Bank & Trust Co. v. Central Bank,[4] Central Bank, RDFI for Murray Distribution Co., missed its midnight deadline on several items. Since all of the transfers occurred after the receiver had filed in Chapter 11, the banks and the Originator had an understandable interest in the finality of the transfers. In a brief opinion, the court held the receiving bank liable; Central Bank had missed its midnight deadline.

Even though the court clearly identified the transactions as "electronic debits," it analyzed the case entirely under Article 4 of the Uniform Commercial Code. Presumably, the transaction occurred through some sort of automated clearing house, although the case does not say so. Evidently the parties argued the case as though it was a check transaction. Because the court treats the transaction only as a check transaction and makes no reference either to the NACHA Operating Rules or to the Federal Reserve Operating Letters, the case is a less compelling precedent than it could be.

It makes some sense to use familiar rules concerning checks as a working basis to approximate the liability of the receiving bank on a debit transfer. Usually the receiving bank has until its midnight deadline and no longer. That result, however, does not arise out of Article 4, but rather from 6.1 and 7.4 of the NACHA Operating Rules as endorsed by the Federal Reserve Operating Letters.[5]

---

3. Mr. Robert Ballen, the general counsel of the Association, tells us that the quoted sentence was adopted with our very problem in mind.

4. 132 B.R. 171, 16 UCC2d 456 (D.Colo. 1991).

5. See   http://www.frbservices.org/ OperatingCirculars/index.html.

§ 7–19   Erroneous and Fraudulent: Introduction

What can go wrong, will. Consistent with this idea, one can imagine a number of variations on erroneous funds transfers. (In all of the following cases assume that the sender acts properly and error is committed by the receiving bank.) First, the receiving bank can send the order to the *wrong person*. This is particularly easy to do when the recipient is identified by number and the money is given either in writing or orally and has to be entered into the electronic system by a sending bank employee who may transpose a digit or make other errors.

The second possibility—one that comes in many colors—is to *transfer the wrong amount*. The amount might be *too small* or *too large*.[1] A particularly unhappy version of this error is to make duplicate transactions in which the receiving bank executes the order on Day 1 and executes it a second time on Day 2.[2]

A third error is temporal. Presumably most orders are issued on the day when payment is to occur. In almost all such cases it is expected that the receiving bank will promptly transmit the order. If it sends the order too late, a variety of untold consequences can occur. An example of a transmission that arrived too late (there is a question whether it was sent too late) is presented by the notorious *Evra* case where the originator lost a very favorable charter of a boat because it did not make its charter payments in time.[3] It is also possible for the receiving bank to send the order *too early*. This might happen when the originator directs its bank to send $1 million to a particular beneficiary on Tuesday, April 26. If by mistake the transmission is made on Monday, April 25, the originator may suffer two injuries. First, of course, it may lose interest on its money for one day, and less likely, but more frightening, it may issue a stop order late on Monday expecting to be able to recall the order not yet transmitted.

In many cases the cause of the error will be obvious and it will rest with clerical personnel at the originator or at the receiving bank. If the authorized clerk of the originator sends an order that it later regrets, it will have earned the loss. After all, the originator is responsible for the acts of its own agents.

Sometimes the error will not be caused by a transposition or other mechanical act by the agents of the receiving bank; the cause will be more remote. For example, error might occur within the

---

§ 7–19

1. An example of the latter problem is illustrated by In re Calumet Farm, Inc., 398 F.3d 555 (6th Cir. 2005).

2. See, *e.g.,* Credit Lyonnais N.Y. Branch v. Koval, 745 So.2d 837 (Miss. 1999); Shawmut Worcester County Bank

v. First Am. Bank & Trust, 731 F.Supp. 57, 11 UCC2d 417 (D. Mass. 1990).

3. Evra Corp. v. Swiss Bank Corp., 673 F.2d 951, 34 UCC 227 (7th Cir. 1982), *cert. denied,* 459 U.S. 1017, 103 S.Ct. 377, 74 L.Ed.2d 511 (1982). See further discussion, *infra* note 4.

receiving bank because the receiving bank chose the wrong system or the wrong bank to execute its order. Some of these issues are resolved by Article 4A; others are not. It is even possible that there will be an argument after the fact about who introduced error into the transaction. This might arise, for example, when the originator gave the order in writing, but the writing was not legible ("I have a gub, give me $"), and the person at the receiving bank reasonably issued the order to the wrong person or in the wrong amount because of the illegibility. In that case the ensuing dispute is likely to deal mostly with who made the error.

Although erroneous orders and erroneous execution of proper orders are likely to abound in the system, they will seldom cause difficulties. Absent fraud or insolvency, an erroneous order can, and almost invariably will, be corrected. In most cases these errors will be found at once and will cause little or no damage. In other cases there may be some modest damage that can be fully satisfied by an interest payment.

But what of the cases like the infamous *Evra* where one party claims that the bank's failure to carry out its order could deprive its customer of a large economic benefit?[4] Even in its time, *Evra* was probably a sport, but for years its facts gave a basis for the banks' fears that they might be held liable for a large loss arising out of a penny ante transaction. Now, however, 4A–305(c) limits a sender's ability to hold a bank liable for consequential damages arising out of a failed funds transfer except if the bank expressly agrees otherwise in an agreement between the parties. For a further discussion of consequential damages under Article 4A, see *infra*.

Due to the significant risk that a bank would assume by signing an agreement with such a provision, we do not expect to see many, if any, banks that would be willing to take on this level of

---

4. In *Evra*, Hyman–Michaels chartered a ship under a contract calling for monthly payments in advance by deposit to the charterer's Swiss bank account. Under the agreement, the charterer could cancel the charter if Hyman–Michaels did not pay on time. Shortly after signing the charter agreement, charter rates skyrocketed. On the day before a scheduled payment was due, Hyman–Michaels instructed its bank to pay the charterer, but the Swiss bank lost the payment order. The charterer then canceled the charter because it did not receive payment on time. After a federal district court in New York upheld an arbitrator's ruling that the charterer was entitled to cancel the charter, Hyman–Michaels brought a tort action against the Swiss bank. Hyman–Michaels' claim included lost profits for the difference between the canceled charter rates and the new charter rates. Finding that Illinois substantive law applied to the transaction, the Illinois Federal District Court found the Swiss bank had been negligent and was liable to Hyman–Michaels for $2.1 million in damages, expenses, and lost profits. The Seventh Circuit reversed, however, finding that Hyman–Michaels had not made the bank aware of the key factors of its arrangement with the charterer, including the date of payment and cancellation terms. Even though the Swiss bank was cleared in this instance, the mere possibility of such large liability resulting from a funds transfer transaction made more than a few banks nervous.

liability without obtaining insurance or requiring additional fees. The rule laid out in 4A–305(c) makes sense, since the sender is the party with better access to information about the importance of having the transfer completed on time, as well as the damages that would arise in the event the transfer is delayed. For especially important transactions, the best solution is for the sender to send the payment order a day early.

Most of the cases with which we are concerned in this section are governed initially by section 4A–303 on Erroneous Execution of Payment Order. The three subsections of 4A–303 are at first confusing, but once one understands the province of each, it is easy to understand the theory of the section. Subsection (a) deals with duplicate payments or payments that are too large. Subsection (b) deals with payments that are too small, and (c) deals with payments to the wrong person.

4A–303. Erroneous Execution of Payment Order.

(a) A receiving bank that (i) executes the payment order of the sender by issuing a payment order in an amount greater than the amount of the sender's order, or (ii) issues a payment order in execution of the sender's order and then issues a duplicate order, is entitled to payment of the amount of the sender's order under Section 4A–402(c) if that subsection is otherwise satisfied. The bank is entitled to recover from the beneficiary of the erroneous order the excess payment received to the extent allowed by the law governing mistake and restitution.

(b) A receiving bank that executes the payment order of the sender by issuing a payment order in an amount less than the amount of the sender's order is entitled to payment of the amount of the sender's order under Section 4A–402(c) if (i) that subsection is otherwise satisfied and (ii) the bank corrects its mistake by issuing an additional payment order for the benefit of the beneficiary of the sender's order. If the error is not corrected, the issuer of the erroneous order is entitled to receive or retain payment from the sender of the order it accepted only to the extent of the amount of the erroneous order. This subsection does not apply if the receiving bank executes the sender's payment order by issuing a payment order in an amount less than the amount of the sender's order for the purpose of obtaining payment of its charges for services and expenses pursuant to instruction of the sender.

(c) If a receiving bank executes the payment order of the sender by issuing a payment order to a beneficiary different from the beneficiary of the sender's order and the funds transfer is completed on the basis of that error, the sender of the payment order that was erroneously executed and all previous senders in the funds transfer are not obliged to pay the payment orders they issued. The issuer of the erroneous order is entitled to recover from the beneficiary of the order the payment received to the extent allowed by the law governing mistake and restitution.

Return to subsection (a). In general it entitles the receiving bank who pays too much or pays twice to receive payment from its sender for the single proper order. Section 4A–303 implies that it is the responsibility of the receiving bank to pursue the beneficiary who presumably holds the overpayment. The last sentence of subsection (a) states that the receiving bank is entitled to recover in restitution to the extent the common law of restitution would allow it to do so. In most of those cases there would be a restitution cause of action; this would be a classic case of payment by mistake.

Where the payment is too small, the receiving bank is entitled under subsection (b) to receive the full amount of the order from its sender if it corrects the error. Otherwise it is entitled to receive payment only to the extent the order was filled and thus to be reimbursed for the money that, by hypothesis, has gone to the right person albeit in a smaller than expected amount.

If the receiving bank pays the wrong person, subsection (c) tells us that the receiving bank is not entitled to payment and that all entities upstream from it are freed from their obligation on the orders they issue. The subsection authorizes recovery in restitution, and it, too, presents a classic case for restitution.

Once the plaintiff-sender claims that it is entitled to the erroneously sent funds under a theory of restitution as a result of mistake, certain defendant-beneficiaries may be able to use the "discharge for value" rule to defend against this claim and keep the money in dispute. When applied, the rule overturns the normal result under restitution—that the plaintiff gets the money back as a result of the mistake. To qualify, a defendant must show that a sender was indebted to it prior to the disputed transfer and the defendant did not know of the mistaken payment. This is different from the "mistake of fact" rule that exists in some jurisdictions, where an unintended payee only keeps the money if it actually changed its position in reliance on the mistaken payment and did not know of the mistake.

Case law has supported the discharge for value rule in the context of Article 4A since 1991 when the New York Court of Appeals and Second Circuit decided Banque Worms v. BankAmerica Int'l.[5] There, Spedley Securities ordered its bank, Security Pacific,

---

5. 77 N.Y.2d 362, 568 N.Y.S.2d 541, 570 N.E.2d 189 (1991). 928 F.2d 538 (2nd Cir. 1991). Although the Second Circuit actually decided the case, that court certified the key question in the case to the New York Court of Appeals.

to send a payment order to Banque Worms' account at BankAmerica in payment of a debt Spedley owned Banque Worms. Before Security Pacific sent the order, Spedley cancelled the first order and requested payment to another one of Spedley's creditors. Security Pacific mistakenly executed the initial payment order to Banque Worms as well as the second order to the other creditor. The court had to decide whether the "mistake of fact" rule or the "discharge for value" rule would apply on these facts.

In holding that the discharge for value rule was more appropriate in the funds transfer context, the New York Court of Appeals looked to the general policies behind such transfers, including the desire for finality and Article 4A's focus on national uniformity. It also noted that 4A–303(c) specifically allows the sender of a mistaken payment order to recover from the beneficiary "to the extent allowed by the law governing * * * restitution," and the discharge for value rule is recognized in the Restatement of Restitution § 14. Furthermore, Security Pacific could have easily avoided the loss here if it had a better procedure to avoid duplicate payment orders. Once the case went back to the Second Circuit, that court applied the decision and held that under the discharge for value rule, Banque Worms was entitled to keep the proceeds from the erroneous payment order.

Much of the same analysis, as well as a desire for national uniformity, supported the subsequent Seventh Circuit decision in GECC v. Central Bank.[6] In that case, a company named Duchow's Marine had a revolving line of credit with GECC and an affiliated blocked account where all of its collections from boat sales were to be directed. GECC would then use the collections to pay down the company's line of credit. Duchow also maintained its general operating account at Central, and in an attempt to circumvent the blocked account agreement, Duchow told a boat purchaser to wire its payment to the company's general account rather than to the blocked account. The attempted fraud was interrupted when an intermediary bank merely told Central to credit Duchow's account and did not include the specific account number to be credited. A clerk at Central then deposited the funds into the first account she saw for Duchow, which happened to be the blocked account.

Duchow noticed the mistake (i.e., that its attempted fraud on GECC had failed) when a check bounced in its general account, and consequently convinced Central to transfer the mistaken funds out of GECC's blocked account into its general account. The district court found for Central, holding that the mistake of fact rule was

Therefore, the main analysis of whether the discharge for value rule existed in New York is contained in the state court opinion.

6. 49 F.3d 280 (7th Cir. 1995).

the law in Wisconsin. Under that rule, GECC could not retain the funds because it did not change its position in reliance on the mistaken payment. The Seventh Circuit reversed, noting that under the reasoning in *Banque Worms*, the mistake of fact rule and the discharge for value rule are not mutually exclusive. The court argued that Wisconsin indicated a desire to conform to national standards in funds transfer transactions by adopting Article 4A, and uniformity is served if Wisconsin follows the law of New York where many funds transfers occur. Like the court in *Banque Worms*, the *GECC* court noted that Central could have avoided the loss by seeking indemnity from the intermediary bank and Duchow when those parties requested that the funds be moved. With two cases on point from these high-profile federal circuits, it is highly likely that future courts will recognize the discharge for value rule in Article 4A cases.

A 2005 Sixth Circuit case, In re Calumet Farm, Inc.,[7] limits the discharge for value rule as a defense to a restitution claim by the payment order's sender. There, Calumet Farm instructed its bank, First National, to wire $77,301.58 to White Birch Farm to cover its loan payment. First National ended up mistakenly transferring $770,301.58. White Birch claimed that it did not have to return the money under the discharge for value rule, and Calumet filed for bankruptcy before the matter was resolved.

The bankruptcy court and district court both held that White Birch satisfied the discharge for value defense, because it did not have notice of the error before its account was credited with the erroneously sent funds. In reversing, the Sixth Circuit adopted the reasoning of an Illinois federal district court judge from a prior case involving checks sent to the wrong beneficiary's lockbox,[8] and held that the beneficiary must actually "give value" by applying the funds to the debtor's account prior to receiving notice of the mistake in order to qualify for the discharge for value defense. The *Calumet Farm* court disregarded White Birch's arguments that the proper times to focus on are either (1) when the beneficiary's account is credited (which would effectively read the notice requirement out of the rule), or (2) when the beneficiary knows that funds are in the account (this would disregard constructive notice of an error in situations where the erroneous payment is quite large).[9] Since it was undisputed that White Birch did not actually credit Calumet's account until after receiving notice of the erroneous transfer, the court held that First National was entitled to the

---

7. 398 F.3d 555 (6th Cir. 2005).

8. NBase Communications, Inc. v. American Nat'l Bank & Trust Co. of Chicago, 8 F.Supp.2d 1071 (N.D. Ill. 1998).

9. Such constructive notice would also presumably include situations where the beneficiary received two payment orders when it only expected one, as in Credit Lyonnais v. Koval, 745 So.2d 837 (Miss. 1999).

funds. The fact that White Birch's owner immediately transferred the additional $693,000 to his personal account also supported the court's decision that White Birch knew the original transfer was erroneous.

While the additional requirement for access to the discharge for value rule in *Calumet Farm* seems correct, the reality of most commercial transactions between debtors and creditors probably means that few cases will arise in this area. Clearly, creditors have an incentive to apply payments to their debtors' accounts as soon as possible, and most companies' accounting systems are set up to perform this task shortly after the creditor receives a debtor's payment. Therefore, even if other circuits or state courts adopt the reasoning from *Calumet Farm*, we do not expect a major impact on creditors, since most of them will post payments to a debtor's account much faster than White Birch did in this case.

§ 7–20   Erroneous Orders

Article 4A distinguishes between "erroneous execution" of payment orders, discussed above, and "erroneous payment orders" dealt with in 4A–205. Later we will meet 4A–205 to the extent it deals with erroneous orders arising out of fraud. We now consider nonfraudulent but erroneous orders and compare the rules in 4A–205 with those in 4A–303.

4A–205. Erroneous Payment Orders

(a) If an accepted payment order was transmitted pursuant to a security procedure for the detection of error and the payment order (i) erroneously instructed payment to a beneficiary not intended by the sender, (ii) erroneously instructed payment in an amount greater than the amount intended by the sender, or (iii) was an erroneously transmitted duplicate of a payment order previously sent by the sender, the following rules apply:

(1) If the sender proves that the sender or a person acting on behalf of the sender pursuant to Section 4A–206 complied with the security procedure and that the error would have been detected if the receiving bank had also complied, the sender is not obliged to pay the order to the extent stated in paragraphs (2) and (3).

(2) If the funds transfer is completed on the basis of an erroneous payment order described in clause (i) or (iii) of subsection (a), the sender is not obliged to pay the order and the receiving bank is entitled to recover from the beneficiary any amount paid to the beneficiary to the extent allowed by the law governing mistake and restitution.

(3) If the funds transfer is completed on the basis of a payment order described in clause (ii) of subsection (a), the sender is not obliged to pay the order to the extent the amount received by the beneficiary is greater than the amount intended by the sender. In that case, the receiving bank is entitled to recover from the beneficiary the excess amount received to the extent allowed by the law governing mistake and restitution.

(b) If (i) the sender of an erroneous payment order described in subsection (a) is not obliged to pay all or part of the order, and (ii) the sender receives notification from the receiving bank that the order was accepted by the bank or that the sender's account was debited with respect to the order, the sender has a duty to exercise ordinary care, on the basis of information available to the sender, to discover the error with respect to the order and to advise the bank of the relevant facts within a reasonable time, not exceeding 90 days, after the bank's notification was received by the sender. If the bank proves that the sender failed to perform that duty, the sender is liable to the bank for the loss the bank proves it incurred as a result of the failure, but the liability of the sender may not exceed the amount of the sender's order.

(c) This section applies to amendments to payment orders to the same extent it applies to payment orders.

Subsection (a) of 4A–205 may be regarded as an exception to the general rule. As a general rule, an order is an order to the receiving bank, and if it follows the order, the bank is free and clear. If it receives an order that is erroneous because the sender intended something else, there will usually be no way for the receiving bank to know that someone not intended by the sender is receiving the money. Section 4A–205 is the exception in that it holds the receiving bank liable, and absolves the sender from an ultimate obligation to pay an erroneous order in the limited circumstance in which the receiving bank failed to use an agreed security procedure, provided that the sender can prove that the use of the security procedure would have avoided the loss. Only time will tell whether such erroneous orders can be ferreted out by security procedures that will be adopted by the parties; to us it seems unlikely that security procedures will reveal these errors.

Section 4A–205(b) requires a sender receiving notification of acceptance from the receiving bank to "exercise ordinary care" in an attempt to discover any error and to notify the receiving bank within a reasonable time not exceeding 90 days. If the sender fails to do that then the sender is liable to the bank but only for the loss "the bank proves it incurred as a result of the failure * * *." This responsibility is similar to the responsibility imposed upon a bank customer under section 4–406.

Turning to events other than simple transposition or copying errors that might themselves cause a loss, section 4A–302 on "Obligations of Receiving Bank in Execution of Payment Order" defines the bank's responsibility. Under subsection (a)(1) the receiving bank has to follow the instruction of the sender concerning the intermediary banks and funds transfer systems to be used. Under subsection (a)(2) it must also use the "most expeditious available means" when instructed to do so.

For an interesting case interpreting a receiving bank's duty to its sender, see Grossman v. Nationsbank, N.A.[1] There, Plaintiff Stephen Grossman's wire instructions to Nationsbank included routing the payment order to a particular account number at Am South Bank and then on to the intended final beneficiary account at First Union. Nationsbank originally sent the funds directly to First Union, but Grossman instructed them to follow his initial instructions to use Am South as an intermediary bank. Thieves took the money once it was deposited into the Am South account, and the Eleventh Circuit affirmed the district court's dismissal of Grossman's claim because Nationsbank ultimately followed Grossman's instructions exactly as given. This is a receiving bank's only duty to a sender under 4A–302(a)(1).

Subsection (b) specifically authorizes the receiving bank to ignore the sender's instructions concerning a particular funds transfer system if the bank in good faith believes it is "not feasible" to follow the instructions or that following them would "unduly delay" the transfer.

Subsection (c) clears up any ambiguity left by (a)(1) by explicitly authorizing the receiving bank to use any means "as expeditious as the means stated" in the sender's instructions. Comment 2 makes it clear that while the receiving bank may use alternative modes of transmission, it is not permitted "the same leeway" with respect to intermediary banks if the sender designates intermediary banks through which the funds transfer are to be routed. The comment gives the following explanation:

> The sender's designation of that intermediary bank may mean that the beneficiary's bank is expected to obtain a credit from that intermediary bank and may have relied on that anticipated credit. If the receiving bank uses another intermediary bank the expectations of the beneficiary's bank may not be realized. The receiving bank could choose to route the transfer to another intermediary bank and then to the designated intermediary bank if there were some reason such as a lack of a

§ 7–20
1. 225 F.3d 1228 (11th Cir. 2000).

correspondent-bank relationship or a bilateral credit limitation, but the designated intermediary bank cannot be circumvented. To do so violates the sender's instructions.

§ 7–21 Erroneous Description of Intermediary or Beneficiary's Bank

If a payment order identifies an intermediary bank or beneficiary's bank only by an identifying number, the receiving bank is entitled to rely on the number, whether or not the number identifies a bank. Furthermore, the sender must compensate the receiving bank for any loss and expenses incurred as a result of reliance on the number in executing, or attempting to execute, the order.[1] Section 4A–208(a) and (b) provide:

(a) This subsection applies to a payment order identifying an intermediary bank or the beneficiary's bank only by an identifying number.

(1) The receiving bank may rely on the number as the proper identification of the intermediary or beneficiary's bank and need not determine whether the number identifies a bank.

(2) The sender is obliged to compensate the receiving bank for any loss and expenses incurred by the receiving bank as a result of its reliance on the number in executing or attempting to execute the order.

(b) This subsection applies to a payment order identifying an intermediary bank or the beneficiary's bank both by name and an identifying number if the name and number identify different persons.

(1) If the sender is a bank, the receiving bank may rely on the number as the proper identification of the intermediary or beneficiary's bank if the receiving bank, when it executes the sender's order, does not know that the name and number identify different persons. The receiving bank need not determine whether the name and number refer to the same person or whether the number refers to a bank. The sender is obliged to compensate the receiving bank for any loss and expenses incurred by the receiving bank as a result of its reliance on the number in executing or attempting to execute the order.

(2) If the sender is not a bank and the receiving bank proves that the sender, before the payment order was accepted, had notice that the receiving bank might rely on

§ 7–21
1. § 4A–208(a).

the number as the proper identification of the intermediary or beneficiary's bank even if it identifies a person different from the bank identified by name, the rights and obligations of the sender and the receiving bank are governed by subsection (b)(1), as though the sender were a bank. Proof of notice may be made by any admissible evidence. The receiving bank satisfies the burden of proof if it proves that the sender, before the payment order was accepted, signed a writing stating the information to which the notice relates.

(3) Regardless of whether the sender is a bank, the receiving bank may rely on the name as the proper identification of the intermediary or beneficiary's bank if the receiving bank, at the time it executes the sender's order, does not know that the name and number identify different persons. The receiving bank need not determine whether the name and number refer to the same person.

(4) If the receiving bank knows that the name and number identify different persons, reliance on either the name or the number in executing the sender's payment order is a breach of the obligation stated in Section 4A–302(a)(1).

If a payment order identifies an intermediary bank or beneficiary's bank by name and by number, and the receiving bank *knows* that the name and number do not coincide, and thus identify different persons, reliance by the receiving bank on either the name or the number in executing the payment order is a breach of the obligation to comply with the sender's order stated in 4A–302(a)(1).[2]

If a payment order identifies an intermediary bank or beneficiary's bank by name and number, the receiving bank may always rely on the name, unless the receiving bank *knows* that the name and number represent different parties.[3] In addition, if the sender is a bank, the receiving bank may also rely on the number, unless the receiving bank *knows* that the name and number represent different parties.[4] If the sender is not a bank, however, the receiving bank may rely on the number, without actual knowledge of a discrepancy, only if the receiving bank proves that, before the order was accepted, the sender had notice that the receiving bank may rely on the number in these situations.[5] If the receiving bank has effectively relied on the name or number, the sender must compensate the receiving bank for any losses incurred as a result of reliance in executing or attempting to execute the order.[6]

---

2. § 4A–208(b)(4).
3. § 4A–208(b)(3).
4. § 4A–208(b)(1).

5. § 4A–208(b)(2).
6. § 4A–208(b)(1).

The misdescription of an intermediary bank will not usually cause any loss if the beneficiary and the beneficiary's bank have been correctly identified.

PROBLEM

General Motors, a non-bank, issues a payment order to JP Morgan Chase instructing that $1 million be credited to account #12345 at National City. General Motors instructs JP Morgan Chase to use an intermediary bank (General Motors intended to use Bank AB, but it mistakenly listed the Bank 2 name on the payment order). Bank 2 is identified by name, but it is Bank AB's identifying number that is listed on General Motors's payment order. Immediately after accepting the order, Bank 2 suspends payments.

a) Regardless of whether General Motors is a bank or not, if JP Morgan Chase has no knowledge that the name and number are different, JP Morgan Chase may rely on the name. General Motors bears the loss.

b) Because sender is not a bank, JP Morgan Chase may also rely on the number if JP Morgan Chase proves that General Motors had notice that JP Morgan Chase may rely on the number, and not verify if the name and number are different, in these types of situations. If so, General Motors bears the loss; otherwise, JP Morgan Chase bears the loss.

c) If JP Morgan Chase relies on the name, or effectively relies on the number, JP Morgan Chase is not liable for breach under 4A–302(a)(1), and is entitled to compensation from General Motors for any loss and expenses resulting from General Motors's error. In other words, General Motors would bear the loss for the routing through the insolvent Bank 2.

d) If JP Morgan Chase knew the name and account number identified different persons, JP Morgan Chase is liable for breach under 4A–208(b)(4) and 4A–302(a)(1) and JP Morgan Chase bears the loss for routing through the insolvent Bank 2.

---

§ 7–22   Erroneous Execution Through Funds Transfer System or Other Communication System

Funds transfer systems—other than those operated by the Federal Reserve Banks—are treated as agents of the sender. Thus, if there is a discrepancy between the order sent by the sender to the funds transfer system, and the order sent by the funds transfer system to the receiving bank, the error of the funds transfer system is the error of the sender and the sender generally bears the risk of loss under Article 4A for errors made by non-Federal Reserve funds transfer systems. Liability for errors made by a non-Federal Reserve funds transfer system is the liability of an agent and is determined by agency law.[1] The sender, however, does not bear the risk of loss of errors made by funds transfer systems operated by the Federal Reserve Banks. According to section 4A–206(a):

> If a payment order addressed to a receiving bank is transmitted to a funds-transfer system or other third-party communication system for transmittal to the bank, the system is deemed to be an agent of the sender for the purpose of transmitting the payment order to the bank. If there is a discrepancy between the terms of the payment order transmitted to the system and the terms of the payment order transmitted by the system to the bank, the terms of the payment order of the sender are those transmitted by the system. This section does not apply to a funds-transfer system of the Federal Reserve Banks.

Under 4A–206, funds transfer systems of the Federal Reserve Banks, like Fedwire, are considered intermediary banks. Thus, Federal Reserve Banks are not merely agents of the sender, but are receiving banks and senders of their own payment orders.[2] These Federal Reserve Banks are independent participants in the funds transfer process and have rights and obligations of a receiving bank and sender of payment orders.[3]

The point is made as follows in Comment 2 to 4A–206:

> In the hypothetical case just discussed, if the automated clearing house is operated by a Federal Reserve Bank, the analysis is different. Section 4A–206 does not apply. Originator's Bank will execute Originator's payment orders by delivery or transmission of the electronic information to the Federal Reserve Bank for processing. The result is that Originator's Bank has issued payment orders to the Federal Reserve Bank which, in

---

§ 7–22

1. *See* M. Spak, The Case to be made for Proposed Article 4A of the Uniform Commercial Code: What's a Trillion Dollars Between Friends?!, 80 Ky. L.J. 167, 174–175 (1992). See also the CHIPS Rules at http:// www.chips.org/reference/docs_rules/docs_reference_rules.php.

2. § 4A–206.

3. 12 CFR § 210.6 states that a "Reserve bank that handles an item shall act as agent or subagent of the owner with respect to the item." On the face of it this would seem to conflict with what we have said above, but it appears that the Federal Reserve has taken the position that it is an agent and not an intermediary bank or an intermediary

bank agent only with respect to checks under subpart (a) of Regulation J and that there is no similar statement in the current version of the subpart (b) dealing with funds transfers. Should the federal government take the position that the Federal Reserve is an agent and not an intermediary bank, that, of course, would override the provisions of 4A–206 to the contrary. *Cf.* R. Stockmann, Liability of Intermediary and Beneficiary Banks in Funds Transfer: A Comparative Study of American and German Law, 8 Int'l Tax & Bus. Law 215 (Winter, 1991). (Beware the references in Stockman to Regulation J are to an earlier version of Regulation J.)

this case, is acting as an intermediary bank. When the Federal Reserve Bank has processed the information given to it by Originator's Bank it will issue payment orders to the various beneficiary's banks. If the processing results in an erroneous payment order, the Federal Reserve Bank has erroneously executed the payment order of Originator's Bank and the case is governed by Section 4A–303.

PROBLEM

1. JP Morgan Chase sends a payment order through CHIPS for $1 million; CHIPS sends the payment order to National City for $10 million. JP Morgan Chase is deemed to have sent a $10 million payment order to National City.

    JP Morgan Chase—>　　CHIPS—>　　National City—>　　Beneficiary
    　　　#1　　　　　　　　　　　　　　　　　#2

    1) JP Morgan Chase is the sender of payment order #2.

    2) National City is the receiving bank of payment order #2.

    3) CHIPS is the agent of JP Morgan Chase.

2. JP Morgan Chase sends payment order through Fedwire for $1 million; Fedwire (FRB) sends the payment order to National City for $10 million. JP Morgan Chase is deemed to send $1 million payment order to FRB via Fedwire.

    JP Morgan Chase—>　　Fedwire—>　National City—>　　Beneficiary
    　　　#1　　　　　　　　　　　　　　#2

    1) JP Morgan Chase is the sender of payment order #1.

    2) Fedwire (operated by Federal Reserve Bank) is receiving bank of payment order #1; sender of payment order #2.

    3) National City is receiving bank of payment order #2.

§ 7–23　Fraud in General

The massive daily flow of money through the global electronics funds system makes the Mississippi look like a trickling stream by comparison. The very size of this river of money might attract a thirsty thief and might encourage the thief to believe that no one would object to his taking a small drink. The fact that the flow is almost entirely within the banking system and among sophisticated participants means that it is difficult for an outsider to commit a successful fraud. The extent of EFT fraud within this system remains a mystery to an outsider. While every UCC Reporter has a handful of cases concerning check fraud, reported cases of fraud in electronics funds transfers are relatively few and far between.[1]

First we can dismiss a fraud that may be frequently practiced but is seldom the cause of litigation. This is fraud committed by the employees of the various banks in the funds transfer systems. Surely there are recurring thefts, perhaps massive thefts by such people. A famous fraud that was made public involved Security Pacific Bank and an intriguing scheme by which the thief procured his money in Switzerland and attempted to launder it by buying Russian diamonds. The thief, computer consultant Stanley Mark Rifkin, used his consultant status to gain entry to Security Pacific's wire transfer room, where he transferred $10.2 million to a bank account in New York. Mr. Rifkin then wired $8 million to a Swiss bank account of the Soviet government's official diamond broker in Zurich. The transfer was not discovered until eight days after it occurred. Mr. Rifkin, possessing thousands of diamonds worth more than $8.14 million wholesale, was arrested almost two weeks after the transfer.[2] Perhaps because it is so clear who is at fault in these cases (or because no bank wishes publicly to admit that such a case has arisen), these cases seldom result in lawsuits. Presumably the bank whose employee does the stealing is also the bank that loses the money. Such a party is not likely to have legal rights against anyone else except its insurer. So *mirable dictu*, we have theft without litigation.

Stating what should otherwise be obvious, Article 4A bars a bank from charging a customer's account for its own employee's fraudulent act:

> If a receiving bank accepts a payment order issued in the name of its customer as sender which is (i) not authorized and not effective as the order of the customer under Section 4A–202, or (ii) not enforceable, in whole or in part, against the customer under Section 4A–203, the bank shall refund any payment of the payment order received from the customer to the extent the bank is not entitled to enforce payment and shall pay interest on the refundable amount calculated from the date the bank received payment to the date of the refund.[3]

§ 7–23

1. As elsewhere in this book, we exclude fraud by the theft or fabrication of debit cards. Those questions are governed not by Article 4A but by the Federal Consumer Credit Protection Act. *See* Bradford Trust Co. v. Tex. American Bank—Houston, 790 F.2d 407, 1 UCC2d 828 (5th Cir. 1986); Securities Fund Serv., Inc. v. American Nat. Bank and Trust Co., 542 F.Supp. 323, 34 UCC Rep.Serv. 607 (N.D.Ill.1982); Merchants Bank North v. Citizens Sav. and Loan Assoc., Inc., No. 87–312–CIV–5, 1988 WL 146591 (E.D.N.C. Aug. 9, 1988).

2. P.G. Hollie, "Police Recount Theft by Wire of $10 Million," N.Y. Times, Nov. 7, 1978, at A–11.

3. § 4A–204(a).

If an embezzling employee at the bank makes a fraudulent payment order that draws on General Motors' account, the bank may not charge General Motors' account and under 4A–204(a) must recredit any amount charged. Frauds of this kind—done by bank employees or by those not associated in any way with a particular customer—doubtless inhabit the nightmares of the bank's security people but they have little importance to the lawyer. A wise bank will devote large resources to prevent their occurrence, but only small resources in an attempt to pass the loss to another when they occur.

For a unique case where a court held a bank liable because payment orders were not "authorized" due to conditional and limited powers of attorney, see Grabowski v. Bank of Boston.[4] There, account holders signed powers of attorney allowing Norman Epstein to send payment orders from their accounts, provided that the account balance was always at least as much as the owner's initial deposit. Bank of Boston ended up allowing Epstein to withdraw all of the money in the customers' accounts, however. The court recognized that banks are not usually held liable for outside information in a transaction, but Bank of Boston was liable here because it had the requisite power of attorney documents in its control and should have seen the restriction when reviewing the powers of attorney as part of the transaction with Epstein.

The cases that the courts will see and that a lawyer must understand are those arising out of fraud by the customer's or sender's employee, or by one who has somehow become a party to the sender's secrets. Because the contact between the originator and the receiving bank is likely to be impersonal, by telephone, telex or computer conversation, the receiving bank needs some electronic way of identifying the sender and it is important for the sender that unauthorized persons not be able to mislead the receiving bank. The relationship between the receiving bank, the sender and the allocation of responsibility for fraud between the two is dealt with extensively by sections 4A–201, 4A–202, and 4A–203. In this vein, consider Centre–Point Merchant Bank, Ltd. v. American Express Bank, Ltd.,[5] where one of Centre–Point's employees sent fraudulent payment orders to American Express via telex that "tested" properly under the agreed upon security procedure between Centre–Point and American Express.[6] The court found that

4. 997 F.Supp. 111 (D. Mass. 1997).

5. No. 95 Civ. 5000 LMM, 2000 WL 1772874, at *1 (S.D.N.Y. 2000).

6. A "tested telex" is an older form of authentication for messages and payment orders between banks where the receiving bank verifies a telex transmission by way of an agreed-upon test key that is exchanged ex ante under an agreement between the individual sending and receiving banks. This form of verification is no longer considered to be truly secure, and many banks now use the SWIFT system in place of tested telexes for such transmissions. For additional information on the security risks

this was a commercially reasonable security procedure under New York's version of 4A–202(c), and that American Express was not liable for sending the fraudulent payment orders under 4A–202(b).

These sections make the sender liable not only for the orders that it authorizes, but also for certain other payment orders that—whether authorized or not—are "verified pursuant to a security procedure."

Authorization can take many forms. At one end of the spectrum are the potentially obvious cases, where the sender signed an actual document authorizing the eventual fraudster to send payment orders from their account—see Sekerak v. National City Bank[7] (funds transfer authorization), Grabowski v. Bank of Boston[8] (power of attorney), and Estate of Freitag v. Frontier Bank[9](decedent's will). At the opposite end are situations where authorization is much less clear—see Skyline Int'l Development v. Citibank, F.S.B.[10] (did not require the sender's employee to actually sign a payment order form in order to hold the sender liable when the transfer was authorized orally).[11]

Section 4A–201 defines a security procedure as:

> a procedure established by agreement of a customer and a receiving bank for the purpose of (i) verifying that a payment order or communication amending or cancelling a payment order is that of the customer, or (ii) detecting error in the transmission or the content of the payment order or communication.

If (1) the sender and the bank have agreed upon a commercially reasonable security procedure and (2) the bank in good faith follows the procedure, the order is treated as though it were authorized even though it is not. The bank may charge the sender's

---

posed by using tested telexes, see John Bryant, Article, SWIFTWorld November/December 1996 (reproduced with permission as: Thales e-Security, White Paper: Fighting Tested Telex Fraud), *available at*: http://www.thalesesecurity. com/Whitepapers/documents/fighting_ tested_telex_fraud3.pdf.

7. 342 F.Supp.2d 701 (N.D. Ohio 2004).

8. 997 F.Supp. 111 (D. Mass. 1997).

9. 118 Wash.App. 222, 75 P.3d 596 (2003).

10. 302 Ill.App.3d 79, 236 Ill.Dec. 68, 706 N.E.2d 942 (1998).

11. When determining which party's intent governs, note that the only focus is on the particular sender of the pay-

ment order at issue. *See* Cmty. Bank v. Stevens Financial Corp., 966 F.Supp. 775 (N.D. Ind. 1997) (addressing a situation where the originator, Stevens Financial, instructed the receiving bank to send a payment order to the originator's account at Chase, but the receiving bank actually sent the payment order to Stevens' account at Community Bank. In holding that Community Bank could accept the receiving bank's payment order, the court held that the receiving bank's intent governed. Since that bank's intent was for the payment order to go to Community Bank, Community could properly accept the order, and Stevens' only recourse was against the receiving bank for sending an erroneous payment order that did not comply with its initial instructions).

account and treat the order as valid even though it is the child of fraud.

Section 4A–201 defines the concept of a security procedure in general terms. The section does not limit the style and complexity of security procedures. As thieves become more clever, security procedures will have to respond. Codes, identifying words, encryption, and procedures whereby one person calls back to confirm, are all possible security procedures. One method that is presumptively not a security procedure is a comparison of the signature on the payment order to an otherwise authorized signature.[12] That said, at least one court has held that verifying a sender's signature in combination with a telephone callback verification is a commercially reasonable security procedure.

An agreed security procedure must be commercially reasonable; commercial reasonableness is only partly defined by 4A–202(c):

> Commercial reasonableness of a security procedure is a question of law to be determined by considering the wishes of the customer expressed to the bank, the circumstances of the customer known to the bank, including the size, type, and frequency of payment orders normally issued by the customer to the bank, alternative security procedures offered to the customer, and security procedures in general use by customers and receiving banks similarly situated. A security procedure is deemed to be commercially reasonable if (i) the security procedure was chosen by the customer after the bank offered, and the customer refused, a security procedure that was commercially reasonable for that customer, and (ii) the customer expressly agreed in writing to be bound by any payment order, whether or not authorized, issued in its name and accepted by the bank in compliance with the security procedure chosen by the customer.

This section was applied in *Centre–Point Merchant Bank*, discussed above, where the court held that the use of a "test key" to verify a telex from the bank's customer constituted a commercially reasonable security procedure.

In subsection (c) one can see the hand of the banks at work. First, reasonableness is a question of "law," not one for the jury. Second, what constitutes a commercially reasonable security procedure will vary depending upon the nature of the customer and receiving bank. For instance, costly security procedures may be commercially reasonable for a customer who frequently issues payment orders in large amounts, but a less sophisticated security procedure may be commercially reasonable for a customer who

---

12. § 4A–201.

transmits payment orders infrequently or in small amounts. Likewise, it may not be commercially reasonable to expect a small rural bank to employ state of the art procedures for its customers, even if the customers are frequently transferring payment orders involving significant amounts.[13]

However, the security procedures employed by the customer and receiving bank must at least meet applicable prevailing standards of good banking practice.[14] Third, the section provides some guidelines and suggests ways in which the bank can increase the likelihood that its procedures will be considered commercially reasonable. Among them is the fact that others "similarly situated" use similar procedures. Another is the fact that the bank offers alternative procedures and that a particular one was chosen by its customer. Where the bank and a sender have agreed on a security procedure and where the person allegedly acting on behalf of the sender and the bank uses the procedure, the order is validated by section 4A–202(b) as follows:[15]

> If a bank and its customer have agreed that the authenticity of payment orders issued to the bank in the name of the customer as sender will be verified pursuant to a security procedure, a payment order received by the receiving bank is effective as the order of the customer, whether or not authorized, if (i) the security procedure is a commercially reasonable method of providing security against unauthorized payment orders, and (ii) the bank proves that it accepted the payment order in good faith and in compliance with the security procedure and any written agreement or instruction of the customer restricting acceptance of payment orders issued in the name of the customer. The bank is not required to follow an instruction that violates a written agreement with the customer or notice of which is not received at a time and in a manner affording the bank a reasonable opportunity to act on it before the payment order is accepted.

---

13. See § 4A–203, Comment 4.

14. § 4A–203, Comment 4.

15. If the order is not authorized and "not effective" as a verified order, the sender is not bound (see § 4A–204(a)), and that is true even if the fraudulent sender knew the code, could have used it, but did not. Put another way, there may be no requirement of a causal connection between the failure to use the security code and the loss in order to render the order ineffective. The text appears to require literal compliance and does not provide that the failure to comply with security procedure must have caused the fraud to go undetected. The comments to 4A–203, however, provide that "if the fraud was not detected because the bank employee did not perform the acts required by the security procedure, the bank has not complied," thus implying that causation is needed. Does compliance mean literal compliance or substantial compliance? See T. McKelvy, Note, Article 4A of the Uniform Commercial Code: Finally, Banks and their Customers Know Where They Stand and Who Pays When a Wire Transfer Goes Awry, 21 Mem. St. U. L. Rev. 351, 368–69 (1991).

Section 4A–203 cuts back slightly on the receiving bank's right to rely upon a properly verified order. Under 4A–203(a)(1) the receiving bank may "limit the extent to which it is entitled to enforce" a properly verified order. One might scoff at the suggestion that a receiving bank might agree *to expand* its liability. But remember, the party requesting such an expansion might be General Motors or ExxonMobil, a person entitled to the careful attention of its banker. With a customer of such importance it is conceivable that a bank would agree to bear more risk under 4A–203 than it would otherwise bear under 4A–202.

Section 4A–203(a)(2) provides the sender (customer) another limited escape. If the sender proves that the thief is not and never was an insider of the customer and did not acquire the information on the security procedure from an insider, then the sender is not bound by the unauthorized but verified order:

> The receiving bank is not entitled to enforce or retain payment of the payment order if the customer proves that the order was not caused, directly or indirectly, by a person (i) entrusted at any time with duties to act for the customer with respect to payment orders or the security procedure, or (ii) who obtained access to transmitting facilities of the customer or who obtained, from a source controlled by the customer and without authority of the receiving bank, information facilitating breach of the security procedure, regardless of how the information was obtained or whether the customer was at fault. Information includes any access device, computer software, or the like.

Cases of outsiders' action alone will be few and far between. By far the most likely thieves are those who are working for or who have worked for the sender, or whose spouses do so, or who one way or another tap into the sender's transmitting facilities.

It is possible that a clever hacker could figure out the proper code from a source unrelated to the sender, and *if* the sender proves as much, then the sender would not be bound by the fraudulent order, but that is a big if. An example of this type of fraud that we are aware of involved Russian thieves who obtained the passwords necessary to gain access to Citicorp's payment order system, and accessed the system over forty times. The thieves then sent unauthorized payment orders from legitimate Citicorp accounts. As the thieves were unrelated to any of the Citicorp customers, 4A–203(a)(2) would presumably have insulated the account holders from any losses in a suit against Citicorp. As secure as Citicorp's computer systems were likely to have been at the time of the thefts, one would imagine they are even stronger today. As such, we continue to believe that this manner of fraud will remain rare in the future.[16]

We suspect that 4A–203(a)(2) will play a modest supporting role in the theatre of fraud. First we suspect that outsider thieves will be few, and even when the thief is an outsider, section 4A–203(a)(2) will not avail the sender unless it can carry the burden of proving that the thief did not acquire the information from the sender.[17]

In general, sections 4A–201, 4A–202, and 4A–203 tell the bank that it can rely on orders transmitted in accordance with a reasonable security procedure and can charge a customer's account even when those orders have been sent by a thief. The rules admonish the receiving bank to set up a good security procedure and to use it. The upshot of all of this is that most of the losses committed by the next generation of embezzlers, namely, those who steal by wire transfer and not by check, will be placed where they generally should be, on the customer (sender) who employs the embezzler. These rules are analogous to the similar rules now found in 3–404 and 3–405 of revised Article 3 on padded payrolls, impostors and the like.

One last point on fraud cases worth mentioning involves situations where customers attempt to hold their bank liable for a fraudulent payment order on a theory of constructive notice of the fraud. In general, courts have generally not been supportive of such theories. An example is Estate of Freitag v. Frontier Bank,[18] where the court held that a deceased account holder's personal representative transferring estate funds into her personal account was insufficient to impute knowledge of the fraud to the bank.

PROBLEM

Thief, an insider at General Motors, originates a funds transfer by electronically transmitting a payment order to JP Morgan Chase. The payment order instructs JP Morgan Chase to transfer $5 million from the account of General Motors to the account of Thief at National City. JP Morgan Chase issues a payment order to Continental Bank instructing that a $5 million credit be placed in

---

16. For an original article describing the fraud, see William M. Carley and Timothy L. O'Brien, Cyber Caper: How Citicorp System Was Raided and Funds Moved Around World, Wall St. J., Sept. 12, 1995, at A1.

17. § 4A–203, Comment 7 also provides that the receiving bank is not entitled to enforce or retain payment of an unauthorized, but effective, payment order if the sender and receiving bank are members of a funds transfer system, and the funds transfer system varies the rights and obligations of the sender and receiving bank.

18. 118 Wash.App. 222, 75 P.3d 596 (2003).

Thief's account in National City. Continental Bank issues a payment order to National City instructing it to credit Thief's account for $5 million. National City credits the account of Thief and notifies Thief. Thief withdraws the funds, and flies to Patagonia, never to be seen again. General Motors refuses to pay JP Morgan Chase, rightfully asserting that neither General Motors nor an agent of General Motors authorized the payment order. Who bears the loss in the following circumstances?

1. What if JP Morgan Chase and General Motors have no security procedure in effect?

    JP Morgan Chase bears the loss. Thief is not an agent of General Motors and has no actual or apparent authority to originate the funds transfer in the name of General Motors.

2. What if JP Morgan Chase unilaterally adopted a commercially reasonable security procedure, and JP Morgan Chase, in good faith, complied with the security procedure?

    JP Morgan Chase bears the loss. A commercially reasonable security procedure must be adopted and agreed upon by both the customer and the receiving bank.

3. What if JP Morgan Chase and General Motors agreed upon a commercially reasonable security procedure and JP Morgan Chase, in good faith, complied with the security procedure?

    General Motors bears the loss.

4. What if General Motors rejected a commercially reasonable security procedure? General Motors and JP Morgan Chase were in the process of negotiating over a security procedure when the fraudulent payment order occurred.

    JP Morgan Chase bears the loss. No security procedure is in effect. In order for General Motors to be liable for rejecting a commercially reasonable security procedure, General Motors must have then chosen its own security procedure and agreed, in writing, to be bound by any payment order accepted by the bank in compliance with the customer's security procedure.

5. What if General Motors and JP Morgan Chase agreed upon a commercially reasonable security procedure requiring JP Morgan Chase to follow through six steps before executing the payment order? For the last step, JP Morgan Chase agreed not to execute General Motors' payment orders before at least one hour expired after JP Morgan Chase received the payment order. JP Morgan Chase received the payment order from Thief at 2:00 P.M. After following the first five steps, JP Morgan Chase executed the order at 2:55 P.M. At 3:50 P.M., GM discovered the unauthorized payment order and called JP Morgan Chase to cancel the payment order. JP Morgan Chase had already accepted at this time, and the Thief had already received the funds and was en route to Patagonia.

The result turns upon whether one reads "in compliance with" in 4A–202 literally. JP Morgan Chase has not literally complied with the security procedure because it executed five minutes early. On the other hand, JP Morgan Chase complied with the first five steps and substantially complied with the last step. More importantly, the failure of JP Morgan Chase to comply with the last step did not cause General Motors to suffer the loss. General Motors did not discover the fraud until after JP Morgan Chase would have executed the payment order if it had complied with the security procedure. We think the loss should fall on GM but we are not sure what the courts will do.

For the most part, banks and customers can modify their responsibilities as they wish by using elaborate or modest security procedures, but there are limits. Bank of Boston's clause that immunized it from liability for executing an unauthorized payment in all cases except where it acted in bad faith did not work.[19]

§ 7–24 Reallocation of Fraud Loss Based on Post Fraud Acts: The Name, Number Discrepancy

There are at least two and possibly three circumstances in which the fraud loss originally charged to the customer (sender) or to the receiving bank under sections 4A–202 through 4A–204 might be reallocated to another because of subsequent events. The first involves a specific kind of fraud that has earned a special place in American case law. This fraud is represented by two pre-Article 4A cases: Bradford Trust Co. v. Texas American Bank—Houston,[1] and Securities Fund Serv., Inc. v. American Nat. Bank and Trust Co. of Chicago.[2]

In *Bradford*, two devious fellows arranged to purchase rare coins and gold bullion from Colonial Coins for $800,000. The thieves and Colonial Coins agreed that Colonial Coins would release the coins and bullion upon receipt of funds wired into Colonial Coins' bank account at Texas American Bank. The thieves then sent a forged letter, purportedly from Frank Rochefort, to Bradford Trust, the agent for his mutual fund account, directing the transfer of funds from the mutual fund account of Rochefort to Rochefort's account at Texas American Bank. Although the instructions named Rochefort as the beneficiary of the funds transfer, the account

---

19. Grabowski v. Bank of Boston, 997 F.Supp. 111, 120 (D. Mass. 1997).

2. 542 F.Supp. 323, 34 UCC 607 (N.D. Ill. 1982).

§ 7–24

1. 790 F.2d 407, 1 UCC2d 828 (5th Cir. 1986).

number (to all appearances Rochefort's at Texas American) was actually the account number of Colonial Coins' bank account at Texas American. In disregard of internal procedures to verify that Rochefort requested this payment order, Bradford Trust instructed its correspondent bank, State Street Bank, to wire the funds to Texas American. Texas American received the funds and, relying on the account number given for the beneficiary (and apparently ignoring the name), credited the account of Colonial Coins. Texas American notified Colonial Coins of the wire transfer, and Colonial released the coins to the two devious fellows.

After receiving notice of the unauthorized withdrawal, Rochefort demanded reimbursement from Bradford Trust. Bradford Trust reimbursed Rochefort's account and then demanded reimbursement from Texas American. Texas American refused and Bradford sued Texas American for reimbursement. Texas American argued that Bradford would have discovered the fraud by following its internal security procedures and that its negligence caused the loss to Bradford Trust. Bradford responded that Texas American had the last clear chance to avoid the loss and was negligent in failing to recognize that the name and number in the payment order did not match, i.e., that the number of the account credited (Colonials) did not bear the name (Rochefort) used in the funds transfer. Thus, Bradford argued that Texas American should bear the loss.

On summary judgment the district court applied the Texas comparative negligence statute and divided the loss equally between Bradford Trust and Texas American. The appellate court reversed. The appellate court declined to apply the Texas comparative negligence statute to the case before it, holding that the statute was intended to apply only to cases of physical harm to persons and property and did not extend to commercial cases.[3] In commercial cases, the court reasoned that the need for fast, efficient, and certain results outweighed the need equitably to apportion loss.

Lacking a comprehensive body of law on electronic funds transfers such as that provided in Article 4A, the court relied by analogy on two factors derived from negotiable instrument fraud cases: "1) which party was in the best position to avoid the loss; and 2) which solution promotes the policy of finality in commercial transactions?"

In light of these two factors, the court held that Bradford Trust should bear the loss. The court emphasized that Bradford Trust was in the best position to avoid the loss. It had dealt directly with the impostor and, in the court's opinion, was the primary law violator. As the court stated:

3.   790 F.2d at 409.

If Bradford had followed procedures it had in place that called for verification of the customer's order, the loss would not have occurred. Instead of following those procedures and verifying Rochefort's order, Bradford set the fraudulent scheme into motion by liquidating Rochefort's account and wiring the funds to Texas American. Although Texas American should have recognized the discrepancy between the account number and name of the owner of the account to whom the wire directed the funds be credited, we are persuaded that Texas American's fault was secondary to that of Bradford's. It is far from certain that the loss would have been prevented even if Texas American had noticed the discrepancy between the account number and the holder of the account and had called this discrepancy to Bradford's attention. To conclude that this action by Texas American would have avoided the loss requires us to assume that such a call to Bradford would have caused Bradford to contact Rochefort and verify his order. On the other hand, it is certain that if Bradford had called Rochefort to verify his purported order to transfer funds to Colonial this scheme would have been discovered and no loss would have been suffered.[4]

In addition, the court noted that placing the loss on Bradford Trust was in accord with the policy of finality in commercial transactions. As the court stated:

Assessing the loss in this case to Bradford and ending the transaction when Bradford paid under Rochefort's forged order rather than inquiring into and upsetting later transactions after the forgery was discovered clearly serves this bedrock policy of finality.[5]

In *Securities Fund Services*,[6] two impostors arranged to purchase diamonds and jewels from Haberkorn by wiring funds into Haberkorn's account at ANB. The two impostors then sent a letter to Securities Fund Services, purportedly from someone named Bushman, instructing SFS to redeem Bushman's shares worth approximately $2 million and to transfer the proceeds to Bushman's account at ANB. Although the instructions named Bushman as the beneficiary of the wire transfer, the account number given was Haberkorn's. SFS processed the redemption by directing NEMB, custodian of Templeton Funds, to make the requested wire transfer. In turn, NEMB instructed ANB to credit the account of "John Bushman, Trustee / / 204471." ANB had no account in the name of John Bushman, either individually or as trustee. Without contacting NEMB, Templeton, or SFS, ANB credited account num-

---

4. *Id*. at 410.

5. *Id*. at 411.

6. 542 F.Supp. 323, 34 UCC Rep. Serv. 607 (N.D. Ill. 1982).

ber 204471 (belonging to Haberkorn). After receiving the funds in his bank account at ANB, Haberkorn released the jewels to the two impostors.

After discovering the fraud, SFS reissued the redeemed shares to the real John Bushman, subrogated itself to the rights of Bushman and Templeton, and sought to recover the amount of the lost funds from ANB. SFS sought to recover from ANB on a number of theories including negligence, bailment, conversion, third party beneficiary and estoppel. On motion for summary judgment, the district court dismissed all of the claims against ANB except the negligence claim and the third party beneficiary claim.

Relying on Article 4 of the UCC, the district court held that ANB, as collecting bank, was an agent of SFS, the initiator of the transfer. Thus, the court precluded dismissal of the negligence cause of action because ANB owed a duty of care to SFS as its agent, and may have breached that duty by failing to recognize the name and account number discrepancy and to inform SFS, NEMB, or Templeton of the discrepancy. The court also held that SFS could seek to recover the funds from ANB as a third party beneficiary of a contract between NEMB and ANB to deliver funds to Bushman's account. Even though SFS was not explicitly named as a third party beneficiary in the contract between ANB and NEMB, the court stated that SFS had rights as a third party beneficiary because the "direct or substantial benefit to SFS [was] the interest in properly transferring the funds to avoid any loss by [its] customer or SFS itself."[7]

In both *Bradford Trust* and *Securities Fund Services*, the thief caused the customer to issue a funds transfer order that identified the customer by name as the beneficiary but also purported to identify the same beneficiary by an account number in the bank to which the deposit was to be made. In some cases this has been done by fooling an honest person in the employment of the originator of the payment order. In other cases the thief has acquired information from the originator and has issued his own fraudulent order directly to the receiving bank. Since the correct name of the customer who owns the account in the receiving bank is identified as the recipient of the order, a bank employee reading the verbal description of the beneficiary is likely to be lulled. (After all, "what could be wrong with a customer transferring funds to itself at another bank?")

In these cases the account number is not the account number of the customer; it is the account number of the thief or, in some cases the account number of an honest person who is an unwitting participant in the thief's scheme. For example, in *Bradford Trust*,

7.   542 F.Supp. at 329.

the person named "in words" was the account owner at Bradford, but the person named "in numbers" was a coin dealer with whom the thieves were doing business. When the money in the proper amount showed up in the coin dealer's account, he assumed that it had come from the persons with whom he was dealing, and he took the money as payment and transferred the coins to them.

Where there is a discrepancy between the name and number of the beneficiary in the payment order, it has sometimes been argued that the receiving bank should compare the name with the number on the account and where they do not match should refuse to accept the order. Indeed, that was the apparent direction of the court's opinion in *Security Fund Services*, though not in *Bradford*.

Because such name-number fraud had become so well known, it received careful and explicit consideration in section 4A–207. The rules there are set out as follows:

> If a payment order received by the beneficiary's bank identifies the beneficiary both by name and by an identifying or bank account number and the name and number identify different persons, the following rules apply:
>
>> (1) Except as otherwise provided in subsection (c), if the beneficiary's bank does not know that the name and number refer to different persons, it may rely on the number as the proper identification of the beneficiary of the order. The beneficiary's bank need not determine whether the name and number refer to the same person.
>>
>> (2) If the beneficiary's bank pays the person identified by name or knows that the name and number identify different persons, no person has rights as beneficiary except the person paid by the beneficiary's bank if that person was entitled to receive payment from the originator of the funds transfer. If no person has rights as beneficiary, acceptance of the order cannot occur.

Basically these rules come to the opposite conclusion as that suggested by *Security Fund Services* and to the same conclusion as that endorsed by *Bradford Trust*. Under 4A–207(b)(1), an ignorant beneficiary's bank may rely on the number and may process the payment order mechanically or electronically without requiring that a person look at the verbal indication of the beneficiary's name. It need not even "determine whether the name and number refer to the same person." This conclusion is consistent with the idea that typical funds transfers should be speedy, inexpensive and not labor intensive. If it is not true already, soon the entire transaction—after it has been mechanically entered into the system—will be completed without the intervention of human eyes or hands. Presumably, therefore, machines will be instructed to read the numbers and to credit the amount represented by the numbers in the numbered account, oblivious to the name on the account. By producing a relatively certain law and stating clearly who bears any loss, the drafters have done all that could be asked of them.

There can be arguments about when a bank "knows" that the name and number refer to different persons, but those too should be minimal. Since "to know" is to have actual knowledge, not notice, and since it is implausible that a bank would "knowingly" make a large payment into a thief's account, this seems a small escape. Even in cases where banks do not process incoming payment orders on a completely automated basis, courts have been reluctant to imply actual knowledge outside of extreme circumstances. First, consider First Security Bank of N.M. v. Pan American Bank,[8] where the Tenth Circuit held that the beneficiary's bank did not have knowledge of a discrepancy between the listed beneficiary and the account holder's name when a wire room employee encountered difficulty in attempting to contact the beneficiary as a matter of the bank's policy to give notice of a payment order's receipt.

A second case on point is TME Enterprises, Inc. v. Norwest Corp.,[9] where the Court of Appeals of California held that Norwest did not have knowledge of a discrepancy even though its wire transfer system required that an employee record the name of the beneficiary when that particular account holder was not a regular recipient of payment orders. Since the name was recorded solely for purposes of complying with the Bank Secrecy Act, and not for verifying that the funds were posted to the proper beneficiary's account, the court held that the bank did not have knowledge of a discrepancy for purposes of 4A–207.[10] Notwithstanding these existing cases, we would imagine that such cases involving actual notice could arise, particularly where a lucky thief does multiple transactions through the same bank.

8. 215 F.3d 1147 (10th Cir. 2000).

9. 124 Cal.App.4th 1021, 22 Cal. Rptr.3d 146 (2004).

10. Only if the "bank personnel handling the transaction are aware that the name of the owner * * * bears no resemblance to, and has nothing in common with, the named beneficiary" would there be the requisite level of knowledge. *TME Enterprises*, at 1025. Furthermore, "[a]ny time a bank's wire transfer system includes any review of the name on the account, the bank's wire operator is almost certain to have actual knowledge that there is some type of mismatch or discrepancy between the name of the beneficiary identified in the wire and the name of the owner of the account designated in the wire.... As a result, the bank should not be exposed to potential liability for accepting a wire unless there is a complete disconnect between the names." *Id.* at 1034, 22 Cal.Rptr.3d 146. Another case confirming that name discrepancies are treated differently is New South Federal Savings Bank v. Flatbush Federal Savings and Loan Ass'n of Brooklyn, No. 01 Civ. 9024(DFE), 2002 WL 31413680 at *1–2 (S.D.N.Y. 2002), and that court's subsequent upholding of a jury verdict for the beneficiary's bank in No. 01 Civ. 9024 (DFE), 2003 WL 1888678 at *1 (S.D.N.Y. 2003).

For originators and other senders, the message embodied in 4A–207(b), and in the other sections of Part 2 of Article 4A, is that they should take steps to see that the numbers on their messages are the correct numbers. They should take no satisfaction in the fact that the proper names appear on the messages.

While most name and number discrepancy cases will be similar to those discussed above, at least one reported case exists that dealt with a payment order requesting credit to a non-existent account number. In Corfan Banco Asuncion Parguay v. Ocean Bank,[11] Corfan's payment order to a beneficiary at Ocean Bank listed the proper beneficiary name, but transposed numbers in the account number, such that the listed account did not match any account actually held at Ocean. Without contacting Corfan, Ocean called its customer (the proper beneficiary) to verify that he was expecting the payment. Upon receiving this verification, Ocean credited his account. The next day, Corfan became aware of the account number error and sent a second payment, this time stating the proper account number. The beneficiary withdrew the proceeds of both payment orders, and this litigation between the banks ensued once the beneficiary was unable to reimburse Corfan for the duplicate payment order.

A Florida state appeals court found for Corfan under a strict reading of Florda's version of 4A–207(a) and (b). The court reasoned that the name and number did not refer to "different persons," as required for 4A–207(b) to apply, because a non-existent account number does not refer to any person. Therefore, 4A–207(a) governed, and the plain language of that section says that if the "account number * * * refers to a nonexistent or unidentifiable person or account, no person has rights as a beneficiary and acceptance of the order cannot occur." The court held that Corfan was not liable to Ocean because the initial payment order from Corfan could not have been accepted, thus Corfan's duty to pay Ocean Bank under 4A–401(b) was not triggered.

In a well-reasoned dissent, Judge Nesbitt noted that 4A–207(a) allows the receiving bank to look at "other information," which indicates that the drafters intended to allow receiving banks to consider items beyond simply the listed name and account number in identifying the proper beneficiary. He also argued that Article 4A was not intended to "abrogate other common law principles applicable to commercial transactions," including the idea that the "party best suited to prevent the loss caused by a third party wrongdoer must bear that loss." Under both of these lines of reasoning, the dissent would have held Corfan liable for the loss. We are persuaded by the dissent's arguments and believe that this case should have resulted in Corfan taking the loss on these facts.

11.   715 So.2d 967 (Fla. Dist. Ct. App. 1998).

A minor change in the language of 4A–207, as suggested by Professors Warren and Walt,[12] would support what we believe to be the stronger reasoning in this dispute. If 4A–207(b) read "If * * * the name and number *do not refer to the same person*, the following rules apply," instead of the current version using the words "refer to *different* persons," this case would arguably have fallen under 4A–207(b)(2) and Corfan would have taken the loss because the person "entitled to receive payment" actually received the funds.

There is one small loophole in 4A–207(c) for non-bank originators, where their banks have not informed them of their potential liability. In the words of the statute, the originator is not liable "unless the originator's bank proves that the originator, before acceptance of the originator's order, had notice that payment of a payment order issued by the originator might be made by the beneficiary's bank on the basis of an identifying or bank account number, even if it identifies a person different from the named beneficiary." Well-counseled banks will give notice to each of their customers and will require that the customer acknowledge in writing that they have notice of their potential liability. Of course, Murphy's Law tells us that some customers will not sign these documents, and as to some of those who have signed them, the bank may be unable to find the notice at the critical time.

In summary, section 4A–207 addresses the name/number discrepancy clearly and explicitly. For the most part, it places the loss back at the beginning of the transaction and leaves the beneficiary's bank free to process the orders by number and in bulk.

§ 7–25 Failure of Depositor to Examine Statements Received From Bank; Possible Reallocation of Fraud Loss

A second way in which subsequent events can alter liability for fraud is familiar to those who remember the consequences of a customer's failure to examine its bank statement under section 4–406 of Article 4. Under Article 4, a customer's failure to discover and report defects often nullifies its right to recover improper payments from a payor bank.

Compared to Article 4, the duty of a customer to examine and report discrepancies is greatly watered down in Article 4A. In rare circumstances, section 4A–205(b) places liability on the customer for failure to find "erroneous payments" represented on its statement. Under section 4A–204(a) the customer who fails to discover

---

12. William D. Warren and Steven D. Walt, Payments and Credits 225 (6th Ed. 2004).

fraud suffers a lesser consequence than one failing to find errors under 4A–205—the loss of interest.

If the customer receives a statement from its bank and the statement of account would have disclosed to a reasonable person that there has been a fraudulent transfer, the customer's failure to give notice within 90 days cuts off its right to interest on the amount taken under 4A–204(a), but no more. In the words of 4A–204's last sentence, "[t]he bank is not entitled to any recovery from the customer on account of a failure by the customer to give notification as stated in this section." The quoted language forecloses the argument that 4A–205(b) (imposing a larger responsibility on the customer in the case of erroneous orders) applies also to fraud cases. If 4A–205(b) applied to fraud cases, there would be an irreconcilable conflict between section 4A–205(b) and the last sentence in 4A–204(a). If 4A–205 is limited only to erroneous but not fraud cases, there is no obvious conflict.

But what about the case in which a thief commits fraud by communicating with an honest employee of the originator who in turn issues an order (stimulated by the fraud of a third party) that directs payment to a person not intended to receive payment by the agent of the customer? Because that order was issued by one authorized to issue and intending to give that order—albeit under the influence of fraud by a third party—it was arguably an "authorized order under 4A–202(a)," not an "erroneous instruction" under either 4A–204 or 4A–205. But one might argue that section 4A–205 covers cases in which the "error" in the payment order was in fact caused by the fraud of someone upstream from the authorized agent. The customer would suggest that it "erroneously instructed payment."[1]

In some limited circumstances a bank can argue that 4A–205 governs even cases where the order is stimulated by fraud. Put another way, some orders might be stimulated by fraud and nevertheless constitute erroneous orders properly issued and covered by 4A–205(b). In that case the loss would be on the bank only if the sender used the proper security procedure and the receiving bank not only failed to do so, but also would have detected the error had it complied with the security procedure. Conceivably this could happen if the bank had a security procedure that specified electronic funds transfers were to be made only to a specified set of banks and to certain numbered accounts. If the numbered account was outside of that field and the bank failed to discover it because it did not use the procedure, conceivably the bank would have liability under 4A–205(a)(1) and (a)(2). Liability under 4A–205 would then

§ 7–25

1. Conversely, if the thief intervenes between the authorized agent and the receiving bank, there is an unauthorized payment order not governed by 4A–205.

cause 4A–205(b) to kick in and could cause a portion of the liability to be shifted back to the sender if the sender failed to exercise ordinary care to discover the error and if the loss could have been prevented if the sender had used ordinary care.

This is a long shot. First, this transaction might not be under 4A–205 at all, at least if the court finds that 4A–205 covers only orders in which the agent of the sender actually made an error (i.e., a transposition of names or numbers). Second, it applies only in the still more unlikely case when the receiving bank fails to follow the security procedure and in which, had it followed the procedure, it would have discovered the error. Finally, 4A–205(b) helps the bank only in the even more remote circumstance in which the ultimate loss is somehow related to the failure of the depositor to examine its statement and report it within 90 days.

It is ironic that the customer's failure to examine its statement could conceivably render it liable for a nonfraudulent, but erroneous debit under 4A–205(b), but the same failure to examine its statement and discover a fraudulent or otherwise unauthorized payment order under 4A–204 will at most cause it to lose interest on the repayment.

One wonders why the banks, who seem to have fought so successfully for the protection of the commercially reasonable security procedure, were not similarly successful in putting losses associated with customer's negligence back on the customer. Perhaps banks hope to achieve the same outcome as in Article 4 but by deposit agreement not by statute. One should compare 4–406 with 4A–204 and 4A–205.

§ 7–26 Preclusion Under 4A–505: The "One–Year" Rule

Even though there is no provision with the bite of 4–406, there is an analog in cases in which a customer waits more than a year after receiving its statement before it reports an error. Section 4A–505 precludes the customer from complaining about a payment under an order "issued in the name of" the customer (sender) and accepted by the bank where the bank gave the customer a "notification reasonably identifying the order" and more than a year passed before complaint and after receipt. The comment describes this as a "statute of repose." This section covers not only cases of erroneous execution of legitimate orders, but also cases of unauthorized and unverified orders, i.e., those done by fraud. The last sentence of the Comment summarizes its consequence: "Under 4A–505, however, the obligation to refund may not be asserted by the customer if the customer has not objected to the debiting of the account within one year after the customer received notification of the debit."

The only reported case to date interpreting 4A–505 in depth is a boon to bank customers' rights. In Regatos v. North Fork Bank,[1] a bank customer discovered that he had been the victim of fraudulent payment orders between four and five months after the transactions actually occurred because his agreement with North Fork provided that the bank would hold his statements and only send them upon request. This particular situation was complicated by a clause in the account agreement purporting to reduce the 4A–505 notice period to fifteen days.

The *Regatos* court held that any modification of the one-year notice provision contained in 4A–505 is prohibited. In support, the court noted that a bank customer has an "invariable" right to a refund under 4A–202 and 4A–204 for unauthorized payment orders. The only limitation on this is 4A–505, which precludes a customer's recovery unless it notifies the bank of the unauthorized order within one year of being notified of the fraudulent order. Although 4A–505 does not explicitly say it cannot be modified by agreement, the court reasoned that to allow a reduction would effectively remove any of the customer's benefit from the "invariable" rights granted under 4A–202 and 4A–204. The court noted that when the drafters wanted to allow the parties to reduce a statute of repose by agreement, they expressly said so (i.e. 2–725).

Even so, this result disregards 4–406(f)—an analogous statute of repose in Article 4 regarding certain fraudulent checks—which some courts have allowed the parties to modify. Furthermore, what of 4A–501, which permits the parties to vary the rights and duties between them "except as otherwise provided [in Article 4A]"? It seems to us that if the drafters truly intended the result that the *Regatos* court reached on this issue, the addition of a single sentence at the end of 4A–505 prohibiting modification would have been an easier way to accomplish the desired end, rather than including a couple of references to 4A–202 and 4A–204 in the official comment.

In addition to the argument under 4A–505, the court gave two more persuasive reasons for its decision. In holding that a fifteen-day period was unreasonably short, the court stated that enforcing such a provision "effectively guts the invariable rights of the consumer under sections 4A–202 and 4A–204." Such a short period could not be construed consistently with 4A–204's discussion of the period of up to 90 days for a customer to obtain interest on unauthorized payment orders. Finally, the court distinguished 4A–505 from 4–406 in holding that 4A–505 requires actual notice of the subject payment order, not just sending the statements (which is all

§ 7–26   2003).

1. 257   F.Supp.2d   632   (S.D.N.Y.

that 4–406 requires). Since North Fork held Regatos' statements until he asked for them, the one-year period did not begin to run until he actually requested a statement (upon receipt of which, he immediately notified North Fork of the unauthorized orders). Therefore, the case would have come out the same even if the court did not reach its first holding prohibiting modification of 4A–505.

§ 7–27 Other Negligence by Parties to an Electronic Transfer

A final issue coming to Article 4A only through section 1–103 involves various forms of negligence that might somehow facilitate loss. Assume, for example, that a thief commits fraud on General Motors and causes it to issue an order to a receiving bank instructing payment to "General Motors, Basel Bank account XYZ7777." Assume further that XYZ7777 is the thief's account number, and that Basel Bank follows the number only rule under 4A–207 and credits the thief's account.

The thief turns out to be not one person, but a group of raucous and brazen drug dealers from South America. These fellows appear in Basel bank on a Friday afternoon with a large bag and demand all of "their" money in American dollars. Many things about their appearance and behavior would put a careful Swiss banker on notice that something is amiss. Their demand for that much money in dollars is most unusual and cannot be met except through courier service from Frankfurt. Assume *arguendo* that one phone call by the Swiss banker or a brief examination of the Bank's paper records would have disclosed that this money belonged to General Motors. Assume further that the failure of the Swiss bank to investigate is "negligence."

Alternatively assume that Basel Bank has the most modern electronic reading machine and that this machinery reads and compares both the number and the name and flags any discrepancies. Or that the Bank has internal controls that make it clear to anyone in the bank that the number XYZ7777 could not be the number of one of its commercial depositors. Assume further that the bank's disregard of this information available to it is itself negligence.

What is the consequence of the Bank's behavior? Does the absence of any provision in Article 4A analogous to 3–406[1] mean that the beneficiary bank's negligence is irrelevant? Or, analogizing to conventional tort law, should one say that the bank has the last

---

§ 7–27

1. Section 3–406 allocates loss due to a forged signature or alteration according to the parties' relative fault.

clear chance to stop the loss and should have liability for failure to do so? Does 1–103 authorize this? Could General Motors sue the bank in common law negligence and recover?

Quaere whether the drafters of Article 4A intended such an outcome. Sections 4A–204 and 4A–205 are a very weak brew and there is nothing like 3–406 here. There is no suggestion that the drafters of Article 4A intend anyone in the shoes of the Swiss banker to have direct liability to the sender for the bank's negligence. Yet the one at the end of the stream in EFT cases holds a position like that of the upstream depositary bank in a check case. It deals face to face with the thief. Moreover, the traditional policies that support the last clear chance doctrine in our tort law might apply.

We are uncertain about the proper outcome. On the one hand, we appreciate the argument for liability; on the other, we recognize that a comprehensive statute that allocates liability quite precisely should not be lightly disrupted.

PROBLEM

Funds transfers can go awry for several reasons. First, a thief employed by the originating customer may get the code and send a "verified" but unauthorized order. Second, one of the customer's employees can make an honest mistake. Third, someone at the receiving bank can make an honest mistake. (We omit the possibility of fraud by a bank employee since it is rare and when it happens rarely results in the bank's trying to put the loss on the customer.)

1. Customer intends to pay $200,000 to BCS Mortgage Co. Misunderstanding her instruction, Employee sends an order to pay $200,000 to Admiralty Mortgage, another mortgage company with whom Customer does business. Admiralty goes bankrupt before the money can be recaptured.

   Easy case. Customer bears the loss and has a restitution claim in Admiralty's bankruptcy.

2. Same facts as problem 1. Customer gives the proper order to bank but bank sends the order on with a transposed account number and the funds wind up in the wrong account and are withdrawn.

   Bank is liable. 4A–302.

3. An embezzler working at Customer gets the security code and directs the payment to an account set up in a fictitious name.

   Customer almost always bears the loss. 4A–202.

> But, what if the security procedure lists only five permitted
> beneficiaries (not including the thief's account) or limits users
> of that particular code to $200,000 and the transfer was for
> $500,000? Now bank bears the loss, 4A–205. Where the
> $200,000 restriction applied, bank could argue that it was
> justified in paying $200,000, but customer will respond that
> bank had a duty to investigate (and possibly stop the transfer)
> when the thief initially attempted to send more than was
> permitted. We think the bank eats it all.

§ 7–28 Fraud in Debit Transfers

Almost every fraud that is somehow accomplished by a debit
transfer will involve a warranty that the ODFI makes to each
RDFI, NACHA Operator and Association. Under the terms of
subsection 2.2.1.1 of the NACHA Operating Rules,[1] the ODFI
warrants that the Originator authorized the transfer, that the
Receiver has approved it, and that any entry is in accordance with
those authorizations. The rule reads as follows:

2.2 *Warranties and Liabilities of Originating Depository Financial
Institutions*

2.2.1 *Warranties*: Each ODFI sending an entry warrants the
following to each RDFI, ACH Operator, and Association:

2.2.1.1 *Authorization by Originator and Receiver*: Except in the
case of XCK entries initiated pursuant to section 2.7 (Destroyed Check Entries), each entry transmitted by the ODFI to
an ACH Operator is in accordance with proper authorization
provided by the Originator and the Receiver.

When an employee of the Originator or the Receiver (or conceivably
even of the NACHA Operator or of the RDFI) steals money by a
debit entry, the ODFI will likely have breached its warranty.
Accordingly it will have liability initially under subsection 2.2.3.
Because the warranty does not run to the Originator or the
Receiver, neither of them could sue on the warranty, but each
might have been an indirect beneficiary of the warranty in receiving or recovering from a party who is covered, who then would
assume the warranty against the ODFI. Initially, therefore, the
ODFI has been given a heavy load to bear. As with a funnel, all of
the potential liability flows to it. But, of course, life is not so simple;
let us turn to the complications.

703–561–1100 or see www.nacha.org.

1. For current information on the
NACHA Operating Rules in general, call

Assume, first, that the employee who caused the theft is employed by one of the beneficiaries of the warranty, an RDFI or an NACHA Operator. Clearly, it would be unfair to require the ODFI to indemnify the receiving bank when the cause of the loss was the fraud of the receiving bank's employee. (We assume that the receiving bank knew or should have known of the problem and could have prevented the loss.) There is nothing in section 2.2, on liability for breach of warranty that explicitly frees the ODFI from liability in such a case. If the innocent ODFI is to escape liability, the courts will have to bend the warranty or turn to the common law and to analogous rules in Articles 3 and 4.

The most obvious analogues are the preclusion rules found in Article 3 and 4 (3–404, 3–405, 3–406, and 4–406). Recall that those rules place the loss on the most culpable party, or, in some cases, require that the loss be shared among those at fault. As we indicated above, how the warranties interact with the comparative negligence standard remains to be seen. Some could argue that the warranty overrides any negligence, but we are doubtful. With respect to the fraud on the part of an employee of the Originator or one who received information from the Originator because of the Originator's negligence, the analogy to Articles 3 and 4 is easy and direct. Section 4–406 might be directly introduced into the transaction because of section 14.1.26 for it makes debit entries into "items" and causes Article 4 to "apply" except when the NACHA Operating Rules are inconsistent. The other sections on negligence, 3–406, and on misbehavior by an originator's embezzling employee, sections 3–404 and 3–405, would have to be applied by analogy. In our view they apply and fit this transaction like a glove.

Where the loss was caused by the negligent supervision of a party who receives the warranty in 2.2, the question is somewhat more complicated. Section 4–208(b) explicitly states that the 4–208 warranties apply notwithstanding the negligence of the plaintiff. There is nothing like that in section 2.2, unless 2.2.2 is similarly stretched.

If the ODFI is able to prove that the theft occurred because of the negligent selection or supervision of an employee of the ACH or of the RDFI, we see no reason why the court should not recognize a common law cause of action by the ODFI against the RDFI or ACH Operator. Where the ACH Operator is the Federal Reserve, one must look at the operating letters and the Federal Reserve rules to see the extent to which they exculpate the Federal Reserve.

In summary, the most directly applicable rules on fraud are found in section 2.2, Warranties and Liabilities of Originating Depository Financial Institutions. These are only a beginning. We expect courts to adopt the rules in Articles 3, 4 and 4A quite liberally to debit fraud. Several other provisions of the NACHA

Operating Rules will have at least tangential relevance for some of these suits. Section 12.3 imposes liability on an association for "Negligence and Willful Misconduct of its ACH Operator." Section 12.4 titled "Protection for the National Association from Frivolous Lawsuits" gives NACHA the right to recover attorneys' fees if it wins in a suit brought by a financial institution. One should also consider section 2.2.3 titled "Liability for Breach of Warranty." Presumably one can recover for breach of warranty only if he has suffered loss. Section 2.2.3 makes the breaching ODFI liable for the other's lawyers' fees and expenses.

To the extent there are differences among the rules of Articles 3, 4 and 4A, courts will have to answer whether the debit transfer more closely approximates Article 4A, or Articles 3 and 4. Because the players are in different positions on the field, the documents are different and the statements provide different information, it would not be sensible to apply all of the sections of Article 3 and 4 willy-nilly to debit transfers. Still we expect they will give sensible and generally useful analogies that can be followed with considerable confidence in most cases.

§ 7–29 Restitution of Amounts Paid by Mistake

If funds are transferred in an amount exceeding the amount intended by the originator of the funds transfer, or the payment is to the wrong person, the participant who originally bears the loss can always seek to recover from the recipient. Many of these are classic "restitution for mistake" cases. It is rare indeed that an unintended beneficiary believes that the money is his or reasonably relies on having it. Usually the recipient will have to give up the funds.

There are at least two exceptional situations where a participant who originally bears the loss for an erroneous funds transfer will not be able to recover from the beneficiary of the erroneous funds transfer. These are the "good faith and for value" exception and the "discharge for value" exception.

a. Good Faith and for Value Exception

If the beneficiary receives in good faith and for value, funds mistakenly paid, the beneficiary will be able to retain the funds. Consider the following example:

> (1) Thief makes an agreement with Colonial Coins to purchase coins worth $2 million. Thief tells Colonial Coins that he will cause a $2 million credit to occur in Colonial's bank account at Bank Texas. Thief, purporting to act as agent of Shill, instructs Bank Bradford to transfer $2 million from Shill's account and cause a credit to occur in Colonial's bank account at Bank

Texas. In contravention of the security procedure in effect between Shill and Bank Bradford, Bank Bradford accepts the order by instructing Bank Texas to cause a $2 million credit to occur in Colonial's account. Bank Texas accepts by crediting Colonial's account for $2 million and notifying Colonial of Colonial's right to withdraw the amount of the payment order. Upon notice of the right to withdraw the payment order, Colonial hands the coins worth $2 million over to Thief. Thief leaves the country, never to be seen again.

Shill(T)—>   Bank Bradford—>   Bank Texas—> Colonial Coins
             $2M $2M $2M

The funds transfer was completed upon acceptance by Bank Texas. Under Article 4A, each sender is obligated to pay because Bank Texas accepted a payment order that mirrored each sender's payment order. Shill will be excused from its obligation to pay the amount of its order because Shill never authorized the payment order and Bank Bradford failed to comply with the security procedure in effect. Thus, Bank Bradford originally bears the loss for the unauthorized payment order.

Furthermore, Bank Bradford will not be able to recover the mistaken payment from Colonial Coins on a restitutionary theory under Texas common law. Colonial Coins received the funds in good faith and gave value in the form of coins, a defense to restitution for mistake under the common law of all states we know of. Certainly in Texas there will be no recovery; that would follow from the law applied in the original *Bradford Trust* case.[1] In some cases there will be difficult fact questions about whether the recipient of the payment acted in good faith. Doubtless the outcomes will vary somewhat from state to state depending upon the nuances of the law of restitution in those particular states. In general, where the party in the position of the beneficiary has acted in good faith and where there is no undue suspicion, we see no reason why that party should not be permitted to keep the payment. After all, that party did part with value.

b. *Discharge for Value Rule*

A beneficiary who is a creditor of the originator of a funds transfer has no obligation to make restitution for payments mistakenly made to that beneficiary in the name of the originator—even if the beneficiary has not changed its position in reliance upon the transfer by giving value—unless the beneficiary obtained the funds

1. 790 F.2d 407, 1 UCC2d 828 (5th   Cir. 1986).

through misrepresentation or had notice of the mistake before receiving the funds.[2] Consider the following example:

(2) General Motors owes $5 million to Goodyear and $5 million to Bridgestone. General Motors instructs JP Morgan Chase to credit Goodyear's account at National City for $5 million. Before JP Morgan Chase accepted the order, General Motors amended the payment order to credit Bridgestone's account at National City for $5 million. By mistake, JP Morgan Chase issued two separate payment orders to National City, causing a $5 million credit to occur in Goodyear's bank account, and a $5 million credit to occur in Bridgestone's bank account. Shortly thereafter, General Motors became insolvent.

In this situation, two funds transfers were completed. Furthermore, under the discharge for value rule, General Motors may not recover from Goodyear on a theory of restitution for mistaken payment. As long as Goodyear received the funds in good faith, the discharge for value rule is a valid defense to the restitutionary theory. But because JP Morgan Chase paid General Motors's debt to Goodyear, JP Morgan Chase would be subrogated to the rights of Goodyear as creditor against General Motors in an action against General Motors for payment of the unauthorized payment order to Goodyear. This subrogation, however, would be of limited value if General Motors were insolvent.

§ 7–30 Damages, in General

The most common damage questions under Article 4A are straightforward. But there are many small questions, and there is at least one large one: When should a bank be liable for consequential damages? That question was addressed in the famous *Evra* case. Because of that case, the issue was well understood and directly confronted by the drafters.

The most common form of liability will be in damages for the full amount of the electronic funds transfer. In one way or another, this liability can be found in section 4A–402(b), section 4A–402(d), and section 4A–404. In addition, there is liability for the full amount in restitution to be found in section 4A–405, under the common law, and arising by implication from other sections of 4A. In most of these cases there will be little or no dispute about the amount of damages once liability has been established.

2. See § 4A–303, Comment 3; Banque Worms v. BankAmerica Int'l, 928 F.2d 538, 14 UCC Rep.Serv.2d 6 (2d Cir. 1991). Using Article 4A as a "point of reference and persuasive authority", the court upheld the discharge for value rule in electronic funds transfers. Note that at least two recent courts required that the mistaken beneficiary actually credit the debtor's account for the amount of the funds transfer before receiving notice. See In re Calumet Farm, Inc., 398 F.3d 555 (6th Cir. 2005); NBase Communications, Inc. v. Am. Nat'l Bank & Trust Co. of Chicago, 8 F.Supp.2d 1071 (N.D. Ill. 1998).

Consider three cases where the defaulting party would have liability for the full amount of the electronic funds transfer. First, under 4A–402(b) and (c) the beneficiary's bank or other receiving bank normally has the right to the full amount of the payment order from its sender once it has accepted. Thus in our ongoing hypothetical, JP Morgan Chase would have a right to $10 million from its sender, General Motors, once it (JP Morgan Chase) had accepted. Second, a sender that has paid the receiving bank, but was not obliged to do so, has a right to the return of its money under 4A–402(d). Finally, section 4A–404 gives the beneficiary a right to payment from its bank once the beneficiary's bank has accepted the payment order. None of these three outcomes is controversial or surprising. In each of them there is privity between the parties and one of the parties would be unjustly enriched if there were no liability for the full amount of the payment.

A fourth case in which one party must pay the full amount of the transfer is specified in 4A–204. That is the case where there has been an unauthorized transfer. In those cases the sender has a right to a "refund" of "any payment of the payment order received from the customer to the extent the bank is not entitled to enforce payment * * *."[1]

§ 7–31   Interest and Other Incidental Damages

Sections 4A–305 and 4A–204 explicitly authorize certain parties to recover interest or lost interest as part of their incidental damages. Under section 4A–305, a receiving bank that improperly executes and thus delays payment of a proper order must "pay interest to either the originator or the beneficiary of the funds transfer for the period of delay caused by the improper execution." This liability for interest runs not merely to persons in privity with the bank, but also to the beneficiary who might not have a contract with the bank.[1]

Section 4A–305(b) provides that the originator may recover "for its expenses in the funds transfer and for incidental expenses and interest losses, to the extent [those resulted] from the improper execution." If, for example, the originator had directed a transfer to a beneficiary who would have paid interest to the originator, but the funds languished for 30 days in a non-interest-bearing account because the execution was incorrect, those "interest losses" would

1. § 4A–204(a).

recovery that the beneficiary would have from the particular bank.

1. This recovery is not properly "incidental" because it would be the entire

have to be made up by the receiving bank that did the improper execution.

Whether the courts here will stretch "incidental expenses" in the way they have sometimes stretched "incidental damages" under Article 2 remains to be seen. As we will see below, Article 4A generally denies the recovery of consequential damages. Assume in our hypothetical case that the originator had directed a payment to Merrill Lynch who was going to purchase General Motors stock for $40 a share. The order was never executed and the stock never purchased. Thirty days later, when the error was discovered, General Motors' stock is at $42. Is the $2.00 difference in the share price an "incidental damage" or is it a consequential damage that cannot be recovered? We suspect that it is the latter. On the other hand, it is ironic that there might be a recovery of lost interest— apparently an incidental expense—when there would be no recovery for lost appreciation (the $2.00 increase in the stock price).

We are certain we have not seen the last of the arguments over the division between incidental and consequential damages. In fact, Article 4A is likely to see the same bending and twisting that has occurred in cases concerning the seller's damages under Article 2 (where a seller is not authorized to recover consequential damages, but may recover incidental damages). Finally, section 4A–204 directs the bank not only to refund payments that were not authorized and were not otherwise enforceable against the customer, but also states that it "shall pay interest on the refundable amount calculated from the date the bank received payment to the date of the refund."

In all of the cases identified above, the rate of interest is fixed by section 4A–506. Under 4A–506(a) the rate of interest will be that agreed by the parties or established by rule in a "funds-transfer system rule." If there is no agreement between the parties, the rate will be the applicable Federal Funds rate established by the Federal Reserve Bank of New York.[2]

---

2. § 4A–506. Rate of Interest.

(a) If, under this Article, a receiving bank is obliged to pay interest with respect to a payment order issued to the bank, the amount payable may be determined (i) by agreement of the sender and receiving bank, or (ii) by a funds-transfer system rule if the payment order is transmitted through a funds-transfer system.

(b) If the amount of interest is not determined by an agreement or rule as stated in subsection (a), the amount is calculated by multiplying the applicable Federal Funds rate by the amount on which interest is payable, and then multiplying the product by the number of days for which interest is payable. The applicable Federal Funds rate is the average of the Federal Funds rates published by the Federal Reserve Bank of New York for each of the days for which interest is payable divided by 360. The Federal Funds rate for any day on which a published rate is not available is the same as the published rate for the next preceding day for which there is a published rate. If a receiving bank that accepted a payment order is required to refund payment to the sender of the order because the funds transfer was not

Interest is also provided for in section 4A–402(d) on amounts to be refunded to the sender and where a refund was made.

§ 7–32   Incidental Expenses

What incidental expenses are recoverable, and in what circumstances, is not always clear. For example, section 4A–305(b) explicitly authorizes the recovery of "incidental expenses" in a case in which a receiving bank has failed to execute a payment order properly. There is no comparable provision for incidental expenses in 4A–402 on the obligation of the sender to pay the receiving bank; nor is there a provision allowing incidental expenses in connection with the obligation to make a refund of an unauthorized payment under section 4A–204. Although incidental expenses are mentioned some places and not in others, we believe the drafters really intended incidental expenses to be paid in all cases where they arise. On the other hand, various provisions do state that "additional damages are not recoverable."[1] Presumably these admonitions are inserted to make doubly clear that banks have no liability for consequential damages. We doubt they were aimed at the incidental damage question, but we could be wrong.

It is hard to imagine the entire range of "incidental expenses" associated with a breach of an obligation under Article 4A. Nevertheless our example arising from the General Motors transaction indicates the kind of argument that might be put forward. If, as we suggest, clever lawyers will try to transform consequential into incidental damages, this could become an important battleground.

§ 7–33   Liability for Improper Execution

Section 4A–305 labeled "Liability for Late or Improper Execution or Failure to Execute Payment Order" is the heart of the 4A damage rules and, presumably, a source of great hope of defendant banks. Improper execution is doubtless far more common than fraud or any of the more gross violations of the obligations under Article 4A. There are many ways for Murphy's Law to apply. The receiving bank can fail entirely to comply with the funds transfer; it can pay the wrong person, it can pay too little, too much, too early, or too late. Some of these failures, namely, nonpayment, or payment to the wrong person, can be cured by the receiving bank merely by executing a new order to the proper person. Where there is delay, section 4A–305(a) specifically obliges the receiving bank to pay interest and explicitly forecloses most other remedies. "Except

completed, but the failure to complete was not due to any fault by the bank, the interest payable is reduced by a percentage equal to the reserve requirement on deposits of the receiving bank.

§ 7–32

1. *See, e.g,* §§ 4A–305(a), 4A–404(b).

as provided in subsection (c), additional damages are not recoverable."

In general, where the improper execution takes a form other than delay, section 4A–305(b) makes the bank "liable to the originator for its expenses in the funds transfer and for incidental expenses and interest losses * * * resulting from the improper execution." Section 4A–305(b) forecloses additional damages not covered by subsection (c). Presumably incidental expenses in this context might include the cost of investigating the transfer, or a modest sum to the beneficiary who now will receive his funds late or who will receive them later because of the use of an inappropriate intermediary bank.

Section 4A–305(e) explicitly authorizes the recovery of reasonable attorney's fees at least if a demand is made and refused before the lawsuit is brought on a claim under 4A–305(a) or (b). Presumably attorney's fees are recoverable only if the originator or beneficiary prevails in the action under 4A–305(a) and (b). Subsection (e) appears to be addressed exclusively to the rights of the originator or beneficiary; it does not authorize the prevailing bank to recover attorney's fees. That is, it seems to contemplate only "an action * * * brought on the claim" (i.e., the beneficiary's or originator's claim under 4A–305(a) or (b), and not the bank's counterclaim or affirmative defense). The presence of 4A–305(e) and the absence of a comparable provision in 4A–204(a) on refund of payments that were not authorized may stimulate lawyers to attempt to squeeze cases under 4A–305 (and thus recover attorney's fees) when the cases in fact belong under 4A–204, or other sections of Article 4A, or the common law.

§ 7–34 Consequential Damages

The possibility that banks would be liable for massive consequential damages caused by an error in executing an electronic message was well understood by the banks at the time Article 4A was drafted. The core of the *Evra*[1] case, discussed above in § 7–19, had to do with the receiving bank's liability for its apparently negligent failure to receive or to receive and transmit an electronic funds message. The charterer of a boat lost its charter (allegedly worth more than $2 million) because one of the banks in an electronic funds transfer failed to move the money quickly enough from the Chicago charter party to the owner of the ship in Europe. On the appeal of the *Evra* case, Judge Posner, writing for the Seventh Circuit, found that the common law doctrine embodied in

§ 7–34

1. Evra Corp. v. Swiss Bank Corp., 673 F.2d 951, 34 UCC 227 (7th Cir. 1982), *cert. denied*, 459 U.S. 1017, 103 S.Ct. 377, 74 L.Ed.2d 511 (1982).

Hadley v. Baxendale[2] protected the banks from liability for consequential damages, even if one concluded, as he apparently did, that they had been derelict in the performance of their duties. Judge Posner held that the Swiss bank had not been put on notice of the special circumstances necessary under *Hadley* to make it liable for consequential damages. The court made the point as follows:

> [Swiss Bank] knew or should have known, from Continental Bank's previous telexes, that Hyman–Michaels was paying the Pandora Shipping Company for the hire of a motor vessel named Pandora. But it did not know when payment was due, what the terms of the charter were, or that they had turned out to be extremely favorable to Hyman–Michaels. And it did not know that Hyman–Michaels knew the Pandora's owner would try to cancel the charter, and probably would succeed, if Hyman–Michaels was ever again late in making payment, or that despite this peril Hyman–Michaels would not try to pay until the last possible moment and in the event of a delay in transmission would not do everything in its power to minimize the consequences of the delay. Electronic funds transfers are not so unusual as to automatically place a bank on notice of extraordinary consequences if such a transfer goes awry. Swiss Bank did not have enough information to infer that if it lost a $27,000 payment order it would face a liability in excess of $2 million.[3]

Although the court in *Evra* protected the bank, Judge Posner's recognition in dictum of the possibility that banks might have liability in a different case for consequential damage under *Hadley* unnerved the bankers. Accordingly the banks argued successfully for an explicit provision in Article 4A that would restrict their liability for consequential damages arising as a result of failure to properly execute electronic funds orders. Comparing themselves to telegraph companies, the banks argued that they should not have responsibility for catastrophic consequences that might arise from the system's failure. Such losses, they argued, should fall on the originators, who fully appreciate the consequences of failure and who, one way or another, can protect themselves against such failure where it is sensible to do so.

Correctly, in our view, the bankers' argument carried the day. This finds expression in the last sentence in 4A–305(a): "[e]xcept as provided in subsection (c), additional damages are not recoverable." Subsections (c) and (d) of 4A–305 allow the recovery of consequential damages only "to the extent provided in an express written agreement of the receiving bank."

2. 9 Ex. 341, 156 Eng. Rep. 145 (1854).   **3.** 673 F.2d at 956.

Subsection (c) reads in full as follows:

In addition to the amounts payable under subsections (a) and (b), damages, including consequential damages, are recoverable to the extent provided in an express written agreement of the receiving bank.

Because consequential damages are not recoverable under (a) or anywhere else except as provided by (c), and because (c) allows consequential damages only to the extent provided in "an express written agreement of the receiving bank," there will be few recoveries of consequential damages because of late or improper execution or failure to execute a payment order. Presumably a receiving bank willing to undertake liability for consequential damages will wish to insure itself, and would at minimum want to be paid enough to enable it to have an investigation by a person with knowledge and authority sufficient to understand the exposure.

By way of summation, we set out section 4A–305 in full below. Note the possibility of recovering reasonable attorneys' fees under 4A–305(e). Note too that this provision is not variable by agreement except for the unlikely case in which a receiving bank might agree to be liable for consequential damages.

Section 4A–305. Liability for Late or Improper Execution or Failure to Execute Payment Order.

(a) If a funds transfer is completed but execution of a payment order by the receiving bank in breach of Section 4A–302 results in delay in payment to the beneficiary, the bank is obliged to pay interest to either the originator or the beneficiary of the funds transfer for the period of delay caused by the improper execution. Except as provided in subsection (c), additional damages are not recoverable.

(b) If execution of a payment order by a receiving bank in breach of Section 4A–302 results in (i) noncompletion of the funds transfer, (ii) failure to use an intermediary bank designated by the originator, or (iii) issuance of a payment order that does not comply with the terms of the payment order of the originator, the bank is liable to the originator for its expenses in the funds transfer and for incidental expenses and interest losses, to the extent not covered by subsection (a), resulting from the improper execution. Except as provided in subsection (c), additional damages are not recoverable.

(c) In addition to the amounts payable under subsections (a) and (b), damages, including consequential damages, are recoverable to the extent provided in an express written agreement of the receiving bank.

(d) If a receiving bank fails to execute a payment order it was obliged by express agreement to execute, the receiving bank is liable to the sender for its expenses in the transaction and for incidental expenses and interest losses resulting from the failure to execute. Additional damages, including consequential damages, are recoverable to the extent provided in an express written agreement of the receiving bank, but are not otherwise recoverable.

(e) Reasonable attorney's fees are recoverable if demand for compensation under subsection (a) or (b) is made and refused before an action is brought on the claim. If a claim is made for breach of an agreement under subsection (d) and the agreement does not provide for damages, reasonable attorney's fees are recoverable if demand for compensation under subsection (d) is made and refused before an action is brought on the claim.

(f) Except as stated in this section, the liability of a receiving bank under subsections (a) and (b) may not be varied by agreement.

Section 4A–404(a) allows consequential damages in the unique situation when the beneficiary's bank stiffs the beneficiary, but even then there are statutory hoops for the beneficiary to jump through in order to recover:

> If the bank refuses to pay after demand by the beneficiary and receipt of notice of particular circumstances that will give rise to consequential damages as a result of nonpayment, the beneficiary may recover damages resulting from the refusal to pay to the extent the bank had notice of the damages, unless the bank proves that it did not pay because of a reasonable doubt concerning the right of the beneficiary to payment.

Note that this liability for consequential damages arises only if the beneficiary gives notice "of particular circumstances that will give rise to consequential damages as a result of nonpayment." The comment states that:

> [This] phrase requires that the bank have notice of the general type or nature of the damages that will be suffered as the result of a refusal to pay and their general magnitude. There is no requirement that the bank have notice of the exact or even approximate amount of the damages, but if the amount of damages is extraordinary the bank is entitled to notice of that fact.[4]

The comment uses *Evra* as an example and suggests that the bank's failure to pay $27,000 in that case would not have been a

---

4. § 4A–404, Comment 2.

basis for a $2 million consequential claim if the only notice given to the bank was one that suggested that the $27,000 payment was necessary "to retain rights on a ship charter." The critical part of the notice was to tell the bank that the loss would be large if it did not make the payment promptly. Why the loss would be large is "a less important circumstance" than the amount of the loss.

Note too section 4A–404(a) gives the bank another out, namely, "that it did not pay because of a reasonable doubt concerning the right of the beneficiary to receive payment." A bank might be uncertain about the beneficiary's right, as for example, where there had been an attempt at cancellation of the order or because there was some doubt about the ownership of the account into which the payment was to be made. In that event, the bank might argue that it failed to pay because it had "reasonable doubt."

The theory restricting the bank's liability for consequential damages is stated in considerable detail in Comment 2 to 4A–305 as follows:

If *Evra* means that consequential damages can be imposed if the culpable bank has notice of particular circumstances giving rise to the damages, it does not provide an acceptable solution to the problem of bank liability for consequential damages. In the typical case transmission of the payment order is made electronically. Personnel of the receiving bank that process payment orders are not the appropriate people to evaluate the risk of liability for consequential damages in relation to the price charged for the wire transfer service. Even if notice is received by higher level management personnel who could make an appropriate decision whether the risk is justified by the price, liability based on notice would require evaluation of payment orders on an individual basis. This kind of evaluation is inconsistent with the high-speed, low-price, mechanical na-ture of the processing system that characterizes wire transfers. Moreover, in *Evra* the culpable bank was an intermediary bank with which the originator did not deal. Notice to the origina-tor's bank would not bind the intermediary bank, and it seems impractical for the originator's bank to convey notice of this kind to intermediary banks in the funds transfer. The success of the wholesale wire transfer industry has largely been based on its ability to effect payment at low cost and great speed. Both of these essential aspects of the modern wire transfer system would be adversely affected by a rule that imposed on banks liability for consequential damages. A banking industry amicus brief in *Evra* stated: "Whether banks can continue to make EFT services available on a widespread basis, by charg-ing reasonable rates, depends on whether they can do so without incurring unlimited consequential risks. Certainly, no bank would handle for $3.25 a transaction entailing potential liability in the millions of dollars."

As the court in *Evra* also noted, the originator of the funds transfer is in the best position to evaluate the risk that a funds transfer will not be made on time and to manage that risk by issuing a payment order in time to allow monitoring of the transaction. The originator, by asking the beneficiary, can quickly determine if the funds transfer has been completed. If the originator has sent the payment order at a time that allows a reasonable margin for correcting error, no loss is likely to result if the transaction is monitored. * * *

The combination of these explicit and limited grants of authority for consequential damages in the statute together with the statement in several places to the effect that "additional damages are not recoverable," surely means that it will be a rare case where an originator or other sender or beneficiary recovers consequential damages from a bank in an electronic funds transaction. As we have indicated above, there may be cases in which the courts stretch the idea of incidental damages to cover some forms of consequential damage, but even that seems unlikely in light of the strong comment and the unambiguous language.[5]

§ 7–35 Miscellaneous Damage Issues

At least two other potentially troublesome damage issues lie around the edges of Article 4A. First, does a party having liability to a sender also have liability to the beneficiary? For an actual example that is partially on point, consider the situation involved in Banco de la Provincia de Buenos Aires v. BayBank Boston, N.A.[1] BPBA was an Argentinean bank that made a loan to Banco Faigan, another Argentinean bank that was not party to this litigation. Argentinean banking authorities suspended Banco Faigan's operations and BPBA put a freeze on Banco Faigan's account that still contained the proceeds of the loan from BPBA. Subsequent to Banco Faigan's operations being suspended, Banco Faigan instructed BPBA to send $245,000 from the account to BayBank Boston, but BPBA refused to execute the payment order. Nearly a month later, BPBA exercised its setoff rights under New York law, and BayBank Boston argued that this was improper because BPBA should have honored Banco Faigan's payment order.

BPBA has violated its duty to Banco Faigan under 4A–302, and would have some liability under 4A–305(b). Of course the liability

---

5. For a case in Article 2 that stretches the idea of incidental damages, see *Union Carbide Corp. v. Consumers Power Co.*, 636 F.Supp. 1498, 1 UCC2d 1202 (E.D.Mich.1986).

§ 7–35

1. 985 F.Supp. 364 (S.D.N.Y. 1997).

would be far less than the total amount of the $245,000 payment order amount if the money had not been moved from Banco Faigan's account and was still available to it.

But what of BayBank Boston's claim against BPBA that it has been injured to the tune of $245,000 (or $245,000 less the claim it has against Banco Faigan's insolvent estate)? Noting that courts have read a certain degree of discretion into 4A–209(a) in allowing receiving banks to reject payment orders, the court stated that a receiving bank simply cannot reject in bad faith or a manner that constitutes an abuse of discretion. Since BPBA had an express right under New York law to setoff against Banco Faigan's account at the time that it rejected the payment order, this was not an act of bad faith, and the court upheld BPBA's actions. Note, however, that this language is dicta in the opinion, as the court had already decided that BPBA was not liable to Banco Faigan for failing to honor the latter's payment order.

Although it was not argued in that case, another obvious answer of BPBA is that it was not in privity with BayBank Boston. Since BPBA had not accepted the order, it might have argued that 4A–212 supports its position: "[bank] does not otherwise have any duty to accept a payment order, or, before acceptance, to take any action, or refrain from taking action, with respect to the order except as provided in this Article or by express agreement." Even if BPBA had accepted the order by erroneously executing (see 4A–301) BPBA could still argue that it was not in privity with Goodyear and therefore had no liability.

On the other hand, BayBank Boston, the beneficiary, might argue that 4A–305 explicitly recognizes that the receiving bank is obligated to the beneficiary, for in an analogous setting the beneficiary is a plaintiff explicitly mentioned in 4A–305(a): "the bank is obliged to pay interest to either the originator or *the beneficiary* of the funds transfer for the period of delay * * * " (emphasis added). This language suggests that at least to the extent of interest payments, a beneficiary such as BayBank Boston, who is deprived of income, is considered a party with a proper claim against a receiving bank, BPBA, despite a lack of privity.

We expect that the receiving bank, BPBA, could also have argued that the language in 4A–305(a)—"additional damages are not recoverable"—forecloses any potential claim. We believe that the receiving bank should win this argument, but we can also think of hypothetical cases that may test the bank's mettle. Assume a case in which a bank knowingly chooses not to execute an order just like BPBA, but does not properly reject, and, in disregard of the order, sets off the sender's account against its own loan. Behavior of this kind by payor banks in check cases has incited the courts to hold payor banks liable even on questionable theories because it appeared the banks were self-dealing. The banks may still be protected by 4A–504 which gives them wide discretion about which items to pay and which not to pay. Although 4A–504 does not extend explicitly to the bank's own setoff, that section might be interpreted to allow the bank to choose to pay its own setoff over other claims.

A second test case might arise under 1–103 for the negligent behavior of the bank in failing to discover fraud or mistake. Recall our example of the Swiss bank that paid even though a small investigation in response to a plain indication of fraud would have uncovered the fraud and stopped the loss. If one assumes liability there, what are the damages? Can the originator whose account was ultimately wiped out by the thieves sue the beneficiary's bank for the negligence in a straight tort suit? This case is different from *Evra* because here there is face-to-face dealing between the thieves and the defendant bank, and by our hypothesis, the bank was negligent.

Pointing to no recovery, of course, is the omission from Article 4A of any section that would impose liability. The bank is sure to argue that the omission of a provision such as 3–406 (imposing liability for negligence in certain Article 3 cases) from Article 4A was intentional, and protects banks from the kinds of claims that could be made under Article 3. If Goodyear does recover, its damages will be for the amount lost as a proximate result of the negligence. In our case, this would be the entire amount of the transfer. We are uncertain about the right answer here.

If litigation becomes more widespread than formerly, there may be pressure on the provisions of Article 4A that exclude consequential damages. There is room to argue about the meaning of the rules on consequential damages set out in 4A–404(a). There is also the possibility of a clever attempt to circumvent 4A by pursuing a cause of action apparently outside of 4A, or by arguing that the damages sought are not consequential, but incidental and therefore not barred. All of this, of course, is wicked speculation. *Evra* may have been an albino leopard.

Chapter 8

LETTERS OF CREDIT

Analysis

---

§ 8–1 Introduction

A seller hesitates to give up possession of its goods before it is paid. But a buyer wishes to have control of the goods before parting with its money. To relieve this simple tension, merchants developed the device known as the "letter of credit" or simply the "credit" or the "letter."[1] Today, letters of credit come in two broad varieties. The "commercial" letter dates back at least 700 years. It is a mode of payment in the purchase of goods, mostly in international sales. The "standby" letter of credit is a much more recent mutant. It "backs up" obligations in a myriad of settings. In the most common standby a bank promises to pay a creditor upon documentary certification of the applicant's default.

§ 8–1

1. The leading treatise on letters of credit today is Dolan, The Law of Letters of Credit: Commercial and Standby Credits (rev. ed. 2003).

For both "commercial" and "standby" letters, this chapter shows how the letter of credit works: how it may be set up, how it is performed, and the remedies when it breaks down. Our discussion will focus upon UCC Article 5[2] and a body of rules known as the "UCP" (Uniform Customs and Practices for Documentary Credits), adopted by the bankers of the International Chamber of Commerce.[3]

a. The Commercial Letter of Credit

While "commercial" letters of credit have domestic uses, they originated in international trade and continue in wide use there. To illustrate: assume an American buyer in Newark, New Jersey wants to buy furniture manufactured by a Danish Seller in Copenhagen. Buyer sends a proposal to Seller which says nothing about payment terms. Seller replies that it will not sell on open credit, and Buyer responds that it will not pay Seller in advance. Buyer then suggests a "documentary sale" by which Buyer would pay "cash against documents," that is, when Seller's American agent tenders documents of title covering the goods to Buyer, plus a "sight draft" calling on Buyer to pay "at sight," Buyer would have to pay then and there, even though the goods themselves were still en route.

A documentary sale is far less risky to Seller than a sale on open credit. Through the bill of lading, our Danish Seller retains title and control over the goods. This keeps the New Jersey Buyer from acquiring possession of or title to the goods without simultaneously paying for them. With cash in hand, Seller does not risk having to sue Buyer in a foreign jurisdiction to force it to pay for the goods. And if Buyer is obligated to pay "blind," Seller runs little or no risk that Buyer will inspect, find defects, and refuse to pay. Even if Buyer for some reason refuses to pay the sight draft, Seller will still have control over the goods covered by the bill of lading and may thus control redisposition of them.

Despite its advantages, the documentary sale has limitations which often prompt one like our Danish Seller to want to *reinforce* that arrangement by using a letter of credit. Where Buyer agrees to pay "cash against documents" (pay a sight draft in exchange for the bill of lading), Seller still remains exposed to major risks. First, our New Jersey Buyer might be insolvent or otherwise unable to pay when the sight draft is presented to Newark Bank for payment. We call this the "insolvency risk." When it materializes, Seller will

---

2. Article 5's current text (the 1995 revision) has been adopted in all U.S. states and jurisdictions except Puerto Rico (including the District of Columbia and the U.S. Virgin Islands). We retain some material on the old 1962 version of Article 5 when it supplies context for particularly important revisions contained in the current version.

3. See UCP 600 (2006), *available at* www.iccwbo.org.

usually be forced to dispose of the goods through agents and in a foreign market. Any damage claim against Buyer for the difference between the resale price and the contract price will be worth little if Buyer turns out to be insolvent. Such a claim would have to be litigated in a court foreign to Seller, with all the uncertainties and expense this entails.

Another risk may be called the "dishonesty" risk. Buyer might wrongfully refuse to pay against documents upon their presentation. For example, Buyer might back out to take advantage of a decline in the market price of goods ordered from Seller.

Then there is the "honest-dispute" risk. For example, Seller's shipment may be one of a series. Buyer may refuse to pay against documents upon presentation because one of Seller's prior shipments was nonconforming or because the present shipment arrived before presentation in Buyer's city and an unauthorized inspection revealed apparent nonconformity.

Assume our Danish Seller insists that New Jersey Buyer procure a commercial letter of credit issued by a bank showing Seller as "beneficiary" with authority to draw drafts on the issuing bank directly, rather than just on Buyer as in the documentary sale. What will this involve, and how can it protect against risks that a documentary sale does not protect against? Having agreed to a payment mode using a sight draft and documents, plus a letter of credit, Buyer goes to its own bank in Newark. There, Buyer ("applicant") applies for issuance of an irrevocable letter of credit which commits Newark Bank ("issuer") to pay a draft drawn by Seller ("beneficiary") upon proper presentation of the draft and any documents required by the letter of credit. These documents must comply with the requirements expressed in the letter of credit. For instance, they must describe the goods in accordance with the description in the letter of credit; they must include any invoice, bill of lading, policy of insurance, certificate of inspection, all as required by the letter; and so on. But if the presented documents comply, the Newark issuing bank must pay—the letter of credit compels it. And this is true even if Buyer, thinking it has hot news of inferior goods shipped, instructs Newark Bank not to pay drafts presented by Seller.[4]

It should be easy to see why a seller might prefer this payment arrangement over one merely requiring buyer to pay "cash against documents." The insolvency risk is reduced, for banks as a class are far more solvent than buyers as a class. The dishonesty risk is much less significant with payor banks than with payor buyers. And while honest disputes may arise over whether documents comply, nonpayment for this reason is less likely where the party to

---

4. This rule which compels the issuing bank to pay despite defective goods has some key exceptions. See, e.g., § 8–9 *infra.*

pay is a bank that has issued a letter of credit than where the party to pay is merely the buyer who has agreed to pay a sight draft against documents. Thus, the money paid under the letter of credit resides in seller-beneficiary's pocket as the dispute grinds toward a judgment or compromise.[5] The seller-beneficiary's convenience and protection become all the greater when, as often arranged, the issuing bank gets a bank in beneficiary's locale to "confirm" the letter of credit.[6]

To summarize, drafts drawn by a seller on an issuing bank are far more certain of payment than drafts drawn on an ordinary buyer who is committed to pay under the terms of an ordinary sales contract. The burden of pursing litigation is also transferred to the buyer since the seller will have money in hand. In effect, the seller has bargained for the right to be the defendant instead of the plaintiff in litigation on the underlying contract. The buyer will bear the burden of litigating, often in a foreign jurisdiction, to recover under the contract.

After paying beneficiary's draft, the issuing bank has the documents which control the goods. These secure the issuing bank's right to get reimbursed by the applicant buyer upon payment to the beneficiary seller under the letter of credit.[7]

b. The Standby Letter of Credit

The commercial letter of credit acts as a payment medium for goods sold. By contrast, the standby letter of credit acts as a "back up" against applicant default on obligations of all kinds, both monetary and non-monetary. Standby letters function somewhat like guarantees, for it is applicant's failing that prompts beneficiary's call on the letter. Yet the standby letter differs from the guarantee in important ways.[8] Even so, this back-up feature in theory more easily and more cheaply available from bankers than from traditional sureties explains the limitless versatility of standby letters and their great growth during recent times.[9] Misconceptions about this feature may also explain the litigation over them.

To show how a standby letter actually "stands by," consider a few examples:[10]

---

5. In practice, he who holds the cash has not only the time value of money but a key advantage over his opponent who must shell out the first costs of litigation.

6. See UCC 5–107 and § 8–12, *infra.*

7. See further, 8–11, *infra.*

8. See 8–2, *infra.*

9. Standby letters of credit can be used in almost any situation imaginable,

where additional security is desired. *See* Julicher v. Internal Revenue Service, 27 UCC2d 244 (E.D.Pa.1995) IRS listed as the beneficiary of a letter of credit entered into to support a taxpayer's delinquent tax repayment plan).

10. Their patterns set the stage for applying the often arbitrary but essential rules governing letters of credit.

1. Construction projects

Builder agrees to perform construction work for Owner. In place of a performance bond from a true surety, Builder (applicant) gets its bank (issuer) to write Owner (beneficiary) a standby letter of credit. In this letter, Bank–Issuer engages to pay Beneficiary–Owner against presentation of two documents: (1) a written demand (typically a sight draft) which calls for payment of the letter's stipulated amount, plus (2) a written statement certifying that Applicant–Builder has failed to perform the agreed construction work.

This three-party arrangement has a four-party variation: Suppose Owner insists on a conventional performance bond from an actual surety. Builder procures one, but now Surety wants protection that Builder will make Surety whole, if Owner calls the bond for Builder's performance failure. So Builder again asks its bank to write a standby letter. Builder is still the applicant and its bank still the issuer, but now the standby letter's beneficiary is Surety. And now Issuing Bank engages to pay Beneficiary—Surety upon its presentation of a sight draft and a statement certifying that Surety's bond stands to be called by Owner (who has no rights under the letter of credit itself).

Aside from non-monetary obligations such as building construction, and like work, a standby letter may back up pure monetary obligations in a construction project. Reversing roles, project Owner or a municipality (applicant) might get its bank (issuer) to write a standby letter naming Builder as beneficiary and engaging Issuer to pay against Beneficiary's installment presentations of drafts and statements certifying successive stages of work progress.

2. Investment programs

A group of marketers put together a limited partnership to drill for oil and gas, or perhaps to buy real estate and develop it. The marketers seek limited partners to invest capital in the partnership by buying fractional interests or units. The marketers will likely manage. The partnership may borrow most of its capital to shelter income from tax. The total price of all fractional interests offered to investors will be high enough to cover this borrowed capital.

Typically the investor does not pay cash for his fractional interest. Instead, each investor makes a small down payment and signs a note to pay the rest in the future. In theory, "the rest" will come from his share of the venture's bounty. But the principal lender wants assurance that investor will pay his share of the borrowing even if the partnership venture goes bust. So Investor (applicant) gets his own bank (issuer) to write a standby letter to the principal lender (beneficiary). In the letter, Issuer engages to pay on presentation of a draft and a statement certifying either that the limited partnership has defaulted on the borrowing from Principal Lender or simply that the rest of Investor's fractional price is due.

In summary, we emphasize that standby letters differ from commercial letters in function, risk to Issuer, and Applicant's underlying obligation. In function, a commercial letter is mainly a payment mechanism for Beneficiary to use by presenting documents that show dispatch of the goods promised to Applicant. Beneficiary's draw is expected in ordinary course.

The standby letter works in two contrary senses to the commercial letter. First, the standby letter typically calls for documents not about Beneficiary's conduct but about *Applicant's*. Second, those documents speak not of achievement but of failure: Customer–Applicant's default on an underlying obligation owed to Beneficiary. Since no one expects failure, no one expects a draw on the standby letter.

By giving Issuer a ready security in goods, the commercial letter minimizes risk. The standby letter does not. After paying Beneficiary under a commercial letter, Issuer often has documents that control the goods. Should Applicant not reimburse it, Issuer may seek satisfaction against the goods. But a standby letter itself begets no ready security. To secure its reimbursement rights against Applicant, Issuer must bargain with Applicant for other collateral.

Finally, standby letters call for a different risk analysis than commercial letters. To write a commercial letter, a banker must judge only Applicant's ability to pay money—the price of purchased goods. Bankers exercise this lender's judgment daily when they make loans. They are thus well suited to issue commercial letters. But when a standby letter backs up Applicant's non-monetary obligation, the banker is not asked just to be a lender, but to be a surety who must predict Applicant's ability to perform its contract by building, selling or manufacturing—matters little known to bankers.[11] Bankers may be ill-suited to analyze the performance risks that sureties routinely bond.

Issuer best manages these extra risks by recognizing that even though it writes the standby letter to Beneficiary, the issuer is really making a loan to Applicant—a "business line of credit" whose sum may be drawn out immediately without "standing by" at all. This loan will be wholly unsecured unless Applicant puts up collateral via a separate reimbursement contract binding Issuer and Applicant. Many bankers have rued the day they issued a standby

---

11. Even where the standby letter purports to back up only a repayment of money, the obligation may embody either a sum resembling "damages" or an accelerated debt, each for an unexpected failing by customer.

letter without assessing and treating it as a true loan or without taking solid collateral as security.[12]

3.   Sample irrevocable letter of credit

One who has never seen examples of the documents described above may find all of the foregoing discussion mysterious. To dispel that we set out examples of the letter of credit draft and demand for payment and other forms here.

To the extent that they can do so at the outset, both the beneficiary and the issuer would like to avoid later uncertainty by being specific in the letter itself. Thousands of cases arise each year in which there is question whether the beneficiary has complied with the letter. Sometimes the beneficiary's demand is not accompanied by the proper documents, sometimes the documents do not say the proper thing, sometimes the documents are not timely presented.

12. Bank regulators eventually awoke to bring standby letters squarely within a bank's loan-booking requirements and all lending limits. See 8–3, *infra.*

NOM DE LA BANQUE EMETTRICE   NAME OF ISSUING BANK
Issuing Bank Limited International Division
23, High Street
London S.W 25
Lieu et date d'émission Place and date of issue
London

13 October 1984

Irrevocable documentary credit
Crédit documentaire irrévocable

Number Numéro
16358

Date and date of expiry Date et lieu d'expiration 30 November 1984
at counters of advising bank

Joan's Boutique
14 Charlotte Street
London W.C.36

The Eastern Trading Company
29, London Road
Hong Kong

Bank "X"
35 Kings Road North
Hong Kong

HK$ 10,000 (Hong Kong Dollars ten thousand)

Shipment/dispatch de not later than
Hong Kong

Heathrow Airport, London

[X] 90 days sight
Bank "X", 35 Kings Road North, Hong Kong

SIGNED INVOICE IN THREE COPIES certifying that the goods are in accordance with Joan's Boutique Order Number 35 dated 14.8.1984.

AIR CONSIGNMENT NOTE evidencing goods dispatched to Joan's Boutique, 14 Charlotte Street, London W.C. 36 marked "Freight Paid".

PACKING LIST IN TRIPLICATE

We are informed that insurance is being arranged by our principals.

covering Ladies Dresses
C and F Heathrow Airport, London

7

Issuing Bank Limited International Division
23, High Street
London S.W 25

1

Note the explicit requirements in the letter and think for a moment how a particular document that appears to fulfill the letter might be found not to do so. Note how carefully the bank (and the drafter of the letter) attempts to limit the beneficiary's acts even by offering examples of the documents which must be presented to earn payment. As we will see, the bank is often in the position of an independent third party who is asked to make difficult choices between its loyalty to its applicant (who does not wish it to pay) and its legal duty to the beneficiary (who asserts a legal right to payment). The bank's discomfort will be inversely related to the care and foresight of its drafter. If the letter is clear, the bank can reject its applicant's plea by pointing to its clear legal duty. As one reads the following section, it might be appropriate to return to the letter and to the demand for payment to see how the language of those might guide one around some of the pitfalls that are disclosed by the cases.

PROBLEM

University is building a new science laboratory. Assume that it has alternatively received one of the following to assure the contractor's performance.

     a.   "Upon contractor's default we promise to pay up to $1,000,000 to complete the project."

     b.   "Upon University's presentation of a certification of contractor's default signed by an executive officer of University, we will pay up to $1,000,000 to complete the project."

1.   Is the statement in "a" a letter of credit?

     No. The promise is not to pay "against documents" but to pay on a particular event, namely default. The statement in "b" is a promise to pay "against a certification of default"—and to do so whether there has been a default or not! The latter therefore is a payment against "documents." 5–102(a)(10).

2.   What name would you give to these documents: guarantee, standby letter of credit, commercial letter of credit?

     The first is probably a guarantee; the second is a standby letter.

3.   What if the document required payment only if the "certificate of default is presented at bank before 4/14/12"? Bank argues that this is not a letter of credit because it has non-documentary conditions, namely that the presentation be before 4/14/12. Does that non-documentary condition change it into a guarantee?

     No. Even in letters of credit, some non-documentary conditions are expected and required. See 5–108(g), Comment 6 to 5–102.

---

§ 8–2   Legal Nature of the Letter of Credit

In the years since the adoption of the Uniform Commercial Code, American courts have seen a steady flow of letter of credit cases. The nature of the defensive positions taken by lawyers and the quality of the draftsmanship of the letters of credit in a number of these cases indicate that the legal nature of the letter of credit is still not as widely understood as it should be. In fact, even a large bank like Citicorp has shown that it is not immune from having one of its branch managers outside of the letter of credit department issue a document that may, or may not, be a letter of credit.[1] In particular, there is an irresistible urge to analogize the letter of credit to other legal arrangements, and this has led to error. The prime purpose of the drafters of Article 5 was to "set a substantive theoretical frame that describes the function and legal nature of letters of credit," a framework independent of contract, of guarantee, of third party beneficiary law, of the law of assignment, and of negotiable instruments. The drafters also indicated a desire "to preserv[e procedural] flexibility through variation by agreement."[2]

The beginning of understanding is to see that the letter of credit transaction is not a two-party, but rather a three-party arrangement. It can be pictured as follows:

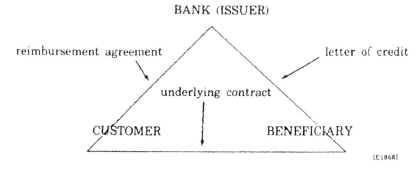

BANK (ISSUER)

reimbursement agreement   letter of credit

underlying contract

CUSTOMER   BENEFICIARY

[E1868]

The arrangement involves two contracts and the letter of credit. In all cases there will be a reimbursement contract between the issuer and the applicant[3] requiring that the applicant reimburse

§ 8–2

1. See Bouzo v. Citibank, 96 F.3d 51, 30 UCC Rep.Serv.2d 913 (2nd Cir. 1996).

2. Comment to 5–101.

3. 102(a)(2) defines the applicant as "a person at whose request or for whose account a letter of credit is issued." While it is usually clear who the applicant is, it can become an issue when the party who requests the letter is not the same as the party for whose account it is issued. *See* In re Enron, 2006 WL 897861, 59 UCC2d 359 (Bankr.S.D.N.Y. 2006). In *Enron* the issuer argued that

both the party who requests the letter and the party for whose account the letter is issued are applicants. *Id.* at *4. The court rejects that argument, stating that, unless otherwise agreed there can be only one applicant. *Id.* at *6. "[T]he party 'for whose account a letter of credit is issued' is only considered the applicant if the requester does not take on an obligation to reimburse the issuer and is a party other than the party for whose account it is issued." *Id.* at *5.

the issuer for payments made on the letter of credit. Usually there will also be a contract between the applicant and the beneficiary. Then there will be the issuer's obligation on the letter of credit itself. The unwashed characterize the letter of credit as a contract between the beneficiary and the issuer, but it is better to call it an "undertaking" and so avoid the implication that contract principles might apply to it.

The most unique and mysterious part of this arrangement is the so-called "independence principle." The principle states that the bank's obligation to the beneficiary is *independent* of the beneficiary's performance on the underlying contract. Put another way, the issuer must pay on a proper demand from the beneficiary even though the beneficiary may have breached the underlying contract with the applicant.[4] Even significant world events, such as the Iraqi invasion of Kuwait in the early 1990s and the resulting Executive Order from President George Bush prohibiting Iraqi government property from leaving the U.S., were not sufficient to stop beneficiaries from drawing on letters of credit. Nor would a beneficiary be kept from drawing even if the issuer violated a cease and desist order in issuing the letter of credit.

Bankers sometimes make the same point by describing the transaction between the bank and the beneficiary as a "paper transaction." By that they mean the issuer's agent should be able to sit in a business suit at a desk in a bank, and by looking at papers that are presented, determine whether the bank is obliged to make payment or not. She is not obligated and, indeed, is foreclosed from putting on overalls and going into the field to determine whether the underlying contract has been performed. We will see that there are some important exceptions to the independence principle, but they are limited.

It should not be surprising that the obligation of the issuer to pay the beneficiary is also independent of any obligation of the applicant to its issuer. If, for example, the applicant goes into bankruptcy after the letter has been issued, but before it has been drawn upon, the issuer must pay despite the fact that the applicant will not be able to pay the issuer.[5] The same would be true if the applicant had repudiated the contract of reimbursement or disputed its terms. Since these are the very risks (applicant's insolvency or

---

4. For such reasons, letters of credit may not always be more attractive to the applicant than standard bonds or guarantees, particularly in situations where the debtor-applicant may want to be able to fight it out in court with the creditor-beneficiary before payment is made.

5. This rule makes perfect sense, as standby letters of credit are expressly designed to insure payment when the applicant cannot pay, which must certainly include situations where the applicant files for bankruptcy and the automatic stay prohibits access to the debtor's assets. A contrary rule would remove the entire value of standby letters in such circumstances.

unwillingness to pay) which the beneficiary sought to avoid by demanding the issuance of the letter of credit, it should not be surprising that the issuer cannot assert them as defenses against the beneficiary. Section 5–108 states the issuer's duty to honor in terms that do not allow for any exception based on the applicant's default on its contract with the bank. The absence of consideration is also expressly ruled out as a basis for dishonor under section 5–105.

In the late 1990s in California, a case arose that had many lenders shaking in their boots, worried that the independence principle was not as absolute as they had initially believed. In Western Security Bank v. Superior Court,[6] Beverly Hills Business Bank made a commercial real estate loan to a customer named Vista Place Associates for the purchase of a retail shopping center. When Vista ran into trouble three years later, the bank required that Vista's principals post three letters of credit that the bank could draw on in the event of a default of the underlying loan agreement. Vista eventually defaulted and the bank attempted to draw on the letters of credit, but Vista threatened to sue the issuer, Western Security Bank, for wrongful honor under the theory that Beverly Hills' draw would violate California's anti-deficiency statute which prohibited collecting a deficiency in cases involving a non-judicial foreclosure.

Beverly Hills responded by citing the independence principle, and claimed that the letter of credit agreement with Western Security was separate from its mortgage contract with Vista. The California Court of Appeals found for Vista and allowed Western to refuse to honor Beverly Hills' presentment. Before the case could be appealed to the California Supreme Court, the state legislature quickly amended the law to abrogate the Court of Appeals decision.[7] The California Supreme Court then remanded the case for consideration under the new law. The Court of Appeals upheld its earlier ruling, holding that the new law did not apply retroactively. Another appeal to the Supreme Court resulted in the final disposition, with the high state court holding that the new law did apply

---

6. 933 P.2d 507 (Cal. 1997).

7. California's anti-deficiency statute is located in Code of Civil Procedure § 580d, and the legislature's modification added §§ 580.5 and 580.7. The first of the two additions makes clear that taking a number of actions related to a letter of credit (such as a beneficiary's documentary presentation or the issuer seeking reimbursement once it pays the beneficiary) do not violate the anti-deficiency provisions in § 580d. § 580.7 contains an important exception to the new rule on letters of credit in this area, however, and protects those mortgagors who are natural persons and pledged owner-occupied property with one to four residential units. In such situations, the standard anti-deficiency rules apply and a mortgagee *cannot* use a letter of credit to collect on a deficiency. As such, the state policy favoring anti-deficiency in cases involving owner-occupied residential real estate remains unchanged.

retroactively and requiring that Western Security honor Beverly Hills' presentment.

Although it took jumping through some procedural hoops on the part of the California legislature and Supreme Court, this case came out the right way.

a. Letter of Credit vs. Guarantee

In a typical guarantee the guarantor agrees to make payments if, and only if, the customer has failed to fulfill its obligation on the underlying contract. If that obligation has been avoided because of the acts of the beneficiary, typically there is no obligation to support the guarantee and thus no duty on the guarantor to pay because the guarantor could assert any defenses to payment that would be available to the original obligor. Letters of credit are different, and they are explicitly and consciously designed to be different in this respect. In effect, the beneficiary under a letter of credit has bargained for the right to be paid upon presentation of documents notwithstanding a default on the underlying contract. This is the principal reason why careful courts and lawyers state that the letter of credit is not a guarantee.

To say that a letter is a guarantee or that the beneficiary is a third party beneficiary of another's contract is to make an inaccurate statement about the letter of credit transaction. (In European practice certain letter of credit-like obligations are sometimes called "bank guarantees," or "independent guarantees." Here we speak of classic American guarantees, i.e., "secondary" guarantees.) A court's characterization of a letter of credit as a guarantee or third party beneficiary contract carries with it implications about kinds of defenses that might be asserted by the bank or by other parties. Those analogies are not accurate with respect to the letter of credit. Perhaps our ranting and raving against improper characterizations makes too much of a simple point. Mostly we fear that a court who describes a letter of credit as a guarantee or as a contract whose benefits run to a beneficiary will then draw improper inferences from that characterization and apply law that should not be applied.

Parties making arguments that letters of credit are really guarantees hope to establish either that (1) the obligor is a "guarantor," and can therefore set up defenses of the principal debtor against the creditor under general suretyship law, or (2) the bank's obligation was *ultra vires* and void on the ground that applicable regulatory law does not permit a bank to issue guarantees.

But a true letter of credit arrangement is not a guarantee, even though the letter fulfills the function of a guarantee. To reiterate, consider the two ways in which a letter of credit is different from a typical secondary guarantee. First, the obligation of the guarantor depends upon the existence of a primary obligation on the part of the guarantor's principal (the debtor) running to the principal's creditor. Thus, the guarantor can often set up defenses of the principal debtor against the creditor. An issuer of a letter of credit cannot do so. In that sense the issuer's obligation to the beneficiary (the creditor) is said to be "primary," i.e., not subject to the defenses the debtor might have against the creditor. Second, the obligation of the guarantor cannot mature unless the principal debtor has actually defaulted. But, as also indicated above, the facts—actual default—are not relevant to the obligation of the issuer under a letter of credit. The issuer's obligation arises upon proper presentation of documents or other papers—no matter that those documents may seem to show a set of facts that do not exist.

Yet an arrangement in the form of a letter of credit may actually be a secondary guarantee and so not a letter of credit when its substance is analyzed. Indeed, this is just what the Ninth Circuit concluded in the celebrated case of Wichita Eagle and Beacon Publishing Co. v. Pacific National Bank.[8] The instrument recited that it was a letter of credit and, among other things, provided that the obligor must pay whatever a lessee owed to a lessor upon lessee's default. The duty of the obligor was premised partly on a determination that the lessee had *actually defaulted*, not upon papers in proper order certifying default. Hence, the court concluded that the arrangement was not a letter of credit but an ordinary guarantee. The court also carefully noted that its decision did not turn on the "stand by" nature of the arrangement, however.[9] To qualify as a letter of credit, an undertaking need not *expressly* require presentation; that can be implied.[10]

A more recent case dealt with the opposite issue: whether an agreement was a letter of credit despite additional language addressing fraud that made it look more like a conditional guarantee.[11] Although the language at issue stated "this letter of credit may not be drawn upon in the case of fraud, misappropriation of funds, misrepresentation or criminal activity," the Seventh Circuit held that this did not preclude the document from being a letter of credit. Instead, the court interpreted the provision as applying to the beneficiary's submission of a fraudulent sight draft, which was required to draw on the letter of credit.

The 1995 revisions to Article 5 made clear that the characterization of an undertaking as a letter of credit is dependent on the

8. 493 F.2d 1285, 14 UCC 156 (9th Cir.1974).

9. *Id*. at 1286.

10. New Jersey Bank v. Palladino, 77 N.J. 33, 389 A.2d 454, 24 UCC 729 (1978).

11. Teleport Communications Group, Inc. v. Barclay Financial Group, Ltd., 176 F.3d 412 (7th Cir. 1999).

presence of documentary conditions. Section 5–102(a)(10) states that a letter of credit is a "definite undertaking * * * by an issuer to a beneficiary at the request or for the account of an applicant * * * to honor a *documentary* presentation * * * "(emphasis added). If the letter of credit contains fundamental non-documentary conditions, the undertaking is not a letter of credit.[12]

For example, Majorette Toys (U.S.), Inc. v. Bank of Shawsville[13] involved a letter of credit having two significant nondocumentary conditions:

> 1. All goods placed for resale at The Kroger Company by Virginia Service Merchandisers, Inc. must have been accepted under the Terms and Conditions of Purchase by The Kroger Company.

> 2. All purchase proceeds for goods purchased and accepted by The Kroger Company from Virginia Service Merchandisers, Inc. must be submitted by The Kroger Company directly to Bank of Shawsville. Bank of Shawsville will not honor any drafts which are for payment for goods which were not accepted by The Kroger Company, or for which The Kroger Company has not fully paid directly to Bank of Shawsville.

> 3. We engage with you that all drafts drawn under and in compliance with the terms of this credit will be duly honored on delivery of documents as specified if presented at this office on or before January 15, 1990. Funds will not be disbursed to honor any drafts prior to January 15, 1990. We confirm the credit and thereby undertake that all drafts drawn and presented as above specified will be duly honored by us.

---

12. Comment 6 to 5–102 reads in part:

When a document labelled a letter of credit requires the issuer to pay not upon the presentation of documents, but upon the determination of an extrinsic fact such as applicant's failure to perform a construction contract, and where that condition appears on its face to be fundamental and would, if ignored, leave no obligation to the issuer under the document labelled letter of credit, the issuer's undertaking is not a letter of credit.

Comment 9 to 5–108 reads in part:

Subsection (g) recognizes that letters of credit sometimes contain nondocumentary terms or conditions. Conditions such as a term prohibiting "shipment on vessels more than 15 years old," are to be disregarded and treated as surplusage. Similarly, a requirement that there be an award by a "duly appointed arbitrator" would not require the issuer to determine whether the arbitrator had been "duly appointed." Likewise a term in a standby letter of credit that provided for differing forms of certification depending upon the particular type of default does not oblige the issuer independently to determine which kind of default has occurred. These conditions must be disregarded by the issuer. Where the nondocumentary conditions are central and fundamental to the issuer's obligation (as for example a condition that would require the issuer to determine in fact whether the beneficiary had performed the underlying contract or whether the applicant had defaulted) their inclusion may remove the undertaking from the scope of Article 5 entirely.

13. 18 UCC2d 1217 (W.D.Va.1991).

Upon presentation of the drafts by the beneficiary, the bank refused payment because the conditions of paragraph 2 had not been met. The court concluded that the bank had a right to rely on the nondocumentary conditions. Under UCP 13c the bank presumably would have been obliged to pay the draft, as that section states that banks should disregard nondocumentary conditions when examining the required documents. However, if the court found the nondocumentary condition to be fundamental to the bank's obligation, the engagement would not be a letter of credit under the UCC (recall 5–102'(a)(10)) and the court's conclusion might still be reached under other law. Where a document promising payment is something other than a letter of credit, the bank would be outside Article 5 and could assert its nondocumentary conditions. Since the only important conditions in *Jak-Pak* were nondocumentary, the court should have concluded that the engagement was not a letter of credit, but a conditional contract.[14]

In nearly all the litigated cases on the question whether an undertaking is a letter of credit or a guarantee, the courts appear to have characterized the arrangement properly. In Republic National Bank of Dallas v. Northwest National Bank,[15] a doubtful characterization of a relationship as a guarantee was reversed. The instrument recited that it was an irrevocable letter of credit and provided for maturity of the issuer's obligation not upon inquiry into actual facts of default but upon presentation of documents.

Why not consider the beneficiary as the third party beneficiary of the contract between the issuer and the applicant? Because of the defenses. A true third party beneficiary's claim is generally subject to the defenses that the promisor could set up against the promisee if the promisee were plaintiff, including failure of a condition, anticipatory breach, certain forms of fraud, and the like.[16] Yet the claim of a beneficiary of a letter of credit is not subject to those defenses. The issuer must honor the drafts even if the issuer's customer has failed to pay agreed fees, has defrauded the issuer, has unequivocally repudiated, and so on.[17]

Similarly, the usual beneficiary of a letter of credit is not an assignee of a contract right, it is also not an assignee of a right of the applicant to require the issuer to honor drafts. The beneficiary acquires that right directly from the issuer. An assignee remains subject to all defenses that an obligor can set up against the

---

14. See also Majorette Toys (U.S.) Inc. v. Bank of Shawsville, 1992 WL 400904, 18 UCC2d 1220 (Va.Cir.Ct. 1992).

15. 566 S.W.2d 358, 24 UCC 939 (Tex.Civ.App.1978), rev'd, 578 S.W.2d 109, 25 UCC 832 (Tex.1978).

16. Restatement (Second) of Contracts § 336 (1981).

17. § 5–108.

assignor,[18] but the beneficiary of a letter of credit cannot be met with defenses the issuer has against the applicant.[19]

Nor is a letter of credit itself a negotiable instrument[20] (although the draft presented under it may be).[21] A letter of credit does not comply with the requisites of a negotiable instrument under section 3–104(1) of the Code. It is not payable to order or bearer, and it is conditional.

In short, a letter of credit is a letter of credit. As Bishop Butler once said, "Everything is what it is and not another thing."[22]

b. Other Related Parties

Additional parties are often added to the three party arrangement discussed above. When buyer and seller are located in different states or countries, the issuing bank may engage other banks to assist in the letter of credit transaction. Nominated banks can take on a variety of roles and attendant legal duties.[23]

An advising bank agrees to inform the beneficiary of the terms of the letter of credit.[24] Upon request by the issuer, a confirming bank agrees to pay upon presentation of the required documents under the letter of credit.[25] The advising bank is not necessarily a confirming bank.[26]

Other parties can also become involved via the beneficiary. If the letter of credit expressly provides, the beneficiary can transfer the duty of performance under the letter to another party.[27] Furthermore, the beneficiary can perform under the letter of credit and transfer its rights to the proceeds to another party.[28]

PROBLEM

1. American Buyer has agreed to buy several thousand copies of several toys manufactured by Chinese Seller. Buyer has given seller a $2 million letter of credit from Bank of America. During an inspection at Seller's plant in China, Buyer discov-

---

18. Restatement (Second) of Contracts 336 (1981).

19. § 5–108.

20. See generally Comment, Letters of Credit—Negotiable Instruments, 36 Yale L.J. 245 (1926).

21. See generally Farnsworth, Documentary Drafts Under the Uniform Commercial Code, 22 Bus.Law. 479 (1967).

22. Somewhere in Bishop Butler's sermons.

23. See 8–12, *infra* for discussion of these duties.

24. § 5–102(a)(1) and 5–107; UCP 7(a).

25. § 5–102(a)(4) and 5–107; UCP 9(b).

26. § 5–107(c); UCP 9(c).

27. § 5–112; UCP 48.

28. § 5–112; UCP 49.

ers that Seller's toys have been painted with lead based paint and do not conform to the contract.

   a. Buyer reports this to Bank of America and asks Bank to dishonor Seller's presentment. When Seller presents complying documents the next day, what does Bank of America do?

     It pays, 5–108(a), 5–103(d). Buyer can duke it out with Seller on his own, but he made a deal to allow Seller to have the money in his pocket during the fight.

   b. What outcome if Buyer had procured a guarantee and not a letter of credit?

     Now guarantor can usually assert Buyer's defenses and refuse to pay.

2. Why couldn't Issuer refuse to pay and then defend by asserting the warranties under 5–110 against Chinese Seller?

   Read 5–110 carefully. The warranties arise only after "payment," so they do not help here. After payment Buyer (or more likely Buyer's parent company who had no contract with Seller but who put up the letter) could sue under 5–110(a)(2).

§ 8–3   Relevant Sources of Law

a.   Authority to Issue

The authority of American banks to issue conventional letters of credit has never been questioned. Though each letter of credit represents a potential liability of the bank (in the form of a promise in effect to make a loan to its applicant by paying money to the beneficiary), the proper treatment of this liability was never the subject of controversy until banks began issuing standby letters of credit. In response to the issuance of thousands of standby letters after 1960, the banking agencies have issued a variety of rules. These rules recognize the right of banks to issue both conventional and standby letters of credit. A regulation of the Comptroller of the Currency, 12 CFR 7.1016, authorizes the issue of letters and states some limitations that should be observed by an issuing bank.

§ 7.1016. Letters of credit.

(a) General authority. A national bank may issue and commit to issue letters of credit * * * within the scope of the applicable laws or rules of practice recognized by law. [a footnote then specifically refers to Article 5 and UCP 500, among other sources of letter of credit law]

(b) Safety and soundness considerations—

   (1) Terms. As a matter of safe and sound banking practice, banks that issue independent undertakings should not be

exposed to undue risk. As a minimum, banks should consider the following:

(i) The independent character of the undertaking should be apparent from its terms (such as terms that subject it to laws or rules providing for its independent character);

(ii) The undertaking should be limited in amount;

(iii) The undertaking should: (A) Be limited in duration; or (B) Permit the bank to terminate the undertaking either on a periodic basis * * * or at will * * *; or (C) Entitle the bank to cash collateral from the applicant on demand * * *; and

(iv) The bank either should be fully collateralized or have a post-honor right of reimbursement from the applicant or from another issuer of an independent undertaking.[1]

However, other regulations[2] require the treatment of standby letters of credit as an extension of credit to the customer and make the extension of credit subject to the lending limits that are specified in the federal law. In a like vein, the Federal Reserve notes that standby letters of credit and ineligible acceptances count toward member banks' lending limits imposed by state law.[3]

The sum of these regulations shows that federal agencies regard conventional commercial letters of credit as different from standby letters of credit. Moreover, it discloses considerable anxiety about banks that issue standby letters of credit without treating them as loans to the customer. In effect, these regulations authorize both kinds of letters but require the potential obligation on standby letters to be treated for some purposes as though they were current loans. More extensive consideration of these questions is beyond the scope of this book. But the lawyer should understand that there is a body of federal rules (and even some state rules) that governs the power of financial institutions to issue letters, and that establishes standards for their issuance and treatment in the issuer's financial statements.[4]

Although almost all issuers are banks, nothing in Article 5 prohibits non-banks from issuing letters of credit. Because the drafters fear that consumers who issued letters of credit would lose their defenses against creditors' claims, Article 5 prohibits consumers from issuing letters of credit. Beyond this limit, there are no

§ 8-3

1. 12 CFR 7.1016.

2. 12 CFR 32.2(f)(iv).

3. 12 CFR 208.24(c).

4. As of May 1, 2006: California, Cal. Financial Code Secs. 1221, 1224; Illinois, 205 Ill. Comp. Stat. Ann. §§ 5/32, 5/34; New York, N.Y. Banking Law.

restrictions and any requirements imposed by the Controller of the Currency or the Federal Reserve would not apply to a non-bank issuer. Conceivably, non-bank financial institutions such as GMAC and General Electric Credit Corporation and possibly industrial corporations will become significant writers of letters of credit in the future.

b. Substantive Law

Because this is a book about the Uniform Commercial Code, we will emphasize Article 5.[5] In the entire universe of letter of credit transactions, Article 5 governs only a limited part. A large share of all letter of credit transactions are international transactions and most of those are governed by the Uniform Customs and Practice (UCP)—a trade practice drafted by commercial law experts from many countries and adopted by the International Chamber of Commerce (ICC).[6] For many, therefore, the UCP will be a more significant source of law than the UCC. Parties routinely incorporate the UCP by a term in the letter of credit. When this is the case, the UCP terms carry the force of law. The UCC still has a place in interpreting cases under the UCP, however, such as when the UCP is silent or ambiguous on the issue and the applicable UCC provision does not conflict with the UCP.

One should also be aware of two sources of law that may govern international letters of credit: the United Nations Convention on Independent Guarantees and Stand-by Letters of Credit, and the International Standby Practices (more commonly referred to as "ISP98").[7] Although the Convention is limited to international letters, nothing in ISP98 restricts domestic parties from agreeing to be held to its terms. Also note that both were specifically drafted with standby letters of credit in mind, to address perceived weaknesses when UCP 500 was applied in standby cases. The significance of the Convention remains unclear due to the limited number of countries that have ratified it.

---

5. Article 5's most recent version (the 1995 revision) has been adopted in all U.S. states and jurisdictions except Puerto Rico (including the District of Columbia and the U.S. Virgin Islands).

6. UCP 600 became effective on July 1, 2007.

7. The U.N. Convention is available at: http://www.uncitral.org/uncitral/en/uncitral_texts/payments/1995 Convention_guarantees_credit.html. The Convention went into effect on January 1, 2000, and has been ratified by Belarus, Ecuador, El Salvador, Gabon, Kuwait, Liberia, Panama and Tunisia—the U.S. has signed the Convention, but not

ratified it. It specifically refers to the UCP and has been endorsed by the ICC. ISP98, on the other hand, has been in effect since January 1, 1999, following its approval by the International Chamber of Commerce. Various publications covering ISP 98 can be found on the websites of the ICC and the Institute of International Banking Law & Practice: respectively, www.iccwbo.org and www.iiblp.org. A comprehensive article surrounding the drafting of ISP98 and its resulting rules is Dolan, Analyzing Bank Drafted Standby Letter of Credit Rules, The International Standby Practice (ISP98), 45 Wayne L. Rev. 1865 (2000).

In addition to the UCC and the UCP, there are other rules. Most important is the language of the letter itself. There is also case law, trade usage, and other law that might be specifically incorporated by the letter.

Most of Article 5's provisions deal with the rights and obligations between the beneficiary and the issuer. A few of the provisions deal with the rights and duties between the applicant and the issuer. However, Article 5 does not much concern itself with the reimbursement contract between the applicant and the issuing bank, nor does it deal at all with the underlying contract between the applicant and the beneficiary.

c. Scope Under Article 5

The principal scope provision of Article 5 is section 5–103 and the associated definitions contained in 5–102:

5–103. Scope.

(a) This article applies to letters of credit and to certain rights and obligations arising out of transactions involving letters of credit.

(b) The statement of a rule in this article does not by itself require, imply, or negate application of the same or a different rule to a situation not provided for, or to a person not specified, in this article.

5–102. Definitions.

(a) In this article: * * * (10) "Letter of credit" means a definite undertaking that satisfies the requirements of Section 5–104 by an issuer to a beneficiary at the request or for the account of an applicant * * * to honor a documentary presentation * * *.

These provisions make clear that something labeled a letter of credit, which calls for nondocumentary determination, is not a letter of credit. That is why 5–102(a)(10) says that a letter of credit must provide for honor of a "documentary" presentation. If the issuer is to test the beneficiary's performance by means other than documentary examination, then the agreement may not be a letter of credit. Comment 6 to 5–102 makes this point clear:

When a document labeled a letter of credit requires the issuer to pay not upon the presentation of documents, but upon the determination of an extrinsic fact such as applicant's failure to perform a construction contract, and where that condition appears on its face to be fundamental and would, if ignored, leave no obligation to the issuer under the document labeled letter of credit, the issuer's undertaking is not a letter of credit.
* * *

It is apparent from the wording of 5–103, from the official comments, and from the drafting process that the Code drafters intended Article 5 to apply to many types of letter of credit transactions besides those involving the sale of goods with an issuer bank obligated to pay drafts on presentment of sales and shipping documents. Furthermore, 5–103's reference to a variety of other "rights and obligations arising out of transactions involving letters of credit" indicates that Article 5 governs, to some extent, the reimbursement agreement, agreements of confirmers, agreements of advisers, and claims of beneficiaries and applicants concerning wrongful dishonor or wrongful honor respectively.

Consistent with the spirit of 5–103, section 5–102 defines terms used in 5–103, and throughout Article 5, expansively. An issuer is defined as "a bank or other person that issues a credit, but does not include an individual who makes an engagement for personal, family, or household purposes."[8] A beneficiary is defined as "a person who under the terms of a letter of credit is entitled to have its complying presentation honored."[9] "Document" means "a draft or other demand, document of title, investment security, certificate, invoice, or other record, statement, or representation of fact, law, right or opinion."[10] The word "document" is far broader in meaning than the phrase "document of title."[11]

Fifteen sections follow the basic scope and definitional provisions of Article 5. A few of these—principally those specifying the formal requisites of creation of a valid letter of credit—cannot be varied by agreement of the parties.[12] The general principle in Article 5, however, is freedom of contract. Section 5–103(c) confirms the parties' right to modify most of Article 5's standard terms: "with the exception of [an enumerated list of seven subsections that cannot be modified by agreement], the effect of this article may be varied by agreement or by a provision stated or incorporated by reference in an undertaking." Any section that can be modified is *a fortiori* a "gap-filler," a provision that supplies a term of the letter of credit arrangement when the parties have left a gap in it (intentionally or unintentionally).

Many letters of credit, domestic and international, state that they shall be governed by the UCP. This incorporation by reference brings a wide range of non-Article 5 "customary law" to bear, and except where there is conflict between *mandatory* provisions of Article 5 and the custom and law incorporated by reference, the custom binds the parties.[13] Nonmandatory Article 5 provisions still

---

8. § 5–102(a)(9).

9. § 5–102(a)(3).

10. § 5–102(a)(6).

11. Compare § 5–102(a)(6) with § 1–201(16).

12. These and other nonvariable provisions will be considered in 8–4, *infra.*

13. Such conflicts should be few and far between, as the comment to 5–101 states: "Article 5 is consistent with and

apply to the letter of credit transaction if they do not conflict with a UCP provision.[14]

Courts sometimes read specific customs and practices into particular letter of credit arrangements. It would be natural for courts to apply Article 1's section on course of dealing and usage of trade in the letter of credit context,[15] especially in domestic transactions. Moreover, court decisions must serve as a source of gap-filler law under Article 5 as well, for the Article does not fill every conceivable gap in a letter of credit arrangement.

Besides Article 5, the agreement of the parties, customs and usage, and court decisions on letters of credit, there are still other possible sources of law. Comment 2 to section 5–103 notes that "Article 5 is supplemented by Section 1–103 and, through it, by many rules of statutory and common law." Moreover, Articles 3 and 4 of the UCC apply to rights and liabilities on a documentary draft, and either Article 7 or the Federal Bill of Lading Act may apply to documents of title involved in a letter of credit transaction. Article 9 will usually govern any security aspects of letter of credit arrangements.

Applicable Uniform Commercial Code law, including Article 5, is generally uniform from state to state. Hence, there are few statutory choice of law problems when a letter of credit transaction has contacts with more than one state.

Article 5 deals explicitly with the choice of law issue. Section 5–116 reads in full as follows:

(a) The liability of an issuer, nominated person, or adviser for action or omission is governed by the law of the jurisdiction chosen by an agreement in the form of a record signed or otherwise authenticated by the affected parties in the manner provided in Section 5–104 or by a provision in that person's letter of credit, confirmation, or other undertaking. The jurisdiction whose law is chosen need not bear any relation to the transaction.

(b) Unless subsection (a) applies, the liability of an issuer, nominated person, or adviser for action or omission is governed by the law of the jurisdiction in which the person is located. The person is considered to be located at the address indicated in the person's undertaking. If more than one address is indicated, the issuer, confirmer, or other person is considered to be located at the address from which the person's undertak-

---

was influenced by the rules in the existing version of the UCP."

14. Integrated Measurement Systems, Inc. v. International Commercial Bank, 757 F.Supp. 938, 14 UCC2d 1167

(N.D.Ill.1991) (bank bound by both UCP 8 and pre-revision UCC 5–107 when provisions are not conflicting).

15. § 1–303.

ing was issued. For the purpose of jurisdiction, choice of law, and recognition of interbranch letters of credit, but not enforcement of a judgment, all branches of a bank are considered separate juridical entities and a bank is considered to be located at the place where its relevant branch is considered to be located under this subsection.

(c) Except as otherwise provided in this subsection, the liability of an issuer, nominated person, or adviser is governed by any rules of custom or practice, such as the Uniform Customs and Practice for Documentary Credits, to which the letter of credit, confirmation, or other undertaking is expressly made subject. If (i) this article would govern the liability of an issuer, nominated person, or adviser under subsection (a) or (b), (ii) the relevant undertaking incorporates rules of custom or practice, and (iii) there is conflict between this article and those rules as applied to that undertaking, those rules govern except to the extent of any conflict with the nonvariable provisions specified in Section 5–103(c).

(d) If there is conflict between this article and Article 3, 4, 4A, or 9, this article governs.

(e) The forum for settling disputes arising out of an undertaking within this article may be chosen in the manner and with the binding effect that governing law may be chosen in accordance with subsection (a).

Section 5–116 gives the parties nearly boundless freedom to choose the law that governs and the forum where they will litigate. Subsection (a) broadly indorses the parties' choice; the jurisdiction chosen need not bear any relation to the transaction. For example, an issuer in Alabama and an applicant in Mississippi can choose the law of New York even though neither the applicant, issuer nor the beneficiary has any association with New York. Note, too, that the section provides a relatively detailed set of rules to determine the "location" of the bank, a question that can present considerable difficulty in the case of a multi-branch or multi-national bank.

The references in subsection (c) to Customs and Practice may seem out of place in a choice of law provision. That reference would have fit better in section 5–103 on variation by agreement, but the friends of the UCP, particularly the United States Council on International Banking (USCIB), argued strongly for the UCP's inclusion under the choice of law section. The reference in 5–116 is a symbolic recognition that, when incorporated, the UCP has the force of law.

Sometimes the express terms of the letter of credit and any relevant agreement will be wholly silent as to the UCP or any other applicable body of law. When this is so, the first issue will be whether relevant course of dealing or usage of trade makes the UCP applicable "in whole or in part." The issue will be one of fact, in light of Code definitions of course of dealing and usage of trade in section 1–303.

Because a large share of all letters of credit are written in international transactions, there is more potential for choice of law arguments here than in almost any area governed by the Uniform Commercial Code. Two cases exemplify the divergence which can occur on the choice of law issue. In *J. Zeevi*,[16] the letter of credit became unenforceable in Uganda by governmental fiat (Idi Amin was angry). Using conventional but rather chauvinistic interest analysis, the court found that New York had an overriding interest as "financial capital of the world" to protect the parties' expectations. In Chuidian v. Philippine National Bank,[17] a federal court in California applied the "most significant relationship" test to find that the foreign law applied under similar circumstances. State-owned Philippine National Bank issued an irrevocable letter of credit to Chuidian who did business in California. The letter was payable at the bank's Los Angeles branch. After President Marcos was overthrown, the government ordered the bank not to pay. Concluding that the Los Angeles branch acted only as an advising bank (and not as a confirming bank with its own obligation), the majority found the place of performance to be Manila. Furthermore, the court found that the Philippines was the jurisdiction with "the most significant relationship to the issues and parties in the case."

These brief descriptions only highlight the divergence problem. There is considerable scholarly literature on choice of law in letters of credit,[18] but we decline to wrestle with the cases and concepts. We justify our hesitance partly because current Article 5 provides no explicit conflict rules[19] and partly out of a fear that even an extensive treatment would not make the rules more certain.

---

16. J. Zeevi and Sons, Ltd. v. Grindlays Bank (Uganda) Ltd., 37 N.Y.2d 220, 371 N.Y.S.2d 892, 333 N.E.2d 168 (1975), cert. denied, 423 U.S. 866, 96 S.Ct. 126, 46 L.Ed.2d 95 (1975). The court also stated that the governmental action was of no force in New York and that the federal act of state doctrine was inapplicable.

17. 976 F.2d 561, 18 UCC2d 1006 (9th Cir.1992).

18. Backus, Foreign Loans, Letters of Credit and Conflict of Laws, 73 Banking L.J. 85 (1956); Funk, Letters of Credit: UCC Article Five and the Uniform Customs and Practice, 11 Howard L.J. 88 (1965); Gewolb, The Law Applicable to International Letters of Credit, 11 Vill.L.Rev. 742 (1966); Note, The Conflicts of Law in International Letters of Credit, 24 Va.J.Int'l Law 171 (1983).

19. Gewolb, The Law Applicable to International Letters of Credit, 11 Vill. L.Rev. 742, 753 (1966). See also Bergsten, A New Regime for International Independent Guarantees and Standby Letters of Credit: The UNCITRAL Draft Convention on Guaranty Letters, 27 Int'l Law. 859 (1993)(discusses choice of law provision in UNCITRAL Draft Convention on Guaranty Letters).

§ 8–4   Establishing, Modifying and Terminating the Letter of Credit

How is a valid irrevocable letter of credit set up under Article 5? When does it become "issued?"

a.   Validity of Letters of Credit and Their Terms

Questions whether a document is a letter of credit or whether a letter has been properly issued are rare. For the most part, letters of credit are stereotypical documents printed by banks or stored in their computers. They announce explicitly that they are letters of credit and, having been drafted by bank lawyers, have all of the attributes necessary under the Uniform Commercial Code, UCP, and under any other applicable law.

Occasionally a stray document is executed by a bank, usually an unsophisticated one, and there is dispute whether it is a letter of credit or whether it is merely some other form of engagement to which different rules of law would apply. Beyond the basic scope requirements listed above in § 26–3(c), Article 5 specifies several formal requirements for a valid letter of credit: the letter must (1) "be issued in any form that is a record," and (2) be "authenticated (i) by a signature or (ii) in accordance with the agreement of the parties or the standard practice referred to in Section 5–108(e)."[1] Notably, these definitions do not require that the document actually be titled "Letter of Credit," and courts have even held documents titled "Guarantee" to be letters of credit where Article 5 or the UCP apply.

The goal is to permit letters of credit in writing, in electronic format, or in any other format that is a "record," i.e., "information that is inscribed on a tangible medium or that is stored in an electronic or other medium and is retrievable in perceivable form."[2] Thus, a letter of credit transmitted electronically from a bank to an adviser and stored in the adviser's computer memory but never printed out would meet the formal requirements of 5–104 (provided the electronic message was properly authenticated) because the computer could be stimulated to show or print out the letter of credit in a "perceivable form."

The pre-revision Code could have been interpreted to prohibit electronic letters. While section 5–104 is not quite *carte blanche*, it is close. It will grant legal effect to letters in every imaginable media provided the letters of credit are authenticated and constitute a record.

Observe that no consideration is necessary[3] and that the credit

§ 8–4

1. § 5–104.

2. § 5–102(a)(14).

3. § 5–105.

itself need not be irrevocable.[4] Comparable provisions are found in the UCP. Article 2 of the UCP provides:

> Credit means any arrangement, however named or described, that is irrevocable and thereby constitutes a definite undertaking of the issuing bank to honour a complying presentation.

The cases that have dealt with whether a particular document or engagement is a letter of credit tend to be the quirky outgrowth of random practices by ill-informed or careless bank officers. To appreciate these cases, consider a few examples.

In United Shippers Co-op v. Soukup,[5] the bank extended a $200,000 line of credit to a buyer to cover crop and operating expenses. In May the buyer and the bank signed a document drafted by the seller in which the buyer stated: "I intend to purchase the following products from United Shippers Cooperative." The document also stated: "To: United Shippers Cooperative. This is to inform you that we have set up an operating credit line to finance the above purchases." That statement was signed by the bank president. Ultimately the buyer exhausted the $200,000 line of credit, but none of the money was used to pay United Shippers. The bank refused to extend more than $200,000. When seller sued, the court properly concluded that the document was not a letter of credit under Article 5, for there was no direct promise by the bank to pay the seller.

In Hendry Construction Company v. Bank of Hattiesburg,[6] a letter to Hendry advising that the Producer's Marketing Association "has applied to Farmers Home Administration for a loan in the amount of $800,000 with Deposit Guarantee National Bank of Hattiesburg acting as the lender" and stating that Producers Association "has asked us to set aside $275,000 for plant renovation" and stating further that "[t]his letter will act as confirmation to you that when all conditions have been met and approval is granted by the Farmers Home Administration for us to fund the loan, a check in the amount of $275,000 will be made payable to Hendry Construction" was not a letter of credit. The court held that this letter merely advised Mr. Hendry and was not a direct promise to advance funds. Cases like *United Shippers Co-op* and *Hendry* are probably sports.

b. *Issuance of the Letter of Credit*

Section 5–106 on issuing, et al., adopts the practice of letter issuers that regards a letter of credit as "issued and enforceable"

---

4. But the default position under both the UCC and UCP is that a credit is irrevocable, unless otherwise stated. 5–106(a), UCP 2.

5. 459 N.W.2d 343, 14 UCC2d 160 (Minn.App.1990).

6. 562 So.2d 100, 13 UCC2d 489 (Miss.1990).

against the issuer when it is "sent" or otherwise transmitted to an adviser or beneficiary.[7] Thus, it is possible to have a binding letter of credit that has never been received by the beneficiary or adviser, but that would be quite unlikely.

Section 5–106 also establishes the credit simultaneously for the applicant and the beneficiary. Regardless of whether the party attempting to invoke the letter of credit is an applicant, issuer or beneficiary, the letter of credit is enforceable when sent.

The primary effect of a letter of credit's issuance is that it can no longer be modified after that point without consent of the beneficiary, issuer, or confirmer whose rights or obligations would be affected by the proposed modification. Note, however, that Comment 2 to 5–106 leaves open the possibility for consent by implication if a party subsequently acts in conformity with the modification.

Does 5–106 mean that once an irrevocable letter of credit is established "as regards the beneficiary," the issuer cannot unilaterally cancel the credit for mutual mistake or fraud? What if its applicant fraudulently induced the establishment of the credit in the first place? The issuer is bound,[8] and presumably it is bound even though the issuer notifies the beneficiary of cancellation long before any reliance by the beneficiary.[9] Does 5–106 also mean that once an irrevocable letter of credit is established as regards the applicant only, the issuer may not unilaterally cancel it for fraud, duress, or mistake? What if the issuer retrieves the letter and thus keeps the applicant (or adviser) from putting it in the hands of a potentially relying beneficiary?

Under the pre–1995 version of Article 5, we think a cancellation would have been effective against the beneficiary in this scenario, as the letter would only be "established" (that version's comparable term for "issued" today) as to the beneficiary when he actually received the letter. The version of Article 5 which is currently in effect, however, is clear to say that the letter of credit is "issued" when it is sent or "otherwise transmitted" to the adviser or beneficiary. A quick look at 1–201(a)(36) confirms that simply putting something in the mail constitutes "sending." Therefore, an issuer's ability to recall a mistaken letter of credit is significantly reduced today—especially in cases where the letter is

7. In re AutoStyle Plastics, Inc., 222 B.R. 812, 36 UCC 2d 172 (Bankr. W.D. Mich. 1998). Although the court was actually interpreting old 5–106, the result would be the same under the current version of 5–106(a).

8. Continental Grain Co. v. Meridien Int'l Bank, Ltd., 894 F.Supp. 654 (S.D.N.Y. 1995). Although the court did not actually find that fraud was present in the subject transaction, dicta indicated that fraud would not have kept the letter of credit from being validly issued.

9. § 5–108(a).

sent electronically, where it would be impossible to recall once the issuer hits the "send" button on his computer.

c. Modification of the Letter of Credit

Once issued, how is a letter of credit modified? Section 5–104 says that the same formalities that applied for a letter of credit to be issued also must be met for that letter to be amended or cancelled. Therefore, one must have the modification embodied in a "record" that is then authenticated by a "signature or in accordance with the agreement of the parties or the standard practice referred to in 5–108(e)."

Section 5–106(b) states whose consent is required for a modification. Amendments, cancellation and the like are binding on beneficiaries, applicants, confirmers or issuers only to the extent each individually agrees. Thus, if the applicant and issuer decide to cancel a letter of credit, the beneficiary is unaffected by the cancellation. Likewise, if the applicant and issuer decide to amend the letter of credit but do not get the agreement of the beneficiary or confirmer, the beneficiary is free to present the documents under the original terms and the confirmer or issuer is bound to honor.[10]

Note, however, that this does not mean that the consent of all possible parties to a letter of credit is required for all modifications. As an example, consider Banca del Sempione v. Provident Bank of Maryland.[11] There, Provident Bank of Maryland issued a multi-year letter of credit to benefit a company called Suriel Finance. Manufacturers Hanover Trust subsequently confirmed the letter of credit for the first year of its existence. Initially, the letter provided that it was in an amount of $750,000 that would revolve on an annual basis, so long as the applicant replenished the collateral pledged to Provident after any draw. This was unsatisfactory to the end transferee of the letter of credit, so Provident and Suriel allegedly agreed to modify the letter of credit such that it would be revolving without requiring the applicant to post additional collateral in the event of a draw. The parties did not obtain Manufacturers Hanover's consent as confirmer.

The federal district court in Maryland held that the assignment was invalid under UCP 10b because the beneficiary did not get the confirmer's consent. In reversing, the Fourth Circuit noted that Manufacturers Hanover's obligation under the letter of credit was limited to the one year period which it had confirmed at the time. Since any effect from the revolving clause's modification would only be felt in future years, Manufacturers Hanover's rights were not

---

10. Peled v. Meridian Bank, 710 A.2d 620, 35 UCC2d 623 (Sup. Ct. Pa. 1998). Although the court was actually interpreting old 5–106, the result would be the same under the current version of 5–106(b).

11. 75 F.3d 951 (4th Cir. 1996).

affected, and their consent was not required for the modification to be effective. The Fourth Circuit then remanded the matter to the district court for consideration of whether the disputed amendment was binding.

What about a complicated case where the actual applicant of the letter of credit is merely itself a supplier of the underlying goods to another party?[12] Should the end user's approval be required for any modifications to the letter, especially if the end user pledged collateral to the issuer in order to secure the letter of credit? On these facts, the Ohio Supreme Court held, and we believe correctly, that the end user was not the "customer" under Article 5 (note that this was a pre-revision case and used the old term "customer" instead of the current equivalent, "applicant").

Note also that an issuer may refuse to modify even though the applicant and beneficiary both seek the modification. For example, the applicant may have become insolvent and willing to waive defects in documents (and presumably the goods) in order to get goods for a quick resale. But the bank will be concerned about reimbursement.[13] Since a modification binds only the parties that have agreed to it, the issuer may be hesitant to recognize any modification where there are third parties who may have rights based on the letter of credit. For example, a bank should hesitate to cancel a letter of credit at the request of the applicant when it knows that the letter has been confirmed and is fearful that documents may already have been negotiated to the confirmer.

Missing from the 5–106 list of protected parties are assignees of proceeds and transferees of letters of credit. Assignees of proceeds are intentionally excluded. They should understand that their rights depend upon the continued rights of their assignors. As persons not protected under 5–106, their rights can be amended out of existence by the assignors. When that happens an assignee may have a cause of action against its assignor, but that cause of action will be of little help if the assignor is insolvent.

Although a transferee of a letter of credit (as opposed to an assignee of proceeds) is not mentioned in section 5–106, the transferee's rights will usually be protected. If the transferee qualifies under section 5–112, it will be a "beneficiary" under 5–102(a)(3)

---

12. Mantua Mfg. Co. v. Commerce Exchange Bank, 75 Ohio St.3d 1, 661 N.E.2d 161, 29 UCC2d 349 (1996).

13. AMF Head Sports Wear, Inc. v. Ray Scott's All–American Sports Club, Inc., 448 F.Supp. 222, 23 UCC 990 (D.Ariz.1978) (issuer not bound by modification agreed to by applicant and beneficiary); Chase Manhattan Bank v. Equibank, 550 F.2d 882, 21 UCC 247 (3d Cir.1977) (modification good against issuer may not be good against applicant when issuer seeks reimbursement); National Bank & Trust Co. v. J.L.M. Int'l, Inc., 421 F.Supp. 1269, 20 UCC 492 (S.D.N.Y.1976) (modification by issuer and applicant repudiation generating beneficiary cause of action).

and will enjoy the rights of a beneficiary under 5–106. We deal with the transfer of the beneficiary's rights in 8–12.

d. Termination of the Letter of Credit

A letter of credit can be terminated by revoking a revocable credit or by expiration of the letter of credit before presentation. Because letters are now presumptively irrevocable under Article 5[14] the careful drafter need only state that the letter is revocable if that is the parties' intent. Article 2 of the UCP concurs. Dicta in one case recited that a revocable letter of credit is "an illusory contract," however.[15] That is wrong. Such a letter is neither a contract nor illusory. It is not illusory, for it cannot be revoked after innocent third parties have negotiated or honored drafts under it before they receive notice of revocation.

Under section 5–106(b), an established revocable credit is excepted from the usual requirement that a beneficiary, applicant, issuer or confirmer whose rights or obligations would be affected by a modification give its consent. However, section 5–106(b) requires the issuer to pay innocent third parties who have negotiated or honored drafts drawn on the revocable letter of credit before receiving notice of the revocation.[16] UCP 10c is comparable.

A letter of credit is also terminated upon its expiration if no qualifying documents have been presented before that date.[17] Article 42(b) of the UCP provides that "documents must be presented on or before [the] expiry date."[18] Should the expiry date pass without a complying presentation, issuer's duty to pay terminates. No later documents, not even documents drawn to perfection, will revive the duty. On this score, courts stand united: the arrival of beneficiary's documents must comply strictly with the letter's time and place requirements. In B.E.I. International, Inc. v. Thai Military Bank,[19] the beneficiary failed to have its letter of credit extended before it drew. An earlier draw had been "suspended" by the beneficiary and the court interpreted the earlier draw to be canceled by the passage of time or act of the beneficiary. The court held that the second draw after the extended expiration date was invalid.

Woe to the beneficiary who relies on the mails. In Consolidated Aluminum v. Bank of Virginia,[20] a delay in the mails caused the

---

14. 5–106(a).

15. West Va. Housing Dev. Fund v. Sroka, 415 F.Supp. 1107, 20 UCC 154 (W.D.Pa.1976).

16. See § 5–106, Comment 3.

17. For timing rules, see UCP 42–45. See also UCP 36 (excusing bank's duty to honor letter of credit which expires during "force majeure" interruption of banking business).

18. See related discussion on non-documentary conditions in Section 8–6(g), *supra*.

19. 978 F.2d 440, 19 UCC2d 256 (8th Cir.1992).

20. 544 F.Supp. 386, 34 UCC 946 (D.Md.1982), aff'd, 704 F.2d 136, 1 UCC2d 193 (4th Cir.1983).

papers to reach issuer four days after the letter's expiry date. The court faulted beneficiary for not hiring a private overnight courier to meet the deadline.

Expiration deadlines present a special problem when standby letters of credit are used to back up obligations of long-term or indefinite duration. Issuers do not like to have a standby letter outstanding for more than three years. How can a beneficiary avoid a gap in protection when a one-year standby letter backs up customer's obligation on a ten-year promissory note? On an appealed judgment that may take anywhere from six months to three years for appeal, rehearing, and perhaps certiorari? A beneficiary might see to it that the underlying bargain compels applicant to get the standby letter renewed and to do so at least 60 days before the letter's expiration. Since the failure to extend the letter of credit will not itself be default on the underlying obligation, it is necessary to make the letter payable on the presentation of documents that either (a) show default or other necessary condition, or (b) show that the date 60 days prior to expiration has passed without renewal. Typically such a letter of credit would have an "evergreen" clause, sometimes called an "extend or pay" clause. That clause might read as follows:

> It is a condition of this letter of credit that it shall be deemed automatically extended without amendment for one year from the present or any future expiry date hereof, unless thirty days prior to any such date we notify you by registered letter that we elect not to consider this letter of credit renewed for any such additional period.

At least one court has held that such notice from the issuer must be "clear and unambiguous."[21] The letter of credit will have to have an additional clause to provide that it can be drawn by the beneficiary's presenting an appropriate draft or demand together with certification that the issuer has failed to renew the letter of credit.

Section 5–106(c) also provides expiration dates as a matter of law for letters of credit in two circumstances. In the absence of an expiration date, a letter of credit expires one year after its stated date of issuance or, if no date of issuance is stated, one year after the date on which it is actually issued. Under 5–106(d) a letter of credit stating that it is perpetual expires five years after its stated date of issuance or, if none is stated, after the date on which it is issued.

It is possible that a clever issuer's lawyer might argue that letters of credit containing evergreen clauses are effectively "perpetual," and are thus limited to a five year duration under 5–106(d)

---

21. 3Com Corp. v. Banco de Brasil, 2 F.Supp.2d 452, 458 (S.D.N.Y. 1998).

regardless of the issuing bank giving notice of nonrenewal.[22] In our opinion, such an argument should be rejected in favor of the parties' ability to contract for an evergreen clause if they so desire. 5–106(d) should apply only to letters that claim to be "perpetual."

e. *Variation by Agreement*

Freedom of contract is the rule in Article 5. The real question is whether there are any exceptions to that rule.

First, consider section 5–108(a) dealing with the issuer's obligation to honor a presentation, which provides:

> (a) * * * an issuer shall honor a presentation that * * * appears on its face strictly to comply with the terms and conditions of the letter of credit.
>
> * * *
>
> (f) An issuer is not responsible for: (1) the performance or nonperformance of the underlying contract, arrangement, or transaction. * * *

A term that altered the issuer's duty to honor might be enforceable and yet "invalid" in the sense that it would change the document into something other than a letter of credit. For example, a promise that the issuer would pay only upon "default" by the applicant would make the agreement something other than a letter of credit, take the parties entirely out of Article 5 and leave them in the common law of contract or suretyship.

In our opinion certain disclaimers that are commonly found in reimbursement agreements do not pass muster under 1–302, which restricts parties from disclaiming the "obligations of good faith, diligence, reasonableness and care prescribed by the UCC." Such questionable disclaimers require the applicant to reimburse the issuer unless the issuer is guilty of bad faith or gross negligence. We believe that such a blanket disclaimer would not be a setting of "standards by which the performance of those obligations is to be measured" under 1–302(b).

Whether the issuer could deprive the beneficiary and the applicant from any remedy provided under 5–111 is an interesting question that is not directly answered by Article 5. Because the market would probably not tolerate letters of credit that explicitly disclaim an issuer's entire liability for wrongful dishonor, that issue is not likely to arise. However, it is plausible and even likely that the reimbursement agreement between the applicant and the issuer will contain limitations of liability. Certainly an issuer could limit

---

22. At least one case arising before the 1995 Article 5 revisions held that evergreen clauses made letters of credit available for an indefinite period. *See* B.E.I. Int'l, Inc. v. Thai Military Bank, 978 F.2d 440 (8th Cir. 1992).

its liability in that contract, but we wonder whether the entire removal of liability for breach of the contract might not render it illusory and might not therefore deprive the issuer also of the benefits of the contract. The Comment to section 2–719 in the analogous context in Article 2 might be brought to bear:

> However, it is the very essence of a sales contract that at least minimum adequate remedies be available. If the parties intend to conclude a contract for sale within this Article they must accept the legal consequence that there be at least a fair quantum of remedy for breach of the obligations or duties outlined in the contract. * * *

So conceivably the issuer could get away with a complete disclaimer of liability, but it may risk a finding of unconscionability (from the common law) or that its contract was illusory and therefore does not entitle it to reimbursement or to the other rights commonly given.

Beyond those few rights that may not be modified, the parties may vary the rights arising from Article 5 under 5–103(c).

The current version of Article 5 is even more generous towards freedom of contract than pre–1995 Article 5. The duty of "care" in old 5–109 that used to apply to the issuer's examination of documents presented under the letter of credit has been removed from its successor 5–108. Current 5–108 imposes a larger duty (the duty not to pay if the documents fail strictly to comply), but since it is not a duty of "care," the parties can clearly change it.

However, current section 5–103(c) restricts the power of the issuer to escape from its liability by boilerplate disclaimers in the reimbursement agreement.[23] Agreements that free the issuer from "all liability except for gross negligence" would be invalidated by 5–103(c). As the Comments to 5–103(c) disclose, the goal of the section is more procedural than substantive. Its purpose is to force the issuer to say in plain words what it will and will not do, so the applicant can decide whether it wishes to deal with that particular issuer on those terms. If the terms are clear enough, the issuer can free itself entirely from examining the documents or can modify its examination obligation in any one of a hundred ways.

§ 8–5 Issuer's Duty to Honor Beneficiary's Draft

The beneficiary's presentation is the legal and practical centerpiece of letter of credit practice. Proper presentation activates the issuer's duty to pay; improper presentation authorizes or, if the applicant does not waive, requires, the issuer to dishonor.

---

23. "A term in an agreement or undertaking generally excusing liability or generally limiting remedies for failure to perform obligations is not sufficient to vary obligations prescribed by this article." 5–103(c).

An issuer's duty actually begins toward its applicant. Section 5–108(e) requires an issuer to "observe [the] standard practice of financial institutions that regularly issue letters of credit." UCP 13a provides that banks must act "with reasonable care * * * as determined by international standard banking practice as reflected in these Articles." But if a strictly conforming presentation is timely and the letter has not been fully drawn, section 5–108(a) requires the issuer to pay. Absent the issuer's showing that these conditions have not been met, issuer wrongfully dishonors if it refuses to pay.[1]

The independence principle refines an issuer's duty: the issuer must deal only in documents. The letter of credit must spell out what documents must be presented, what they must recite, and in what medium (written, electronic or otherwise). Events or circumstances outside the presented documents and the letter itself must not determine whether the issuer has a duty to pay in any given case. Unless certain narrow exceptions apply, the issuer must disregard what it cannot glean from carefully examining the face of required documents as presented. Beyond that examination, an issuer has no duty to look deeper for forgeries, falsifications, inaccuracies, or other defects in the documents. Nor is an issuer bound to look beyond the four corners of presented documents for facts that might cure discrepancies, omissions, or inconsistencies in the papers.

To put it as courts often do, the issuer has neither the duty nor the right to police the underlying bargain between the beneficiary and applicant. Under 5–108(b) and UCP 14, the issuer has only a short time to decide whether to honor. Issuer thus does not commit to the time-consuming and risky business of deciding what is a material discrepancy, or what significance should be given to non-banking norms and practices within beneficiary's and applicant's circles. For the limited fee it receives, issuer commits only to the ministerial duty of checking presented documents carefully against the letter. Though this duty runs to the applicant and beneficiary under 5–108 and comment 7, it always remains separate from both the beneficiary-applicant contract and the applicant-issuer reimbursement agreement.[2]

In most cases, the issuer's basis for dishonor will be noncomplying presentation. However, the defect in the document may not be the principal motivation for the issuer's refusal to pay. Instead the issuer's valued applicant may have filled the president's ear with reasons why the beneficiary is a scoundrel and why, if the

§ 8–5

1. Apart from the Code's bar against disclaimer of good faith and reasonable care (see 1–302(b)), by agreement the parties could enlarge or narrow the applicant's claim upon wrongful dishonor.

2. See 5–108(f)(1); UCP 4.

issuer pays, the money will never be seen again. Or the applicant may have filed bankruptcy and the issuer believes that reimbursement will fail. Either way, the issuer may examine the documents microscopically and may assert small discrepancies to excuse its duty to pay.

a. Whether the Documents Comply—The Strict Compliance Standard

Prior to the 1995 revisions to Article 5, determining whether a presentation complied with the terms of the letter of credit was not always easy. The drafters of original Article 5 deliberately chose to leave this matter to case law and practice;[3] for the first time, in 1995, the UCC specified a "strict" standard for compliance.[4] A small minority of pre-revision cases held that a beneficiary's "reasonable" or "substantial" compliance would do, but 5–108 and comment 1 explicitly overrule this view. In an attempt to create even more certainty with letter of credit transactions, 5–108(e) states that determining what constitutes "standard practice" is a "matter of interpretation for the court."

The UCP still does not express a choice in explicit terms, although Articles 2 and 14d refer to compliance with international banking standards, which arguably constitutes strict compliance in today's world. Certain sections of the UCP, such as Article 18 on commercial invoices and the practice under the UCP are also widely interpreted to indorse the "strict compliance" standard.

Despite the fact that Article 5 adopted the strict compliance standard, the comments explicitly embrace the holding in New Braunfels Nat. Bank v. Odiorne:[5] "strict compliance means something less than absolute, perfect compliance." Visionaries claimed that the explicit adoption of the strict compliance doctrine and careful reference to standard practice would cause litigation over wrongful dishonor to wither away. Realists were skeptical, and that view appears to have been correct in looking at the number of reported cases where parties have questioned whether a presentation strictly complied with the letter's requirements. One should not underestimate lawyers' cleverness; as we suspected in the previous edition of this treatise, yesterday's controversies about strict versus substantial compliance turned into today's argument about the meaning of "standard practice" and about the difference between strict compliance and perfect compliance. No statute or published practice, however detailed, can completely resolve legiti-

---

3. See 5–108(a) and (e) and Comment 8.

4. § 5–108(a) and (e).

5. New Braunfels Nat. Bank v. Odiorne, 780 S.W.2d 313, 10 UCC2d 1352 (Tex.App.1989).

mate arguments among document checkers, much less disagreements between plaintiffs' and defendants' lawyers.

Following the UCP, section 5–108(g) directs the issuer to disregard nondocumentary conditions. The comments to 5–108(g) and 5–102 differentiate between fundamental nondocumentary conditions and conditions which are not fundamental. If the letter is premised on a fundamental nondocumentary condition, then it is not a letter of credit, and ordinary principles of contract law should apply to the transaction because it is completely outside Article 5. If the nondocumentary conditions are not fundamental, then those conditions should be disregarded. If a letter of credit provided that the issuer should pay upon "applicant's default in the underlying contract," that would not be a nondocumentary condition that would be so substantial that the undertaking would not constitute a letter of credit and would not be governed by Article 5. Comment 6 to 5–102 also clarifies this issue:

> When a document labeled a letter of credit requires the issuer to pay not upon the presentation of documents, but upon the determination of an extrinsic fact such as applicant's failure to perform a construction contract, and where that condition appears on its face to be fundamental and would, if ignored, leave no obligation to the issuer under the document labeled letter of credit, the issuer's undertaking is not a letter of credit. It is probably some form of suretyship or other contractual arrangement [such as a secondary guarantee] and may be enforceable as such. * * * Therefore, engagements whose fundamental term requires an issuer to look beyond documents and beyond conventional reference to the clock, calendar, and practices concerning the form of various documents are not governed by Article 5. Although Section 5–108(g) recognizes that certain nondocumentary conditions can be included in a letter of credit without denying the document the status of letter of credit, that section does not reach cases where the nondocumentary condition is a fundamental part of the issuer's obligation. * * *

In addition to setting standards for dealing with nondocumentary conditions, specifying the notice requirements on dishonor, and stating the legal result that follows failure to comply with those notice requirements, section 5–108 contains the routine disclaimer concerning knowledge of usage in a particular trade (in (f)) and carries forward the obligation to return documents upon dishonor (in (h)).

Subsection 5–108(i) ties up a few loose ends. It states the issuer's right to reimbursement (as if that were not already covered by agreement). Most important, it cuts off an honoring issuer's right of recourse under 3–414 or 3–415 on a draft presented to it. It also bars the issuer from recovery when the issuer has paid despite an apparent discrepancy in the documents. In effect, 5–108(i)(4) closes the back door that an issuer who has missed a discrepancy might otherwise use. Subsection (i)(4) keeps the issuer from dressing its discrepancy argument in clothes of restitution.

Subsection (i)(5) states a final and mysterious consequence of honor. It is unremarkable that honor discharges the obligation of the issuer. The interesting part of (i)(5) is the "unless" clause: there is discharge "unless the issuer honored a presentation in which a required signature of a beneficiary was forged." Beneficiaries expect the issuer to remain liable even though the issuer has paid a third party because of that person's forgery of the beneficiary's signature. This is so even though the issuer might be entitled to reimbursement from its applicant notwithstanding the forgery and to reimbursement a second time from its applicant on a later but legitimate draw.

Note the difference from the case where the issuer pays the beneficiary over forged documents. In that case the issuer is discharged and typically the applicant must reimburse the issuer. In effect, 5–108(i)(5) is a special rule for draws on the letter of credit by a stranger.

In summary, revised 5–108 is the guts of the new Article 5. It is complex and detailed; it bears close study by every user of the Article.

b. Applicant's Ability to Waive Document Non–Conformance

When the beneficiary is unable to present documents on time or when some of the documents contain a description that is not consistent with the description of the goods in the letter, the issuer may consult the applicant to seek a waiver. If the applicant authorizes payment, however, the issuer will typically pay despite the defects. This, of course, is nothing more than a modification of the agreement to which all the parties—the applicant, issuer, and beneficiary—have agreed. It may be sensible for the applicant and issuer to tell the beneficiary that it has "agreed to pay despite deficiencies," but there are few interesting legal issues involved in such a straightforward transaction.

A recurring question prior to the 1995 revision of Article 5 was whether the applicant's waiver in one case (and the issuer's payment in that case without notifying the beneficiary that the presentation was defective) was a silent modification of the terms of a letter of credit. If so, the beneficiary would have earned a right to payment on its next identical, but still defective, presentation. Most pre-revision courts found that the waiver of a defect in one presentation was not a waiver of that defect in another, and comment 7 to

5–108 concurs. The message for the beneficiary is to beware. If the beneficiary makes repeated presentations of the same kind, it will be wise to determine whether its early presentations were paid because they were complying or because of the applicant's waiver.

Note finally that the issuer has no duty to seek a waiver from the applicant.[6] Technically it is the issuer and the issuer alone who determines whether the presentation is complying. Even though the issuer may use its discretion to ask whether the applicant wishes to waive, there is no duty to ask. Under the terms of both the revised UCC and the UCP the beneficiary has no right to expect that the issuer's discretion will be routinely exercised in its favor. So, the issuer is not obligated to honor a discrepant presentation following a waiver by the applicant and can still exercise its option to require strict compliance.[7]

PROBLEM

A letter of credit calls for "Imported 100% acrylic yarn." On five occasions seller presents invoices that describe the product as "acrylic yarn." In each case, unbeknownst to the seller, Issuer asks buyer to waive the discrepancies in the presentation.

1. In the first four cases the buyer waives, but in the last case the "buyer" is the trustee in bankruptcy because buyer has filed for bankruptcy. In the last case the buyer refuses to waive and the bank dishonors. The seller argues that the bank is bound by its prior behavior. Who wins?

   Bank, comment 7 to 5–108.

2. Assume that applicant/buyer asked the bank to waive in the fifth case too. Bank refuses (because it is afraid that applicant/buyer will not reimburse it). Seller sues. Who wins?

   Bank, comment 7 to 5–108.

---

c. Ambiguities in the Terms of the Letter of Credit

Compliance arguments are sometimes exacerbated by ambiguity in the letter of credit. When so, no compliance standard will help until the letter's terms are cleared up. Courts usually supply the needed clarity through ordinary rules of judicial interpretation or construction.[8]

---

6. See comment 2 to 5–108 ("the decision to honor rests with the issuer and it has no duty to seek a waiver") and UCP 16b.

7. *See* comment 7 to 5–108.

8. When the letter's terms are precise and an ambiguity appears in a *presented document,* the question is not how to resolve the ambiguity but whether the presented document with the am-

Classic ambiguity occurs when, with equal plausibility, words can be read more than one way. Consider, for example, a letter of credit stating:

> This credit is revolving and becomes reinstated only by the issuing bank's authenticated amendment for further two times at the same amount and same quantity for shipment during July and August, 1988 * * *.[9]

The beneficiary successfully argued that the language was ambiguous since it indicated "automatic" revolution as well as "conditional" revolution. The ambiguity led the court to deny summary judgment.

Another standby letter stated its maximum drawing amount like this:

> This credit shall be automatically reinstated from time to time for any sum or sums up to $145,000.00 upon presentation of described documents.[10]

Did this mean "any sum or sums up to $145,000" in the aggregate, or "any sum or sums up to $145,000" per presentation? If "in the aggregate," then beneficiary could present multiple partial drafts totaling $145,000. But if "per presentation," then beneficiary could present (as beneficiary actually did) several drafts, each up to $145,000. The court admitted extrinsic evidence to ascertain the parties' intent. Aided by this evidence, the court resolved the ambiguity against the party who created it.[11] Most often this will be the issuer (perhaps with the applicant's help) as author of the unclear language. But here it was the beneficiary who composed the muddy "$145,000" language.[12]

Ambiguity can arise from the use of inappropriate forms with language meant for other cases. In one case, for example, issuer wrote a standby letter of credit on a printed form designed for commercial letters. The standby letter was intended to back up a builder's obligation to maintain a Completion Assurance Fund for a federal apartment project. But the standby letter spoke of documents covering invoice value of merchandise to be described in an invoice as: Project #115–44050 LDP.[13] Worse, issuer dishonored for beneficiary's failure to accompany his draft with some document

biguity on its face strictly meets the concededly precise terms in the letter.

9. Timber Falling Consultants, Inc. v. General Bank, 751 F.Supp. 179, 13 UCC2d 1230 (D.Or.1990).

10. Philadelphia Gear Corp. v. FDIC, 751 F.2d 1131, 40 UCC 240, 242 (10th Cir.1984), rev'd on other grounds, 476 U.S. 426, 106 S.Ct. 1931, 90 L.Ed.2d 428 (1986).

11. *Id.* at 40 UCC at 249 and n.5.

12. See Hill v. Mercantile First Nat. Bank, 693 S.W.2d 285, 42 UCC 247, 249–50 (Mo.App.1985).

13. See East Girard Sav. Ass'n v. Citizens Nat. Bank & Trust Co., 593 F.2d 598, 26 UCC 475, 477 (5th Cir. 1979).

showing applicant-builder's default in the construction. The court found the dishonor wrongful.[14]

Finally, ambiguity may arise from the letter's inclusion of trade terms. Doubts may arise over their special meaning or how the parties understood them.

Sometimes parties claim "ambiguity" to open the door to testimony about intention. As evidence of the parties' "real" intent, issuer may try to exploit flaws in the letter's wording or may even try to dredge up matters outside the papers. Most courts repel these efforts either by finding no true ambiguity (thereby resolving the dispute without extrinsic evidence), or by resolving real doubts against the issuer as author of the letter's unclear language. After all, if the beneficiary must comply strictly, the letter of credit should tell precisely what is expected.

Beneficiaries too may cry "ambiguity" when their papers seem doomed to flunk strict compliance.[15] As with issuers' claims, most courts disregard false ambiguities and rigorously apply the strict compliance test.

§ 8–6 Compliance of Beneficiary's Presentation

The standard of "strict compliance" leaves "no room for documents which are almost the same or which will do just as well."[1] But even if one adopts the standard of strict compliance, there are still questions. Does a misspelled word or the abbreviation of a name "Company" to "Co." render a document noncomplying? What about words that accurately describe the commodity but are different from the words on the letter of credit? If the letter of credit calls for the Venus de Milo, will an invoice describing the commodity as "badly damaged statue" be satisfactory? Can raisins be described as shriveled grapes? These questions are not easy to answer and there are many more where they came from. This section identifies some of the compliance disputes from American cases of the last 40 years.

a. Description of Goods

When the letter of credit calls for an invoice covering goods, the invoice must describe the goods exactly as the letter prescribes. Under UCP 18c: "[t]he description of the goods ... in the commer-

---

14. *Id.* 26 UCC at 480. See 8–6(b), *infra* discussing Banco Espanol de Credito v. State Street Bank & Trust Co., 385 F.2d 230, 4 UCC 862 (1st Cir.1967).

15. Applicants as well may use this ploy when they wish to defeat issuer's reimbursement rights after issuer has honored wrongfully in applicant's view.

§ 8–6

1. Courts often quote this remark of Lord Sumner's from Equitable Trust Co. v. Dawson Partners, Ltd., 27 Lloyd's List Law Rep. 49, 52 (H.L.1927).

cial invoice must correspond with that appearing in the credit." Article 5 has no similar provision that is so specific, beyond the "strict compliance" standard of 5–108(a) discussed in § 8–5(a), *supra*.

In this category, courts face the issue whether minor variations in the invoice description should justify the issuer's dishonor. In general, courts do and should hold that insignificant deviations (Co. for Company) do not render documents noncomplying, even under the strictest standards. On the other hand, accurate but deviant description of goods ("raisins" as "shriveled grapes") do not comply under UCP 18c or under the provisions in the UCP and the UCC that states that the document examiner need not know the custom of any particular trade. The examiner is not expected to understand that description A is actually the same as description B in the farm or oil and gas business. For example, "Imported Acrylic Yarn" is not "100% Acrylic Yarn."[2] One letter spoke of "white Java refined granulated sugar."[3] Two invoices, one omitting "refined" and the other "granulated", failed.

In another case, refusal to honor was upheld even though the beneficiary complied with the underlying contract by supplying sweet oil.[4] Because of a clerical error, the letter of credit erroneously contained the requirement that the oil be identified as sour oil. The court concluded that the beneficiary had the burden of seeing that the letter of credit conformed to the underlying contract.

As Article 18c of the UCP makes plain, the invoice is usually the most important document in the presentation under a commercial letter of credit. The invoice is prepared by the beneficiary and provides whatever assurance is to be found in the documents that the beneficiary has complied with the underlying contract. For that reason the applicant is understandably concerned that the invoice accurately describe the goods. The UCP imposes a heavy burden on the beneficiary and on the issuer to insure that the description on the invoice conforms to the terminology on the letter of credit.

As we have indicated above, here is the principal place where the UCP and UCC rules absolving the document examiner of the need to know the underlying trade come into play. One in the trade might instantly recognize that a description inconsistent with the words on the letter of credit was nevertheless a synonymous description of the same goods. The examiner need not know this and, absent a waiver by the applicant, can and should dishonor. The UCP explicitly recognizes that other documents in a commer-

---

2. See Courtaulds North America, Inc. v. North Carolina Nat. Bank, 528 F.2d 802, 18 UCC 467 (4th Cir.1975).

3. Crocker First Nat. Bank v. De Sousa, 27 F.2d 462 (9th Cir.1928), cert. denied, 278 U.S. 650, 49 S.Ct. 94, 73 L.Ed. 561 (1928).

4. In re Coral Petroleum, Inc., 878 F.2d 830, 9 UCC2d 184 (5th Cir.1989).

cial presentation (such as inspection certificates and packing lists) can have somewhat deviant descriptions as long as they are not inconsistent with the description in the invoice or other documents.

b. Inspection Certificate Discrepancies

Letters of credit calling for inspection certificates are inherently troublesome. Assume that the letter of credit requires a certificate of inspection stating that "all goods meet minimum safety standards." In a shipment of 100,000 identical toys, must the inspector examine all toys in order to certify that "all" goods meet the safety standards? Or, can the inspector examine a representative sample? Surely a sample is enough where there are 100,000 items, but that might not be true if there were only 20 pieces. How closely must the inspection certificate track the language of the letter of credit? Consider a case in which the letter of credit required an inspection certificate that shipped steel be, "Ribbet Flange in accordance with sample and buyers drawing No. 19865." If the presented inspection certificates speaks of steel "as per shippers pro forma invoice of November 9th, 1977," the certificate will fail to comply.[5]

A celebrated First Circuit case, Banco Espanol de Credito v. State Street Bank & Trust Co.,[6] arose out of a dispute over an inspection certificate. The letter of credit required a certificate stipulating "that the goods are in conformity with the order"[7] for the purchase of clothing from a Spanish beneficiary-seller. But applicant-buyer sent beneficiary-seller "stock sheets" which were really purchase orders and "orders" which were merely preliminary papers.[8] Worse, as the inspection process got underway, applicant-buyer sent the inspector a barrage of contradictory telegrams about how the goods should be inspected, what samples should be used, and when the inspection certificate should issue.[9] Confused and caught on the eve of a shipping deadline, the inspector issued a certificate of inspection which did not literally track the commercial letter's wording "that the goods are in conformity with the order." Instead the certificate said that "a ten percent random sample had been taken" from the goods about to be shipped and that the whole sample was "found conforming to the conditions estipulated [sic] on

---

5. See Eximetals Corp. v. Guimaraes, 73 A.D.2d 526, 422 N.Y.S.2d 684, 28 UCC 157 (1979), aff'd mem., 51 N.Y.2d 865, 433 N.Y.S.2d 1019, 414 N.E.2d 399, 30 UCC 657 (1980). Also required was the "countersignature" of customer-buyer's president. Even though the president signed the inspection certificate, it failed to comply strictly: since the inspector himself had not signed, the president's signature had not been added to someone else's as the word "countersignature" required.

6. 385 F.2d 230, 4 UCC 862 (1st Cir.1967), appeal after remand, 409 F.2d 711, 6 UCC 378 (1st Cir.1969).

7. Id. 4 UCC at 863.

8. Id. at 870.

9. Id. at 865–66.

the Order–Stock-sheets."[10] Those "sheets" seemed to represent applicant-buyer's "order" and spoke of "COATS or JACKETS TO BE AS SAMPLE INSPECTED IN SPAIN"—the sample at the heart of customer's contradictory telegrams.[11]

Issuer dishonored because the certificate did not track the commercial letter's language about the goods being "in conformity with the order." Though it acknowledged that strict compliance was the prevailing standard, the First Circuit noted "some leaven in the loaf" of strict compliance.[12] As the court saw it, the problem lay at applicant-buyer's feet for having created so much ambiguity in the inspection process which it was best able to control.[13] In the end, the First Circuit refused to let the blameworthy applicant-buyer and the letter's issuer defeat compliance of beneficiary's inspection certificate.

Banco Espanol may be criticized for not hewing more rigorously to the strict compliance norm, yet we see it more as an "ambiguity" case whose bad facts left the court little choice but to resolve the ambiguity against those who created it, applicant and issuer.[14]

c. *Inconsistencies in Presented Documents*

If the invoice matches the letter of credit in describing the goods, UCP 14 permits every other document to describe the goods with only enough particularity to link them to the letter. To benefit from this distinction, however, the general description must be consistent with the letter's description of goods[15] and the presented documents as a whole must not show any inconsistencies among one another.[16] UCP 14e states that documents other than the invoice, are okay as long as they describe the goods "in general terms not conflicting with their description in the credit." Remember, however, that banks are not allowed to go beyond the express requirements of the letter of credit in finding discrepancies. For example, see Automation Source Corp. v. Korea Exchange Bank,[17] where the bank improperly dishonored a presentation containing two invoices for the exact same number of goods, but showing different weights. Since the letter was silent on the proper weight of each shipment, the bank exceeded its permitted bounds in calling this a discrepancy.

---

10. *Id.* at 866.

11. *Id.*

12. *Id.* at 867–68.

13. *Id.* at 869, 870, 872.

14. Sometimes courts use "substantial compliance" terminology or cite *Banco Espanol*'s "leaven in the loaf" remark when referring to flyspeck discrepancies which could not possibly mislead any document examiner. See, e.g.,

First Nat. Bank v. Wynne, 149 Ga.App. 811, 256 S.E.2d 383, 26 UCC 1273, 1276, 1278 (1979).

15. Talbot v. Bank of Hendersonville, 495 S.W.2d 548, 13 UCC 310 (Tenn.App.1972); UCP 37(c).

16. UCP 14e, "not conflicting."

17. 249 A.D.2d 1, 670 N.Y.S.2d 847 (1998).

In S.B. International, Inc. v. Union Bank,[18] the letter required documents covering a shipment of goods that were to be "claded three ply stainless steel circles with 55% to 60% iron $1300/-per ton cif Calcutta." The beneficiary presented invoices that properly described the goods to be shipped, but also bills of lading containing various descriptions. One of the bills of lading described the goods as "BXS–STEEL SHEETS (SECONDARY DEFECTED SCRAP) STEEL CIRCLES." Acknowledging the possibility that the description on the bill of lading might (according to trade practice) conform to the description in the letter of credit and recognizing that the UCP required absolute conformity only in the invoice and not in the other documents, the court still held that the terms of the UCP requiring that the general terms not be "inconsistent" made the presentation defective.

Clearly the effect of a complying invoice may be destroyed by something said in another document. Does the reverse apply? Can one document cure a discrepancy in another? Some cases, usually addressing trivial discrepancies, permit inter-document cure. Others refuse this zen approach and require each document to face judgment on its own against the commandments in the letter of credit.

Courts routinely disregard minute discrepancies in invoices or other documents as so insignificant that no document examiner could possibly be misled by them.[19] Arguably, this is a retreat from

---

18. 783 S.W.2d 225, 11 UCC2d 171 (Tex.App.1989).

19. No banker's list would be complete without these example discrepancies:

(1) letter of credit requires beneficiary's draft to bear legend "Drawn under NEMNB Credit No. 18506," but draft says only "No. 18506" or omits legend entirely. See Flagship Cruises, Ltd. v. New England Merchants Nat. Bank, 569 F.2d 699, 704, 24 UCC 745 (1st Cir. 1978) (held: complying). See also E & H Partners v. Broadway Nat'l Bank, 39 F.Supp.2d 275 (S.D.N.Y. 1998) (use of ZIP Code 10001 instead of 10010 did not mean that required notice did not reach the applicant and including extra digits in invoice numbers (i.e. showing "VCR3002–NG" on a purchase order and "VCR3002" on the associated invoice) did not create sufficient confusion. Both were complying.), American Airlines, Inc. v. FDIC, 610 F.Supp. 199, 41 UCC 192, 196 (D.Kan.1985) (typo on beneficiary's draft showed letter's number as "GO391" instead of correct "G–0391," but bank neither was nor could

have possibly been misled by presented documents as a whole; held: complying); Travis Bank & Trust v. State, 660 S.W.2d 851, 38 UCC 300, 306–07 (Tex. App.1983) (disregarding omission of words "drawn under" from remaining legend which referred to irrevocable letter of credit by its correct number; held: complying); Tosco Corp. v. FDIC, 723 F.2d 1242, 37 UCC 1660, 1664–65 (6th Cir.1983) (minute defects in draft's legend disregarded: "No." instead of "Number"; lower case instead of capital "L" in "Letter"; words "Clarksville, Tennessee" added after "Bank of Clarksville"; and legend placed on draft by beneficiary instead of negotiating bank). See also, First Nat. Bank v. Wynne, 149 Ga.App. 811, 256 S.E.2d 383, 26 UCC 1273, 1276 (1979) (held: complying).

(2) letter of credit requires six copies of presented documents, but only five come. See Bank of Cochin Ltd. v. Manufacturers Hanover Trust Co., 612 F.Supp. 1533, 41 UCC 920, 933 (S.D.N.Y.1985) (held: complying), aff'd

strict compliance,[20] but we see no real retreat as long as the court disregards a discrepancy only after beneficiary shows that no reasonable document examiner could possibly have been misled by it.[21] For example, listing a letter as "G0391" instead of "G–0391" did not render the document discrepant[22] and the change of "Number" to "No." together with a lower case "l" instead of an upper case letter in "Letter" or the addition of the words "Clarksville, Tennessee" after the words "Bank of Clarksville"[23] did not render the

on waiver/estoppel grounds, 808 F.2d 209, 3 UCC2d 1489 (2d Cir.1986).

(3) corporate beneficiary's draft comes signed by an individual whose authority to sign for corporation is not shown on face of draft. See American Airlines, Inc. v. FDIC, 610 F.Supp. 199, 41 UCC 192, 196 (D.Kan.1985) (held: complying). Compare Flagship Cruises, Ltd. v. New England Merchants Nat. Bank, 569 F.2d 699, 704, 24 UCC 745 (1st Cir.1978) (draft drawn by corporate agent Flagship, *Inc.* instead of corporate principal beneficiary Flagship, *Ltd.,* but discrepancy unmistakenly cured by accompanying document) with Far Eastern Textile, Ltd. v. City Nat. Bank & Trust Co., 430 F.Supp. 193, 195, 197 (S.D.Ohio 1977) (where letter of credit required *purchase order* to be signed by "Larry Fannin," *purchase order* which came signed by "Larry Fannin by Paul Thomas" as agent violated strict compliance standard).

(4) beneficiary's required certification omits use of the magic word "certify." See Brown v. United States Nat. Bank, 220 Neb. 684, 371 N.W.2d 692, 41 UCC 1765, 1777–78 (1985) (held: complying).

(5) a presented document misspells a name common in the community where issuer, beneficiary, and customer operate—for example, "*Smithh*" for "Smith." See Beyene v. Irving Trust Co., 762 F.2d 4, 40 UCC 1811 (2d Cir. 1985). But see *id.* 40 UCC at 1813 (strict compliance standard was violated where foreign name "So*f*an" was misspelled "So*r*an"; held: noncomplying).

(6) letter of credit requires beneficiary's draft to come with a statement that the "draft is in conjunction" with a certain agreement; statement accompanies draft, as does the letter itself, but statement says that the "Letter of Credit [not the draft] is in conjunction." See Flagship Cruises, Ltd. v. New England Merchants Nat. Bank, 569 F.2d 699, 703, 705, 24 UCC 745 (1st Cir.1978)

(held: complying when subsequent receipt of letter was timely).

See also Integrated Measurement Systems Inc. v. International Commercial Bank, 757 F.Supp. 938, 14 UCC2d 1167 (N.D.Ill.1991) (description in the airbill was consistent with the invoice; held: complying); Exotic Traders Far East Buying Office v. Exotic Trading U.S.A., Inc., 717 F.Supp. 14, 9 UCC2d 698 (D.Mass.1989) (court disregarded discrepancies in shipping documents misstating date of telex and "F.O.B. Korea" rather than "F.O.B. Seoul" as hypertechnical and not misleading); Continental Casualty Co. v. Southtrust Bank, N.A. 933 So.2d 337, 58 UCC2d 372 (Ala. 2006) (sight draft identifying beneficiary by name but omitting address was held complying).

See also Datapoint, Corp. v. M & I Bank, 665 F.Supp. 722, 4 UCC2d 829, 833–34 (W.D.Wis.1987) (missing logo "Drawn under [issuer's] letter of credit no. _____;" court leaves question open whether concededly non-misleading discrepancy like this would justify dishonor, because issuer failed to notify the dishonor diligently under UCP 16(d)).

20. See generally Dolan, The Law of Letters of Credit: Commercial and Standby Credits (rev. ed. 2003), Para 6.05 (criticizing cases like *Flagship* and *First Nat. Bank v. Wynne* along with others).

21. For example, if some legal error unquestionably occurs during trial but the error could not possibly have misled the jury, the error is deemed "harmless" and disregarded as a matter of law.

22. American Airlines, Inc. v. FDIC, 610 F.Supp. 199, 41 UCC 192, 196 (D.Kan.1985).

23. Tosco Corp. v. FDIC, 723 F.2d 1242, 37 UCC 1660, 1664–65 (6th Cir. 1983).

document noncomplying. Strict compliance to the letter of credit does not require slavish conformance.[24]

An example of a minor discrepancy regarding identification of the letter of credit arose in New Braunfels National Bank v. Odiorne.[25] The case reminds one of the Woody Allen movie, in which the thief comes to the teller's window with a note that says "give me your money, I have a gub." The teller and the thief then argue about the meaning of the word "gub." The thief insists the note says "gun" and the teller insists it says only "gub" and therefore no money needs to be given up.

In *New Braunfels* the demand was under credit number "86–122–5," but the true letter of credit number was "86–122–S." Because the demand included the numeral "5" instead of the letter "S", the bank refused to pay, even though it was obvious to everyone under which letter the beneficiary was demanding payment. The court reasoned that strict compliance does not mean perfection when dealing with standby letters of credit; it correctly found the demand proper and ordered the bank to pay. The case is correct. This did not call for the banker to know practices in the steel or some other industry. To the extent that the court limits its holding to standby letters of credit we think it is being too reticent. We believe that strict compliance means something less than "absolute, perfect compliance" in every case.

Discrepancies may also arise between the actual parties' names and those that are listed in the actual letter of credit document. In at least two instances, courts have held that the misspelling of a name by just one letter meant that strict compliance was violated. In Beyene v. Irving Trust Co.,[26] a required bill of lading spelled the party's name "Mohammed Soran" rather than the proper name, "Mohammed Sofan." In dicta, the court noted that if "Smith is spelled Smithh," this would not rise to the level of non-compliance because the mistake is obvious. Still, Soran would not be obviously recognized as a misspelling of Sofan in the Middle East, but Smithh would obviously be recognized as Smith in the U.S. A subsequent case, Hanil Bank v. Pt. Bank Negara Indonesia,[27] relied on the reasoning in *Beyene* and held that "Sung Jin" as specified in the letter of credit itself did not comport with "Sung Jun" as shown on the presented documents, and the issuing bank properly dishonored the presentation.

But, on similar facts, a federal district court in Texas held that inverting parts of a beneficiary's name did not give the issuing bank a right to dishonor the presentation.[28] In that case, the

---

24. Comment 1 to 5–108.

25. 780 S.W.2d 313, 10 UCC2d 1352 (Tex.App.1989).

26. 762 F.2d 4 (2nd Cir. 1985).

27. 41 UCC2d 618 (S.D.N.Y. 2000).

28. *See* Voest–Alpine Trading USA Corp. v. Bank of China, 167 F.Supp.2d 940 (S.D. Tex. 2000).

presentation documents all contained the name "Voest–Alpine Trading USA," but the actual letter of credit named the beneficiary as "Voest-Alpine USA Trading." The court distinguished this case from *Beyene* because here it was an "inverted name," and not a "misspelling or outright omission." We are not sure that the misspellings in those cases really could have, or did, mislead any issuer.

PROBLEM

Which of the following presentations strictly comply?

1. The letter calls for the presentation of a "sight draft," but the beneficiary presents a letter on its letterhead demanding payment.

   This is a complying presentation. Article 5 has no definition of sight draft and there was no chance of confusion about the request.

2. Contract between seller and buyer calls for delivery of a quantity of "sweet crude" (i.e., crude with little sulfur). By mistake the letter calls for an invoice showing "sour crude" (with sulfur). Seller delivers sweet crude that complies with the contract and presents an invoice showing delivery of "sweet crude." Strict Compliance?

   No. So what should the seller have done? Get the letter amended if there is time. If no time? Put in a "sour crude" invoice.

3. Letter requires "aluminum scrap" and invoice says "aluminum punchings."

   This is a close one but the court said there was compliance.

4. Letter and invoice say "100% imported acrylic yarn" but the packing list says "acrylic yarn."

   Okay. UCP requires the invoice to be exact but allows variation in other documents as long as they are not inconsistent with the invoice.

5. Seller presents an air way bill when Issuer knows the goods have not yet been shipped?

   Okay. The court says that Issuer's knowledge does not matter here. However, this could mean fraud and if so, the Issuer can probably still pay but the applicant might argue bad faith.

6. Letter requires that documents show that freight has been paid. Beneficiary presents a shipping document that shows the word "CASH" with a strike through the word. Beneficiary tells Issuer that, in the carriage trade, the strike through shows that cash has been paid. Issuer dishonors. What result?

Not conforming; remember the document examiner need not know any trade usage.

7. The product to be shipped is described in the letter as GO–391. The documents presented show G–0391 as shipped.

   Okay. The court found no possibility of misleading or error.

8. The document in a standby required the signature of John Summers. The documents were signed "by John Summers, by Evelyn Larsen, agent."

   Not complying. The court interpreted the letter to require Summers' signature not that of an agent. (Note that if the parties contemplated the signature of a corporate agent, they would usually identify him, e.g., "Treasurer.")

9. Letter requires documents to show shipping "FOB Japan," and the documents showed "FOB Tokyo." Complying?

   Yes. Even someone who needs to know no trade practice should know that Tokyo is in Japan.

Be careful generalizing here. Some of the above cases would have come out otherwise another day in another court.

d. Beneficiary's Merger, Consolidation, Change of Name or Death

Because the applicant has negotiated with the beneficiary for performance, the applicant expects performance from the beneficiary and not from another. Unless the letter is transferable, only the beneficiary can present documents and receive payment under the letter of credit. How does one proceed when the beneficiary's name changes or the beneficiary is merged after the letter of credit is issued? Assume that First National issues a letter of credit to "Oliver Chemicals." After the letter is issued, Oliver Chemicals is merged into "Acme Chemicals." If Acme presents documents in the name of Acme Chemicals, the issuer will dishonor because the documents are nonconforming. In that case a clever beneficiary would present documents in the name of "Oliver Chemicals" and so be paid upon "strict" if "immaterially fraudulent" compliance.

Section 5–113 specifically permits this, governing the rights of the transferee "by operation of the law," and allowing a beneficiary's successor to draw in the name of the beneficiary. By revising this section, the drafters resolved a conflict among the courts regarding whether a receiver or trustee can draw against a nontransferable letter of credit. For a more detailed discussion of the cases, see 8–11, *infra*.

At least one court has recognized a limited exception to strict compliance when the beneficiary has been dissolved. In Temple–

Eastex, Inc. v. Addison Bank,[29] the beneficiary of a letter of credit had been dissolved and the parent company, Temple–Eastex, attempted to draw on the letter. The bank dishonored the demand. The Supreme Court of Texas found that the circumstances and the presented documents should have put the bank on inquiry as to the rights of Temple–Eastex, and that on further inquiry the bank would have discovered that Temple–Eastex, as the sole shareholder of the now dissolved beneficiary, had the right under Texas law to demand payment on the letter.[30]

Parties to a letter of credit transaction should be careful not to provide more specificity than necessary on exactly which individuals are required to sign in order to draw on a letter of credit. For example, in Samuel Rappaport Family Partnership v. Meridian Bank,[31] the letter at issue required the signature of a Mr. Orleans on a certificate stating that an event of default occurred on the underlying contract. Mr. Orleans died before the letter was to be drawn on, and the purchasers of the lease and letter of credit attempted to make a presentation by including documents to indicate the transfer from Mr. Orleans to the current owners. The court properly upheld the bank's decision to dishonor the presentation.

e. *Missing Documents*

Failure to present a document listed in the letter of credit justifies dishonor. Commercial and standby letters typically require a "draft" as the beneficiary's payment demand. When beneficiary fails to submit any draft along with the other required papers, its presentation fails. The ordinary "collection letter" of a collecting bank will not do. Nor will it do for beneficiary to present a sight draft when the letter of credit requires a time draft. In some cases the invoices failed.

Many letter of credits will also require that the beneficiary submit the original Letter of Credit document when making a presentation. In one such situation, covered in Airlines Reporting Corp. v. Norwest Bank, N.A.,[32] the beneficiary lost the original letter and "orally asked Bank to update its files on the letter and received from Bank . . . a copy of the letter of credit . . ." In a short opinion, the court held that the strict compliance standard was not met, as only the original letter of credit document would suffice. The court also rejected the beneficiary's estoppel argument, noting

---

29. 672 S.W.2d 793, (Tex.1984).

30. The Court of Appeals of Texas refused to extend this exception to apply to two companies that shared common ownership. Cobb Restaurants, L.L.C. v. Texas Capital Bank, N.A., 201 S.W.3d 175, 60 UCC2d 469 (Ct.App.Tx.2006).

31. 441 Pa.Super. 194, 657 A.2d 17 (Sup. Ct. Pa. 1995).

32. 529 N.W.2d 449 (Ct. App. Minn. 1995).

that Norwest did nothing to indicate that it did not expect the letter of credit's terms to be adhered to. We would imagine that this case is a bit of an outlier, especially given the beneficiary's communication to the bank about the lost original document. That said, it should serve as another reminder to beneficiaries that "strict compliance" demands exactly what the term says.

The 1995 revision to 5–104's formal requirements for letters of credit was designed with the continuing movement towards electronic transacting in mind by only requiring that a letter take the form of a "record." How, then, would a beneficiary meet a requirement that the original letter of credit document be a part of the documentary presentation? The most obvious answer, and one specified in comment 3 to 5–104, is that parties will typically print off the original electronic document and submit that along with the other documents. So long as a number of the presentation documents are likely to exist in paper form, this solution will suffice. If, as we expect, these documents begin to move to electronic format as well, parties to letters of credit will have incentive to make the entire process electronic. This would likely require some type of "authentication" software to verify that the various electronic documents are originals from the proper party that meet the letter's requirements.

f. Certifications and Other Statements Required by Standby Letters of Credit

Standby letters of credit typically require some type of certification of default or entitlement. Like invoices, these certification statements must "strictly comply" with the terms of the letter of credit. For example, a standby letter in an order for steel required the invoice to mention "#0046." Beneficiary and applicant later agreed to a change in this order, which they evidenced via new purchase orders, #0060 and #0064. Beneficiary presented invoices mentioning the new numbers but without referring to "#0046." The issuer dishonored and won.[33]

In Occidental Fire and Casualty Co. v. Continental Bank N.A.,[34] the letter of credit required the draw to state it was for "the express purpose of reimbursing any incurred liabilities of the aforementioned bonds." Certification that the beneficiary was drawing for the purpose of reimbursing "any incurred liabilities for any bonds" was not sufficient. In another case,[35] beneficiary's certifica-

---

33. See Dubose Steel, Inc. v. Branch Banking and Trust Co., 72 N.C.App. 598, 324 S.E.2d 859, 41 UCC 187 (1985), review denied, 314 N.C. 115, 332 S.E.2d 480 (1985).

34. 918 F.2d 1312, 13 UCC2d 289 (7th Cir.1990).

35. Waidmann v. Mercantile Trust Co., N.A., 711 S.W.2d 907, 2 UCC2d 252 (Mo.App.1986).

tion that the applicant "defaulted pursuant to the terms of the said note and stock purchase agreement" failed for lack of strict compliance when the letter required beneficiary to certify that the applicant had defaulted "in the payment of [a promissory] note." In a third example, the letter called for invoice-like statements covering oil runs "during the month of August, 1982." The letter's expiry date was extended twice or so beneficiary apparently thought to cover oil runs in later months. Still, the prescription about "August, 1982" was not changed. When beneficiary presented oil run statements for July, August, September, and October 1982, it failed to comply.[36]

At least one court has suggested that courts should police issuers' behavior more closely in standby cases than in commercial cases.[37] While we do not agree that there should be a different standard for standby letters than for commercial letters, we think it appropriate to recognize that an issuer may have larger incentives to dishonor a standby letter than a commercial letter. By hypothesis, a draw on a standby means that the applicant has failed to perform. That failure may also mean that the applicant is incapable of performing its reimbursement agreement. Unless it is adequately secured, the issuer then runs the risk of paying its own money without hope of reimbursement. While we do not advocate a different standard for standby and commercial credits, courts should be especially skeptical of an issuer's justification for dishonor in a standby letter where the flaws in the presentation are *de minimis*.

g. *Nondocumentary Conditions*

Nondocumentary conditions in letters of credit can be divided into three parts. First certain nondocumentary conditions, present in every letter of credit, are intended to be there. These are conditions concerning time and place of presentation. Clearly, they are not documentary and clearly they must be complied with or the presentation is improper.

Second are conditions that are so fundamental and serious that they deprive the document of its status as a letter of credit. We discussed those earlier in § 8–2. An example would be a case in which the letter of credit did not require the presentation of a document showing default, but required the bank "to pay upon default by Applicant on its contract with beneficiary * * *." That condition makes the core requirement "nondocumentary" and so renders the issuer's undertaking not a letter of credit under 5–

---

36. Westwind Exploration, Inc. v. Homestate Sav. Ass'n, 696 S.W.2d 378, 42 UCC 271 (Tex.1985).

37. New Braunfels Nat. Bank v. Odiorne, 780 S.W.2d 313, 10 UCC2d 1352 (Tex.App.1989).

102(a)(10). It leaves the parties on the street, outside of Article 5 just where they belong.

Third are nondocumentary conditions that are not fundamental, but go beyond time and place of presentation. An example might be a requirement that shipment be in "ships less than 15 years old" or that goods arrive "before Halloween." Both Article 14h of the UCP and section 5–108(g) require (*require* not authorize) issuer to ignore such nondocumentary conditions and treat them as though they were not stated.[38] When it meets a nondocumentary condition from this third group, the issuer is to treat the letter as though the condition were not present and to act upon the documents presented and irrespective of compliance with the conditions. Necessarily there will be disagreement about which conditions fall in part two (so fundamental that the engagement is no longer a letter of credit) and which in part three (incidental and to be disregarded), but that is life.

Turn now to the first condition: the requirement of time and place. Article 6d.i. of the UCP and section 5–108 require presentation before expiration. Certain letters may also require presentation within a fixed period after some event, i.e. shipment of the goods in question.[39] Note that compliance is measured at the time of presentation even though it may take several days thereafter for the issuer to determine whether the presentation complies. As we indicate below, the issuer will have a reasonable time—perhaps extending beyond the expiration—to determine whether to dishonor, but that does not change the fact that compliance has or has not occurred at the instant of presentation. Put another way, the fact that the expiration date occurs within a reasonable time after presentation and while the issuer is still inspecting the documents, does not change the beneficiary's right to have his presentation honored if its presentation was complying or the right of the issuer to dishonor, if not.

In a negotiation credit, sometimes called a "freely negotiable" credit, or other credit identifying "nominated persons," the beneficiary need only present the documents to a nominated person who takes them up prior to the expiration. By the same token, a complying presentation to a confirmer prior to the expiration satisfies the timing condition. To restate, the documents need not

---

38. See 8–2, *supra*.

39. *See* Banco General Runinahui, S.A. v. Citibank Int'l, 97 F.3d 480 (11th Cir. 1996) (interpreting a requirement that the presentation be made within 15 days of shipment, but recognizing that the letter of credit specified an actual expiration date that was later than the shipment date. The court held that these provisions meant that the benefi-ciary had to make a conforming presentation within the 15 day period, it could not make a non-conforming presentation and cure the defects after the 15 day period, but before expiration. To hold otherwise would be to encourage benefi-ciaries to make discrepant presentations.).

get to the issuer prior to the expiration date provided they have been presented prior to the expiration date to a nominated party who takes them up or to a confirmer.

Where the issuer or other person to whom presentation is to be made is a multi-branch bank, the beneficiary must present at a place identified in the letter of credit or, if none is identified, must use reasonable care to present at the proper place within that system.

In well-drafted letters of credit, the exact hour of expiration may also be included along with a date. Such a provision would have settled the confusion that arose in Carter Petroleum Products, Inc. v. Brotherhood Bank & Trust Co.[40] There, the beneficiary made the documentary presentation at the required bank branch just after the regular 5:00 p.m. closing time, but a bank employee allowed the beneficiary in and accepted the documents. The bank ended up dishonoring the presentation for being late, claiming that the bank had a posted 2:00 p.m. cutoff time for transactions to occur on the particular day, and alternatively, that the letter of credit expired at 5:00 p.m. with the close of the bank's regular business hours. In disregarding these outside times, the court held that presentation was timely because the letter of credit did not specify a particular expiration time on the applicable date.

Turn now to the second condition: nondocumentary conditions other than those having to do with time and place of presentation. When the issuer tolerates nonpaper requirements, it risks (and deserves) to be stuck in the crossfire between the beneficiary and the applicant. Because the documents no longer control the issuer's duty to honor, it makes little sense to ask whether they conform strictly. Where the documents commit the issuer to assess facts and events outside the documents presented, they disable the independence principle and topple the wall that separates presented documents from beneficiary-applicant disputes. Sometimes issuers who tolerate such conditions will be saved by 5–108(g), but the protection from this section is limited.

Where the applicant can show it truly relied on the nondocumentary conditions and that they were fundamental to the issuer's duty, a court may find that the undertaking is not a letter of credit, yet conclude that the issuer remains bound. In that case the issuer will stand naked before the common law, unprotected by the cover of the UCC or UCP. Even where the UCP and revised UCC direct the issuer to ignore the nondocumentary conditions, neither the UCP nor the UCC insulate the issuer from liability to its applicant for disregarding those conditions.

---

40. 33 Kan.App.2d 62, 97 P.3d 505 (Ct. App. Kan. 2004).

h. Issuer's Request for Additional Documents

The strict compliance approach keeps issuers in check by preventing them from exacting more than the letter of credit unambiguously requires. For example, when the issuer demands extra documents or insists that beneficiary's papers reflect something not spelled out in the letter of credit, courts have protected the beneficiary by finding that dishonor could not be justified for non-compliance with those demands. And once beneficiary presents the right documents in the way the letter requires, issuer may not further condition honor upon matters outside the papers.

i. Issuer's Ability to Contact Applicant Regarding Discrepancies

Recall § 8–5's discussion of an issuer's express ability to contact the applicant and obtain a waiver of the beneficiary's deficiencies in presentation of documents. Exactly how far can this conversation extend before the applicant provides so much information to the issuer about the underlying transaction that the issuer is deemed to have exceeded its restriction on making the honor/dishonor decision solely based upon the documents? The issue is dealt with nicely in E & H Partners v. Broadway Nat'l Bank.[41] There, the evidence showed that the applicant made multiple requests for the issuer to dishonor the beneficiary's presentation, and even went so far as to hire an attorney to investigate possible discrepancies in the presentation. In the words of the court, "the purpose of the multiple communications * * * was not to discuss waiver of the alleged discrepancies."

Noting that this plainly violated the independence principle, and may have also violated the general obligation of good faith and fair dealing, the court estopped the issuing bank from asserting any non-compliance against the beneficiary. In similar situations, issuing banks must keep in mind that they owe a primary duty to the beneficiary, not the applicant.

§ 8–7 Warranties

Warranties were among the most contentious issues in the revision of Article 5. Banks writing international letters of credit argued for the removal of the warranties on the ground that the warranties were foreign to the Europeans and Asians and tended to make the American letters of credit appear less certain of payment. This, they argued, put the American banks at a competitive disadvantage. Applicants, on the other hand, argued strongly for warranty. They pointed out that the applicants are the principal beneficiaries of warranties and since the applicants must reimburse the

---

41. 39 F.Supp.2d 275 (S.D.N.Y. 1998).

bank, the applicant, not the issuer, needs a way to get money back from a beneficiary. In addition to these arguments, there was a continuing debate among various parties on the question whether the warranties should deal only with apparent defects (those sufficiently apparent on the face of the documents), with latent defects (those not apparent on the face of the documents) or with both of them. On the eve of final adoption of the revised Code by the National Conference of Commissioners on Uniform State Laws in August, 1994, the drafting committee agreed on revised section 5–110 that currently reads in full as follows:

(a) If its presentation is honored, the beneficiary under a letter of credit warrants:

(1) to the issuer, any other person to whom presentation is made, and the applicant that there is no fraud or forgery of the kind described in Section 5–109(a); and

(2) to the applicant that the drawing does not violate any agreement between the applicant and beneficiary or any other agreement intended by them to be augmented by the letter of credit.

(b) The warranties in subsection (a) are in addition to warranties arising under Articles 3, 4, 7, and 8 because of the presentation or transfer of documents covered by any of those articles.

Note first that no warranty is given unless the presentation is honored. This is critical, for it prohibits the warranty from being used as a defense by an issuer who has not honored or by an applicant when the issuer has failed to honor. This makes sense, as the availability of warranties as a defense would undermine the certainty of payment and would degrade the independence of the letter of credit. If the issuer dishonors, no warranties are given under 5–110(a). Neither the issuer nor the applicant may defend the issuer's dishonor on the ground the beneficiary broke a warranty in its presentation.

If the presentation is honored, the issuer under 5–110(a)(1) may recover the payment where there is fraud or forgery of the kind identified in revised 5–109(a).[1]

Warranty under section 5–110(a)(2) goes only to the applicant and is broader than the warranty under 5–110(a)(1). Yet, it too is conditioned upon honor by the issuer.

The beneficiary warrants to the "applicant" that the "drawing does not violate any agreement between the applicant and beneficiary or any other agreement intended by them to be augmented by the letter of credit." What does that mean? In the most obvious

§ 8–7

1. *See, infra,* § 8–9.

case it means that a beneficiary who has breached the underlying contract in a commercial case has broken its warranty to the applicant. It is possible, but unlikely, that a beneficiary could have "broken the underlying contract" but not "violate[d] any agreement" between the parties by drawing. We believe that it is an express or an implied condition of the typical underlying commercial contract, but not of the letter of credit itself, of course, that the beneficiary have properly performed in order for it to have a right vis à vis the applicant to draw under a letter of credit.

It is important to note that this part of 5–110 clarifies the fairly contentious issue under pre-revision 5–111 of whether a violation of the underlying contract also constituted a warranty violation. Remember that most warranty cases were decided under the substantially different pre-revision version of the Article.

The second clause of 5–110(a)(2) concerning violation of "any other agreement intended by them to be augmented by the letter of credit" is aimed principally at standby letters. Even a conforming draw on a standby would violate the explicit or implicit term of the underlying agreement when the beneficiary had not complied with the terms that gave it a right to draw.

In most commercial letters of credit cases the warranty will not give the applicant more than it already has. In those cases the very same act that will be a breach of the warranty is likely also to be a breach of an underlying contract and so give the applicant a claim under Article 2 of the UCC or other law. Note, however, that the applicant's rights under Article 5 are unlikely to be coextensive with those under Article 2. For example, Article 5 does not allow consequential damages but Article 2 does; Article 5 has a one-year statute of limitations, Article 2 has a four-year statute; Article 5 authorizes the recovery of lawyer's fees, Article 2 does not.

We expect 5–110(a)(2) to be most important with standby letters of credit. In many standbys the applicant will not have a direct contractual claim against the beneficiary. That applicant would not have a contract claim even when the beneficiary's draw was not authorized by the underlying deal. Consider Mellon Bank v. General Electric Credit Corporation.[2] In that case, GEEC presented complying documents that certified a default. It had a right to draw on the letter of credit only if there was a default on the underlying loan. The court found there had been no default and that GEEC's certification to the contrary broke its warranty under pre-revision 5–111. The same result would follow under 5–110(a)(2) for the drawing would be a violation of the "agreement * * * augmented by the letter of credit." We believe that most beneficiaries, who draw under standby letters of credit when they are not

2. 724 F.Supp. 360, 10 UCC2d 946 (W.D.Pa.1989).

authorized to draw—by certifying as true what is false—would have broken their section 5–110(a)(2) warranty by "violat[ing] any agreement * * * intended * * * to be augmented by the letter of credit." To be certain, applicants' lawyers should make any improper draw a violation of the "agreement" that underlies the standby letter of credit.

Note that virtually every warranty claim requires the court to dig into the underlying transaction. Because no warranty arises until the beneficiary has been paid, we do not believe that this digging offends the independence principle. Once the beneficiary has left the bank with money in his pocket, that principle has been served, and we think it appropriate to allow the applicant or any other party to sue either on the underlying contract or on the warranties under 5–110.

Lastly, 5–110(b) continues the rule of the pre-revision Code; warranties that would otherwise arise under other articles also arise on presentation and transfer of documents under a letter of credit.

§ 8–8   Preclusion for Issuer's Failure to Notify of Defects

The cases in the foregoing sections tell that there are hundreds of cases annually in which a good faith presentation fails the strict compliance test. Some assert that as many as fifty percent of all presentations of commercial letters of credit are somehow defective. In most of those cases, the customer, willing to pay despite the deviations in the documents, waives (see § 8–6(b), *supra*). So payment is made despite a noncompliance.

Here we deal with a different avenue that sometimes also leads to payment over nonconforming documents. Under the UCP and Article 5, an issuer that fails to give timely notice of discrepancies is precluded from later asserting those discrepancies as a defense to its action. When the issuer dishonors but fails to give notice, the beneficiary will often have a right to damages for dishonor despite the fact it has failed strictly to comply with the terms of the letter. It is tempting but incorrect to say there is a right to "payment"—alà the "final payment" rule in Article 4. That may be the consequence of suit, but it is not the correct articulation of the beneficiary's rights. If there is a discrepancy and if the issuer fails to give notice of that discrepancy within a reasonable time not to exceed seven days, the issuer has still dishonored—silence is dishonor. The consequence of the issuer's silence is denial of a particular defense (namely, that the presentation was discrepant) when it is sued for wrongful dishonor by the beneficiary. Since the beneficiary's most likely recovery is the full amount of the draw, recovery is likely to be equal to the amount of that draw, which in many cases will equal the full amount of the letter.

a. *Issuer's Preclusion*

For the lawyer, the important cases are those where the issuing bank's failure to notify of discrepancies somehow deprives it of the right to justify its dishonor on discrepancies not specified. Most of the cases arise from the bank's failure to give timely notice of discrepancies when it dishonors a draft drawn under the letter of credit. Under Article 5–108, the "issuer is precluded from asserting as a basis for dishonor any discrepancy if timely notice is not given, or any discrepancy not stated in the notice if timely notice is given.[1] Similarly, UCP 16c requires the issuing bank to "state each discrepancy * * *."

In full, the relevant provisions of 5–108 are as follows:

(b) An issuer has a reasonable time after presentation, but not beyond the end of the seventh business day of the issuer after the day of its receipt of documents:

(1) to honor,

(2) if the letter of credit provides for honor to be completed more than seven business days after presentation, to accept a draft or incur a deferred obligation, or

(3) to give notice to the presenter of discrepancies in the presentation.

(c) Except as otherwise provided in subsection (d), an issuer is precluded from asserting as a basis for dishonor any discrepancy if timely notice is not given, or any discrepancy not stated in the notice if timely notice is given.

(d) Failure to give the notice specified in subsection (b) or to mention fraud, forgery, or expiration in the notice does not preclude the issuer from asserting as a basis for dishonor fraud or forgery as described in Section 5–109(a) or expiration of the letter of credit before presentation.

The UCP spells out these obligations in an equally precise manner in Articles 14a, 14b and 16.

In effect, these sections are the *quid pro quo* for the strict compliance requirements. While the beneficiary must strictly comply in its presentation, so too must the issuer give notice of the deficiencies in a prescribed manner or forever waive the right to raise the issue of defective presentation. These notice requirements are an offsetting balance for the strict compliance requirements.

§ 8–8

1. 5–108(c).

Courts have disagreed over exactly what an issuer must give "notice" of in order to avoid preclusion in these situations. Some courts deciding cases under the UCP 500 have held that the language of 14(d)(ii) (now 16) requires actual notice of dishonor, not simply a list of discrepancies. On the other hand, any extension of these holdings to current UCC cases is arguably foreclosed by 5–108(b)(3) which only requires "notice * * * of discrepancies." One thing is certain, the notice must specifically include all discrepancies that the issuing bank is relying on in dishonoring the presentation.

Although the strict preclusion rules of 5–108(c) and UCP 16f (and its predecessor, 14(e)), have been in existence for over a decade, the lawyer must still be careful here. Some older cases interpreted earlier versions of the UCP and pre-revision 5–112, neither of which applied the flat preclusion that is the law today. Furthermore, many pre-revision courts deciding UCC cases used to require some level of detrimental reliance on the beneficiary's part before finding preclusion. In the previous edition of this treatise, we argued that such holdings were incorrect, and the new provisions on strict preclusion in the UCC and UCP indicate that the drafters agreed. Many of the old holdings are irrelevant under current law, for the word "preclusion" was consciously and carefully chosen to make it clear that there would be no reliance requirement under revised Article 5. Another example of an old case that is no longer good law is a holding that the preclusion rule applied even though presentation was knowingly made after the letter's expiry date. Note that 5–108(d) expressly overrules this result.

Failure to act within the time permitted constitutes a dishonor under section 5–102(a)(5). The practical consequence of a dishonor without notice may be the same as honor in the sense that the liability the issuer will have to the beneficiary for dishonor may equal, or in rare cases, exceed what would be due to the beneficiary upon honor.

Lastly, under 5–108(d) preclusion does not apply to fraud, forgery or expiration. The presenter has no right to expect and the issuer has no obligation to give notice of fraud, forgery or the letter's expiration date. The beneficiary, as much as anyone else, can determine whether it has met the expiration rules.

b. Time of Notice

Other issues present themselves when the bank's dishonor and notice obligations interact with the letter's expiry date. Assume, for example, that the demand for payment is presented by the beneficiary shortly before the expiration of the letter. If the letter of credit is governed by either the UCC or the UCP, the issuer has the shorter of a "reasonable time" or seven *banking* days (in the case of the UCP), or seven *business* days (under the UCC) to decide. One thing is clear, the seven day period does not serve as a safe harbor under either the UCP or UCC.

Neither Article 4 nor the UCP defines a banking or business day. Because most issuers are banks, we suggest that one refer to Regulation CC for guidance. Section 229.2 of regulation CC (12 CFR 229.2(f)) defines banking day as "that part of any business day on which an office of a bank is open to the public for carrying on substantially all of its banking functions." Business day is defined in 12 CFR 229.2(g) as:

> [A] calendar day other than a Saturday or a Sunday, January 1, the third Monday in January, the third Monday in February, the last Monday in May, July 4, the first Monday in September, the second Monday in October, November 11, the fourth Thursday in November, or December 25. If January 1, July 4, November 11, or December 25 fall on a Sunday, the next Monday is not a business day.

When a business day is not a banking day, the outside limit might be longer under the UCP than the UCC. Because a "reasonable time" for document examination is normally less than seven days, the distinction between business and banking day is not likely to be important. When presentation consists of only a few documents and examination is straightforward, the reasonable time for examination might be only one or two days after which the issuer would be obliged to give prompt notice of dishonor.

Note also that under 5–108(b) the issuer's duty to give notice arises upon the beneficiary's presentation. Therefore, expiration during the examination period does not relieve the issuer of a duty to give notice. The rights of the parties are fixed upon presentation (absent waiver) and the duty to the beneficiary arises as soon as the issuer determines there is a deficiency.

Assume that documents are presented within one or two days of the letter's expiration date. In the first case, the bank takes no action until the letter has expired. In the second case, the bank makes an immediate examination and promptly determines not to pay. Must the second bank send notice under the UCP? Under the UCC?

The focus in such situations is primarily upon the reasonableness of the issuer's behavior in light of how other banks in the industry would act under similar circumstances. It is not "interpreted ... to mean [that the issuer must give notice] 'early enough to allow the beneficiary to cure and represent the documents before the presentment deadline.' "[2] In other words, if the beneficiary

---

2. Banco General Runinahui, S.A. v. Citibank Int'l, 97 F.3d 480, 487, 30 UCC2d 1163 (11th Cir.1996) (holding that the issuer notified the beneficiary

presents documents close to the deadline, then the beneficiary takes the risk that the issuer's "reasonable" time to give notice will extend past the letter's expiration date, at which time the beneficiary would not be able to cure any of the discrepancies.

Several things should be clear to the parties involved. First, the beneficiary runs considerable risk that it will be denied the benefit of a preclusion or estoppel if it waits until shortly before the expiration to make presentation. Second, the bank may or may not be entitled to keep its mouth shut until the end of the period if presentation is made shortly before the expiration date. The bank's risk is substantially greater if it communicates its intention to dishonor to the beneficiary and thus loses any claim that it had not yet made its decision to dishonor until shortly before or even after the expiration.

An issuer's attempt to obtain a waiver of deficiencies from the applicant does not extend the issuer's time beyond seven days.[3] While contacts with the applicant to obtain a waiver may extend the reasonable time, in no case can the time of review and notice exceed the seven day limit (unless, of course, the beneficiary has also agreed to an extension). The fact that the applicant has insufficient funds on account to reimburse the issuer is not a basis for extending the "reasonable time."

PROBLEM

Issuer declines to pay on a presentation because the invoice incorrectly describes the goods and because the bill of lading (documents required by the letter) is missing. In its notice of dishonor, Issuer mentions only the invoice.

1. Within the time available under the letter, Seller brings a complying invoice the next day. On the following day, the letter expires and Issuer declines to pay because the bill of lading is still missing.

   Does Issuer have liability for dishonor? Yes. Since it did not list the missing bill of lading, it cannot use it as a basis for dishonor.

2. What if Issuer had defended on the ground that its notice did not cause the loss since Seller could not have gotten a comply-

---

in a reasonable time when it took two days to give notification and the beneficiary made its presentation one day before the letter of credit's expiration date).

3. UCP 16b. Despite the lack of an express statement on this point, Article 5 arguably includes it by the language of comment 3 to 5–108, which states that Article 5 was modeled after the UCP in this area.

> ing bill of lading within the time available even if it had given notice?
>
> Issuer loses. This is hard edged law, not wimpy waiver and estoppel. 5–108(c), comment 3 to 5–108.

c. Preclusion of Restitution

In addition to the 5–108(c) preclusion of defenses to dishonor, the issuer is also precluded from asserting a defective presentation as a basis for restitution once it has paid. Section 5–108(i)(4) states:

> (i) An issuer that has honored a presentation as permitted or required by this article:
>
>   * * *
>
> (4) except as otherwise provided in Sections 5–110 and 5–117, is precluded from restitution of money paid or other value given by mistake to the extent the mistake concerns discrepancies in the documents or tender which are apparent on the face of the presentation * * *.

This section specifically precludes restitution only in those cases where the issuer paid despite "apparent" discrepancies in the presented documents. If the applicable state law permits, restitution may still be available from the beneficiary when there has been fraud or forgery, or in other cases based on events that did not constitute apparent discrepancies.

Preclusion from restitution claims when the issuer pays over a patently defective presentation seems fair. For example, assume that the beneficiary presents nonconforming documents ten days before the expiration of the letter of credit. Despite the nonconforming presentation, the issuer pays and receives title to a shipload of clothing. The applicant refuses to reimburse the issuer because of the wrongful honor. If the issuer sues the beneficiary on a restitution theory, the beneficiary could respond that issuer had an obligation to notify the beneficiary of defects so that a conforming presentation could have been made. Because the issuer did not advise the beneficiary, it should not now be able to recover from the beneficiary since the beneficiary was willing and able to correct the presentation before the letter's expiration date.[4]

What if the beneficiary submits facially nonconforming documents on the letter's expiration date? Assume again that the issuer pays, cannot obtain reimbursement from the applicant, and subsequently the issuer sues the beneficiary in restitution. While 5–

---

4. In this case, the issuer may also try to sue the beneficiary for breach of warranty. This would raise the question of whether the beneficiary's presentation constituted "material fraud" under 5–109(a). See § 8–9, *infra*.

108(i)(4) precludes restitution in this case as well, the underlying justification is not as obvious. Even if the issuer had advised the beneficiary of the problems with the presentation, beneficiary could not have corrected because the letter would have expired. Nonetheless, we believe that the drafters were correct in denying issuer's claim for restitution. In the absence of fraud, forgery or the like, the beneficiary will not be unjustly enriched by the issuer's payment under a commercial letter. The beneficiary has given up title to valuable goods in exchange for payment under the letter of credit. Moreover, it is the issuer who has contracted to provide its expertise in determining that the documents are conforming.

Exactly when restitution is permitted is more difficult than the question when it is precluded. An issuer that has paid but has not been reimbursed by its applicant will have three possible routes to recovery against the beneficiary. First is for breach of warranty, although the warranty given to the issuer under 5–110(a)(1) is quite narrow. It covers only material fraud and forgery of the type described in 5–109(a).[5]

Second, the issuer may pursue its rights of subrogation under 5–117. Those rights are discussed below in section 8–14. Whether the 5–117 rights will prove important depends also on the issuer's need for them. Every careful issuer is adequately covered by a reimbursement agreement and by collateral supporting that agreement. If the cases where issuer seeks recovery of money paid to beneficiaries are few, there will be little need for or pressure upon rules of subrogation. Since the issuer has only the right it would have if it were a secondary guarantor and since those depend upon the common law of each state, it is hard to predict exactly how broad or narrow those rights will be.

The third way to recover money paid to the beneficiary is in restitution. Except when precluded by 5–108(i)(4) as discussed above, this right is available to the issuer wherever applicable common law grants it. Under that law an issuer will need to prove the requisite payment by mistake or on fraud and show the appropriate equities. That may be easy where there is fraud.

Where the beneficiary has taken money which it arguably did not deserve because it broke its underlying contract, one soon arrives at a place where the equities give no guidance. Consider a case. Assume that ABC Corporation submits conforming documents indicating that the goods are "A" grade. ABC Corporation actually ships goods that are "B" grade. After the issuer pays ABC Corporation, the applicant is insolvent and is unable to reimburse the issuer. Does the issuer have a claim for restitution despite 5–108(i)(4)? This case is different from one where the issuer is

---

5. *See* § 8–9, *infra.*

presented with nonconforming documents. There, 5–108(i)(4) would arguably bar a restitution claim.

Here, however, the issuer may argue that the shipment of "B" grade goods was fraudulent but this argument will often fail in the face of the beneficiary's ignorance or good faith. No issuer is expected nor required to travel to the port to inspect the goods to insure they are "A" quality before paying under the letter of credit. If the "equities" balance properly between the beneficiary and the issuer, we think this is a fair case for restitution.

§ 8–9 Injunctions Against Honor by Fraud and Forgery

Applicants often have second thoughts about the wisdom of having established a letter of credit for the benefit of their seller beneficiaries. Yet the independence principle instructs the bank that it must pay on the letter of credit despite troubles with the underlying contract. The bank is obliged to pay on the letter if the documents submitted conform to the terms of the letter.

A celebrated 1941 New York case, Sztejn v. J. Henry Schroder Banking Corp.,[1] now codified and perhaps expanded by 5–109, permits the issuing bank to refuse to pay notwithstanding the presentation of proper documents in certain situations if, in the words of 5–109(a), a "required document is forged or materially fraudulent, or honor of the presentation would facilitate a material fraud by the beneficiary on the issuer or applicant." One man's breach of contract is another's fraud, and routinely applicants seeking to enjoin their banks from paying argue that there is "fraud in the transaction" and thus the court should enjoin payment.

To set the stage, consider the Sztejn case and a few of the many cases that have applied 5–109 and its pre-revision counterpart, 5–114(2). In Sztejn, plaintiff (applicant and purchaser) sought to restrain the payment of drafts under the letter of credit, to enjoin their presentation and asked also for a declaratory judgment that the letter of credit and the drafts were null and void. In denying the defendant's motion to dismiss, the court recognized that the independence principle could be overridden where there was "active fraud on the part of the seller." It was alleged in that case that the seller had not shipped merchandise that was "merely inferior in quality" but rather merchandise that consisted of "worthless rubbish."[2] The court concluded that an injunction would be proper if those facts were proved.

§ 8–9

1. 177 Misc. 719, 31 N.Y.S.2d 631 (1941).

2. Id. at 719, 31 N.Y.S.2d at 635.

Like 5–114(2) of the pre-revision Code, section 5–109 codifies the *Sztejn* case and goes beyond it:

(a) If a presentation is made that appears on its face strictly to comply with the terms and conditions of the letter of credit, but a required document is forged or materially fraudulent, or honor of the presentation would facilitate a material fraud by the beneficiary on the issuer or applicant:

(1) the issuer shall honor the presentation, if honor is demanded by (i) a nominated person that has given value in good faith and without notice of forgery or material fraud, (ii) a confirmer who has honored its confirmation in good faith, (iii) a holder in due course of a draft drawn under the letter of credit which was taken after acceptance by the issuer or nominated person, or an assignee of the issuer's or nominated person's deferred obligation that was taken for value and without notice of forgery or (iv) material fraud after the obligation was incurred by the issuer; and

(2) the issuer, acting in good faith, may honor or dishonor the presentation in any other case.

(b) If an applicant claims that a required document is forged or materially fraudulent or that honor of the presentation would facilitate a material fraud by the beneficiary on the issuer or applicant, a court of competent jurisdiction may temporarily or permanently enjoin the issuer from honoring a presentation or grant similar relief against the issuer or other persons only if the court finds that:

(1) the relief is not prohibited under the law applicable to an accepted draft or deferred obligation incurred by the issuer;

(2) a beneficiary, issuer, or nominated person who may be adversely affected is adequately protected against loss that it may suffer because the relief is granted;

(3) all of the conditions to entitle a person to the relief under the law of this State have been met; and

(4) on the basis of the information submitted to the court, the applicant is more likely than not to succeed under its claim of forgery or material fraud and the person demanding honor does not qualify for protection under subsection (a)(1).

Under this section, the issuer may withhold payment to certain beneficiaries who are not holders in due course or did not act in good faith and without notice of the fraud or forgery.

Section 5–109 requires the issuer to pay certain parties, e.g., confirmers and other bona fide payors, despite fraud. As to those not entitled to special treatment, an issuer acting in good faith may "honor or dishonor the presentation."

It is easy to understand what documents are "forged," hard to know when a document is "fraudulent," and harder still to decide the boundaries of "material fraud." The *Sztejn* case presents the question whether a presentation of an invoice showing conforming goods by a seller who has shipped "trash" is a "fraudulent" document. Presumably if there is at least passing compliance with the contract, even a knowing presentation is not fraudulent; clearly a presentation made in ignorance of the defect in the goods would not be.

The addition of the adverb "materially" and the adjective "material" are intended to raise the applicant's burden of proof. Compare this language to former 5–114(2) which focused on whether there was "fraud in the transaction."

Sections 5–109(b)(1)-(4) contain additional barriers to injunctive relief. These inclusions rest on the hypothesis that injunctions should be few and far between, that injunctions are injurious to the vitality of the letter of credit, and that the cases in which an injunction is sought far exceed those where an injunction is deserved. The revision's drafters were convinced that most injunction cases were brought by disappointed applicants whose complaints about the underlying contract may be justified but do not rise to fraud. The drafters of 5–109 concluded that the threat to letters of credit is greater from false claims of fraud than it is from those who commit fraud.

What constitutes "material" fraud is for the courts. Two years' effort by one of us produced no definition of fraud suitable for inclusion in 5–102. By indorsing Judge Breyer's articulation from Ground Air Transfer v. Westate's Airlines,[3] the comments to 5–109 give some guidance:

> We have said throughout that courts may not "normally" issue an injunction because of an important exception to the general "no injunction" rule. The exception * * * concerns "fraud" so serious as to make it obviously pointless and unjust to permit the beneficiary to obtain the money. Where the circumstances "plainly" show that the underlying contract forbids the beneficiary to call letter of credit * * * where they show that the contract deprives the beneficiary of even a "colorable" right to do so * * * where the contract and circumstances reveal that the beneficiary's demand for payment has "absolutely no basis in fact" * * * where the beneficiary's conduct has "so vitiated

3. 899 F.2d 1269, 1272–73 (1st Cir. 1990).

the entire transaction that the legitimate purposes of the independence of the issuer's obligation would no longer be served" * * * then a court may enjoin payment.

Because revised Article 5 has been in effect for less than ten years in most jurisdictions, it took some time for most state legislatures to enact its provisions. As such, there are few cases that directly interpret the new "material fraud" standard. One of those is *In re Tabernash Meadows, LLC*,[4] dealing with a letter of credit that was set up to secure a buyer's obligation to purchase residential lots in a new subdivision from the land's developer. Prior to the debtor's filing a bankruptcy petition, the buyer-applicant, Lakeside, allegedly attempted to purchase the lots, but developer-beneficiary, Tabernash, avoided this by claiming that the underlying contract was invalid. Following bankruptcy, Tabernash continued to argue that the underlying contract was unenforceable, but also attempted to draw on the letter because Lakeside had not purchased the lots. The court granted an injunction because it found sufficient evidence to support Lakeside's claim that the only reason it did not purchase the lots was because of Tabernash's actions to thwart the sale. In addition, by the time of this decision, the bankruptcy court had lifted the automatic stay on the lots, and they were currently under foreclosure proceedings by Tabernash's bank, which was another reason that Lakeside had not yet completed its purchase.

The court in *Mid–America Tire, Inc. v. PTZ Trading Ltd.*[5] also found that the beneficiary committed "material fraud" when it misrepresented the amount and type of tires that the applicant would be buying. The buyer-applicant, Mid–America, was interested in purchasing blemished Michelin tires from Europe for importation to the U.S. PTZ, seller-beneficiary, claimed that it could provide 50,000–70,000 summer tires that it would sell to Mid–America, provided that Mid–America also take some leftover (and less desirable) winter and mud tires. As negotiations proceeded, it became clear that PTZ could provide, at most, 12,000 summer tires. In addition, 2,500 of those tires were not even eligible for sale in the U.S. Despite Mid–America's revocation of its offer to buy, PTZ unilaterally shipped the winter tires and drew on the letter of credit. The Ohio Supreme Court held that PTZ's actions constituted material fraud because they did not meet the agreed-upon level of summer tires that were a condition of the contract between Mid–America and PTZ. As such, the court upheld an injunction prohibiting a draw under the letter.

As an example of a pre-revision case that we are confident would constitute "material fraud," consider Prairie State Bank v.

4. 56 UCC2d 622 (Bankr. D. Colo. 2005).

5. 95 Ohio St.3d 367, 768 N.E.2d 619 (2002).

Universal Bonding Ins. Co.[6] The letter of credit at issue in that case was set up to secure applicant Bauer Floor Covering, Inc.'s contingent liability to beneficiary, Universal Bonding, in the event that Universal paid on an underlying bond securing Bauer's work on a construction project. At the time of the draw, Universal had not paid out any amounts on Bauer's behalf under the bond, so there was no underlying debt owed to it from Bauer to support the presentation. Although this case was decided under the old "fraud in the transaction" standard, we are confident that this would constitute material fraud if decided today since Universal had no reason to draw on the letter without an outstanding debt from Bauer.

Finally, consider Roman Ceramics Corp. v. Peoples Nat'l Bank,[7] which is cited approvingly in comment 1 to 5–109 in an attempt to delineate what constitutes "material fraud." There, the letter of credit required invoices to be presented that were "certified as unpaid." When Roman, the beneficiary, submitted invoices that it claimed were unpaid, but had actually been paid, the applicant informed the issuer, Peoples National Bank, of the discrepancy and the bank refused to honor the presentation. The court held that this was sufficient to constitute "fraud in the transaction," which was the applicable standard at the time of the case.

A few cases have held that certain discrepancies in the underlying agreement did not reach the level of material fraud. For a recent one, see New Orleans Brass v. Whitney Nat'l Bank.[8] There, a hockey team that applied for a letter of credit was not entitled to an injunction against the beneficiary-arena owner's draw under the letter for disputed rental amounts just because certain items in the arena, such as jacuzzis, showers, and lighting, did not meet the standards of the lease, especially since the team was still able to play its games at the arena. Another case worth considering is Intraword Industries, Inc. v. Girard Trust Bank,[9] which is cited approvingly in comment 1 to 5–109 when it attempts to define "material fraud." There, a dispute arose on whether the beneficiary made a proper declaration of the applicant's default under the lease agreement between the parties. The applicant claimed that this was fraudulent because the lease had been terminated, so it did not owe any money to the beneficiary. In denying an injunction, the court cited *Sztejn* and held that this was a breach of contract issue for another court to decide—not an action that rose to the level of material fraud.

6. 24 Kan.App.2d 740, 953 P.2d 1047, 35 UCC2d 241 (1998).

7. 714 F.2d 1207.

8. 818 So.2d 1057 (Ct. App. La. 2002).

9. 461 Pa. 343, 336 A.2d 316 (Pa. 1975).

Limiting the use of the 5–109 defense to instances where the beneficiary actively commits material fraud is necessary to preserve the independence principle, and puts the burden of investigating the propriety of the underlying transaction on the applicant, where it belongs. Note that the section requires either forgery or material fraud "by the beneficiary." If the fraud is perpetrated by someone else, an injunction is not authorized. To that extent the section adopts the position taken in Cromwell v. Commerce and Energy Bank.[10]

Section 5–109 also warns against injunction substitutes. Courts are prohibited from granting an injunction or "similar relief" absent satisfaction of the conditions in 5–109(b). "Similar relief" might constitute an injunction against presentation, garnishment of the proceeds, or the issuance of other legal processes that would forestall payment. Clearly the limits on injunctive relief should not be avoided by use of other and equally deleterious legal remedies. At least one court has held, however, that the applicant may seek an injunction in a different jurisdiction from the one that is hearing the underlying dispute.[11]

Finally, before an injunction is issued, section 5–109(b)(2) requires that one who may be adversely affected by the injunction be protected against loss that may be suffered due to the injunction. Adequate protection might be a bond. This provision requires the enjoining applicant to put his money where his mouth is. If he is unwilling to put up some security, one ought to question his right to an injunction. In the same vein, section 5–111(e) authorizes lawyers' fees for the winner in the injunction action.

Some issuers have hidden from injunction actions by interpleader. By playing Pontius Pilate, can and should an issuer avoid not only the responsibility of deciding who is entitled to the money but also the cost and grief of injunction suits? The answer to "can it" is maybe; the answer to "should it" is no.

Assume that a beneficiary presents documents to the issuer. Before honor, the applicant informs the issuer that there has been material fraud in the underlying transaction. Under section 5–109(a)(2) the issuer "may honor" unless a court enjoins the payment. By paying, the issuer risks suit from the applicant for wrongful honor. By not paying, the issuer risks suit from the beneficiary for wrongful dishonor. Can the issuer forego all liability

10. 464 So.2d 721, 40 UCC 1814 (La. 1985).

11. Hendricks v. Bank of America, N.A., 398 F.3d 1165 (9th Cir. 2005) (allowing the Central District of California to issue a 5–109(b) injunction against honor even though the underlying complaint was pending in the Northern District of Illinois).

by filing an interpleader action? This question was answered nega-tively in Royal Bank v. Weiss[12] as follows:

> Certainly the * * * interpleader provisions are not properly employed as a means for the issuer to avoid the risks of dishonor so purposefully allocated by the UCC.

Having decided not to honor the demand for payment, the bank cannot "gratuitously characterize itself as a mere stakeholder * * *." We endorse these views. The utility of the letter of credit depends upon quick payment or, at minimum, quick decision whether to pay. Banks should not be permitted to hide behind the court's skirts in an interpleader action.

§ 8–10 Wrongful Honor and the Reimbursement Contract

Often an applicant who procured a letter of credit in happy times wishes that it not be paid in desperate times. If the applicant is unable to procure an injunction under 5–109(b) and the issuer pays, the applicant is likely to find itself a plaintiff, not a defendant, in any ensuing lawsuit with the issuer or the beneficiary. This is because the careful issuer will have procured the applicant's funds or other collateral or will debit the applicant's account when it makes payment on the letter. Unless the applicant chooses to pursue the beneficiary on the underlying contract, it will be left with a suit against the issuer for breach of duty under Article 5 or under the reimbursement contract.

Under section 5–108, unless otherwise agreed, the same strict liability standard runs to the beneficiary as well as the applicant. Section 5–108 provides that "an issuer shall honor a presentation that * * * appears on its face strictly to comply" and "unless otherwise agreed with the applicant, an issuer shall dishonor a presentation that does not appear so to comply." This represents a change from pre-revision Article 5 law, where some courts applied a "strict compliance" standard to the bank's honor/dishonor decision against the beneficiary, but a more generous "substantial compliance" standard in any resulting wrongful honor/dishonor suits from the beneficiary.[1] Comment 1 to 5–108 confirms that the bifurcated standard is no longer supported under the Code.

Returning to current 5–108, an issuer will be liable to the applicant if it honors a presentation that does not strictly apply,

12. 172 A.D.2d 167, 567 N.Y.S.2d   (S.D.N.Y.1982).
707, 14 UCC2d 1186 (1991).

§ 8–10

1. Transamerica Delaval, Inc. v. Citibank, 545 F.Supp. 200, 34 UCC 1296

unless the strict compliance standard is varied by agreement of the parties. Comment 1 to 5–108 recognizes that the issuer may restrict its liability to the applicant:

> Although this section does not impose a bifurcated standard under which the beneficiary's right to honor is more limited than the issuer's right to reimbursement from the applicant, many issuers substantially restrict their liability to the applicant. Where that is done, the beneficiary will have to meet a more stringent standard of compliance as to the issuer than the issuer will have to meet as to the applicant.

Notwithstanding this recognition, issuers are required to write the reimbursement agreement so that terms modifying the UCC requirements are understandable to the applicant and not buried in a boilerplate. Section 5–103(c) states that:

> A term in an agreement or undertaking generally excusing liability or generally limiting remedies for failure to perform obligations is not sufficient to vary obligations prescribed by this article.

Further clarification is provided in Comment 2 to 5–103 as follows:

> * * * The last sentence of subsection (c) limits the power of the issuer to achieve [variations of the issuer's obligation] that result by a nonnegotiated disclaimer or limitation of remedy.

> What the issuer could achieve by an explicit agreement with its applicant or by a term that explicitly defines its duty, it cannot accomplish by a general disclaimer. * * * Where, for example, the reimbursement agreement provides explicitly that the issuer need not examine any documents, the applicant understands the risk it has undertaken. A term in a reimbursement agreement which states generally that an issuer will not be liable unless it has acted in "bad faith" or committed "gross negligence" is ineffective under section 5–103(c).

The applicant's basic argument in wrongful honor cases is that the issuer violated its obligation under 5–108(e) to "observe standard practice of financial institutions that regularly issue letters of credit" by paying over documents that did not strictly comply with the credit. In addition the applicant may throw in a series of fraud or common law negligence claims, but ultimately they will add up to no more than an allegation of breach of the 5–108 duty. If the applicant accepts the documents from the issuing bank and uses them to get the goods, the applicant may have lost its claim.

Two significant obstacles confront the customer in asserting a violation of the 5–108 duty. First is the courts' sympathy for the middleman bank and interest in the integrity of the letter of credit transaction in general. The second is the reimbursement agreement. This contract will contain little that increases the applicant's rights and much that limits the issuing bank's liability.

For several reasons we believe it should be an unusual case in which the applicant successfully recovers from the issuing bank for wrongful honor under 5–108. In the usual case the bank's bias and its selfish interest run exclusively toward dishonor. In the normal case the issuer's most obvious and intense interest will be in its applicant as against a diffuse and remote interest in the integrity of the letter of credit system. If we are to preserve the independence principle and bolster the utility of letters of credit, the law must encourage banks to act in a relatively disinterested way, namely to pay. Moreover, one should have some sympathy for the bank in this position. The bank earns only a small fee, has a limited amount of time to make a decision and, at least when it acts in good faith, courts should be sympathetic to its judgment about beneficiary's compliance with the credit.

If suits by applicants against issuing banks have been unproductive, suits against more remote advising and confirming banks have been even less so. Representative of these cases is Auto Servicio San Ignacio, S.R.L. v. Compania Anonima Venezolana De Navegacion.[2] In that case the beneficiary of the letter of credit presented forged documents which portrayed the shipment of more than $100,000 of tires. In fact, none had been shipped. The Hibernia Bank in New Orleans, labeled by the court as "advising, confirming and paying bank," paid and was sued by the Venezuelan customer of Banco de Maracaibo, the issuing bank. Applying old 5–109, the court rejected the issuer's argument that an advising or confirming bank had liability under Louisiana tort principles, or any contractual duty arising out of 5–109. The court found that Hibernia owed a duty to Banco de Maracaibo, not to Maracaibo's applicant. Accordingly, the case by the applicant was dismissed.

The denial of a cause of action against a nominated bank on behalf of the applicant might be significant for several reasons. First, the customer might have no cause of action against the issuer because the reimbursement agreement exculpated the issuing bank. There is also the possibility that the applicant may have forsaken its rights against the issuing bank in other ways. In those circumstances, it doubtless makes sense to say that the applicant cannot give up its rights against its friend, the hometown bank, and at the same time assert those rights against a distant and unrelated bank.

a. The Reimbursement Contract

In § 8–2, *supra* we point out that the letter of credit transaction involves three parties: two contracts and one "undertaking."

---

2. 765 F.2d 1306, 41 UCC 554 (5th Cir.1985).

The interaction between the reimbursement contract and the letter of credit defines the roles that the issuing bank plays in paying demands under the letter of credit and that the applicant plays in reimbursing the issuing bank. The issuer's obligation to pay under the letter of credit is governed by the UCC, the UCP and common law on the letter of credit. This means that the beneficiary's presentation of documents must "strictly comply" with the terms of the letter of credit.

Once the issuer has paid under the letter of credit, the applicant's obligation to reimburse the issuer is governed by the reimbursement contract between the applicant and the issuer. Because this contract is separate and independent from the letter of credit, courts and commentators sometimes apply normal contract standards of substantial compliance to the performance of this transaction.[3]

Because the issuer-applicant relationship is governed by any reimbursement agreement, the language of that agreement often determines the issuer's liability to the applicant for wrongful honor.

At one extreme, reimbursement agreements often provide that the issuer shall never be responsible for the "form, sufficiency, accuracy, genuineness, falsification, legal effect, correctness or validity of any documents."[4] Nothing in Article 5 says that such a clause is invalid, but 1–302(b) regarding disclaimers of "good faith, diligence, reasonableness and care" might invalidate it. The obligation of 5–108 to examine documents carefully calls not only for good faith, but also for diligence, reasonableness and care. Thus, a broad reading of the reimbursement clause would conflict with the issuer's duty under 5–108 and might cause the clause to be invalid under 1–302(b). While such broad exculpatory provisions are of doubtful validity, clauses of more limited application should withstand the test of 1–302(b).[5]

---

3. See Dolan, The Law of Letters of Credit: Commercial and Standby Credits, Para. 9.03[1][a](rev. ed. 2003) "The strict compliance standard recognizes the unique nature of credits; the substantial compliance standard recognizes that the credit application is just another contract."

4. Overseas Trading Corp. v. Irving Trust Co., 82 N.Y.S.2d 72, 74 (Sup.Ct. 1948). Some of this language tracks portions of UCP 15, but as a whole suggests a broader disclaimer than that section. Article 5 no longer contains any express reference to an issuer's lack of a duty to detect fraud in the documents, but this is arguably included in the issuer's obligation to "observe standard practice of financial institutions that regularly issue letters of credit." Compare UCP 15 with Harfield, Bank Credits and Acceptances, 5th ed.1974, at 315 (Paragraph 13(d) in reimbursement agreement for commercial letter) and McCullough, Letters of Credit App. A, Form [7] (Paragraph (6) in reimbursement agreement for standby letter).

5. Overseas Trading Corp. v. Irving Trust Co., 82 N.Y.S.2d 72, 74 (1948). See generally Harfield, Bank Credits and Acceptances, 5th ed.1974; McCullough, Letters of Credit, Appendix A, Form [7]. See also Kozolchyk, Commercial Letters of Credit in the Americas, 15.01 (suggesting that pre-Code cases generally upheld such clauses when circumscribed to avoid total disclaimer of care).

Beyond exculpatory clauses, what other kinds of clauses might the issuer and applicant include in a reimbursement agreement? Consider the following:

(1) Security interest provisions just as would appear in a security agreement. (This emphasizes that writing a letter of credit is like making a loan; applicant's reimbursement obligation to issuer should thus be secured with well-described collateral; events of default should be spelled out; issuer may wish to be put in funds at first hint of an injunction; and issuer should include other self-help remedies.)

(2) A contractual "bifurcated standard" provision permitting issuer to honor a presentation which substantially performs the letter's conditions, even though issuer could require strict compliance from beneficiary. (Issuer must be careful here not to play too loose with discrepancies in the presentation.)

(3) Provisions permitting issuer to act on oral waivers from applicant, and also requiring applicant to speak up promptly if applicant spots other discrepancies after getting his hands on beneficiary's presented documents, or be automatically deemed to have waived these as well. (These provisions will be especially handy when discrepancies in beneficiary's presentation stem from ambiguities in the required-document descriptions supplied by applicant in the application which then found their way into the letter itself.)

(4) Warranties from applicant concerning legality of applicant-beneficiary deal, applicant's own corporate authority to act, and the like. (These may vary from simple to intricate, depending on the complexity of the deal.)

(5) "Choice of law" provisions concerning Article 5 and the UCP.

(6) Provisions giving issuer letter-issuance or commission fees, imposing interest on applicant's unpaid reimbursement obligation, and authorizing issuer to charge one or more accounts of applicant's as necessary for issuer to realize reimbursement. (These are perhaps dearest to issuer.)

(7) Anti-injunction provisions. (These may spare issuer from being sucked into the vortex of an applicant-beneficiary dispute.)

Even the most carefully drafted reimbursement agreement will be of no avail if the applicant is insolvent. In a commercial letter of credit with an insolvent applicant, the issuer can retain the title to the goods. With the standby letter of credit, the issuer has nothing unless the reimbursement agreement provided for a security interest in applicant's collateral. Even if the issuer retains the goods or a security interest in the collateral, the value of these assets may be far less than the amount paid to the beneficiary. If the goods are nonconforming, is the issuer subrogated to the applicant's rights to sue for breach of warranty?[6]

What about subrogation from another angle: the beneficiary attempting to take advantage of the reimbursement agreement between a failed issuer and the applicant to make itself whole when the issuing bank did not honor a proper presentation? That unusual occurrence was the issue at bar in Colonial Courts Apartment Co. v. Proc Associates, Inc.[7] Proc Associates obtained a letter of credit from Marquette Credit Union to back up promissory notes issued to Colonial Courts related to the sale of some apartment buildings. In addition to its reimbursement agreement with Proc, Marquette also took personal guarantees of Proc's principals as additional security. In the interim, Marquette failed and was taken over by a receiver. When the subject letters of credit were not extended, Colonial made a presentation on the letters. The parties stipulated that this was a proper presentation which Marquette was obligated to honor.

Colonial made a settlement with Marquette's receiver for a $500,000 cash payment and an assignment of Marquette's interest in the reimbursement agreement and personal guarantees. In denying Colonial's claim against Proc and its principals, the First Circuit stressed the language of the reimbursement agreement. Proc became liable under the reimbursement agreement only if Marquette was "required to make payment." Since the bank never actually paid, Proc had no liability to Marquette which could be assigned to Colonial. Similarly, the principals' guarantees were conditioned upon Proc's non-payment of a liability, so they, too, had no obligation for Marquette to assign.

But why was Marquette not "required to make payment" at the moment that Colonial made a proper presentation under the letter of credit (all parties stipulated to a proper presentment)? We are not sure.

This case illustrates the risk that a beneficiary takes in accepting a letter of credit from a potentially insolvent bank. Although the *Colonial* relies mostly on the agreement's language, the court did consider the independence principle. While the Code now contains express provisions on subrogation in 5–117,[8] the independence principle will likely keep courts from reaching beyond the statutory

---

6. See also revised § 5–117 and the discussion in 8–14, *infra*.

7. 57 F.3d 119, 26 UCC2d 1207 (1st Cir.1995).

8. See § 8–14, *infra*.

language to assist parties in these situations. Beneficiaries should remember that their recourse under a letter of credit will typically only run to the issuing bank.

§ 8–11 Transfer of Rights and Assignment of Proceeds

a. *Types of Letters of Credit*

There is considerable confusion about the practical distinctions among three attributes of letters: (1) transferable letters of credit, (2) negotiation credits, and (3) assignment of the proceeds from a credit.

1. *Transferable letters of credit*

A transferable credit allows one other than the beneficiary to perform and draw on the credit. Section 5–112 provides that the letter must specifically state that it is "transferable" in order for the right to draw to be transferred.[1] These provisions of the UCP and UCC are intended to authorize a beneficiary to transfer its benefits and burdens *qua beneficiary* to its own supplier.[2] That transfer carries with it not only the right to sign the draft, but also the right to present invoices of the transferee as opposed to those of the beneficiary. Section 5–112 reads in full:

(a) Except as otherwise provided in Section 5–113, unless a letter of credit provides that it is transferable, the right of a beneficiary to draw or otherwise demand performance under a letter of credit may not be transferred.

(b) Even if a letter of credit provides that it is transferable, the issuer may refuse to recognize or carry out a transfer if:

(1) the transfer would violate applicable law; or

(2) the transferor or transferee has failed to comply with any requirement stated in the letter of credit or any other requirement relating to transfer imposed by the issuer which is within standard practice referred to in Section 5–108(e) or is otherwise reasonable under the circumstances.

Under this provision, drawing rights can be transferred only if the letter so provides and then only if the prospective transferee complies with the requirements that the issuer establishes. The issuer, of course, is fearful of possible multiple transfers or that a beneficiary will later show up and demand payment after the bank has paid a person it believed was the transferee. To protect itself, the issuer will typically require that any beneficiary who wishes to

---

§ 8–11   2. Comment 1 to 5–112.
  1. Accord UCP 48(b).

transfer a letter procure the bank's agreement so that it knows who will be presenting documents. It appears to us that transfers of letters of credit are so tightly controlled and so infrequent that they cause only limited problems.

To make the same point another way, consider a case where a party appears at the issuing bank's window with invoices that correctly describe the goods identified on the letter and with a draft for the amount specified on the letter together with other necessary documents, but assume that the invoice is that of the assignee and the draft is drawn by the assignee. If the letter is transferable and, the parties have complied with any requirements of the issuer, the issuing bank is obliged to pay. If the letter is not transferable, there is no obligation to pay because the applicant has in effect bargained for invoices of its beneficiary, not of a third party, and has a right to the benefit of its bargain.

2. Negotiation letters of credit

To turn to a more mysterious question, what is the distinction between a "negotiation" credit and one that is not a negotiation credit? Even if the letter of credit is not transferable, its proceeds may be assigned under 5–114 or UCP 39. Proceeds may be assigned whether the letter is a negotiation credit or not, but if the letter is not a negotiation credit, some issuers expect the beneficiary to be present at the draw unless they have specifically agreed otherwise. Unlike the transfer of the letter of credit, the assignment of proceeds does not delegate any duty. That is a subtle distinction and one that ultimately may or may not be recognized by American courts. Henry Harfield,[3] one of the leading commentators on American letter of credit law, and at least one case have distinguished the two. The "straight" letter specifies in effect that no third party *claiming on its own behalf* may make the presentation and therefore that there can be no holder in due course or other person with greater rights than the beneficiary.

To illustrate, assume a case in which a bank makes presentation of beneficiary's invoices together with the beneficiary's draft that has been negotiated to the bank under a negotiation credit. If the bank has given value and taken without notice, it will be a holder in due course of the draft and, under 5–109(a)(1)(iii), can argue that it has a right to payment notwithstanding fraud in the underlying transaction. This is because such a bank would qualify as a "nominated person" under 5–102(a)(11), assuming that the credit authorized other parties to negotiate its presentation. If the credit is *not* a negotiation credit, however, the bank cannot claim

3. See Harfield, Identity Crisis in Letter of Credit Law, 24 Ariz.L.Rev. 239, 246–8 (1982); Dolan, The Law of Letters of Credit: Commercial and Standby Credits, Para. 10.02[3], [4] (rev. ed. 2003).

that status and can be no better than an assignee of the beneficiary's rights to payment, whatever those rights are. If, on the other hand, the credit is a negotiation credit, all would agree that the bank—meeting the tests of the holder in due course statute—would have a right to insist upon payment from the issuer notwithstanding fraud in the underlying transaction.

Another distinction between the negotiation and nonnegotiation of letters of credit is that the former permits presentation to someone other than the issuer. For example, negotiation credits known in the industry as "freely negotiable" typically authorize presentation at any bank. Under those credits every bank is a nominated person and presentation to any bank that takes up the documents would be an effective presentation and satisfy the condition that presentation occur prior to expiration.

How does one identify a negotiation credit? There are at least two ways in which a credit may be identified as a negotiation credit. A common way in American letters of credit is to add a sentence to the letter such as the following: "We hereby agree with drawers, indorsers, and bona fide owners of drafts drawn under and in compliance with the credit, the same will be duly honored on presentation to the drawee bank as specified above." A second possibility is to have a series of blocks on the face of the letter of credit in which to put a check mark where appropriate. For example, such blocks might say that the credit was available by sight payment or by acceptance or by negotiation. Presumably, if the negotiation block was checked, the document would be a negotiation credit, but not otherwise.[4]

3. *Assignment of proceeds*

To reiterate—issues about negotiation or transfer should not be confused with the beneficiary's right to "assign proceeds." Regardless of the type of credit, section 5–114 provides that the beneficiary can "assign its right to part or all of the proceeds of a letter of credit" if done before presentation of the credit. Note, however, that Article 5 does not strictly require that assignment only occur before presentation. At least one court has read 5–114 in conjunction with 5–103(b)'s prohibition against negative inferences and held that an assignment made after a beneficiary's right to payment had accrued was valid.[5]

Here the beneficiary is not attempting to give a right to some other person to draw on a letter of credit but is only assigning

4. For additional information on negotiation credits, see Dolan, The Law of Letters of Credit: Commercial and Standby Credits, Para. 1.02[3], [4] (rev. ed. 2003).

5. In re XYZ Options, Inc., 154 F.3d 1276, 36 UCC2d 839 (11th Cir.1998).

rights to proceeds. "Proceeds" will exist only if the beneficiary itself prepares the proper documents and draws. The right of the assignee to the proceeds is precarious, for its rights are dependent upon beneficiary's performance and presentation under the letter of credit. In a significant concession to the issuers, section 5–114(c) allows an issuer or nominated person to disregard an assignment of proceeds to which it has not consented. However, 5–114(d) provides that the issuer's consent cannot be unreasonably withheld if the "assignee possesses and exhibits the letter of credit and presentation of the letter of credit is a condition to honor."

Section 5–114 serves as a significant restriction of the rights that beneficiaries and their assignees had under old 5–116. It comes quite close to granting the bank the right to behave like Marie Antoinette in the face of supplicant assignee's pleas. The lesson to be gained from 5–114 for prospective assignees is that they should not count on payment from the issuer unless the issuer itself has acknowledged and consented to the assignment.

The section runs smack into issues involving Article 9 and the secured creditor. The right of the assignee secured creditor vis à vis third parties is governed by "Article 9 or other law." Its rights against the issuer and against transferee beneficiaries of a nominated person are governed by 5–114.

One way of looking at 5–114 is to think of it as an extensive protection of the issuer against the prospect of multiple claims. In a sense it is like 9–405 through 9–406, but it is more protective of the obligor's rights. It does not purport to govern the rights of certain third parties fighting over the proceeds (e.g., rights of a trustee in bankruptcy versus the rights of a secured creditor). Those rights are to be fought out under bankruptcy law and Article 9.

b. *Transfer by Beneficiary of Rights to Proceeds as Security for a Loan*

Assume that the buyer-applicant is unwilling to have a transferable letter of credit issued and that the seller needs to borrow money to get the goods from its supplier. Assume further that the seller's financer, a local bank, is unwilling to take an assignment of the seller's unearned rights under its furniture sale contract with the buyer as security for a loan.[6]

The seller as a beneficiary under a letter of credit could assign its right to the proceeds to its bank as security for a loan under section 5–114(b). The seller can do so even where the letter of credit is not transferable and is not a negotiation credit. With the loan the seller could then pay its own supplier, procure the neces-

---

6. See Gilmore, The Assignee of Contract Rights and His Precarious Securi- ty, 74 Yale L.J. 217 (1964).

sary documents under the letter of credit, present the same to the issuer, and remit the amount owed to the lending bank. The foregoing arrangement can take other forms too. For example, the seller's bank might take an assignment of proceeds, but instead of disbursing the loan to the seller, it could notify the seller's supplier that the supplier may draw drafts on the bank for goods supplied.[7] The seller might even assign the right to proceeds to its supplier as security for an extension of credit by the supplier itself.

Lastly, if the letter of credit that was issued to the seller is a negotiation credit, the seller could negotiate the drafts over to the local bank, enabling the bank to present the beneficiary's drafts to the issuer and to apply the proceeds towards the seller's outstanding loan. The bank becomes a holder in due course and will not be affected by any 5–109(a)(1) defense asserted by the buyer.

What of risks to the assignee financer who lends or extends credit against an assignment of proceeds from the seller-beneficiary as collateral security? Or, how good is this security? First there are risks of assignor double-dealing. After making the assignment the assignor might procure forged documents, negotiate or present them with a properly drawn draft to a third party or to the issuer, and pocket the entire proceeds. Section 5–114(d) allows the assignee to protect itself against assignor double-dealing. By the terms of that section the assignee of proceeds may take possession of the letter of credit. As noted above in § 8–11, 5–114(c) provides that the issuer "need not recognize an assignment of proceeds of a letter of credit until it consents to the assignment;" 5–114(d) provides the assignee a measure of protection, however, as such "consent may not be unreasonably withheld if the assignee possesses and exhibits the letter of credit and presentation of the letter of credit is a condition to honor." While not required under Article 5, comment 3 to 5–114 notes that "it has always been advisable for the assignee to obtain the consent of the issuer in order better to safeguard its right to the proceeds." This section represented a departure from old Article 5, as a pre-revision assignment would have been binding on the issuer once the assignee took possession of the letter and provided reasonable notice of the assignment to the issuer.

Is there any way to protect the assignee against a double dealing assignor who, after assignment, nonetheless wrongfully negotiates a draft (with forged documents) drawn under the credit to an innocent third party? Here if the issuer is obligated to honor the draft presented by the third party, it should not also remain obligated to the assignee. The assignee therefore needs protection against this possibility. One way to provide it is as follows. The letter of credit and drafts can be drawn (or amended) to provide

---

7. But see Ufford, Transfer and Assignment of Letters of Credit Under the   Uniform Commercial Code, 7 Wayne L.Rev. 263, 271 (1960).

that *no draft* drawn under it is to be honored by the issuer unless accompanied by the letter of credit itself. A third party who bought such drafts and documents from the double dealing assignor would not be a party taking "under circumstances which would make it a holder in due course" within subsection 5–109(a)(1)(iii). The issuer would, therefore, not be required to honor the drafts even though the documents complied.

The use of a nonnegotiation credit discussed above may also help. If courts ultimately adopt the position taken by Henry Harfield, an issuing bank that paid over a fraudulent document could conceivably retrieve that money from the presenter and then pay on the true documents presented by the assignee. If the issuer did not pay, it could not be forced to do so because presenter would not be a holder in due course. If the idea of the nonnegotiation credit is accepted, the assignee could himself draw on the credit only if he had previously procured properly signed drafts and properly prepared documents of the assignor.

So much for risks that the assignor will double deal. How is the assignee protected against creditors of the assignor beneficiary who seek by garnishment or the like to reach the beneficiary's rights under the letter of credit? 5–114(f) states that this section only affects rights between the assignee and the "issuer, transferee beneficiary or nominated person," and leaves all questions on "the mode of creating and perfecting a security interest" to "Article 9 or other law." Comment 1 to 5–114 refers you to the operative sections of Article 9, which are 9–203(b)(3)(D) (the assignee must have "control" of the "letter-of-credit right") and 9–107 ("control" is present "if the issuer or nominated person has consented to an assignment of proceeds of the letter of credit under Section 5–114(c) or otherwise applicable law or practice.")

c. Beneficiary's Use of Its Rights Under Letter of Credit to Procure Issuance of a Second Letter of Credit in Favor of Its Lender or Supplier

So called "back-to-back" letters of credit are sometimes used in international trade. In the immediately preceding discussion, we canvassed a variety of risks incurred by the assignee of proceeds (a lender or supplier of the beneficiary) under a non-transferable letter of credit. A prospective assignee might refuse to become an assignee and insist on being a beneficiary of a second letter of credit procured by the beneficiary of the first ("prime") letter of credit. For example, a Georgia financing institution or the Georgia furniture supplier might demand that the Georgia seller have a second letter of credit issued naming the financer or the supplier as beneficiary. With this status, the Georgia financer or supplier would not incur many of the risks otherwise incurred by a mere assignee of proceeds. Indeed, the Georgia financer or supplier would be assured of payment upon drawing and presenting the drafts (and accompanying documents) called for by the terms of the second letter of credit.

But how could the beneficiary of the "prime" letter of credit, the Georgia seller, induce a Georgia bank to issue a second letter of credit naming its financer or supplier as beneficiary? The prospective issuer of the second letter would likely be willing to issue it on the security of an assignment by the Georgia seller of its right to proceeds under the prime letter. That issuer incurs the risks and has the protection of the assignee discussed in the preceding subsection. The issuer of the second letter should also see that documents required under the prime letter are procured prior to the time for expiration of the Georgia seller's status as beneficiary of the prime letter. Usually, this poses no problem and the issuer of the second letter simply pays off the beneficiary of the second letter (the seller's financer or supplier) by honoring drafts accompanied by the very documents that the issuer of the second letter will (as assignee of the rights of the beneficiary of the prime letter) forward with further drafts to the issuer of the prime letter for honor.

d. *Assignment and Transfer by Operation of Law*

Prior to the 1995 revision of Article 5, a beneficiary's insolvency or merger with another entity raised some interesting issues regarding the rights of the beneficiary's trustee in bankruptcy or successor entity to draw under the letter of credit. Technically, a nonbeneficiary presenting under a nontransferable letter of credit would fail strict compliance. However, for reasons of commercial necessity (and logic), such successors should have the same rights under a letter of credit as the original named beneficiary. Prior to the revision, two lines of cases developed—one recognized an exception to strict compliance and allowed the successor entity to draw on the letter, while a second line held that strict compliance should not yield (at least in the bankruptcy context). Revised 5–113 adopted the former view:

> (a) A successor of a beneficiary may consent to amendments, sign and present documents, and receive payment or other items of value in the name of the beneficiary without disclosing its status as a successor.

> (b) A successor of a beneficiary may consent to amendments, sign and present documents, and receive payment or other items of value in its own name as the disclosed successor of the beneficiary.

(c) An issuer is not obliged to determine whether a purported successor is a successor of a beneficiary or whether the signature of a purported successor is genuine or authorized.

In effect, section 5–113 authorizes what one of the drafters described as "immaterial fraud." For example, assume that American Motors is the beneficiary under a letter of credit. Subsequently, American Motors is merged into Chrysler Corporation. If Chrysler is American Motor's successor by operation of law, section 5–113(a) or (b) allows Chrysler to draw in the name of American Motors even though that is no longer the beneficiary's true name—so an "immaterial fraud." One becomes a successor by operation of the law by merger or consolidating with another, and by bankruptcy. Section 5–113 codifies the rules set out in FDIC v. Bank of Boulder,[8] *as noted in comment 1.*

Section 5–113 also recognizes the legitimate concerns of the issuer to be able to pay without worrying about a second draw by the beneficiary or by a third party. The issuer's obligation is fulfilled upon payment to the transferee by operation of the law and there is no requirement that the issuer investigate whether the purported successor is a successor of the beneficiary or whether the signature is genuine or authorized.

§ 8–12   Confirmers, Nominated Persons and Advisers

Above we note that issuers of letters of credit involving parties in different states or countries frequently request assistance from other banks. What are the duties and liabilities of advising, confirming and nominated banks? The answers lie in the definitions of each party in 5–102 and the duties of those respective parties in 5–107.

a.   Confirmers

A confirmer "undertakes * * * to honor a presentation under a letter of credit issued by another."[1] 5–107(a) defines a confirmer's rights and obligations as follows:

(a) A confirmer is directly obligated on a letter of credit and has the rights and obligations of an issuer to the extent of its confirmation. The confirmer also has rights against and obligations to the issuer as if the issuer were an applicant and the confirmer had issued the letter of credit at the request and for the account of the issuer.

Unlike a nominated person or an adviser, a confirmer itself promises to pay a letter of credit. It, therefore, has the same rights when

---

8.   911 F.2d 1466 (10th Cir. 1990).

§ 8–12

1.   5–102(a)(4).

there is a presentation by a beneficiary as if it were the issuer of the letter of credit. It has the same duties and is subject to the same preclusion as an issuer would be under 5–108(c) and the UCP. Furthermore, after payment under the letter of credit, the confirmer has a right to reimbursement irrespective of any underlying fraud. Comment 1 to 5–107 expands on this point as follows:

> A confirmer that has paid in accordance with the terms and conditions of the letter of credit is entitled to reimbursement by the issuer even if the beneficiary committed fraud * * * and, in that sense, has greater rights against the issuer than the beneficiary has.

Just like an issuing bank, a confirming bank also remains subject to the independence principle. They cannot defeat the beneficiary's claim to the letter's proceeds by claiming that they will not be reimbursed by the original issuing bank.

The obligations of the confirming bank do not generally extend to the applicant. Neither the confirming bank's right of reimbursement from the issuer nor its duty of care to the issuer extends to the applicant. In Confeccoes Texteis de Vouzela, Lda v. Riggs National Bank,[2] the beneficiary presented documents to Riggs as a confirming bank. Riggs paid and forwarded the documents to the issuing bank even though they were conceded to be nonconforming. In fact, the goods were worthless to the buyer. Riggs debited the issuer's account and the issuer presumably got reimbursement from the plaintiff (applicant). The court held that the confirming bank's duty is to the issuing bank and not to the applicant. This is the clearest statement in modern American law that a confirmer has no responsibility to a remote applicant for wrongful honor. It conforms to the belief of most banks, but it comes to the ironic conclusion that the confirmer has no liability for its bad acts. The court suggests that Riggs would have liability to the issuing bank, but if the issuing bank's reimbursement contract allows it to charge the applicant's account, the issuing bank may have no incentive to sue Riggs in an expensive lawsuit in a foreign country. See, however, the last sentence of comment 1 to 5–107, which allows the possibility of a claim by the applicant against the confirmer under 5–109 (material fraud), 5–110 (warranties) or 5–117 (subrogation).

Free of liabilities to the applicant, confirmers are special types of "nominated banks" that have only limited warranty liability to the issuer. Section 5–110(a)(1) states that the beneficiary warrants "that there is no fraud or forgery of the kind described in Section 5–109(a) [i.e. no material fraud]," as noted in § 8–7, *supra*, on warranties. This section expressly applies to "the issuer and any other person to whom presentation is made," which arguably

2. 994 F.2d 851, 20 UCC2d 1034 (D.C.Cir.1993).

includes confirming banks and nominated persons. However, a negotiating, advising, confirming, collecting or issuing bank presenting or transferring a draft or demand for payment is subject only to the warranties of a collecting bank under Article 4. These Article 4 warranties generally provide that the nominated bank is entitled to enforce the draft and that there have been no forgeries or alterations.

Lastly, the UCC specifically requires that the confirmer obtain its authority to act in that capacity under "designation or authorization of the issuer."[3] In the typical confirmation, the issuing bank will contact the confirming bank directly—although usually this is done at the request of the beneficiary, and not on the issuer's own initiative. Situations where the beneficiary approaches the potential confirming bank without contacting the issuer are called "silent confirmations," and the only known case to address this issue is Dibrell Bros. Int'l v. Banca Nazionale Del Lavoro.[4]

Silent confirmations arise in situations where the issuing bank does not want to approach another bank to act as a confirmer.[5] Although it was a pre-revision case, *Dibrell Bros.* applied an ABA Task Force's recommendations by analogy, and held that silent confirmations were not true Article 5 "confirmations." This holding means that the silent confirmer has no right of reimbursement from the issuer, although it may have duties to its beneficiary created by the separate contract between the silent confirmer and beneficiary. Similarly, the beneficiary would not have a statutory Article 5 wrongful dishonor claim against the silent confirmer, and would have to rely on a general contract claim, provided that they could prove an underlying contract (unless, of course, the contract between the silent confirmer and beneficiary incorporated Article 5 or the UCP). To borrow the *Dibrell Bros.* court's language: "the silent confirmer's engagement appears more like a surety agreement rather than an extension of [a letter of] credit."[6]

b. Nominated Persons

The issuer may also "nominate" another bank and so authorize that bank to accept documents and give value (negotiate) under the letter of credit.[7] As noted in 5–102(a)(4), confirming banks are a special subset of nominated persons who have the right and obligation to honor a beneficiary's presentation. 5–107(b) defines the nominated person's rights and obligations succinctly:

---

3. Comment 1 to 5–102.

4. 38 F.3d 1571, 25 UCC2d 196 (11th Cir. 1994).

5. *Id.* at 1575, n.4.

6. *Id.* at 1581.

7. 5–102(a)(11); UCP 10(b).

A nominated person who is not a confirmer is not obligated to honor or otherwise give value for a presentation.[8]

A nominated person has three options available. First, the person nominated can refuse to act as a nominated person. Second, the nominated person can agree to act on the beneficiary's behalf with an implicit or explicit agreement that the beneficiary should not rely on the actions of the nominated person. Third, the nominated person can examine the documents and charge a fee thereby encouraging the beneficiary to rely on the nominated person's examination of the documents.

To see how this might work, assume that the beneficiary brings the documents to a nominated person. The nominated person reviews the documents and sends them on to the issuing bank. If the issuing bank denies payment because of deficiencies in the presentation, the beneficiary may look to the nominated person. The beneficiary will assert that it relied on the nominated person's review of the documents and had it known of the deficiencies it could have corrected them before the letter's expiration date. Although the statutory preclusions do not apply to nominated persons (see UCP 16f), the nominated person may have liability in tort or contract to the beneficiary, particularly if it charged a fee for reviewing the documents.

c. Advisers

Section 5–102(a)(1) of the UCC defines an adviser as one which "notifies * * * the beneficiary that a letter of credit has been issued, confirmed, or amended." Under 5–107(c), an adviser's rights and obligations are as follows:

> (c) A person requested to advise may decline to act as an adviser. An adviser that is not a confirmer is not obligated to honor or give value for a presentation. An adviser undertakes to the issuer and to the beneficiary accurately to advise the terms of the letter of credit, confirmation, amendment, or advice received by that person and undertakes to the beneficiary to check the apparent authenticity of the request to advise. Even if the advice is inaccurate, the letter of credit, confirmation, or amendment is enforceable as issued.

> (d) A person who notifies a transferee beneficiary the terms of a letter of credit, confirmation, amendment, or advice has the rights and obligations of an adviser under subsection (c). The terms in the notice to the transferee beneficiary may differ from the terms in any notice to the transferor beneficiary to

---

8. Accord UCP 10(c).

the extent permitted by the letter of credit, confirmation, amendment, or advice received by the person who so notifies.

The advising bank does not incur obligations to pay under the letter of credit, but it does assume an obligation for the accuracy of statements made to the beneficiary. Under letters governed by the UCP, the advising bank must use reasonable care to check the authenticity of the letter.[9]

Where the advice is inaccurate, the document is enforceable according to its original terms. For example, assume the original letter of credit calls for invoice stating "3XZ–55S" but the adviser informs the beneficiary that invoices must state "3XX–SSS55." In this case, the beneficiary's presentation of invoices stating "3XX–SSS55" to the issuer will flunk strict compliance. If the adviser is also a confirming bank, it would have to honor the beneficiary's presentation but might not be entitled to reimbursement from the issuing bank.

§ 8–13　Damages

a.　*Beneficiary's Remedies for Wrongful Dishonor*

By far the most common damage suit in letter of credit law is a suit by a spurned beneficiary who claims that the issuer wrongfully dishonored. Opinions in wrongful dishonor cases deal mostly with right to honor not with the amount of the damages. Section 5–111(a) provides that the beneficiary may recover the face amount of the draft plus incidental damages and interest, but cannot recover consequential damages.[1] However, the comments point out that the bar to consequential damages will not protect the defendant from consequential damages that may be available under Article 4. The plaintiff may also obtain specific performance when the issuer's obligation is for something other than the payment of money. Punitive damages are *a fortiori* prohibited under the bar against consequential damages, which conforms to the pre-revision case law where such damages were almost never given.

In addition to covering wrongful dishonor cases, section 5–111(a) specifies the same damages when the issuer repudiates: the beneficiary may recover incidental damages, interest and attorney fees, but no consequential damages. Repudiation claims are slightly different, however, in that the beneficiary must also be able to prove that they were ready, willing and able to perform the obligations under the contract with the applicant.

---

9. UCP 7(a).

§ 8–13

1. § 5–115(1). Other provisional

remedies may be appropriate, too.

One significant departure from pre-revision case law to the current Code is that attorney fees are now expressly provided for under 5–111(e). One exception to the rule on recovery of attorney fees is that they are not awarded in actions for injunctive relief under 5–109 against an issuer.

Although the revised Code leaves the basic liability for wrongful dishonor as "the amount that is the subject of the dishonor or repudiation," it also addresses the possibility that the issuer's performance would be the delivery of an item of value instead of the payment of money.

b. Mitigation

Mitigation of the beneficiary's damages was another disputed issue that was resolved by the 1995 revision to Article 5, as the current Code specifies that the claimant has no duty to the issuer to mitigate damages. The drafters of 5–111 realized that allowing an issuer who wrongfully dishonored to require the suing beneficiary to mitigate its damage might give issuers an incentive to dishonor conforming presentations.

Assume a case where the issuer is faced with an insolvent applicant and an outstanding letter of credit for $1 million. When the beneficiary presents conforming documents, the issuer is faced with two alternatives. First, the issuer can pay the beneficiary and obtain title to the goods. Because the applicant is insolvent, the issuer will have to sell the goods itself. In the alternative, the issuer could dishonor the beneficiary's presentation. If the beneficiary has a duty to mitigate the issuer's loss, the issuer would have an incentive to dishonor because the burden of disposing of the goods would be shifted to the beneficiary. To remove that incentive, the drafters have minimized the beneficiary's duty to mitigate. Specifically, 5–111(a) states:

> The claimant is not obligated to take action to avoid damages that might be due from the issuer under this subsection.

The language is an attempt to require the issuer to pay upon beneficiary's conforming presentation and bear the burden of disposing of the goods. Exactly how this will work or whether it will work at all when the issuer joins the applicant (and the applicant asserts its underlying claims against the beneficiary) remains to be seen.

What if the beneficiary throws the conforming documents across the counter, walks away and the goods rot? Is the loss of the value of the goods the beneficiary's or the issuer's? We think that the loss falls on the issuer, who had better pick the documents up off the floor, and resell the goods before they rot. But of course the issuer, having failed to act, may still be able to recover on its reimbursement agreement and then send the applicant to do its work in court. We are certain we have not seen the last of this issue, but a court, in interpreting 5–111(a), should be sensitive to the problem. The law should not give the issuer a motive to dishonor conforming presentations.

It will be interesting to see if courts are willing to extend Article 5's lack of a mitigation requirement to the underlying transaction. This would obviously conflict with the general contract law requirement that the damaged party mitigate its damages for breach of contract. For a case that did not address this issue, but had facts under which the argument might arise, see Clark Oil Trading Co. v. J. Aron & Co.[2]

c. Wrongful Honor

The second most common damage in one sense is not an Article 5 claim at all, but a breach of contract claim by the applicant against the issuer for wrongful honor.[3] This is a claim that the presentation was defective and the issuer broke its contract with the applicant by paying under that defective presentation. The lawsuit will depend heavily on the reimbursement contract which will likely contain a variety of disclaimers. The lawsuit may include claims for restitution when the issuer has already debited the account of the applicant and the applicant is suing for a return of the money.

Unlike its predecessor, current Article 5 clearly provides for applicant's action against the issuer for wrongful honor. Section 5–111(b) reads:

> If an issuer wrongfully dishonors a draft or demand for payment presented under a letter of credit or honors a draft or demand in breach of its obligation to the applicant, the applicant may recover damages resulting from the breach, including incidental but not consequential damages, less any amount saved as a result of the breach.

This section clarifies that the applicant has no action unless actual damages resulted from the issuer's breach of contract. In the event that the underlying contract has been fully performed, no action can be pursued by the applicant against the beneficiary. Note the different rule that applies here compared to suits by beneficia-

---

2. 256 A.D.2d 196, 683 N.Y.S.2d 12, 38 UCC2d 414 (N.Y. Sup. Ct. 1998).

3. Though less common, the applicant can also have a breach of contract claim against the beneficiary for wrongful draw. *See* Alstom Power, Inc. v. RMF Indus. Contracting, Inc., 2006 WL 1580254, 60 UCC2d 136 (W.D.Pa.2006) (affirming dismissal of wrongful draw claim because plaintiff could not show a loss and questioning plaintiffs standing because plaintiff was not the applicant and was not primarily liable on the letter).

ries for wrongful dishonor—in wrongful honor lawsuits, the applicant *is* required to mitigate.

Sometimes an applicant who has suffered wrongful honor deserves no damages. Assume a beneficiary who complies with the underlying contract but submits noncomplying documents. If the applicant got exactly what it bargained for, its expectations are fully satisfied. It might argue, of course, that the market has changed and that it now would like to get out of the bargain because the subject goods are worth less than they were at the time of contracting. Further, it might maintain that it could have gotten out of the bargain if the issuing bank properly declined to pay. To us this argument is unpersuasive. Since the applicant was seizing on a technical detail to escape a deal with which the beneficiary is willing to comply, we see no reason to be generous with the applicant. Moreover, it is not certain that the applicant would have escaped the bargain had the issuing bank failed to pay. In that event the beneficiary might have chosen to sue on the underlying contract and, by hypothesis, would have recovered.

There are also intermediate cases in which both the documents and the goods are defective in some respects, but in which the goods still have some value. In such circumstances, presumably, the applicant should not be free to recover the entire value of the letter, but only the difference in value between the goods as delivered and the goods as promised.

Because applicants are so infrequently successful in suing issuing banks for wrongful honor, the law here is undeveloped. Presumably the outcome should normally be the same whether the applicant is the defendant seeking to forestall the obligation to reimburse or whether the applicant is the plaintiff seeking to recover an amount already paid to the bank. If the outcomes in the two cases are to be consistent, it may sometimes be necessary to recognize the right of restitution when the issuing bank pays by mistake.

d. *Breach by Other Parties*

Section 5–111 also deals with the less significant event of breach by an adviser or nominated person failing correctly to advise or otherwise breaking the contract. All of these suits are "under Article 5" and are covered by 5–111 even though they are also contract claims. Because of the special rules concerning attorney fees and consequential damages, the damages under 5–111 are likely to be different from those that would be granted for breach of a similar contract not governed by 5–111.

§ 8–14 Subrogation

The claims of the issuer or applicant to subrogation to the rights of the beneficiary stirred a lively judicial debate prior to the

1995 revision of Article 5. Now, however, section 5–117 specifically provides for subrogation in certain circumstances as follows:

(a) An issuer that honors a beneficiary's presentation is subrogated to the rights of the beneficiary to the same extent as if the issuer were a secondary obligor of the underlying obligation owed to the beneficiary and of the applicant to the same extent as if the issuer were the secondary obligor of the underlying obligation owed to the applicant.

(b) An applicant that reimburses an issuer is subrogated to the rights of the issuer against any beneficiary, presenter, or nominated person to the same extent as if the applicant were the secondary obligor of the obligations owed to the issuer and has the rights of subrogation of the issuer to the rights of the beneficiary stated in subsection (a).

(c) A nominated person that pays or gives value against a draft or demand presented under a letter of credit is subrogated to the rights of:

(1) the issuer against the applicant to the same extent as if the nominated person were a secondary obligor of the obligation owed to the issuer by the applicant;

(2) the beneficiary to the same extent as if the nominated person were a secondary obligor of the underlying obligation owed to the beneficiary; and

(3) the applicant to same extent as if the nominated person were the secondary obligor of the underlying obligation owed to the applicant.

(d) Notwithstanding any agreement or term to the contrary, the rights of subrogation stated in subsections (a) and (b) do not arise until the issuer honors the letter of credit or otherwise pays and the rights in subsection (c) do not arise until the nominated person pays or otherwise gives value. Until then, the issuer, nominated person, and the applicant do not derive under this section present or prospective rights forming the basis of a claim, defense, or excuse. Assume an issuer and applicant agree to provide a standby letter of credit in favor of the beneficiary. In the underlying transaction the beneficiary takes a security interest in assets of applicant or of applicant's company. The applicant or its company defaults and the beneficiary presents conforming documents to the issuer. After the issuer pays the beneficiary, the issuer will argue that it should be subrogated to the beneficiary's security interest in the collateral belonging to applicant.

The section balances the claimant's right to subrogation and the letter of credit independence principle by precluding any defenses or rights until after payment is made under the letter of credit. This is critical, as one of the key justifications for disregarding the independence principle under these circumstances is that there is no reason to apply the principle once its primary objective (that the beneficiary be paid quickly) is met by the issuer's honor.

A pre-revision case, Colonial Courts Apartment Co. v. Proc Associates, Inc.,[1] (mentioned in § 8–10, *supra*) illustrates some of the limitations of 5–117. There, Colonial Courts sold a number of apartment buildings to an entity affiliated with Proc Associates. Proc obtained a letter of credit from Marquette Credit Union to back up promissory notes issued to Colonial. In addition to its reimbursement agreement with Proc, Marquette also took personal guarantees of Proc's principals as additional security. In the interim, Marquette failed and was taken over by a receiver. When the subject letters of credit were not extended, Colonial made a presentation on the letters. The parties stipulated that this was a proper presentation which Marquette was obligated to honor.

Colonial entered into a settlement with Marquette's receiver for a $500,000 cash payment and assignment of Marquette's interest in the underlying reimbursement agreement and personal guarantees. In denying Colonial's claim against Proc and its principals, the First Circuit found that the language of the reimbursement agreement did not make Proc liable under the reimbursement agreement because Marquette never actually made payment. Proc had no liability to Marquette that could be assigned to Colonial.

Would 5–117's express permission of subrogation under letters of credit result in a different outcome if the same case was brought after the revision? For at least two reasons the result would be the same. First, Marquette never honored the presentation, so the threshold requirement for 5–117 to apply would not be met. Secondly, the party seeking subrogation in this situation is the beneficiary, and 5–117 only provides subrogation rights to "an issuer that honors a beneficiary's presentation" or "an applicant that reimburses an issuer." Although one might argue that a beneficiary lost out in the transaction by shipping goods for which it was never paid, denying subrogation may still be the proper result, for denial encourages the beneficiary to bargain directly with its customer for additional security rather than relying upon collateral or guarantees obtained by other parties to the letter of credit transaction.

When the subrogee is in bankruptcy, the courts look to 11 U.S.C. 509 of the Bankruptcy Code to determine if the claimant can be subrogated to another's rights. Section 509(a) provides:

§ 8–14

Cir.1995).

1. 57 F.3d 119, 26 UCC2d 1207 (1st

* * * an entity that is liable with the debtor on, or that has secured, a claim of a creditor against the debtor, and that pays such claim, is subrogated to the rights of such creditor to the extent of such payment.

Note that some courts reviewing this provision of the Bankruptcy Code have held that the claimant, as one principally liable, was not "liable with the debtor on" or did not "secure a claim of the creditor against the debtor." As all of these are pre-revision cases, it is unclear how courts will address this issue now that 5–117 provides for subrogation in letter of credit situations. Clearly, subrogation would be permitted in non-bankruptcy cases, but what of the potentially competing ideals of bankruptcy? In our opinion, 5–117 should be read to mean that the issuer was "liable with the debtor on" the underlying claim as a "codebtor," thus allowing subrogation in the bankruptcy context under § 509. Although the Bankruptcy Code is federal law, there are many instances where state law is used to determine the meaning of undefined words included therein, and we feel that this is one such situation where 5–117 should be used to interpret the Code.[2]

§ 8–15　Statute of Limitations

If the letter of credit is not a contract, what statute of limitation governs? At least one court[1] has found that the action by the beneficiary against the issuer is subject to "contract" statute of limitations which begins to run on the issuer's dishonor of the beneficiary's first request. Revised section 5–115 deals with this question as follows:

An action to enforce a right or obligation arising under this article must be commenced within one year after the expiration date of the relevant letter of credit or one year after the [claim for relief] [cause of action] accrues, whichever occurs later. A [claim for relief] [cause of action] accrues when the breach occurs, regardless of the aggrieved party's lack of knowledge of the breach.

The statute of limitations governs not only suits against the issuer for wrongful dishonor but also claims against nominated persons, advising banks, and others whose rights arise from or are associated with the letter of credit transaction. It also governs the

---

2. *See* James J. White, Rights of Subrogation in Letters of Credit Transactions, 41 St. Louis U. L.J. 47 (1996). *See also* In re Mirant Corp., 2005 WL 2589162 (Bankr. N.D. Tex. July 21, 2005) (holding that section 509 was ambiguous and whether there were subrogation rights was a question for the jury).

§ 8–15

1. Century Fire and Marine Ins. Corp. v. Bank of New England–Bristol County, N.A., 405 Mass. 420, 540 N.E.2d 1334, 10 UCC2d 1370 (1989).

applicant's claim for wrongful honor, since that claim arises out of a letter of credit transaction and even though it is essentially a suit on a written contract, the reimbursement agreement. The one-year statute of limitations should be widely applied so that no part of the same dispute finds it way outside of Article 5 while another portion of the same dispute is foreclosed by the one-year statute of limitations.

Table of Cases

D

S

Index

---

†